THE
CAMBRIDGE ANCIENT HISTORY

VOLUME II
PART 2

THE
CAMBRIDGE
ANCIENT HISTORY

THIRD EDITION

VOLUME II
PART 2

HISTORY OF THE MIDDLE EAST AND
THE AEGEAN REGION c. 1380–1000 B.C.

EDITED BY

I. E. S. EDWARDS F.B.A.
Formerly Keeper of Egyptian Antiquities, The British Museum

THE LATE C. J. GADD

N. G. L. HAMMOND F.B.A.
Professor Emeritus of Greek, University of Bristol

E. SOLLBERGER F.B.A.
Keeper of Western Asiatic Antiquities, The British Museum

CAMBRIDGE UNIVERSITY PRESS

CAMBRIDGE

LONDON   NEW YORK   NEW ROCHELLE

MELBOURNE   SYDNEY

Published by the Press Syndicate of the University of Cambridge
The Pitt Building, Trumpington Street, Cambridge CB2 1RP
32 East 57th Street, New York, NY 10022, USA
296 Beaconsfield Parade, Middle Park, Melbourne 3206

This edition first published 1975
First paperback edition 1980

Printed in Great Britain at the
University Press, Cambridge

British Library Cataloguing in Publication Data
The Cambridge ancient history – 3rd ed.
Vol. 2. Part 2: The Middle East
and the Aegean Region *c.* 180–1380 B.C.
1. History, Ancient
I. Edwards, Iorwerth Eiddon Stephen
930   D57   75–85719
ISBN 0 521 08691 4 hard covers
ISBN 0 521 29824 5 paperback

CONTENTS

CHAPTER XVII

THE STRUGGLE FOR THE DOMINATION OF SYRIA
(1400–1300 B.C.)

by A. GOETZE

CHAPTER XVIII

ASSYRIA AND BABYLON
c. 1370–1300 B.C.

by C. J. GADD, F.B.A.

[v]

CONTENTS

(b) CYPRUS IN THE LATE BRONZE AGE

by H. W. CATLING

CHAPTER XXIII

EGYPT: FROM THE INCEPTION OF THE NINETEENTH DYNASTY TO THE DEATH OF RAMESSES III

by R. O. FAULKNER

CHAPTER XXIV

THE HITTITES AND SYRIA (1300–1200 B.C.)

by A. GOETZE

CHAPTER XXV

ASSYRIAN MILITARY POWER 1300–1200 B.C.

by J. M. MUNN-RANKIN

CHAPTER XXXI

ASSYRIA AND BABYLONIA
c. 1200–1000 B.C.

by D. J. WISEMAN

CHAPTER XXXII

ELAM AND WESTERN PERSIA,
c. 1200–1000 B.C.

by RENÉ LABAT

CHAPTER XXXIII

SYRIA, THE PHILISTINES, AND PHOENICIA

by W. F. ALBRIGHT

CHAPTER XXXIV

THE HEBREW KINGDOM

by O. EISSFELDT

CHAPTER XXXV

EGYPT: FROM THE DEATH OF RAMESSES III TO THE END OF THE TWENTY-FIRST DYNASTY

by J. ČERNÝ

CHAPTER XXXVI

THE END OF MYCENAEAN CIVILIZATION AND THE DARK AGE

(a) THE ARCHAEOLOGICAL BACKGROUND

by V. R. D'A. DESBOROUGH

(b) THE LITERARY TRADITION FOR THE MIGRATIONS

by N. G. L. HAMMOND

CONTENTS

CHAPTER XXXVII

THE WESTERN MEDITERRANEAN

by GLYN DANIEL

and J. D. EVANS

CHAPTER XXXVIII

GREEK SETTLEMENT IN THE EASTERN AEGEAN AND ASIA MINOR

by J. M. COOK

CHAPTER XXXIX(*a*)

THE PREHISTORY OF THE GREEK LANGUAGE

by JOHN CHADWICK

BIBLIOGRAPHIES

MAPS

TEXT-FIGURES

PREFACE

FOR very different reasons the two kings who lived at the beginning of the period to which this part of the *History* is devoted have received more attention in modern times than any of their predecessors or successors on the Egyptian throne: Akhenaten, on account of his religious and artistic innovations, and Tutankhamun, on account of the chance survival of his tomb at Thebes with its fabulous contents untouched since antiquity until its discovery in 1922. Neither of them was accepted as having been a legitimate ruler worthy of inclusion in the king-lists of the Nineteenth Dynasty kings Sethos I and Ramesses II, as recorded in their temples at Abydos. While they and their successors until the end of the Twenty-first Dynasty occupied the throne of Egypt, important events were happening in Western Asia, the course of which is traced in this volume. The long Kassite rule in Babylonia came to an end and the rivalry between Assyria and Babylonia began. The Hittite empire reached its peak, declined and fell, as did the Elamite kingdom in Persia. The Phrygians appeared on the scene for the first time. Along the Mediterranean shores, in Phoenicia and in Ugarit new forms of writing were developed. Palestine emerged from its long period of anonymity with the rise of the Hebrew kingdom culminating in the reign of Solomon. Inevitably some of these events and others too, such as the southern movement of the so-called Sea Peoples, affected Egypt either directly or indirectly and she was fortunate in having on the throne a succession of warrior-kings who were able to ward off the worst of the threats to their country's independence either by military action or by judicious diplomacy. Indecisive battles between the Hittites and the Egyptians under Sethos I and Ramesses II ended with a peace-treaty which was honoured by both nations until the Hittites had ceased to be a power in Western Asia and the Sea Peoples had taken their place as the most serious menace to Egypt. The first clash came in the reign of Merneptah when the Sea Peoples, in alliance with the Libyans, invaded the western Delta but were beaten in a six-hour battle in which they suffered heavy losses. Further battles on land, outside Egyptian territory to the north-east, and in one of the mouths of the Nile, fought by Egypt's last great pharaoh, Ramesses III, proved more conclusive and the danger of invasion from the

north was removed. The Libyans, however, in spite of being
driven back by Ramesses III, continued to encroach on Egyptian
soil and ultimately, under his weak successors of the same name,
they set up communities in the Delta and at Heracleopolis, near
the entrance to the Faiyūm. Their relations with the native population are not easy to understand. On the one hand Libyan bands
are reported as harrying workers in the royal necropolis as far
south as Thebes, and on the other hand Libyans served as mercenaries in the Egyptian army. Not very many years after their
arrival a descendant of one of the chiefs of the Libyan community
at Heracleopolis named Sheshonq was able to establish himself
on the throne as king of Egypt, but his reign lies outside the scope
of this volume.

The central theme in the Aegean region is the spread of
Mycenaean civilization. Although deeply influenced by Minoan
culture, the rulers and the upper classes of the Mycenaeans imposed their own pattern upon the outlook and the art of the
peoples of the mainland. They built strongly fortified castles,
organized their realms into powerful kingdoms and made conquests overseas. In the fourteenth century, when the Mycenaean
civilization was at its zenith, the overseas settlements extended
from Acragas and Syracuse in Sicily to Miletus in Asia Minor
and to Cyprus. At this time when the civilizations of the Near
East enjoyed a high level of prosperity and the resources of
Europe and the Western Mediterranean were being developed,
especially in minerals, the Mycenaeans held the intermediate
zone through which most of the seaborne traffic passed between
Europe, Africa and Asia. Mycenaean objects and Mycenaean
traders reached many distant parts of the world, and the Greek
language was enriched by contact with many peoples. Mycenaean experiences were incorporated in the myths which were to
be transmitted to the Classical world and to modern times, and the
foundations of Greek religion were laid in a Minoan–Mycenaean
context which was itself influenced by the other religions of the
Near East.

The decline of the Mycenaean civilization was a result of a
general deterioration of trade and a dislocation of political conditions, to which the Mycenaean states themselves contributed by
attacking one another and by destroying Troy. The Aegean
Bronze Age drew to its end with the migrations of less civilized
peoples into the Balkan peninsula and Asia Minor, which led in
their turn to the migrations of Greek-speaking peoples from the
North into Greece and from Mycenaean Greece to Crete, Cyprus,

Asia Minor and other places. It was in this final stage of the Mycenaean world that the expedition of Agamemnon against Troy took its place in Greek legend and provided Homer, centuries later, with the theme of the *Iliad*. The prehistoric cultures of the Western Mediterranean region, including the islands and the coastal lands, are described in Chapter xxxvii, and the account is carried down to the arrival of migrants and colonists from the Eastern Mediterranean in the Early Iron Age.

Four contributors wish to express their gratitude to other scholars for giving them assistance: Dr R. D. Barnett to Dr J. Chadwick, Dr M. and Dr T. Dothan and Professor O. R. Gurney in his revision of Chapter xxviii, and to Professor Gurney, Mr J. D. Hawkins and Dr G. I. Martin in his revision of Chapter xxx; Professor D. J. Wiseman to Professor J. A. Brinkman for generously placing at his disposal the manuscript of his doctoral thesis (see the bibliography to Chapter xxxi, G, 2 and A, 3), and allowing him to use it freely when writing Chapter xxxi; Professor J. M. Cook to Mr R. V. Nicholls; Professor W. K. C. Guthrie and the Editors to Mrs Helen Hughes-Brock for additions to the bibliography of Chapter xl. The Editors are also indebted to Dr Chadwick for the generous help which he has given in matters deriving from the decipherment of Linear Script B.

The task of the Editors has been greatly facilitated by the friendly cooperation which they have received from the staff of the Cambridge University Press and they wish to thank them both for the readiness with which they have given it and for their patience in enduring the delay which has attended the submission of the text to the printer. Several contributors have availed themselves of the invitation of the Syndics to revise their chapters, and they, as well as the Editors, are grateful for the opportunity thus afforded to make use of information which was not available when the chapters appeared in fascicle form.

It is with sadness that the Editors record the deaths of no fewer than seven contributors since the publication of the previous part: Professors W. F. Albright, J. Černý, O. Eissfeldt, C. W. Blegen, A. Goetze, R. Labat and R. de Vaux.

Chapters xxix and xxxii by Professor Labat were originally written in French and were translated into English by Mr D. A. Kennedy of the Centre national de la recherche scientifique, Paris.

I.E.S.E.
N.G.L.H.
E.S.

CHAPTER XVII

THE STRUGGLE FOR THE DOMINATION
OF SYRIA (1400–1300 B.C.)

I. MITANNIANS AND HITTITES—TUSHRATTA
AND SHUPPILULIUMASH

SYRIA lies at the crossroads of the Near East between Mesopotamia in the east, Anatolia in the north and Egypt in the south. Both Mesopotamia and Anatolia are lacking in indispensable raw materials which they must acquire by trade. For them, then, Syria means access to world trade. Through Syria pass the overland communications that lead from one to the other. More significant still, Syria possesses ports where merchandise from far-away countries is received and exchanged for whatever Asia has to offer. By land and by sea Syria is also linked to Egypt, another important centre of ancient civilization. For these reasons all political development in the Near East tends toward the domination of Syria by its neighbours. In antiquity possession of this key position assured supremacy in the world as it then existed. The fourteenth century, a period of intensive interrelations among all parts of the world, was no exception. In fact, the struggle for the domination of Syria was never more marked than during this period.

The efforts of the various powers involved in the struggle were facilitated by the ethnic and social conditions which they encountered when they invaded Syria. The Amorite rule over the country had created a large number of small city-states which were organized along feudalistic lines. This had become more accentuated when the Hurrians, revitalized by Indo-Aryan dynasts, had expanded from Upper Mesopotamia toward the west. Hurrian knights had then replaced the Amorite princes, taken over the best parts of the land for themselves and their liegemen (*mariyanna*), and now formed a caste of their own. Thus the rift between the rulers and the ruled was not only economic and social, it was ethnic as well. Anyone who gained the co-operation of the upper class could easily dominate their countries.

Egyptian power had been omnipotent in Syria in the days of

* An original version of this chapter was published in fascicle 37 in 1965.

the great Tuthmosis III. During the reigns of his successors it was definitely on the decline, until under Amenophis III (1417–1379) Egyptian domination was only nominal. The most important source illustrating these conditions is the Amarna letters, the remnants of the political archives of Amenophis III and IV. Found in the ruins of Amenophis IV's palace at Amarna they have given the name 'Amarna Age' to the whole period which they cover. The Amarna letters consist of the messages, mostly composed in Akkadian and all of them written in cuneiform script on clay tablets, which had been sent to the Egyptian court by the contemporary rulers of the great powers in neighbouring Asia and by the numerous independent princes of Palestine and Syria. At the period in question Egyptian officers, appointed to supervise and control the local princes and to collect the tribute which these had to pay to the pharaoh, still resided in the area. The Akkadian sources call such an officer *rābiṣu*, literally 'watcher, observer', the corresponding word in the Semitic vernacular of the country being *šākinu* (Canaanite *sōkinu*). During our period, the cities of Kumidu and Ṣumura served as residences for these 'commissioners' or 'regents' of Syria. Both these cities are strategically located. The former blocks the passage through the Biqāʿ, the narrow plain between the Lebanon in the west and the Anti-Lebanon and the Hermon in the east; it is close enough to Damascus to control it as well. The latter is situated on the coastal highway, near the mouth of the Eleutheros River, and also dominates the road which leads eastward along that river to the Orontes Valley. Along the coast Egyptian control was firmer than inland. When roads were disrupted there was always the sea route to maintain communications with Egypt.

The Mitanni kings ruled in Upper Mesopotamia with their capital Washshuganni probably near the Upper Khabur River, and the influence which they exercised upon Syria no doubt depended on the fact that since the days of the Hurrian expansion many, if not most, of the small states there had passed into the hands of Hurrian princes. In the days of Egyptian weakness, the Mitannian kings used this circumstance to create a kind of Hurrian confederacy which was controlled from their capital. Mitannian power was at its height at the beginning of the fourteenth century.

It had then taken the place of the Hittites as the dominating factor. With the decline of Egyptian might after the death of Tuthmosis III the Hittites had, with considerable success, tried to re-establish themselves in Syria where they had ruled during their 'Old Kingdom'. But when their homeland on the Anatolian plateau had been attacked from all sides in the times of Tud-khaliash III, they had been forced to withdraw from Syria. Yet their power continued to loom in the background as a factor with which to reckon.

The interplay of all these forces—the Egyptians, the Mitannians with their Hurrian partisans and finally the Hittites—determined the fate of Syria in the fourteenth century.

Since the middle of the second millennium the dynasty which called itself 'kings of Mitanni (Maitani)' had become dominant among the Hurrians.[1] From Washshuganni it exercised power eastward over Assyria and the East Tigris regions, northward over the country which later became Armenia, and westward into Syria.

Within the Hurrian realm there existed a rivalry between the kings of Mitanni and those who called themselves 'kings of the Khurri Land'. This must refer to a Khurri Land in the narrower sense of the term. The border dividing this Khurri Land from the Mitanni kingdom apparently ran along the River Mala, i.e. the Euphrates (Murad Su?). It seems that the Khurri Land had been the older of the two, but that Mitanni had overtaken it in power and political importance. Tushratta, the younger son of a Shuttarna who had been an older contemporary of Amenophis III,[2] had acquired kingship over Mitanni in irregular fashion. Shuttarna had first been succeeded by his son Artashuwara. He was slain, however, by a certain Utkhi (UD-ḫi), a high officer of the state, and Tushratta (Tuišeratta), a younger brother, then still a minor, was installed on the throne.[3] Artatama of Khurri apparently did not recognize Tushratta as his overlord; on the contrary he seems to have claimed at least independence if not more. Judgement on the situation is rendered difficult by the circumstance that the earlier relations of the two rivalling states are not known to us. According to the beliefs of the time, the struggle which ensued between Tushratta and Artatama was conceived as a lawsuit between the two opponents pending before the gods.[4]

The date of Tushratta's accession to the throne falls within the reign of Amenophis III (1417–1379), more precisely into its second half. The Amarna archive has yielded seven letters from Tushratta to Amenophis III,[5] an indication that their friendly

---

[1] See *C.A.H.* II[3], pt. 1, pp. 422 ff.

[2] EA 17, 21. [For brevity, EA in footnotes to this chapter refers to the Amarna letters (and their lines) as numbered in G, 12.]

[3] *Ibid.* 1–20. [4] §1, 8, no. 1, obv. 48 f.

[5] EA 17–21; 23 (Amenophis III, year 36); 24.

relationship was maintained over a number of years. We may estimate that Tushratta's reign is to be counted from about 1385.

Whatever territory Artatama of Khurri may have controlled,
Tushratta was able to maintain himself in the Mitanni kingdom
for the time being. This included, in addition to Assyria and the
adjoining provinces in the east, Upper Mesopotamia and parts of
Syria. There, more specifically, the following territories were under
his overlordship. Farthest north, in Cilicia and bordering on the
Mediterranean lay Kizzuwadna.[1] For a long time it had shifted
its allegiance back and forth between Khatti and Mitanni. The
collapse of Hittite power under Tudkhaliash III had driven it
again into the arms of the Mitannians.[2] Something similar may
have happened to Ishuwa, farther east,[3] although nothing precise
is known about it. In Syria proper the kingdoms of Carchemish
and Aleppo were most important; in the circumstances, neither
can have been independent of Mitanni. For the first this is confirmed by the role it played in the later Hittite war of conquest;
for Aleppo there is documentary proof that it once formed part of
the Hurrian system of states.[4] Further to the south were located
the countries of Mukish (with its capital at Alalakh) and Ugarit.
Formal relations with the Mitanni state are assured for the
former;[5] for Ugarit this remains doubtful. Its position on the
coast may well have resulted in conditions different from those
which prevailed inland; under the protection of Egypt, Ugarit
may have maintained a precarious kind of independence. The
Nukhash Lands, between the bend of the Euphrates and the
Orontes, definitely belonged to Tushratta's realm.[6] In the Orontes
valley we find Neya (Ne'a), Arakhtu, and Ukulzat ruled by
Hurrian dynasties[7] which no doubt maintained friendly relations
with the Mitanni king. Finally there are, in the far south of
Syria, Qatna, Kinza (Kidsa = Qadesh on the Orontes), and
Amurru. Here Mitannian influence was counterbalanced by the
Egyptians, and local princes found it necessary to play the dan-
gerous game of aligning themselves on one side or the other, as
circumstances required.

Tushratta at first experienced no unpleasantness in his relations
with the Hittite kingdom. As long as the Hittites remained re-
coiled upon their Anatolian homeland and maintained themselves
with difficulties, there was no opportunity for friction.

[1] §1, 4.   [2] §1, 8, no. 7, i, 7, 38.
[3] §1, 8, no. 1, obv. 10 ff.; no. 7, i. 8.   [4] §1, 8, no. 6, obv. 23; cf. §1, 3.
[5] §1, 9, nos. 13 and 14.   [6] §1, 8, no. 3, i, 2 ff.; §1, 6, i, 4 ff.
[7] §1, 8, no. 1, obv. 31 ff

The relations of Mitanni with Egypt were friendly. Friendship with Egypt had been a traditional policy of the Mitanni kings for several generations. A number of marriages had taken place between the royal houses. Artatama, Tushratta's grandfather, had sent one of his daughters to the pharaoh,[1] and Shuttarna, his father, had given his daughter Gilu-Kheba in marriage to Amenophis III[2] (an event which falls into that king's tenth year,[3] i.e. about 1408). Tushratta himself was to continue this policy by sending one of his daughters, Tadu-Kheba, for the pharaoh's harim.[4]

The inactivity of the Egyptians in Syria made it possible for Tushratta to remain on friendly terms with Amenophis III during all of the latter's reign. When it is realized that this was so in spite of the expansionist tendencies of Mitanni in Syria, one is led to assume that a formal understanding must have existed by which the coast of Syria and all of Palestine, including the region of Damascus, was recognized as an Egyptian sphere of influence, the rest of Syria being considered as Mitannian domain. During the later part of Tushratta's reign, good relations with Egypt became more and more a necessity, because a powerful personality had in the meantime ascended the Hittite throne and had initiated a period of Hittite renascence.

Probably not long after the events which brought Tushratta to the throne of Mitanni (c. 1385), a shift of rulership also took place in the Hittite country. Under Tudkhaliash III the previously mighty kingdom had shrunk into insignificance from which it had only partially recovered before the king's death.[5] If some of the lost territory, especially along the eastern border had been regained, this had been due to the military leadership of the king's son, Shuppiluliumash.[6]

Upon his father's death Shuppiluliumash became king as the next in line. In him there came to the throne a powerful man who was destined to restore the might of his country and to secure for it a position second to none. The ambitions which must have spurred Shuppiluliumash from the outset made him cast his eyes almost automatically upon Syria, where earlier Hittite kings had won glory. Hence an armed conflict with Tushratta became inevitable. It was postponed for some time only because Shuppiluliumash had to reorganize his homeland before he could think of embarking on a war of conquest in Syria.

---

[1] EA 24, iii, 52 ff.; 29, 21 ff.   [2] EA 17, 26 ff.; 29, 21 ff.
[3] G, 17, sect. 866.   [4] EA 19, 17 ff.; 22, iv, 43 ff.
[5] G, 4, vi, 28, obv. 6 ff. (cf. §1, 4, 21 ff.).
[6] See below, p. 117.

This was done with comparative ease, for the Hittite system of government was more firmly knit than that of the Mitannians. The ruling class among the Hittites had long since become amalgamated with the Anatolian population. Strong feudalistic tendencies still lingered on, but as a whole the Khatti Land proper was now governed by officials who were appointed by the king, preferably members of the royal family. Around this inner core of the kingdom an outer ring of vassal states had been formed. Their rulers had concluded formal treaties with the 'Great King' and received back their lands from his hands. They had surrendered to him part of their sovereignty, above all the right to conduct an independent foreign policy. There was a marked trend toward assuring the loyalty of these vassals by tying them to the royal house of Khatti by intermarriage.[1]

The accession of Shuppiluliumash to the Hittite throne can be dated only approximately. It falls within the reign of Amenophis III[2] (c. 1417–1379), and probably later than the beginning of Tushratta's reign which was estimated above as having taken place c. 1385. It can be set at approximately 1380.

The first clash between the two adversaries must have occurred soon after Shuppiluliumash ascended the throne. Tushratta, in one of his letters to Amenophis III, tells about a victory in which he claims to have crushed an invading Hittite army.[3] The letter in which the report is contained is very likely the first of the letters directed to that pharaoh which have been preserved. It seems, then, that Shuppiluliumash failed in his early attempts at expansion toward the south. One may well doubt, however, that it was anything more than a testing raid.

The military situation was not yet such as to encourage Shuppiluliumash to conduct operations on a larger scale. At the beginning of his reign, the Khatti Land and the country of Mitanni had only a comparatively short border in common. It became more extended when Shuppiluliumash recovered Ishuwa which his father had lost.[4] But even then, for the larger part of the distance between the Upper Euphrates and the Mediterranean Sea, the two countries were separated by Kizzuwadna. It must have been one of the first tasks of the young king to come to terms with this buffer state. The result of his efforts is contained in the treaty which he concluded with Shunashshura, the king of Kizzuwadna.[5]

[1] G, 22, 99 ff.   [2] EA 41, 7.
[3] EA 17, 30 ff.; 45.
[4] §1, 8, no. 1, obv. 10 ff.; G, 4, vi, 28, obv. 12 (cf. §1, 4, 21 ff.).
[5] §1, 8, no. 7; cf. §1, 4, 36 ff.

Large parts of an Akkadian version and parts of a parallel Hittite version have survived. The salient fact in the treaty is that Kizzuwadna renounced its affiliation with the Mitanni kingdom and forthwith returned to the Hittite sphere of influence.[1] Shunash-shura was treated by Shuppiluliumash with some consideration and granted certain privileges. This does not alter the fact that he had to surrender essential parts of his sovereignty, especially the right to maintain such relations with foreign countries as suited himself. The common frontier was revised.[2]

Shuppiluliumash also reached an agreement with Artatama, the king of the Khurri Land.[3] In view of the enmity that existed between Tushratta and Artatama—their law-suit was still pending before the gods—this must have been comparatively easy. From Artatama's point of view, Tushratta was a rebel and a usurper. The text of the treaty has not come down to us, but there is every reason to believe that Shuppiluliumash treated Artatama as a 'Great King', i.e. his equal; there is certainly no doubt that the treaty was directed against Tushratta. In all likelihood, Artatama promised at least benevolent neutrality in the impending conflict. This relieved Shuppiluliumash of the fear that the Hurrian might try to interfere in favour of the Mitannian; it thus enabled him to concentrate all his might against the latter. No wonder then that Tushratta considered the conclusion of the treaty as a *casus belli*.[4]

The relations of Shuppiluliumash with Egypt at that moment conformed with the diplomatic customs of the time, but were rather cool. The Hittite had good reason for keeping them correct. He had exchanged courteous messages with Amenophis III; we possess the letter which he wrote to Amenophis IV (1379–1362) when the latter assumed kingship.[5] It betrays a certain tension between the two countries. This is easily understandable when it is recalled that family ties existed between the pharaoh and Tushratta, Tadu-Kheba his daughter having been given in marriage to Amenophis III from whose harim she was transferred to that of Amenophis IV. Furthermore, the Egyptians must gradually have grown apprehensive of the Hittite's intentions. One may rather feel surprised that relations between Khatti and Egypt remained as undisturbed as they apparently did for so long. The situation suggests that Amenophis IV had no desire whatever to become involved in what he considered the internal affairs of Syria and to provide Tushratta with more than nominal support. Tushratta may

---

[1] §1, 8, no. 7, i, 30 ff.
[3] §1, 8, no. 1, obv. 1 ff.
[5] EA 41.

[2] §1, 8, no. 7, iv, 40 ff.
[4] §1, 8, no. 1, obv. 2 f.

have hoped for more active assistance, and, when none was forth-coming, his feelings toward the pharaoh became increasingly cool. His three extant letters to Amenophis IV[1] show a growing ani-mosity, and it may well be that after the third the correspondence was actually discontinued.

II. THE FIRST SYRIAN WAR OF SHUPPILULIUMASH

When the Hittite attack finally came, Tushratta proved unable to keep his hold on Syria. Shuppuliumash moved at will, and all the country between the Euphrates and the Mediterranean Sea as far south as the Lebanon fell prey to the invader.[2] One may assume that see-sawing battles took place before a firm frontier was finally established. As a matter of fact, existing reports—if they belong here—suggest that Tushratta conducted a counter-campaign in Syria. He is said to have reached Ṣumura (which had been before, and was later, an Egyptian stronghold) and to have tried to cap-ture Gubla (Byblos), but to have been forced to retreat by lack of water.[3] Was this a mere show of force or was it an attempt at creating a line which made it possible for him to maintain contact with the Hurrian princes in southern Syria and ultimately with Egypt? If so, it was of no avail; the Hittite king's might proved overpowering. The most loyal partisan whom the pharaoh had in Syria, Rib-Adda of Gubla, sums up the result of the campaign in the following words:[4] 'The king, my lord, should be advised that the Hittite king has taken over all the countries affiliated(?) with the king of the Mita(nni) land, i.e.(?) the king of Nakh(ri)ma' (probably meaning Naharina, the name under which the Mitanni country was known in Egypt).

This move had brought Shuppuliumash right to the border of the territory over which Egypt not only claimed, but in some fashion also exercised sovereignty. Shuppuliumash halted here. He could not wish to antagonize the pharaoh unnecessarily at a time when Tushratta was far from completely defeated. To be sure, the Mitanni king was no longer undisputed ruler of Syria. But he may still have held open a line of communication with Egypt by way of Kinza. At any rate, Kinza defied the Hittites for a long time to come and was considered by them, even after Tushratta's down-fall, as part of Egypt's sphere of influence (see below, pp. 15 f.). At

---

[1] EA 27 (Amenophis IV, year 2); 28; 29.
[2] §1, 8, no. 1, obv. 4 ff.   [3] EA 85, 51 ff.; cf. 58, 5 ff.
[4] EA 75, 35 ff.

the present moment Tushratta still ruled over his homeland in Upper Mesopotamia as well as all his eastern provinces.

Moreover, there existed a treaty of long standing between the Hittites and Egypt. It had been concluded when people of the Anatolian town of Kurushtama had been transferred (in a somewhat mysterious way) to Egyptian territory to become subjects of the pharaoh.[1] It is unknown who precisely had been the contractants, but the political situation suggests that on the Egyptian side it must have been one of the pharaohs who still controlled Syria, and on the Hittite side a king who still held at least the Taurus frontier, i.e. a king reigning before the rebellion against Tudkhaliash, father of Shuppiluliumash. It must go back to the time before the Mitannians had come on to the scene and separated the two great western powers. The treaty had almost been forgotten; it acquired new actuality only when conquest reconstituted a common frontier between them.

It is difficult to assign an exact date to this first great success of the Hittite king. It seems clear, however, from the sources that the event took place during the lifetime of 'Abdi-Ashirta of Amurru (see below) whose death occurred late in the reign of Amenophis IV, perhaps about 1365.

The Hittite victory upset the order in Syria; it destroyed Mitannian control, but it did not replace it as yet with an equally firm Hittite rule. Some of the Syrian states became Hittite vassals, a development which made them susceptible to Mitannian vengeance. Others were freed from their old obligations and thus enabled to follow their own particularistic ambitions.

To safeguard access to his Syrian dependencies Shuppiluliumash installed, perhaps at this time, his son Telepinush as the local ruler ('priest') in the holy city of Kumanni (Comana Cappadociae). The pertinent decree has come down to us in the name of the great king, his second queen Khenti, and the crown prince Arnuwandash.[2]

The Syrian states in the north, the territories of which were contiguous with former Hittite possessions, were reduced to vassalage. The most important among them was the state of Aleppo (Khalap). So far we have no direct testimony for a treaty between Shuppiluliumash and the king of Aleppo. We may take it for granted, however, that such a treaty must have existed.[3] The same can be assumed for Mukish (Alalakh).[4] The treaty between Shuppiluliumash and Tunip, remnants of which have survived,[5] may belong

1 §II, 5, 208 ff.; §II, 1; 7; 8; 9; 10.
2 G, 1, xix, 25 (cf. §I, 4, 12 ff.).   3 §I, 8, no. 3, ii, 14.
4 *Ibid.*   5 §I, 8, no. 10.

to this period. As far as Ugarit on the coast is concerned, it is unlikely that it submitted at that time. Protected as it is by mountain ranges toward the plains of the north, it could feel reasonably safe. There are indications that Ammishtamru remained true to his obligations toward Egypt.[1] His son Niqmaddu who later had to submit to Shuppiluliumash still corresponded with the pharaoh[2] and even seems to have married an Egyptian princess.[3] A treaty between Shuppiluliumash and the Nukhash Lands, the territories south of Aleppo, is definitely attested; the ruler of that region was at that time Sharrupsha.[4]

It goes without saying that Tushratta could not accept without a fight the loss even of northern Syria. In fact, we know that he reacted violently. He could not but regard the conclusion of a treaty with the Hittites on the part of the king of the Nukhash Lands as a treasonable action. Aided by a local pro-Mitannian party, an armed invasion of Nukhash by a Mitannian army was temporarily successful, but was ultimately repulsed.[5]

In other countries, e.g. in Neya and Arakhtu, partisans of the Mitannians must also have existed. After all, the ruling class was largely Hurrian in origin. Shuppiluliumash proved his deep mistrust of them when later, after his final conquest, he exiled most of these families to Anatolia. He probably had experienced difficulties with them. Of course, the position in which these dynasts found themselves was in no way enviable. They were caught between the three parties to the conflict: Tushratta, Egypt, and now the Hittites. The bolder among them tried to exploit the situation for their own ends and avoided commitments and eventual submission to any of the great powers. Such men were to be found particularly in southern Syria. There Mitannian supremacy had been broken, Egyptian domination was an empty claim, but Hittite influence was still too weak to demand unquestioned recognition. The princes of Amurru in particular took advantage of the opportunity that presented itself.

The kings of Amurru, 'Abdi-Ashirta and his son Aziru after him, were easily the most restive personalities in Syria at this time. A country Amurru had existed there at least since the Mari Age; it apparently lay west of the middle Orontes. Reactivated by Ḥapiru people it now showed a marked tendency to expand toward the Mediterranean coast; gradually it gained a foothold between Ṣumura in the south and Ugarit in the north. This had

---

[1] EA 45 (cf. Nougayrol, J., *Le Palais royal d'Ugarit*, III, p. xxxvii). See below, pp. 137 ff.   [2] EA 49 (cf. Nougayrol, *loc. cit.*).
[3] G, 16, 164 ff.   [4] §1, 8, no. 3, i, 2 ff.   [5] *Ibid.* 4 ff.

happened before Shuppiluliumash appeared on the scene. Already Amenophis III had had to recognize 'Abdi-Ashirta as the Amurrite chief; he had even tried to use him as a tool of Egyptian policy in order to check Tushratta's Syrian schemes.[1] Rib-Adda of Gubla (Byblos), who was to become the foremost victim of the Amurrite, dates the beginning of his troubles from a visit that Amenophis III had paid to Sidon.[2] The Hittite conquest of northern Syria did not make Rib-Adda's situation any less dangerous. On the contrary it removed every restraint that had held back 'Abdi-Ashirta. Egyptian control had ceased for all practical purposes. Pakham-nate, the Egyptian 'commissioner', had to give up his residence Ṣumura and probably returned to Egypt.[3] 'Abdi-Ashirta stepped into the gap thus created; in doing so he seems to have obtained the official sanction of the pharaoh.[4] He used his enhanced position to expand inland toward Damascus and to get a firmer hold on the coast, to the dismay of Rib-Adda of Gubla. The territory con-trolled by this tragic champion of Egyptian rule began to dwindle; his ever-repeated complaints and his incessant demands for help were not taken seriously by the pharaoh. Neither did his southern neighbours comply with his calls for help. In consequence, Ṣumura fell.[5] Then the rulers of the town of Irqata and Ambi were murdered at the instigation of 'Abdi-Ashirta, and these places, together with Shigata and Ardata, were taken by the Amurrite.[6] The appointment of Kha'ip (Ḫa'api) as the new Egyptian com-missioner[7] did not arrest this development. 'Abdi-Ashirta, Rib-Adda says, acted as though he were the Mitanni king and the Kassite king all in one.[8] Gubla itself was seriously threatened.[9] It was saved at the last moment when, after Bīt-Arkha[10] and Batruna,[11] the last possessions of the prince of Gubla, had fallen, the Egyptian general Amanappa finally appeared with some troops.[12]

Ṣumura and the other towns just mentioned are later in Egyp-tian hands again.[13] Their recapture perhaps took place in con-nexion with the events that led to 'Abdi-Ashirta's death. This fierce fighter, whose activities in the interest of Amurru, his country, had been troublesome for many of his contemporaries, was at last slain, no matter in what way.[14] His death did not, however, change the situation materially. After a temporary set-

[1] EA 101, 30 f.
[2] EA 85, 69 ff.
[3] EA 62; cf. 67.
[4] EA 101, 30.
[5] EA 83, 11 ff. (cf. 67, 17 f.); 91, 6.
[6] EA 74, 23 ff.; 75, 25 ff.
[7] EA 71, 7 ff.
[8] EA 76, 9 ff. (cf. 104, 19 ff.).
[9] EA 78, 11 ff.
[10] EA 79, 21; 83, 29; 91, 8 f.
[11] EA 87, 18 ff.; 88, 15 f.; 90, 14 ff.
[12] EA 79, 7 ff.; cf. 117, 23.
[13] EA 106; 107; 112.
[14] EA 101, 2 ff.; cf. §1, 5, 27 f.

back, the people of Amurru, now led by Aziru, 'Abdi-Ashirta's son, resumed their activities with renewed vigour. Very soon Irqata, Ambi, Shigata and Ardata were reoccupied by them.[1] Ṣumura did not fall at once; it was besieged and could for some time be reached only by boat.[2] The Egyptians made an effort to hold it, and the commissioner of Ṣumura was killed in the fight.[3] But the Egyptians finally had to evacuate their troops from the city.[4] Rib-Adda, now left alone, faced a hopeless situation, particularly when Zimredda of Sidon allied himself with Aziru.[5] Finally Gubla alone was left in his possession,[6] and it too fell[7] when intrigues compelled Rib-Adda to flee his hometown; he met a—probably violent—death in exile.[8] At the same time Aziru took possession of Neya.[9] All this seems to have taken place shortly before, or at the very beginning of, the second war in Syria.[10]

It is quite likely that already at that time some understanding had been reached between Shuppiluliumash and Aziru.[11] It need not necessarily have consisted of a formal treaty. At repeated times Aziru calls the pharaoh's attention to the fact that the Hittite stands in the Nukhash Lands,[12] as though to remind him he might be forced to throw in his lot with the northerners. But, at the height of the threatening crisis, and before Shuppiluliumash was able to advance further to the south, the pharaoh called the Amurrite to Egypt.[13] The correct interpretation of this act is probably an attempt at removing from the scene at the decisive moment the potentially most dangerous man. The pharaoh may even have hoped to draw Aziru over to his side, assigning him a role in a scheme for the preservation of Egyptian influence in Syria. Be this as it may, Aziru complied and, once there, played his ambiguous game with political skill and cleverness. His son, left at home, had to listen to accusations that he had sold his father to Egypt.[14] But Aziru eventually returned from the court of the pharaoh unharmed. His treaty with Niqmaddu of Ugarit,[15] which greatly strengthened his position in Syria, may have looked as though inspired by Egypt. It revealed its real import only when

[1] EA 98, 10 ff.; 104, 10 ff.; 40 ff.; 140, 14 ff.
[2] EA 98, 12 ff.   [3] EA 106, 22; 132, 45.
[4] EA 103, 11 ff.; 132, 42 f.; 149, 37 ff., 67.
[5] EA 103, 17 ff.; 106, 20; 149, 57 ff.
[6] EA 126, 37 ff.   [7] EA 136–138.
[8] EA 162.   [9] EA 59, 27 f.
[10] EA 126, 51 ff.; 129, 76   [11] §II, 3, no. 1, obv. 2 f.
[12] EA 164, 21 ff.; 165, 18 ff.; 166, 21 ff.; 167, 11 ff.
[13] EA 161, 22 ff.; 164, 20; 165, 14 ff.
[14] EA 169, 17 ff.   [15] G, 15, 284 ff.

shortly thereafter,[1] it seems, he also entered into a formal pact with Shuppiluliumash.[2] Thereby he took finally his place in the Hittite system of states.

At about the same time Shuppiluliumash took another step of a highly political nature: he married a Babylonian princess. Assuming the name Tawannannash, a name which the first queen of the Hittites had borne in the old days, she also became reigning queen.[3] The purpose is clear: in anticipation of the attack on Tushratta of Mitanni, Shuppiluliumash sought protection of his rear. Burnaburiash must then have been king in Babylon.

III. THE SECOND SYRIAN WAR OF SHUPPILULIUMASH

His rival's earlier successes had alerted Tushratta to the things to come. Naturally he had tried to reassert his power. We know of two counter-measures he took. He interfered in the Nukhash Lands deposing Sharrupsha;[4] he also initiated an anti-Hittite action further toward the north in Ishuwa.[5] This gave Shuppiluliumash the pretext for his final attack. He declared that the Nukhash Lands were 'rebels'—neighbouring Mukish and Neya were likewise involved[6]—and that the Mitannian had acted with arrogant presumptuousness.[7]

At the same time he had prepared himself with circumspection. Approaching Ugarit beforehand he proposed a treaty of mutual peace which, in the circumstances, can only have been favourable to the small country where Niqmaddu, the son of Ammishtamru, then reigned.[8] In this way he kept his right flank secure; sending a detachment to the Nukhash Lands,[9] he himself crossed the Euphrates into Ishuwa where Tushratta had threatened him. Having obtained King Antaratal's permission he passed through Alshe and appeared on the north-western border of the Mitanni land proper. Having there captured the forts of Kutmar and Suta, he made a swift stab at Washshuganni, the Mitannian capital. When he reached it, he found, however, that Tushratta had fled.[10]

[1] §II, 2, 380 f.
[2] §I, 8, no. 4; §II, 4; cf. §II, 3, no. 1. obv. 3 ff.
[3] §II, 6, vol. I, 6 ff.; G, 16, 98 ff.   [4] §I, 8, no. 3, i, 2 ff.
[5] §I, 8, no. 3, i, 14; no. 1, obv. 17 ff.
[6] G, 15, dossier II A 3; cf. dossier II A 1 and 2.
[7] §I, 8, no. 1, obv. 17, 45; §II, 7, frgm. 26, ii, 11 ff.
[8] G, 15, II (29 ff.).   [9] §I, 8, no. 3, i, 9.
[10] §I, 8, no. 1, obv. 17 ff.; cf. §II, 7, frgm. 26, ii, 21 ff.

He did not bother to pursue him, but turned westward; Syria was of much greater importance to him. He entered it recrossing the Euphrates from east to west, probably south of the strongly fortified Carchemish. Once on Syrian soil, one country after another fell to him. Everywhere he removed the Hurrian city-rulers who had been the mainstay of Mitannian domination and replaced them with men of his own choice. The list of the rebellious countries which Shuppiluliumash gives himself includes Aleppo, Mukish, Neya, Arakhtu, Qatna, Nukhash and Kinza,[1] the sequence most likely indicating the order in which he defeated them. The campaign ended in Apina (Damascus), i.e. in clearly Egyptian territory.[2] The negative fact is noteworthy that the report does not mention Carchemish, Ugarit and Amurru. The first probably remained independent; the two others were already bound by treaty to the Hittites.

This war had profoundly changed the overall political picture. Above all it meant the end of Tushratta and his empire. He himself may have held on for a while after his flight from Washshu-ganni; in the end he was murdered by conspirators among whom was his own son Kurtiwaza.[3] In accordance with the beliefs of the times, his death was interpreted as the final decision of Teshub (the Mitanni Land's highest god) in the long-pending lawsuit between him and the king of the Khurri Land.[4] It was now considered proven that Tushratta had usurped a throne which had not been rightfully his.

To be sure, the immediate advantage of Tushratta's downfall was not Artatama's, but went to Alshe and above all to Assyria. These two countries, freed by the Hittite victory from Mitannian overlordship, divided most of the Mitannian territory between themselves,[5] Alshe taking the north-western part and Assyria the north-eastern. The liberation of Assyria, where Ashur-uballit was then king, was an event which, unwished for and of little consequence at the moment, became of great significance later on. However, the Mitanni kingdom, although greatly reduced in area, did not entirely cease to exist; Kurtiwaza remained its ruler. A serious rival to him arose in the person of Shutatarra (Shuttarna), apparently son and successor of Artatama, who maintained, so it seems, that the Mitanni Land was now a vacant fief of the Khurri king.[6] Kurtiwaza, expelled by Shutatarra (Shuttarna) sought refuge in Kassite Babylonia; finally he appeared at the court of

---

[1] §1, 8, no. 1, obv. 30–43.
[2] §1, 8, no. 1, obv. 43 f.
[3] §1, 8, no. 1, obv. 48.
[4] §1, 8, no. 1, obv. 49 f.
[5] §1, 8, no. 2, obv. 1 ff.
[6] §1, 8, no. 2, obv. 28 ff.

Shupppiluliumash and tried to enlist the help of the Hittite king for the recovery of his throne.[1]

Of greater immediate significance for the Hittites was the new order which Shuppiluliumash, after the destruction of the Mitanni Empire, created in Syria. It was based on the system of vassal states. In northern Syria some treaties already existed, with the successors to the vanquished rebels new ones were concluded. Soon the south was also reorganized. This time Ugarit was firmly included in this system. Niqmaddu came to Alalakh, the capital of Mukish, to pay homage to Shuppiluliumash. He received his country back as a fief, the frontier toward Mukish being regulated in detail, and assumed, as usual in vassal treaties, the duty of furnishing troops in wartime and paying a yearly tribute to his overlord. The documents written out then and handed to Niqmaddu bear the seal of Shuppiluliumash and sometimes that of the Great King and his third queen Tawannannash.[2]

The treaty with Aziru of Amurru was confirmed; parts of a copy have survived.[3] Aziru proved a loyal vassal of the Hittite king for the rest of his life which lasted into the reign of Murshilish, the son of Shuppiluliumash. The treaties no doubt concluded with Mukish and Neya have not come to light. Further inland and in the south the reorganization seems to have taken somewhat longer. At first Shuppiluliumash merely removed the reigning families to Hittite territory, Eventually, however, he brought them back; probably a few years later.

Thus in the Nukhash Lands, where Tushratta had started his last war, he replaced Sharrupsha, who had lost his life in the upheaval, by his grandson Tette. The treaty concluded with him is partly preserved.[4] In Kinza Shuppiluliumash had not wanted to interfere. However, attacked by the local king, Shutatarra, and his son, he had been forced to engage himself. Defeated, they were deported, but the son, Aitakama, was eventually brought back. No doubt a formal treaty, not recovered as yet, was concluded also with him. Abi-milki of Tyre reports to Amenophis IV the fact of his restoration with obvious misgivings;[5] he may have had good reasons. For Aitakama, backed by Hittite power and seconded by Aziru, immediately sought to extend his own borders by attacking the nominally Egyptian territory on his southern frontier.[6] Not far east from Kinza, in Qatna, Aitakama found another target for his attempt at expansion. In a way not clear to

1 §1, 8, no. 2, obv. 14 ff.   2 G, 15, 30.
3 §1, 8, no. 4; §11, 2.   4 §1, 8, no. 3.
5 EA 151, 58 ff.   6 EA 140, 25 ff.

us a certain Akizzi had gained possession of the small kingdom which had been listed only a short while ago as conquered by Shuppiluliumash; this Akizzi, as his letters show,[1] recognized Egyptian overlordship. He reports to the pharaoh that Aitakama had tried to persuade him to take part in an anti-Egyptian conspiracy.[2] He also reports that Aitakama's advances had been more successful with Teuwatti of Lapana and Arzawiya of Ruhhizzi.[3] Indeed, reinforced by Hittite troops, he attacked Qatna,[4] apparently capturing it and compelling Akizzi to flee.[5] Aitakama was even able to attack Apina (Damascus) where Piryawaza, the 'commissioner' of Kumidu, represented the pharaoh.[6]

The advance of Hittite partisans as far south as the Biqā', the valley between Lebanon and Anti-Lebanon, and further east as far as Damascus ought not to have left the Egyptians indifferent; this was undisputed Egyptian territory. However, they either were unwilling or unable to help their friends in southern Syria. The letters of Akizzi—like those of Rib-Adda—are vivid testimony to Egyptian impotence.

A word remains to be said on chronology. The precise date of Tushratta's downfall is not ascertainable. Tushratta once mentions that friendship had prevailed between Amenophis IV and himself for four years.[7] All his letters keep the memory of Amenophis III alive as though he had passed away only a short while ago. On the other hand, all of Aziru's struggle with Rib-Adda of Gubla must fall before the victory of Shuppiluliumash. The latter occurred early in the reign of Ashur-uballit of Assyria and certainly before Kurigalzu became king of Babylon, i.e. during the reign there of Burnaburiash. Therefore, one will be inclined to propose a date about 1360 or a little later.

IV. THE HURRIAN WAR OF SHUPPILULIUMASH

The summaries of the Hittite conqueror's reign list—allegedly after twenty years of war against the Kaska (Gasga) people[8]—six years of campaigning in the Khurri Lands, i.e. in northern Syria.[9] The combined evidence from various surviving sources makes at least a tentative reconstruction possible.

---

[1] §III, 3, 8 ff.   [2] EA 53, 1 ff.
[3] EA 53, 35 ff.; 54, 26 ff.; 56, 23 ff.
[4] EA 53, 8 ff., 174–176. See G, 14, 94 f.
[5] EA 55, 40 ff., 56 f.   [6] EA 53, 24 ff., 56 ff.
[7] EA 29, 113.
[8] G, 1, xix, 9, i, 8 ff. (cf. §iv, 4, ii/1, 10).
[9] G, 1, xix, 9, i, 7 ff. (cf. §iv, 4, ii/1, 10).

The first link in the series of campaigns is probably a Hittite attack on Amqa, the land between Lebanon and Anti-Lebanon which was considered an Egyptian dependency. The attack was commanded not by the king himself, but by one of his generals.[1] The second year of this campaign[2] saw serious fighting on the Euphrates frontier; the main adversary there was Carchemish which—surprisingly—had so far not been conquered. The city must have had helpers from further east. The military leader on the Hittite side was Telepinush, the king's son, who held the position of the 'priest' in Kumanni. His quick success resulted in the submission of the countries of Arziya and Carchemish; only that city itself continued to resist. The victorious army took up winter camp in Khurmuriga (or Murmuriga). When Telepinush had to go home in order to attend to urgent religious duties, the command was entrusted to the general Lupakkish. The prince's departure precipitated an attack of Hurrian troops on Khurmuriga, which was enveloped and besieged. At the same time, Egyptian troops—probably reacting to the Hittite raid on Amqa which had just been mentioned—invaded Kinza. It was probably then that Kinza and Nukhash, as other sources relate, 'revolted' against Shuppiluliumash. Aziru of Amurru, however, remained loyal to his overlord.[3]

Shuppiluliumash prepared his counter-stroke carefully.[4] He gathered a new army in Tegarama and with the arrival of spring (this then is the third year of this series of campaigns) he sent it to Syria under the joint command of the crown-prince Arnuwandash and Zidash, the major-domo. Before he could join this army himself, it defeated the Hurrians and lifted the siege of Khurmuriga. He could at once proceed to laying siege to the city of Carchemish, and still had sufficient troops at hand to send a column under Lupakkish and Tarkhunda-zalmash against the Egyptians. They promptly drove the Egyptians from Kinza and re-entered Amqa, the Egyptian border province.[5]

While Carchemish was under siege and this second army stood in Amqa, news reached Shuppiluliumash that a pharaoh, whom our source calls *Piphururiyaš*, had died. His identity has been much discussed;[6] the publication of a new fragment[7] in which the name

---

[1] §II, 5, 208 ff.   [2] §II, 7, frgm. 28.
[3] §II, 3, no. 1, obv. 3 ff.   [4] Main source again §II, 7, frgm. 28.
[5] Also EA 174, 14 ff.; G, 1, xxxi, 121 *a*, ii, 8 f. (cf. §IV, 4, 11/1, 23 ff.; §II, 8, 59 ff.).
[6] Above all §IV, 7; §IV, 2, 14 f.; §IV, 8.
[7] G, 5, xxxiv, 24, 4 (cf. §II, 7, 98, l. 18).

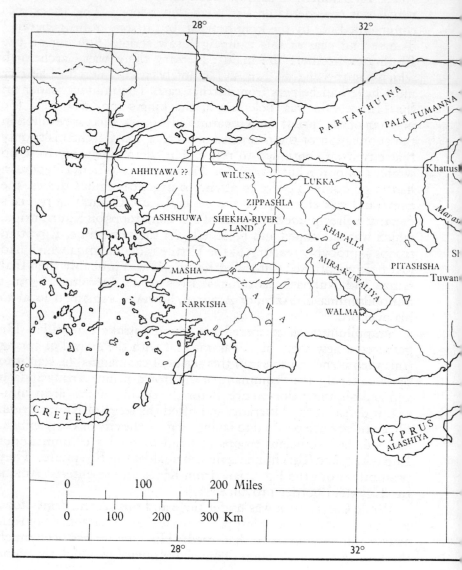

Map. 1. Ancient Asia Minor and Northern Mesopotamia.

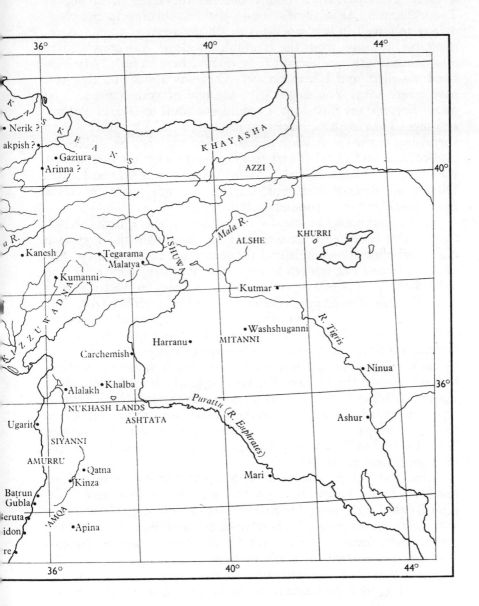

is given as *Niphururiyaš* finally decides the issue in favour of
Tutankhamun, Akhenaten's son-in-law. According to the chronology followed in this work his death occurred *c.* 1352. A remarkable message from the pharaoh's widow[1] was conveyed to
Shuppiluliumash. It deserves to be quoted here in full: 'My husband has died, and I have no son. They say about you that you
have many sons. You might give me one of your sons, and he
might become my husband. I would not want to take one of my
servants. I am loath to make him my husband.' This offer was so
surprising to the Great King that he called together his noblemen
into council and decided first to investigate whether the request
was sincere. A high official, Khattusha-zitish was sent to Egypt.
During his absence in Egypt, Carchemish was taken by storm
more quickly than anyone expected.

At the beginning of the following year—the fourth—Khattusha-zitish returned with a second message from the Egyptian
queen, who bitterly complained about distrust and hesitancy. She
added: 'I have not written to any other country, I have written
only to you..... He will be my husband and king in the country of
Egypt.' This time Shuppiluliumash complied with her wish. He
sent Zannanzash[2] to Egypt, but the prince never reached the goal
of his journey. He was murdered on the way,[3] probably by the
'servants' of the queen who did not wish a foreigner to ascend the
throne of the pharaohs. Thus, by over-cautious hesitation Shuppiluliumash missed the chance of making one of his sons pharaoh of
Egypt. All that he was able to do then was to send Hittite troops
on a new expedition against Amqa.[4] This seems to be counted as
the fifth campaign in the series. On their return they carried
home to the Hittite country a plague which harassed the people
for a long time to come.[5]

After the fall of Carchemish Shuppiluliumash reorganized
northern Syria: he elevated his two sons Piyashilish and Telepinush (until then 'priest' of Kumanni) to kingship in Carchemish
and Aleppo respectively.[6] Thereby he assured firm control of the
Taurus and Amanus passes and Hittite domination of the two
most important states in northern Syria.

The downfall of Tushratta had set free Assyria, a result which
was not altogether desirable from the Hittite point of view. Shup-

---

[1] §IV, 3.   [2] §II, 7, frgm. 31.
[3] §II, 5, 210 f.; §II, 7, frgm. 31; G, 1, XIX, 20 (cf. §IV, 4, II/1, 28 ff.).
[4] §II, 5, 210 f.   [5] *Ibid.*
[6] G, 4, VI, 28, obv. 19 ff.; G, 1, XIX, 9, i, 17 ff. (cf. §IV, 4, II/1, 10); G, 1, XIX, 20
obv. 13 (cf. §IV, 4, II/1, 28 ff.).

piluliumash was not oblivious of the danger inherent in this development. To counteract it, he decided to make use of the presence of Kurtiwaza, the Mitannian prince, at his court. Piyashilish, the new king of Carchemish—now known as Sharre-Kushukh[1]—was entrusted with the task of re-establishing him as king in Washshuganni. This may be counted as the sixth Hurrian campaign; it involved a serious armed expedition. The two princes set out from Carchemish, crossed the Euphrates, and attacked Irrite. The people of this city and the surrounding country, after some fighting, recognized that resistance was useless and surrendered. The next objective was Harran, which was quickly overrun. Further advance toward Washshuganni brought about some interference from the Assyrian, i.e. Ashur-uballiṭ, and from the king of the Khurri Land. But the Hittite troops, acclaimed by the populace, were able to enter the former capital. The advance east of Washshuganni, however, proved to be difficult, mainly for lack of supplies. Nevertheless, the Assyrians did not risk battle and withdrew. Shuttarna retired beyond the Upper Euphrates and only insignificant skirmishing took place beyond that line.[2] It became the north-eastern boundary of Kurtiwaza's new kingdom. The two versions of the treaty which Shuppiluliumash concluded with the new king are preserved.[3] By taking one of the overlord's daughters in marriage, Kurtiwaza had previously been made a member of the royal family.

Either simultaneously with this campaign in the Mitanni country or in the following year, Arnuwandash, the crown prince, was sent out against 'Egypt'.[4] Nothing beyond the mere fact is known.

When the reign of Shuppiluliumash drew toward its end—he must have died soon afterward, i.e. about 1346, the victim of the plague which Hittite soldiers had imported from Amqa—he was the undisputed master of Syria and wielded more power than any one of his contemporaries. The Egyptians, at the end of the Amarna period, were for internal reasons in no position to challenge the Hittites, and remained unable to do so for the next fifty years. The Assyrians, still in process of reorganization after their liberation from Mitannian overlordship, were not yet ready to oppose them seriously. Thus the struggle for Syria had ended for

---

[1] §II, 7, 120 f.

[2] §I, 8, no. 2, obv. 35 ff.; G, I, VIII, 80+xxiii, 50+G, 2, 21 (cf. in part §IV, 5); G, I, XIX, 9, i, 13 ff. (cf. §IV, 4, II/I, 10); §II, 7, frgm. 34 ff.

[3] §I, 8, nos. 1 and 2.   [4] §II, 7, frgm. 34 ff.

the time being and a balance of power had been established. Despite the efforts of the pharaohs of the Nineteenth Dynasty, and also despite the intermittent resurgence of Assyrian might, this remained essentially unchanged down to the great migrations toward the end of the thirteenth century.

CHAPTER XVIII

ASSYRIA AND BABYLON,

c. 1370–1300 B.C.

I. RECOVERY IN WESTERN ASIA

THE pages of this history have had little to tell about Assyria or Babylonia since the reigns of Shamshi-Adad I and of his son Ishme-Dagan in the former, and since the end of Hammurabi's last successor in the latter. The intervening space of nearly three centuries was occupied by the invasions and retarding influences which affected the whole of Western Asia and Egypt as well, and had produced a similar dimness in the view of all that vast area. In Egypt the invaders were the Hyksos,[1] in Syria, Mesopotamia, and eastward the Hurrians, in Babylonia the Kassites; all of them peoples of origins as obscure as their cultural levels were generally low, and all alike destined to lose their individuality, partly by conquest, but mostly by absorption, before they had attained a distinctive civilization or much history of their own. For this dark age modern research has therefore to depend partly upon survivals and intermittent gleams of the old. The point now reached in the story is that where the gloom is everywhere receding—it had been dispelled from Egypt with the ejection of the Hyksos and the counter-invasion of Syria by the kings of the Eighteenth Dynasty, but these had never approached near enough to the old seats of the Babylonian culture to exercise a direct influence there or to break (if such had been the effect) the deadening spell which still overpowered them. The greatest of Egyptian conquerors, Tuthmosis III, was indeed able, at the farthest point of his penetration into Syria, to include among the spoils of his campaign a tribute from Ashur, which his fame if not his armies had reached.[2] Little affected by this distant intruder, and not at all by his successors, the Assyrian nation had far more to fear and to suffer from the nearer oppression of the Hurrians, represented by kings of the states called Mitanni and Khanigalbat, whose history up to the present point has been

* An original version of this chapter was published as fascicle 42 in 1965.
[1] See *C.A.H.* ii³, pt. 1, pp. 54 ff., 289 ff.
[2] *C.A.H.* ii³, pt. 1, pp. 452 f.; G, 28, 227 ff.

related in the foregoing chapters.[1] The Kassites had begun to
raid and settle in Babylonia under the son of Hammurabi, and
had at length established themselves in the capital, filling the void
left after the Hittite raid which ended the Amorite Dynasty there.[2]
Yet despite violent interferences the two lands had lost little of
their respective identities. Throughout all these years the line of
Assyrian kings was never broken, and the invaders of Babylonia
had come, like so many of their forerunners, to be accepted as
merely a new dynasty in a country seemingly gifted with an
inexhaustible capacity of absorbing the most intractable elements
and reshaping them in its own mould.

In Assyria the line of kings is preserved unbroken to us only
by lists of their names and reigns.[3] Of the thirty-six counted
between Ishme-Dagan I and Ashur-uballiṭ several occupied an
uneasy throne for a moment only, and the rest have left no more
than a few records of local building activity in the city of Ashur,[4]
coupled with a genealogical notice. Their inscriptions occupy not
half-a-dozen pages in modern books, and where they have told
nothing of themselves it is not surprising that the outside world
has told, in general, no more. There is no doubt that most of
these reigns were passed under the shadow of foreign domination,
projected partly from Babylonia, where the equally obscure early
Kassite kings seem to have claimed a certain sovereignty over the
northern neighbour. But a much more menacing cloud impended
from the west, from the various rulers of the Hurrian peoples,
who, if they never supplanted the Assyrian kings in their own
small domain, at least extended their power and occupied districts
which more naturally belonged to the Assyrians, even on the
side remote from the principal seats of the Hurrian kingdoms. It
chances that we are very amply informed upon the population,
the institutions, language, and life of a district centred upon
Arrapkha (modern Kirkuk) with an important outlying subsidiary
at Nuzi, only a few miles away. The towns were then inhabited
by a mostly Hurrian population, which rather awkwardly affected
to use the Akkadian language[5] for its legal business and public
records, but spoke its own uncouth vernacular[6] and acknowledged
the rule of Saustatar, king of Mitanni.[7] The city of Ashur hardly
appears at all in these voluminous documents,[8] but Nineveh is

---

[1] *C.A.H.* II³, pt. I, ch. x; and above, ch. XVII.
[2] *C.A.H.* II³, pt. I, pp. 224 f.   [3] *C.A.H.* I³, pt. I, pp. 194 ff.
[4] G, 3, 20 ff; G, 8, 28 ff; G, 22, vol. I, 47–57.
[5] §I, 5; 7; 10, 9 ff.; 20.   [6] §I, 4; 18; 19; 23.
[7] §I, 4, 1; §v, 32, 54; §VI, 4, 202.   [8] §I, 11, 20.

prominent, especially in personal names,[1] and may probably be considered a Mitannian possession, containing a strong blend of Hurrian inhabitants at this time. Arrapkha, lost to Babylonian rule since the days of Samsuiluna,[2] passed into the domain of the Hurrians, not of the Assyrians, despite its comparative proximity to Ashur; the Nuzi tablets give sufficient indication that the kings of Assyria must, in these generations, have been no more than vassals of the Hurrian monarchs who controlled the country far and wide around the city on the Tigris.[3] In these circumstances it is not surprising that what little is known about Assyria, even in the time which directly preceded her great recovery, is derived incidentally from the history of Mitanni, itself fragmentary and partly dependent upon still other records.

II. EXTERNAL RELATIONS

The restorer of the power of Assyria was, beyond doubt, Ashur-uballiṭ who was destined to become a leading figure of his day, but he has told us nothing to the purpose about himself. Half-a-dozen short inscriptions[4] concern the repair of two temples and some work upon a well in his city of Ashur, no more than the least distinguished of his predecessors. The Assyrian kings had not yet learned[5] the art of appending to their building-inscriptions those notes of contemporary events which were soon to expand themselves into the detailed annals of later reigns. A first mention of the great king's deeds is made, in his own family, by his great-grandson, looking back over the glories of his line and taking Ashur-uballit as the inaugurator of these.[6] In the general documentation of his age he makes a better appearance, though sometimes anonymously. His own most interesting relics are two letters[7] found in distant Egypt among the celebrated archive of Amarna. These two despatches clearly belong to different periods of his reign and power. The first is addressed 'to the king of Egypt from Ashur-uballit, king of Assyria', and its contents are suitable to this modest beginning—the writer sends his messenger to make contact with the potentate, 'to see you and your land', and to offer a suitable present, a fine chariot, two horses, and a jewel of lapis-lazuli, in lauding which he observes that his father had never sent such gifts, a remark which is amplified in the

---

[1] §1, 4, 106, but the connexion is questioned, *ibid.* 239.   [2] §IV, 2, 54 ff.
[3] §1, 15, 191 ff.   [4] G, 8, 39 ff.; G, 22, vol. I, 58–63; G, 3, 26 ff.
[5] Below, pp. 217 f.; but also pp. 295 ff.
[6] G, 8, 62 ff.; §1, 26; G, 3, 37.   [7] G, 20, nos. 15, 16; §1, 9, 212 ff.; §II, 1, 43.

second letter. This is longer and more interesting; Ashur-uballit, writing later in his reign, has now become 'the king of Assyria, the great king, your brother', and addresses Amenophis by the corresponding titles, including 'my brother'. The gifts are repeated, even increased, but it is made very clear that they are sent strictly upon the understanding *do ut des*, for the writer goes on to say he is informed that 'gold in your land is dust, they pick it up'. So, as he has to sustain the expense of building a new palace, let his brother send all the gold it needs. This is reinforced by an interesting appeal to the past, 'when Ashur-nādin-ahhē my father [second predecessor] sent to Egypt they returned him twenty talents of gold, and when the Khanigalbatian king sent to your father they sent him also twenty talents. Send me as much as to the Khanigalbatian.' In the same ungracious strain he churlishly dismisses the favour already accepted—'(what you have sent) does not even suffice for the expense of my messengers going and coming'. This is, of course, only one example of the greed for Egyptian gold which pervades the letters of the Asiatic princes, who evidently saw nothing unworthy in such bartering of presents. It has been observed[1] that, for uncertain reasons, gold had at this period temporarily replaced silver as a medium of exchange, and that the mutual gifts, massive and carefully inventoried, passing between these courts, may be considered a form of state trading; as gold was the particular export of Egypt so were lapis-lazuli and horses the Asiatic valuables traded in return. In any case, princes had never been restrained in criticizing their correspondents' gifts with unblushing candour.[2] The letter of Ashur-uballit ends with some words about the difficulties of communication, 'we are distant lands, and our messengers must travel thus', subject to hindrances. There had been complaints on both sides about undue retention of messengers; some of the Egyptians had been kept prisoners by the Sutu, the desert nomads, and the Assyrian king writes that he had done everything possible to effect their release. But this misfortune, he adds, is no reason for the Assyrian messengers to be detained as a reprisal—why should they die in a far land? If this brought any advantage to the king, so be it, but since there is none, why not let them go?

There is nothing to show that the pharaoh took all this in particularly ill part—the style was too familiar. But there was another who thought it worth while to send him (or his successor)[3] a sharp protest against these negotiations, the contemporary

---

[1] §II, 3.   [2] §IV, 1, vol. v, no. 20.   [3] §I, 2, 14 f.; §II, 1, 54, 62 ff.; §I, 9, 213.

Kassite king Burnaburiash, the second of that name in the dynasty.[1] This indignant letter[2] recalls that Kurigalzu, his father,[3] had been tempted by the Canaanites to make a league with them for a raid upon Egypt, and Kurigalzu had repulsed these overtures. 'But now the Assyrians, subjects of mine, have I not written to you how their mind is? Why have they come to your country? If you love me, let them accomplish nought of their purpose, but send them away empty.' The ancestors of Burnaburiash may indeed have claimed and even exercised a certain supremacy over the shadow-kings of Ashur, pent in their small domain between the hordes of a nearer oppressor. But not only was there now a man of different temper upon the Assyrian throne; the oppressors had been repulsed and every circumstance changed. Protest from Babylon was in vain, for the pharaoh was too well advised to ignore reality. To be noticed, it would have had to come from another quarter, and there all was silence.

Burnaburiash was a regular correspondent with the Egyptian court, and had much more to write than complaints about the Assyrians. In a first letter[4] to Amenophis IV he was garrulous about his health and his vexation that no condolences had been sent to him; he peevishly enquired whether it was a long way to Egypt and, hearing that it was, he condescended to forgive his 'brother' such neglect. Burnaburiash too wanted much gold,[5] but advised his royal correspondent not to entrust the despatch of this to any knavish official, for the last time when it arrived the weight was short, and on another occasion there was less than a quarter of the due tale.[6] More serious subjects (if there could be any more serious than the gold supply) figured also in these letters: caravans from Babylon to Egypt had been stopped by the lawless Canaanites, some merchants robbed and murdered, others mutilated and enslaved. 'Canaan is your land ... and in your land have I been outraged. Arrest them, therefore, make good the money they plundered, slay those who slew my servants and avenge their blood!'[7] There were also marriage treatments between the two kings; Burnaburiash promised to send a daughter to Egypt, but was not at all disposed to let her go without due attention.[8] He complained that the delegation from Egypt to fetch her had only five carriages, and imagined to himself the comments of his courtiers if a daughter of the great king

[1] C.A.H. I[3], pt. 1, pp. 206 f.; §1, 9, 212 differs. [2] G, 20, no. 9.
[3] Or grandfather, §1, 9, 201, 213. [4] G, 20, no. 7; §1, 9, 213.
[5] G, 20, no. 7, ll. 63 ff.; §11, 3, 47. [6] G, 20, no. 10.
[7] G, 20, no. 8. [8] G, 20, no. 11.

travelled with such a paltry escort. However, the marriage came to pass in the end, for there are two interminable lists of costly presents[1] which were probably the mutual compliments of the two monarchs upon that occasion.

Nothing of more than such minor interest occurs in the dealings between Babylonia and Egypt at this time. Parted by a distance so great that Burnaburiash had no idea of it, the two kings did not even co-operate in dealing with the menace which afflicted them both alike, the lawless condition of Syria, and they had no other object in common. The most urgent topic in the letters from Babylon was the protest against recognizing the Assyrians, a matter of some weight to Burnaburiash, who saw his nominal supremacy passing rapidly into the real dominance of his rival, Ashur-uballit. The moment of destiny for Assyria in its relation with the Hurrian kingdoms which had long oppressed her was undoubtedly the murder of Tushratta,[2] king of Mitanni, by one of his sons. This wealthy monarch, who had corresponded at great length with Amenophis III, lived to continue the same relation with Amenophis IV,[3] but disappeared soon after the latter's accession. The events of this time are related in some detail by the preambles of two versions of a treaty made between Tushratta's son Kurtiwaza and the great king of the Hittites, whose patronage he obtained and sealed by marriage with a daughter.[4]

At Tushratta's death the throne of Mitanni was occupied by Artatama, the king of the Khurri land, who had long been his opponent and had as such enjoyed support from the Hittite king. But he had other supporters as well, particularly the lands of Assyria and Alshe, and he was accused of dissipating in bribes to these allies the riches gathered in the palace of earlier kings. If such were offered no doubt they were readily enough accepted by the avaricious Assyrian, but he had reasons of defence and ambition which in themselves would have ensured his hostility to Tushratta. When Artatama became king of Mitanni he left his son Shuttarna (called elsewhere Shutatarra) as his successor in the Khurri land (these realms are, however, ill-defined), and the latter completed the surrender to Assyria which his father had begun—this according to the hostile account which alone survives.[5] He destroyed the palace built by Tushratta, broke up the precious vessels stored therein, and gave away these rich materials

[1] G, 20, nos. 13, 14.   [2] See above, p. 14.
[3] *Ibid.*   [4] See a full account above, ch. XVII, sects. III and IV.
[5] §1, 25, 36 ff.

to the Assyrian who had been his father's servant, but had revolted and refused tribute. Above all, Shuttarna restored to Assyria a splendid door of silver and gold which had been carried off by a former king of Mitanni and used to adorn his own palace at his capital Washshuganni. He made the same lavish sacrifices of his paternal wealth to the land of Alshe, he destroyed the houses of his Hurrian subjects, and delivered certain obnoxious nobles to the same enemies, who promptly impaled these hapless captives.

There can be no doubt that the Assyrian king who plays so prominent a part in this account was Ashur-uballit, although he is never named. How humble was his position at the beginning of his reign is proved by the definite claim that he was the tributary servant of the Babylonian king, and hardly less clearly by his own reference to a 'Khanigalbatian king' as, in a sense, his own predecessor.[1] At a favourable moment he cast off allegiance to Mitanni, but instead of incurring punishment, received from his master's successor not only the trophies of earlier conquest, but the wealth, the princes, and even the territory of his former sovereign. The reason for this strange behaviour on the part of Artatama and his son can only be supposed the necessity in which they found themselves to win allies against an external danger, and that danger could be only the Hittites. Nevertheless, this too is strange, for it is clear that upon the death of Tushratta, who had been his enemy, the Hittite king viewed with indulgence the succession of Artatama. Estrangement soon occurred, however, and the Mitannian kings knew they must face the hostility of the powerful Shuppiluliumash, who found ready to his hand an opposition headed by Kurtiwaza, son of the murdered Tushratta. This young man's situation soon became dangerous; he was constrained to flee, first to Babylon, and thence to the Hittite, with whom he threw in his lot and married his daughter. The course of a campaign which Kurtiwaza was now enabled to conduct against the Mitannian, and subsequently the Assyrian, powers has been sketched from available evidence in the preceding chapter.[2]

What happened to Kurtiwaza in the end is not known, but that he finally suffered defeat from the Assyrians may be gathered from the testimony, some fifty years afterwards, of the great-grandson of Ashur-uballit, that the latter 'scattered the hosts of the widespread Subarians'.[3] Yet even if he did so this was no

---

[1] See above, p. 24.   [2] See above, ch. XVII, sect. IV.
[3] G, 8, 64 f.; §1, 26, 93 ff.

more than a bare victory, for his descendants found a kingdom of Khanigalbat still in existence under the family of Shattuara and of his són Wasashatta,[1] probably related to the old ruling house, and had to wage against these enemies repeated wars, which continued into the reign of Shalmaneser I; as the outcome of these the territory of Khanigalbat was annexed to the Assyrian Empire.[2] In addition to victory over the Subarians in the west, the only other specific conquest attributed to Ashur-uballiṭ is that he 'subdued Muṣri'.[3] If, as some think, Muṣri lay to the east of Assyria, beyond Arrapkha (Kirkuk), or even to the north-east of Nineveh, this claim would be an indication of success upon another front, but there is no certainty where this land was situated,[4] for others would place it in the nearer or farther west of Assyria, and this is perhaps favoured by the discovery near Aleppo of an Aramaic treaty (eighth century B.C.) which proves the existence at that time of a Muṣri[5] in the vicinity of the north Syrian city of Arpad; if this was meant, the conquest of Muṣri would have been no more than a part of Ashur-uballiṭ's campaign against the Subarians.

III. THE ASSYRIANS IN BABYLONIA

In the south, Ashur-uballiṭ's relations with Babylonia were intimate and dramatic, and are fairly well known. He achieved power in the reign of the Kassite king Burnaburiash II, whom we have seen above complaining bitterly to the Egyptian court of the notice accorded to his presumptuous vassal. No attention having been paid to this, Burnaburiash no doubt nursed his grievance for a time, perhaps for the remainder of his life. But a complete change of policy, spontaneous or forced, set in before long. Muballiṭat-Sherua, daughter of Ashur-uballiṭ, married the king of Babylon, and with the backing of her formidable father and her own spirit, evidently became a leading figure in that country. Owing to discrepancies in the two authorities[6] which have preserved the history of this time it is uncertain whether she married Burnaburiash himself or his son Karakhardash; the

[1] G, 3, 36, 38.   [2] G, 8, 116 ff.; G, 3, 38 f., 57; see below, p. 281.
[3] G, 8, 62 f.; G, 3, 57.
[4] G, 28, 389, n. 13; cf. below, p. 460 and n. 2.   [5] §11, 2, 223 f.
[6] The records of this time, called the 'Synchronistic History' and 'Chronicle P' (on which see *C.A.H.* 1³, pt. 1, p. 196, n. 5), differ as to the names and order of these Kassite kings, and modern historians differ accordingly; see G, 2, 365 f.; G, 28, 263; G, 19, 242 f.; §1, 9, 201, 212; §1, 22, 4 f.

latter may be thought the more likely. The reign of Karakhardash was short in any case, and he was succeeded (according to the Babylonian version,[1] which is followed here) by Kadashman-Kharbe, his son by his Assyrian queen. This young king[2] undertook a campaign in the desert country of the middle Euphrates against the nomads called Sutu whom he used with great severity. After operating against them over a wide area 'from east to west' he built a fort, dug a well and a cistern, and established there a permanent garrison to pacify the country. Not long afterwards his reign came to a violent end, for his Kassite subjects revolted, murdered him, and exalted to the throne one Nazibugash, otherwise called Shuzigash, a person of common birth. This revolt, the murder of his grandson, and the insult to his house called for the speedy revenge of Ashur-uballit; he marched forthwith into Babylonia, defeated and slew the usurper, and set upon the throne Kurigalzu 'the young', son of Kadashman-Kharbe (according, again, to the more probable Babylonian version), who would thus have been his great-grandson, and doubtless no more than a child.

The jejune accounts of these two chronicles certainly refer to events of great moment at the time, the most dangerous of which was the invasion of the Sutu, or Aramaean tribes, continuing the age-old pressure from the north-west which, as ever, had behind it the remoter outflow of the deserts, and invariably ended in Babylonia. The letters both of Burnaburiash and of Ashur-uballit to the king of Egypt describe lawless molestation of their emissaries by the nomads and townsmen of the upper Euphrates and Syria, too remote from either power to be effectively controlled. The depredations of these robbers account sufficiently for the campaign of Kadashman-Kharbe who, like other Babylonian kings before him, had to take up the hopeless burden of holding an indefensible frontier on the Euphrates. But his operations were certainly instigated and supported by Ashur-uballit, who suffered no less from the Sutu, and a letter found at Dūr-Kurigalzu[3] seems to witness this close touch kept with the Assyrians. Whatever success was obtained (and it could have little lasting effect upon so evasive a foe) the effort was a severe strain for Babylon, for it coincided with other afflictions. The result was public detestation of the Assyrian alliance, concentrated upon its representative Muballitat-Sherua, whose prominence in the scanty records of the time leaves no doubt that she was a

[1] I.e. 'Chronicle P'.
[2] The following actions have otherwise been ascribed to an earlier Kadashman-Kharbe (I), §1, 9, 210.   [3] §III, 5, 149, no. 12; §1, 9, 252.

masterful and probably hated figure. Her son was struck down as the agent of servitude and disaster, but the rash impulse only brought on the heavier vengeance of the outraged Assyrian mother and grandfather.

In the dearth of historical records for this period, indirect illumination has been sought from two works of literature which seemed to have possible reference to the age of Ashur-uballiṭ. These have the added interest of coming respectively from Assyrian and Babylonian sources, being thus parallel with the two prose-chronicles which have been drawn upon hitherto. The Assyrian poem[1] is very inadequately preserved but its character is fairly clear. It is an epical description of a war between Assyria and Babylonia, written in a spirit of undisguised chauvinism; the Assyrians are acclaimed throughout as righteous victims of aggression and as heroes in battle, fighting with the aid of indignant gods against a faithless and cruel foe, who had set at nought the sanctity of treaties. Their respective leaders were the kings Tukulti-Ninurta of Assyria and Kashtiliash the Kassite. Thus the main part of this action would belong to a time more than a century later. But there is a passing reference to earlier reigns,[2] and although a supposed mention of Ashur-uballiṭ himself does not exist,[3] some very fragmentary evidence survives[4] that the war between Tukulti-Ninurta and Kashtiliash was only the last episode in a series of armed clashes between the powers, in the course of which both Adad-nīrāri I and his father Arik-dēn-ili had opposed Nazimaruttash and, still earlier, Enlil-nīrāri of Assyria had fought with Kurigalzu of Babylon.

A close predecessor of this Kurigalzu 'the young' had led an expedition against the Sutu,[5] and from this a connexion has been inferred with some passages in a composition known to the Babylonians as 'King of all Habitations' and to modern scholars as the 'Epic of the Plague-god Erra'. The general purport of this poem, which is strongly marked by the elaborate and prolix style of the Kassite period, is the affliction brought upon the land at a certain time by the wrath of Erra and the hand of his divine minister Ishum. It is needless to resume here the contents, beyond its description of a raid by the Sutu upon Uruk,[6] and the denunciation of vengeance upon these nomads; one day Akkad, now humbled, will overthrow the proud Sutu.[7] Weakness and

---

[1] §III, 2; §III, 8, 45, no. 39A; see below, pp. 287, 298.
[2] §III, 2, 20 ff., ll. 29–33.   [3] §III, 7, 40.
[4] §III, 9.   [5] See above, p. 11; G, 28, 263.
[6] §III, 4, 28 f., ll. 51 ff.   [7] *Ibid.* 34 f., l. 27.

affliction, depicted in the poem as the present lot of the Babylonians, would not be inappropriate to the days when alien, short-lived, and feeble kings held Babylon under the sway of its northern neighbour, but it is now the general opinion[1] that these attacks of the Sutu and the poem itself belong to a later age.

IV. ENLIL-NĪRĀRI AND ARIK-DĒN-ILI

The Kurigalzu who was set upon the throne of Babylon by Ashur-uballiṭ was destined to enjoy a long if not always fortunate reign of twenty-two years, not only outliving his benefactor but continuing into the tenure of the next Assyrian king as well. But their relations were soon embroiled, for the national feelings of the southern kingdom could not tolerate equality with a nation which they were accustomed to regard as subject. Before long it came to war between the two countries, in which Assyria under Enlil-nīrāri, the son of Ashur-uballiṭ, was successful, whereby he won fame in the words of a successor[2] as he who 'slew the hosts of the Kassites'. Enlil-nīrāri reigned for ten years, and nothing more is known about him than this general description and a few details of the Babylonian wars given by the chronicles relating to this time. The two principal authorities, which have already differed concerning Kurigalzu's parentage, continue to give divergent accounts of what were clearly the same affairs. The Assyrian document, called the 'Synchronistic History', places this war in the reign of Enlil-nīrāri of Assyria,[3] whereas the Babylonian ('Chronicle P') postpones it until the reign of his second successor Adad-nīrāri I.[4] The former (Assyrian) version is undoubtedly correct here, for Kurigalzu did not in fact survive into the reign of Adad-nīrāri, and other fragments of inscriptions and chronicles[5] confirm that the opponents were indeed Enlil-nīrāri and Kurigalzu. It would appear, in fact, that wars between the Assyrians and Kassite kings lasted indecisively through all these reigns, and were brought to a stop only by the more complete victory of Tukulti-Ninurta I.

As to the course of these conflicts little is known. A recently published fragment reveals[6] that in the time of Enlil-nīrāri and Kurigalzu there occurred a battle at a spot not far from Irbil, and thus close to the Assyrian centre, which indicates that

[1] §III, 4, 85 ff.; §III, 3, 164, 176; §III, 6, 398, 400.
[2] G, 8, 62 f.; G, 28, 268; G, 3, 37.   [3] G, 7, pt. 34, pl. 38, 18 ff.
[4] §III, 1, 45, ll. 20 f.   [5] §III, 9   [6] §III, 9, 115 f.

fortunes were wavering. The two main authorities continue to diverge; the Assyrian claims a victory for its own side, whereas the other seems to ascribe it to Kurigalzu. There is some indication that two battles took place, the last at a place called Sugaga on the Tigris, and they were probably hard-fought without a very decisive issue. The succeeding settlement was in accord with this equilibrium of forces. The 'Synchronistic History' has some obscure phrases which relate, in general significance, that an equal division was made of certain territory stretching from the land of Shubari to Karduniash (Babylonia), and a boundary traced between the shares of the two powers. The Babylonian chronicle precedes its brief mention of this war with a longer account of Kurigalzu's quarrel with a rival, one Khurpatila,[1] whom it calls 'king of Elammat'. The final battle between them at Dūr-Shulgi, in which Kurigalzu prevailed, followed a verbal challenge from Khurpatila which suggested the place of the encounter almost as if it had been a duel between the two kings, a picturesque incident[2] exactly matched many centuries later (A.D. 224), when the last of the Arsacid kings replied to a challenge from the usurping Ardashīr 'I will meet you in a plain which is called Hormizdaghan on the last day of the month of Mihr': if the battlefields were known it might prove that they were less separated by distance than by time.

Enlil-nīrāri of Assyria was succeeded by his son Arik-dēn-ili, whose reign lasted for twelve years. War continued with the Kassites, now under their king Nazimaruttash, whose design, as in the preceding reign, was to mount flank-attacks with the alliance of the eastern hillmen, rather than direct assaults upon the Assyrian centre.[3] Consequently the efforts of Arik-dēn-ili appear more as the usual offensive-defensive operations against the highlands than as moves in a conflict with Kassite Babylonia. In a summary of his father's exploits the next king of Assyria divides his victories into two—the first group was achieved against the districts of Turukku[4] and Nigimti[5] and 'all the chiefs of the mountains and highlands in the broad tracts of the Qutu (Gutians)'. This description makes it clear that the opponents dwelt in the Zagros; the general appellation of 'Gutians' is familiar enough, and Turukku was an old enemy of Hammurabi,[6] as also

---

[1] See below, p. 381.
[2] Ṭabarī, tr. Nöldeke, Th., *Geschichte der Perser und Araber zur Zeit der Sasaniden*, p. 14; *C.A.H.* XII, 109.   [3] §III, 9, 113, 115.
[4] §IV, 3, 17.   [5] G, 8, 52, n. 5.
[6] G, 9, vol. II, 181, no. 139; §IV, 1, vol. XV, 136.

the neighbour of Assyria with whom, in former days, Ishme-Dagan had confirmed peace by a marriage-alliance.[1] Some further details of this campaign were given by Arik-dēn-ili himself in a document[2] of which very little now remains—it was rather a chronicle than the earliest example of Assyrian annals. According to this fragment the opponent of Arik-dēn-ili in Nigimti was Esinu, whose land the Assyrian invaded and burned his harvest. In revenge Esinu attacked a district belonging to Assyria and killed many of the inhabitants. In a second invasion Arik-dēn-ili laid siege to a town named Arnuna, where Esinu was confined among the defenders. Gate and walls were laid in ruins and Esinu surrendered on terms of allegiance to Assyria and of bearing a tribute. The inscription continues with mention of a great victory by the Assyrian king and enormous booty, but it is not clear whether Esinu was again the enemy. Among a number of places named in this campaign is apparently Tarbiṣu, a very short distance north-west of Nineveh itself, from which it appears that serious danger was at one moment threatened to the very centre of the Assyrian kingdom.

The other scene of Arik-dēn-ili's wars, according to the summary of his son,[3] was the land of Katmukh, a district lying on the western side of the upper Tigris, between the river and a line roughly drawn through the present towns of Jazīrah-ibn-'Umar, Nisibis and Mārdīn. Here he encountered the local hillmen, who were in alliance with the Aramaean nomads called Akhlamu and Sutu, and another tribe the Yauru, probably cognate with these but otherwise unknown. The Assyrian was successful in this campaign, much as the Babylonian king Kadashman-Kharbe had been in his against the same elusive foes, but the Assyrian victory was more effectual, conquering 'the picked warriors of the Akhlamu, the Sutu, the Yauru, and their lands', since it apparently halted a direct incursion of the nomads into the lands north of Assyria, and directed their pressure southwards to the Babylonian district where they were to establish themselves gradually as the predominant element. With this episode, at whatever period of his reign, ends our knowledge of Arik-dēn-ili, a worthy maintainer of the great tradition established by his grandfather, though destined to be outshone by the military glory of his son. In the south the throne was occupied by Nazimaruttash, son of Kurigalzu, throughout the reign of his northern neighbour.

---

[1] §iv, 3, 17, 73. [2] G, 8, 52 f.; G, 22, vol. i, 68–71; G, 3, 31.
[3] G, 8, 60 f.; G, 28, 269, 390.

V. SOCIETY IN THE MIDDLE KASSITE PERIOD

Both in the northern and in the southern kingdoms the foreign repressions which had so long stifled their normal development were withdrawn at about the same time, although the processes were different in their outward aspects. Assyria, or rather its innermost core, ceased to suffer the domination of the Hurrians, embodied in the kingdoms of Khanigalbat or Mitanni. These either came to an end or languished, and with them disappeared even so vigorous and highly organized a Hurrian community as that which occupied the neighbouring territory of Arrapkha, the ample documents of which have been found to extend over four or five generations[1] and then stop, doubtless at the end of the Hurrian ascendancy. That the local population changed much is unlikely, but Arrapkha's whole future, from the thirteenth century onward, was to be that of a provincial Assyrian capital, and little more is known about it,[2] for when the Hurrian mainspring was broken it ceased to have a movement of its own. In Babylonia it was not the removal of external pressure so much as the advance of assimilation which now allowed native forces again to become operative and the general pattern of life in the south to be re-established. When this growth becomes visible after the long night of the earlier Kassites what reappears is largely familiar as the old life under the First Dynasty and its contemporary kingdoms. But the changes are significant, and certain influences which induced them can perhaps be traced in resurgent Assyria as well.

It happens that the evidence in both countries lies principally in the domain of law and society; in both there are official enactments and a body of semi-official or private documents. In Babylonia here began the age of the 'boundary-stones', famous since the beginning of modern studies, when their fine preservation, strange symbols, and elaborate inscriptions made them objects of strong and immediate interest.[3] The earliest of these[4] bears the name of Kadashman-Enlil, father of that Burnaburiash (II) who was the contemporary of Ashur-uballit. The inscription of this monument purports to confirm a grant of land already made by Kurigalzu (I) in the preceding generation, which is enough to show that the legal usage consecrated by these stones,

---

[1] §v, 18, 61.   [2] G, 9, vol. i, 154.

[3] G, 25, 77; §v, 24; 27; 44; G, 19, 245 ff.; G, 6, vol. ii, 896 ff.; G, 12, pl. 71.

[4] §v, 27, Introd. ix and pp. 3 ff.; §v, 44, no. 1; a different position in §1, 9, 253 (no. 181). See Plate 132 (a).

and probably the stones themselves, may be traced back at least so far. The purpose of these monuments was to record and ratify grants of land made by the king to trusted officers and subjects. There was nothing new in this, but the process of conveyance exhibits certain peculiarities which were unknown in the First Dynasty. The external form of the monuments is novel, and their most striking peculiarity is the presence of sculptured religious symbols which represent those gods under whose protection the grant is placed, whose curse is to be incurred by any who should presume to violate or question the donations. This introduction of penalties against offenders has been regarded[1] as a relic of the recent state of society when insecurity of life and property was the rule under the barbarian invasions, but it may be observed that invocation of the divine wrath against violators of monuments was a much older feature in Babylonian inscriptions, being especially prominent under the Dynasty of Agade.[2] What is new is the introduction of civil penalties against non-observers of the contract or donation. Such penalties consist usually in a manifold delivery of the goods purported to be sold,[3] or in a monetary fine (frequently to be paid in gold),[4] but sometimes a cruel physical sanction is menaced—a bronze peg shall be driven into the mouth of the deceiver.[5] The idea of severe forfeits is thus common to Babylonia and Assyria at this time, and physical mutilations had earlier been inflicted by Elamite justice.[6] Both of these innovations seem therefore to be a sign of foreign, apparently eastern, customs invading the Babylonian world at this period. Another mark of this might be seen in the definition of lands as belonging to certain 'houses' or territorial districts, defined as the property of tribes. This reveals that great tracts of land were owned collectively by communities, and it is natural to see in this the effect of settlement by tribes such as produced the various 'Houses' found in the history of Sennacherib's wars against Merodach-baladan II.[7] On the other hand it has been observed[8] that a like system of ownership may appear already in the ancient Obelisk of Manishtusu, and even earlier,[9] so that perhaps nothing was new in this tenure except the owners.

Certain other peculiarities which mark the legal practice of the boundary-stones have been noticed as not only novel in them-

---

[1] G, 19, 247.   [2] Many examples in §v, 26, 37 ff.
[3] §v, 35, 269.   [4] §11, 3, 40; §v, 7, 39 f.   [5] §1, 10, 11.
[6] C.A.H. 11³, pt. 1, p. 281; §v, 25, 89 f.; §v, 28, 307.
[7] §v, 4, 234; §v, 5, 7 f.   [8] G, 19, 250; §v, 11; G, 21, 75 ff.
[9] C.A.H. 1³, pt. 2, pp. 131 and 449; §v, 10, 24 f.

selves but as having parallels in the contemporary practice of the
northern country. Thus in one place[1] there is a reference to the
practice of official proclamation of the sale of land between
private persons, after which, when there had been no objection
raised by third parties, the transaction was officially registered
and the document placed in the archives. A similar requirement
appears in the Assyrian law concerning the sale of land;[2] when
the bargain had been arranged between two parties it was
necessary for the buyer to employ a crier who had to proclaim
three times in a full month, within the city of Ashur, or within
any other place where the ground was situated, that the prospec-
tive buyer was about to acquire such and such lands, and calling
upon any person who conceived himself to have a claim upon, or
rights concerning, those lands to produce his written documents
of title before the magistrate and town-clerk of Ashur, or before
the mayor and elders of another city, within that month. Any
claim so substantiated was admitted and the proposed sale thereby
voided, but if no claim was made within the appointed period
the sale proceeded, the buyer took possession, and the transaction was officially registered. The same custom of public
proclamation is at least implied in the Assyrian contracts of this
period[3] (i.e. the age of Ashur-uballiṭ) where transfers of land,
in order to be absolutely legal, were subject to the issue of a
'valid tablet' by the seller to the buyer, and this could be given
only after proof that there had been no appearance of anybody
laying rival claims to the land. Furthermore, the custom of
public proclamation was well known also at Nuzi and Arrapkha,
where it was called by a word meaning 'information', and this
procedure was ordained not only in transfers of land but in a
variety of other transactions such as sales of slaves, and even in
such matters as marriage, divorce, and adoptions.[4] Without need-
ing to discuss here the formal aspects of this requirement, it is
sufficient to note the introduction of a peculiar act of legal
publicity in the practice both of the south country, of Ashur,
and of Arrapkha.

Yet one more common feature has been pointed out in the
formalities of the boundary-stones and of the northern peoples;
this is the appearance of an accurate survey of the site and
especially the mensuration of the properties conveyed by the
respective documents concerning land-tenure. In the boundary-
stones, when the king was making a grant of estate, the phrase

---

[1] §v, 27, no. III, col. iii, 30 ff.; §v, 35, 270.
[2] §v, 12, 312 ff. (Tablet B, sect. 6).   [3] §I, 10, 80 f.   [4] §I, 10, 77 ff.

ran commonly 'he (the king) measured the field and conferred it upon (the recipient)', or even more explicitly 'the king sent (certain individuals) and these measured the field'.[1] In the Middle-Assyrian contracts for the sale of land the regular form is, after acknowledging receipt of the price, that the seller undertakes to meet any outstanding claims, and then 'he will measure the field with the royal tape and will write a valid tablet before the king'.[2] Since this procedure might seem superfluous between the parties once the bargain had been agreed and the price paid, the subsequent measurement 'with the royal tape' and the writing of a 'valid tablet' must be considered as another act, like the proclamation described above, giving official status to the transaction. All of these changes in the law governing transfers of land mark a notable departure from the practice of the First Dynasty of Babylon, and a distinct growth of officialdom. And since they are shared, in varying degrees, by Babylon under the Kassites, Assyria under isolation in a world of foreigners, and Arrapkha with its alien population, it is necessary to look for some common influence which produced these likenesses. Importation of eastern custom has been suggested, and colour might be given to this possibility by the appearance upon Kassite tablets of nail-marks[3] imprinted by the parties to deeds of sale, hire, loan, and pledge as (apparently) a more personal form of attestation than the traditional seal-impression, a practice virtually unknown to tablets of the First Dynasty in Babylonia, but on the contrary frequent in the legal documents found at Susa, which were contemporary with these.[4] It might seem therefore that the custom had spread from Elam and been adopted thence in Kassite Babylon. But a curious difference appears here in the lands hitherto seen as using similar innovations in legal practice, for the nail-marks are unknown to the Nuzi tablets and to the Middle Assyrian contracts.[5]

The boundary-stones are only one kind of legal document from the Kassite period. Side by side with them exist many less solemnly preserved records and letters, such as have been seen to throw so much light upon the life of the Old Babylonian period. In comparison with those, however, the Kassite tablets[6] seem disappointing, the contents being mostly of a very humdrum tenor. This is due to the fact that nearly all belong to a single find at Nippur, which yielded simply the contents of one administrative office, and consequently they are mainly occupied by a single subject, records of rent from temple estates and lists of wages and allowances to officials. Occasional tablets refer to sales, guarantees, and legal proceedings, and the latter are more frequent in a small find at the city of Dūr-Kurigalzu.[1] These documents from Nippur begin at about the time when this chapter opens, in the reign of Burnaburiash II, and continue through the next seven or eight kings to Kashtiliash IV, a century which may be regarded as the most flourishing of Kassite rule. The Assyrian contracts[2] are somewhat earlier, for, although there is no list of the eponyms by whom they are dated, allusions to the names of kings reveal that they were written under Ashur-nīrāri II, Ashur-bēl-nishēshu, Erība-Adad, Ashur-uballiṭ, and Enlil-nīrāri, a few being even later.[3] These Assyrian documents are more interesting than the Kassite, for their contents are much more varied; there are sales of land, houses, and slaves, the payments for which are made in lead, the usual medium of exchange. Some of the legal practices described in these contracts have been noticed above, and another which is of much juristic interest is the custom for joint heirs of a landed property to sell their portions before the details, especially the position, of their shares in the inheritance had been defined[4]—a mortgage of expectations. The buyer acquired the right to 'choose and take' whichever part of the estate should fall to the lot of the heir in a certain territory. A modification of this was the practice of selling the deed-tablet which gave title to a property, the buyer of such a tablet obtaining the right to 'demand and take possession'. Even princes thus disposed of ground which had become the 'share of the palace'[5] by titles which are unexplained or by confiscation. They also accepted payment for transferring the deed of title to a royal fief from one holder to another.[6] Loans too are common among the Assyrian private documents, the commodities borrowed being usually lead or barley, and after the short period of the loan had elapsed interest was charged if payment was delayed. Meanwhile a pledge had been given by the debtor,[7] either land or slaves, from the use of which the lender might in certain circumstances compensate himself for the lead or barley taken out of his capital. Not only the debtor's house but his own person or his children[8] might serve as security for the loan.

The letters[9] found with the Kassite administrative tablets

---

[1] §vi, 2; §iii, 5.   [2] §v, 8; 13; 14; 15; 17; 29; 49; §i, 3; 10, 6 ff.

[3] §i, 3, 42 ff.   [4] §i, 10, 39 f., 149 f.; §v, 49.

[5] §i, 10, 43 ff.; §v, 41.   [6] §i, 10, 44 f.

[7] §i, 10, 96 ff.   [8] §i, 10, 117 ff.   [9] §v, 36; §v, 34, nos. 15–86.

and covering about the same period of time are of greater interest, though perhaps more often because of their form than their matter, which is frequently difficult of interpretation. They preserve the Old Babylonian (and indeed Sumerian) form of introduction 'to X say, thus Y...', assuming that a scribe will read out the contents to a perhaps illiterate recipient. But the salutations which follow this[1] show a characteristic increase of formality over those of the Hammurabi period; one official writing to another adds after his name 'your brother', and the phrase 'be it well with you!' which is ubiquitous in the Amarna and the late Assyrian letters. Not only this, but the greeting is extended 'to your house and your office' and the blessing of the gods who were patrons of the writer's city is added, 'may they protect your life, make your path perfect'. In addressing higher officials or even the king himself the compliments are naturally multiplied— 'to your house, your city, your territory, guards, forts, chariots, cattle, harvests, canals, craftsmen'; an almost fantastic phraseology of submission, indeed of servility, to the great king of Egypt is affected by some of the writers of the Amarna letters. An especially frequent phrase in the Kassite letters to a superior is 'I will go as the substitute of my lord',[2] which expresses the sender's readiness to take upon himself all evil which may threaten his master; this locution, sometimes preceded by 'I cast myself down',[3] is shared by a few Assyrian letters of the same period. The contents of these missives are not frequently of much interest, for many are reports of minor officials to the heads of their departments in the temples of Nippur.

Some topics of interest fall, nevertheless, to be discussed in them, such as weavers and their work, the progress of building operations[4] in a temple or upon an official house for which thousands of bricks have to be prepared,[5] irrigation, reed-cutting for use in canals and buildings, repair of flood damage, and maintenance of watercourses.[6] In the course of these appear complaints against royal commissars who are accused of misusing the city levies of workmen,[7] of giving arbitrary orders for tasks not authorized,[8] and of misappropriating temple property and personnel:[9] there is overt collision between the king's authority and the hardly less powerful interests of the great temples.[10] A highly curious group of letters from the Nippur archives concerns the conduct of a temple hospital or sick-room[11] of a special kind.

[1] §v, 36, 18 ff.; §v, 46, 6.   [2] §v, 46, 20 ff.; G, 5, vol. 3, 149.
[3] §v, 43, 369.   [4] §v, 46, 45 f.   [5] Ibid. 66 f.   [6] Ibid. 44 ff.
[7] Ibid. 59.   [8] Ibid. 60.   [9] Ibid. 59.   [10] Ibid. 61.   [11] Ibid. 25 ff.

The patients found in this were all female and belonged to the class of temple-singers, the hospital itself being established in the house of the goddess Gula, the divine physician, in the city of Nippur. About a dozen cases were under treatment at the same time, and frequent reports upon the condition of these were sent off, even at midnight, to a superior who occasionally gave directions himself about the cures to be administered. The prevalent diseases were fevers and coughs with various consequences, and the remedies given were medicinal drugs compounded from the plants which abound in the later medical texts, but also externally oil and bandages were applied. Nothing is heard about that other regular ingredient of healing, the incantation, doubtless because this was the business of a different specialist.

Two documents, of which considerable fragments exist in later copies, throw a baleful light upon the temper and institutions of the Assyrians in the renascence begun under Ashur-uballit I. The 'Middle-Assyrian laws' are only chance survivals of what must have been a larger collection, the legal character of which is not clear.[1] Of the two principal tablets, the first deals with offences generally concerning women, which involve incidentally such subjects as sacrilege, theft, enticement, slander, and murder, as well as rules concerning marriage and the conduct of women in public places, but most of these laws are directed to the punishment of sexual offences. In the other principal tablet the general subject is land-holding, with regulations concerning inheritance, sale, and irrigation-rights. Apart from the wealth of detail which these laws supply upon the life of the period, their cultural interest may be thought to lie in the general impression they give of a hard and primitively-minded society, not at all out of accord with the cruelties wreaked upon public enemies which so disfigure the later Assyrian annals.[2] These laws abound, in almost every section, with heavy fines and convict-labour, superadded to savage beatings and ghastly physical mutilations, inflicted upon men and women alike, to which the death-penalty, also freely awarded, can seem only an alleviation. It must be owned that the insistence upon such barbarities, coupled with the accident that some of the offences concerned are themselves of the more repellent kind morally, makes the 'Assyrian laws' disagreeable reading.

No less unpleasing a picture of a more private life, that of the king, is drawn by a series of regulations,[3] collected in the reign of Tiglath-pileser I, and issued by himself and by eight of his

---

[1] §v, 12, 12 ff.; see below, 475 ff.
[2] See, however, a palliation of these, §v, 37, 154.   [3] §v, 48.

predecessors. These regulations governed the conduct of the royal household in Ashur. Sons and brothers of the royal family dwelt there, but also a troop of courtiers and underlings, and especially the numerous women, pining and quarrelling through the idle days in their own quarters, which they hardly ever quitted, having their own ill-used maidservants, and being more distantly waited upon by eunuchs and royal officials, whose access was jealously measured and spied upon. The whole establishment was under the rule of a major-domo and a hierarchy of subordinates, admission to which was gained by passing a rigorous if undefined examination before a board of higher mandarins, who applied a meticulous test, and made errors or omissions at their peril, for the whole system rested upon a compulsory sycophantism, under which the non-informer suffered as severely as the offender. It is again the despotic spirit, the harsh discipline, the jealous seclusion, enforced by the same unmerciful sanctions, which give their whole tone to these decrees; the Assyrian royal residence was more of a prison than a palace. That a more enlightened régime could exist within the conditions and the mentality of that age is suggested by the almost contemporary instructions for officials among the Hittites.[1] Not only are these much wider in their range of interests, more concerned with the interests of a state than of an individual, but they stress rather the impiety of disloyal acts, and are content to leave their punishment to the offended gods, omitting the abominable man-inflicted cruelties. Shamshi-Adad I, in an earlier generation, had sharply rebuked his son at Mari for not keeping a better rule in his household.[2] It was perhaps only because the old tyrant had found ruling there a temper more humane and civilized than was ever allowed to penetrate the Assyrian court.

In literature the creative power of the Kassite period has been underestimated as compared with others, which pass for more glorious. Babylonian and Assyrian texts as a whole are anonymous, and their age can be determined, if at all, only by internal evidence, making much necessary allowance for alteration in the process of transmission through many centuries.[3] The Old Babylonian period, to which is due the preservation of so great a part of the literature now available certainly did not originate most of that which it committed to writing.[4] The succeeding period of the Kassites has hitherto been reckoned the age of

[1] §v, 40, esp. 6 f.
[2] §iv, 1, vol. i, no. 73. The reproach itself was undeserved, *ibid.* vol. xi, 120 ff.
[3] §v, 42, 17 f. [4] *C.A.H.* ii³, pt. i, pp. 210 ff.

collection and arrangement of this literary heritage. Such a contrast does indeed seem to be reflected in the diverse image of scribes belonging to these two epochs. The Old Babylonian scribe, for all his pretensions, is an everyday figure. Emerging from the hurly-burly of his school life, passed under the tutelage and the hands of very human, not to say vulgar, educators, the finished scribe shows little sign of having altered much of his adolescent habits. He was at pains to advertise himself as an adept in all trades, even if he specialized in some.[1] A man of letters indeed, and able to recommend himself to kings,[2] he was more often busied in very ordinary affairs as arbitrator, surveyor, cost-expert, businessman, engineer, and even craftsman, in all of which accomplishments he proclaimed his own merits as loudly as he denounced the ignorance and falsity of his rivals. This stirring and mundane figure seems (to us at least) quite absent from the scene in the Kassite period. It is true that scribes still perused the chequered experiences of their forebears in the pursuit of learning, but now as lesson-books provided with a translation into Akkadian,[3] in which guise they were found in the library of Ashurbanipal. But the Kassite scribes, who begin to take on a degree of individuality, are far different characters. Shadows appear of great names, authors and scholars, whose memory was kept alive and honoured by descendants in the same professions. To such men can be attributed not merely the study, the textual fixation, and the exegesis of traditional works, but more original authorship than can be actually identified with any other age. The 'epic' concerning the wars between Tukulti-Ninurta I of Assyria and Kashtiliash IV of Babylon dates itself to the latter half of the thirteenth century B.C. The epic of Erra, the Plague-god, composed (or, as he affirms, divinely received) by one who appended his own name to the composition is clearly dated by internal evidence and language to a time still later.[4] And finally the Babylonian 'Theodicy', also signed by its author in the acrostic form of its verses, was in one document provided with an actual date, which may be the reign of Adad-apla-iddina (1067–1046 B.C.).[5]

Nevertheless, it is clear both from the material itself and from the above-mentioned tradition of master-scribes that in this period was carried forward with great zeal the collection of classes of literature, the revision of their contents, their arrangement into series of numbered tablets, scarcely begun hitherto, and the translation of Sumerian texts into Akkadian, only half-

[1] §v, 19, 31 f.   [2] §v, 19, 37; §v, 20, 261.   [3] §v, 20.
[4] Upon these see above, pp. 30 f.   [5] §v, 31, 66 f., 76.

necessary in the Old Babylonian period, when much of the old language and learning was still living. These labours were accompanied by writing of gloss and comment, designed to expound the meaning of Sumerian originals to a body of students now almost wholly Akkadian-speaking. The desire to extract more refined and more comprehensive significance from the words and names of the tradition led to the common result of some misplaced ingenuity and overstrained etymologies being mingled with genuine interpretation, well exemplified in the often-fanciful commentary upon the 'fifty names of Marduk' which conclude the Creation Epic.[1] At this time began also the arrangement of large works of lexicography and of divination,[2] the supreme science of the Babylonians, into the series which embody the principal subjects of extispicy, astrology, and omens from signs upon earth, as they are found fully shaped and named in the late Assyrian kingdom. Authors and scholars with such accomplishments as these do honour to their age, and are entitled to be regarded as the Alexandrians of Babylonian literature.

Strong influences of culture emanating chiefly from the centres of Babylon and Borsippa undoubtedly began to prevail in Assyria about the time which is the subject of this chapter, and under the influence of Ashur-uballiṭ himself. In his reign occurs the first mention in Assyria of the god of Babylon,[3] who, it is revealed, already had a temple in the city of Ashur itself. The source of this information is a remarkable inscription[4] written by a private, if highly placed, individual named Marduk-nādin-ahhē, who declares himself the blessed of god and king, the favourite, the renowned, who rejoices the heart of his lord. He relates that he was granted the right to build for himself a dwelling 'in the shadow of the house of Marduk my lord'. This private residence is described as built with especial cunning and lasting materials, having a well of cold water and rooms for esoteric uses. Marduk and his divine spouse were besought to make it a place of repose for the builder and continue it as the dwelling of his posterity for evermore; the inscription ends with a cordial blessing upon Ashur-uballiṭ the king 'who loves me'. Nothing more is said of the relation, evidently close, between the Assyrian king and this highly favoured foreigner, but the purport of the inscription suggests that Marduk-nādin-ahhē was a man of particular accomplishments, and that he was in Assyria

[1] §v, 2, 198; §v, 30, 36.　　　　[2] §v, 42, 22, 24. See Plate 132 (c).
[3] §v, 39; §v, 38, 203 f; C.A.H. ii³, pt. 1, p. 210.
[4] G, 4, 388 ff.; G, 8, 38 ff.; §1, 3, 109.

by special invitation, for the purpose of inaugurating the cult of Marduk; so much is implied by his description of his house as built in the expectation of handing it on as the official residence for the priest of Marduk in each generation. A further interest may be found in the name of this individual, for he was the son of a certain Marduk-uballiṭ, son of Ushshur-ana-Marduk, and these latter names are one identical and the other closely similar to those connected with the writer who has left a curious treatise upon the making of glass.[1] Being dated in the reign of Gulkishar, this tablet is presumably earlier[2] than the age of Ashur-uballiṭ, but it may be that the protégé of the Assyrian king was a person of celebrated skill, the contemporary head of an old and famous family (he refers proudly to his forefathers), attracted to Assyria by its enlightened ruler in order to bring the real and imagined benefits of his Babylonian arts to the capital of the northern kingdom. But doubtless the strongest testimony to the prevailing Babylonian influence in the north, before the time of Ashur-uballiṭ, is found in the tablets of Nuzi already mentioned. There is exhibited the whole legal and official business of a completely foreign and heterophone community couched in the language and writing of Babylon, with a fraternity of native attorneys bearing professional Babylonian names[3] striving to cast their institutions as well as their documents as best they could into the medium solely recognized as the authentic vehicle of culture.

VI. NEW INFLUENCES IN ART

If in literature and all things of the intellect Babylon was at this time supreme it was not so in the material arts. The antiquities of this age are neither common nor particularly distinguished, but their general characteristic is a strong alien tinge. Apart from the boundary-stones, which display as marked innovations in the use of their sculptures as in legal ideas, the principal remains of this period are buildings and cylinder-seals. As concerns the first, the new Kassite foundation of Dūr-Kurigalzu, so far as it has been explored,[4] does not indeed reveal anything which is out of keeping with the Babylonian scene. But at Uruk there stood, on the north-east side of the great enclosure surrounding the stage-tower, a temple of peculiar form and decoration,[5] identified by brick-inscriptions as the work of a Kassite king Karaindash

---

[1] *C.A.H.* II[3], pt. 1, pt. 227. See Plate 132 (b).   [2] §v, 32, 68, n. 174 (d).
[3] §I, 20; §I, 10, 13.   [4] §vi, 2. See Plate 133 (a).
[5] G, 17, 1, 30 ff., pls. 11, 15–17.

(*c.* 1420 B.C.). The ruin of this temple was marked by two unusual features, first the form of the sanctuary, which was of the lengthwise shape, having the cult-image at one of the ends, not in the middle of a long wall, as was the custom in Babylonia; and this itself is evidence of some influence from the north or east, where this disposition of the image prevailed.[1]

Still more remarkable than this planning exception was the structure of the burnt-brick walls. As restored by the discoverers[2] (since no part was preserved for more than a few courses high) the walls carried on their outer side a series of deep niches, each the breadth of one whole brick, separated by spaces of the like width at the surface of the walls. The niches were occupied by figures in high relief, moulded on the edges of the bricks in such a way that the figure was wholly withdrawn behind the outer surface of the wall. All of these were divine; they wore low flat caps decorated with the single pair of horns which marked inferior or servant deities. Alternately they were male and female, the males bearded, the females wearing a necklace, and the two differing in the patterns of their skirts which fell full-length to the ground concealing the feet. Both alike held in the right hand, and supported with the left, a round-based vase from which sprang a double stream of water flowing outwards to each side, and combining with the streams from the next figure on either hand so as to fall in regular waves down the fronts of the panels separating the niches. In these figures and the streams which they pour out there is indeed nothing un-Babylonian; both the costume of the gods and their symbolic action of bestowing water[3] had been familiar long before the days of Karaindash. But as with the boundary-stones it was not the figures themselves which were novel but the use made of them. No earlier building is known in which these symbolic figures surround the whole outside, and a further innovation is the use of moulded bricks as a medium for producing a decoration in relief upon the surface of a wall.

If the pattern of this temple's exterior seems to have found little favour afterwards it was otherwise with this moulded brickwork which was destined to achieve great fame and popularity; the vast stately buildings of Nebuchadrezzar in Babylon made impressive use of it, so did the Assyrians, and so did Darius in his palace at Susa, recording that the brickwork was executed by the Babylonians.[4] Of all these monuments notable remains are still

---

[1] §VI, 1, 22 f.; §VI, 8, 304 ff.; §VI, 12.
[2] G, 17, 1, pls. 15, 16; G, 12, 63 f., pl. 70A.; G, 6, vol. IV, 2132 ff.
[3] §VI, 26. See Plate 133 (*c*).   [4] §VI, 13, 142 ff., ll. 28–30. See Plate 133 (*b*).

in existence, resplendent in the coloured glazes of which apparently there was no trace upon the building of Karaindash. It is perhaps significant that the only other such figures in moulded brick relief around a temple wall[1] have been found in pre-Achaemenid Susa. There they adorned a temple dedicated to the principal god In-Shushinak by two kings who reigned successively[2] in the twelfth century B.C. In this case too the figures were alternate, but not withdrawn into niches, as at Uruk. The first was a group of two subjects, the half-man, half-bull, divinity bearded and wearing a crown with multiple horns. His arms reached out to the side and touched the trunk and top of a stiffly fashioned palm with pendent dates. The other figure, less well defined, was apparently a standing goddess clasping her hands before her face in the posture of supplication. Above the figures seems to have run a band of quadruple zig-zag pattern, and inscriptions[3] were carried across the middle. It is not inviting to draw a confident conclusion from these two examples. Since they are at present the only two known it would seem logical to trace the influence from the earlier (at Uruk) to the later (at Susa), remembering the constant dependence of Susa upon Babylonian culture and fashions, and also that there is nothing un-Babylonian, but quite the contrary, in any of the subjects depicted. But as the arrangement and the technique were both novel it has been supposed that the temple walls at Uruk were created by an eastern inspiration due to the Kassite origin.[4] As to this, more evidence is required.

There can be no such doubt of the foreign influences prevailing in the cylinder-seals of this period—indeed, for the first time, the most numerous as well as the most characterized of these were not made in Babylonia at all and have nothing more than certain reminiscences of the land which invented them and by its prestige imposed their use upon foreigners. In the homeland itself the Kassite style was distinctive, but is so well known that it needs no description here.[5] Ornamental gold mounts at each end of the cylinders, if not unknown before,[6] became at least more common,[7] perhaps in consequence of the increased gold supply which was noticeable in this period.[8] The materials preferred for the cylinders were brightly coloured stones, chosen

---

[1] §vi, 25; G, 6, vol. ii, 932 f., but see now §vi, 29, 3.
[2] See below, pp. 437 f.   [3] §vi, 11, 57, no. 29.
[4] §vi, 1, 22; §vi, 12.
[5] G, 11, 180 ff.; §vi, 23, vol. i, 63; G, 6, vol. ii, 906 f.; §vi, 5; §vi, 19, 126 f., 140.
[6] §vi, 6, 47.   [7] §vi, 5, 267.   [8] See above, p. 24.

doubtless for supposed amuletic virtues,[1] the engraving was often shallow and rough. Single figures were the rule, accompanied by symbolic devices such as the familiar 'Kassite cross'. Another novel introduction was the long Sumerian inscription, filling most of the surface, generally prayers to a tutelary god, and often obscure in expression,[2] which may be regarded as another manifestation of the literary and learned interests of the period. But whereas these seals, apart from the importation of a few secondary motives, remained very much in the exclusive Babylonian tradition, there were flourishing at about the same time two other 'schools' which, since they occupied the geographical area of Assyria, must be noticed here. The first is amply illustrated by cylinders found at Nuzi,[3] and the numerous impressions upon the tablets from that town. The second is that which produced the class of seals called 'middle Assyrian',[4] but the title has a misleading implication, since they were in fact the first cylinders of native Assyrian style, formed in the age of national revival symbolized by the name Ashur-uballiṭ.

Much of the répertoire of the Nuzian artists was taken over by the Assyrians, but upon this material they imprinted a strongly individual stamp.[5] Inscriptions are rare and figures few, but these are chosen and combined with a new effectiveness which makes vigour and physical activity the keynote. Their favourite theme was combat,[6] the usual participants demons and monsters. Thus, two seals which bear the names of the kings Erība-Adad and Ashur-uballiṭ himself[7] represent winged demons of fearful aspect overcoming or dispatching smaller creatures or a lion; such winged apparitions, dragons, griffins, lions, and scorpions, in all postures of struggle, fill the Assyrian seals with a world of fantastic vigour which seems untrammelled with any purpose to tell a story but only to picture the clash of mythological terrors against daemoniac champions of the human kind, for, as their later literature shows, the Assyrians were subject to a gloomy cast of religious thinking, dominated by the fear of devils and the threat of ill omens. The seals often depict, likewise, a human figure probably of divine nature which shoots or slays a raging monster[8] and thus is conceived as protecting the owner of the seal. This idea contrasts strongly with the older Babylonian, where the amuletic virtue of the seal lay in its picture of the

[1] §vi, 18, 74, 88; §vi, 10.
[2] §vi, 3; 9; 14.
[3] §vi, 22.
[4] §vi, 5, 266 ff.; §vi, 18.
[5] §vi, 4, 200 ff.
[6] §vi, 4, 209.
[7] §vi, 4, 142 ff., Abb. 2, 17, 22.
[8] §vi, 18, 52 ff.; §vi, 5, 266 ff.

owner being led up to his god and recommended to his blessing, while in Assyria the whole emphasis was upon protection from the assault of hostile powers. The other principal subject of the Middle Assyrian seals is the group of animals or monsters ranged symmetrically on each side of a tree or plant,[1] an effective composition which, in addition to whatever religious significance attached to it, probably owed its favour as much to its artistic effect and to its peculiar suitability for the diminutive spaces which the craftsman had to fill.

The most significant distinction between the seals of this period is into two kinds which have been called the elaborate or well-cut, and the common style.[2] What principally gave rise to the rough execution of the latter was the use of a new material, in place of various kinds of stones. This was frit,[3] a composition of powdered silicious grains fused together and coated with coloured glaze—a substance which could be produced in quantity and shaped in moulds, with designs ready-made. The distribution of such seals in the Near East at this time was very extensive,[4] and evidently corresponded with a demand spreading far beyond the official class which had hitherto possessed them. This demand was both occasioned and supplied by a new technique of glass-working,[5] capable of providing cheap substitutes for the individual products of the stone-engravers, although at the sacrifice, as usual, of quality and design.

[1] §vi, 18, 73 ff.; §vi, 4, 160 f., 210; §vi, 5, 274.
[2] §vi, 22, 12, 107; §vi, 5, 274 ff.
[3] G, 11, 5, 278; §vi, 4, 186, 207; §vi, 23, 139; §vi, 15, 341.
[4] §vi, 5, 274, n. 95.
[5] *C.A.H.* II[3], pt. 1, p. 227. Yet in Egypt the use of this material for small objects, including seals, was much older, §vi, 15, 342.

CHAPTER XIX

EGYPT: THE AMARNA PERIOD AND THE END OF THE EIGHTEENTH DYNASTY

I. THE PROBLEM OF A CO-REGENCY BETWEEN AMENOPHIS III AND AKHENATEN

LETTERS from Tushratta of Mitanni and Shuppiluliumash of Hatti[1] show that on the death of Amenophis III his eldest surviving son, Neferkheprure Amenhotpe (Amenophis IV), who later in his reign took the name of Akhenaten, was accepted by these foreign princes as the new pharaoh. The problem remains whether he had been recognized by the Egyptians as the co-regent of his father for some time previously. The matter has been much discussed in recent years, one body of opinion maintaining the orthodox view that Amenophis IV acceded only after the death of his father and ruled for his full term of seventeen years alone, the other interpreting ambiguous evidence, much of it recently uncovered, as revealing that the son had ruled with his father for a decade or more. No side has produced conclusive proof to convince the other, and a final decision will have to await the emergence of further evidence, perhaps in the field of comparative chronology.

The scheme of chronology adopted in this History admits of no overlap in the reigns of Amenophis III and his son;[2] a co-regency, however, must allow for a joint rule lasting some eleven years.[3] The independence of the two courts and their officials would permit these alternative interpretations, but adjustments would have to be made in the case of certain events which are treated here as occurring consecutively, whereas they may have been coeval. Thus it should be borne in mind that tendencies in art and religion, for instance, which appear in the reign of Amenophis III and are described as anticipating the innovations of Akhenaten, may in fact be contemporary with them.

---

* An original version of this chapter was published as fascicle 71 in 1971; the present chapter includes revisions made in 1973.

[1] E.A. 27, E.A. 41.

[2] *C.A.H.* II³, pt. 1, pp. 316 n. 9, 322 nn. 7 and 10. See also §I, 1–21; A, 9.

[3] §I, 4, 110; §I, 5, 29; §I, 10, 37.

II. THE CHARACTER OF THE AMARNA 'REVOLUTION'

The new king was a pharaoh whose monuments have won for him, among modern scholars, the reputation of being the most remarkable king to have occupied the throne in the history of Egypt. Wide claims have been made for him as a thinker, religious reformer, artistic innovator, revolutionary and individualist.[1] It seems probable, however, that such opinions, based upon inadequate evidence, have led to many ill-founded conclusions about his originality and personal qualities. Few would now maintain that his outlook was any more international than that of other pharaohs whose sandals traditionally trod upon captive figures of the Nine Nations,[2] and who claimed to rule as gods over all that the sun encircled.

Akhenaten has also been credited with modern pacifist principles in his conduct of foreign policy that are difficult to reconcile with the testimony from damaged temple reliefs in which he appears as the conquering king smiting the age-old foes of Egypt.[3] Other scholars have seen him as a social revolutionary who chose his high officials and entourage, not from the old scribal families, but from new men of humble origins, free from hereditary traditions and orthodox habits of thought.[4] In the absence of a system of universal education in Egypt, however, it is doubtful whether the king could have found any trained personnel outside the small hereditary scribal caste who were capable of dealing with the essential paper-work by which the Egyptian bureaucratic machine functioned. Some at least of his high officials were clearly the sons of men who had held like offices during his father's reign, and it is to be suspected that many more affiliations lurk under non-committal names and titles.[5] It was a polite convention during the dynasty that such courtiers should occasionally refer to their king as having advanced them from humble origins. Thus Yuya, who was influential enough to arrange for his infant daughter to be married to Amenophis III when that king was a mere boy, refers to himself as one whom 'the pharaoh promoted and made great'.[6] Such protestations of lowli-

---

[1] G, 2, 356, 292; §II, 13, 207; §VIII, 14, 126–7.
[2] §I, 20, pl. 107 B; §IV, 5, vol. I, 119; §VIII, 14, pl. XI.
[3] §II, 5, fig. 19; §VIII, 11, 47, nos. 50–51 a; A, 9, 190–1.
[4] G, 6, 223–4; G, 8, 297–8; §II, 13, 207; §VI, 5, 539.
[5] §I, 4, 103–4; §VI, 1, 34.
[6] §II, 6, xv–xvi.

ness, like many official pronouncements in ancient Egypt, need not be taken at their face value.

The most striking of Akhenaten's innovations, and one that has gained for him the most attention in modern times, is a style of art which he instigated and which indeed seems revolutionary in its more bizarre forms, but which on closer examination is seen to be a mere distortion of the traditional manner of representing the royal family. The naturalism or realism that has been claimed for it[1] had already appeared in his father's reign.[2] Its true novelty is rather more subtle and lies in an iconography which was new and was created by artists having a non-traditional conception of spatial relationships.[3]

In only one aspect of his religious thinking is Akhenaten seen to be original—in his insistence on a true monotheism, as distinct from the henotheism of the sun-cult, which he embraced with such fervour as to arouse the strong suspicion that he was a religious fanatic. It is significant that the first great event of his reign should be a decree marshalling all the resources of the land for building temples to his god whom he identified by a didactic name which was his profession of faith—Re-Harakhte who rejoices on the horizon in his aspect of the light which is in the Aten (or Sun-disk).[4] This deity first appeared in the traditional iconic form of Re-Harakhte as a falcon-headed god, but was soon symbolized by the elaborated glyph for sunlight, a disk having a dozen or more rays emanating from it ending in hands, some of which hold the sign of life to the nostrils of the king and queen, but to no one else.[5] At the same time the enhanced divinity of the pharaoh, 'the beautiful child of the Aten',[6] is emphasized by the appointment of his own ritual priest or prophet, by the protestation or abasement of his followers when they are in his presence, and by the fact that prayers can be addressed to the god only through him as intermediary. Figures of the king and his family are substituted for Re-Harakhte at the entrance to the tombs of his officials, as indeed they replace representations of the owners themselves in all the principal scenes.[7] The old gods of burial were banished and Akhenaten's favourites prayed that in

[1] *E.g.* §II, 13, 214, 218–19; §III, 37, 33; §VIII, 21, 28.
[2] G, 7, fig. 142; §I, 20, 154, 180 (cf. Cairo Museum No. 33900).
[3] §VIII, 21, 11, 15. See below, sect. VIII.
[4] §III, 6, 209; §III, 24, 176.
[5] §II, 1, 24–5.
[6] G, 6, 228; §II, 13, 223–4; §IV, 17, 28; §IV, 20, 16; §VIII, 19, 91 ff.
[7] §II, 12, 84–5, 89; §III, 14, 35.

death they might rest eternally near him and behold him daily, for he was now the patron of the dead as well as of the living.[1]

In this respect, so far from being revolutionary, Akhenaten was reverting to beliefs current in the Old Kingdom when the dead in their mastaba-tombs were clustered around the pyramids of the sun-kings whom they had served in life. There is a distinct antiquarianism in this return to an earlier and more exalted status for the pharaoh which was already a feature of the preceding reign when the records of the past had been diligently searched in an endeavour to find the tomb of Osiris at Abydos and also to revive the proper ritual for the king's first jubilee.[2] It is perhaps significant in this context that a fragment of a predynastic or early archaic slate palette should survive, reworked on its reverse in the reign of Amenophis III with the name of his chief queen.[3]

This increase in the power and glory of the kingship was the inevitable political concomitant of Akhenaten's religious ideas. Such absolutism might have been effective if the king had busied himself with the *minutiae* of government, but it would seem that, absorbed as he must have been in his religious schemes, he left most of the vastly increased business of state to be carried on by his officials.[4] The introduction of monotheism into Egypt necessarily wrought changes in local affairs. The economy of Egypt was almost wholly dependent upon the utilization of land, and this was cultivated on behalf not only of the Crown and various corporate bodies, such as the royal harims, but also of the great temples of Thebes, Memphis and Heliopolis, and the local temples as well.[5] Even such a modest foundation as that of Khnum at Elephantine enjoyed income from estates which it owned as far afield as the other extremity of the country,[6] and although our information refers to conditions during the twelfth century B.C. there is no reason to believe that they differed essentially in the Eighteenth Dynasty. The dispersal of local priesthoods or the closing of the temples would have had the effect of transferring all their domains to the ownership of the pharaoh,[7] doubtless to the advantage of his deity, the Aten.

The administration of this great accession of property evidently ceased to be in the hands of the many local officials, particularly

---

[1] §II, 13, 223–4; §III, 13, Pt. I, 46.
[2] §II, 8, 462, ll. 9–10 of inscription; §II, 11, 17.
[3] Brooklyn Mus. No. 66. 175; §II, 3, 1–4.
[4] §II, 7, 156–7.   [5] §II, 9, 9–25.
[6] §II, 10, 61.
[7] *Ibid.* 23; §II, 9, 165–7, 189.

for fiscal purposes, and became the responsibility of the king's high officers of state, who may well have called upon the army as the only source of manpower able to enforce the payment of taxation. Without proper supervision the inevitable malpractices would have obtained a firm hold. Over-centralized government was doubtless to blame for the corruption, arbitrary exactions and mismanagement which Horemheb later had to suppress with a heavy hand in restoring the traditional form of government.[1]

The rapid building of the new capital city at El-Amarna and temples to the new god in every major centre must have drained the land of its labour and economic resources, and the lavish offerings to the Aten that were such a feature of the worship in the Great Temple at El-Amarna,[2] and probably elsewhere also, could only have been made at the expense of other cults. The fiscal system of Egypt had developed over the centuries and, by adjusting the claims of small local shrines, the larger temples and the departments of the Palace, had produced a system that operated without intolerable exploitation. But it must now have been overturned by new arrangements that poured the nation's resources into the coffers of the king and his god. It was doubt-less the chaos caused by the economic consequences of Akhen-aten's religious reforms that brought about a complete reversal to the old order as soon as he was dead. The recollection of the misery of such times was strong enough to bring upon him the odium of later generations.

III. THE REIGN OF AKHENATEN

The first important record of the new reign to have survived is a stela hewn on the east bank of the Nile at Gebel es-Silsila showing the (erased) figure of Amenophis IV wearing the Upper Egyptian crown and offering to Amon-Re.[3] The damaged text speaks of the opening of a quarry in the vicinity for extracting stone for the erection of a great benben sanctuary at Karnak for 'Re-Harakhte (who rejoices on the horizon) in his aspect of the sunlight which is in the Disk (Aten)'. For this purpose the king ordered that a muster should be made of all workmen from one end of the country to the other and that the high court officials should be put in charge of the work of cutting and transporting the stone. The quarry was evidently opened in a different place from the region

---

[1] §II, 7, 157; G, 6, 244–5; §V, 12, 311–18.
[2] §I, 18, 15, pls. VIa, VIb.
[3] G, II, v, 220; §III, 30, 261 ff.; §VIII, 40, fig. 1.

whence came the large blocks of fine sandstone used for the great temple of Luxor, which was left unfinished on the death of Amenophis III.[1] The small size of the new blocks was probably determined less by the shallow depth of the strata from which they were prised than by the ease with which they could be handled by a large, unskilled labour force.

The impressment of workers by *corvée* shows the importance that the new king placed upon the swift fulfilment of his plans. The remains of dismantled temples to the Aten recovered from the interior of several pylons and other parts of the main temple at Karnak betray distinct signs of the haste with which they were built, particularly in the often careless and summary cutting of the reliefs in the somewhat coarse granular stone.[2] The fact that the stela at Gebel es-Silsila does not bear a date doubtless points to its being carved in the very first months of the reign. Included in the king's titulary is the designation 'First Prophet of Re-Harakhte', but, since the pharaoh was *ex officio* the chief priest of every god in the land, the special emphasis given to the sacerdotal office here probably means that he had elected to celebrate the daily ritual in the temples of the Aten and in no other.

A series of temples was built at Karnak, mostly in sandstone, but, until their dismantled parts have been studied and published in detail, it is idle to speculate on the size and nature of these edifices. While they were doubtless built in a remarkably short time, their decoration must have taken much longer to complete. A temple to the Aten apparently existed at Karnak in the time of Amenophis III, if not earlier, to judge from blocks, much greater in size than those used in Akhenaten's constructions, which have been found in the core of the Tenth Pylon.[3]

Early in the reign, perhaps by the second year,[4] the Aten ceased to appear in the traditional therioanthropic form of Re-Harakhte and was represented by the symbol of the rayed disk. At the same time its didactic name was enclosed in cartouches and it acquired a titulary like a pharaoh's and an epithet to indicate that it had celebrated a jubilee.[5] Coincident with this epiphany of a heavenly king is the appearance of a new style of art which has been described as 'expressionistic' and 'realistic',[6] but the most prominent feature of which is a grotesque manner of

---

[1] *C.A.H.* ii³, pt. 1, pp. 395–6.

[2] §i, 20, 178–9; §iii, 16, 113–35; §iii, 41, 24 ff.

[3] §iii, 38, 28–9; §viii, 40, pl. 4; §viii, 46, 114; §i, 20, 179, n. 18.

[4] §ii, 1, 24.   [5] §iii, 24, 170–2.

[6] §i, 20, 179; §iii, 39, 57 ff.; §viii, 21, 28.

representing the royal family, particularly the king himself, as
though he suffered from a malfunctioning of the pituitary
system, with an overgrown jaw, receding forehead, prominent
collar-bones, pendulous breasts and paunch, inflated thighs and
spindle shanks.[1] Such a marked departure from the heroic and
idealistic traditions of royal portraiture could only have been
taken at the instigation of the king himself, and this is made clear
in the inscription of his chief sculptor Bak who claims that he
was 'an apprentice whom the king himself instructed'.[2]

Temples to the Aten appear to have been raised in most of the
principal towns of Egypt during these early years of the reign;[3]
but however vast and numerous they may have been, the Aten
could only be a parvenu on sites which had belonged to gods
since they had first manifested themselves during the creation of
the universe. The next ambition of Amenophis IV, therefore, was
to find the 'place of origin' of the Aten and to establish there a
great city dedicated to him, an ambition in which he claims to
have been directed by 'Father Aten' himself.

The favoured spot selected by the king under this divine
guidance proved to be a natural amphitheatre about eight miles in
diameter lying on the east bank of the Nile half-way between
Memphis and Thebes. To this site the modern name of Tell el-
Amarna has been rather loosely applied,[4] and this in turn has
been used to describe the period covered by the reign of Akhenaten. The king claimed that when found it was virgin ground
which belonged to no god, goddess, prince, princess nor indeed
to anyone. This may well have been the case, since no definite
traces of earlier occupation have been found at El-Amarna[5] and
its previous neglect was probably due to the extreme scantiness
of the living that could be scratched from the strip of cultivation
that bordered the river. Even today the villages on the site are
comparatively recent and among the poorest in Egypt. The City
of the Aten had to be sustained from the cultivation on the
opposite bank, and doubtless from the rest of Egypt, as its
population grew steadily during the reign.

In his fourth regnal year the king, accompanied by Queen
Nefertiti and his retinue, paid an official visit to the chosen site
and offered a great oblation to Re-Harakhte on the festal day of

[1] §III, 3, 305; §III, 2, 60–1; §III, 22, 29 ff; A, 1, fig. 12.
[2] §III, 25, 86.
[3] *E.g.* G, 11, III, 220, 222, 224; IV, 61, 63, 113, 121, 168, 259; V, 129, 144, 158,
196; VII, 73, 172–4.
[4] §III, 13, Pt. I, 1; §III, 35, 2.   [5] §I, 18, 4.

demarcating Akhetaten, 'the Horizon (seat) of the Aten', as the new township was called. After summoning his courtiers and high officers to him, he showed them the site and declared that it was the Aten alone who had revealed it to him. He then swore a solemn oath that he would make Akhetaten in that place and nowhere else, even though the queen and others might try to persuade him to build it elsewhere. He went on to name the various buildings that he proposed to construct there, among them a House of the Aten, a Mansion of the Aten, a House of Rejoicing for the Aten and palaces for himself and the queen.[1] It seems likely that in this respect he was erecting the counterparts of buildings that had already been raised in Thebes and elsewhere. He also stipulated that a tomb should be cut in the eastern hills for the burial of himself, the queen and the eldest daughter, Merytaten, and that, if any of them should die in another town of Egypt, he or she should be brought to Akhetaten for burial there. The burial of the Mnevis-bull, the sacred animal of the sun-cult, should be made in the eastern hills, thus indicating that Akhetaten was to replace Heliopolis as the chief centre of sun-worship. He then promised that the tombs of his high officials should also be hewn in the same hills and, since this proposal may well have caused consternation among his followers, who would have had to abandon their family burial-grounds, he was at pains to emphasize what an evil thing it would be if they were not interred near their king.[2]

All these declarations are contained in a proclamation, unfortunately imperfectly preserved, inscribed on three heavily damaged stelae hewn into the cliffs at the northern and southern extremities of the site.[3] The royal family paid another state visit to Akhetaten in Year 6 of the reign on the second anniversary of the first demarcation and set up landmarks in the form of additional great stelae on each side of the river, giving the precise dimensions of the township and defining its boundaries, which the king swore he would not go beyond.[4] This oath has been interpreted as indicating that the king shut himself up in his holy city and did not venture beyond its confines again,[5] but this is clearly a misunderstanding and the vow appears to be no more than an affirmation by the king that he would not extend the limits of the town beyond the boundaries he had stipulated, probably for

---

[1] §I, 18, 190. [2] §VI, 5, 300, n. 7.
[3] §III, 13, Pt. v, pls. XXIX–XXXII.
[4] *Ibid.* pls. XXVI–XXVIII, XXXIII.
[5] *E.g.* G, 3, 64; G, 8, 295; §II, 13, 215.

taxation purposes.[1] The entire area so designated was dedicated to the Aten, together with all its produce including its human inhabitants.

During the two years that had elapsed between the early and later proclamations, much of the central part of Akhetaten had been built and from that moment its occupation by the official classes began, if we are to judge from the incidence of dated dockets inscribed on the many sherds from broken wine-jars found on the site.[2]

The official quarters in the Central City were laid out on a fairly well-planned system, the large estates of the wealthy fronting upon two or three main thoroughfares.[3] Behind them the houses of the lesser officials were built on vacant lots and the hovels of the poor, usually sharing a common courtyard, were squeezed in wherever there was space. No system of drainage is evident and rubbish was dumped in any convenient pit or midden. The city spread northwards as its population grew and was still in process of being built when it was abandoned in the next reign. The South City housed the more important officials and was distinguished by a Maru-Aten[4] or so-called pleasure-palace, gay with a lake and basins and decorated with painted pavements and coloured inlays. Here were the kiosks or 'sunshade temples' dedicated to the daily rejuvenation of the queen and some of the princesses.[5]

The Central City contained the main official buildings such as the Great Palace, which extended for over 750 metres along one side of the principal thoroughfare and ran westwards to a frontage on the river. On its eastern boundary was the Great Temple (the 'House of the Aten') set within a huge enclosure about 750 metres long by 250 metres wide and containing several structures, notably the sanctuary and the 'House of Rejoicing' leading to the 'Gem-Aten' ('Aten is found').[6] Further south rose a smaller temple (the 'Mansion of the Aten') which appears to have been similar in design to the sanctuary of the Great Temple.[7] Both buildings appear to have been elaborations of the primitive sun-temple,[8] being a series of courts, open to the sky, with the focal point as an altar before a stela which took the place of the benben-

---

[1] G, 2, 365; §II, 2, 233–4. [2] §I, 18, 160.
[3] §I, 16, 35–45; §I, 20, 186–204; §III, 17, 32 ff.
[4] §III, 32, 109–24; §III, 5, 58 ff.
[5] §I, 18, 200–8.
[6] Ibid. 5–20. [7] Ibid. 92–100.
[8] §III, 36, 233, 237–8, 240–2.

stone pyramidion, as in the sanctuary of Re at Abu Ghurāb.[1] The stela, however, was an icon of the king and queen worshipping the Aten and not a sacred object of worship in itself. Because the Aten was not in tangible form, the daily ritual was of the simplest kind and centred around the presentation of lavish offerings. A later feature of the worship appears to have been the erection of a dense mass of altars in a vast area lying to the south of the 'House of Rejoicing'.[2]

Between these two temples lay such official quarters as the 'King's House', with its magazines and gardens connected by a bridge over the main road to the Great Palace.[3] Also in the vicinity were the 'House for the Correspondence of Pharaoh', where the celebrated Amarna Letters were found,[4] the Office of Works and the Police Headquarters. Half a mile downstream was the North Suburb containing the less pretentious houses of the merchants and minor officials, standing cheek by jowl with the slums of the poor.[5] The chief quays of the city appear to have been situated here and received the produce brought over daily from the cultivation on the west bank and from elsewhere. Further downstream at the extremity of the site was the North City, which has not been fully excavated or published. It contained other palaces and official quarters.[6]

The temples and the offices of the Great Palace were built of limestone, apparently quarried locally, and supplemented in certain parts with blocks of alabaster, quartzite and granite. All the domestic building, however, was in mud-brick, sometimes coated with plaster and painted. The mansions of the wealthy had stone thresholds, door-jambs, lintels, column-bases and window-grilles; bathrooms were fitted with stone splash-backs and lustration slabs.[7] Columns and doors were of wood. Such domestic architecture appears to have differed little in style and methods of construction from the palace-city of Amenophis III at Western Thebes,[8] but a novel feature of the Amarna buildings was the use of inlays of coloured stones, glass and faïence, often applied in a kind of mosaic.[9]

Particulars of the topography and architecture of Akhetaten

[1] §III, 7, vol. I, 7–56.   [2] §I, 18, pl. VIA.   [3] *Ibid.* 86–105.

[4] *Ibid.* 113–30; §III, 35, 23–4; §VII, 5; §VII, 7.

[5] §III, 19, 1–4.

[6] §III, 34, vol. XVII, 240–3, vol. XVIII, 143–5.

[7] §III, 19, 98–100; §I, 20, 198–204; §III, 32, 37–50.

[8] *C.A.H.* II³, pt. I, p. 341 n. 2.

[9] §III, 35, 10–12, 28, pl. VI; G, 8, 288–307.

have been recovered by archaeological missions from Britain, France and Germany,[1] which have dug much of the site in the present century. The tombs of the officials hewn in the cliffs and foothills on the northern and southern flanks of the eastern boundary have, however, been available for study since the days of the early Egyptologists. Their sculptured walls are the main source of our knowledge of events at El-Amarna during the king's reign and of the character of the new teaching of Akhenaten.[2]

The later boundary stelae show that, by the time they were carved in Year 6, the king had changed his *nomen* to Akhenaten, while the name of Queen Nefertiti was inflated to include the epithet Neferneferuaten. The titles of the Aten were also altered to indicate that it had celebrated a further jubilee.[3] Probably all three changes took place at the same moment. The later boundary stelae bear a codicil dated to Year 8 in which it is stated that royalty was again in Akhetaten for the purpose of inspecting the boundaries on the south-eastern frontier of the city. A more explicit reference on two of them repeats the oath of the king in fixing the limits of the city and dedicating the entire region to 'Father Aten'.[4]

At some time between this date and the pharaoh's twelfth regnal year, the didactic name of the Aten was altered from its earlier form so as to remove the last vestiges of the old therio-anthropic concept from the idea of the sun as a deity.[5] The falcon-symbol, which had been combined with the hieroglyph of the sun's disk to indicate Re in his aspect of Harakhte (i.e. at his rising and setting on the eastern and western horizons) was replaced by a shepherd's crook, thereby changing the name to an abstract phrase meaning 'Re, the ruler of the horizon'. This change probably coincided with other changes of a similar kind, such as the substitution of phonetic spellings for words like 'truth' and 'mother' which had formerly been determined by hieroglyphs in the shapes of the vulture (the symbol of the goddess Mut) and the figure of a squatting woman with a feather on her head (the symbol of the goddess Maet). The new form of the name of the Aten appears at the same time as changes in its epithets, suggesting that it had celebrated a third jubilee.[6] The exact date when this development occurred is not known with certainty, but

[1] §III, 32; §III, 19; §I, 18; §III, 8; §III, 10.
[2] §III, 9; §III, 13.
[3] §III, 24, 172; §II, 1, 24–31. [4] §III, 13, Pt. v, pl. xxxiii.
[5] §III, 24, 174–6; §III, 6, 208–9. [6] §II, 1, 30–1.

there appears to be no reason to dispute the conjecture that it was in Year 9.[1]

The later form of the name of the Aten appears in the reliefs of private tombs in the northern group at El-Amarna, which were among the last in the series to be hewn. Two scenes in these tombs give differing versions of the presentation of gifts to the pharaoh and are dated by the text to his twelfth regnal year.[2] The representations show the king and queen being carried in their state palanquins to their thrones set up under a great baldachin at Akhetaten. With their six daughters beside them they receive gifts presented by delegates who, according to the accompanying text, came from 'Syria and Kush (the North and the South), the East and the West, and from the Islands in the Mediterranean, all countries being united for the occasion so that they might receive the king's blessing'. Representations of such ceremonies with similar texts are common in tombs of the Eighteenth Dynasty, and it has been argued that they record an event which took place on the occasion either of the king's accession to the throne or of his jubilee, and not the reception of annual tribute or plunder from successful wars, as has generally been supposed.[3] If this be so, the ceremony of Year 12 at Akhetaten must have marked either Akhenaten's accession to sole rulership or his jubilee. The alternative explanation, that Akhenaten arranged a great parade of tribute from his vassals in order to impress his followers at Akhetaten with the power and influence that he exerted abroad,[4] is difficult to reconcile with the apparent collapse of the Egyptian 'empire' in Asia during his reign.[5]

In about the same year the Queen-Mother Tiy either paid a state visit to Akhetaten with her young daughter Baketaten or took up residence there. Evidence of the visit is provided by pottery jar-dockets found at El-Amarna which mention her house and that of Baketaten.[6] Moreover her steward, Huya, was granted a tomb in the northern group, one of the last to be hewn at El-Amarna.[7] Representations in its chapel show Tiy being given a sunshade temple at Akhetaten by her son, who also furnished her with new burial equipment, perhaps intending that, like her courtiers, she should be buried near him.[8] A fragment of red granite inscribed with her name and with the praenomen

---

[1] §III, 40, 116; §I, 18, 153.　　　[2] §III, 13, Pt. III, pl. XIII; Pt. II, pl. XXIX.
[3] §VII, 3, 105–16.　　　[4] §I, 16, 20–1; §III, 13, Pt. II, 43.
[5] §I, 16, 22–7; G, 2, 389. See, however, below, p. 82 ff.
[6] §I, 18, 164, nos. 4, 14, 200(d), (ii), (iii).　　　[7] §III, 13, Pt. III, pl. VIII.
[8] §IV, 11, pls. XXVII–XXIX, XXXI, XXXII.

of Amenophis III has been found in the Royal Tomb at El-Amarna, but probably belongs to the shattered sarcophagus of Meketaten.[1]

This tomb, in a wādi among the eastern hills at El-Amarna, was prepared as a family sepulchre in accordance with promises on the early boundary stelae. Some reliefs in the subsidiary rooms show the king and queen mourning over the bier of their second daughter, Meketaten, who died some time after the ceremony of Year 12. The presence of a nursemaid holding a baby in these scenes of poignant grief has provoked the suggestion that the princess died in childbirth,[2] which, if true, appears to indicate that the reliefs could hardly have been carved before Year 14 at the earliest. It was soon after this event that Queen Nefertiti too disappeared from the scene, her place being taken by the eldest of her six daughters, Merytaten. This change in her fortunes has been attributed to her fall from the king's favour. The evidence is largely contained in reliefs from the *maru*-temple in the southern part of the city, where a 'sunshade' dedicated to her originally has had its inscriptions and reliefs re-cut to refer to Merytaten.[3] It seems much more probable, however, that this usurpation followed on the death of Nefertiti soon after Year 14, when her sunshade was adapted to serve the needs of her eldest daughter. If she had been disgraced, much more evidence would have been forthcoming in the wholesale excision or alteration of her name and figure in the many representations of her that have survived.[4] The archaeologists who re-excavated the royal tomb in 1931 found evidence that led them to believe that the main chamber had been prepared for her burial.[5]

The place of the queen was taken for a time by her daughters, first by Merytaten and then by the latter's eldest surviving sister Ankhesenpaaten.[6] These two princesses must have played influential rôles at the court of Akhenaten in the last four years of his reign, the elder being mentioned under a hypocoristicon by foreign correspondents in some of the Amarna Letters.[7]

A notorious incident of the reign, and one that has left its mark on not a few of the standing monuments of Egypt, is the

---

[1] *Cf.* §iv, 16, 102, n. 2; A. 6.

[2] §iii, 9, 21, pls. vii–ix; §viii, 14, 153; §vi, 7, 208; §iii, 31, 229; For other views, see §iii, 40, 116; §iv, 28, 174, n. 44.

[3] §iii, 32, 154–6; §i, 5, 56–7.   [4] §ii, 2, 242.

[5] G, 15, 88–9.

[6] §vii, 1, 191–3; §iii, 11, 104–8; §vii, 4, 12.

[7] E.A. 10, 44; E.A. 11, rev. 26; E.A. 155, *passim*.

iconoclastic fury which the king unleashed against other cults, particularly that of the influential Amun of Thebes. His agents were active throughout the land in destroying effigies of the gods and excising their names from objects great and small. Even the cartouche of his father, which bore the hated name of Amun in its composition, did not escape the hammers of these zealots. Some at least of the extensive damage which they wrought was not repaired until the reign of Ramesses II. The precise point in the reign of Akhenaten when this campaign of persecution was instigated is difficult to place. The king's name is still given in its Amenophis form in a letter from Ghurāb dated to Year 5,[1] but on the boundary stelae of Year 6 it has changed to Akhenaten. It has been supposed, therefore, that the excisions were made about the time of the *hijrah* to Akhetaten, and later references to Amun in the reign must represent a compromise in the king's views and a partial recognition of the old proscribed cults.[2] But there is evidence that the iconoclasm may belong to the very last years of his reign.

Among the jewellery found in the vicinity of the royal tomb in 1883 and presumed to have belonged to one of the royal women who was buried there after Year 14 is a finger-ring, bearing on its bezel an inscription 'Mut, Lady of Heaven', which shows no signs of any attempt at alteration or obliteration.[3] Since such small items as scarabs often had the name of Amun excised during this period,[4] it is surprising to find that a finger-ring worn by royalty late in the reign could preserve the name of the equally ostracized Mut.

Another piece of evidence is afforded by the shrine made by Akhenaten for Queen Tiy, which bore the names of the Aten in their late form showing that it was made after Year 9 and most probably after Year 12. The words for 'truth' and 'mother' appear in its inscriptions in those phonetic forms which came into use as Akhenaten's ideas of godhead developed along more abstract and monotheistic lines. Yet it seems that when it was first carved the *nomen* of her husband had appeared on it with the Amun element intact.[5] It had subsequently been excised by the iconoclasts and the praenomen substituted in red paint. This evidence, if reliable, would support the theory that the campaign of excision and suppression took place in the last years of Akhenaten's life.

---

[1] §III, 21, 343–5.
[2] *E.g.* §I, 16, 28.
[3] §II, 2, 3, 156, pl. XII; §IV, 3, 45.
[4] §I, 18, pl. LXXVII, 6.
[5] §IV, 11, 14; §IV, 31.

The latest known date of the reign is Year 17 contained in dockets on jars found at El-Amarna, and this would appear to indicate that he died before the grape-harvest in his 18th regnal year.[1]

IV. THE IMMEDIATE SUCCESSORS OF AKHENATEN

Who the immediate successor of Akhenaten was presents a problem. In the tomb of Meryre, the Chief Steward of Nefertiti at El-Amarna, there appears a scene sketched in ink on a wall of the main hall showing the owner being rewarded for his services by a king and his queen whose names in cartouches are given as Ankhkheprure Smenkhkare and Merytaten.[2] Since the contiguous wall has an elaborate relief showing the tribute of Year 12 being received by Akhenaten and Nefertiti, the presumption is that soon after that date Smenkhkare was made king and married to the eldest daughter of Akhenaten, by which alliance he strengthened any claim he may have had to the throne. Meryre evidently continued in office as steward under the new queen, though he was unable to complete the decoration of his El-Amarna tomb, probably because the Court moved elsewhere.

A dated graffito scribbled in a tomb at Thebes[3] shows that by his third regnal year Ankhkheprure had adopted the nomen of Neferneferuaten in place of Smenkhkare, or as an alternative to it.[4] This change presumably did not take place until the death of Nefertiti who had previously added this same name to her own by Year 6 of her husband's reign.[5] The graffito also mentions the funerary temple of Neferneferuaten as being in the estate of Amun, indicating that by that date at least the site of the royal tomb had reverted to the necropolis at Thebes. Merytaten certainly played an important rôle at El-Amarna after the death (?) of her mother and is believed to have borne a daughter, Merytaten-tasherit, while still a princess.[6] Since Akhenaten appears to have advanced the next of his surviving daughters, Ankhesenpaaten, to her sister's position of favour before his death,[7] the evidence suggests that Smenkhkare was made co-regent and married to Merytaten before the end of the reign of Akhenaten.[8] Monuments have

---

[1] §III, 18, 108–9.   [2] §III, 13, Pt. II, pl. XLI, cf. pls. XXXIII. and XXXVII.
[3] §IV, 18, 10–11.   [4] For a contrary opinion see §VI, 8.
[5] See above, p. 59.   [6] A, 8, 288.
[7] §III, 11, 104–8; §VII, 4, 12 n. 1; cf. §I, 20, 278 n. 4; A, 8, 289, 4a.
[8] §IV, 23, 3–9.

survived which reinforce this view. An unfinished stela from El-Amarna shows two kings seated on thrones side by side in affectionate intimacy, and another represents a young king pouring wine into an elder king's cup, much as Nefertiti was earlier shown performing that office for her husband.[1] Although the cartouches on both unfinished stelae are not inscribed, it seems clear on stylistic grounds that Akhenaten and a younger co-regent are seen together, as also appears to be the case on a sculptor's model relief excavated at El-Amarna showing differing official portraits of the two kings side by side.[2] A fragmentary stela in London is inscribed with the names of Akhenaten, followed by those of Neferneferuaten, above a scene which may have shown both kings together.[3] A box-lid found in the filling of the tomb of Tutankhamun bears the titularies and names of Akhenaten, Neferneferuaten and Merytaten, suggesting that they were all ruling together.[4] Moreover, Neferneferuaten incorporated into his cartouches epithets to show that he was 'beloved' of Akhenaten, and his assumption of the other name of Nefertiti suggests that he had in some way filled the position formerly occupied by Akhenaten's chief queen.

The evidence is therefore strongly circumstantial that Smenkhkare was specially favoured by Akhenaten and appointed his co-regent. As such he would have dated the years of his rule from the time of his accession.[5] The question remains whether he survived his senior partner or died before him. The recent publication of an inscription from Hermopolis has given grounds for believing that Merytaten predeceased him, whereupon he married the next heiress, her sister Ankhesenpaaten.[6] This has been accepted as warrant for thinking that Akhenaten, who in his time had also taken Ankhesenpaaten as his consort in place of Merytaten, must have died before him.[7] The argument, however, is far from being conclusive. If Smenkhkare enjoyed any independent rule it could have lasted no more than a few months since a docket on a honey-jar from El-Amarna with Year 1 written below a partly expunged Year 17 is against the view that Smenkhkare ruled alone, and most probably belongs to the successor of Akhen-

[1] §IV, 23, 7; §VIII, 40, pls. 30, 31; cf. §III, 13, Pt. II, pl. XXXII.
[2] §I, 18, 19, pl. LIX, 1; §III, 34, vol. XIX, 116; §IV, 14, 103; §II, 2, pl. 68.
[3] §I, 18, 231–2; A, 11, 104.   [4] §IV, 23, 5 (Carter Cat. No. 1 K).
[5] §IV, 19, 23.
[6] A, 9, p. 169, 5d (826–VIIA). It should be noted, however, that she is not given a queen's titles; nor is her name enclosed in a cartouche like Merytaten's, which could suggest that she filled a subsidiary role while her elder sister was still chief queen.   [7] A, 3, 16.

aten, who in that case must be the boy-king Tutankhaten.[1]
This view is reinforced by another docket from a wine-jar, excavated from the Central City at El-Amarna, reading 'Year 1,
wine of the house of Smenkhkare, deceased...',[2] which can only
mean that, in the first regnal year of an undisclosed king,
Smenkhkare was dead, although wine from his estate was still being bottled. The king in question must be the same Tutankhaten.

Very few of the monuments of Smenkhkare have survived. No
representation in relief or statuary bears his indisputable name,
and a recent attempt to identify his portraits among the Amarna
sculptures has further complicated the problem by confusing his
features with those of Nefertiti, Tiy, Amenophis III and Akhenaten.[3] The most reliable portrait of this king must be sought in
the canopic coffinettes of Tutankhamun, which were originally
made for Smenkhkare since they were inscribed with his name,
still visible under the cartouches of the later king on the interior
surfaces of their gold shells.[4] In adapting them for his successor,
it is to be presumed that a minimum of alteration was made, and the
portait mask on each coffinette was left untouched. Some items at
least of his burial furniture were not used for his interment and
appear to have been adapted for his successor, Tutankhamun.[5]

This latter king was little more than nine years old at his
accession.[6] Nevertheless he was married, as custom required, to
the heiress Ankhesenpaaten, the third daughter of Nefertiti and
presumably the eldest surviving princess. For a time at least the
pair appear to have resided in a palace in the northern quarter
at El-Amarna,[7] but a decision was soon taken to abandon
Akhetaten as a Residence and to make the palace quarters at
Memphis, which had still been used in the previous reign, their
main seat of government.[8] They evidently also refurbished the old

---

[1] §I, 18, pl. xcv, no. 279.

[2] *Ibid.* 164, no. 8, pl. LXXXVI, 35; §IV, 27, 55, D, III, 4.

[3] *Ibid. passim*; A, 1, *passim*.

[4] Roeder's denial (§IV, 27, 71) is unjustified. §I, 7, 137, pl. XXIII; §IV, 17, 39; §VIII, 20, pl. 46; §IV, 5, vol. III, pl. LIV; §VIII, 14, pl. XXXIV; A, 2, no. 9. See Plate 134 (*a*).

[5] §IV, 5, vol. II, 84–5; §I, 7, 136, 138; §IV, 29, 642 ff.; see also p. 70, n. 5.

[6] This deduction is based on the estimated length of his reign and his age at death, as revealed by his mummy. See §IV, 5, vol. II, 158–60.

[7] §III, 34, vol. XVII, 243; §I, 16, 29.

[8] G, 8, 173–6; §IV, 2, 12 n. 25; §II, 2, pls. 8, 9; §IV, 23, 8; §VI, 5, 538–9. It should be noted that this decision appears to have been taken very early in the reign. Pendlebury found houses in the northern suburbs in process of building at the time of their abandonment with little or no evidence of stonework inscribed after Akhenaten. The ring-bezels of post-Akhenaten date were inscribed for Tutankh*amun* (§III, 19, 3, 71). *Cf.* G, 6, 236.

palace of Amenophis III at Medīnet Habu for use whenever their presence was required at Thebes.[1] The artificial town of Akhetaten with its inflated population of officials, craftsmen, priests and workers and its essential garrison could not be sustained from the local resources alone, and when the Court was moved elsewhere it was inevitable that Akhetaten would no longer be able to support itself, but would dwindle to the status of a mere village. In fact, the evidence uncovered by the spade suggests that the entire area had been deserted by Ramesside times in favour of Hermopolis across the river.

The reign of Nebkheprure Tutankhaten (Tutankhamun) was comparatively short. His ninth regnal year is inscribed on two wine-jars from his tomb, and in addition four other dockets bear a Year 9 which is almost certainly his.[2] Another wine-jar, dated to Year 10, also probably refers to his reign and suggests that he ruled for a full nine years.[3] Despite the finding of his burial, however, with its great wealth of golden treasure virtually intact,[4] the monuments of his reign which yield historical data are regrettably few. The most important of them is the so-called Restoration Stela, found near the Third Pylon of the temple of Amun at Karnak, which had been usurped by Horemheb.[5] It is exceptional in Egyptian annals for its confession of past sins and the frank statement of the situation that faced the young king at his accession, with the temples from one end of the country to the other fallen into neglect and the land in a state of confusion through the indifference of the offended gods. Foreign ventures met with no success and the prayers of suppliants went unanswered. The stela goes on to relate the measures which the king was taking to restore confidence in the nation and to propitiate the gods. These included the fashioning of new statues and sanctuaries of the chief deities in gold and precious stones, the repairing of their neglected shrines, the re-establishment of their daily services and offerings, and the restoration of their sequestered treasure and revenues. New priesthoods were created to re-establish the lapsed rituals, and to these were nominated the sons and daughters of notables who commanded the respect of the local populace. Most of the temple serfs and musicians were appointed from the palace staff and their upkeep was made a charge on the king's revenues. In this we may perceive a complete reversal of the policy which had been pursued by Akhenaten, whereby the local

[1] §I, 10, 177, 242. [2] §IV, 6, 3, nos. 18–23. [3] Ibid. no. 24; §IV, 7, 39, §3.
[4] §IV, 5; §VIII, 20; §VIII, 14; §IV, 6; §IV, 29; A, 2. See Plate 134(c).
[5] G, 9, no. 34183; G, 13, 2025 ff.; §IV, 2, 8–15; §V, 12, 128–35, 235–7.

temple revenues had doubtless been diverted into the treasury of the Aten and the pharaoh.

Since the king was still a minor when these decrees were promulgated, it is clear that they were made at the suggestion of his advisers, the most prominent of whom was the vizier and regent Ay, who had served Akhenaten as a Master of the Horse and who must now have counselled a return to traditional policies that had worked well in the past.[1] The reins of government were picked up from the point where they had been dropped by Amenophis III, and a start was made on completing that king's monuments as at Luxor and Sulb.[2] The worship of Amun was restored. The royal pair changed their names so as to honour the god of Thebes, where a tomb was begun or extended for the young king, probably in the western branch of the Valley of the Kings, near the sepulchre of Amenophis III.[3] The mortuary temple on the west bank at Thebes is known from at least one reference[4] and this was probably in the Medīnet Habu area, though its remains have not been identified. The colossal statues destined for this temple were unfinished at the time of the king's death and were usurped by his successors.[5]

The removal of the Court from Akhetaten to Memphis, accompanied by its large retinue of officials and chamberlains, would certainly have been followed by the exodus of most of the remaining professional classes with their valuables and house-fittings.[6] Some activity was still carried on in the town, largely at the faïence- and glass-works attached to the Great Palace.[7] The withdrawal of the town garrison would have invited the looting of the local cemeteries. Those who had died there must in the main have been removed to family burial-grounds in other parts of the country, since no cemeteries, apart from a few poor burials, have been found at El-Amarna.[8] No doubt the royal burials were also transferred elsewhere. In 1907 a small tomb, No. 55, was uncovered in the Valley of the Kings at Thebes, which contained a decayed mummy in an elaborate coffin of the royal type and the remains of funerary furniture, including the dismantled parts of the large gilded wooden shrine made for Queen Tiy by Akhenaten.[9] The burial had been desecrated and the names on the coffin excised before the tomb was re-sealed in antiquity. The mummy has recently been re-examined with the aid of modern techniques by medical experts whose findings leave little room for

[1] §IV, 24, 50–2; §V, 19, 58.   [2] §IV, 15, 3–9; §I, 21, 278.
[3] G, 15, 89–90, 92.   [4] G, 7, fig. 191.   [5] §V, 15, 101–5.
[6] §III, 19, 3.   [7] §III, 35, 44.   [8] §III, 32, 95; §III, 8.   [9] §IV, 11.

doubt that it is of Smenkhkare, who died in his twentieth year.[1] A reappraisal of the objects left in Tomb No. 55 and the circumstances in which they were found has also recently sought to show that, before desecration, this small tomb-chamber housed the burials of Queen Tiy, Akhenaten and Smenkhkare, and that it was under Tutankhamun that their remains were deposited here.[2] It would seem that from the first there was no intention of burying Akhenaten in the tomb he had designed for himself at El-Amarna. Fragments of his alabaster canopic chest, found in the royal tomb, show no signs of the staining by the sacramental oils that would have been poured into it if it had ever been used.[3] It is virtually certain that other burials of the royal family, including those of Nefertiti and Meketaten were also transferred to Thebes during the reign of Tutankhamun, though their heavy stone sarcophagi were left behind, to be smashed into thousands of fragments and scattered far and wide in Ramesside times. During the transfer of the burials from the royal tomb some items of personal jewellery belonging to one of the royal women were apparently stolen and hidden nearby, to be found again in 1883 by natives during their illicit operations in the royal wādi.[4]

Certain objects of no intrinsic value were, however, left behind at El-Amarna, notably the master-portraits, model reliefs, plastercasts and half-completed studies found during this century in the ruins of several sculptors' studios in the town.[5] These works represented defunct persons, particularly members of the royal family, whose portraits were no longer being carved. In the Bureau of the Correspondence of Pharaoh, too, was a mass of cuneiform tablets, comprising despatches from the great kings and vassal princes of Asia, which had been received during the reign and filed away in the archives. These clay tablets, the famous Amarna Letters,[6] were also not removed, though there is some evidence that they had been buried in a hole dug beneath the office floor.[7] It is to be presumed that the Egyptian clerks did not trouble to take away these cumbersome and weighty records, since they would probably have had copies of them written in Egyptian on easily portable papyrus, according to age-old Egyptian office procedure.[8]

[1] §III, 27, 95–119.
[2] §II, 2, 140–62; §III, 2, 41–65; §IV, 17, 25–40; §IV, 20, 10–25; §IV, 31, 193–9.
[3] §III, 26, 537.   [4] §II, 2, 243, pls. XII, 109; §IV, 3, 45.
[5] §I, 18, 34, 80, 81; §IV, 14, 96–101, 106; §III, 8, no. 52; §VIII, 39; §VIII, 13, pls. 12–19; A, 1, ch. III. See Plate 134 (b).
[6] See below, ch. XX, sect. 1.
[7] §I, 18, 114; §III, 35, 23–4; cf. §I, 5, 34, 35.   [8] §II, 2, 203–4.

Tutankhamun did not live long enough to see his policy of a return to the orthodox traditions of his dynasty take full effect. He died in his nineteenth year, perhaps as the result of a wound in the region of his left ear which penetrated the skull and resulted in a cerebral haemorrhage.[1] How this lesion was caused must remain a mystery, but the nature and seat of the injury make it more likely to be the result of a battle wound or an accident than the work of an assassin.

He left no children to succeed him. Two mummified human foetuses found in his tomb in coffins inscribed with his name are generally taken to be his children, born prematurely and subsequently buried with him.[2] It was at his death that his widow, Queen Ankhesenamun, wrote to the Hittite King Shuppiluliumash asking him to send to Egypt one of his sons, whom she would marry and so make him pharaoh. The suspicious Shuppiluliumash hesitated too long, and when at length he despatched Zannanzash the young prince was killed while making his way to Egypt.[3]

The reason for Ankhesenamun's extraordinary request can only be surmised, but it would seem that Tutankhamun was the last male in the line of descent, and with him the family of Amosis, the virtual founder of the Eighteenth Dynasty, came to an end. Whomsoever his widow married would *ipso facto* be the next pharaoh, and in this quandary it is probable that Ankhesenamun and her advisers sought the hand of powerful foreign royalty rather than that of a native commoner, in conformity with the ideas of the age regarding the divinity of kings. There had been a tradition of intermarriage between the ruling houses of Egypt and the Mitanni for the previous three generations at least; since at this time the Hittites were in the process of absorbing the Mitanni (see p. 83 below), perhaps it was thought politic to transfer the marriage alliance to them. The death or murder of Zannanzash, however, put an end to this scheme. The new pharaoh was the Vizier Ay, who is shown in a painting on the wall of the burial chamber of Tutankhamun's tomb officiating as the dutiful successor at the last rites.[4]

Recent attempts to interpret the inscriptions on damaged architraves retrieved from the Third Pylon at Karnak as demonstrating that Ay served for a time as the co-regent of Tutankhamun have been shown to be mistaken; such a joint rule of a young king

[1] *The Times*, Science Report, 25 October 1969: *Nature*, 224 (1969), 325–6.
[2] §IV, 5, vol. III, 88, 167–9.   [3] See above, pp. 17 f.
[4] §IV, 29, 647–8, 659–60, fig. 90, pl. CXVI; §I, 20, 141 A.

with an aged co-regent is by its very nature exceedingly improbable.[1] There is some evidence that Ay secured the throne by marrying the royal widow in the same way as was planned for Zannanzash, since a blue glass ring, formerly in the possession of a Cairo dealer and seen by Professor Newberry in 1931, had the cartouches of Ay and Ankhesenamun engraved on its bezel, suggesting the alliance of these two persons.[2] Ankhesenamun, however, disappears from the scene after the death of her husband and the consort who is represented in the Theban tomb of King Ay is that same Tey who had appeared at El-Amarna as his wife and Nefertiti's nurse.[3]

Ay buried Tutankhamun in the main eastern branch of the Valley of the Kings in a small tomb which does not appear to have been the one he was preparing for himself.[4] Nevertheless, the funerary furniture that was crammed into its confined space was exceptionally rich and incorporated some of the equipment prepared for Smenkhkare's burial and evidently part of Akhenaten's also.[5]

The ill-documented reign of the aged Ay, who had served Akhenaten at least twenty years earlier as Master of the Horse, must have been short. Regnal Year 4 is his highest recorded date,[6] and he probably ruled for a little longer if the entry in Josephus for *Harmais* refers to him.[7] He presumably followed the same policy of rehabilitation that he had doubtless persuaded his predecessor to adopt. He built his mortuary temple at Medīnet Habu at the southern end of the row of such structures at western Thebes and incorporated in it a palace used during religious festivities, a feature of subsequent Ramesside mortuary temples, if indeed it had not already been anticipated by Amenophis III.[8] The entire complex was, however, taken over and extended by his successor Horemheb.

Ay prepared a tomb, No. 23, for himself in the western branch of the Valley of the Kings, near that of Amenophis III,[9] but it is

---

[1] §iv, 28, 179; v, 12, 177–8. In a recently published inscription from Hermopolis, Tutankhaten is already described as a king's son before he came to the throne. Cf. i, 15, 317 n. i. See A, 8, pl. 106 (831–viii–c).   [2] §iv, 24, 50.

[3] §iii, 13, Pt. vi, pls. xxxi, xxxviii, xxxix. See Plate 135 (a).

[4] G, 15, 89; §iv, 28, 179.

[5] See above, p. 65, nn. 4 and 5. According to Gardiner's note *apud* Carter's Catalogue, pectoral No. 261 P(1) [*q.v.* §iv, 30, No. 43] was inscribed for Akhenaten originally.

[6] On a stela in Berlin. G, 11, v, 22.

[7] G, 16, 103.

[8] §v, 15, 75–82; §iv, 10, pls. i, ix, x, xiv.   [9] G, 11, i², Pt. ii, 550–1.

probable that it had originally been started for an earlier pharaoh.[1] In the sarcophagus chamber is a wall-painting which is unique for a royal tomb and shows Ay, in company with his wife Tey, spearing a hippopotamus and fowling in the marshlands.[2] The names of the royal pair and their figures, however, have been mutilated, and the red granite sarcophagus, similar in design to those of Tutankhamun and Horemheb, has been smashed to pieces.[3] A thorough clearance of the tomb might uncover evidence to show whether Ay was ever buried there: so far his mortal remains have not come to light.

V. THE REIGN OF HOREMHEB

Ay apparently died without living male issue and was succeeded by the Great Commander of the Army, Horemheb, who had exercised supreme power as the King's Deputy under Tutankhamun during the latter's minority.[4] It would seem that Horemheb continued to enjoy high office under Ay, and the 'Weepers Relief' in Berlin, showing a funerary procession in which the figure of a King's Scribe, Heir and Commander of the Army takes precedence over all other high officials, may date to this period.[5] The Coronation Inscription on the back of a seated dyad of himself and his wife, Queen Mutnodjme, in the Turin Museum[6] recounts the steps in his early career up to his appointment as king, and gives the impression of a smooth transfer of power from his predecessors to himself. But for ambiguous references to Horus (the ruling king) and Horus of Hnes (his divine sponsor), a critical passage in the text could be interpreted to imply that Ay accompanied Horemheb to Karnak in order to induct him as co-regent, their participation in the Festival of Southern Ope being made the occasion of obtaining the recognition of the gods.[7] At least the unusual phrase in which he is referred to as 'the eldest son of Horus' suggests that he had been appointed the heir of Ay.[8] The fact that Horemheb considered himself in the proper line of descent and not as a usurper or the founder of a new dynasty is to be inferred from the formation of

---

[1] G, 15, 92.

[2] §IV, 5, 246–7, pl. XXI; §I, 20, 141 B.

[3] §III, 26, 542, pl. LVI(6); §III, 38, 3–4, pl. I[6, 7]; §VIII, 40, pl. 57.

[4] §V, 23, 1–5; V, 12, 45–9; A, 6, 11–21.

[5] §V, 21, 56–8; §V, 12, 63–4; §V, 19, 59–61; §II, 2, pl. 78; §III, 29, pls. 54–5. See Plate 135 (b).   [6] §V, 10, 13–51.

[7] *Ibid.* pl. II, ll. 4, 12–14.   [8] *Ibid.* l. 12; §V, 12, 211 n. 198.

his praenomen with the 'kheperu-re' element, in which he followed the fashion set by nearly all the kings of the Eighteenth Dynasty and certainly by his Amarna predecessors.

The dated documents of the reign are scanty, Years 1, 3, 7 and 8 only having been preserved for certain, so that recently the view has been challenged that Horemheb enjoyed a long rule of between 25 and 30 years,[1] which follows if the date recorded in the inscription of Mes is accepted.[2] A hieratic graffito found at Medinet Habu and mentioning a Year 27 must be regarded as too ambiguous to be admitted alone to consideration.[3] It has been argued that the absence of any date after the first eight years, which are consistently documented, is significant. The paucity of the monuments of Horemheb which have survived is also taken as an indication of the shortness of his reign. This is not the place to discuss those arguments, which are made largely *ex silentio*; suffice it to say that the chronology followed in this work demands a reign for Horemheb of some 27 years determined by the Mes date.

Horemheb has often been identified with the King's Scribe, Steward, Master of Works and Commander of the Troops of the King (Akhenaten), Paatenemheb, who had started to cut a tomb among the southern group at El-Amarna, but the equation cannot be proved and remains doubtful.[4] Horemheb makes his first unequivocal appearance at the beginning of the reign of Tutankhamun, and, despite the high military rank which he held, he must be classed as a staff officer rather than a field commander.[5] It may have been his organizing ability which first marked him for preferment. In the tomb which he constructed for himself at Memphis as a private person, he makes a passing reference to having accompanied his lord (doubtless the young Tutankhamun) on the battlefield in Asia,[6] which may refer to some parade of force early in the reign in the disaffected areas of Palestine.

Another early inscription on the Zinzinia fragment[7] almost certainly refers to a diplomatic mission that he undertook to secure the allegiance of the Nubian and Kushite native governors at the accession of the same boy-king, rather than to some military expedition in those regions.[8] We are also to infer from his

---

[1] §v, 13, 95–9; *cf.* §v, 6, 33.   [2] §v, 8, 3; §v, 12, 405–9.

[3] §v, 15, 106–8; §1, 18, 157–8; §v, 12, 354–5; §v, 13, 96.

[4] §v, 12, 35–6, 41; §v, 19, 60; G, 4, 350.

[5] §vi, 4, 43, 78–84; §vi, 5, 371–4, 486–7.

[6] §v, 16, 16. See below, pp. 84–5.

[7] §v, 12, 64–8; §v, 9, 3.

[8] §vii, 3, 108.

Memphite tomb-reliefs that he acted as the mouth-piece of the king in dealings with foreign legates and Egyptian provincial governors alike.[1] On the death of Tutankhamun he appears to have continued in office under Ay, being accepted as the heir apparent and probably being created co-regent in the last years of the reign. During this period he must have played a key rôle in the rehabilitation of the country, for in the Coronation Inscription he claims to have renewed the temples from one end of the land to the other, fashioning statues of the gods and re-establishing their endowments and services, in much the same way as Tutankhamun in his Restoration Stela speaks of his work of reparation a decade or so earlier. It is perhaps significant that Horemheb should in his lifetime have usurped this stela of the king he had once served.[2]

During his sojourn with the court at Memphis he built a tomb in the nearby necropolis decorated with fine reliefs now dispersed among several museums.[3] An uraeus has been added later to the brow of Horemheb in these reliefs, though no alterations to the texts and other figures appear to have been made.[4] A second tomb, however, was cut for him in due course in the royal necropolis at Thebes in which he appears to have been buried, though no part of his human remains has been identified among the débris found there.[5]

As has been mentioned above, his surviving monuments are relatively few having regard to the length of time he is presumed to have ruled; but this is true for all the immediate post-Amarna kings, and the presumption is that they were so fully occupied with the re-building and re-endowment of the temples up and down the country that they had little resources of labour and treasure to expend on new constructions. In this context it is significant to note that in his nine years of rule Tutankhamun was able only to finish the companion to the granite lion of Amenophis III in the temple of Sulb, and it was left to his successor, Ay, to transport it from the quarry to the site.[6] Nevertheless, apart from his restorations, the building enterprises of Horemheb were far from inconsiderable. He enlarged the mortuary temple of Ay for his own use, or their joint cult, until it assumed gigantic proportions,[7] though it has now almost totally disappeared. At

---

[1] §v, 9, 5, 7–8; §v, 10, pl. II, l. 7; §v, 12, 113–14; §vi, 5, 373.
[2] §v, 12, 130.
[3] §v, 12, 69–125; §v, 5, 2 ff.; §viii, 11, 23–4; §v, 3, 31 ff.; §viii, 13, 27–31.
[4] §v, 2, 49–50.   [5] §v, 6; G, 15, 92–6.
[6] §iv, 15, 9.   [7] §v, 15, 78.

Karnak he seems to have planned and begun the great Hypostyle Hall of the Temple of Amun and the Second Pylon, using in their foundations and cores blocks from the Aten temples of Akhenaten in the vicinity, though it was left to his successors in the following dynasty to complete these works.[1] He also raised other pylons, the Ninth and Tenth on the processional way to the south of the temple, and joined them by walls forming a large court enclosing on the east side the jubilee temple of Amenophis II.[2] The towers of these great gateways were also filled with thousands of small blocks from the dismantled temples of the Aten.[3] Both pylons were usurped by later kings and are now greatly ruined. Before them stood a total of six colossi in red quartzite of the king, with Queen Mutnodjme on a much smaller scale. It is probable, however, that some at least of these statues were already lying on the site, but still unfinished, from the days when Amenophis III planned the erection of the Tenth Pylon.[4] The great avenue of crio-sphinxes that connected this latter gateway to the temple of Mut also appears to be the work of Horemheb, though usurped by others.[5]

At Gebel es-Silsila he cut and decorated with fine reliefs a *speos* in the cliffs on the western bank.[6] A similar rock temple, but on a smaller scale, was hewn out of the cliffs at Gebel Adda in Nubia and dedicated to Amun and Thoth.[7] At Memphis he erected buildings in the precincts of Ptah, as a damaged stela bearing a version of the Coronation Inscription proclaims, and these included a temple furnished with the usual cedar flag-poles and embellished with gold and Asiatic copper.[8] It is also certain that similar constructions were raised in Heliopolis.[9]

The tomb that the king cut at Thebes is among the largest in the Valley of the Kings and followed the fashion introduced into the design of such royal hypogea by Akhenaten at El-Amarna, being virtually a long corridor driven into the hillside and leading to the burial vault.[10] It is decorated in those parts which it was customary to embellish in the Eighteenth Dynasty, but it differs from earlier examples in having its scenes cut in relief and not painted on plaster. It also introduces for the first time in a royal

[1] §v, 20, 7 ff.; §v, 12, 329.   [2] G, 11, 11, 59–63; §v, 12, 331–7.

[3] §III, 16; §III, 12; §III, 41; A, 11.

[4] G, 11, 11, 62. It is difficult to see otherwise why the statues of Amenophis son of Hapu should have been placed here; (but cf. §v, 12, 256–7).

[5] §v, 12, 282–3.   [6] G, 11, v, 208–13; §v, 12, 359–70.

[7] G, 11, vii, 119–21.   [8] §v, 10, 30, 31.

[9] §v, 12, 289–92, 386; §G, 11, iv, 63, 70.

[10] A, 5; §v, 6.

tomb extracts from *The Book of Gates* which are inscribed on the walls of the pillared burial hall.[1] The decoration is almost complete except for some reliefs in the latter chamber which are in various stages of being sketched, carved and painted. It would be rash, however, to draw inferences as to the length of the king's reign from this circumstance. The paintings, for instance, in the tomb of Amenophis III, who had a long reign, are also incomplete.[2] Doubtless all kings depended upon the piety of their successors for finishing off their tombs before they were buried in them. Horemheb was unfortunate in being followed by a king who had the briefest of reigns.[3]

It may well have been that Horemheb did not begin to cut his Theban tomb until his later years. There is some evidence that the workmen's village at Deir el-Medīna, on the west of Thebes,[4] was only being re-established in this reign.[5] The policing of the Valley of the Kings, at all events, appears to have been negligent during his earlier years, for tomb-robbers were active in the Valley at this period and had evidently broken into several tombs including those of Tuthmosis IV and Tutankhamun.[6] It was in his Regnal Year 8 that Horemheb had to renew the burial of the former and it was probably at the same time that the violated tomb of the latter was cleared up. It seems incredible that Horemheb's tomb could have been in process of construction about 150 metres from the spot where another royal tomb was being violated, and the inference is that it had not at that time been started.

This pillaging is but one indication of a general lawlessness that seems to have prevailed since the end of the reign of Akhenaten, and suggests that the disorder referred to by Tutankhamun in his Restoration Stela had by no means been curbed. The great granite stela which Horemheb erected against the north face of the western tower of the Ninth Pylon at Karnak bears other witness to this general unrest.[7] The woefully damaged text which is usually referred to as 'The Edict of Horemheb' appears to be a selection of the ordinances which the king issued 'to seek the welfare of Egypt' by suppressing illegal acts.

[1] G, 15, 94–5; G, 11, 1², Pt. II, p. 568.
[2] §v, 18, 116.   [3] §v, 1, 102 n. 1; see below, pp. 77, 217 f.
[4] See below, pp. 620 ff.
[5] Verbal communication by the late Prof. Jaroslav Černý.
[6] §v, 4, XXXIII–IV, figs. 7, 8; §v, 12, 393, pl. LX; §IV, 5, vol. I, 54, 93; vol. III, 85–6.
[7] §v, 12, 302–18; G, I, III, §§45–67; §v, 17, 260–76; §v, 14, 109–36; §v, 22, 230–8.

It seems clear from this Edict that the central authority of the Crown had grown considerably, presumably at the expense of the religious foundations both local and national, and much of the administration had in consequence fallen into the hands of court officials, notably of the army, so removing any local checks and balances that the former system may have enjoyed. The result had been widespread corruption, the oppression of freemen by fraudulent tax-collectors, and arbitrary exactions and requisitions by an undisciplined soldiery in the name of the king. Both the tax-paying populace and the crown had been cheated by this extortion, and the enactments were designed to protect the interests of both. In his edict Horemheb quotes examples of abuses that had developed, and threatens future transgressors with savage punishments. At the same time he announces that he has appointed reliable men as supreme judges (viziers) in the two capital cities of Memphis and Thebes and has adjured them to hold themselves aloof from other men and not to accept bribes or presents from them. The district tribunals were also re-organized to consist of the headman of the region and functionaries and ritual priests of the local temples. If any member of these councils should be accused of practising injustice, he would have to answer a capital charge. On the other hand, those judges who performed their duties conscientiously were to have the honour of being rewarded periodically by the king in person.

Despite the numerous lacunae in the edict, several facts emerge from its study, such as the organization of the army into two main divisions, one serving in Upper and the other in Lower Egypt, a system which still prevailed when Herodotus visited the land some nine hundred years later and which probably dated from the beginning of the New Kingdom. Nevertheless, the plundering of the inhabitants by a rapacious army implies that a reform of its command was a necessary preliminary to Horemheb's measures to restore justice, and is already implicit in his statement in the Coronation Inscription that the priesthoods had been re-established from the 'pick of the army', presumably referring to its administrators, a rather different method of recruitment from that employed a decade earlier, when they were drawn from the families of local worthies.[1] Remarkable, also, is the return of supreme judicial power to the viziers in Memphis and Thebes, presumably in place of favourites of the king such as the High Stewards and Butlers, to whom royal authority had so often been delegated in the Eighteenth Dynasty from Hatshepsut onwards.

[1] §v, 10, pl. II, l. 25, p. 21 n. 3j; §IV, 2, 10, l. 17.

The success of Horemheb's reforms must have owed not a little to the tours of inspection which he claims to have made throughout the length and breadth of Egypt to ensure that his new measures were enacted with vigour, and that fresh abuses had no chance to develop. But whether he acted thus on behalf of the kings he served in his early career or only when he came to the throne is obscure, since the Coronation Inscription does not specifically mention these activities and the edict lacks its critical date.[1]

If Horemheb had any sons by his principal queen, Mutnodjme, they do not appear to have survived him and he was succeeded by a Ramesses whose claim to the throne is uncertain, but whose former identification with the Vizier and deputy, Pramesse, has apparently to be abandoned.[2] Ramesses, the first of that name, evidently hailed from the Delta and was regarded as founding a new dynasty, his praenomen setting a new pattern in royal nomenclature. His reign was too brief to decide whether it was he who instituted the policy which his son and grandson followed of execrating the Amarna pharaohs, destroying their monuments and suppressing their records.[3] He must have been of advanced years when he ascended the throne, for his son, Sethos, was then a man in the full vigour of life. A fragment of a model obelisk giving part of the titularies of Horemheb and Ramesses I suggests that the former king had associated the latter on the throne with him for some years before his death.[4]

VI. THE ROYAL FAMILY AT THE END OF THE EIGHTEENTH DYNASTY

It is clear that around the kings of the Fourth Dynasty, for instance, there clustered many officials who were closely related to them,[5] but, because our documentation is far less complete for other periods, it is generally assumed that the custom of appointing viziers and other high officers of state from the circle of the royal family was abandoned in the later Old Kingdom. Thus the title 'King's Acquaintance' was not regarded then as signifying that its owner was a relation of the pharaoh.

In the Eighteenth Dynasty, however, sufficient evidence has survived to encourage the view that many of the king's entourage were related to him, either directly or by virtue of some less

---

[1] But cf. §v, 12, 307–8.   [2] §v, 11, 23–9.
[3] §v, 12, 167; §viii, 11, 2; §iii, 2, 59; §v, 13, 96 n. 9.
[4] §v, 1, 100–3.   [5] G, 8, 62.

exalted familial bond.[1] Apart from the junior sons and daughters who all had to be brought up to wear the purple, in case it should fall to their lot, as it so often did, by the premature demise of elder brothers and sisters,[2] there were also collateral descendants from earlier reigns, foster-brothers whose mothers had acted as wet-nurses of the kings[3] and high officials whose daughters had entered the royal harims[4] or who had been honoured by the gift of a wife brought up in such an institution.[5] In exceptional circumstances men who were not in the direct line of descent, such as Tuthmosis I,[6] or even commoners without evidence of royal blood in their veins, such as Ay,[7] might marry the heiress daughter of the pharaoh.

It is difficult to trace such relationships in detail because, for the most part, the officials are extremely reticent in mentioning their connexions with the royal house, but there is little doubt that such kinsmen must have formed veritable dynasties around the dynasties of the kings and queens whom they served, and the ramifications of one or two influential families can be traced to show the interdependence of the ruling caste of Egypt at this period.[8]

A notable case in point is the family of Queen Tiy, the chief wife of Amenophis III, who is usually regarded as a commoner whom the King married as the result of a 'love-match'.[9] As Amenophis III could not have been more than eight years old at his accession, it can be presumed that romantic passion played no part in this alliance and that the infant Tiy must have had influential supporters. Her father Yuya was an experienced officer of chariotry and the Master of the Horse. It is to be suspected that he was related to the Queen Mother, Mutemwiya, and was perhaps the uncle of the young king.[10] He was in any case sufficiently important and well known to have his name and that of his wife mentioned in the rescript of the infant king's accession.[11] He came from the provincial city of Akhmīm, where he and his wife held important and lucrative sacerdotal positions and in the vicinity of which Tiy acquired large estates.[12] One of

[1] §vi, 5, 254, 279–80; cf. §vi, 4, 31 n. 2, 66–71; G, 8, 268; §vi, 1, 30–1.
[2] For deceased eldest sons see §vi, 3, 15; C.A.H. ii³, pt. i, pp. 316 and 320.
[3] C.A.H. ii³, pt. i, p. 315; §vi, 4, 66–73; §i, 10, 238.
[4] G, 5, i, no. 127; §vi, 1, 35–6.   [5] §vi, 9. no. 51005 passim.
[6] C.A.H. ii³, pt. i, p. 315; §vi, 1, 30–1.
[7] Ibid. 35–7.
[8] E.g. §vi, 5, 435 (4), 499 (8); §vi, 1, 30.
[9] E.g. §vi, 5, 538.   [10] §ii, 2, 40, 42, 88–9.
[11] §vi, 2, 5, pls. i–ix.   [12] §vi, 13, 23–33.

his sons, Anen, held the office of Second Prophet of Amun in Thebes and Chief Seer in the temple of Re in Karnak.[1] It is also likely that Yuya had another son, Ay, who held his father's office of Master of Horse under Akhenaten and who as king built a rock-temple to Min in the family seat of Akhmīm at a time when little new constructional work was undertaken.[2]

Like his father before him, Akhenaten appears to have married a cousin as his chief wife, for Nefertiti has been identified as the daughter of Ay.[3] It was probably by virtue of this relationship, if not some closer ties with the royal house, that Ay eventually ascended the throne on the extinction of the direct line.

In addition to the many foreign marriages which Amenophis III made for diplomatic reasons, he also wedded several of his daughters,[4] a practice which appears to have been followed by Akhenaten, and although these incestuous unions seem to have been as much permitted to the pharaohs as to the ancient Hebrews, for instance,[5] the custom has been dismissed as no more than a symbolic rite enabling the princesses to act as deputies of the queen in ceremonies in which she played an essential rôle, even though they were mere infants.[6] Since Akhenaten's daughters, however, are known to have had children while they were still princesses, not having their names enclosed in cartouches, it is difficult to accept these marriages as purely nominal.[7] The custom in fact may have been more general than is supposed, our documentation on the subject being a little fuller for this period than for nearly all other reigns, though it is noteworthy that Ramesses II also married some of his own daughters.[8]

Some ambiguity exists about the exact relationship of Smenkhkare and Tutankhamun to the ruling house. That they legitimized their claims to the throne by marrying the eldest surviving heiress queen is certain, but it is to be suspected that they had strong rights of their own. In the case of the latter king there is little doubt in the matter, since he was only eight or nine at his accession, and a newly published inscription from Hermopolis names him, while still uncrowned, as the son of a king 'of his loins'.[9] As he had been born at least four years before Smenkhkare came to the throne, his claims would not have been passed over, young as he was, if his predecessor too had not been the

[1] §VI, 1, 32; §I, 19, 137; §I, 21, 275.   [2] §VI, 1, 33.
[3] §II, 2, 89–92; §VI, 1, 37–9; §V, 12, 171–4; §V, 1, 105–6.
[4] §VI, 12, 36–54.   [5] Lev. 18, 6 ff., 20, 10 ff.; Deut. 27, 20 ff.
[6] §VI, 6, 24.   [7] §III, 11, 104–8.   [8] Cf. §III, 31, 229.
[9] See above, p. 70, n. 1. Cf. §IV, 28, 178, 179.

son of a king. The mortal remains of these two pharaohs have such close physical resemblances that they have long been regarded as brothers, a view that has recently been strengthened by the recognition that they belong to the same blood groups, A_2 and MN.[1]

The problem remains of the identity of the king whose sons these brothers are. Tutankhamun states that Amenophis III is 'his father' (as distinct from 'the father of his father'),[2] but most Egyptologists refuse to accept this claim and dismiss it as merely implying that Amenophis III was his ancestor. If, however, Akhenaten the only other possible claimant was the father of these two princes, Smenkhkare must have been born at the latest soon after he had come to the throne, and more probably three years before. In the latter event, it is doubtful whether Smenkhkare would have taken precedence over a younger brother who had not been born until his father had been consecrated as a pharaoh. If, on the other hand, Akhenaten had fathered both these princes only after he became king,[3] their mother, who would have held an extremely influential position at his Court as the mother of the heirs apparent, has not been disclosed. She is unlikely to have been the Chief Wife Nefertiti, since that queen is never shown as the proud mother of his sons despite her paramount importance and the unprecedented way in which her domestic life with the king and her daughters is frankly depicted. Despite, too, the intimacy in which Smenkhkare is shown with Akhenaten, calling himself 'beloved' of the older king, he never pretends to be his son, which was the closest relationship that it was possible for him to claim. While, therefore, it remains doubtful whether Akhenaten was the father of Smenkhkare and Tutankhamun, the paternity of Amenophis III can only be admitted in their case if there was a long co-regency between him and Akhenaten,[4] since Tutankhamun must have been born in Akhenaten's seventh regnal year at the very earliest.

Ay certainly gained the throne on the death of Tutankhamun, but that he married the royal widow is denied by some historians,[5] the evidence of the ring inscribed with his name and that of Ankhesenamun being considered too flimsy for admission.[6] It seems inevitable, however, that Ay would have confirmed his

---

[1] A, 4, 13. Also see above, p. 69, no. 1.   [2] §IV, 21, 76; §I, 21, 279.

[3] In view of the jar-dockets mentioned above (pp. 64 f.), this is impossible in the case of Smenkhkare since he died in his 20th year and Akhenaten's highest regnal year was 17 (pp. 63, 68).

[4] See above, p. 49.   [5] G, 6, 236; §IV, 28, 180.   [6] See above, p. 70.

shaky right to the throne by the time-honoured custom of marrying the royal heiress, even though in his case she may have been his grand-daughter, since this was to have been the means by which the prince Zannanzash was to be made pharaoh. Ay, the putative father of Nefertiti, almost certainly had other children, including that Mutnodjme who at El-Amarna is described as the 'sister' of Nefertiti.[1] From the early days of Egyptology she has been identified as the woman who later married Horemheb, and as the royal heiress furnished her husband with his right to the throne. Whether Horemheb married her in his early years and by this alliance climbed to a position of influence at the court, or only espoused her on his nomination to the crown is problematic.[2] It is also doubtful whether the family of Ay succeeded in maintaining its position in the next dynasty. A faience knob, however, bearing his cartouche and evidently from a piece of furniture deposited as an heirloom in the tomb of Queen Nefertari-merymut may be not without significance.[3] This queen was the chief wife of Ramesses II during his early years and must have been given to him in marriage on his appointment as co-regent. She bears a name not unknown in the family of Ay, who were devoted to the worship of Mut,[4] and she may therefore have been a connecting link between the two dynasties.

VII. FOREIGN AFFAIRS

The victory of Megiddo, won by Tuthmosis III in his twenty-third regnal year over a confederation of Asiatic princelings, asserted Egyptian claims in Syria which had been challenged in the earlier years of the Eighteenth Dynasty by the vigorous and rising power of the Mitanni.[5] The successors of Tuthmosis III, however, were unable or unwilling to maintain their pretensions over vassal states in North Syria and came to an understanding with other Great Powers in the Near East to define their spheres of influence.[6] A treaty with the Khatti was arranged early in the career of Tuthmosis III[7] and was apparently still in force during the reign of Amenophis III.[8] Babylonia also had a pact of mutual assistance with Egypt and invoked it to warn the Canaanites from attacking the territory of its ally.[9]

---

[1] §vi, 1, 39, 41; §v, 12, 171–6; §v, 1, 103–6.   [2] §vi, 1, 41; §v, 12, 78, 232.
[3] §vi, 11, 55, 103, fig. 82.
[4] §vi, 1, 33 n. 1; §ii, 2, 88, pl. 66; §vi, 10, 66–8.
[5] C.A.H. ii³, pt. 1, p. 671.   [6] Ibid., p. 676.   [7] Ibid., p. 671.
[8] E.A. 41; §vii, 4, 22 n. 1.   [9] E.A. 9; see above, pp. 24–5.

Such treaties were cemented by marriages between the daughters of the royal houses and the pharaoh, the most documented of such alliances being the series of marriages between princesses of the Mitanni and Tuthmosis IV, Amenophis III and Akhenaten.[1] The daughters of less exalted princes, however, also entered the royal harims in Egypt and played their part in the diplomacy of the age.[2]

Within its Asiatic sphere of influence, Egypt hardly exercised any Roman *imperium*, despite some ambiguous indications of its exploitation of the region.[3] The pharaoh as the traditional vanquisher of the Nine Nations was the divine overlord whom vassals in Palestine and Syria addressed as 'my sun', 'my god', 'my lord' and in similar terms of subservience.[4] Apart from this spiritual leadership, however, it is doubtful whether anything like an empire existed[5] and the scenes of foreigners bearing tribute to lay before the mercy-seat of the pharaoh are capable of other interpretations than the mercantile development of the region.[6]

The many vassal states kept up interminable internecine squabbles, their main objective being to preserve their own autonomy, to extend their frontiers and power at the expense of their weaker neighbours and to enlist the military might and resources of their overlord, ostensibly to protect his interests, but actually to advance their own ambitions.[7] They therefore set up a constant clamour for help to preserve the town or state they were so loyally defending, coupled with assurances of their own honesty and fidelity and the treachery and ruthlessness of their rivals.[8]

Despite the remoteness of these quarrels from the centre of government in Egypt, it seems highly probable that the Egyptians, informed by despatches from their own commissioners and garrison commanders, had a good idea of what was afoot and took the action that seemed best to them, though modern observers of the partially revealed scene have not been slow to level charges of supineness and muddle against the Egyptian administration.[9]

The treaties between the Great Powers of the Near East, however, brought a period of comparative calm and stability to

[1] E.A. 17, 26 ff.; E.A. 19, 17 ff.; E.A. 22, IV, 43 ff.; E.A. 24, iii, 9 ff.; E.A. 29, 16 ff.; §VI, 2, pl. XXIX.

[2] E.A. 31; E.A. 31 *a*; §VII, 9, 41, 47.   [3] See below, pp. 105–7.

[4] *Cf.* E.A. 60, 1–7; E.A. 76, 1–6; E.A. 176 *a*, 1–6; E.A. 270, 1–8.

[5] G, 6, 230; §VII, 3, 111.   [6] *Ibid.* 105–16.

[7] See below, pp. 104–5; §VII, 4, 14.   [8] §VII, 8, 60–3.

[9] G, 2, 379, 385–6; §II, 13, 207, 230–1.

Palestine and South Syria during the reigns of Tuthmosis IV and Amenophis III, when the Egyptian garrisons in key cities such as Gaza, Beth-shan, Joppa, Sumura, Rehōb and Megiddo were able to reinforce local levies in checking the pretensions of the more turbulent dynasts and in repressing the Shasu bedawin and the Apiru freebooters who posed a constant threat to law and order.[1]

With the accession of Shuppiluliumash to the Hittite throne, however, about the second decade of the reign of Amenophis III,[2] a new actor appeared on the scene who was to remould decisively the political structure of the region during the following century. The struggle that now developed between the Khatti and the Mitanni for supremacy involved the vassal states of Egypt on her borders with these two powers and ultimately led to the wars of attrition between Egypt and the Khatti in the early Nineteenth Dynasty.[3]

The Egyptian records from the death of Amenophis III to the accession of Sethos I are too scanty and incomplete to give any coherent picture of the foreign scene as viewed through Egyptian eyes. The outlines have therefore to be sketched from the cuneiform archives found at El-Amarna and Boğazköy, and the situation prevailing when Sethos I began his Asiatic campaigns in his first regnal year.[4]

The protracted struggle between Tushratta of the Mitanni and Shuppiluliumash of the Khatti is recounted elsewhere.[5] The Egyptians had treaties with both nations and appear to have shown little inclination to intervene, a policy which has been accredited to the neglect by Akhenaten of the affairs of his 'empire' rather than to the preservation of a strict neutrality. It may have been immaterial to the Egyptians which of the two rivals had suzerainty in North Syria, since they themselves were evidently unwilling to exercise any dominion over the region. Their efforts appear to have been reserved for trying to maintain their influence in the coastal area stretching from Byblos in the south to Ugarit in the north. In this policy they found themselves dealing with the astute and turbulent princes of the Amurru, whose domains straddled the region and who found the confusion caused by the wars between the Khatti and the Mitanni congenial to their own expansionist aims.[6]

Abdi-ashirta, the first of these Amurru princes, made a show of

---

[1] *C.A.H.* ii³, pt. I, pp. 27–8; see below, pp. 110–16.
[2] See above, pp. 6–7; §vii, 4, 39.　　　[3] See below, pp. 226–9.
[4] G, 6, 252–5.　　[5] See above, pp. 1–16.　　[6] *Ibid.*, pp. 10–13.

recognizing Egyptian suzerainty on the North Syrian coast, but his intrigues eventually exhausted Egyptian patience and he was slain by a task-force of marines in the last years of Amenophis III or early in the reign of Akhenaten.[1] His equally troublesome successor, Aziru, was summoned to the Egyptian court to give an account of himself and to serve as hostage for the good behaviour of his state.[2] Though he eventually returned to the Amurru with the confidence of the pharaoh, the pressure of events left him no option but to become the faithful vassal of Shuppiluliumash.[3]

By the end of the reign of Akhenaten, Egypt had proved a broken reed in its failure to support the independent states of South Syria with effective military aid. Qatna, Nukhash, Qadesh and above all the Amurru passed into Hittite vassalage.[4] It is doubtless this loss of influence which is referred to in the Restoration Stela of Tutankhamun when it is admitted with rare candour that, if in the days of his predecessor an army was sent to Syria to extend the boundaries of Egypt, it met with no success.[5] It would appear, however, that some attempt was made during the reign of Tutankhamun to recover lost ground, a more aggressive policy being promised to the king's District Commissioners in an inscription in the Memphite tomb of Horemheb, where the owner is spoken of as 'the guardian of the footsteps of his lord on the battlefield on this day of smiting Asiatics'.[6] The cuneiform records reveal that the Hittites raided Amqa between the Lebanon and Antilebanon, which was a violation of Egyptian-held territory. As a riposte the Egyptian forces captured Qadesh on the Orontes and doubtless encouraged the revolt of Nukhash.[7] Their triumph was shortlived, however, for in the following year a Hittite force drove the Egyptians from Qadesh and re-entered Amqa. It was at this point that Tutankhamun died and his widow petitioned Shuppiluliumash to give her one of his sons in marriage.[8] After the murder of Zannanzash, Shuppiluluimash again attacked Amqa, defeated the Egyptian forces and brought back prisoners who carried with them a plague which spread among their captors and became endemic among the Khatti for years afterwards.[9]

Evidently the Hittites realized that by their aggression they had broken the terms of their treaty with Egypt, a pact which had

[1] §vii, 4, 27–8.
[2] E.A. 161, 22 ff.; E.A. 164, 14 ff.
[3] See above, pp. 12–13; §iv, 4, 17–18.
[4] See above, pp. 15–16; §iv, 4, 46.
[5] G, 13, 2025 ff.; §iv, 2, 9, l. 9.
[6] §v, 16, 16; §v, 9, 7.
[7] See above, p. 17; §iv, 4, 47.
[8] See above, p. 69.
[9] §viii, 34, 395.

been sealed by oaths to the gods, probably of both powers,[1] who were now accredited in their anger with visiting the plague upon the violators. Shuppululiumash himself died of the disease early in the reign of Horemheb and his successor, Murshilish, undertook penances to deflect the wrath of the gods, making restitution and returning prisoners to Amqa.[2] It seems probable therefore that the frontiers of Egypt and of the Khatti were stabilized at the Lebanon throughout the reign of Horemheb and that Egyptian policy was confined to trying to exert the claims over the Amurru and Ugarit which it had exercised in the prosperous days of Amenophis III. In this it appears to have enjoyed some temporary success, but was defeated by the superior skill of Murshilish.[3]

Further south in Palestine the task of the Egyptians in maintaining their influence was simpler, since here they were not opposed by a unified great power commanding trained military forces and enjoying interior lines of communication. This area was also in a constant state of unrest caused by the rivalries and feuds of local princes, whom it was not difficult to divide and rule. In the reign of Akhenaten a more serious threat developed in Central Palestine through the ambitions of the 'Apiru Chief' Labaya of Shechem, who, however, was killed in a skirmish with loyalist forces.[4] He was succeeded by his sons, who proved no less fractious.[5] Towards the end of the reign unrest at Gezer imperilled the whole Egyptian position in Central Palestine, and it would seem that forces and supplies were being marshalled for a more serious campaign which may have been mounted early in the reign of Tutankhamun.[6] Whatever threat may have developed to the Egyptian position here, it had evidently been dispersed by the time Sethos I set out on his first foreign campaign, and there is no reason to doubt that under the successors of Akhenaten Palestine was as firmly held as it had ever been, despite the fissiparous nature of its politics, the constant jockeying for power by its princelings and the disorder caused by the operations of the Shasu and the Apiru.

Nubians and Kushites are represented on the monuments as equally prostrate beneath the feet of pharaoh as the Asiatics or the adoring *rekhyt* populace of Egypt, but during the greater part of the Eighteenth Dynasty the African dependencies were peaceful and well-ordered, being governed through an administration

---

[1] *Cf.* §VII, 6, 197.   [2] §VIII, 34, 396.
[3] See below, pp. 139–40; §IV, 4, 36.   [4] See below, pp. 114–16; §I, 5, 104, 110.
[5] *Ibid.* 103, 109; E.A. 289, 5; E.A. 287, 29–31.   [6] §VII, 8, 63–4.

modelled on that of Egypt itself.[1] Punitive expeditions against nomad disturbers of the peace on the unsettled borders were undertaken by the Viceroys of Kush as part of their duties and were no more than police actions.[2] The processions of manacled prisoners in some of the representations of the time give a misleading picture of events in Africa, since these captives are often not prisoners of war, but the traditional 'black ivory' of the region, captured in slave-raids or trafficked together with the elephant tusks, ebony logs and gold dust as part of the native produce. The visit of Heknufer, the Prince of Mi'am (Aniba), and the Sudani princess with their retinues to the court of Tutankhamun, presumably at his accession, as represented in the tomb of the Viceroy Huy,[3] is a peaceful occasion and not a scene of conquest.[4] Similarly the victory over Kush depicted in the *speos* of Horemheb at Gebel es-Silsila is doubtless pure bombast, if it is not merely heraldic, showing the pharaoh as all-conquering in his southern domains as elsewhere.[5] If it has any basis in historical reality, it almost certainly refers to slave-raids or police action undertaken by the viceroys in his name.

The reliefs on the east wall of the court between the Ninth and Tenth Pylons at Karnak, showing delegates from Punt bringing gifts to Horemheb,[6] may, however, represent an historical event, since here the Puntites are hardly likely to represent the southern peoples in an equipoise of the foreign nations that owed allegiance to the pharaoh. This scene may therefore indicate that at the end of the Eighteenth Dynasty trading relations with the mysterious spice-lands of Punt had once more been re-established.

VIII. RELIGION, LITERATURE AND ART

A feature of religious thought during the Eighteenth Dynasty is a preponderance in the influence of the sun-cult, whose centre at Heliopolis, the Biblical On, was the chief seat of its theologians. These traditional 'wise men' of Egypt had radically overhauled their doctrines and re-interpreted old beliefs, perhaps as a result of seminal ideas from other sun-cults imported from Asia in Hyksos times.[7] The interpenetration of the new thought can be seen not only in the solarization of the old cults, which hastened to add the name of the supreme sun-god Re to the name of their

[1] *C.A.H.* II[3], pt. I, pp. 348–50; §G, 12, 186 ff.   [2] *Ibid.* 162–7.
[3] §IV, 9, pls. XXVII, XXVIII.   [4] §VII, 3, 115.
[5] G, 11, V, 211 (34)–(36); *cf.* G, 12, 107–8, 163 ff.
[6] G, 11, II, 61 (56).   [7] §VIII, 8, 113–14.

local divinity, but also in the royal tombs at Thebes where the Pyramid Texts used in the Old and Middle Kingdoms were replaced by extracts from such sacred works as *The Book of What is in the Underworld*, *The Litany of the Sun* and *The Book of Gates*.[1] In these writings a new interest is revealed in a monotheistic syncretism of ancient beliefs. In them Re becomes the sole god who has made himself for eternity. He is invoked in *The Litany* under his 'seventy-five names which are his bodies, and these bodies are the other gods'.[2] He is hailed as 'the sole god who has made myriads from himself: all gods came into being from him'.[3] He is also invoked as 'he whose active forms are his eternal transformations when he assumes the aspect of his Great Disk'.[4] This disk, or *Aten*, which illumines the world of the dead as well as the living, and daily brings both to life from death or sleep,[5] is the constant element in these transformations, and the power immanent in it, Re, is the supreme god of whom the pharaoh is the offspring on earth.

The sun-worship of Akhenaten, which most modern observers have accepted as a new and revolutionary religion, differed from these re-edited doctrines of the Re-cult by a mere nuance, by placing a little more emphasis upon the Aten, or visible manifestation of godhead, than upon Re, the hidden power that motivated it.[6] It would seem that, as far as theological thought was concerned, there was little to choose between Atenism and the cults that it displaced. Amon-Re, the influential god of the dynasty, for instance, was also a 'hidden' force like Re, who might manifest himself in some tangible form, *e.g.* a ram (*cf.* the Mnevis bull of Re) rather than a remote and celestial body like the sun-disk. But his identification with Re weakened his ancient primal aspect of an ithyphallic god of storm, air and fertility, like his counterpart Min of the Eastern Desert, and he became purely the sun-god under the name of the god of Thebes, sailing over the waters above the earth in a divine bark, contending with the cloud-dragon Apophis and being worshipped as the creator and sustainer of all living things.[7] In Papyrus Bulaq 17, written about the time of Amenophis II,[8] all these aspects are praised in terms which differ little from similar phrases in the Great Hymn to the Aten, and it is doubtful whether a devotee of Amun of Thebes in the reign of Akhenaten would have found anything

---

[1] §VIII, 30, 121–2.   [2] §VIII, 31, 207–8.   [3] *Ibid.* 208 n. 5.
[4] *Ibid.*   [5] §VIII, 16, 21 ff.   [6] §VIII, 31, 218; §IV, 26, 12–13.
[7] §VIII, 18, 49 ff.; §VIII, 29, 7–14; §VIII, 41, 35; §II, 12, 87.
[8] §VIII, 34, 365–7.

heretical in the doctrines being propounded by the new prophet at Akhetaten. In fact there is evidence that the personnel required for staffing the temples of the Aten at Karnak were drawn initially, at least, from the priesthood of Amun.[1]

Kings from the time of Ammenemes I had been spoken of as departing at death to the horizon and uniting with the Aten.[2] In the reign of Amenophis II a symbol of the sun-disk had appeared with a pair of embracing arms,[3] and under Tuthmosis IV the Aten is mentioned on a scarab as a great universal god whose exalted position in the sky entitles it to rule over all that it shines upon.[4] In the reign of Amenophis III it became even more important, being attached to the name of the king's palace, his state-barge and one at least of his children, if not of himself.[5] Under Akhenaten, this deity became the supreme state-god, gradually achieving the position of a heavenly pharaoh who, like his earthly counterpart, had his names inscribed in two cartouches, assumed titles and epithets and celebrated jubilees. Where the Aten of Akhenaten differed from the Re of the new sacred books was that, instead of incorporating all the old deities in a comprehensive henotheism, it rigidly excluded them in an uncompromising monotheism.[6] This is seen as early as the Great Hymn to the Aten inscribed in the tomb of Ay before Year 9.[7] In this work, which has often been compared with Psalm 104, sentiments and phrases are included which can be found in earlier hymns to Amun and Osiris; where it differs from them is in ignoring completely the existence of other deities.

Later in the reign of Akhenaten this passive disregard of the other gods changed to an active antagonism which manifested itself in the excision of their names wherever they appeared, and the changing of the word for 'gods' to its singular form only. Just as remarkable, also, is the complete neglect of the old mortuary cults such as that of Osiris, with whom dead kings had become identified, and which had enjoyed an enormous expansion since the end of the Old Kingdom. The sun-god and his incarnation, the pharaoh, had taken over the care of the dead, and the new eschatology is seen in such features as changes in burial customs and funerary furnishings and the excision of the old

---

[1] §viii, 25, 5, 6 n. 1; G, 13, 1935, l. 18; §vi, 5, 390–1.
[2] *Sinuhe*, R, 7; *cf.* G, 13, 54.
[3] §viii, 27, 53 ff.   [4] *C.A.H.* ii³, pt. 1, p. 343.
[5] §i, 10, 179; §iii, 13, Pt. iii, pl. xviii; §iii, 35, 33; §iii, 19, 108; §vi, 2, pls. xxx–xxxi; §i, 18, 164, no. 13.   [6] G, 3, 63; G, 6, 227.
[7] §iii, 13, Pt. vi, pl. xxvii; §viii, 34, 369–71; G, 6, 225–7.

setem-priest from the scenes of the last Osirian rites before entombment.[1] It is perhaps significant that special emphasis should have been placed upon the restoration of this scene in the wall-paintings in the tomb of Tutankhamun, where Ay officiates at the burial of his predecessor.[2]

Where Akhenaten's ideas of monotheism came from in a world which widely tolerated so many diverse forms of godhead is unknown, but the inference is that they were his own, the logical outcome of regarding the Aten as a heavenly king, whose son was the pharaoh. Like the latter, he could only be regarded as 'unique, without a peer'. It was, as has already been stated, the insistence by Akhenaten on a rigid monotheism in state affairs which proved disastrous for Egypt, since it destroyed the old system by which the lives of all the populace, from the lowest to the highest, had been regulated. In the world of the Late Bronze Age, religion and government were as inextricably mixed as they had ever been.

On the return to orthodoxy initiated by Akhenaten's successors, the old gods improved their position by the force of reaction, and that 'pagan' delight in the sunlit world of the living was in the ensuing dynasty to be excluded from the scenes painted on the walls of private tomb-chapels.[3] Nevertheless, it is probable that the faith of the mass of the Egyptian people was untouched by Akhenaten's religious reforms. They evidently continued to worship their old gods and godlings in the manner of their ancestors, for references to Bes, Toeris, Shed, Isis and even Amun were found in the workmen's village at El-Amarna.[4] The prayers and appeals of such humble folk, which show that a direct personal relationship was felt to exist between the petitioner and his god, are in marked contrast with the optimistic and complacent utterances of the official religion.[5] This spirit of self-abasement is more Hebraic than Egyptian in its concept of a merciful god who forgives the transgressor, and it may have owed something to the influence of the many Semites who had found an occupation in Egypt during the Eighteenth Dynasty. What has been called 'the religion of the poor' is better known from prayers written by the workmen at Thebes in Ramesside times,[6] but examples exist to show that such humble petitions were already being made as early as the reign of Amenophis III.[7]

---

[1] §VIII, 16, 24–5; §VIII, 22, 21, 24, 58.
[2] See above, p. 69, n. 4.   [3] §I, 20, 226.
[4] §III, 32, 25, 60, 65–6, 95–8.   [5] See below, p. 248.
[6] §VIII, 26, 87 ff.   [7] §VIII, 23, 188 ff.; cf. §IV, 18, 10–11.

Such minor compositions have often by their very unobtrusiveness survived unscathed the passage of time, but it is one of the ironies of chance that the Eighteenth Dynasty, which was one of the most prolific and imaginative periods of Egyptian art, has bequeathed us scarcely anything of its great literature. Hints exist in fragments of a story about the insatiable greed of the sea,[1] a book on the pleasures of marsh sports and a poem on the joys of spring,[2] to suggest that the elegance, good proportions and high technical accomplishment of the plastic arts would have found their counterparts in contemporary writing; if so, it was a style of composition that made little appeal to the schoolboy copyists, or rather their teachers, whose scribbles have bequeathed us almost all that we now possess of earlier Egyptian literature.[3] Nothing original exists, moreover, of the sapiential writings of Amenophis son of Hapu, whose wise sayings were treasured throughout the centuries, though a fragment of the *Instruction of Amonnakhte*[4] shows that this class of wisdom literature was not neglected in the Dynasty.

That literary composition was moulded by the same influences that shaped the progress of the other arts is suggested by the utterances inscribed in the temple of Queen Hatshepsut at Deir el-Bahri accompanying reliefs inspired by Theban models of the early Middle Kingdom, and quoting from the classical *Story of Sinuhe*.[5] As the dynasty wears on and art becomes freer, its lines more flowing and its compositions more adventurous, particularly in such a non-royal genre as the paintings in the private tomb-chapels at Thebes, the language also changes to express a more flexible and vernacular manner of speech. New grammatical tendencies and idioms, foreign words and a different orthography characteristic of Late Egyptian began to replace classical Middle Egyptian about the reign of Tuthmosis III for less formal writings, but at El-Amarna they had already entered the monumental texts.[6]

It is from its official inscriptions, in fact, that any appreciation of the literary achievement of the Eighteenth Dynasty has to be gleaned. The Annals of Tuthmosis III, inscribed on walls adjacent to the innermost shrine of the temple of Amun at Karnak, are remarkable for their terse, methodical record of events, with so little of the bombast that passes for the writing of

[1] §VIII, 24, 74 ff.; §VIII, 32, 461 ff.
[2] §VIII, 9, 1–21; §VIII, 17, 252–3; §VIII, 12, pl. LXX.
[3] *Ibid.* 185 ff.   [4] §VIII, 33, 61 ff.
[5] §VIII, 17, 14 n. 4.   [6] *E.g.* §II, 13, 220–1.

history in ancient Egypt that they can be accepted with some confidence.[1] The stelae which describe the Homeric prowess of the pharaohs as sportsmen also, in their vivid hyperbole and the elegance of their diction, are surely indicative of a not unhappy striving on the part of their authors for a literary excellence which would match the marvellous feats of the royal paragons.[2] By the end of the dynasty literary artifice had almost triumphed over clarity of expression, as in the Coronation Inscription of Horemheb, where the historical facts of his accession have been obscured by elaborate flowers of speech.[3] This may, however, be a deliberate glossing over of the means by which the king attained a throne to which he had no strong claim.

Such records are the prose of the period. The poetry has to be sought in the hymns written to Amun of Thebes and the Aten of Akhetaten. The great triumphal hymn celebrating the victorious might of Tuthmosis III, inscribed on a magnificent stela of polished black granite from Karnak,[4] contains an apostrophe by Amun which is clearly cast in a poetical form, the balanced strophes being emphasized by the disposition of the hieroglyphs:

I have come
> that I may cause thee to trample upon the great ones of Phoenicia; that I may strew them under thy feet throughout their lands; that I may cause them to see thy Majesty as the Lord of Radiance,
> > when thou shinest in their sight like my image.

I have come
> that I may cause thee to trample upon them that are in Asia; that thou mayest strike the heads of the Asiatics of Syria; that I may cause them to see thy Majesty equipped with thy panoply
> > when thou seizest the weapons in thy chariot...

This composition was evidently considered a masterpiece, for phrases from it inspired similar triumphal hymns written for later kings.[5] Thus Amenophis III set up a great black granite stela at Medīnet Habu which recounted his achievements based upon a phrase taken from the earlier inscription:

I turn my face towards the south,
> that I may perform a wonder for thee;
> causing the great ones of Kush to
> > hasten to thee bearing all their gifts upon their shoulders.

[1] G, 13, 645–756; G, 1, vol. II, §§407–540.
[2] §VIII, 34, 243–5; C.A.H. II³, pt. 1, p. 333
[3] §V, 10, 21.
[4] G, 9, no. 34010; G, 13, 610–19; §VIII, 34, 373–5.   [5] Ibid. 373.

I turn my face towards the north,
  that I may perform a wonder for thee;
  causing the nations to come from the ends of Asia,
  bearing their gifts upon their shoulders and giving
  themselves to thee, together with their children,
  that thou mayest grant them in return the breath of life.[1]

The hymn to Amun written on Papyrus Bulaq 17 has already been mentioned as a forerunner of the Great Hymn to the Aten. In it Amun is hailed as a pharaoh and in phrases that recall those of the later hymn is referred to as 'the Solitary One with many hands, the Sole One who made all that exists' and is identified with the Creator 'who made mankind, distinguished their nature and made their life...Who made that on which the fish in the river may live and the birds soaring in the sky...Who gives breath to that which is in the egg and gives life to the offspring of the worm.'[2] The Great Hymn to the Aten, however, is justly praised as the masterpiece of psalmodic writing in the Eighteenth Dynasty, and its unknown author is often identified as Akhenaten himself, though it should be noted that the only known full-length copy appears in the Amarna tomb of Ay.[3] Many of its sentiments can be paralleled in other hymns, as has been mentioned, but the organic succession of its thought and expression demonstrates the difference between the mechanical stringing together of resounding phrases, culled from a corpus of such passages, and the inspired work of a true poet:[4]

Thou it is who causeth women to conceive and maketh seed into man; who giveth life to the child in the womb of its mother; who comforteth him so that he cries not therein, nurse that thou art, even in the womb! Who giveth breath to quicken all that he hath made.

When the child cometh forth from the womb on the day of his birth, then thou openest his mouth completely and thou furnishest his sustenance.

When the chicken in the egg chirps within the shell, thou givest him the breath within it to sustain him. Thou createst for him his proper term within the egg...

How manifold are thy works! They are hidden from the sight of men, O Sole God, like unto whom there is no other!

We shall have occasion to observe the same sensibility at work in the creation of Amarna pictorial art, where a unified composition replaces the old assemblage of diverse parts. Some of the shorter hymns at Amarna also contain passages of poetic beauty,

---

[1] G, 9, no. 34025; §viii, 34, 375–6.
[2] *Ibid.* 365–7; §viii, 17, 282–8.   [3] See above, n. 1.   [4] §ii, 12, 90.

particularly in their loyal praise of Akhenaten and his queen,[1] and the same original phraseology is found in the substitutes for the old Osirian funeral formulae. A notable example of this is the prayer on the foot-board of the coffin in which Smenkhkare was buried, but which originally was made for a daughter of Akhenaten,[2] who addresses him thus:

I shall breathe the sweet air that issues from thy mouth. My prayer is that I may behold thy beauty daily; that I may hear thy sweet voice belonging to the North Wind; that my body may grow young with life through thy love; that thou mayest give me thy hands bearing thy sustenance and I receive it and live by it; and that thou mayest call upon my name for ever and it shall not fail in thy mouth.

The modernization of Amarna hymnody is here complete. Instead of the conjuration of the god by his suppliant with propitiatory praises that had varied little since archaic times, the relationship of worshipper to deity is one of mutual affection. It is perhaps significant that this prayer of a faith that spoke much of love[3] should contain sentiments which find their echo in the secular love poetry of the following dynasty, though the fragment from the tomb of Nebamun in the British Museum[4] shows that some of it could have been composed in the Eighteenth Dynasty.

The same vulgarization is seen in the plastic arts which, during the reign of Amenophis III, were characterized by the weakening of the idealism of the official style in favour of a more sensuous naturalism. The rather prim and precise drawing of the reigns of Tuthmosis III and Amenophis II is replaced by a more dashing line and adventurous use of colour, though the craftsmanship is still meticulous.[5] The change is most marked in the last decade of the reign, by which time a new generation of artists must have succeeded their fathers.[6] The sculpture of this period is much more realistic. The torsos of the king found at Medīnet Habu and the statuette in New York[7] show him in all the obesity of his later years, while the little head of Tiy from Sinai is no less frank in revealing her features as sharp and lined.[8] At the same time iconography is brought up to date to reveal fashions of dress that had replaced the traditional garments of both kings and

---

[1] §III, 13, Pt. I, pl. xxxvi; Pt. II, pl. xxxvi; Pt. III, pl. xxix; Pt. vi, pl. xxv.
[2] §IV, 17, 35–6.   [3] §III, 13, Pt. I, 45; §v, 5, 8.
[4] §VIII, 12, pl. LXX; §VIII, 17, 252–3.
[5] Cf. §VIII, 12, pls. XVII, XXXV, XXXVI, LII, LXI, LXX.
[6] §VIII, 3, 78.   [7] See above, p. 51, n. 2.
[8] §VIII, 2, nos. 83, 84; §II, 2, pls. 21, 22.

commoners. This tendency towards 'modernism' continues unabated in the reign of Akhenaten and is found in such stylistic details as a more natural setting of the eye within its socket, the delineation of the lines that run from the corners of the eyes and nose, the folds in the neck, the large perforations in the ear-lobes and the contemporary modes of dressing the hair.[1] The innovations, however, were not accepted wholesale, and the finished reliefs in the tomb of the vizier Ramose at Thebes and one or two statues of private persons are completely in the style of the preceding reign.[2]

The great departure of Akhenaten's reign, however, and the one that has been responsible for accrediting him with a new 'realism' in Egyptian art, is his choosing to have his family and himself represented as though they suffered from some physical abnormality. Akhenaten's faithful courtiers followed his example in claiming similar diseased physiques, though the common folk were spared such marks of the elect. The distortion that Egyptian drawing now underwent is so gross as to verge on crude caricature in its more extreme and less accomplished examples,[3] but it cannot be denied that the colossal statues from Karnak, presumably the work of his master-sculptor Bak, still have a power to move the spectator by their inner spiritual malaise.[4] This revolutionary style erupts early in his reign, perhaps in his second regnal year, but it becomes more refined with the passage of time, presumably as his artists became more experienced and the less expert among them were replaced.

Apart from this new mannerism, Akhenaten inspired no fundamental change in age-old Egyptian conventions of drawing the human figure, but his artists did introduce a new space-concept in which to represent the new subjects for illustration which he must have specified. We have already remarked that in the Amarna tombs traditional themes for decoration are banished in favour of representations of events in the life of the royal family. During the dynasty there had been a steady growth in the popularity of a trinity consisting of a pair of deities and their male offspring, an idea that appealed particularly to the Egyptian with his strong love of family. This tendency received a considerable stimulus

[1] A, 1, chs. IV, V; §VIII, 1, 141 ff.; cf. §VIII, 21, 29 n. 3. This stela (G, 9, no. 34023), however, is a posthumous representation of Tuthmosis IV belonging to a later period in the dynasty.

[2] §III, 15, pls. XLVI–XLVIII; §VIII, 6, 79 ff.; §VIII, 7, 167 (reg. no. 69·45).

[3] §VIII, 13, 10; §IV, 14, 105.

[4] §II, 2, pls. 2–4; §VIII, 2, nos. 107–9; §IV, 14, pl. 95; §VIII, 28, pls. 176, 177.

when the new sun-god could no longer be exhibited in iconic form, and scenes of religious import were replaced by compositions in which his incarnation in the person of the pharaoh with his wife and daughters enacted incidents from their lives—the worship of the Aten,[1] the investiture before the palace balcony,[2] the visit to the temple[3] and so forth.[4] Stelae used like triptychs in the chapels connected with private houses show the royal family in even more intimate scenes with the queen seated in the king's lap, or playing with their children.[5]

There were no precedents in Egyptian religious art for such subjects, and the artists therefore took their inspiration from the vernacular art that had already appeared in the scenes of everyday life in the Theban tomb-paintings. The royal family and the courtiers are now grouped in the same poses that had hitherto been reserved for the lowly and the vulgar.[6] They express emotions of unction, joy, pride and sorrow not by a symbolic gesture, but by pose and facial expression, like the mourners before the tomb-door or the dancers at the feast.[7]

These new subjects are depicted in a novel manner in the Amarna tomb-reliefs. Instead of a selection of standard scenes taken from pattern-books and assembled haphazardly according to the taste of the patron, each wall of the chamber is considered a complete entity and decorated with a single composition. Indeed, in a chamber in the royal tomb, one scene is spread over two adjacent walls.[8] A room in the Northern Palace was decorated apparently with one continuous scene of bird-life among the papyrus thickets.[9] The same readiness to regard space as a totality is revealed in the sarcophagus of Tutankhamun, where the goddesses stand at the corners, each with her spine in alignment with the edge where two adjacent sides meet.[10] The disposition of Nefertiti on a fragment of a corner of a sarcophagus from the royal tomb shows that this pose was an innovation of the preceding reign.[11] That it was felt to be outside the natural instincts of the Egyptian artist is seen in the similar sarcophagi of Ay and Horemheb, where the four goddesses have been so placed

[1] §III, 13, Pt. II, pls. V, VII, VIII; Pt. IV, pl. XXXI.
[2] *Ibid.* Pt. VI, pls. XXIX, XLII.   [3] *Ibid.* Pt. I, pl. XXV; Pt. III, pl. VIII.
[4] *E.g. ibid.* Pt. I, pl. X; Pt. II, pls. XVIII, XXXVII; Pt. III, pl. XXXIIA; Pt. IV, pl. VI; Pt. VI, pl. VI.
[5] §III, 35, pl. I, 16; §VIII, 13, pls. 8, 9, 11; §VIII, 40, pl. 22; §VIII, 35, pl. 51.
[6] *Cf.* §VIII, 11, 29; §VIII, 28, 147.
[7] §VIII, 21, 8, 9; §VIII, 10, 11–12.   [8] §III, 9, pl. I.
[9] §VIII, 21, 58–9.   [10] §VIII, 2, no. 161.
[11] §III, 38, 5; §VIII, 40, pl. 56.

that two are fully revealed on each long side, one only of their winged arms being on each short end.[1] Nevertheless, many of the Amarna novelties remained in the repertoire of Egyptian art-forms, such as the 'caryatid' figures of the pharaoh standing against a pillar in the costume of the living[2] and the decoration of Ramesside walls and pylons.[3] In the unified compositions of Amarna art we can see at work the same influences that are manifest in a monotheistic conception of godhead and in the progression of thought in the Great Hymn to the Aten, although such tendencies are already present in the reign of Amenophis III.[4]

The excesses of the earlier Karnak style, still evident in the Boundary Stelae and other reliefs from Amarna, had been modified by the later years of Akhenaten, though the casts found in the sculptors' studios at El-Amarna tend to give an unbalanced view of the 'naturalism' of the period, since for the most part they appear to be portrait studies modelled from the life in wax or clay to catch a likeness and be cast in plaster for working over to an accepted standard.[5] To this period belongs the famous painted bust of Nefertiti modelled in plaster over a limestone core.[6]

This restrained style was more sympathetic to the temper of the post-Amarna age when a return was made to the traditions of Amenophis III, though the artists did not discard all they had been allowed to express under Akhenaten. The statuary of the end of the dynasty is among the finest produced in its noble proportions, high technical excellence and the individualism of its portraiture.[7] A group of sculptors working at Memphis produced reliefs for the private tombs, notably that of Horemheb, which show the same qualities in their lively scenes, splendidly conceived and executed.[8] These are among the last expressions of that delight in the world of the living and pride in worldly success which is the special contribution of the Eighteenth Dynasty to Egyptian art.

The decoration of tomb walls at El-Amarna and Memphis with carved reliefs broke the traditions of the Theban tomb-

[1] §II, 2, pl. III; §v, 6, pls. LXV, LXVIII, LXXIII.
[2] As, for instance, in the first courts of the great temples at Abu Simbel and Medīnet Habu (Ramesses III). [3] §I, 20, 209, 222-4.
[4] Cf. scenes of the owner before his king in Theban tombs nos. 48 and 57, G, 11, 1², Pt. II, p. 88 (4), 89 (7); p. 115 (11), 116 (15). [5] §VIII, 36, 145 ff.
[6] §VIII, 5; §VIII, 4; §VIII, 13, pls. 13, 14; §II, 2, pls. VIII, 7.
[7] E.g. §II, 2, pls. 56, 63-6; §VIII, 13, pls. 7, 24; §VIII, 28, pls. 196-9; §VIII, 2, no. 175.
[8] §VIII, 2, nos. 144-8; §v, 3, pls. V-VII; §VIII, 13, pls. 4, 5, 22, 23, 27-31.

painters and they never recovered the assurance and mastery that they had demonstrated under Amenophis III. The painting in the tomb of Huy and others is often poor in its drawing and proportions and crude in its colouring, and many of the mannerisms of the Ramesside style are already anticipated.[1] The same loss of confidence is seen in the wall-paintings in the tombs of Tutankhamun and Ay.[2]

The Amarna age showed no falling-off in its appetite for exotic objects of great luxury, particularly in gold, glass and polychrome faïence, that had characterized the reign of Amenophis III. The specimens found in the tomb of Tutankhamun give an unparalleled conspectus of the applied arts of the period, and while some of them seem hasty in execution and over-exuberant in taste, certain items may be singled out for their high technical excellence, such as some of the wooden furniture, an ivory bracelet exquisitely carved in coin-like relief with a frieze of horses, and the great head-rest of rich blue glass.[3] A novelty of the age is the gold tinted in tones from pink to purple by a metallurgical process,[4] but as Tushratta of the Mitanni speaks of sending the pharaoh gold ornaments 'through which blood shines',[5] we may presume this to have been an Asiatic invention, like his iron dagger-blade.[6]

---

[1] §IV, 9, 3; §I, 20, 210.　　　　　[2] §IV, 25; §IV, 29.
[3] §IV, 5, vol. I, pl. XLIX; §VIII, 14, pls. XII, XLIA, L.
[4] *Ibid.* pl. XXIIA.
[5] E.A. 22, I, ll. 20, 25; II, ll. 8, 15.
[6] E.A. 22, I, l. 32; II, l. 16; III, l. 7; §VIII, 14, pl. XXIB; §IV, 5, vol. II, 135–6.

CHAPTER XX

THE AMARNA LETTERS
FROM PALESTINE

I. THE TABLETS AND THEIR CHRONOLOGY

IN 1887 an Egyptian peasant woman accidently discovered a large collection of tablets at El-Amarna in Middle Egypt; they were dug out by the local inhabitants and sold to various dealers. Eventually more than 350 cuneiform tablets, some complete, some broken, were purchased by various museums and private collectors. More than half of them were acquired by the Berlin Museum. Smaller collections found their way to the British Museum and the Egyptian Museum in Cairo. In 1915 the publication of all then available Amarna Tablets, begun by J. A. Knudtzon in 1907, was completed.[1] Since then another seven important tablets belonging to the original find have been published by F. Thureau-Dangin[2] and G. Dossin,[3] while a dozen additional tablets and fragments were recovered still later by German and British excavators at the same site.[4] These tablets are mostly letters from the royal archives of Amenophis IV or Akhenaten (1379–1362 B.C.) and his father, Amenophis III (1417–1379 B.C.);[5] only about twenty-five of the texts are not epistolary in content. About 150 of the letters either are written directly from or to Palestine, or are so immediately concerned with Palestinian affairs that they fall within the scope of the present survey.

Some similar documents have also been discovered in Palestine. In 1892 F. J. Bliss found a well-preserved tablet of the Amarna Age at Tell el-Ḥesi.[6] So far twelve tablets and fragments have been excavated at Taʻanach, near Megiddo,[7] one at Gezer,[8] two at Shechem,[9] one at Jericho,[10] one at Megiddo,[11] and one at Hazor.[12]

---

* An original version of this chapter was published as fascicle 51 in 1966.
[1] §1, 35.   [2] §1, 50.   [3] §1, 25.
[4] §1, 46; §1, 31. See also A. R. Millard in *P.E.Q.* (1965), 40 ff.
[5] I should prefer to date their reigns *c.* 1365–1348 and *c.* 1401–1365, respectively.
[6] §1, 5.   [7] §1, 9; §1, 44, 490.   [8] §1, 8.   [9] §1, 4; §1, 36, 59, n. 121.
[10] §1, 49, 116 ff. I am inclined to date this piece in the early sixteenth century B.C. (Alalakh VII period).   [11] §1, 30.
[12] Fragments of liver models; see now *I.E.J.* 14 (1964), 201 ff.

Most of these documents from Palestine belong to the period between 1450 and 1350 B.C.; at least nine of them are letters.

The interpretation of the letters concerning Palestine is relatively difficult because the scribes who wrote them were nearly all Canaanites, with a few Egyptians. None had a native command of Akkadian (Babylonian), and most of them had learned their cuneiform from local teachers, who had themselves learned it from other local teachers. This we infer from many facts. The recent discovery of a fragment of the Gilgamesh Epic at Megiddo, written in a local Phoenician hand of the early fourteenth century, demonstrates the existence of a scribal school in that area.[1] A letter written by a teacher to a patrician of Shechem says: 'What is my offence that thou hast not paid me? The boys who are with me continue to learn; their father and their mother every day alike am I.'[2] School texts were found at El-Amarna, and some of these texts show the same lack of familiarity with Akkadian grammar and phonetics which we find in the letters. The Akkadian of the letters contains many archaisms which are no longer to be found in contemporary Babylonia, but do occur in Old Babylonian, especially in the letters written by Amorite scribes of the eighteenth and seventeenth centuries in Syria and Upper Mesopotamia. Most significant is the fact that the letters abound with Canaanitisms in vocabulary, syntax, morphology and phonology, proving a Canaanite substratum in the mind of the scribe.[3] Moreover, many grammatical forms which recur constantly in these letters are neither Akkadian nor Canaanite but a mixture of both, showing a formalizing of mistakes which must themselves have been taught in the schools. In short, the language of the Amarna Letters was a scholastic and diplomatic jargon, the use of which had become acceptable for written communication between Canaanites and foreigners, as well as among Canaanites who did not wish to use either of the native consonantal alphabets which we know to have been current at the time. Because of the nature of this jargon, it is not enough for the would-be interpreter to know Akkadian; he must also be a specialist in Hebrew and Ugaritic, and above all he must be so familiar with all the letters that he knows what to expect from their writers.

The chronology of the Amarna Letters is gradually being cleared up, though it will perhaps never be possible to give each

[1] §1, 30.
[2] §1, 4. Contrast §1, 36, 59, n. 121, where the fact is overlooked that in all Canaanite letters voiced and voiceless stops are sharply distinguished.
[3] §1, 7; 5; 6; 14.

letter a date exact to the year.[1] Since all the letters from foreign princes which contain the official name of the reigning pharaoh are addressed either to Amenophis III or to his son, Akhenaten, with the possible exception of one letter that may be addressed to Tutankhamun,[2] it is obvious that they must be limited to a period of little over half a century. Moreover, it is possible to limit them more closely than that. Akhetaten, the new city built by Akhenaten at El-Amarna, was occupied from the fifth to the seventeenth year of Akhenaten, in the first and second years of his successor Smenkhkare, and apparently during the first four years of Tutankhamun, as indicated by hundreds of inscribed portable objects, mostly dated jar-sealings, which were excavated at the site. To what extent the regnal years of Smenkhkare over-lapped the end of Akhenaten's reign, is uncertain. When the royal archives were brought to Amarna they included documents from the latter part of Amenophis III's reign, probably going back at least to the latter's thirty-second year.[3] We may safely allow a minimum chronological scope of twenty-seven years and a maximum of just over thirty for the correspondence—about 1389–1358 B.C.[4]

Inside these limits we can fix the relative chronology of most of the letters within about five years, by relating their contents to external evidence from other sources, mainly Egyptian.[5] The most important group of letters consists of some 67 (or 68) letters from and to Rib-Adda, prince of Byblos. These may be divided into two main groups, EA 68–96 and 102–138,[6] dating from before and after the death of 'Abdi-Ashirta, prince of Amurru. Subdivisions may also be set up within the groups, particularly the second. In Palestine the role of 'Abdi-Ashirta was filled to a certain extent by Labaya (Lab'ayu), prince of Shechem, who was equally involved in happenings in northern and southern, western and eastern Palestine. Fortunately we have a hieratic docket, written in ink on one of Labaya's letters to the pharaoh, which probably mentions the thirty-second year of the king, 1385 B.C.[7] After Labaya's death his place was taken by his sons, who played an even more active part than their father in Palestinian

----

[1] §1, 18.   [2] §1, 18, 49, 53 ff.

[3] §1, 18, 69 ff., 103, 109 n.

[4] I should prefer the dates c. 1375–1344.   [5] §1, 18; 34.

[6] §1, 18, 79 ff. groups them as follows: 71–95 and 68–70; 101–138; 362. (For brevity, EA in footnotes to this chapter refers to the Amarna Letters (and their lines) as numbered in §1, 35.)

[7] c. 1370 in my system of chronology. On the situation of Labaya at that time see below, pp. 114 f.

politics. We have several such local dynastic sequences, which are very helpful in fixing relative chronology; thus Milkilu of Gezer was followed by Iapakhu and Ba'lu-shipti, in uncertain order; Zimredda of Lachish was followed by Shipti-Ba'lu and Iabni-ilu.

Knowledge of the succession of Egyptian commissioners and other high officials involved in Palestinian affairs is also very helpful. The Canaanite Iankhamu, who attained the high rank of 'Feather-Bearer on the Right of the King', figured prominently in the affairs of Byblos and Palestine in the middle period of the Amarna correspondence; his name is rare until after Labaya's death but it is very common for some years thereafter; similarly it does not appear in the earliest or the latest Byblos correspondence. Iankhamu is never mentioned in the latest letters of all from Tyre or Palestine. Since there is no trace of his name among the officials of Akhenaten mentioned in the Egyptian inscriptions from Amarna, and since he is never mentioned together with Egyptian officials belonging to the Aten circle, we may safely infer that he held power during the first years of Amenophis IV, being removed from office after the Aten revolution.[1] Maya followed Iankhamu; his name is never mentioned in a letter of the Iankhamu period, and his official role coincides well with that of a high military officer of Akhenaten bearing the same name. The representation of only three royal princesses in his unfinished tomb at Amarna establishes a date for his *floruit* between the eighth and twelfth years of Akhenaten's reign; we may place his rise after the sixth year and his downfall about the eleventh year. The Amarna references to him would then fall roughly between 1374 and 1368 B.C.[2]

While many more illustrations of the chronological evidence could be given, a single example of combinatory character must suffice. Piryawaza, prince of the region of Damascus, was a contemporary of Akhenaten and of Burnaburiash II, king of Babylon, who complains about him in a letter to the former.[3] He was also contemporary with the sons of Labaya, whose father had written to Egypt in the thirty-second(?) year of Amenophis III.[4] He was, further, still alive and engaged in an otherwise unknown war with Aziru, son of 'Abdi-Ashirta of Amurru, at the very end of Akhenaten's reign, as we know from a letter of Abi-milki of

[1] §1, 18, 90 ff.; §1, 33, 259.
[2] §1, 18, 75 ff., 126 ff.; §1, 33, 260, 266. My date would be between *c.* 1360 and 1354.
[3] EA 7.   [4] See above, p. 100.

Tyre.[1] The relative date of the last-mentioned letter is fixed by the fact that Abi-milki's reign in Tyre came after that of Iapa-Adda, who flourished until late in the reign of Rib-Adda of Byblos, and by the references to Akhenaten's daughter Mayate (Merytaten) as queen (of Smenkhkare) in one of Abi-milki's letters.[2] Piryawaza's correspondence is thus relatively as late as any.

II. POLITICAL ORGANIZATION OF PALESTINE IN THE AMARNA AGE

During the two centuries of Egyptian occupation of Palestine since the conquest under Amosis and Amenophis I, its political organization had become more or less normalized. As far as practicable the Egyptians had left the local princely houses in control of their own territories, but under the close supervision of Egyptian agents whom we may conveniently designate as 'commissioner' (Akkadian *rābiṣu*, Canaanite *sōkinu*, Hebrew *sōkēn*)[3] and 'envoy' (Egyptian *uputi* [*wpwty*]). These agents were generally Egyptians, but they were not infrequently Canaanites of Semitic stock, as in the case of Iankhamu and Addayu. Sometimes native princes played an important role in Egyptian administration, as in the case of Iapa-Adda, who was probably prince of Tyre,[4] or Piryawaza, prince of the Damascus region. The chief centres of Egyptian administration in Palestine were Gaza and Joppa on the coast;[5] Gaza is mentioned several times as the residence of an Egyptian commissioner in one letter,[6] and it appears already in that role in an earlier letter from Ta'anach.[7] There were also Egyptian outposts at strategic points through the country, such as Beth-shan,[8] where excavations have brought to light a series of Egyptian fortresses from the fifteenth to the twelfth centuries.

In addition to Egyptian commissioners, whose military functions seem to have been subordinated to their administrative duties, there were also military officers, such as the *ākil tarbaṣi*, or 'inspector of the stable',[9] who was a commander of chariotry, and the *wē'u* (Egyptian *w'w*), 'petty officer', often in charge of a detachment of archers (*pitate*, Egyptian *pḏtyw*). The contrast

---

[1] EA 151. Cf. §1, 34, 17, 45.   [2] §1, 18, 70 ff.
[3] Gloss in EA 256, 9; 362, 69.
[4] §11, 1, 10 n.; §1, 33, 178, 193; §1, 18, 92 n. The last two favour Berytus.
[5] EA 296, 32 ff. On the Egyptian administration in general see §1, 34, 256 ff.
[6] EA 289.   [7] Ta'anach no. 6, 12 ff.; see §1, 9.
[8] EA 289, 20.   [9] §11, 2, 38; §11, 1, 11.

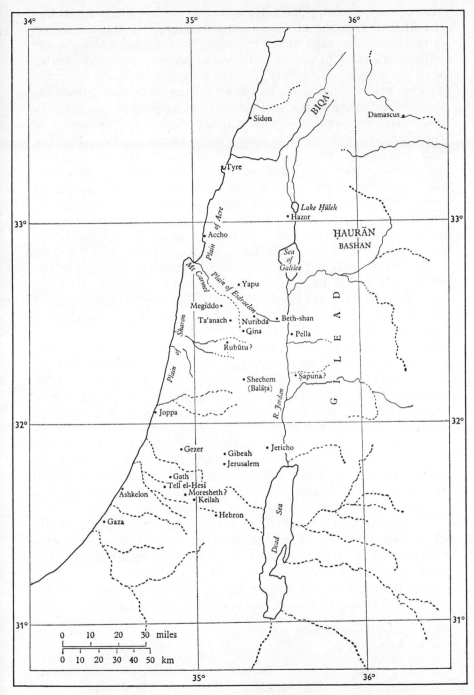

Map 2. Political geography of Palestine, about 1400–1200 B.C.

between the multifarious titles of the Egyptian inscriptions and the limited number of expressions employed in the cuneiform letters shows that the Canaanites found the intricacies of Egyptian officialdom hard to define. Often the scribe contented himself with the word *rabū*, 'officer' (literally, 'great one').

The native chieftains, in spite of their excessive grovelling before Pharaoh, which sometimes occupies over half their letters, were patricians, proud of their ancestry.[1] A high proportion of the Palestinian chiefs bore Indo-Aryan names.[2] Officially their title was *awilu*, 'free man', 'chief' (of such-and-such a place), and their office was that of *ḫaziānu* (*ḫazānu*), 'governor' (literally, 'inspector'). In Canaanite circles, however, the prince was called 'king' (Akkadian *šarru*, Canaanite *milku*); in one letter to the pharaoh the prince of Hazor forgot himself so far as to apply the term 'king' to himself at the beginning of his salutation.[3] Elsewhere, Mut-Ba'al, prince of Pella, does the same thing farther on in his letter,[4] while Piryawaza of Damascus uses the term 'king' of the chiefs of Buṣruna and Khalunnu in Bashan,[5] and Abi-milki of Tyre calls the princes of Sidon and Hazor 'kings'.[6] The Canaanite chieftains are also spoken of more than once as 'kings' in the plural. The later use of the same expression in the Book of Joshua to designate local princes was, therefore, quite normal. The extent of the territory over which these chieftains held sway varied greatly. The princes of Hazor, Shechem, Jerusalem, and the southern hill-country of Judah controlled among them almost all the areas of western Palestine which were in Israelite hands during most of the period of the Judges. Other chieftains with extensive lands were the princes of Gezer and Megiddo. Though details are generally lacking, there seems to be no doubt that certain princes exercised acknowledged feudal rights over other weaker chieftains; e.g. Tagu was the immediate suzerain of the chief of Gath (Jett) in Sharon.[7]

The Amarna letters exhibit very frequently the unhappy results of this organization. The princes were continually at war with one another; each accused his neighbour of being a traitor to the crown. In the Tell el-Ḥesi letter, from the end of the reign of Amenophis III or the beginning of his successor's,[8] a minor

---

[1] Cf., for example, EA 224, 17 from Shamu-Adda of Shamruna in Galilee (so read). The name of his ancestor Kuzuna is identical with the Ketjun (*Ktwn*) of a Hyksos scarab (§11, 3, pl. xxiii, 28).

[2] See below, p. 109. [3] EA 227, 3.

[4] EA 256, 8. [5] EA 197.

[6] EA 147; 148. [7] See EA 289, 18 ff., compared with EA 249.

[8] §1, 5. On the date of this letter (EA 333) see also §1, 18, 101, 134.

Egyptian officer, Pa'apu, accuses the prince of Lachish and his brother (who later became prince himself) of disloyalty to the crown. Pa'apu is particularly indignant because Shipti-Ba'lu has had the effrontery to accuse the writer himself of disloyalty to the king. Similarly, 'Abdi-Kheba of Jerusalem accuses his neighbours, Milkilu of Gezer and Shuwardata of the Hebron area, of being traitors and rebels,[1] an accusation which they return with interest.[2] The extraordinary extent of such recrimination in the Amarna letters, which far exceeds anything found in other comparable archives, shows the extent to which Canaanite morale had deteriorated after nearly two centuries of Egyptian domination. The demoralization of Canaanite ethos was, moreover, not much worse than that of Egyptian. Bribery and corruption were rampant among the Egyptian officials of the time, as we learn from contemporary Egyptian documents. Most instructive in this connexion is the edict of Horemheb, which was issued only a few years after the last of the Amarna Letters was written.[3] In it we find the most stringent penalties invoked against corrupt or oppressive officials, and instructions for the complete reorganization of the local *qenbe* (*knbt*) courts by the appointment of well-born and respected priests to judicial posts. Moreover, these judges were thenceforth to receive salaries, evidently in order to make it less necessary for them to take bribes so as to live in proper style.

Additional evidence from Egyptian sources is abundant, but we do not have to go beyond the Amarna Letters themselves to hear of exactions by Egyptian officials, especially by military officers. For example, late in the reign of Akhenaten, Ba'lu-shipti of Gezer complains that Pe'eya, a minor Egyptian official stationed at Joppa,[4] not only appropriates for himself the services of the men of Gezer sent there to work on the *corvée* and to guard the royal granaries, but even holds them for ransom. The prince of Gezer asserts that 'from the mountains people are ransomed for thirty (shekels) of silver, but from Pe'eya for one hundred (shekels) of silver'.[5] In other words, the bandits from the hill-country of Palestine asked as ransom only the conventional price (which was also the normal price of an able-bodied male slave), but the rapacious Egyptian official is said to have demanded over three times as much!

[1] EA 287; 289; 290.   [2] EA 280.
[3] See §II, 4, 260 ff.; §II, 5, Übersetzung zu den Heften 17–22, 416 ff.
[4] §II, 1, 19.
[5] EA 292; 294 (assuming that the illegible name of the sender of EA 294 [see §I, 18, 101, n. 73] is a form of *Ba'lu-shipti*).

The extent to which both official and irregular exaction went is almost unbelievable. The regular tribute alone must have been a terrific burden. The grain-lands of Megiddo and Sharon were all considered as crown property, and the harvest was stored in royal granaries (Akkadian *maškan[āti]*,[1] Egyptian *šunut [šnwt]*).[2] Thus Biridiya, prince of Megiddo, complains to the pharaoh (about the end of the reign of Amenophis III or early in that of Akhenaten): 'Behold, I am working in the town of Shunama, and I bring men of the *corvée*, but behold, the governors who are with me do not as I (do): they do not work in the town of Shunama, and they do not bring men for the *corvée* from the town of Yapu (Yafa, near Nazareth). They come from Shu[nama], and likewise from the town of Nuribda (Nuris near Zer'in).'[3] The chief of Gath (Jett) in the northern part of Sharon complains bitterly: 'And let (the king) know that my m[en] have gone [to] Mil[kilu]. What have I done to Milkilu (of Gezer) that he oppresses my men because of his subservience to Tagu, his father-in-law, (to whom) he has rendered his service. But what can I do?'[4] In addition to regular tribute and the *corvée* there were also all kinds of exactions for the feeding and clothing of troops and fines for real or imaginary crimes. Levies for the support of troops, especially of garrisons and of armies on their way to Syria, were normal practice; we have a number of copies of letters written from Egypt to local princes demanding supplies of cattle, grain, oil, etc., for the troops. Frequently a local chieftain tries to persuade the central authorities in Egypt that his neighbours should do more than he, for reasons duly set forth. Milkilu of Gezer writes complaining that the Egyptian commissioner Iankhamu demands two (or three) thousand shekels from him. Until he gets it the luckless Milkilu is to hand over his wife and children as surety, besides being flogged if he cannot scrape the amount together.[5]

The Egyptian garrisons in Palestine and Syria were mainly composed of Egyptian and Nubian archers. In his extant letters, Rib-Adda of Byblos asks at least a dozen times for troops, nearly always specifying equal numbers of Egyptians and Nubians (men of Kashu, biblical Cush, which alternates with Meluhha, an archaic designation for Negro Africa). When they were not provided with rations, owing presumably to official corruption, they resorted to robbery or brigandage. The local chieftains complain bitterly of the depredations of the troops. Even 'Abdi-Kheba,

---

[1] EA 306, 31.   [2] EA 294, 22.   [3] EA 365.
[4] EA 249, 5 ff.   [5] EA 270.

who unceasingly repeats his request for garrison troops, complains that the Nubians almost killed him when they broke into his quarters on the terrace of his palace.[1]

III. PALESTINE: DEMOGRAPHY AND SOCIETY

The population of Palestine in the Amarna age was small; it was mostly concentrated on the coastal plains and the adjacent low hills, the plain of Esdraelon and the Jordan valley. The hill-country of western Palestine was sparsely settled; its population was mostly concentrated around well-watered centres such as Shechem, Jerusalem and Hebron. Eastern Palestine (Transjordan) was occupied by a sedentary population only in the Jordan valley and the extreme north, between the wooded hills of Gilead and the Syrian desert, just south of Bashan (southern Ḥaurān). Otherwise it was occupied chiefly by nomadic tribes which did not begin settling down until the following century. This situation has been demonstrated by the exhaustive surface surveys of Nelson Glueck, made possible by the fact that there are very few stratified mounds in southern and central Transjordan. Virtually all sites exhibit only one or two superimposed layers of occupation, and many sites which were reoccupied in different periods were never walled, so sherds of different ages may be found either mixed together or in different parts of a given site. His discovery that there was a long period of abandonment in the eighteenth to thirteenth centuries sandwiched between two periods of relatively heavy sedentary population, has been confirmed by the explorations and excavations of others. It is instructive to note that only a single town of all those mentioned in the Amarna Tablets and in the New-Kingdom Egyptian lists of conquered places can be plausibly identified with any site in Transjordan south of latitude 32° 20′ (Pella); this town is Ṣapuna (Zaphon),[2] some 12 miles in a straight line south of Pella (which is mentioned frequently). And both Zaphon and Pella were in the Jordan valley.

By combining evidence from archaeological surveys and excavations with written evidence, we are able to give a rough

---

[1] EA 287 translated in §1, 44, 488. Mention of their breaking through the roof is vividly illustrated by Dame Kathleen Kenyon's excavations, which prove that most of Late Bronze Age Jerusalem was built in terraces rising from the original edge of the Kedron Valley.

[2] §1, 7, 15 ff. The identification of Zaphon with Tell es-Saʿidiyeh, excavated by J. B. Pritchard, seems probable to the writer.

estimate of the population. Archaeological indications point to the contemporary existence in the fourteenth century of not over a score of fortified towns, large and small, in the entire region which later belonged to the kingdom of Judah, but was at this time divided among three major chieftains. Besides these fortified towns, some of which were exceedingly small, there were villages and hamlets at points which were watered by nature (since the technique of lining cisterns with watertight lime plaster had not yet become widely known). The sedentary population cannot have exceeded a rough total of 20,000 and the nomadic population must have been under 5000, since the hills were then densely wooded with scrub timber and bush. Proceeding through the country, district by district, we reach an approximate total of 200,000 for all Palestine, eastern and western. In no case can the population at this time have exceeded a quarter of a million. It is interesting to note that this was the approximate population of the country at the lowest ebb of its prosperity under the Turks, about A.D. 1800. The population of Egypt in about 1800 was also very low, and was estimated at about two millions by the members of the French scientific mission brought out by Napoleon. The same average ratio between the population of Egypt and that of Palestine has been maintained until recently; Egypt first gained proportionately under the *pax Britannica*, and Palestine gained subsequently as a result of British rule and Jewish immigration. In the early fourteenth century B.C. Egypt was enjoying its period of greatest prosperity before Hellenistic times, while Palestine was at a very low ebb. Assuming a ratio of twenty to one as in 1914, when Egypt had been governed by the British for some two decades and Palestine was still ruled by the Turks, we obtain the reasonable figure of four million for the population of Egypt (two-thirds of the probably inflated figure which Diodorus gives for Egypt in the first century B.C.). When we glance through the Amarna letters, we cannot but be impressed with the smallness of the garrisons which were considered adequate by the local princes when clamouring for aid; the prince of Megiddo wants a hundred men,[1] but three other chieftains, including the princes of Gezer and Jerusalem, are satisfied with fifty each.[2] Even the prince of wealthy Byblos, who constantly asks for assistance, is generally satisfied with two hundred to six hundred infantry and twenty to thirty chariots. Piryawaza of the Damascus region also wants two hundred men.[3]

Ethnically Palestine was very mixed, though dialects of

[1] EA 244. [2] EA 237; 289; 295. [3] EA 196.

Canaanite or of a closely related Amorite were spoken everywhere, as is proved by the language of the letters.[1] Not a single letter from Palestine shows any trace of the Hurrian substratum which appears everywhere north of the region of Damascus and the Biqā' in central Syria. Nor is there any trace of the Egyptian substratum which characterizes the letters of the scribe of the prince of Tyre.[2] If we turn to the non-Egyptian names in the Amarna letters proper we find the following situation:[3]

Clear north-west Semitic names	32
Certain or probable Indo-Aryan names	20
Certain or probable Hurrian names	3
Miscellaneous or uncertain, but not Egyptian	6

In the case of the twelve earlier tablets and fragments from Ta'anach, owing to their broken condition and the defective copies which we have, most of the seventy-five names are incomplete or cannot be read with confidence. Omitting the Egyptian names, we have the following picture:

Clear north-west Semitic names	14
Certain or probable Indo-Aryan names	5
Certain or probable Hurrian names	4

The two tablets from Shechem contain eight certain or probable north-west Semitic names, two certain or probable Indo-Aryan names and one uncertain name.

Evidently the proportion of Indo-Aryans decreases as we go downward in the social scale (most of the Amarna names belong to native princes, whereas the lists from Ta'anach and Shechem are of miscellaneous persons). Moreover, we find traces of the symbiosis of Hurrians and Indo-Aryans which was already well known from Nuzi, Mitanni and northern Syria. In all these areas the highest-ranking patricians (*mariyanna*) tended to have Indo-Aryan names, while the common people were overwhelmingly Hurrian in name.[4] At Ta'anach two of the five clear Indo-Aryan names are borne by a 'king' and a 'prince' (both carefully labelled as such); Indo-Aryan names are also borne by the princes of Ta'anach and Megiddo mentioned in the Amarna Tablets. The patrician to whom was addressed a letter found at Shechem bore an Indo-Aryan name also known from Nuzi. The Indo-Aryan

---

[1] See above, p. 99.   [2] §III, 1, 196 ff.

[3] There is a certain amount of fluidity in our numbers, since it is often hard to tell whether a given place belongs in northern Palestine or southern Syria. For convenience Ḥaurān has been included.

[4] §1, 43, 56 ff., 149 ff.

ruling class was scattered over northern, central and eastern Syria; it was particularly strong in the Damascus region and Ḥaurān, and appears to have been well represented in the plains of Acre and Esdraelon, where the princes of Accho and Achshaph, Megiddo and Taʿanach were all Indo-Aryan in name. Indo-Aryans were also represented at Shechem and in the Hebron region (Shuwardata). There can be little doubt that they were bracketed in Hebrew tradition with the Hurrians (Horites). According to the Septuagint, the prince of Shechem (who was also called 'father of Shechem') and the Canaanites of Gibeon were also Horites. Similarly the Boğazköy texts call both Indo-Aryans and Hurrians by the latter name. Evidently the Indo-Aryans migrated into south-western Asia in such small numbers that they became submerged in the Hurrian mass, in spite of their obvious pride of family and their preservation of Indo-Aryan names as a token of nobility—much as happened to the Visigoths in Spain. It is likely that there was a somewhat comparable situation at Jerusalem whose prince, ʿAbdi-Kheba, bore a name formed with that of a Hurrian goddess, while Araunah the Jebusite, who is said to have sold the site of the future Solomonic temple to David, appears to have the same Indo-Aryan name as Ariwana or Arawana, a prince of the Damascus region in the Amarna age.

The evidence of the Amarna Letters is confirmed by excavations, which show a striking contrast between the spacious, well-built houses of the patricians and the hovels of the poor during the Late Bronze Age. The letters from Palestine exhibit little interest in the downtrodden peasants except as material for *corvées*; there is no appeal on behalf of an individual of humble origin and it is doubtful whether a single native outside the patrician class is ever mentioned by name. The generic Canaanite word for 'peasant' or 'serf' does not appear at all in the letters from Palestine; it is known from the Byblian correspondence and from Ugarit to have been *ḥupšu*, Ugaritic *ḥpt*, a word also employed in Assyria for 'half-free person', or the like. By a very interesting shift of meaning Hebrew *ḥopšī*, 'free', is derived from it.

There was also a large and apparently increasing class of stateless and reputedly lawless people in Palestine and Syria to whom the appellation ʿ*Apiru* was given. It has now become certain that they were a class of heterogeneous ethnic origin, and that they spoke different languages, often alien to the people in whose documents they appear.[1] The cuneiform spelling *ḥapiru* (formerly read *ḥabiru*) appears in the letters of ʿAbdi-Kheba, prince of Jeru-

[1] §1, 16; §1, 32; §1, 33, 526 ff.

salem; elsewhere it is always written ideographically as *SA.GAZ* or the like, employing a logogram also used for *ḫabbātu*, 'bandit'. For a long time it remained uncertain whether there was any direct connexion between the two expressions; Hugo Winckler discovered that they were synonymous in Hittite documents of the same general age. Finally, in 1939, Ch. Virolleaud found that the same logogram had the Ugaritic alphabetic reading '-*p*-*r*, with a medial *p* which had been surmised from Egyptian transcriptions of the word. The problem of the 'Apiru is complex and many different solutions have been suggested; it is rendered even more elusive by the fact that it recurs in cuneiform texts from different parts of Mesopotamia, Syria, Egypt and Asia Minor, all dating between the Dynasty of Agade and the eleventh century B.C. The problem took a new turn with the publication of a triumphal inscription of Amenophis II (1450–1425 B.C.), at the end of which is a list of captives, including especially the following four groups: '3600 'Apiru; 15,200 Shasu; 36,300 Hurrians; 15,070 men from Nukhashshe in northern Syria.'[1] Other entries in the same text include 550 patricians (*mariyanna*), 640 merchants (*Kinaʿnu* = Canaanites),[2] 217 princes of Syria and Palestine, together with many sons and daughters, wives and concubines, and brothers of the princes. At the end of the second list all the wives (or 'relatives')[3] are mentioned without details. In order to understand the above collocation we turn to a letter of Piryawaza, prince of the Damascus region, who writes: 'Behold, I am in front of the royal archers, together with my troops and my chariots, and together with my brethren, and together with my 'Apiru, and together with my Sutu.'[4] Since the term Sutu is used as a generic term for 'bedawin' in the Amarna Tablets, following Babylonian usage in earlier centuries, we have exactly the same terminology as in the Amenophis text, where the 'Apiru are also followed by the bedawin (Shasu). We must accordingly differentiate sharply between the two groups: both were donkey nomads, but the 'Apiru were less nomadic than the Sutu.[5]

In the Amarna Tablets the 'Apiru generally appear as the foes of both native princes and Egyptian officials, as men who raid and destroy settled areas. Each prince accuses his enemies of being in league with the 'Apiru, and it would seem from a number

---

[1] §I, 39, 9; §II, 5, Übersetzung zu den Heften 17–22, 32 ff.
[2] §I, 39.   [3] §II, 5, Übersetzung zu den Heften 17–22, 40.
[4] EA 195.
[5] See below, p. 112, on the Curse of Agade and on a composition from the reign of Shulgi.

of passages that they sometimes call their most hated enemy by the same opprobrious term. In one passage, a Canaanite chieftain named Dagan-takala begs the king to save him 'from the hand of the 'Apiru, the bandits (ḫabbātu), and the bedawin (Sutu)'.[1] This passage again shows that the 'Apiru were distinct from both bandits and bedawin, though obviously similar in some respects to both. One letter says that Zimredda of Lachish had been killed by slaves who had become 'Apiru.[2] Similarly we read in a fifteenth-century text from Alalakh that the king Idrimi found refuge among the 'Apiru, and in thirteenth-century documents from Ugarit we hear of men of Ugarit, including slaves, who had escaped to the 'Apiru in Hittite territory.[3]

There are many sidelights on the background of the 'Apiru now available which were still unknown when Bottéro and Greenberg published their syntheses in 1954–5.[4] It is now virtually certain that ḫabbātu, one of the standing equivalents of the logogram SA.GAZ, meant originally 'tramp, wanderer, roving agricultural worker, donkey driver', etc., from the verb ḫabātu, 'to tramp', 'rove', 'cross over', and that the meaning 'robber', 'bandit', with the derived verbal sense, 'to rob', is secondary.[5] The Neo-Sumerian literary texts confirm this view. In the Lipit-Ishtar code SA.GAZ activity obviously refers to smuggling or similar illegal pursuits, since it is carried on by a boat's crew,[6] and in the 'Curse of Agade' the SA.GAZ were thrown out of work on the caravan routes when the empire of Agade collapsed.[7] A composition from the reign of Shulgi, towards the end of the third millennium, is even more informative, since we read that 'the rebellious people, the SA.GAZ...their men go where they please, their women carry spindle and spinning bowl.[8] They pitch their tents and their camps, they spend their days in the fields, and they do not obey the laws of Shulgi, my king.'[9] Evidently they refused to pay the proper tolls and taxes—in other words

---

[1] EA 318.   [2] EA 288, 43 ff.

[3] §III, 10, 107, 161 ff. The latter document is otherwise extremely interesting, since it explicitly states that certain men of Siyannu were not the Ḥapiru who had smitten a certain fortress.

[4] §I, 16; 32.   [5] See under these words in §III, 5 and §III, 13.

[6] For the original publication see §III, 14.

[7] §III, 9, 62 ff. My translation of the relevant passage is partly based on the obvious fact that when the cities lay in ruins, the caravan roads would be abandoned anyway. See now A. Falkenstein in Z.A. 57 (1965), 43 ff.

[8] The Sumerian word is GIŠKEŠDA. This must surely mean a wooden spinning bowl, which was necessary in spinning, and could be used for many other purposes. On the spinning bowl in the Ancient Near East see §III, 7, 97 ff.

[9] §III, 8, 286.

they engaged in smuggling, as well as in other reprehensible activities. But they were far superior in culture to the nomads of the Arabian desert (the Martu), who are said to have lived in tents, had no houses, eaten their food raw, raised small cattle but no grain, left their dead unburied, and otherwise behaved like savages.[1]

Some of the most instructive passages relating to the 'Apiru come from recently published Old Hittite texts; they date from about 1500 B.C. Here the *SA.GAZ* troops are mentioned together with the Hittite troops and they are given a pledge not to be mistreated. Then are mentioned successively the 'men of the desert tribes' (bedawin)[2], the grooms (literally, 'the dusty men', *LŪ.SAḪAR*),[3] 'the...*SA.GAZ* troops'.[4] Here again they are distinguished sharply from the bedawin and the grooms. They share with the latter, however, the interesting designation 'dusty ones'. It has been pointed out that the word 'Apiru must mean 'dusty one' in north-west Semitic.[5] It has since been observed that the word still appears in Syriac with the same meaning,[6] and that the international pedlars and hucksters of the Middle Ages also bore the name 'dusty feet' (*pies poudres*, which passed into Anglo-Norman law as 'pie-powders').[7] Characteristic of all these terms is the common fact that the bearer of the designation trudges in the dust behind donkeys, mules or chariots. In 1961 I collected the then available archaeological and documentary material bearing on the caravan trade of the twentieth to nineteenth centuries B.C. and the organization of donkey caravans; I found far-reaching correlations with early Patriarchal tradition in Genesis.[8] It became particularly obvious that the previously enigmatic occupational background of Abraham becomes intelligible only when we identify the terms '*Ibrī*, 'Hebrew' (previously '*Aḫiru*) with '*Apiru*, later '*Aḫiru*, literally 'person from across or beyond'.

This is not the place for a detailed treatment of the involved question, but it may be observed that after the catastrophic decline of caravan trade at the end of the Dynasty of Agade and again

---

[1] §III, 9, 253, 278, etc.

[2] The word is *līm ṣēri* (*līmu* is a synonym of *kimtu*, 'single family', 'clan'). It corresponds with the usual Akkadian designation *Sutū*.

[3] Akk. *kizū*, W. Sem., *kāziy[u]*, Eg. *kudji* or *kutji* (*kṯ* and *kṯn*).

[4] §III, 11, 216 ff.

[5] §III, 6, 261.

[6] §III, 4, 131. Cf., for example, E. Lipson, *The Economic History of England*, 1 (The Middle Ages), 221 ff., 250 ff.

[7] This analogy was first suggested to me by Dr P. F. Bloomhardt.

[8] §III, 2, 36 ff. Cf. also §III, 3, 5 ff., 11 ff.

after about 1800 B.C., when there were perhaps even more violent disruptions of caravaneering, the donkey caravaneers were forced into other occupations in order to exist. Among available means of gaining a livelihood were banditry, service as mercenaries, and more peaceful activities such as peddling and viniculture.[1] But donkey caravaneers continued to ply their ancient trade in the Amarna period,[2] and their mode of life is still described in the Song of Deborah from the twelfth century B.C.[3] It is interesting to note in this connexion that in the above-mentioned list of captives[4] there are five or six times as many 'Apiru as Kina'nu, 'merchants', which seems to be a very plausible ratio. It is obvious from the respective contexts that the Kina'nu were much more highly respected than the 'Apiru. Though the 'Apiru were generally just as nameless in the Amarna Letters as other people of the lower classes, we can follow the career of one 'Apiru and his apparently nameless sons. This fortunate exception is Labaya (Lab'ayu) 'the lion man', who controlled the hill country of central Palestine during the first half of the Amarna period. Characteristically, however, he is anonymous in the first letter of Shuwardata which mentions him.[5] In this letter, which probably belongs to the beginning of the reign of Amenophis IV,[6] Shuwardata writes from southern Judaea: 'The 'Apiru chief[7] has risen in arms against the lands which the god of the king, my lord, gave me, but (thy servant) has smitten him. Also let the king, my lord, know that all my brethren have abandoned me and that it is I and 'Abdi-Kheba who fight against the 'Apiru chief. And Zurata, chief of Accho, and Endaruta, chief of Achshaph

---

[1] The first three kinds of activity are well attested in our sources; viniculture as an 'Apiru occupation is known from Egyptian sources (see §III, 12, 1, 5 ff., and G. Posener in §1, 16, 166 ff.). There is additional evidence from the north-eastern Delta and a very striking parallel in Hebrew tradition (see §III, 3, 11 ff.).

[2] §1, 53. See also EA 227, 11, where the prince of Hazor writes to the king that his donkey caravan has escaped intact (§III, 2, 40). Cf. also §III, 10, 176 ff., which mentions 400 donkeys belonging to caravans of merchants which had been seized by the king of Ugarit. From this letter it follows that the current price for a caravan donkey was ten shekels.

[3] §III, 2, 43, 53.

[4] See above, p. 111.

[5] Published in §1, 50, 98 ff., 106, now listed as EA 366. For my translation see §1, 44, 487.

[6] The following excerpt contains several major changes in rendering which are explained briefly in the following notes. See §1, 18, 134 and *passim*.

[7] The expression *awil ḫapiri* must surely mean "'Apiru chief". That it is not to be taken as collective is certainly suggested by its use twice with the following singular verb.

pretended[1] to come to my help in return for fifty chariots—
I have been robbed (!)[2]—and now they are fighting against me.'
Obviously the area menaced by the 'Apiru chief lay between later
Judaea and the Plain of Acre—which is precisely the territory
held or directly threatened by Labaya. In a later missive[3] Zurata
is again portrayed as a traitor to the king because of his friendship
with Labaya.

That the latter's beginnings were insignificant also appears in
one of the earliest letters from him to the pharaoh,[4] which was
written by a scribe so untutored that he wrote the second half of
the letter in almost pure Canaanite, obviously not knowing enough
Akkadian to translate it even into the strange jargon taught in
the schools. The truculence of Labaya's tone in writing to the
court contrasts oddly with the grovelling subservience of most
Palestinian chieftains. In another semi-literate early letter,
probably written in the 32nd year of Amenophis III,[5] he is
much more conciliatory, ending with a drastic statement of his
obedience to the king.[6] Immediately before, he writes: 'The
king has written about my father-in-law.[7] I did not know that
my father-in-law was continuing to make raids with the 'Apiru.
And truly I have delivered him into the hand of Addayu.' This
statement does not necessarily mean that the unknown father-
in-law—or Labaya himself for that matter—was not originally
an 'Apiru; it may merely be an effort to prevent the bad reputation of the latter among the Egyptian officials and the Canaanite
princes from interfering with his own ambitious plans. We read
in another letter:[8] 'I will resist my foe(s), the men who captured
the "city of god", the despoilers of my father.' The term *āl ili*[9]
may well refer to the temenos (sacred enclosure) of Shechem,
excavated by Sellin and Wright,[10] in which case Labaya was presumably a native of the city like Abimelech over two centuries
later. His father may even have been prince of Shechem, in

---

[1] *Šunima* can scarcely be identical with normal Amarna Akkadian *šunu-mi* in this
context, but is probably the same word as Biblical Hebrew *šōnīm* (Prov. xxiv. 21)
which seems to refer to duplicity (i.e. shifting of purpose), as understood in the
Syriac version.   [2] *bazzāku* (Hebrew *bzz*).

[3] EA 245.   [4] EA 252.   [5] EA 254.

[6] See the translation in §1, 44, 486 and Campbell's version in §1, 52, 196 ff.

[7] I see no escape from rendering *i-mu-ia* as father-in-law, corresponding to normal
Middle Babylonian *e-mu-ia*; *imišu*, 'his father-in-law', appears in EA 249 with
reference to Tagu, the father-in-law of Milkilu.

[8] EA 254, 28 ff.

[9] Contrast the renderings of the text in §1, 44, 486 and §1, 52, 196 ff.

[10] See especially §1, 52, 87 ff. and *passim*.

which case he (like Idrimi) presumably joined the 'Apiru after his father's ruin.

By one means or another Labaya was able to extend his control from the Mediterranean to the hills of Gilead and from the plain of Esdraelon to the frontiers of Jerusalem. Milkilu of Gezer and Tagu of Gath in Sharon were more or less faithful allies of his, and he kept the princes of Megiddo and Jerusalem in a perpetual state of apprehension. A son of his (?), Mut-Ba'al, became chief of Pella on the eastern side of Jordan south of Beth-shan.[1] After his violent death early in the reign of Amenophis IV, his sons continued in his footsteps and were just as fervently denounced to the king as their father had been.

Shechem appears in a letter of 'Abdi-Kheba[2] in the following passage:[3] 'And now Jerusalem—if this land does belong to the king, why like the city of Gaza[4] does it [not] concern the king? See, the land of Ginti-kirmil belongs to Tagu and (yet) the men of Gintu (Gath in Sharon) are on garrison duty in Beth-shan.[5]— Or shall we do like Labaya and [his sons who] have given the land of Shechem to the 'Apiru men?—Milkilu (of Gezer) has written to Tagu and the sons of Labaya, "As for you, go on and give all they want to the men of Keilah,[6] and let us break away from the city of Jerusalem".'

It has not infrequently been suggested that the episode apparently referred to here may also be reflected in the tradition of Gen. xxxiv. This is possible, especially since the events alluded to[7] probably include the capture and plundering of the city. And yet we cannot go beyond the possibility of such a connexion. It is clear, however, that the Hebrews of central Palestine gained the upper hand in Shechem about this time and that they still held it at the time of the Israelite conquest, over a century later.[8]

---

[1] §1, 52, 205 ff. Judging from Schroeder's copy of the Berlin original, the reading La-ab-aya is virtually certain.   [2] EA 289, 14 ff.

[3] For a recent translation see my rendering in §1, 44, 489, and Campbell's still later in §1, 52, 200 ff. The following translation shows a number of significant changes in detail.

[4] Gaza was held by an Egyptian governor and was the administrative capital of Palestine at that time, as we know from the Ta'anach and Amarna letters.

[5] The mound of Beth-shan was then occupied by an Egyptian fortress. 'Abdi-Kheba's point seems to be that the Egyptians trusted Tagu sufficiently to man the fortress with his subjects.

[6] The men of Keilah were followers of Shuwardata, whose capital was probably at Hebron. The use of such an expression for the followers of Shuwardata seems to be rather contemptuous. At the end of line 26 we should read ṣa-mi at-tu-nu, 'as for you, go on'.

[7] In EA 254.   [8] See §1, 52, 139 ff.

CHAPTER XXI (*a*)

ANATOLIA FROM SHUPPILULIUMASH TO THE EGYPTIAN WAR OF MUWATALLISH

I. THE RESTORATION OF HITTITE POWER

THE condition in which Shuppiluliumash found the Hittite country when he began to take part in state affairs as crown prince and as military leader is summarized by a Hittite historiographer in a dry but impressive enumeration. He states that on every frontier the enemies of Khatti were attacking. The Kaska people (in the north) had invaded the Khatti Land proper and occupied Nenashsha; they had burned down the capital Khattusha itself. The people of Arzawa (in the south-west) had invaded the Lower Land and occupied Tuwanuwa and Uda; the Azzians (in the east) had invaded the Upper Lands and occupied Shamukha. Smaller inroads had been made by raids from Arawanna (in the north-west) and from Ishuwa and Armatana (in the south-east); they had reached respectively the country of Kashshiya and the country of Tegarama and the city of Kizzuwadna (i.e. Comana Cappadociae).[1] In other words, the Hittite realm had been severely trimmed around the edges and reduced to its very core. All the outlying dependencies—not only in Syria but also in Asia Minor—had been lost.

Shuppiluliumash had already as crown prince succeeded in stabilizing the situation during the later part of the reign of Tudkhaliash, his father. He had led the Hittite armies skilfully and successfully and had restored the frontier, particularly in the north and in the east.[2] After his accession to the throne he continued these activities with increasing vigour.

In the east the country of Azzi required close attention.[3] Not only had the relationship of that country (also called Khayasha) to Khatti to be regularized for its own sake, this was also necessary as a preliminary to re-establishing the Hittite position in Syria which must have been in the prince's mind already then. His campaign

---

* An original version of this chapter was published in fascicle 37 in 1965.

[1] G, 2, VI, 28, obv. 6 ff.; §1, 2, 21 ff.

[2] Above, ch. XVII, sect. IV.   [3] §1, 4, frgms. 10 and 13.

(or campaigns) in the east of Anatolia, the details of which escape us, culminated in the treaty with Khukkanash of Khayasha-Azzi and his chieftains, the text of which has come down to us.[1]

The Kaska people, who, since their first appearance during the Old Kingdom in the days of Khantilish, the son of Murshilish I, had incessantly harassed the districts along the northern border, and who were the most dangerous of the enemies enumerated in the just-quoted text, must have caused the Hittites no small worries. It was fortunate that they were loosely organized and, as is occasionally stated, did not possess the institution of kingship.[2] Being mostly swineherds and weavers[3] they were considered as inferior by the Hittites. Nevertheless, they had seriously interrupted important state-cults, above all in the city of Nerik, cutting off that city from the capital. A prayer of Arnuwandash I and his queen Ashmu-Nikkal, composed about half a century before Shuppiluliumash, vividly shows the inconveniences and distress which this caused the responsible leaders.[4] The capital Khattusha itself was within striking distance of the border and had—as mentioned before—just been raided when Shuppiluliumash began to reign.

The summaries of his achievements which we possess state that it took him twenty years to restore the northern frontier as it had existed before.[5] The length of this 'war' alone illustrates the effort that had to be exerted. There is hardly any doubt that it was guerrilla warfare[6] in which success and failure quickly alternated. The long absence of the king in Syria and the ensuing weakness of the Hittites in their home country aggravated the situation. In the circumstances, it is not surprising that the town of Tumanna had to be abandoned to the Kaska people, and that the Hittite troops in Pala under the command of Khutupiyanzash, the governor of that province, were barely able to hold their own.[7]

The Arzawa Lands—Arzawa in the narrower sense, Mira-Kuwaliya, Khapalla, Shekha-River Land—filling the west of Asia Minor were independent during most of his reign. This is best illustrated by the fact that Tarkhunda-radu of Arzawa corresponded with Amenophis III and could discuss with him marriage questions as they were customary between equals.[8] This, of course, does not mean that Shuppiluliumash did not try to assert his influence in the Arzawa Lands; he certainly did. According to his

[1] §1, 1, vol. ii, 103 ff.

[2] G, 2, iii, 4, iii, 74 f.; §ii, 5, 88 f.

[3] G, 1, xxiv, 3, ii, 39; §1, 3, 28 f.

[4] G, 1, xvii, 21 (see G, 6, 399 f.).

[5] See above, p. 16.

[6] §1, 4, frgms. 10–14.

[7] G, 2, v, 8, ii, 8 ff.; §ii, 5, 152 ff.

[8] G, 3, 1 = G, 4, 31; §1, 5, 334.

annals he campaigned, probably based on Tuwanuwa, in Kha-palla.[1] In connexion with Wilusa—a country on the (northern) fringes of Arzawa—it is stated that the Arzawa Land (in the nar-rower sense) revolted while Wilusa under Kukkunnish remained loyal. The Arzawa Land was subjugated.[2] It seems obvious, then, that Wilusa had a common border with the Khatti Land and that a treaty regulating the relationship of at least Wilusa with the Hittite king must have existed. In other words, the Hittites were more successful in the north-west than in the south-west.

Toward the end of the Great King's reign, when he was fully occupied with the 'Hurrian War', the Arzawa Lands again re-volted. The southern Arzawa front was then guarded by Khanut-tish, the governor of the Lower Land;[3] on the northern Arzawa front Wilusa again kept true to its obligations.[4] It was probably then that Uhha-zitish of Arzawa—who in the meantime must have replaced Tarkhunda-radu—entered into relations with the country of Ahhiyawa.

The latter, met from now on again and again as a main western adversary of the Hittites, makes at this point its first appearance in history. Its identity has been much discussed with little positive result.[5] The similarity in name with that of the Achaeans is not sufficient reason to seek its capital in Mycenae, as has been done. The texts we possess furnish no valid argument for looking out-side of Asia Minor. If Ahhiyawa, then, is an Anatolian country, the chances are in favour of a location in the north-western part of the peninsula.

Uhha-zitish of Arzawa persuaded the city of Millawanda to make also a bid for independence and to seek likewise the support of Ahhiyawa.[6] The neighbouring country of Mira became, prob-ably at the same time, restive. Mashkhuiluwash of Mira rejected a suggestion on the part of his brothers to join the revolt and as a result had to flee to the Hittite court. He was well received: he married the king's daughter Muwattish and was promised re-instatement in his principality. Shuppiluliumash, however, was too deeply engaged in Syrian affairs to fulfil his promise.[7] In the Shekha-River Land things had developed in a similar manner. Here Manapa-Tattash had been driven into exile by his brothers

---

[1] §1, 4, frgms. 18–20.   [2] §1, 1, vol. II, 42 ff. (sect. 3).
[3] G, 1, XIX, 22.   [4] §1, 1, vol. II, 42 ff. (sect. 4).
[5] Selected bibliography below (pp. 931 f.) as Appendix.
[6] G, 1, XIV, 15, i, 23 ff.; §II, 5, 36 ff.; cf. 232 ff.
[7] G, 1, XIV, 15, iv, 38 ff. (see §II, 5, 72 f.); G, 1, IV, 4, iv, 56 ff. (see §II, 5, 140 ff.; also §1, 1, vol. I, 95 ff., sect. 2).

and found a refuge in Karkisha where Hittite influence protected him.[1] He eventually returned to his country. Mashkhuiluwash of Mira was later used by Murshilish, successor to Shuppiluliumash, when he reasserted Hittite power in that part of Asia Minor.

There is no doubt that the endless campaigning in Syria, first against Tushratta and later against the Egyptians, the Assyrians and whatever other forces tried to resist the Hittite conquest, taxed the king's resources to the utmost. At the end of his reign, to be sure, Syria was firmly in his hands, but home affairs, both political and religious, had been sorely neglected. On the political side, even the cults of the main goddess of the country 'who regulated kingship and queenship' were not properly attended to.[2] When death came to the king, all the outlying countries revolted; besides Arzawa, the list[3] includes Kizzuwadna (in one copy of the respective text its name has been erased, however, and, in fact, his successor held it firmly in his possession), and Mitanni (i.e. the part of it that had been restored to Kurtiwaza[4] and his descendants), furthermore Arawana and Kalashma in the north-west of Asia Minor, Lukka and Pitashsha in its centre, and above all the Kaska people in the north. To judge from the troubles encountered by his successor in his attempts at making his empire secure, the general state of affairs at the king's death was no less serious than it had been at the time of his accession to the throne.

II. THE HITTITE EMPIRE UNDER MURSHILISH

Immediate successor to Shuppiluliumash was his son Arnuwan-dash.[5] The potentially dangerous situation created by the death of the conqueror was aggravated by the circumstances that the new king was seriously ill and, therefore, could not demand the authority which was needed. Syria, on possession of which the Hittite claim for world leadership rested, was naturally the critical danger spot. Arnuwandash made haste to confirm his brother Piyashilish as king of Carchemish and also appointed him to the position of the *tuḫkantiš* (a high rank in the government).[6] He was apparently the mainstay of Hittite domination in the provinces south of the Taurus, and is known from then on by the (Hurrian) name Sharre-Kushukh.[7] With some justification one may consider it fortunate that the reign of Arnuwandash was only of short

---

[1] §1, 1, vol. II, 1 ff. (sect. 1).　　　　[2] G, 2, III, 4, i, 16 ff.; §II, 5, 20 f.

[3] G, 1, XXIV, 4, obv. 17; §1, 3, 28 f.　　[4] See above, p. 19.

[5] G, 2, III, 4, i, 3 ff.; §II, 5, 14 f.; G, 2, XII, 33.

[6] G, 2, I, 28; §II, 3, fasc. I/2, 101.　　[7] §1, 4, 120 f.

duration. Murshilish,[1] a younger son of Shuppiluliumash, who now assumed kingship, was still very young but in the full possession of his powers. He proved himself an extremely able and energetic ruler.

When he ascended the throne, the Lower Lands, the province on the Anatolian plateau guarding the frontier toward the Arzawa lands, were administered by Khanuttish.[2] Unfortunately, he also died immediately after the accession of Murshilish. This resulted in a precarious situation on this frontier too; it was counteracted by the despatch of reinforcements to the new governor (whose name remains unknown).[3]

In Syria interference from the side of the Assyrians was feared. One might have expected that Ashur-uballit would choose the change over for an attack. To forestall any untoward developments Murshilish strengthened the hand of Sharre-Kushukh, his brother, the king of Carchemish. He assigned to him another army under the command of Nuwanzash.[4] The Assyrian attack did not materialize, but no doubt the Mitanni state as it had been restored for Kurtiwaza fell into Assyrian hands. The claim of Ashur-uballit that he 'scattered the hosts of the far-flung country of the Subarians' (i.e. the Mitannians)[5] seems quite justified. It was this conquest that entitled him to assume the title of 'Great King'.[6]

Egypt might have made the situation still more embarrassing for the Hittites. However, it never seriously entered the strategic picture. It is safe to assume that it had not sufficiently recovered as yet from the strife that followed after Amenophis IV and the restoration under Horemheb.

The efforts of the first ten years of Murshilish were concentrated upon the reassertion of Hittite power, mainly in Asia Minor. His main object was the subjugation of Arzawa (south-western Asia Minor). But, before he could devote himself to his great task, he had to secure his rear. In other words he had first to punish the unruly and rebellious Kaska people.[7] This was accomplished during the first two years and part of the third year of his reign. Only then Murshilish felt sufficiently prepared for the attack on Arzawa.[8]

His main adversary was Uhha-zitish of Arzawa; he had aligned with himself most of the other Arzawa states: Khapalla, Mira-

---

[1] For the rest of this section see mainly §11, 5.
[2] G, 1, XIX, 29, iv, 11 ff.; §11, 5, 19.   [3] G, 1, XIX, 22.
[4] G, 1, XIV, 16, i, 13 ff.; §11, 5, 26 f.   [5] §11, 2, 56 f.
[6] G, 4, 16.   [7] §11, 5, 22 ff.   [8] §11, 5, 44 ff.

Kuwaliya, and the Shekha-River Land. Wilusa, it seems, once more
—as under Shuppiluliumash—remained loyal to the Great King.
But Uhha-zitish had previously persuaded the city Millawanda—
apparently an important centre—to desert the Hittites and to seek
the protection of the king of Ahhiyawa. Hence a preliminary step
taken by Murshilish was an expedition against Millawanda; it
was successfully carried through.

In the third year the main expedition could then begin. For it
Sharre-Kushukh, the king of Carchemish, joined Murshilish with
a corps from Syria. The opposing forces of the Arzawa people
were led by Piyama-Inarash, a son of Uhha-zitish; the latter had
entrusted the command to him because of ill health. Murshilish
defeated him in a battle near Walma on the River Ashtarpa.
Pursuing the fleeing enemy he entered Apasha, the capital of
Arzawa. But Uhha-zitish, he found, had fled 'across the Sea'.

This left two centres of resistance to be dealt with: the mountain
fortresses of Arinnanda and of Puranda. The former was captured
before the third year came to a close; the latter had to be left for
the next year. For the time being the Hittite king retreated to the
river Ashtarpa and established camp there for the winter; the
Syrian corps, it seems, went home.

When the season suitable for the resumption of warfare arrived,
the final attack against Puranda was mounted. During the winter
Uhha-zitish of Arzawa had died, but Tapalazanaulish, another of
his sons, had organized resistance. When asked to surrender he
declined, an assault was launched; it resulted soon in the fall of the
fortress. Tapalazanaulish escaped and sought refuge with the king
of Ahhiyawa. It seems that Murshilish demanded his extradition
and that it was granted. If so, we must assume that between the
Hittites and Ahhiyawa a treaty existed which made provisions for
the extradition of fugitives.

Thus Murshilish emerged as the victor over Arzawa. The
princes of the other Arzawa states drew quickly the consequences
and surrendered without further resistance. Both Targashnallish
of Khapalla and Manapa-Tattash of the Shekha-River Land were
generously treated and reinstated as Hittite vassals. The affairs of
Mira, long unattended to, were also settled when Murshilish
passed through on his way home; the new ruler was to be Mashkhuiluwash, who, since his flight to Shuppiluliumash, had fought
on the Hittite side.[1] The treaties which at that time were concluded
with Manapa-Tattash[2] and Targashnallish[3] are preserved. What

[1] §1, 1, vol. 1, 95 ff. (sect. 2 f.).
[2] §1, 1, vol. 11, 1 ff.   [3] §1, 1, vol. 1, 51 ff.

provisions were made with the Arzawa Land proper is unknown; since it is later found in the Hittite camp, the assumption seems safe that a willing member of the Arzawa dynasty swore an oath of allegiance to Murshilish.

The fifth, sixth, and probably also seventh years again required the king's presence on the Kaskean frontier.[1] Beginning with the seventh year, operations shifted to Azzi-Khayasha in the far east of Anatolia.[2] Before Anniya, king there, could be dealt with decisively, grave complications arose. The beginning of the ninth year[3] brought alarming news from Syria: the Nukhash Lands and Kinza had revolted. Suspicion seems justified that Egypt, now firmly reorganized under Horemheb, was behind the unrest. Sharre-Kushukh, the Hittite viceroy in Syria, had to invoke the treaty with Niqmaddu of Ugarit and ask for military help from him.[4] At the same time the enemy from Khayasha had invaded the Upper Land, taken the town Ishtitina and laid siege to Kannuwara. Murshilish himself was obliged to go to Kumanni in order to perform long-delayed religious duties. Sharre-Kushukh was able to restore order in Syria sufficiently so that he could come up and join his brother, the Great King, in Kumanni. However, he fell ill there and died quite unexpectedly. With him Murshilish lost his ablest helper, also the man to whom the task of protecting Syria would naturally have fallen.

His death was the signal for new disturbances in Syria. More serious still, it moved the Assyrians to make an attack on Carchemish. Thus Murshilish was faced with weighty decisions of a military kind. He finally dispatched the general Nuwanzash to take command on the Khayasha front and sent another general Inarash to deal with the Nukhash Lands and with Kinza. He himself went to Ashtata on the Euphrates, and Inarash was ordered to meet him there on his return. They both were then to go together to Aleppo and Carchemish.[5]

Matters went according to plan. The Syrian rebels were punished. It was at that time that Aitakama of Kinza who had played a part in Syrian affairs during the days of Shuppiluliumash[6] met his death. He had revolted, it seems, because he saw a chance for regaining his independence. However, his son Ari-Teshub (NÍG.BA-Teššub) opposed his father's step and had him murdered. Ari-Teshub was brought back by the victorious general to face Murshilish, who had in the meantime reached Ashtata; he was

---

[1] §II, 5, 76 ff.
[2] §II, 5, 96 ff.
[3] §II, 5, 108 ff.
[4] §II, 9, 53 ff.
[5] §II, 5, 110 ff.
[6] See above, pp. 15 f.

reinstalled by the Great King as the prince of Kinza.[1] Murshilish then went to Carchemish and installed there [...]-Sharruma, the son of Sharre-Kushukh, his dead brother. At the same time Talmi-Sharruma, a son of Telepinush, was made king in Aleppo.[2] The treaty concluded with the latter has survived.[3] It is noteworthy that Carchemish, at that time, had clearly overtaken Aleppo as the most important centre of Hittite power in Syria. It was the king of Carchemish who played the role of something like a viceroy of Syria.

It was probably then that Murshilish confirmed Niqmepa, the king of Ugarit. He renewed with him the treaty which his father Shuppiluliumash had concluded with Niqmaddu, Niqmepa's father. The new treaty contains a detailed description of the frontier between Ugarit and Mukish.[4]

While Murshilish was in Syria, Nuwanzash in the north had accomplished his mission. The king of Khayasha who had invaded the Upper Land had been forced to retreat and the siege of Kannuwara lifted. The way for a campaign against Khayasha was thus free. However, the season was too far advanced for any serious operation in this mountainous region. Therefore, only small raids were executed and a larger campaign prepared for the coming spring.[5] The king's tenth year passed before Khayasha was brought to its knees.[6] Although its actual submission did not take place before his eleventh year, the Great King could consider the task of reasserting himself as completed with the end of the tenth year. The so-called 'Ten-year Annals'[7] depict matters in this light.

It would be untrue to assume that Murshilish was saved the necessity of making incessant efforts through the rest of his reign for maintaining the position he had won. In fact it is known that in his twelfth year a new uprising in the Arzawa lands took place. It was instigated by a man named É.GAL.KUR (Hittite reading unknown)[8] about whom nothing further is known, but who may well have been a successor of Uhha-zitish and Piyama-Inarash. Mashkhuiluwash of Mira-Kuwaliya was implicated and had to flee when Murshilish undertook a punitive expedition. Kupanta-Inarash, his adopted son, who, on the occasion of his father's first feoffment, had been designated crown-prince became his successor. The text of the treaty concluded with him is known.[9]

It is very likely that here again, as before,[10] the king of Ahhi-

---

[1] §II, 5, 120 f.   [2] §II, 5, 124 f.
[3] §II, 11, 80 ff.   [4] §II, 9, 59 ff.
[5] §II, 5, 124 ff.   [6] §II, 5, 130 ff.
[7] G, 1, III, 4; §II, 5, 14 ff.   [8] §I, 1, vol. 1, 128 f.
[9] §I, 1, vol. 1, 95 ff.   [10] See above, p. 119.

yawa played a sinister role in the background. It is certain that he pretended to be an equal of the Great King of the Khatti Land; one also has the impression that the power of Ahhiyawa was on the upswing. This is important for the overall view. For it indicates that the Hittite kings had, from this time on, to be alert to developments in the west also. As though it had not been enough of a strain to keep a constant eye on Egypt and Assyria!

The Euphrates frontier was far from being stable. The pressure from the Assyrians was incessant and their attempts at conquering as much of the former Mitannian territory as they could never slackened. If Murshilish was to continue the role in world politics on which his father had embarked he had no choice but to maintain a firm hold on Syria. As before, much of the burden fell upon the ruler of Carchemish, now Shakhurunuwash, another son of Sharre-Kushukh.

One can also discern a tendency to curtail the power of the Syrian vassals as though the overlord was not entirely certain of their loyalty. The secession of Siyanni from Ugarit, which halved the territory controlled by Niqmepa, was recognized by the Hittite overlord and Shiyanni was placed under supervision from Carchemish.[1] When Abirattash of Barga raised old claims to the city of Yaruwanda against the Nukhash Land, the case was decided in favour of the former. He was thereby rewarded for the support he had given the Hittite king when Nukhash had risen against him.[2] The Hittites adhered, wherever the occasion presented itself, to a policy of *divide et impera*.

Further south Amurru developed into a champion of Hittite domination. The fact that the once so unruly Aziru, now rather advanced in age, had remained true to his oath of loyalty[3] when Nukhash and Kinza revolted, must have been a source of satisfaction to Murshilish. He reaffirmed his friendship with Amurru by installing Aziru's son *DU*-Teshub as his successor and soon thereafter also his grandson Tuppi-Teshub.[4]

It is quite possible, though not specifically attested, that Murshilish undertook himself another campaign in Upper Mesopotamia or at least sent one of his generals there. Muwatallish, his successor on the Hittite throne, counts Mitanni as one of his vassal states. It seems to have been regained from the Assyrians in the preceding reign.

What we possess of annals from the later years of Murshilish—

[1] §11, 9, 71 ff.   [2] §11, 1; §11, 4, 19 ff.; §11, 7.
[3] §1, 1, vol. 1, 1 ff.   [4] §1, 1, vol. 1, 1 ff. (sect. 3 f.).

it is unfortunately incomplete[1]—does not relate any large-scale
military operations anywhere. In quite detailed manner it speaks
about never-ending guerrilla warfare on the Kaskean frontier.
These expeditions were routine to the king and had the nature of
police actions. If considerable space was given to them in the
royal annals it seems to indicate that nothing of greater importance
was to report. Later on, we find firm military control established
all along the Kaskean border, a veritable *limes*.[2] We do not know
who first built it, but since from the time of Murshilish onwards
the scheme worked with some measure of success, we may infer it
was he who initiated it.

In a long reign Murshilish succeeded in firmly organizing the
empire which he had inherited from his father. As in the days of
Shuppiluliumash it spread from the Lebanon and the Euphrates in
the south to the mountains of Pontus in the north and to the
western reaches of Asia Minor. It was a continental power in the
sense that it only accidentally, so to speak, reached the sea, and
certainly did not extend beyond it. The negative fact should be
stressed that the island of Cyprus—Alashiya[3] as it was then called
—did not form part of the Hittite realm. Its kings had corresponded as independent rulers with Amenophis IV, and it served
as asylum for all those who, in danger of their lives, had to flee from
the continent.

Little is known about the internal affairs of the Hittite Empire
during the reign of Murshilish. Worthy of note is his conflict with
Tawannannash, last queen of Shuppiluliumash. She had survived
her husband and was reigning queen also during the first part of
the following reign. She was accused of various offences, above
all of having caused the death of the young king's wife by black
magic. The incident is mentioned in prayers which seek to determine the reasons for divine anger and the ensuing misfortune.[4]
There seems to have been some doubt as to whether the steps
taken against Tawannannash had been entirely legitimate. The
affair had political overtones, since Tawannannash was originally
a Babylonian princess.[5]

A word remains to be said about the chronology of the reign of
Murshilish. Its beginning is approximately fixed by the death of his
father Shuppiluliumash, which took place several years after that
of Tutankhamun (*c.* 1352), i.e., about 1346.[6] The preserved
parts of the annals of Murshilish justify the assumption that his
reign covered more—and probably not much more—than twenty-

[1] §ıı, 5, 146 ff.   [2] §ıı, 10, 36 ff.   [3] G, 4, 33–39.
[4] §ıı, 6, vol. ı, 12 ff.; §ıı, 8, 101 ff.   [5] See above, p. 13.   [6] See above, p. 19.

two years. If we estimate that it lasted about twenty-five years, we come down for its end to about 1320, or a few years before that. The Syrian campaign of the pharaoh Sethos I may fall in the very end of his reign, or when his son Muwatallish had recently succeeded him.

III. ASIA MINOR UNDER MUWATALLISH

The sources at our disposal for the reign of Muwatallish are rather poor. Moreover, they are most of them not impartial toward the king. Much of the little we do know must be culled from the texts of Khattushilish, his younger brother and rival,[1] which make it abundantly clear that he had personal ambitions irreconcilable with the position held by his brother. The information thus gathered hardly does justice to Muwatallish. At least it gives a one-sided picture which belittles the king's achievements and unduly stresses those of the younger brother.

At first the relations between the brothers were cordial. As soon as Muwatallish assumed kingship, he made his brother not only Great Majordomo (*GAL ME-ŠE-DI*) but also field-marshal of the Hittite armies. In addition he appointed him governor of the Upper Land which included the important town Shamukha. In this capacity Khattushilish replaced Arma-Tattash, who as the son of Zidash, a former Great Majordomo, was cousin to the late king. The power thus vested in the prince was quite extraordinary. No wonder then that his enemies—and above all Arma-Tattash and his friends—grew envious and denounced him to the king; they asserted that Khattushilish nursed ambitious plans, in fact aspired himself to the kingship over the Khatti Land. Whatever truth might have resided in such accusations, Muwatallish trusted his brother and rejected them as malicious slander.

As field-marshal of the Hittite armies Khattushilish claims to have conducted numerous campaigns for his brother, both offensively and defensively. Nothing specific is known of these military activities, but, as far as we can see, they were limited to the northern frontier area where Khattushilish ruled as governor. Later in the reign of Muwatallish, when the Great King personally undertook a campaign to the Arzawa Lands, his brother had to concentrate his efforts on the Kaska people. The king's absence, as was to be expected, provoked serious raids on their part. Khattushilish speaks of ten years of warfare he had to go through. There is every reason to believe that the unruly neighbours continued their

---

[1] §III, 1; 2.

harassment indefinitely, although the territory affected at one and the same time always remained small. The so-called Kaskean War can hardly have been more than an annoying series of small-scale raids and counter-raids.

Neither do we know details of the king's campaign against Arzawa, but we can at least recognize some of its results.[1] At that time the term Arzawa Lands comprised four principalities: Arzawa proper, Mira-Kuwaliya, Khapalla and Wilusa. In the end, it seems, all four of them remained Hittite dependencies, their rulers vassals of the Great King.[2] King of Arzawa was probably Piyama-Inarash, either the same person who had fought against Murshilish or a younger member of the same dynasty. In Mira-Kuwaliya the kingship was still held by Kupanta-Inarash, who had been installed by Murshilish. In Khapalla we find one Ura-Khattushash as ruler. And in Wilusa Muwatallish placed Alakshandush upon the throne; the customary treaty, then concluded, has come down to us.[3] The Shekha-River Land is no longer counted as an Arzawa Land; its legal status must have changed in the meantime. Manapa-Tattash who also had been a vassal of Murshilish was in control there when Muwatallish became king. When he died his son Mashturish succeeded him, and the Great King gave his sister in marriage to him.[4] Thus domination of the most important countries adjacent to Hittite territory was complete.

On the northern frontier, even after the successful conclusion of the Arzawa campaign, conditions remained unsettled. The Kaska must have made dangerous inroads. For Kahha, where Khattushilish, despite depleted forces, claims to have won an important victory over the Kaska people lies far to the south. He was also able, so he says, to repel a dangerous attack which had been launched from the town of Pishkhuru.[5]

While all this was going on, Muwatallish began to prepare for a major war in Syria. As will be pointed out later,[6] war in the south became inevitable when Egypt, reorganized by the pharaohs of the nineteenth dynasty, resumed its traditional policy of domination there. This test, Muwatallish foresaw, would be crucial. Wise strategist that he was, he therefore had to concentrate as many troops as he could possibly muster. With this goal in mind he saw to it that the far-flung system of fortifications which already existed along the Kaskean frontier was strengthened so that he could

---

[1] §1, 1, vol. II, 42 ff. (sect. 6).   [2] §1, 1, vol. II, 42 ff. (sect. 17).
[3] §1, 1, vol. II, 42 ff.
[4] G, 1, xxiii, 3, 1, ii, 14 ff. (see §iii, 3).
[5] §iii, 1, 16 ff.   [6] Below, ch. xxiv, sect. 1.

withdraw most of his troops from the area. As a precautionary measure he moved his capital from Khattusha, which was considered too close to the border, to Tattashsha and had the state deities and also the *manes* of the royal family brought there for safe-keeping. In the north Khattushilish was left in command. To the territory which he had administered so far the whole frontier zone—largely devastated and depopulated—was added, including Palā and Tumanna. Furthermore, he was made king in Khakpish, the territory of which included the important cult centre of Zippalanda, a town holy to a Storm-god who, as the son of the Sun-goddess of Arinna, was highly venerated. The power of Khattushilish, very considerable before, was thus still further increased, and no doubt he was now the most powerful man in the Khatti Land, second only to the Great King himself. After the Syrian campaign, in which Khattushilish took part as a military commander of the army contingent raised in his province for the event, his prestige rose further by his marriage to Pudu-Kheba, the daughter of Bentibsharre, the local king of Lawazantiya.[1]

Khattushilish was doubtless ambitious; the power he had accumulated might have led a lesser man into temptation. Thus a situation had been created which led to internal strife soon afterwards.

[1] §III, 1, 18 ff.

CHAPTER XXI(*b*)

UGARIT

IV. UGARIT IN THE FOURTEENTH AND THIRTEENTH CENTURIES B.C.

In previous chapters, frequent reference has been made to the city of Ugarit, the North Syrian coastal town whose site, the modern Ras Shamra, meaning 'Fennel Cape', is situated some seven miles north of Latakia. More is known about Ugarit during the two centuries before her downfall, in about 1200 B.C., than about any other Syrian city of the second millennium. The reasons are twofold. First, whereas most excavators of ancient mounds in Syria have been forced to concentrate on the central area only, where public buildings were likely to be found, at Ras Shamra over two-thirds of the site have been systematically explored, and the nearby port installation has also been uncovered. Secondly, a wealth of documentary evidence is becoming available with the gradual publication of some thousands of tablets found in private and public buildings in various parts of the city.[1] Some of these tablets are the letters and memoranda of merchants and private individuals, written in the local dialect and script;[2] others deal with matters of domestic administration: lists of towns and country districts, for instance, furnishing contributions to the government in the form of silver, produce or *corvée* labour, lists of bowmen and slingmen, or payrolls and tax receipts. There are diplomatic archives written in Akkadian, the language of international intercourse,[3] and legal texts which are for the most part also in Akkadian. Large tablets in Ugaritic contain mythological and liturgical texts, invaluable for our knowledge of Canaanite[4] religion, and there are lists of offerings and omen texts for the use of priests. Glossaries and lexicographical

---

* An original version of this chapter was published as fascicle 63 in 1968; the present chapter includes revisions made in 1973.

[1] §iv, 30; §iv, 44; §iv, 30; A, 19.

[2] §iv, 11, 63 ff.; *C.A.H.* ii³, pt. 1, pp. 506 ff.   [3] *C.A.H.* ii³, pt. 1, p. 468.

[4] The extension of the term 'Canaanite' to include the North-West Semitic peoples of the Syro-Palestinian littoral in the second millennium B.C. needs no excuse (§v, 44, 16), though it should perhaps more properly be applied to the inhabitants of the Egyptian province Kana'an (§iv, 31, 105 f.)

texts for scholastic use, and tablets in Hurrian,[1] Hittite[2] and Cypro-Mycenaean,[3] are also included in the miscellany.

The importance of these archaeological and textual discoveries may, it is hoped, justify the present attempt to trace briefly the part played by one of the richest and most powerful cities in the Near East during the latter part of the Bronze Age, in spite of the fact that in doing so, some repetition of historical narrative becomes inevitable.

The kingdom of Ugarit possessed many natural advantages which her rulers turned to good effect. Augmented, thanks to the good sense and careful diplomacy of King Niqmaddu, by territory in the hinterland taken from Mukish,[4] it included a long stretch of fertile coastal plain, hills clad with olive groves and vine terraces, and thickly wooded mountains; behind, the steppe afforded both grazing and hunting.[5] The thirty odd miles of its coastline contained at least four ports,[6] that of Ugarit itself—the bay today called Mīnet el-Beidha, the 'White Harbour'—being capable of accommodating ships of a considerable size.[7] The most southerly port was probably Shuksi, the modern Tell Sūkās, south of Jebeleh, where a tablet in the Ugaritic script has been found.[8] Ugarit, situated as she was at the intersection of land and sea routes, was destined from the beginning to become a commercial power. Within easy sailing distance of Cyprus and the Cilician coast, and the most northerly of the chain of ports which served coastal traffic to the Lebanon, Palestine and Egypt, she was the natural link between the Aegean world and the Levant. Ships from Beirut and Byblos and Tyre,[9] from Alashiya, and from far-away *Kptr* or Crete (the Biblical Caphtor)[10] and *Hkpt*, which is usually associated with it,[11] unloaded their cargoes at her ports. She also commanded the caravan route from the coast through the 'Amūq plain to Aleppo, and thence by way of Emar and Carchemish to join the riverine Euphrates route to Babylonia or the road eastwards to Assyria by way of the Upper Khabur region.[12] Another road ran northwards through the territory of Mukish to the Beilān pass, giving access to central Anatolia.[13]

---

[1] §IV, 44, vol. 5, 447 ff.   [2] *Ibid.* 769 ff.   [3] *Ibid.* vol. 3, 227 ff.
[4] §IV, 30, vol. 4, 11 ff., 48 ff.; §IV, 10, 261 ff.; A, 4, 398 ff.
[5] §IV, 44, vol. 2, 17; §IV, 30, vol. 2, xxxviii f.   [6] §IV, 7, 255; A, 20, vol. 3, 6 f.
[7] §V, 55, 165; A, 28; §IV, 44, vol. 1, pl. VIII. Miss Honor Frost (*ibid.* vol. 6, 235 ff.) estimates, from the size of stone anchors found, that some Ugaritic ships were of at least 200 tons.   [8] §IV, 33, 215; A, 15, 538 no. 502; A, 27, 4.   [9] §IV, 7, 253.
[10] §IV, 30, vol. 3, 107 = *RS*.16.238.
[11] §V, 25, 169; §V, 77, 192 f.; §IV, 30, vol. 2, 162 = *RS*.16.399, l. 26.
[12] *C.A.H.* I[3], pt. 2, p. 333.   [13] §IV, 56, 20.

In addition to her activity in middleman trade, Ugarit was herself a centre of considerable industrial activity and exported her products far and wide. Metal workers had their foundries in the port district and in the town,[1] and the fine bronze weapons and vessels they turned out were in more than local demand.[2] Linen and wool, obtained from the large flocks of sheep and goats grazed in the hinterland, were dyed red-purple or blue-violet[3] in the same quarter, where heaps of crushed murex shells were found,[4] and made into bales or finished garments for export.[5] Merchantmen carried grain to Alashiya and Cilicia, and olive oil, produced in commercial quantity in large presses,[6] was shipped abroad in amphorae, some of which were found in the quay warehouses.[7] The wine of Ugarit, too, was exported,[8] and salt from the numerous salt-pans along the coast,[9] while fine woods, such as box and juniper,[10] as well as the coarser pine,[11] were in demand. A flourishing trade in scented oils and cosmetics is attested by the presence in Ras Shamra of locally made containers of ivory and alabaster modelled on Egyptian originals,[12] perhaps because Egypt was the original home of the industry.

Little is known of the early history of the kingdom of Ugarit. The city was already flourishing in the eighteenth century B.C., and on a tablet from the palace,[13] unfortunately much damaged, the names of about thirty of the deified kings of Ugarit are listed in two columns, the first of which ends with YQR, perhaps the 'Yaqaru son of Niqmaddu' whose dynastic seal, in the style of the Old Babylonian period, was treasured by later kings of the dynasty as an heirloom and employed to give ancient authority to their decrees.[14] Either Yaqaru or Niqmaddu may have been the unnamed ruler of Ugarit who wrote to the king of Aleppo expressing his desire to visit Mari in order to see for himself the renowned palace which Zimrilim, the king of Mari, had built.[15] The foundations of a large building, probably a palace, of the Middle

---

[1] §IV, 30, vol. 2, xxxiv ff.   [2] §IV, 7, 253; A, 34.
[3] A, 11, 231 ff.   [4] §IV, 30, vol. 2, xxvi, pl. xiv; §IV, 35, 38; §IV, 36, 2.
[5] §IV, 44, vol. 4, 142 = RS. 19.28. See C.A.H. II³, pt. 1, pp. 510 f.
[6] §IV, 44, vol. 4, 421, figs. 6, 7; §IV, 30, vol. 5, 117 f. = RS.18.42.
[7] §IV, 44, vol. 1, 30 f., pl. ix.   [8] §V, 66, 44.
[9] §IV, 30, vol. 5, 118 f. = RS.18.27, 18.30.
[10] EA (the Amarna letters), 126, ll. 4–6; §IV, 26, 126 f.; §IV, 30, vol. 4, 196 = RS.17.385 ll. 11 ff.
[11] C.A.H. I³, pt, 2, pp. 346 f.
[12] §IV, 44, vol. 1, 31, figs. 21, 22.   [13] §V, 65, 214 f.
[14] §IV, 30, vol. 3, xl ff., pls. xvi, xvii; §IV, 52, 92 ff.; §V, 63, 260 ff. Plate 136 (c).
[15] §IV, 44, vol. 1, 16, n. 2, 15; C.A.H. II³, pt. 1, pp. 11 f.

Bronze period, were discovered in 1969;[1] many of the large ashlar blocks from this building had been re-used in the later palace.

After a long lacuna in which even the names of the dynasts are
lost, the history of the royal house of Ugarit begins in the early
fourteenth century with Ammishtamru I.[2] At this time Ugarit
was 'on the water' of Egypt, as the Egyptians themselves would
have phrased it; that is to say, within the Egyptian sphere of influence and almost certainly bound by a treaty to keep her ports
open to Egyptian shipping for both commercial and strategic
purposes. In a previous chapter[3] it has been argued that the
theory that Tuthmosis III or Amenophis II conquered Ugarit is
based on the mistaken identification of the name of an otherwise
unknown town in the Biqā' captured during the latter's return
from North Syria. It is more reasonable to suppose that during
the early part of the fifteenth century Ugarit came for a time
under the protection of Saustatar of Mitanni who, as has been
seen, controlled both Mukish and Kizzuwadna.[4] His successors
were forced to withdraw over the Euphrates, but in that age of
power politics no country could long remain neutral and un-
committed,[5] and early, perhaps, in the reign of Amenophis, or even
sooner, Ugarit must have yielded to diplomatic pressure and joined
the other cities of the east Mediterranean seaboard, some of which
had been under Egyptian control since the 1580s. Egyptian resi-
dents paid homage to the local deities; a treasury official named
Mami, who later dedicated a stele inscribed in hieroglyphics to the
city god, Ba'al Sᵉphōn,[6] may have been stationed there to secure the
collection and dispatch of tribute due under the terms of a treaty;
the style of the carving is Ramesside.

One of the letters from Ugarit found among the Amarna correspondence bears the name of Ammishtamru.[7] In it the king
declares himself a loyal vassal of the Sun, Amenophis III, and
asks for Egyptian aid against an enemy who may be either the
neighbouring state of Amurru[8] or else perhaps the Hittite king
Shuppiluliumash,[9] whose intervention in North Syria had already
begun. Other Amarna letters from Ammishtamru or his son, Niqmaddu II, make it clear that during the lifetime of Amenophis
III Ugarit was faithful to her allegiance, a state of affairs which

[1] A, 30, 524 f.   [2] §iv, 26, 23 ff.; §iv, 30, vol. 4, 6 ff., 27 f.
[3] C.A.H. ii³, pt. 1, pp. 460 f.
[4] C.A.H. ii³, pt. 1, p. 436.   [5] §iv, 28, 110.
[6] §iv, 44, vol. 1, 39 ff., 40, fig. 30; vol. 4, 133 ff. and fig. 101; §iv, 26, 31.
[7] EA 45, ll. 22 ff.; G, 4, 309 ff., 1097 ff.; §iv, 3, 30.
[8] §iv, 26, 24.   [9] §iv, 21, 34 f.; G, 4, 1098.

must go back at least to the earliest years of the pharaoh's reign, since one of the scarabs issued to commemorate his marriage with Queen Tiy in his second year was found at Ras Shamra[1] and the cartouches of the royal pair were on fragments of alabaster vases uncovered in the palace ruins.[2] Akhenaten and Nefertiti sent similar diplomatic gifts in the early years of their reign[3] and Nefertiti must have been the queen of Egypt to whom the Ugaritian queen sent a present of a pot of balm.[4] At about this time, a disaster overtook the city in which at least part of the palace, and quarters of the town, were destroyed by fire. The passage in the letter in which the king of Tyre informed Pharaoh of the news[5] is of doubtful interpretation[6] and leaves it uncertain whether the destruction of the palace was due to enemy action of some kind or whether it was rather, as the excavator himself maintains, the result of a violent earthquake of which signs can be discerned in the masonry.[7] However this may be, the damage was made good and the palace rose again, more splendid than before.[8]

At its greatest extent, in the fourteenth and thirteenth centuries, this palace covered some two and a half acres and must have been one of the largest in western Asia; its fame was great among the Canaanites; according to the king of Byblos, only the palace at Tyre could rival it in size and magnificence.[9] The original building had not been very large: it consisted essentially of an entrance hall and staircase leading to a large courtyard with rooms around it, under one of which was the royal hypogeum with three corbelled vaults.[10] As time went on, and with increasing prosperity, the administration grew more complex and the court more numerous. The palace was accordingly repeatedly enlarged and rebuilt;[11] over ninety rooms have been excavated, and there are eight entrance staircases, each with a pillared portico, and nine interior courtyards. Rooms were panelled with cedar and other precious woods, and flights of stairs led to an upper floor. In the eastern part of the palace was a large walled garden with flower beds and a pavilion,[12] and in one of the courtyards a piped water supply led to an ornamental basin.[13]

---

[1] §IV, 44, vol. 3, 221 ff., fig. 204.   [2] *Ibid.* vol. 4, 97; §IV, 40, 16; §IV, 37, 112.

[3] §IV, 44, vol. 3, 167, fig. 120; §IV, 38, 41; §IV, 21, 36.

[4] EA 48; G, 4, 315 ff.   [5] EA 151, ll. 55 ff.; G, 4, 625, 1251 ff.

[6] §IV, 26, 28 ff.; §IV, 1, 203; A, 20, vol. 2, 356 ff.

[7] §IV, 44, vol. 1, 35 ff. and fig. 29; §IV, 43, 9; §IV, 42, 7.

[8] §IV, 44, vol. 4, 7 ff.; §IV, 30, vol. 3, xii f.

[9] EA 89, ll. 48 f.; G, 4, 425; §IV, 44, vol. 4, 9; §IV, 4, 164.

[10] §IV, 42, 16 and fig. 8.   [11] §IV, 44, vol. 4, 9 ff. and fig. 21.

[12] *Ibid.* 15 ff.   [13] *Ibid.* 27 ff., 42, fig. 29, 47, fig. 31.

The palace was the centre of great scribal and administrative activity. Here were drawn up the contracts to which the king set his name as witness and affixed his stamp, the dynastic seal of Yaqaru. When written and sealed, the documents were taken to a bell-shaped oven in one of the courtyards for baking;[1] they were then stored, according to their category, in one of several archive rooms in various parts of the palace.[2] Most of the diplomatic correspondence was kept together, and here the scribes who could read and write Babylonian learned their craft[3] with the help of school exercises and glossaries. Some of the more important letters were translated on receipt into Ugaritic for greater convenience.[4]

Craftsmen, too, worked in the palace. Ivory was lavishly used in the decoration of furniture in the royal throne room and private apartments, and an ivory-carvers' workshop contained some fine pieces, perhaps brought for repair, including a series of panels which must have adorned the headpiece of a couch or bed.[5] A circular table-top more than a yard in diameter, elaborately fretted,[6] a carved elephant tusk[7] and a large ivory head from the chryselephantine statue of a queen or deity,[8] with inlaid eyes and curls in silver-and-gold niello work, were also among the objects found in the garden near this workshop.

The spacious houses of the well-to-do, some of them minor palaces for high officials and members of the royal family, lay grouped in large *insulae* to the east and south of the palace; that of Rap'anu, for instance, who held a high position at court, had no less than thirty-four rooms on the ground floor alone; his library contained both private and official correspondence.[9] Most of the houses were provided with bathrooms and lavatories and had a well-planned drainage system.[10] Below each was the family vault, a corbelled chamber with an arched roof in the Mycenaean manner,[11] in which the bodies of successive generations were laid on the flagged floor, surrounded by rich grave-goods—vessels of alabaster and lapis lazuli and metal, and painted pots of Aegean manufacture. Similar tombs were found in the residential quarter of the port,[12] where rich merchants had their houses and warehouses.[13] Smaller houses in the north-eastern and

---

[1] §IV, 44, vol. 4, 31 ff., 91, figs. 35–39.
[2] *Ibid.* 45 ff.; §IV, 30, vol. 3, xi ff.   [3] §IV, 50; §IV, 30, vol. 3, 211 ff.
[4] §IV, 44, vol 4, 91.   [5] *Ibid.* vol. 4, 17; §IV, 38, pl. VII.
[6] §IV, 44, vol. 4, 30, fig. 22; §IV, 38, 59.
[7] §IV, 38, 62 and fig. 9.   [8] §IV, 44, vol. 4, 25 f., figs. 24–6. Plate 136(*a*).
[9] §IV, 39, 233 f.   [10] §IV, 44, vol. 4, 30, pl. VI.
[11] §IV, 44, vol. I, 30, figs. 75–80, pls. XVI, XVII; *ibid.* vol. 4, 30, pl. XVI, 2; §IV, 35, 49 ff.   [12] §IV, 44, vol. I, 30 ff. See Plate 137.   [13] §IV, 44, vol. 4, 30 f.

north-western sections of the town were densely grouped on each side of narrow, winding streets, much like those of the older quarters of oriental towns today.[1] The artisans' quarter was to the south: here goldsmiths and silversmiths, seal-cutters, sculptors and workers in bronze had their dwellings,[2] their houses grouped around an open square overlooked on the south side by an imposing stone building which had housed a library of texts in Babylonian cuneiform, some astrological and some literary, perhaps used for teaching purposes.[3] On the highest part of the hill rose the two main temples, one, dedicated to the god Dagan, very massively built, that of Ba'al being to the west of it;[4] between them was the residence of the high priest, in which most of the large mythological tablets in alphabetic cuneiform were found.[5] The city was surrounded by a rampart of formidable proportions, with a postern gate in Hittite style.[6]

Pottery models of huts[7] suggest that some of the houses, perhaps those in the surrounding villages, may have had a conical 'sugar-loaf' roof similar to those in parts of North Syria today. Judging by the large number of town and village communities listed for administrative purposes, the kingdom must have been comparatively densely populated. Many different nationalities were represented in Ugarit.[8] The official language was a local dialect of North Canaanite, which was spoken by the largest group among the population, but for the benefit of the large Hurrian-speaking minority,[9] many of them soldiers and craftsmen in the king's service,[10] who maintained their identity and their cult practices, a number of bilingual glossaries were compiled,[11] and one lexicographical tablet from Rap'anu's library contains equivalents in no less than four languages: Hurrian, Ugaritic, Sumerian and Babylonian.[12] Akkadian legal terms, too, were translated into Hurrian for administrative purposes.[13] The presence of Minoan and, at a later date, Mycenaean colonists at Ugarit has been inferred[14] from the numerous figurines and fine pottery vessels, some in the Cretan 'palace' style, found in the tombs together with local imitations of such objects.[15] Tablets in

[1] §iv, 39, 235. [2] §v, 65, 206 ff. [3] §iv, 39, 235; §iv, 30, vol. 3, fig. 21.
[4] §v, 64, 154 ff. and pl. 36. [5] §iv, 11, 63; §iv, 20, 7 ff.
[6] §v, 67, 289 ff., pls. xlii, xliii, figs. 12, 13. See Plate 104.
[7] §iv, 44, vol. 2, 194 f., fig. 79 and pl. xxx. [8] A, 16, 4 f.
[9] §iv, 44, vol. 1, 28; vol. 4, 51, 83 f.; §v, 76, 24. [10] A, 10, 188 ff.
[11] §v, 52; §iv, 44, vol. iv, 87, 136, fig. 119; §iv, 30, vol. iii, 311 = RS.13.10.
[12] §iv, 44, vol. 4, 87 = RS.20.123+149. [13] §iv, 50, 264; §iv, 44, vol. 1, 28 f.
[14] §iv, 44, vol. 1, 53 ff., 67.
[15] Ibid. 77, fig. 68; otherwise §iv, 26, 53 f.; §iv, 6, 354.

the Cypro-Mycenaean script betray the presence of Alashiyans from Cyprus,[1] and large quantities of *bilbil* jars and other characteristic wares found stacked in the sheds of Mīnet el-Beidha suggest that the Cypriots, too, were there for commercial reasons.[2] Hittite and Egyptian merchants and envoys, too, had their residence in Ugarit,[3] and objects of Egyptian and Anatolian workmanship were in demand.[4] Travellers and traders from Tyre, Byblos, Beirut and other neighbouring kingdoms, as well as neighbouring Amurru, frequented the city,[5] and mention in the texts of the Kassite deities, Shuqamuna and Shumalia,[6] and of the Moabite Chemosh[7] suggests that Babylonians and Palestinians from over the Jordan contributed to this cosmopolitan community.

A fragment of an alabaster vase found in the rebuilt palace is incised with a scene of great interest: it depicts an Egyptian lady of noble or royal rank (her name is unfortunately missing), in the presence of 'Niqmad, the king (*wr*) of the land of Ugarit'.[8] The scene has been dated on stylistic grounds to the Amarna or immediately post-Amarna period[9] and the royal marriage which it appears to imply may have been prompted by the desire of Akhenaten or one of his immediate successors to cement the bond which linked Ugarit and Egypt,[10] an alliance not only profitable for commercial reasons but also of great strategic value in the face of Shuppiluliumash's threatening aggression. The Hittite king was even now making preparations for his great offensive in Syria.[11] Niqmaddu, cut off from the help of Egyptian troops stationed at Byblos by the hostile activities of Aziru of Amurru and his brothers,[12] found his kingdom endangered on two fronts. A treaty was accordingly negotiated with Aziru[13] by the terms of which the latter was bribed by a large payment of silver[14] to renounce all claims on Siyanni, Ugarit's most southerly dependency, which the kings of Amurru had long coveted,[15] and to promise help to Ugarit in case she were attacked. The pact between Aziru

[1] §IV, 44, vol. 3, 227 ff., 247; *ibid.* vol. 4, 131 ff., 122, fig. 100.

[2] §IV, 44, vol. 1, 72, figs. 69–74; *ibid.* vol. 3, 227 ff.; *ibid.* vol. 4, 30 f., fig. 20, *cf.* §IV, 7.

[3] E.g. §IV, 30, vol. 4, 103 ff. = *RS*.17.130; *ibid.* vol. 3, 19 = *RS*.15.11; *ibid.* 142 = *RS*.16.136 (Egyptians); §IV, 41, 199 f. (Hittite merchants).

[4] E.g. §IV, 44, vol. 4, 30 ff.; §IV, 39, 235; §IV, 41, 199.

[5] E.g. §IV, 44, vol. 4, 140 = *RS*.19.42.   [6] §V, 30, 88; §IV, 14, vol. 2, 528 ff.

[7] §IV, 54, 96.   [8] §IV, 44, vol. 3, 164 ff., 179 ff., figs. 118, 126.

[9] *Ibid.* 179 ff.   [10] §IV, 21, 34 f.   [11] See above, pp. 13 ff.

[12] EA, 126, ll. 4–13; G, 4, 539.

[13] §IV, 30, vol. 4, 284 ff. = *RS*.19.68; EA 98, ll. 5–9; §IV, 28, 11.

[14] A, 20, vol. 2, 349; but see §IV, 44, vol. 5, 259 ff.

[15] §IV, 26, 33; §IV, 30, vol. 4, 282.

and Shuppiluliumash,[1] however, which must have been negotiated soon after,[2] revealed the policy of the Amorite ruler in a clearer light and Niqmaddu was forced to accede to the pressing demands of the Hittite king: he had first to promise to withhold aid from the 'rebel' kingdoms, Nukhash and Mukish,[3] and subsequently to accept the terms of a treaty imposed upon him by the Great King in Alalakh.[4]

Instead of the rays of the pharaoh, the Egyptian 'Sun', the Sun of Khatti-land now shone upon Ugarit. By the terms of the treaty, Niqmaddu recognized Shuppiluliumash as his overlord; he was required to send large annual tribute, in specified amounts of silver and of blue- and purple-dyed wool and garments,[5] for the Hittite king and queen and various members of their court.[6] In return for his loyalty, the frontiers of his kingdom were delimited and guaranteed,[7] and, contrary to the usual practices of international law,[8] Niqmaddu was accorded the right to retain at his disposal fugitives from the defeated rebel kingdoms, Mukish and Nukhash.[9] The tablets on which the frontier territories are enumerated are somewhat broken, but, judging by the complaints of the people of Mukish,[10] it appears that Ugarit's new frontiers included land taken from both Mukish and Neya, districts which had long been the subject of disputes between the Ugaritians and their neighbours. If the identifications of place-names proposed by one scholar[11] can be accepted, the size of Niqmaddu's territory must have been increased by nearly four times, and his eastern frontier extended beyond Idlib to Afis, 95 miles inland.

Niqmaddu remained faithful to this alliance for the remaining years of his long reign, and when Sharre-Kushukh, the viceroy appointed by Murshilish II to rule at Carchemish,[12] summoned the aid of the Syrian vassals against Tette of Nukhash, who had once more risen in revolt against his Hittite overlord,[13] there is no reason to suppose that the king of Ugarit failed in his obligation. Unlike Alalakh, the city of Ugarit shows no sign of Hittite occupation,[14] but appears to have retained its role as a wealthy port, affording the Hittites an outlet for maritime trade which

---

[1] §IV, 15, 377 ff.; §IV, 26, 36 ff.
[2] §IV, 8, 45; §IV, 22, 456. [3] §IV, 30, vol. 4, 35 ff. = $R\mathcal{S}$.17.132.
[4] §IV, 30, vol. 4, 40 ff. = $R\mathcal{S}$.17.227 etc.; §IV, 23, 68.
[5] §IV, 30, vol. 4, 37 ff. = $R\mathcal{S}$.17.227 etc.; §IV, 14, vol. 3, 75 ff.; §IV, 17, 128.
[6] §IV, 16.
[7] §IV, 30, vol. 4, 63 ff.; $R\mathcal{S}$.17.340; 17.62, 17.399A; 17.366; §IV, 26, 48 f.
[8] §IV, 22, 456. [9] §IV, 30, vol. 4, 52 = $R\mathcal{S}$.17.369A.
[10] §IV, 30, vol. 4, 63 ff. = $R\mathcal{S}$.17.237, ll. 3 ff. [11] A, 4, 399 ff.
[12] See above, pp. 120 f. [13] §IV, 30, vol. 4, 53 ff. = $R\mathcal{S}$.17.334. [14] §IV, 32, 54.

they valued too highly to reduce by excessive interference.[1] The reign of Niqmaddu appears to have been a prosperous one in which literary texts were copied[2] and the palace enlarged and embellished.[3] It may even be that the city maintained her position as a commercial intermediary between Egypt and the Hittite empire, for Egyptian influence continued to be strong in his reign and that of his successors. A queen named Sharelli, whose name appears on several documents and on a stele dedicated to the god Dagan,[4] had a seal engraved not in cuneiform but in Egyptian hieroglyphs;[5] though it is tempting to equate her with Niqmaddu's nameless bride,[6] the style of the writing indicates a somewhat later date.[7] It may however be significant that Sharelli appears to be the exact Hurrian equivalent of Akhat-milki, 'sister of the king', which would suggest a title rather than a proper name.[8]

Two of Niqmaddu's sons in turn succeeded to the throne. Ar-Khalba, the elder of the two, reigned for nine troubled years at the most.[9] Sharre-Kushukh was now dead. Syria rose again in revolt against Hittite rule, and so serious was the peril that Murshilish II himself was forced to march against Nukhash and Kinza (Qadesh); even Carchemish itself may for a time have been lost.[10] Ugarit too seems now for a time to have thrown in her lot with the rebels, for a subsequent treaty between Murshilish and Niqmepa, the second son of Niqmaddu,[11] makes it clear that he was set on the throne by the direct intervention of the Hittite king. Ugarit was punished by the loss of two of its most valuable territories, Siyanni and the neighbouring kingdom of Ushnatu, on the south-eastern frontier,[12] both of which were handed over to Carchemish. This reduced the kingdom of Ugarit to two thirds of its former size[13] and must have been a great blow to the country's economy; a fresh assessment of tribute had to be made on the basis of her reduced revenues.[14] The presence in the palace at Ras Shamra of alabaster vases inscribed with the cartouches of

[1] §IV, 23, 73.   [2] §IV, 26, 56, n. 111; §V, 72, 31, n. 1; A, 20, vol. 2, 357.
[3] §IV, 44, vol. 4, 13 ff.
[4] §IV, 44, vol. 3, 81; §IV, 30, vol. 2, xix; §IV, 26, 138 f., 30 f. = RS.15.08; §V, 43, 117 f.
[5] §IV, 44, vol. 3, 85, fig. 106.   [6] Ibid. 168.   [7] Ibid. 81, n. 3 (by J. Vandier).
[8] §IV, 44, vol. 5, 261 f.
[9] §IV, 30, vol. 4, 57; §IV, 26, 58, Klengel (A, 20, vol. 2, 359 f.) argues for a reign of not more than two years.   [10] See above, p. 123.
[11] §IV, 30, vol. 4, 84 ff.; A, 20, vol. 2, 362 ff.; §IV, 23, 68 f.
[12] §IV, 30, vol. 4, 16 f., 71 ff. = RS.17.335, 17.344 and 17.368; §IV, 26, 75 ff.
[13] §IV, 22, 459.   [14] §IV, 30, vol. 4, 79 ff. = RS.17.382 + 380; §IV, 23, 68.

Horemheb,[1] the Egyptian contemporary of Murshilish II, suggests that it may have been the pharaoh who attempted to woo Ugarit away from her Hittite allegiance, since such gifts usually accompanied a diplomatic mission.[2] What happened to Ar-Khalba is not known. He may have had a premonition of disaster, for, in a legal document executed in his name,[3] he willed that, according to the levirate custom, his wife should marry his brother Niqmepa after his death, thereby ensuring the continuance of the hereditary line.[3] The presence at Ugarit of an actual seal of Murshilish II[4] suggests that it was brought here by the Hittite envoy who negotiated the deposition of Ar-Khalba and set Niqmepa on the throne.

Henceforward Ugarit appears to have remained loyal to her Hittite overlord. In common with many of the kingdoms of Anatolia and North Syria, she sent a contingent to the aid of Muwatallish when, in the year 1300, he encountered the army of Ramesses II at Qadesh.[5] At this time, as a later treaty indicates,[6] Amurru had deserted her alliance and was fighting on the Egyptian side. A letter found at Ugarit[7] appears to be a dispatch from a general Simiyanu (or Simitti) operating against Ardata, an important town in Amurru;[8] he speculates on the likelihood of Egyptian intervention, and asks for more troops. This letter may have been written shortly before the battle of Qadesh, when an Egyptian army may have been reconnoitring in the area; after the battle, Amurru surrendered to the Hittites and its king Benteshina was deposed. Other documents from the reign of Niqmepa belong to the period after the accession to the Hittite throne of Khattushilish III.[9] Relations between monarch and vassal appear to have remained cordial: when complaints were received at Khattusha of the overbearing behaviour of Hittite merchants from Ura in Cilicia,[10] a fair compromise was agreed.[11] Another royal edict lays down that fugitives from Ugarit will not be allowed to settle in the land of the *Ḥapiru* of the Hittite king,[12] that is to say, in nomad

[1] §IV, 40, 16.
[2] §IV, 26, 61 f.; §IV, 22, 458. Ugarit appears with Tunip, Qadesh and Qatna in a topographical list of the reign of Horemheb in the temple of Karnak (§IV, 47, 50 ff., no. XII, *a*, 12). [3] §IV, 17, 130; §IV, 51; A, 22, 108.
[4] §IV, 44, vol. 3, 87 ff., 161 ff., figs. 109–112; §IV, 26, 63 f.
[5] See below, p. 253; A, 20, vol. 2, 369. [6] K.U.B. 23, 1, vs. 1, 28 ff.
[7] §V, 56, 80 ff. = RS.20.33; §IV, 28, 119 f.
[8] C.A.H. II³, pt. 1, pp. 454 and 459; §IV, 44, vol. 5, 69 ff. [9] §IV, 26, 80 ff.
[10] §IV, 30, vol. 4, 103 ff. = RS.17.130; §IV, 24, 270; §IV, 23, 70.
[11] C.A.H. II³, pt. 1, p. 507; A, 20, vol. 2, 370.
[12] §IV, 30, vol. 4, 107 f. = RS.17.238.

country,[1] but shall be returned to Niqmepa. When Kadashman-Enlil of Babylonia complained to Khattushilish that merchants of his were being killed in Amurru and Ugarit,[2] the Hittite countered by declaring that such things could not happen in his territory;[3] an argument based on a different understanding of the text, that Khattushilish was denying that Ugarit was within his jurisdiction,[4] must be rejected in view of the overwhelming documentary evidence that, while refraining as far as possible from interference in internal matters, the Hittite kings of the time were the ultimate arbiters of Ugarit's destiny. At the same time, after the peace treaty of 1284 or thereabouts which finally put an end to hostilities between the Hittites and Egypt,[5] there was nothing to prevent the resumption of diplomatic relations between that land and Ugarit, and an alabaster vessel fragment bearing the name of Ramesses II, found at Ras Shamra,[6] may be a witness to the *rapprochement*. A letter,[7] unfortunately fragmentary, hailing the king of Egypt as 'puissant king...master of every land, my master' and couched in the language of a vassal to his overlord, is thought on other grounds to be addressed to Ramesses II. It appears to refer to the settlement of some dispute between people of Canaan—Egyptian territory in southern Syria?—and people of Ugarit.

After a long reign of perhaps more than sixty years,[8] as the vassal of four successive Hittite sovereigns, Niqmepa was succeeded in about 1265 B.C. by his son Ammishtamru, the second of the name.[9] Although he must have been a middle-aged man at the time of his accession, it would appear that the affairs of the state were managed for a short time by the dowager queen Akhat-milki,[10] the daughter of King *DU*-Teshub of Amurru. An impressive list of her personal ornaments, vesture and furniture, which she presumably brought with her as her dowry at the time of her marriage to Niqmepa, has survived among the palace archives.[11] As queen of Ugarit, she was the arbitrator in a dispute between her sons, Khishmi-Sharruma and *ARAD*-Sharruma, and

---

[1] §iv, 9, 215; §iv, 5, 70 ff.; §iv, 22, 459, n. 1.
[2] *K.Bo.* 1, 10, vs. ll. 14–25; §iv, 13, 130 ff.
[3] §iv, 44, vol. 1, 41.
[4] §iv, 46, 134, n. 3; §iv, 32, 54 ff., 63, n. 35.
[5] See below, pp. 256 and 258 ff.; A, 20, vol. 2, 373.
[6] §iv, 44, vol. 3, fig. 121; §v, 67, 287 f., fig. 10.
[7] §iv, 44, vol. 5, 110 ff. = *RS*.20.182.
[8] §iv, 26, 67.   [9] *Ibid.* 99 ff.; §iv, 30, vol. 4, 113 ff.
[10] §iv, 26, 99 f.; §iv, 30, vol. 3, 178 ff. See above, p. 139.
[11] §iv, 30, vol. 3, 182 ff. = *RS*.16.146; *ibid.* vol. 4, 10 and 120.

their brother or half-brother, Ammishtamru himself,[1] and her seal appears also on a legal document of the latter's reign.[2] An Assyrian envoy to the Ugaritic court, on receipt of a letter from Ashur, was directed to read it to the Queen.[3]

The renewed *entente cordiale* between Amurru and Ugarit had been strengthened yet again by the marriage of Ammishtamru to the daughter of Bente-shina, the grandson of *DU*-Teshub and nephew of Akhat-milki.[4] The union of the two houses was this time less happy, however, in its outcome, for the Amorite queen, whose name the documents are careful to omit, after having borne her husband a son, was accused of 'having sought evil [? sickness] for Ammishtamru'. A bill of divorcement was accordingly drawn up,[5] the Hittite king, now Tudkhaliash IV, acting as arbitrator, for the matter had the nature of a dispute between vassals. Following the usual custom in divorce proceedings, it was decreed that the woman repudiated was to take her dowry and depart; everything she had acquired at Ugarit since her marriage, however, belonged to her husband and must be left behind.[6] A knotty problem remained to be solved, for her son, Utri-Sharruma, was the heir to the throne of Ugarit. Tudkhaliash gave his decision: if the prince should elect to stay in Ugarit with his father, he might inherit the kingdom; but, if he chose to return to Amurru with his mother, then he forfeited the right to the throne and Ammishtamru must nominate as his heir a son by another wife.[7] This was not the end of Ammishtamru's marital troubles, however, for further divorce proceedings appear to have been taken against another of his wives, called 'the daughter of the noble lady [*rabītu*]';[8] since she, too, came from Amurru it is tempting to identify her with Bente-shina's daughter[9] but there are reasons for supposing that a different wife was involved[10] and that the 'great sin' of which the second was accused was adultery.[11] Condemned to death by Ammishtamru, she fled to Amurru and took refuge with Bente-shina's son and successor, Shaushga-muwash. Hard words and a military exchange between Ugarit and Amurru over this affair led again to the intervention

---

[1] §iv, 30, vol. 4, 121 ff. = *RS*.17.352.
[2] §iv, 30, vol. 3, 150 f. = *RS*.16.197.   [3] §iv, 49.
[4] §iv, 26, 104 f.; A, 20, vol. 2, 307.
[5] §iv, 30, vol. 4, 126 f. = *RS*.17.159 and 127 f. = *RS*. 17.396; §iv, 57.
[6] §iv, 30, vol. 4, 126 f. = *RS*.17.159, ll. 8–18.   [7] *Ibid*. ll. 31–39 and *RS*.17.348.
[8] §iv, 30, vol. 4, 129 ff. = *RS*.16.270, 17.372A + 360A, 17.228.
[9] §iv, 44, vol. 3, 31 f.
[10] §iv, 30, vol. 4, 131; §iv, 26, 108; A, 20, vol. 2, 224 ff., 323.
[11] §iv, 27, 280 (*cf*. Gen. xx. 9); A, 22, 104.

of Tudkhaliash,[1] and it was finally agreed that the erring wife must be returned to her husband; Ammishtamru might carry out the sentence of execution, as was his legal right,[2] but had to pay Shaushga-muwash a large sum of money by way of compensation.[3]

The tablets, sent from Khattusha, which conveyed the decisions of the Great King on these matters of more than domestic importance[4] were sealed with the royal seal of Tudkhaliash himself,[5] but his son, Ini-Teshub, was now viceroy at Carchemish, and as the Hittite governor responsible for affairs in North Syria his name and seal appear frequently on documents of the reign of Ammishtamru and his son Ibiranu.[6] It was he who decided what might be taken by Bente-shina's daughter after her divorce,[7] arbitrated in cases of dispute affecting merchants travelling from kingdom to kingdom in the area under his jurisdiction,[8] and settled claims for compensation made by individuals of one kingdom against those of another. The verdicts appear to have been delivered without bias: in one case a Hittite merchant convicted of theft was condemned to make triple restitution to the Ugaritian from whom he had stolen.[9] Sometimes the disputes were over border incidents between kingdom and kingdom. Ugarit and her neighbour and erstwhile vassal Siyanni quarrelled over relatively unimportant local incidents involving acts of hooliganism, a tower destroyed and vines chopped down, and the smuggling of wine or beer through Ugaritian territory to Beirut;[10] a complaint from the king of neighbouring Ushnatu that Ugaritians had violated his frontiers and captured a town called forth a sharp reproof from the viceroy.[11]

From such documents the figure of Ini-Teshub stands out with dignity. In these latter days, when the Hittite empire was hard pressed and the Great King was often occupied with urgent military matters in the west of his wide realm, it was the Syrian viceroy, resident at Carchemish, to whom the kingdoms of Syria turned for guidance in their affairs[12] and the protection of their commerce. The close contact maintained thus between Hittites

[1] §IV, 30, vol. 4, 137 f. = RS.18.06 + 17.365; §IV, 23, 71.
[2] §IV, 26, 109; §IV, 23, 71.
[3] 1400 shekels of gold (RS.17.228, ll. 30 ff.).   [4] §IV, 28, 115; §IV, 57, 23 f.
[5] §IV, 44, vol. 3, 14 ff.; §IV, 30, vol. 4, 126 = RS.17.159.
[6] §IV, 44, vol. 3, 21 ff., figs. 26–35; §IV, 26, 115 ff.
[7] §IV, 30, vol. 4, 127 f. = RS.17.396; §IV, 57, 26.
[8] E.g. §IV, 30, vol. 4, 169 ff. = RS.17.158; 171 f. = RS.17.42; 172 f. = RS.17.145.
[9] §IV, 30, vol. 4, 179 = RS.17.128.
[10] Ibid. 161 ff. = RS.17.341; §IV, 26, 118 ff.
[11] §IV, 44, vol. 5, 90 f. = RS.20.174A.   [12] §IV, 23, 74 ff.

and Canaanites resulted in a lasting influence: the rulers of North Syria were known to the Assyrians of the first millennium as 'the kings of Khatti-land'.[1]

Ugarit itself was still enjoying a fair measure of autonomy. A letter addressed to Ammishtamru by Shukur-Teshub, on the latter's installation as Hittite representative in Mukish, assured his new neighbour that his friendly intentions would be cemented by an exchange of gifts.[2] The carved orthostat found in the palace of Alalakh, depicting Tudkhaliash and his queen,[3] is not paralleled by any monument yet found in Ugarit. Commercial contact with Egypt was maintained. Egyptians resident in Ugarit were given land by the king,[4] and a bronze sword engraved with the cartouche of the pharaoh Merneptah, found in a private house at Ras Shamra, was probably commissioned by him but for some reason never delivered.[5] In the emergency produced by the advance of the Assyrian army led by Tukulti-Ninurta I[6] to the Euphrates, however, the vassals in Syria were called upon by Tudkhaliash to show their loyalty and lend assistance. Among them were Ugarit and Amurru, with whose ruler, Shaushgamuwash, the Hittites had recently signed a new treaty.[7] The danger was great, and the war needed costly preparation:[8] while Amurru was called upon to furnish troops, wealthy Ugarit's aid took the form of a heavy monetary contribution in gold;[9] the royal coffers had to be replenished for this purpose by means of a special tax levied on the towns and villages of the realm 'for the tribute of the Sun'.[10]

Ammishtamru's successor on the throne of Ugarit was not his first heir designate, Utri-Sharruma, who had presumably chosen to return with his mother to Amurru, but Ibiranu, a son by another wife.[11] During his reign the close relationship between Carchemish and Ugarit continued, but the judgements which have been preserved are not delivered in the name of Ini-Teshub, the king of Carchemish, or of his son and successor Talmi-

---

[1] E.g. G, 6, 279, 281, 291.

[2] §IV, 28, 115.　　　　　　　　　[3] §IV, 55, 241 and pl. 48.

[4] §IV, 30, vol. 3, 142.　　　　　　[5] §IV, 7, 253.

[6] A, 20, vol. 2, 380; §IV, 26, 110 f. M. Nougayrol (§IV, 30, vol. 4, 150) places these events in the reign of Shalmaneser I.

[7] §III, 3, 113 ff.; §IV, 47, 320 f.

[8] The view is expressed below, p. 291, that the Assyrian threat was nothing more serious than a border raid.

[9] §IV, 30, vol. 4, 149 ff. = RS.17.59; §IV, 23, 70.

[10] §IV, 44, vol. 4, 73 = RS.19.17; §IV, 30, vol. v, 75 f.; §v, 66, 42.

[11] §IV, 26, 125 f.; A, 20, vol. 2, 388 ff.

Teshub, but in that of a prince Armaziti;[1] it was he who stabilized the frontiers of Ugarit after some border incident.[2] A certain coolness appears to have sprung up at this time between the court at Boğazköy and that of Ugarit.[3] Ibiranu was sharply reprimanded for not having presented himself at the Hittite capital,[4] perhaps to do homage on his accession, and for sending no messages or presents.[5] Since he had also failed to meet his obligations in sending a contingent of foot soldiers and chariotry when urgently requested to do so, a Hittite officer had to be sent to make a personal inspection. Already, it may be surmised, the Hittite hold on North Syria was weakening.

Ibiranu was a contemporary of Tudkhaliash IV and probably also of his successor Arnuwandash III. The next king of Ugarit, Ibiranu's son Niqmaddu III, can have had only a brief reign;[6] whether 'Ammurapi, who followed him, was of the royal line or no is uncertain, for, contrary to the usual custom, his parentage is nowhere mentioned;[7] he is likely to have been of the same generation as his predecessor.[8] Divorce at this time ended the marriage of an Ugaritic prince, perhaps the son of 'Ammurapi, to a Hittite princess;[9] and Talmi-Teshub, who adjudicated in the affair, allowed her to keep her dowry but ordered her to give up a royal residence which she had, it seems, been reluctant to leave.[10]

Shuppiluliumash II now ascended the Hittite throne and, facing a mounting tide of threatening disaster, found himself relying more and more on the fleet of his most important vassal on the Levant coast. The blow was not long delayed. In the ruins of the latest level of the palace at Ras Shamra, the kiln used for baking tablets was found to be packed full of documents,[11] a batch of about one hundred brought by the scribes when freshly written; many are transcriptions into alphabetic Ugaritic of letters and despatches which must have been received in the weeks—even the days— before the fall of the city: there had been no time to take them from the kiln.[12] The immediacy of the danger facing Ugarit is implicit in the wording and content of some of these and other tablets.[13] The Hittite king asks urgently for

---

[1] §iv, 25, 143; A, 20, vol. 2, 394. [2] §iv, 30, vol. 4, 188 = RS.17.292.
[3] §iv, 30, vol. 4, 187; §iv, 26, 127 f. [4] §iv, 30, vol. 4, 191 = RS.17.247.
[5] §iv, 30, vol. 4, 192 = RS.17.289.
[6] §iv, 30, vol. 4, 199 ff.; §iv, 26, 129 ff.; cf. §iv, 44, vol. 5, pp. 102 ff. = RS.20.237.
[7] §iv, 30, vol. 4, 8; §v, 74, 76.
[8] §iv, 22, 461; A, 20, vol. 2, 403. [9] §iv, 30, vol. 4, 209 f. = RS.17.355.
[10] §iv, 30, vol. 4, 208 = RS.17.355. [11] §iv, 44, vol. 4, 31 ff., figs. 35–39.
[12] §iv, 30, vol. 5, 81 ff.; §iv, 44, vol. iv, 31 ff.
[13] A, 21, 29 ff.; §iv, 28, 120 f.; §iv, 7, 254 ff.

a ship and a crew to transport grain from Mukish to the Hittite town of Ura in Cilicia, as a 'matter of life and death' since there is famine in the area.[1] In making this demand, the Hittite refers to an act of liberation whereby he has formally released the king of Ugarit (probably 'Ammurapi) from vassalage, but he makes it clear that Ugarit has not yet been absolved from all her obligations towards her former overlord. Famine may also have afflicted Alashiya at this time: a certain Pagan whose letter to the King of Ugarit was one of those found in the kiln, calls the Ugaritian 'my son', perhaps indicating that a dynastic marriage linked their houses; he asks for a ship to be sent with food supplies for the island.[2] In reply,[3] 'Ammurapi informs his 'father', the king of Alashiya, that he has not a ship to spare, since the enemy has plundered his coasts, while his own fleet is in the Lukka lands and his troops in the land of the Hittites.

Only one known situation fits this predicament: the approach of the 'Peoples of the Sea' whose destructive progress by way of Qode (Kizzuwadna), the Khatti-land, Carchemish, Alashiya and Amurru is all too briefly related by Ramesses III in his inscription on the north wall of the temple of Medīnet Habu.[4] At the approach of the enemy, Shuppiluliumash must have summoned his vassals in North Syria to his aid, and Ugarit, loyal to the last, must have sent her whole army. One of the letters found in the kiln[5] appears to be an urgent dispatch sent to the king in Ugarit from the commander of the army in Lawasanda (Lawazantiya) in Cilicia,[6] which his troops had fortified in anticipation of attack. The enemy is nowhere mentioned by name, probably because so motley a horde had no collective name. Their presence in Mukish, only a few dozen miles from Ugaritian territory, is indicated in a letter of Ewir-Sharruma, another of the Ugaritian generals in the field, to the queen or queen-mother,[7] in the absence of the king at the front. Part of the letter is unfortunately damaged, but it sounds the note of extreme urgency and makes reference to Mount Amanus, though a contingent of two thousand horses (equivalent to a thousand chariots, a very formidable force[8]) is apparently still at the king's disposal. Other letters which may well date from this time of crisis tell of looting and burning.[9]

---

[1] §iv, 44, vol. 5, 105 ff., 323 f. = RS.20.212, 26.158.　　[2] §iv, 28, 120.
[3] §iv, 28, 121; §iv, 7, 255 = RS.20.238.
[4] G, 6, 262; see below, pp. 242 ff.
[5] §iv, 30, vol. 5, 90 = RS.18.40; §iv, 7, 256 f.
[6] §iv, 7, 257; see below, p. 514.
[7] §iv, 30, vol. 2, xviii, 25 ff. = RS.16.402.　　[8] §iv, 7, 257 f.
[9] E.g. §iv, 30, vol. 5, 137 = RS.19.11.

Of the anxiety of the king and people of Ugarit in the face of impending danger the tablets leave us in no doubt. Whether or not the destruction of the city was due to enemy action is less certain. M. Schaeffer, the excavator of Ras Shamra over more than forty years, who long held the view that the Peoples of the Sea were responsible for the final pillage and burning of Ugarit,[1] has now reached a different conclusion.[2] Ugarit, he suggests, may have come to terms with the invaders and persuaded them to by-pass the city. The letter mentioned earlier,[3] addressed to the king of Ugarit by a general operating in the field near Ardata, was in fact found among the archives of Rap'anu, who held office under the last four kings of Ugarit.[4] 'Half my chariots', he says, 'are drawn up on the shore of the sea, and half at the foot of the Lebanon'; Ardata has been hard pressed; he speculates on the likelihood of the Egyptian king intervening, presumably against Ardata, and complains that he has been awaiting reinforcements for five months. If, as M. Schaeffer now argues,[5] the pharaoh in question is indeed Ramesses III (since he would be the only Egyptian king likely to have been engaged in Amurru during Rap'anu's lifetime) the situation must have been one in which the Egyptian army was preparing for its final decisive action against the Sea Peoples on the coast of Amurru, and a possible reason for the delay of the king of Ugarit in sending troops might be his desire to maintain a neutral attitude and not to provoke either his old friends the Egyptians or his new neighbours and potential enemies. There are however many obscurities in this letter and its interpretation must remain in doubt; moreover in script and language it differs from the other tablets in the archive[6] and its date is therefore problematical.

The excavator attributes the final destruction of Ugarit to natural causes: a terrible earthquake, or series of shocks, which must have overwhelmed the city very shortly after the events mirrored in the tablets from the kiln. The disaster, he thinks, was sudden and complete. Fire swept the city, covering it with a thick layer of ash. The inhabitants had apparently had enough warning to escape, for no skeletons were found in streets or houses other than those buried in the tombs. *Objets d'art* were left half-finished on the workshop benches, others were hidden in walls or beneath floors, in the vain hope that they might one day be recovered.[7]

---

[1] §IV, 44, vol. 1, 45 f.; §IV, 35, 27 f. Schmidtke (§IV, 45) attributes the destruction to the army of Ramesses III.　　[2] §IV, 44, vol. 5, 760 f.
[3] See above, p. 140.　　[4] §IV, 44, vol. 5, 69.
[5] §IV, 44, vol. v, 666 ff.　　[6] *Ibid.* 76 ff.　　[7] §V, 65, 206 ff.; §IV, 39, 235.

Pillagers, prowling soon after among the ruins, prised open the family vaults and carried off their treasures, but there was no attempt to rebuild the houses. Fragments of the large, beautifully written mythological tablets were used later in the construction of small walls[1] by a people who had no reverence for, or understanding of, their contents. The alphabetic script of Ugarit was forgotten and the city abandoned by those who could read it. Ugarit's history was ended.

V. CANAANITE RELIGION AND LITERATURE

Until the discovery of the cuneiform texts of Ras Shamra, little was known of the mythology and religious beliefs of the peoples of Syria–Palestine in times preceding the Iron Age. The *Phoenikikē Historia* attributed to a priest named Sanchuniathon, who was supposed to have lived before the Trojan war and to have derived his knowledge from a perusal of the archives of the temple at Byblos, his native town, was preserved in Greek translation in the works of Philo of Byblos,[2] who wrote in the first century A.D., but the latter's text survives only in an abridged and altered form in the *Praeparatio evangelica* of Eusebius, written three centuries later;[3] moreover, the account of the Phoenician pantheon there given is coloured both by Greek elements (much uncertainty arising, for instance, from the custom common among classical writers on oriental religion of substituting for the names of Semitic deities their imagined equivalents in Greek mythology) and also by the glosses of the Christian commentator.[4] Until recently, therefore, the account was generally dismissed as late and untrustworthy. The publication of the Ugaritic epics, however, has thrown revealing light on Philo's statements, and has rendered the existence of Sanchuniathon himself as a figure of history more probable,[5] though his date is still in dispute.[6]

Similarly, the Phoenician account of the creation of the world, preserved by Damascius from the writings of Mochus of Sidon,[7] has a ring of authenticity,[8] and Lucian of Samosata, writing in the middle of the second century A.D., gives a plausible account of

---

[1] §iv, 11, 31.
[2] §v, 32, 75 ff.; §v, 20, 3 ff.
[3] §v, 34; Eusebius i, 9, 20–1, 10, 28; iv, 16, 11.
[4] §v, 31, 31 ff.; §v, 44, 119.   [5] §v, 19, 77; §v, 33, 68 f.
[6] O. Eissfeldt (§v, 32, 70 f.) suggests *c.* 1000 B.C., but W. F. Albright (§iv, 2, 24) argues for a later date, between 800 and 500 B.C.
[7] §v, 20, 310 ff.   [8] §v, 19, 33 ff.

the cult of one Phoenician deity, the goddess of Hierapolis, the modern Membij.

Apart from these literary sources, the ritual and cult practices of the early Canaanites are known mostly from the polemic directed against them by Old Testament writers[1] and from the material legacy of these rites, the standing stones and altars, incense-burners and similar cult paraphernalia which are found in the majority of archaeological sites in Palestine and Syria, in levels of the later Bronze Age as well as those of the first millennium.[2]

The Canaanite temple of the Late Bronze Age was a simple building in comparison with its grandiose contemporaries in Egypt and Mesopotamia. It consisted essentially of an anteroom, a larger pillared room or open courtyard, and a sanctuary beyond, usually on a higher level reached by a short flight of steps; in this sanctuary was the altar. Storage rooms were sometimes built around, to contain the offerings and the trappings of the cult.[3] The two large temples at Ugarit, on a grander scale than most, as befitted the wealth and size of the city, were similar in plan;[4] built on the highest part of the *tell*, their towers must have dominated the town. The temple of Ba'al had a large forecourt with an altar on which sacrifices must have been offered in the sight of the assembled worshippers.[5] References in the Ugaritic texts[6] to the sacred courtyard (*hzr*), the 'table of gold', and the Holy of Holies suggest that the Solomonic temple built by Tyrian workmen may have followed traditional Canaanite design.[7] The reconstruction of buildings thought to be temples or shrines is, however, often in doubt, and rooms with pillars which were in reality parts of private houses have sometimes been taken to be shrines with *maṣṣēbōt* or standing stones.[8] Such stones were, however, found in the Bronze Age shrine at Hazor;[9] and in one of the temples at Byblos they were a striking feature of the sanctuary.[10]

Many of the technical terms employed in the Old Testament for the different sacrificial rites are found also in the texts from Ras Shamra;[11] it may be assumed that the Israelites adopted much of their ritual of offering from the Canaanites, and also some of

[1] §v, 48, 45 ff.; §v, 44, 15, 119; §v, 2, 158 ff.; §iv, 35, 59.
[2] §v, 11, vol. 2, 375 ff.; §v, 2, 42 ff., 64 ff.
[3] §v, 66, 84 ff.; §v, 11, vol. 2, 355 ff.; §v, 68; §v, 62, 6 ff., pl. vi.
[4] §iv, 44, vol. 1, 15 f.; §v, 62, 1 ff.   [5] §v, 64, 154 ff.   [6] §v, 49.
[7] §v, 11, vol. 2, 436 ff., fig. 348.   [8] §v, 68, 83.
[9] §v, 84, vol. 1, 90 f. and pls. xxviii–xxx; §v, 6, 254 ff.
[10] §v, 24, vol. 2, Atlas, pls. xxii–xxxii; §v, 44, pl. 25.
[11] §v, 48, 63 ff.; §iv, 11, 180 ff.; §v, 47, 143 ff.; §v, 26.

their festivals, for references to seasonal rites in the poems correspond with those performed at early Hebrew festivals such as the Autumnal Festival[1] (*hag hāāsīp*) and the Feast of Weeks.[2] It has been further suggested that certain of the Ugaritic epics contain sections of the liturgy accompanying the rites performed at such festivals,[3] and that one, at least, may even contain the text, with stage directions, of a religious drama enacted in mime and accompanied by music.[4] Another poem,[5] in which the Kotharoth, the goddesses of song,[6] appear, has been thought to be a wedding hymn.[7] The fragmentary nature of many of the tablets, however, and imperfect understanding of many of the words and phrases used make the interpretation of the texts a matter of great difficulty.

Similar uncertainty clouds the question whether it is possible to see, in the Ras Shamra texts, references to the practice of sacred prostitution and infant sacrifice, both said to have been characteristic of Phoenician religion at a later date and to have survived among the Carthaginians. The mention of votaries (*qdšm*) of both sexes as members of professional guilds at Ugarit[8] has been thought to furnish proof that the former practice, against which the Hebrew prophets of the eighth century B.C. thundered their denunciations,[9] was an ancient institution in Canaan;[10] there is, however, no proof that the term *qdš*, 'sacred', had this particular connotation in the second millennium B.C.[11] Similarly, a handful of references to the sacrifice called *mlk*[12] (not, as was once supposed, to the non-existent god Moloch[13]), contain nothing which would indicate that the terrible sacrifice of newborn infants was a Canaanite practice, though this is sometimes assumed.[14]

Priests with various ranks and functions appear frequently in the administrative texts from Ugarit,[15] and the house of the chief priest (*rb khnm*), which lay in the heart of the temple quarter, was one of the largest and richest in the city.[16] It contained a library of mythological and religious texts, including some in the Hurrian

---

[1] §v, 38, 37 ff.; 65 ff.; §v, 36, 72 f. [2] §v, 38, 232; §v, 48, 58.
[3] §v, 11, vol. 2, 337; §v, 38, 72, 235 ff.; §v, 52, 128 ff.
[4] §v, 36, 49 ff.; §v, 38, 225 f. [5] §v, 25, 23 ff. ,125 ff.
[6] §v, 21, 81; T. H. Gaster (§v, 37, 37 f.) translates 'swallows'.
[7] §v, 37; §v, 32, 76 f. [8] §v, 69, 166; §v, 80, 147 ff.
[9] Deut. xxiii. 18. [10] §v, 5, 234 f.; §v, 11, vol. 2, 341; §v, 69, 168 f.
[11] §iv, 11, 179; §v, 66, 44 f.
[12] §iv, 44, 77 ff.; §v, 75, 67; §v, 76, 168 f.; §iv, 30, vol. 5, 7 = *RS*.19.15.
[13] §v, 31, 31 ff.; otherwise §v, 22; §v, 2, 163 f.
[14] §v, 65, 44 f.; §v, 2, 75, 179.
[15] §v, 80, 135 ff.; §v, 69; §iv, 30, vol. 5, 75 ff. = *RS*.19.17; §iv, 11, 76 and 179.
[16] §iv, 44, vol. 1, pl. 24.

language, as well as vocabularies, syllabaries and school exercise tablets, showing that the house also filled the function of a seminary for the training of priestly scribes.[1] Another priest's house, on the southern edge of the city, also contained a library; this man was probably a diviner, for inscribed models were found in it of the lungs and liver of sheep.[2] In common with other peoples of the ancient Near East, the Canaanites evidently set great store by divination; inscribed models of sheep's livers found also at Hazor[3] and Alalakh[4] were used by apprentice diviners to learn the ancient Babylonian science of hepatoscopy, as popular in Syria–Palestine as it was in Anatolia.[5] Other tablets contained medico-magical texts, incantations intended to ward off disease, which also derived from Babylonia.[6]

The Canaanites do not seem to have acquired from the Egyptians belief in the survival of the soul after death. Aqhat, tempted by the goddess 'Anath with promises of immortality, professes disbelief, declaring that death is the lot of all men, and none may escape the grave.[7] Yet few graves were without their complement of grave-goods, and at Ugarit each of the well-to-do houses had its family vault below the floor of the living-room: a vaulted tomb reached by a flight of stone steps and closed by a door, in which successive generations of the family were buried.[8] Not only were the tombs richly furnished, but the dead were thereafter carefully tended by their relatives, for provision was made for their sustenance, in the shape of a baked clay pipe leading vertically down from ground level; through this channel libations could be trickled down into a receptacle or pit in the ground below, to which the dead could have access through a window cut in the wall of the vault.[9] Thus they could be supplied with food and drink. Mention of the *rp'um* in the alphabetic texts[10] has suggested the Rephaim, the ancestral shades of Hebrew tradition,[11] but *rp'um* appear in the administrative texts to be priests,[12] and may have been members of a clan of noble descent with special ritual functions.[13]

Stelae erected in the temples by devotees, and figurines of bronze or terracotta found in a number of sites, appear to depict Canaanite deities with their several attributes. The horned head-

---

[1] §IV, 20, 5 f.   [2] §V, 77, 94; §IV, 21, 5 f.; §IV, 44, vol. 6, 91 ff., 165 ff.
[3] §V, 83, vol. III–IV, pl. 315; §V, 44, pl. 47.   [4] §IV, 54, 256 ff., pl. LIX A–C.
[5] §IV, 19, 158 f.; *C.A.H.* II³, pt. 1, p. 522. *Cf.* §V, 72, 118.
[6] §V, 57, 41 f.   [7] §V, 25, 55 = *Aqhat*, II, vi, ll. 33 ff.
[8] §IV, 44, vol. 1, 77 ff. and pls. XVI, XVII. See Plate 137.
[9] §IV, 35, 49, fig. 11 and pl. 38.
[10] §IV, 18, 161, texts 121–4; §V, 25, 9f., 67 ff.
[11] §IV, 35, 72.   [12] §V, 47, 154.   [13] *Ibid.* 92 f.; §V, 45.

dress worn by some of these figures derives from the tiara of the Mesopotamian gods;[1] others reflect Anatolian influence in their pointed helmets, dagger worn at the waist, or shoes upturned in the Hittite manner.[2] The stance and proportions of many of the figures recall Egyptian prototypes and the elaborate crowns worn by some deities also derive from those worn by Egyptian gods.[3] A few of the stelae were dedicated to Canaanite deities by Egyptians visiting or resident in Syria or Palestine; unlike the purely local stelae, which are usually anepigraphic, these usually bear hieroglyphic inscriptions which identify not only the worshipper but also the deity portrayed; it is thus possible to distinguish the attributes of Resheph, the Syrian war-god, who brandishes a fenestrated axe in one hand and holds shield and spear in the other,[4] and of Mekal, the Annihilator, the local god of Beth-shan,[5] who like Resheph wears the horns of a wild goat on his brow in place of the royal uraeus of Egypt.[6] His tall helmet with streamers and his thick Syrian beard proclaim his nationality, but he proffers the Egyptian symbol of life and prosperity to his worshipper. Similarly, 'Anath, Lady of Heaven, Mistress of all the gods', wears in Beth-shan a typically Egyptian crown of high feathers.[7] The Egyptian royal scribe Mami, 'Overseer of the House of Silver', who at Ugarit dedicated a fine stela to Seth of Ṣapuna,[8] was a worshipper of the local Ba'al Ṣᵉphōn, the personification of Mount Khazi (Mons Casius),[9] whose peak, thrusting through cloud on the northern horizon, was understandably thought to be the seat of the storm-god.[10]

Ba'al is the central figure of many of the Ugaritic poems, the majority of which concern the loves, rivalries and wars of the various deities of the West Semitic pantheon, called 'the assembly of the children of El'.[11] In spite of difficulties of interpretation such as those already mentioned, the fragmentary nature of many of the tablets, and consequent uncertainty concerning the sequence of fragments (so that the order of episodes in some of the myths cannot with any certainty be established), these poems are in-

[1] §iv, 44, vol. 1, 128 ff., pls. 28–30; vol. 2, 83 ff., pl. 20, 121 ff., pls. 23, 24.
[2] §iv, 44, vol. 2, pl. xxii. See Plate 138 (a).   [3] E.g. §iv, 44, vol. 2, pl. 22.
[4] §v, 44, pl. 19; §v, 12, 638.   [5] §v, 62, frontispiece.   [6] §v, 44, 52.
[7] Ibid. pl. 23; §v, 62, pl. xxxv, 3.
[8] §iv, 44, vol. 1, 39 ff., 40 fig. 30; §iv, 36, 10 f. and pl. 6. See Plate 101.
[9] The modern Jebel Aqra'.
[10] §iv, 55, 178, 182; §v, 28, 5 ff.; §v, 25, 21, n. 1; §v, 51, vol. 2, 217 ff.; §iv, 41, 203; §iv, 44, vol. 5, 557 ff. = RS.24.245. See §iv, 14, vol. 4, 53 ff. for the theory that Ba'al Ṣᵉphōn was the head of the state pantheon, the counterpart of Amun in Egypt.   [11] §v, 21, 66; Baal, ii, ii, 13; iv, i, 3.

comparably rich sources of information about the religious beliefs and ritual practices of the people of Ugarit in the second millennium B.C. They leave the impression, moreover, that the tradition they embody is not exclusively local, but rather one in which the whole of Canaan may at one time or another have participated, since many of the deities who form the *dramatis personae* of the myths are known to have been worshipped in a number of cult centres from Mount Casius in the north to Egypt, from the Mediterranean coast to the banks of the Euphrates.[1]

Chief among these was the god Baʻal himself, whose worship was widespread, indeed universal, in Canaan.[2] In the Ugaritic mythological texts, he appears as a warrior god, 'the Prince, Lord of Earth', and 'the Victor (Aliyan)'. As 'Rider on the Clouds', he is the storm-god of the mountains, manifest in lightning and thunder, who sends rain and snow on the earth[3] and causes the growth of vegetation. His daughters are Mist and Dew,[4] and his father, Dagan, the personification of corn;[5] elsewhere, however, Baʻal is said to be the son of El.[6] A well-cut stela found in the temple of Baʻal at Ras Shamra without doubt depicts the god holding a thunderbolt in one hand and lightning in the other.[7] On his head he wears a horned helmet, symbol of divinity throughout the Near East and, in its peculiar North Syrian form, recalling the bull, the embodiment of male potency, to which Baʻal is often likened.[8] His feet tread the mountain tops. The name Baʻal means 'Lord', and the local gods of individual city states of Canaan were often referred to as 'the Baʻal of City X'. Some had special epithets: Melqart (King of the City), for instance, was the Baʻal of Tyre. As the lord *par excellence* of the early Semitic peoples of North Syria, Hadad the storm-god is identified in the texts with Baʻal,[9] and it has been suggested that the worship of Baʻal may have originated in the old Amorite cult of Hadad centred in Mari, Tirqa and Aleppo.[10]

The high deity of the Ugaritic pantheon, however, was not Baʻal but El, sometimes called *Luṭpan*, the 'Kindly One',[11] who

---

[1] §v, 2, 71 f.; §v, 21, 68 f.; A, 2.   [2] §v, 50; §v, 30, 80 ff.; §v, 27, 362 f.
[3] *Baʻal*, v, i, ll. 6–9; A, 1, 280 f.   [4] *Baʻal*, i, v, l. 10; ii, i, l. 11.
[5] §v, 25, 154; §v, 27, 364; §v, 23, 746; §v, 2, 74; otherwise §v, 21, 79 f.
[6] *Aqhat*, ii, iv, l. 28; §v, 25, 6, n. 3, 13, n. 2.
[7] §iv, 44, vol. 2, 121 ff., pls. xxiii, xxiv; §iv, 35, 68; A, 32. See Plate 100. A text describing Baʻal's enthronement (A, 13 = *RS*.24.245) calls his sceptre 'the tree of lightning'.
[8] §v, 25, 19, 117, n. 3; §iv, 20, 44; §iv, 44, vol. 4, 45; A, 31.
[9] §v, 25, 10, 71 ff.; §iv, 18, 258.   [10] §v, 50, 136; §iv, 20, 35 f.
[11] §v, 25, 159; §v, 60, 25, 44 f.; A, 24, 15 ff.

is described as an old man with white hair and beard.[1] He was believed to live in or upon a mountain, at a place where 'the two rivers join the two oceans'.[2] His epithets 'creator of creatures' and 'father of mankind' proclaim his function.[3] Most of the other deities are counted among his progeny and he entertains his sons, the seventy gods, at a banquet in his palace.[4] In this creative aspect he is called 'the bull El'.[5] In spite of his pre-eminent position, however, he plays little part in the myths and is a somewhat remote and mysterious figure;[6] he is not invoked in treaties or referred to in texts other than literary, and no priest or temple of his is mentioned in the administrative tablets. El may perhaps be the god represented by a relief, in rather clumsy style, found at Ras Shamra in the level of the fourteenth century B.C., which depicts an elderly bearded figure seated on a throne and footstool of Egyptian type and wearing a crown which derives from the curious crown of horns and feathers worn by Egyptian divinities and known as the *atef*.[7] Over his head, and that of the king who performs a ceremony of offering before him, the winged sun-disc hovers. The central figure in a group of bronze statuettes found together[8] wears a similar *atef* crown; he is an elderly god, seated between two identical youthful Ba'als. The fourth figure of the group is, significantly, that of a bull. The iconography is again Egyptian: the bull wears between his horns a sun-disc engraved with the hieroglyph for 'life' (ʿnkh).

The question of the relationship between Ba'al and El has been much discussed. Ba'al is a youthful, vigorous god, and a considerable part of the cycle of myths concerning him is devoted to the building of his temple, since he alone of the great gods has no fitting abode.[9] Does this point to a comparatively late introduction of the cult of the storm-god from elsewhere?[10] A theory has been put forward that the Ugaritic texts contain hints of a struggle, the account of which may one day be unearthed, between El and Ba'al, a struggle[11] which finally ended in the victory of the young god over the old (just as in Hurrian mythology Kumarbi was replaced by the storm-god, the Babylonian Enlil

---

[1] *Aqhat*, II, i, l. 25; *Ba'al*, II, v. l. 4; etc.

[2] §v, 77, 110 f. Pope, who translates 'the two deeps' (§v, 60, 72 ff.), suggests Afqa at the source of the Adonis river. Cf. A, 24, 106 ff.

[3] *Aqhat*, II, i, l. 25; *Ba'al*, II, ii, l. 11; iii, l. 31; etc.; §IV, 20, 54 ff.; §v, 21, 73 ff.

[4] §IV, 44, vol. 5, 545 ff.; §v, 78, 111 = *RS*.24.258.

[5] §v, 21, 73; §v, 60, 35 ff.; A, 29; A, 32, 129 f., 161.   [6] §v, 60, 28.

[7] §IV, 35, pl. 31; §v, 65, 213; §v, 60, 46. See Plate 138(*b*).

[8] A, 31, 1 ff. and pls. 11f.   [9] §v, 58, 5 ff., 52 ff., 84; A, 7, 58 ff.   [10] §IV, 35, 8.

[11] §v, 50, 75 ff., 86 ff., 130 ff.; §IV, 21, 58 f.

gave place to Marduk, and Kronos was deposed by Zeus),[1] and that El was thereafter banished to the nether world.[2] There is no doubt, however, that, at the time when the majority of the Ugaritic texts were composed, El was still one of the high gods.

It must be admitted that there are reasons for supposing that a gap of some centuries separates the composition of the texts and their copying or redaction in the fourteenth century B.C. The hierarchy of the gods who play the chief roles in the myths which survive does not fully correspond with the pantheon of fourteenth- and thirteenth-century Ugarit as it may be compiled from lists of some fifty or sixty deities drawn up by the priestly scribes for ritual purposes,[3] and from some hundreds of personal names compounded with those of deities, found in the administrative and economic texts.[4] Babylonian and Hurrian deities, who played an important part in the daily life of Ugarit and Alalakh,[5] are absent from the myths. Dagan, who is mentioned in the literary texts only as Ba'al's father,[6] was accorded the honour of having one of the two major temples in the heart of the city dedicated to him.[7] Similarly, the Syrian god Resheph[8] is rarely mentioned in the poems: once, in the legend of Keret, his role as a god of pestilence is emphasized,[9] and in a fragment he is called Resheph the Archer, referring to his warlike character.[10] On the strength of such evidence it has been claimed that the mythological poems of Ugarit are of very ancient origin, some perhaps antedating the second millennium altogether,[11] or at least that they were some hundreds of years old at the time when our copies were made by King Niqmaddu's scribes.[12]

Of the leading position of Ba'al at Ugarit throughout the period covered by the textual and archaeological remains there is, at any rate, no doubt. His was the largest and richest temple in the city;[13] oaths were sworn before the king in his name.[14] In the myth which is called after him, he vanquishes his enemies. One of

---

[1] §v, 21, 77, n. 4; §v, 60, 29 ff. [2] §v, 60, 72 ff.

[3] §v, 82, 170; §v, 65, 214; §iv, 18, 132, text 9; §iv, 44, vol. 5, 42 ff.; A, 5; §v, 56, 82 f. = RS.20.24.

[4] §v, 73. [5] §v, 52, 152 f.; §v, 82, 70; §iv, 18, 139, text 50.

[6] §v, 25, 31, n. 1. [7] §v, 64, 156 ff., pls. 31, 36; §v, 21, 78 ff.

[8] §v, 54; §v, 21, 84 f.; §v, 46, 28. [9] §v, 25, 28 f. = Keret, i, i, 1.19.

[10] §iv, 30, vol. 2, 5 = RS.15.134, l. 3. [11] §v, 5, 175; §v, 8, 38.

[12] §v, 25, 115 = Ba'al, iii, vi, l. 16 ff. See also A, 24, 143 ff. for the view that Ba'al-Hadad was introduced by Amorites in the nineteenth or eighteenth centuries B.C., replacing the Canaanite El.

[13] §v, 64, 154 ff. and pl. 36.

[14] §iv, 30, 84 = RS.16.143, l. 27; 76 = RS.16.144, l. 9 f.

these enemies is Yam, Beloved of El, the personification of the ocean which loomed understandably large in the myths of sea-bordered Canaan. The taming of the ocean of chaos may be mirrored in Ba‘al's defeat of Prince Yam in single combat,[1] and the latter's epithet 'Judge River' perhaps shows him in the role of arbiter of the destiny of human souls[2] and reminds us, too, that the ordeal by water was an accepted form of trial in criminal cases.[3] The same poetic cycle relates Ba‘al's struggle with his antithesis Mōt, the god of dryness and death,[4] to whom he is for a time forced to submit, with disastrous consequences to the fertility of earth and its creatures,[5] and his subsequent return from the underworld and reinstatement. Once explained as part of an allegorical drama of the annual death of vegetation and its re-awakening, enacted to ensure the continuation of the cycle of sowing and harvest,[6] the episode perhaps rather emphasizes the function of Ba‘al as the rain-god, bringer of fertility;[7] while he is temporarily vanquished by drought,[8] 'Athtar, the god of springs and irrigation waters, attempts to take over, but is too small (inadequate[9]) and Ba‘al must be revived by his sister, the virgin 'Anath. In another part of the poem 'Anath appears in the guise of a goddess of battle, familiar from her Egyptian mani-festations:[10] like the Indian Kali, she revels in destruction and wades in blood.[11] A fragment tells of her battle with the dragon Tannin.[12] In a milder role, as mother of the child-king, she may be depicted in a striking ivory panel from the palace of Ugarit.[13]

Ba‘al's consort 'Athtarat, or 'Ashtoreth, the West Semitic form of Ishtar,[14] appears in various guises at Ugarit and Alalakh. As 'Ashtoreth of the Field,[15] she was, like 'Anath, a goddess of battle, and thus rides on horseback in Egypt, as the patron of horses and chariots.[16] Ishtar of Khurri is invoked in Ugarit[17] and the same aspect of the goddess was paramount at Alalakh.[18] In

[1] §v, 25, 12 ff., 20 f. =Ba‘al, III*A; §v, 38, 123; §v, 50, 39 ff.; §v, 47, 71.

[2] §v, 25, n. 7.

[3] §IV, 30, vol. 3, 311 ff.=RS.15.10, l. 3; §v, 11, vol. 2, 339; §v, 42, 99; §v, 8, 19 f.

[4] §v, 21, 81 f.; §v, 38, 154 ff.; A, 7, 81 ff.; A, 18; A, 33, 62.

[5] §v, 25, 111 ff.=Ba‘al, III, ii, l. 17* ff.; III, iv, l. 1 ff.; cf. §v, 25, 10, 71 ff.

[6] §v, 49, 17 f.   [7] A, 7, 65 ff.   [8] §v, 43, 3 ff.   [9] §v, 25, 20 ff.; §v, 21, 88 f.

[10] §v, 12, 37 f.; §v, 61, 76 ff.   [11] §v, 25, 14; §v, 17; §v, 74, 183; A, 9.

[12] §v, 78, 187 ff.   [13] §v, 18, 54 ff.; see Plate 136(b).

[14] §v, 21, 87; §v, 1, 246.

[15] §IV, 30, vol. 4, 122 =RS.17.352, l. 12; §IV, 26, 104, n. 18.

[16] §v, 12, 55 ff.; A, 3, 116 f.; A, 26; see C.A.H. II³, pt. 1, p. 482.

[17] §IV, 30, vol. 3, 171 =RS.16.173, ll. 4–5.

[18] §v, 83, 16 f.; §IV, 30, vol. 4, 52 =RS.17.340, l. 20.

her astral form she personified the planet Venus, as did the Babylonian Ishtar,[1] and her male counterpart 'Athtar, who, as we have
seen, aspired to the kingship during Ba'al's absence, appears in
South Arabia later as a stellar deity.[2] He is called the son of
another goddess, Athirat, or Asherah, who, as the wife of El and
Mistress of the Gods, plays a more important part in the myths
than her spouse or her son.[3] Her epithet 'Dame Athirat of the
Sea'[4] emphasizes her connexion with the coastal cities: she is
called Athirat of Tyre[5] and at Sidon was known as Elat, the female
aspect of El.[6] Qadesh, the Holy One, who is depicted on stelae
from Egypt[7] and on a pendant from Ras Shamra[8] as a naked
goddess standing on the back of a lion, may represent an aspect of
one of these goddesses, whose personalities and attributes merged
and interchanged against a background of common belief.
Which, if any, of them is represented by the numerous crudely
formed plaques and pendants found in Syrian and Palestinian
sites[9] cannot be determined.[10] The emphasis placed upon the
female parts suggests that they were amulets worn by women to
aid fertility or protect in childbirth. On a plaque from Alalakh,
the nude goddess holds in each hand a dove, symbol in Mesopotamia of the goddess Ishtar.[11]

The importance of Horon, god of the underworld, is attested
in Canaanite place-names and personal names.[12] In Egyptian texts
he is equated with the god Horus, and it is possible that figurines
of hawks found at Minet el-Beidha represent this god.[13] His
adventures are described in a large mythological text recently discovered, in which his home is said to be the City of the East.[14] The
chief role in this text, which appears to be an incantation against
snake-bite,[15] is played by the goddess Shapash, 'the lamp of the
gods',[16] who personified the sun as did her counterpart Yerakh,
'the Illuminator of Heaven', the moon—while Kushukh, their
own moon-god, was invoked by the Hurrians in Ugarit.[17] Divine

---

[1] §v, 16, 57.   [2] §v, 21, 85; §v, 15, 57.   [3] §v, 59, 38 f.; §v, 1, 42.
[4] §v, 25, 93 = Ba'al, ii, i, l. 19, etc.   [5] §v, 25, 33 = Keret, i, iv, ll. 35, 38.
[6] Ibid. ll. 36, 39.   [7] §v, 12, 362 f.; C.A.H. ii[3], pt. 1, p. 483.
[8] §iv, 44, vol. 2, 36, fig. 10.
[9] §v, 3; §v, 61; §v, 11, vol. 1, 401, fig. 149; vol. 2, 395.   [10] §v, 30, 79.
[11] §iv, 55, 247, pl. liv, no. o; §v, 10, 42.
[12] §v, 2, 81; §v, 21, 82 f.; §v, 35, 61 f.; §iv, 44, vol. 2, vii f.
[13] §iv, 44, vol. 1, 32, fig. 24; §v, 44, 177 f.
[14] §v, 79, 108; §v, 65, 213, Abb. 33.
[15] §iv, 44, vol. 5, 564 ff.; §v, 78, 106 = RS.24.244; A, 6.   [16] §v, 16.
[17] §iv, 30, vol. 3, 316. For the Hurrian pantheon at Ugarit, see E. Laroche in
§iv, 44, vol. 5, 518 ff.

pairs such as Dawn and Sunset[1] (or Morning Star and Evening Star[2]) and Mist and Dew[3] bear the stamp of mythopoeic imagination and reflect, too, that deeply rooted love of symmetry which was manifest in literature as well as in art. So, too, some beings have composite names and are treated in the poems sometimes as one deity, and sometimes as two: such are Gupan-and-Ugar, the messenger of the gods, apparently a personification of vine yards and fields,[4] Qodesh-and-Amurr, a compound perhaps of the separate gods of Qadesh and Amurru, by a process of syncretization,[5] and the craftsman god Kathir-and-Khasis, 'Skilful and Clever',[6] who comes to the aid of the gods whenever something is to be fashioned with skill, and was said to hail from far-off Caphtor,[7] an indication that the people of North Syria recognized the debt owed by their craftsmen to the inspiration and techniques of Minoan Crete.[8] He must be the Khusor to whom Philo, quoting Sanchuniathon, ascribes the invention of iron.[9]

The fragmentary text containing the myth of Aqhat, son of King Danel,[10] again contains the theme of dying vegetation.[11] At the instigation of 'Anath, who covets his wonderful bow, Aqhat is murdered and the bow shattered. Drought follows, the crops fail, and Danel rides about his kingdom seeking the cause of the disaster, aided by his daughter Pughat (Perfume):

'Hear, O Pughat, who carriest the waters on thy shoulders,
Who sprinklest the dew on the barley, who knowest
The courses of the stars; saddle the he-ass,
Yoke the donkey, put on my trappings of silver,
My saddle-cover of gold.' . . .
Forthwith she saddled the he-ass,
Forthwith she yoked the donkey; forthwith
She lifted up her father (and) put him on the back of the he-ass,

[1] §v, 25, 22 f., 121 ff.; §v, 21, 91; A, 12, 7 ff.
[2] §v, 36, 70 ff. Cf. A, 5, 281 f.
[3] §v, 25, 85. Sometimes Ba'al has a third daughter, perhaps 'Earth'. Aistleitner (§v, 1, 254) associates *Pdry* rather with the thunderbolt of Ba'al, and Neiman (A, 23) with lightning.   [4] §v, 25, 146, n. 26; *Ba'al*, II, vii, l. 54.
[5] §v, 1, 26 no. 289, though J. R. Kupper (*L'iconographie du dieu Amurru*, Acad. royale de Belgique, Lettres LV/1, 1961) doubts the authenticity of Amurru as a god of a city or region. Alternatively 'Holy and Blessed' (§v, 30, 787).
[6] §v, 38, 154 ff.; §v, 21, 81 f.; §v, 47, 97.
[7] §v, 25, 91 = *Ba'al*, v, vi, ll. 14–16. He is also said to come from *Hkpt* (*Ba'al*, v, VI, 13), possibly Egypt (from Egyptian *ht-k3-pth*, Memphis; §v, 47, 137), but perhaps rather a name of Crete, or some place in Crete (§v, 25, 169).
[8] §v, 34, vol. I = Eusebius, I, 10, 11.
[9] §v, 25, 12 n. 1 and 169; §v, 47, 95; A, 8, 35 f.
[10] §v, 25, 5 ff.; 48 ff.; §v, 72, 125 ff.; 186 ff.; 217 ff.   [11] §v, 47, 84 ff.

On the fairest part of the back of the donkey.
Danel approached, he went round his parched land(?)
That he might descry green corn in the parched land(?), might descry
Green corn in the scrub, might embrace the green corn
And kiss (it saying): 'May, ah! may green corn shoot up in the parched
    ground(?), may green corn shoot in the scrub
(Blasted) with heat, may the hand of Aqhat the Hero
Gather thee (and) put thee within the granary!'[1]

Aqhat's body is found and mourned for seven years, and Pughat girds on her armour and sets out to avenge her brother. The end of the story, which is lost, must have told of the resurrection of the dead hero and the consequent revival of vegetation upon earth.[2]

Another of the texts, entitled by the scribal copyist 'Of Keret',[3] purports to relate the deeds of a hero or demigod. As the poem opens, Keret, king of 'well-watered Khubur', is bemoaning the loss of his wife, the destruction of his sons and the ruin of his palace. El appears to him in a vision and promises him success. In obedience to the god's instructions, Keret sacrifices to the gods and prepares a great army, which overruns the countryside. On the third day's march he comes to a large shrine where the goddesses of Tyre and Sidon promise him success. The following day he reaches Udum, whose King Pabil[4] attempts to buy him off; the latter insists only that he shall be given Pabil's beautiful daughter Ḥuriya to wife, for El has promised that she will bear him sons. The request is granted, and Keret, with divine blessing, begets seven sons and eight daughters. Later in the tale he falls sick, and at a feast prepared by his queen the nobles of Khubur are bidden to pray for him; bread, wine and oil, which depend on the king's well-being, begin to fail. One of the king's sons, Yaṣṣib, supposing the sickness to be mortal, attempts to seize the throne, but the king is restored by the intervention of El and threatens his rebellious son with the vengeance of the gods.

The latter half of the story follows a familiar pattern but the opening narrative has been interpreted as embodying the memory of some historical invasion of Edom and the Negeb by an army from North Syria.[5] The names Keret and Pabil, however, have not so far been found in any inscription or text and the theory, in whole or in part, has been rejected by most scholars.[6] Alterna-

---

[1] §v, 25, 61 = *Aqhat*, I, ii, ll. 1–5, 8–18.   [2] §v, 25, 8.

[3] §v, 25, 2 ff.; 28 ff.; §v, 39; §v, 41, 142 ff.; §v, 43, 66 ff.; §v, 46; §v, 70; §v, 71.

[4] §v, 25, 5, n. 7.   [5] §v, 70; §v, 51, vol. 2, 105 ff.; §v, 49, 38 ff; §v, 52, 147 f.

[6] §v, 25, 5; §v, 47, 14 f.; §v, 39, 6 ff. Albright (A, 3, 103 and n. 19) suggests that the name Keret may be the Indo-Aryan *Kirta*, the ancestor of the Mitannian royal house.

tively, the story has been interpreted as a social myth pertaining to the rise of the dynasty of Ugarit.[1]

The language of this earliest Canaanite literature is full of metaphor and poetic imagery.[2] Many of the stylistic conventions of later epic poetry are employed.[3] Statements are made twice or three times in parallel terms for greater emphasis:

> Ba'al opened a window in the mansion,
> A lattice in the midst of the palace,
> He opened a skylight in the roof.[4]

The effect of emphasis is frequently achieved by the cumulative use of numbers in progression;[5] the poet thus describes the conquests of Ba'al:

> He did seize six and sixty
> Cities, seven and seventy towns,
> He became lord of eight and eighty,
> Lord of nine and ninety.[6]

Similarly, the countless army of King Keret is described as

> Going by thousands like rain,
> By tens of thousands like drops of rain.[7]

Set phrases recur, as they do in Hebrew literature of the Old Testament[8] and in the Homeric poems.[9] The close similarity between the phraseology of the Ugaritic texts and that used in certain poetic passages of the Pentateuch, the Song of Deborah, for instance, and some Psalms,[10] has led some to suggest an early, perhaps even second millennium, date for the latter.[11] Similarly, there is reason to think that the epics of Homer derive their inspiration, and even part of their text, from an ancient tradition, oral or written, of Mycenaean heroic poetry, a tradition which may go back at least to the fourteenth century B.C.[12] Mycenaean merchants at the court of the kings of Ugarit, must have listened to the priestly musicians singing their lays of Ba'al and of 'Anath and Astarte. Such contacts, in countries throughout the eastern Mediterranean, gave birth to that interchange of forms and themes which was the literary heritage of the Late Bronze Age.[13]

[1] §v, 46, 3 ff.; §v, 47, 14 f.　　[2] §iv, 18, 102 ff.; §v, 1, 9 f.; A, 15, 111 ff.
[3] §v, 50, 80 ff.; see below, pp. 566 ff.
[4] §v, 25, 101 = Ba'al, ii, vii, ll. 25–28.　　[5] §v, 47, 211 f.; §v, 1, 11; §iv, 18, 104.
[6] §v, 25, 101 = Ba'al, ii, vii, ll. 9–12.　　[7] Keret, i, iv, ll. 17–18.
[8] §v, 2, 15 f.; §iv, 18, 108; §v, 47, 189 ff.; §v, 50, 80 ff.; see below, p. 566.
[9] §v, 14, 81 ff., 91 ff.; §v, 42, 102 ff.
[10] §v, 38, 73 ff.; §v, 29, 134 ff.; §iv, 18, 114 f.; §iv, 2, 23.
[11] §v, 7, 27 ff.; §v, 8, 38.　　　　　　[12] §v, 13, 14, 19 ff., 33; §iv, 80, 37, 66.
[13] A, 8, 44 f.; A, 14.

CHAPTER XXI(c)

TROY

VI. TROY VII

Under this designation Dörpfeld grouped two layers of very different character, and called them VII 1 and VII 2 respectively (our VII*a* and VII*b*). See Fig. 1.

Settlement VII*a* represents a direct continuation after the earthquake of the culture that flourished in Troy VI. The fortress walls were repaired where needed and most of the earlier gateways were re-used. Inside the citadel the old streets were cleared and new houses were erected; they were built in a characteristic masonry that, along with rough unworked material, re-utilized many squared blocks that had obviously been shaken down from the structures of the Sixth Settlement. The houses themselves, for the most part small, were numerous; they were crowded closely together, often with party walls, and they seem to have filled the whole area inside the fortification, where they were superposed over the earlier buildings, as well as the considerable spaces that had previously been left open. Another distinctive feature is the presence in almost every house of large *pithoi* or storage jars: ranging in number from one or two to eight or ten or even twenty, they were sunk deeply beneath the floors so that the mouth, covered by a stone slab, projected only an inch or two above the ground.[1]

The minor objects and pottery clearly attest a continuity in all branches of craftsmanship. Grey Minyan Ware, for the most part indistinguishable from that of Troy VI, occurs in abundance; alongside it are found in large quantities Red and Tan Wares closely resembling those of the preceding period, though the Tan Ware especially is often coated with a distinctive orange-tan glaze. Some changes in the pot shapes may also be noted, though the repertory as a whole conforms to that of Troy VI. Imported Mycenaean pottery in the style of Late Helladic IIIa still occurs, but that of IIIb is much more common, being found along with Cypriote White Slip II Ware. The incidence of Mycenaean imports, however, has fallen off greatly since the time of Troy VI,

---

* An original version of this chapter was published in fascicle 1 in 1964.
[1] See Plate 139.

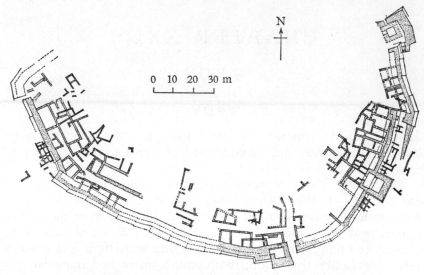

Fig. 1. Buildings of Troy VII. (From C. W. Blegen, C. G. Boulter, J. L. Caskey and M. Rawson, *Troy* IV 1 (Princeton, 1958), fig. 321.)

and the number of imitations in local Trojan fabric has grown proportionately. The evidence seems to indicate that relations with the Aegean had lost much of their intensity and importance. No objects were found that could be identified as importations from Central Anatolia.

The layer of accumulated deposit of Period VII*a* had an average thickness of little more than 0·50 m.; but in streets and certain other places debris from the final destruction was heaped up to a height of 1–1·5 m. In some houses two successive floor levels were noted. One, or at the most two, generations would seem to be a reasonable estimate of the duration of the settlement. It came to its end in a devastating conflagration that swept over the entire citadel and reduced all the houses to ruins. Under the masses of stones that fell into the streets inside the South Gate were found remnants of the skeletons of two human victims of the catastrophe, which has the appearance of the handiwork of man. The crowding together of a great number of small houses within the fortress and the installation of innumerable huge storage jars to lay up a supply of provisions are factors that suggest preparations for a siege, and the final holocaust was the usual accompaniment of the capture, sacking and burning of an ancient town. The general agreement of this evidence with the accounts preserved in Greek tradition cannot safely be disregarded: if a Troy of Priam, besieged and taken by an Agamemnon, ever actually existed in fact, it must be identified with the settlement called VII *a*.

The exact date of the capture and destruction of Troy by the Achaeans has not been definitely fixed in terms of absolute years. The Greek chronographers, who based their conclusions on computations of genealogies, reached many different results, ranging from the fourteenth century through the thirteenth and on down to 1184 B.C., as calculated by Eratosthenes. The latter date has been more or less tacitly accepted by numerous scholars. Archaeological research has now shown that the event took place at a time when imported pottery in the style of Mycenaean III b was in common use on the site, though the style of III a had not yet been wholly abandoned. The fashion of Mycenaean III c was still altogether unknown. These observations give a plausible fixed point in the sequence of ceramic styles, but to convert it into a specific year B.C. is another matter on which one finds no close agreement among the specialists. The evidence from contacts with Egypt is still, particularly for the later Mycenaean phases, woefully inadequate. There is, however, a fairly general belief that the style of Mycenaean III a prevailed through most, if not all, of the fourteenth century, whereas that of III b flourished during the greater part of the thirteenth century, coming to its end shortly before 1200 B.C. If this view is approximately right, the fall of Troy and the end of Settlement VII *a* should be placed about 1250 B.C.,[1] coinciding with the estimate of Herodotus. In any event the expedition against Troy must surely have been carried out about the middle of the ceramic phase III b when Mycenaean Greece stood at the height of its wealth as well as of its political and military power.

In Settlement VII *b*, which seems to have been built without an interval after the fire, two successive strata have been recognized. The objects recovered from the lower stratum (VII *b* 1) make it clear that some part of the Trojan population survived the disaster and in their reconstructed houses they continued to maintain the same culture that had flourished in Period VII *a*. This is especially evident in the pottery which in all respects carries on the local tradition of the past. Grey Minyan, Red-washed and Tan Wares continue to be made in large quantities and in forms which, except in small but distinctive variations, can scarcely be differentiated from what had gone before. Exactly how long this phase lasted has not been determined, but it can hardly have been less than a generation and may have been more.

[1] For a later date, *c.* 1200 B.C., see *C.A.H.* 1³, pt. 1, p. 246.

The pottery found in strata of Troy VII*b* 1 offers a little evidence for sequence dating. The imported Mycenaean ware includes some pieces in the style of Furumark's category IIIb and others that must be assigned to IIIc. It thus appears that the settlement overlapped the phase during which the ceramic change from IIIb to IIIc was working itself out. This carries us down, in accordance with most current views, to a time near the end of the thirteenth century.

The upper stratum of Troy VII*b* reveals an abrupt change in culture which unmistakably signifies the arrival of a new people on the scene. The most conspicuous innovation makes its appearance in the pottery, known as *Buckelkeramik*, or Knobbed Ware, a rude, handmade, black polished fabric in a wholly new repertory of shapes. In broad general lines the closest analogy for this pottery is to be found in the Late Bronze Age in Hungary, and it is from that region that many archaeologists believe the migration to have started which brought the *Buckelkeramik* folk to Asia Minor, probably by way of Thrace. Certainty has not yet been reached regarding details of this problem, nor is the extent of the diffusion, if any, which this rude culture attained in Anatolia yet adequately known.

The minor objects which come from the stratum of VII*b* 2 at Troy also exhibit a break with the past of the site; and the architecture, too, has a stamp of its own. Many small houses were built throughout the citadel, and a fairly consistent feature in the masonry is the setting of rough orthostates along the lower edges of the walls. In some parts at least the old fortification walls seem to have remained standing above ground and were evidently re-used; in other places the settlement now spread out over the earlier walls.

Not all the previous inhabitants were exterminated. Some pottery in Grey Minyan and Tan Wares still continues to be made, and this fact suggests that there were survivors familiar with the old culture.

A few sherds of imported Mycenaean ware of the Granary Class have been found: they indicate that some relations were still maintained with the Aegean, and they also give ground for concluding that Settlement VII*b* 2, following immediately after VII*b* 1, continued to exist for some time, presumably lasting on well into the twelfth century while the pottery style of Mycenaean IIIc prevailed. How much longer the settlement endured has not been ascertained. It was destroyed in a conflagration, perhaps in connexion with the disorders that attended the long and troubled transition from the Late Bronze Age to the Iron Age.

CHAPTER XXII(a)

THE EXPANSION OF MYCENAEAN CIVILIZATION

I. THE ECLIPSE OF THEBES

THE destruction of the Minoan palace centres about 1400 B.C., whatever its cause,[1] left the leadership of the Aegean world thenceforth to Mainland Greece; and for nearly two centuries the Mycenaean civilization was free to develop and enjoy a remarkable prosperity, founded in part on the heritage of Minoan culture which it had already absorbed, in part on new opportunities, vigorously exploited, of commercial and cultural relations with all parts of the eastern Mediterranean. The chronology of the period[2] is based on the typological sequence of Mycenaean pottery styles;[3] and that a reliable dating sequence can be established is due to the remarkable degree of uniformity of style throughout the area in which Mycenaean pottery occurs, a uniformity obviously bound up with the frequent and easy communications that characterize the period. Absolute dating, in turn, depends on the occurrence of Mycenaean pottery in datable contexts in Egypt, Palestine, and Syria, which is evidence of regular traffic with those parts. In these two centuries of maturity Mycenaean Greece becomes, as we shall see, part of a much larger cultural area, comprising the whole eastern Mediterranean, and exists on virtually the same level as the older civilizations in that area. It is, until well into the thirteenth century, a period of prosperity and of peace. There is no observable major event, natural or political, that separates Myc. III a from Myc. III b; the two phases may be treated as a continuum. Some hostile encounters abroad the Mycenaean Greeks must surely have had; but we shall find but little trace of them either in the written history of their neighbours or in the archaeological record. In Crete the destruction of the palaces (oddly, if Mycenaeans were the destroyers) is not followed by any obvious or considerable signs of Mycenaean settlement;

---

* An original version of this chapter was published as fascicle 26 in 1964, the present chapter includes revisions made in 1970.

[1] See *C.A.H.* II³, pt. 1, pp. 558 and 656.

[2] See *C.A.H.* I³, pt. 1, p. 245.   [3] See Plate 144.

indeed the divergence between Late Minoan III and Late Helladic III is much greater than between Late Helladic II and the last phase of the palace at Cnossus. In Rhodes, though Trianda may have been destroyed by Mycenaeans, actual Mycenaean settlement[1] had begun before this. At Miletus, however, on the coast of Asia Minor, the first Mycenaean pottery, of III a style, occurs above the destruction by fire of the preceding Minoan settlement;[2] we have here, perhaps, early evidence of the increased freedom and strength of Mycenae.

In the history of events, then, it is primarily the destruction of the Cretan palaces that marks off Late Helladic II from Late Helladic III. Yet the period of maturity was not achieved without some further adjustments at home, some of which involved hostilities between the various kingdoms of Greece, to judge from tradition, though these conflicts are but doubtfully tied to the archaeological data. We have already seen in L.H. II the growth of a united Argolis, with its palace-capital established by Perseus at Mycenae;[3] of Laconia we hear little as yet; Pylus to the southwest is a formidable kingdom, though we cannot be sure for this period where its capital lay: the beehive tombs of Kakovatos imply a palace site in that area,[4] and we know that Messenian Pylus (Ano Englianos) had at least a citadel, and so probably a ruler's palace, by L.H. I;[5] Elis, the home of Pelops and his line, completes the picture of the Peloponnese, for the more rugged areas of Achaea and Arcadia were not sufficiently productive or populous to be of political importance. Attica we may think of as a separate state, shortly to achieve greater prosperity now that it is free of the Minoan yoke.[6]

Further north the most important state is the city of Cadmus, the later Thebes, so important indeed as to be a rival of Mycenae for the supremacy of Greece. Its eminence at this time may need a word of explanation, though the reasons for it are in part the same that were operative in the days of its classical greatness. It is not simply that it lies in a productive territory; it also controls important routes. Obviously it sits in the path between Attica and northern Greece; less obviously, to the modern traveller, it is at the crossing of this route with another which ran by sea from the coasts near Corinth or Sicyon to the north-eastern inlets of the Corinth-

---

[1] See *C.A.H.* ii³, pt. 1, p. 644. [2] §v, 17, vol. 7, 131 f.
[3] See *C.A.H.* ii³, pt. 1, p. 650
[4] Cf. *C.A.H.* ii³, pt. 1, p. 642.
[5] §1, 2, vol. 64, 156; A, 2, 31–3 and 420.
[6] See *C.A.H.* ii³, pt. 1, p. 657.

ian Gulf and so from the later Thisbe or Creusis straight across Boeotia to Chalcis, Euboea, and the Aegean. A Peloponnesian power was as sure to be involved with Thebes in the fifteenth century B.C. as in the fifth. Tradition was well aware that this had been so. The greatness of Thebes in the first heroic age left a wealth of legends which provided the themes of many a classical Greek tragedy; and it was indeed a fit subject for tragedy. Here was a city most remembered for its fall. First there was the great siege which to us is most familiar through the drama of Aeschylus, the *Seven against Thebes*—a siege indecisive in its outcome; then, in the latter age of heroes, the final destruction by the Epigoni, the sons or successors of the Seven. Hesiod mentions the Theban War and the Trojan War in the same breath, as the greatest events of heroic times, and as the most disastrous, by which the race of heroes was brought to an end:

$$\tau o \grave{v} s \ \mu \grave{\epsilon} \nu \ \pi \acute{o} \lambda \epsilon \mu \acute{o} s \ \tau \epsilon \ \kappa \alpha \kappa \grave{o} s \ \kappa \alpha \grave{\iota} \ \phi \acute{v} \lambda o \pi \iota s \ \alpha \grave{\iota} \nu \grave{\eta}$$
$$\tau o \grave{v} s \ \mu \grave{\epsilon} \nu \ \grave{\epsilon} \phi' \ \grave{\epsilon} \pi \tau \alpha \pi \acute{v} \lambda \omega \ \Theta \acute{\eta} \beta \eta, \ K \alpha \delta \mu \eta \ddot{\iota} \delta \iota \ \gamma \alpha \acute{\iota} \eta,$$
$$\grave{\omega} \lambda \epsilon \sigma \epsilon, \ \mu \alpha \rho \nu \alpha \mu \acute{\epsilon} \nu o v s \ \mu \acute{\eta} \lambda \omega \nu \ \grave{\epsilon} \nu \epsilon \kappa' \ O \grave{\iota} \delta \iota \pi \acute{o} \delta \alpha o \ldots .[1]$$

Here the occasion of the war is given as the flocks of Oedipus, a characteristic bone of contention among early peoples. To us the version used by the tragedians is more familiar, the quarrel between Polynices and Eteocles who disputed the throne after the death of Oedipus. Eteocles seized the government, and Polynices fled to the court of Adrastus of Argos. It is significant that the Argolid is the natural refuge for a Theban exile. At Argos Polynices was joined by Tydeus, also an exile, from Calydon. (Both the man and the place confirm that this is an event of the first heroic age.) Adrastus espoused their cause, and in due course an army led by these and four other heroes—the famous Seven— marched against Thebes. It was essentially an Argive expedition; the surviving first line of the *Thebaïs*, beginning Ἄργος ἄειδε, θεά..., makes that clear; and the *Iliad* agrees that Mycenae took no part, though invited to do so.[2] This seems, historically, strange; it may be that as with the stories of Danaus and Perseus we have here some distortion resulting from rival traditions.[3] To return to the story, Thebes withstood a long siege, until in the final desperate assault Eteocles and Polynices each fell by the other's hand; the city was saved, and the attackers were obliged to withdraw. A generation later, however, the attack of the Epigoni was more successful, and Thebes was destroyed. Both campaigns were the

---

[1] *Works and Days*, 161 ff.   [2] *Iliad* IV, 376 ff.
[3] See *C.A.H.* II³, pt. I, p. 650.

subject of epics now lost, and are referred to frequently from Homer[1] onwards; and there is no reason to suppose the tale was not based on fact. We have noticed Hesiod's allusion to it; and when, much later in time, Pausanias comments[2] that in his opinion the Theban War was the most important internal conflict in Greece in all the heroic period, he is but echoing the general testimony of antiquity. In Homer, references to the War of the Seven are linked with the praise of Diomede's father Tydeus, who had been one of them, and it is cited as an outstanding exploit of the previous age, an example to live up to. The campaign of the Epigoni (which the son of Capaneus remarks was a yet greater exploit, since it was successful) is ascribed to the generation of the Trojan War heroes. This, as observed before,[3] need not represent the true chronological interval between the two campaigns; but if it does not, where are they to be dated?

On the interpretation which we have advanced, the campaign of the Seven, as an event of the first heroic age, belongs not later than L.H. II. It need not have left any trace in the archaeological record. The eventual sack of Thebes, however, should be identifiable by a destruction level on the site. Unfortunately the Mycenaean palace lies most unfavourably for excavation, beneath the modern town; but such investigation as has been possible[4] when parts of the site have been cleared for rebuilding showed clearly that the palace had been a structure of some magnificence, decorated with frescoes and carved stonework, and with extensive store-chambers in which lay wine or oil jars with brief painted inscriptions in Linear B. Certain place-names in the inscriptions, together with analysis of the clay, suggest that at least some of the jars were imports from Crete.[5] Fragments of carved ivory attest the elegance of the palace furnishing, and a few Linear B tablets survive from its administrative records. The whole was destroyed by a fire of unusual intensity, which left a thick burnt layer on much of the site. What the earlier excavators published of the pottery found in this burnt stratum consisted largely of plain cups and *kylikes* (stemmed goblets), which are harder to date than decorated wares but have usually been ascribed to L.H. III a.[6] The more recent investigations, however, have distinguished two successive palaces, both destroyed (on the evidence of the pottery) within the L.H. III b period. A treasure of semi-precious stones discovered in the later palace includes thirty-nine inscribed

[1] *Iliad* iv, 376 ff.; v, 801 ff.; x, 284 ff.
[2] Paus. ix, 9.
[3] *C.A.H.* ii³, pt. 1, pp. 646 f.
[4] §1, 3 and 4; A, 16; 17; 20.
[5] A, 7.
[6] §1, 1, 118.

cylinders of lapis lazuli, of Kassite Babylonian style, which as a
possible royal gift raise interesting speculations on Theban contacts with the Near East. They do not, however, assist us with the
dating; none of them, nor of other associated cylinder-seals, can
be later than the fourteenth century B.C.,[1] and they are therefore
older than the L.H. IIIb pottery which gives the destruction
date. Without more detailed study it is wiser not to try and translate this into years B.C., though it falls within the thirteenth
century. The site lay vacant thereafter right down to Christian
times, which agrees with the evidence of Strabo[2] that the Cadmea,
the palace-citadel of Thebes, was not rebuilt after the sack. Pausanias similarly records that in the *agora* at Thebes the sometime
site of the House of Cadmus was still left as an ἄβατον, a place
taboo.[3] It also agrees with the evidence of the Homeric *Catalogue
of Ships*, which does not even mention Thebes or Cadmea among
the cities of Boeotia, though *Hypothebai* in that list, *Nether Thebes*,
was by some ancient authorities interpreted as referring to the
unwalled lower town.[4]

The sack of Thebes may then be regarded as one of the certain
events of Mycenaean history; and the elimination of this rival has
an obvious bearing on the development of the Mycenaean power
in the Peloponnese. Perhaps, too, it contributed to the prosperity
of Attica in L.H. III, which is archaeologically well attested by a
wide distribution of large cemeteries of well-furnished Mycenaean
tombs.[5] Whether such prosperity was due to or combined with the
political maturity implied by the ascription to Theseus of the
συνοικισμός, the political unification of Attica, is not certainly
established. Some modern scholars are indeed reluctant to admit
that the synoecism could have occurred so early; yet the tradition[6]
is unanimous; and there are hints that it may be true in the
archaeological remains. The citadel that in L.H. II was the castle
of 'Cephalus' at Thoricus seems not to have been occupied in the
succeeding period;[7] and at Brauron too the L.H. III remains seem
confined to the open lower slopes of the citadel hill.[8] Were these
strongholds in fact dismantled voluntarily as part of the scheme
of unification that made the Athenian acropolis the citadel of all
Attica?

[1] A, 18; 19.   [2] Strabo 412.   [3] Paus. IX, 12, 3.
[4] Strabo 412.   [5] §1, 6.
[6] Thuc. II, 15; Plutarch, *Life of Theseus*, 24.
[7] §1, 5; cf. §1, 1, 109.   [8] Personal observation.

II. THE RISE OF THE PELOPIDS

If the sack of Thebes took place, as the remains imply, within L.H. III b, it may or may not have been the work of literally the same generation of men who fought at Troy. But that the Homeric epic does date it in the same generation must at least imply that it belongs in some sense to the same period, a period regarded already as historically separate from the first heroic age. The implication is that for the generation of the Trojan War the campaign of the Seven was already 'past history', matter perhaps for epic; that of the Epigoni was not: it was part of the current era. This break in tradition we probably ought to connect, for Mycenae at least, with the change of dynasty from Perseids to Pelopids which is so firmly attested by the legends.

The coming of Pelops and his establishment in Elis has already been discussed.[1] The acquisition by his descendants of the kingdom of Mycenae itself, and so of the supremacy of Greece, is represented as subsequent to and to some extent consequent upon the death of Heracles and of his rival Eurystheus. Perhaps that is only another way of saying that it marks a new era. Thucydides tells us briefly that on setting out on a campaign against the sons of Heracles in Attica, Eurystheus had entrusted the kingdom of Mycenae to Atreus, being his mother's brother; and when Eurystheus was killed the people of Mycenae invited Atreus to take over the throne permanently.[2] Thus the Pelopids became more powerful than the Perseids. Later versions of the tale[3] are more elaborate, but do not alter the basic facts of the dynastic change, which there seems no reason to doubt. It is noticeable that Attica is represented as an independent territory; this is always so in the legends. The only hint of connexion with the Argolid that we come across is that Aethra, the mother of Theseus, is said to have been of the family of Pelops; and that Theseus was brought up by her on the further side of the Saronic Gulf, at Troezen. It might be plausible to suggest that the tale of Theseus' 'home-coming' to claim his birthright as the heir of the Athenian king Aegeus, killing brigands and monsters in the Megarid as he came, is but a patriotic Athenian disguise for the annexation of Attica by a Peloponnesian prince. But this remains speculation, and if Attica was ever part of the Peloponnesian kingdom in Mycenaean times Athenian tradition has successfully eliminated the record of it. More probably it really was independent.

[1] *C.A.H.* II³, pt. 1, pp. 638 f.
[2] Thuc. I, 9, 2.   [3] E.g. Diod. IV, 58; Apollodorus 2, 4, 5, 2 ff.

Accepting the truth of a major change of dynasty at Mycenae we may find in this the crucial event which separates the first heroic age from the second. No other in the traditional records of heroic dynasties bears any comparable importance. The new establishment in the Peloponnese endured to the end of the Bronze Age; it is the descendants of Atreus—Agamemnon at Mycenae and Menelaus at Sparta—who virtually control the Peloponnese at the time of the Trojan War, and therefore lead the expedition. The kingdom of Pylus never came under the Pelopids' rule, but it was well-disposed towards them. Other parts of Greece, though they might like Attica be independently governed, could be rallied to the Mycenaean standard if the interests of Hellas as a whole were at stake. But though the Pelopids had achieved the supremacy, the rival house, the sons and descendants of Heracles, still sought opportunity to regain it. They figure in this role in the legends right down to the end of the heroic age, when they eventually attained their aim with the help of the Dorian Greek tribes. Thus the dynastic change at Mycenae from Perseids to Pelopids was bound up in the Greek memory with inner racial conflict.

When, in terms of our archaeological chronology, the change took place, is difficult to decide. If it is a fact that the people of Mycenae accepted their new ruler voluntarily, we shall not expect to find there any marks of sack and pillage such as might have confirmed or dated a conquest by violence. We do however know that at some time in Mycenaean IIIa much of Mycenae was rebuilt. The palace whose remains lie on the citadel is the successor of earlier Mycenaean II structures;[1] so are some of the large houses outside the citadel.[2] But not enough is known of the earlier buildings to determine when and why they were replaced. In the absence of more particular clues we need assume no more than rebuilding and improvements prompted by growing economic prosperity. But we may reasonably consider this new era to have been as much the creation of the new dynasty as the result of the removal of the Minoan obstacle to expansion. Which of the two came first, the fall of Crete or the establishment of the Pelopids, we cannot surely tell. Within Mainland Greece, however, we may feel fairly confident that the destruction of Thebes was the work of the new masters of Mycenae. Perhaps that is why it is a clear event in the tradition, while the fall of Cnossus is not.

---

[1] §III, 34, 189 f.; §III, 35, 266 ff.; A, 13, 59.   [2] III, 38.

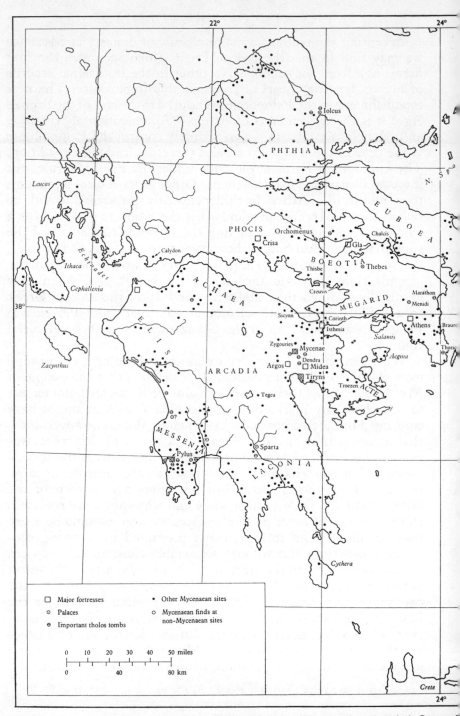

Map 3. Distribution of Mycenaean sites and remains in Greece and

Legend:

□ Major fortresses   • Other Mycenaean sites

⊙ Palaces   ○ Mycenaean finds at non-Mycenaean sites

⊖ Important tholos tombs

Scale: 0 10 20 30 40 50 miles

0 40 80 km

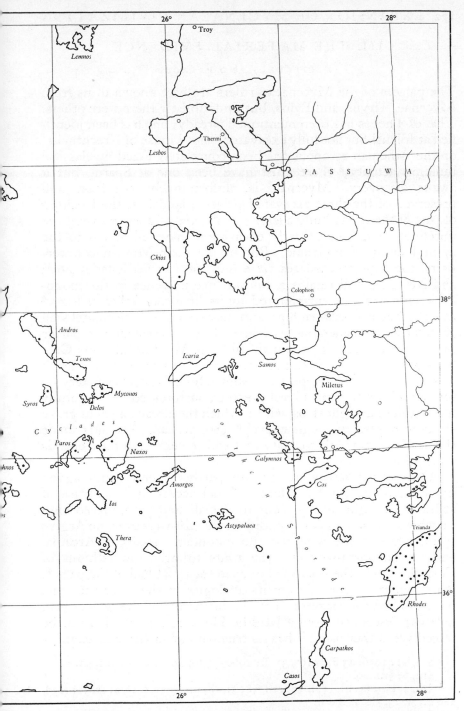

(Based on R. Hope-Simpson, *Gazetteer and Atlas of Mycenaean Sites*.)

III. THE MATERIAL EVIDENCE

(a) CITADELS AND PALACES

The palaces of the Mycenaean rulers are best known to us from Mycenae, Tiryns, and Pylus, but undoubtedly there were others. That of Thebes has been mentioned already; one has been identified at Iolcus[1] but not fully excavated; the 'House of Erechtheus' on the Athenian acropolis has been completely razed by classical building activity;[2] there must have been one at Sparta, but it awaits discovery. Mycenae[3] is, unfortunately, the least well preserved of the three excavated palaces; landslips, the levelling of part of the site to build a later temple, and to a lesser extent the unrefined technique of early excavation, have all added to the natural decay of millennia. But unlike their Minoan counterparts, the mainland palaces were built on fortified citadel sites; and Mycenae still retains a colossal magnificence in the monolithic entrance gate surmounted by its limestone relief of lions,[4] and approached between high and massive walls. The citadel wall contained a considerable area in addition to that of the palace proper which occupied the main hill-top. West of the Lion Gate it swings out expressly to include the Grave Circle; and when it was built yet further respect was shown for this royal cemetery by terracing it up to form a level precinct, surrounded by a carefully made wall of upright slabs, within which the already ancient grave stelae were reset at the new level.[5] (So, perhaps, Pelopids made themselves acceptable to a city that still remembered the Perseids with pride.)

Ahead of the gate, a broad ramp, partly preserved, zig-zagged up towards the royal residence. Final access by a staircase of at least two flights brought one to a small courtyard, placed high up where it commands a splendid view south-west over the Argive plain, while to the west rise the mountain massifs of Arcadia, and to the north-west lies the route towards the Isthmus of Corinth. On to the courtyard opened the great hall of the palace, what modern scholars, from its analogies in the Homeric epic, have dubbed the *megaron*. This is distinctive of the Mycenaean palaces; descended from a Middle Helladic type (which can be traced yet farther back) it has no true parallel in Minoan arrange-

---

[1] §III, 21: 1956, 43 ff.; 1957, 31 ff.; 1960, 55 ff.; 1961, 55 ff.; §III, 32.

[2] §III, 8; §III, 20.

[3] §III, 27; III, 34; III, 35; III, 37; III, 38; III, 18; III, 19; IV, 1; IV, 2; IV, 5; III, 39, 386 ff.; A, 13, chs. II and III.

[4] See Plate 140 (a).   [5] See Plate 140 (b); A, 13, 15–35.

ments. It is the nucleus and focus of the whole; other parts of the building are subordinated to it and lead up to it.

This is yet more obvious in the plan of the Tiryns[1] citadel. There a long history of building and expansion resulted in a final fortified circuit of dimensions unusual even in Mycenaean times. In Homeric epic τειχιόεσσα is a standard epithet of the town, 'Tiryns with its walls'. The blocks are so huge that tradition ascribed the building to giants, the Cyclopes,[2] specially invited over from Asia Minor, and so gave to such masonry the name of 'Cyclopean', which is still used. That tradition has a particular interest in that the nearest parallels to such fortifications are in fact those of the Hittites, which may well have been known to the Mycenaean builders.[3] The latest defences at Tiryns on east and south are pierced by a series of embrasures linked to each other by a tunnel, corbel-vaulted, within the twenty-foot thickness of the walls. This forbidding mountain of masonry admitted the visitor indirectly, from an exterior ramp through monolithic gateways like that of Mycenae and by a long corridor leading eventually to a more decorative gate, with columns on either side, opening into a courtyard about thirty yards across. From this a second columned gateway opened into the smaller inner court, surrounded by a colonnade, with on the far side the megaron. This consisted of a shallow porch with two columns, an anteroom of similar dimensions, and the main hall, almost square, with a large circular hearth in the middle around which stood four timber columns supporting the roof. On the right, facing the hearth, stood the king's throne. It is a standard plan, repeated at Pylus,[4] and at Mycenae, though in these the courtyard is much smaller, and without continuous colonnades. It is repeated again on a smaller scale within the Mycenae citadel in the House of Columns[5] (east of the palace), which was perhaps the residence of some high officer of state. A smaller megaron at Tiryns, alongside the chief one, known as the 'Queen's megaron' has a parallel, though not on the strict megaron plan, at Pylus. In both cases the secluded siting lends colour to the idea that these are the women's quarters, but this should not be taken to imply an oriental segregation of women in Mycenaean society, for which there is no evidence.

The megaron, rising to the height of two ordinary floors, with its great hearth and throne, was clearly a ceremonial as much as a

---

[1] §III, 17; III, 26; III, 11; III, 33; A, 13, 11–15 and 46–52. See Plate 141 (*a*).
[2] Paus. II, 16 5; II, 25, 8; Apollodorus 2, 2, 1, 3; Strabo 373.
[3] §III, 15, 193.   [4] §III, 1; III, 2; III, 39, 422 ff.; A, 2. See Plate 141 (*b*).
[5] §III, 37, 91 ff.; A, 14, 11 ff.

domestic centre. Other living-rooms were perhaps often on an upper level, for many of the ground floor rooms that cluster round the megaron were used only for storage and service. At Pylus there were large separate buildings for storing jars of wine and oil, and the subordinate rooms and corridors were particularly compact and orderly in plan. At Tiryns or Mycenae the irregularity may be due to a longer history of building or to the unevenness of the site.

The basic structure, of stone or unbaked brick, with timber framing, is common to the Aegean Bronze Age; but decorative features and refinements show specifically Minoan origins. From Crete comes the use, and the form, of columns. Though they were of wood we know their appearance from representations in fresco and ivory carving,[1] as well as from stone half-columns in the façade of one or two beehive-tombs.[2] The fresco decoration of the principal rooms is Minoan in technique; but in L.H. III the style and subjects are more peculiar to the mainland. At Mycenae[3] was a battle scene, with warriors storming a building, and a group of armed men with horses; at Tiryns a lively boar-hunt,[4] with spearmen and dappled hounds in pursuit of the wounded beast; at Pylus[5] lions and griffins, a frieze of dogs, a lyre-player, and a fight between Mycenaean warriors and 'barbarians' clad in skins. The decorative use of gypsum or carved stone for the floors and facings of entrances, as we noted earlier,[6] was another Minoan feature. But floors were more often of plaster, which could be painted in chequerboard schemes to imitate decorative flagging. Sometimes, as in the Tiryns megaron and in a smaller room at Pylus, the squares were filled with motifs of octopus or dolphins— Minoan in origin, but unmistakably Mycenaean in their stylized treatment.[7]

Normally the Mycenaean citadel was not merely a royal residence; it was a military stronghold.[8] At both Mycenae and Tiryns the fortified area included a considerable space that was not built on, presumably to provide accommodation in time of danger for extra forces and perhaps cattle and people from the surrounding countryside. In case of siege, protected access to water was provided: both citadels had hidden rock-cut passages

[1] E.g. §III, 35, pl. 33; §IV, 2, fig. 73; §III, 38, vol. 49, 241 and pl. 40. See Plate 143 (b).

[2] §III, 37, 29 and 36, fig. 51. See Plate 148 (b).

[3] §III, 25. See Plate 142 (a).   [4] §III, 26, p. 13. See Plate 142 (b).

[5] A, 9.   [6] C.A.H. II³, pt. 1, p. 644.

[7] §III, 26, 222 ff. and pls. XIX–XXI; §III, 2, vol. 57, 61; vol. 61, 132 and pl. 45. See Plate 142 (c).   [8] Cf. §III, 37, 111; §III, 39, 352 and fig. 17.

and stairs leading to a cistern or other supply.[1] But clearly the bulk of the population in peacetime lived outside the citadels, nearer to their fields and their work. At Mycenae the location of their cemeteries suggests several separate groups of dwellings.[2]

(b) ARTS AND CRAFTS

Few private houses have yet been explored; but remains at Mycenae show that they could be substantial and luxurious.[3] On a smaller scale we find the same building methods, with well-plastered walls and floors, and even fresco decoration, as in the palaces. They too had their cellars of wine and oil, their stores of painted pottery. Movable furniture has perished, leaving little trace; but a scrap or two of carved wood[4] and numerous fragmentary inlays of ivory,[5] carved in relief, show how delicate and sophisticated was the decoration of tables, chairs, or footstools,[6] in these houses, and *a fortiori* in the palaces. Ivory was used also for carved boxes[7] and the ornamental handles of large mirrors, for parts of lyres,[8] and occasionally for carving in the round, as in an exquisite group of two women and a small boy found at Mycenae.[9] Favourite subjects in ivory carving include griffins and sphinxes, monsters probably borrowed from the repertory of the eastern countries from which the ivory itself came;[10] others, such as the heart-shaped ivy-leaf, and the figure-of-eight shield, are also familiar in Minoan art.

Jars and lamps of carved stone[11] were sometimes used, but not with the figured reliefs such as are known from the preceding age in Crete. Repoussé work in gold and silver, however, was still current, as we can tell from the splendid cup from Dendra (Midea) in the Argolid.[12] So was the technique of metal inlay; Dendra

---

[1] §III, 10; §III, 33. [2] §III, 36, 121 ff.

[3] §III, 38; §IV, 1; §IV, 2; §IV, 5; §III, 22.

[4] §III, 38, vol. 50, 184 and pl. 27; cf. §III, 5, 166 and fig. 164.

[5] §IV, 2, figs. 11–17, 70–3; §III, 38, vol. 48, 8 and pl. 5; vol. 49, 235 ff. and pls. 33–6, 38–40; vol. 50, 182 and pls. 25, 26, 30; vol. 52, 197–9; A, 17. See Plate 143.

[6] §IV, 7, 332–46. [7] E.g. §III, 13, pl. VII; §III, 29, 283 ff. See Plate 148.

[8] §III, 34, pls. 55–6; §III, 35, 369 f.; pl. 59; cf. §III, 3, 283; and for lyre §III, 13, pl. VIII, 6 and 10.

[9] §III, 37, 83 f., 86, pls. 101–3; §III, 40. See Plate 143 (a).

[10] Cf. §V, 1 and 2.

[11] E.g. §III, 37, fig. 86; §III, 38, vol. 50, 182 f., pls. 23–4; §IV, 2, figs. 18–23; §III, 35, pl. 52a; §III, 24, fig. 77. See Plate 145.

[12] §III, 24, 31 f., 43 f., frontispiece and pls. IX–XI; 33 f., 50 f., pl. XVI; §III, 23, 89 ff., frontispiece and pls. IV, VI. See Plate 146 (a).

again provides a fine example, a silver cup ornamented with bulls' heads (which has a parallel, even more beautiful, from Enkomi in Cyprus); and other pieces are known from Mycenae and the Pylus area.[1]

Vessels of bronze were doubtless common. They are fairly often found in tombs;[2] and a further indication is the frequency with which pottery imitates obviously metallic shapes and finishes.[3] Though less often found, bronze tools must equally have been plentiful. Axes, adzes, saws, chisels, and hammers were essential to the Mycenaean builders, whether working in wood or stone, as were hoes, ploughshares, and sickles to the farmer.[4] Finer tools were needed by carvers of wood and ivory, and by the engravers of signets of semi-precious stone, which the Mycenaean officials, like the Minoans, used to authenticate the sealing of wine or oil or other valuable goods.[5] Weapons and armour too were of bronze. Swords, daggers, and spearheads are reasonably familiar to us from Mycenaean graves;[6] protective arms are less so, but we have several surviving examples of bronze greaves,[7] and one magnificent suit of bronze body armour found in a grave at Dendra.[8] Comparatively few bronze objects of any kind survive, and it is easy to see why; the metal was valuable, and things doubtless went to the smiths as scrap when broken or worn out. But the importance of metal in the everyday life of the Mycenaeans can hardly be exaggerated; all their surviving works attest the need of a large supply, and the Linear B tablets from Pylus fill in some local detail. In them we find at least 270 smiths (*ka-ke-we*) mentioned by name, and allowing for the incompleteness of the records we may suppose there were up to 400 in the two dozen or so towns of the area governed from Pylus. The tablets record the distribution from the palace of over a ton of bronze, in individual lots averaging about seven pounds; but we do not know how frequent such distributions were, and since not all smiths received such allotments there were possibly other channels also for the supply of raw metal. This palace issue may have been for the manufacture

---

[1] §III, 24, 38 and 48 ff., pls I, XII; §III, 39, pl. 36(c); §III, 14, pls. XXXVIII, 196. See Plate 146(b).

[2] E.g. §III, 3, 352 f.; §III, 24, pls. XXX–XXXIII.

[3] Cf. §III, 31, 60 ff.; §III, 24, 135 ff.

[4] §III, 3, 342 ff.; §III, 30, especially p. 296, with references; §III, 16, 152 ff. See Plate 147 (a).

[5] Examples in §III, 14, pls. 208–11; §IV, 2, 103 f.

[6] E.g. §III, 3, 330 ff.; §III, 24, pls. XX–XXII.

[7] §III, 4; cf. §III, 39, 505 f., and fig. 55.

[8] §III, 9, 9 f., and figs. 8, 9; A, 17. See Plate 147 (b).

of special requirements (perhaps arms), a kind of government contract, perhaps to be associated with certain remissions of tax which the tablets show some smiths enjoyed.[1]

Much the most plentiful Mycenaean product to survive is of course the pottery.[2] Pottery is a staple of the archaeology of most ages, but it has special importance here. It was manufactured in great quantities, and this, together with good communications, made for a standardized style—the Mycenaean *koine* as it has been called. The comparative absence of local variation makes typological study the more valid, and this provides the basis of our relative chronology for the period. L.H. III pottery is interesting, too, as reflecting the general trends of the art and culture of the times. The continuity of both shapes and patterns from L.H. II is readily traceable; but with the removal of Minoan sources of inspiration the decoration becomes increasingly stylized. The use of horizontal stripes (painted mechanically as the pot revolved on the wheel) is very frequent; and motifs that had once been naturalistic became wholly linear, and were used for the construction of new abstract patterns.[3] This is typical of Mycenaean art; it seems not to grow, but to be built; it reflects the high organizing capacity of its producers. Technically, the pottery is of the highest quality. It is a skilful feat to throw on the wheel in one piece either the wholly closed globular or piriform 'stirrup-jar' type, or the tall-stemmed shallow goblet or *kylix*.[4] Yet these are among the commonest and most characteristic of a wide and attractive range of shapes. The clay is excellently refined, and fired at a higher temperature than most ancient pottery, which gives practical as well as aesthetic advantages.[5] As a result, it was traded all round the eastern Mediterranean, and the surviving examples thus give invaluable clues, as will be shown later, for the history of Mycenaean commerce and foreign relations.

(c) TOMBS

Most of the Mycenaean pottery to be seen in the world's museums has been found not on habitation sites, but in tombs. So well-equipped a world as the Mycenaean was not lightly to be left, and these people took considerable care over their funeral arrangements. Burial was, for ordinary folk, in rock-cut chamber-tombs, many of them already in use in L.H. II, and continuing so, as family vaults, for the remainder of the Bronze Age. Pottery

[1] A, 10.   [2] §III, 6 and 7.   [3] See Plate 144.
[4] See Plate 144, (c, d, f).   [5] §III, 13, especially 109, 119.

vessels, personal ornaments, sometimes tools, weapons, or other metal utensils, were laid with the dead. A farewell toast was drunk outside the tomb door, and the goblet smashed. Yet there seems to have been no thought that the departed would continue to use or need the grave-gifts, and when the tomb was opened for later burials they were often unceremoniously pushed aside, along with the mortal remains.[1]

For the rulers, the stone-built beehive-tomb was their final resting-place and monument; and we can trace, especially at Mycenae, a growing skill and refinement in their construction.[2] The 'Treasury of Atreus' at Mycenae,[3] one of the latest, dating from the fourteenth century, is much the grandest and best-preserved example of Mycenaean architecture. The heavy sawn blocks of conglomerate that line the entrance passage, the doorway sixteen feet high with its hundred-ton lintel, the vast and still perfect stone chamber, nearly fifty feet wide, and as high, are even now awe-inspiring. No stone-roofed building of equal size was constructed between this and the Pantheon at Rome. In its pristine state, it would have impressed by the skilful finish as well as the mass; the entrance was flanked and surmounted by carved columns and relief decoration in stone; great bronze-mounted doors pivoted on the threshold; ornaments of bronze adorned the surface of the vault. The name of 'treasury' that had attached to these structures by the time of Pausanias[4] bears witness to the splendour of the grave-goods that would have accompanied a royal burial; and it is confirmed by the riches of even a much smaller beehive tomb found unplundered at Dendra.[5] Beside the precious objects laid in the actual grave-pit, others were heaped on a pyre and burned within the tomb chamber. Animals too might be sacrificed—dogs or horses: at Marathon[6] two horse skeletons lay stretched outside the tomb door. Sometimes there may even have been human victims; the practice of suttee is suggested by the remains at Dendra, though it cannot be proved. These royal tombs, obviously constructed in the ruler's lifetime, were doubtless in the main intended (unlike the family chamber-tombs) as monuments to individuals. Enormous and extravagant expenditure of time and labour and material went to their construction; they imply an extreme exaltation of the monarch, even to the extent of raising the question, which remains at present

---

[1] §III, 3, ch. VI; §III, 36, 121–46; §III, 37, 14 f. See below, p. 898.
[2] §III, 37, 16, 26–46.
[3] §III, 37, 28–33; §III, 35, 338 ff. See Plate 148 (b).   [4] Paus. II, 16, 6.
[5] §III, 24, 1–70.   [6] §III, 21, 1958, 23–7.

unsolved, whether more than mortal status was ascribed to him, either in life or after his death.[1] They imply too a remarkable economic prosperity; and it is hardly surprising that they did not continue to be built throughout the Myc. III period; the ordinary tombs remain in uninterrupted use till the twelfth century, but it is doubtful whether any beehive at Mycenae itself can be dated as late even as the thirteenth, though one at Menidi[2] outside Athens belongs to Myc. III b. It may be that in this phase the labour forces available were employed rather on the great works of fortification.

IV. MYCENAEAN SOCIETY

The high level of social and economic organization that must have prevailed in a society that could construct the beehive tombs is amply confirmed and illustrated by the palace records that survive, scratched in the Linear B script on tablets of unbaked clay.[3] That no such tablets were found in the palace at Mycenae is clearly an accident of time and excavation, for a number have survived in houses outside the citadel.[4] At Pylus the excavators were lucky to find (in their first trial trench) some 600 tablets lying in the ruins of a little office near the palace entrance, and many more have come to light since.[5] They are all administrative records. It is likely, but not provable, that other types of document may have been written on different material; but to judge from the tablets the chief purpose of writing was to record those matters of daily business which in themselves are difficult to remember with accuracy, and concerning which an objective record will obviate dispute and inefficiency. A large proportion are lists of persons, some indicating their duties or occupations, their tenancy of land, or the produce due from them or delivered by them; others the provisions issued to the palace servants and dependants; offerings sent to the sanctuaries of the gods; inventories of domestic chattels or military equipment; the disposition of troops. Above all we get a picture of the palace itself, with hundreds of men, women and children busied over their domestic or administrative tasks.

The palace controls everything; it is the main channel of economic distribution; and the territory of Pylus was conceivably regarded as fundamentally the personal estate of the *wa-na-ka* (king). But two categories of land-holding are referred to, *ki-ti-me-na* and *ke-ke-me-na*, which in effect (though not in etymology) seem to

---

[1] Cf. *C.A.H.* II³, pt. 2, pp. 35 f.   [2] §III, 13.

[3] §IV, 7; §IV, 4; A, 15.   [4] §IV, 1; §IV, 2; §IV, 5.   [5] §IV, 3.

refer to private and communal lands respectively. It is possible (though no more) that the two categories reflect a dual society, an original distinction between a native population and its conquering overlords; if so, the *ki-ti-me-na* would have been originally the demesnes assigned to individual immigrants. The king's special portion or *te-me-no* of land is presumably that which was farmed for his direct use. Similarly there is a *te-me-no* of the *la-wa-ge-ta*—'leader of the people'—an important office, tentatively explained by some as commander-in-chief of the army, but not necessarily military; he might be a sort of *tribunus plebis*. We can identify too some other grades of society: the *e-qe-ta* ('followers' or 'companions' of the king), whose names are distinguished by patronymics and who seem to have important military duties; and the *qa-si-re-we* (= βασιλῆες), who are governors of subordinate towns. Other minor offices or ranks also are named. There was a developed specialization of labour: carpenters, masons, shipwrights, bronze-smiths, potters, and goldsmiths, might have been assumed from other archaeological evidence; but the tablets tell also of workers who have left no visible products of their crafts, of spinners, weavers, and fullers, of perfume-makers, doctors, and heralds. The tablets prove also the existence of slaves, some privately owned, but more of them 'slaves' of a god or goddess, a term which may conceal some different status.[1] The gods appear in the tablets only as recipients of offerings; these are business documents, not ritual texts or temple records. The information indirectly provided about Mycenaean religion is, however, important, and will be discussed later in this volume.[2]

We shall not be far wrong in reading into the tablets a system of administration in which members of the ruling class govern and enjoy allotments of territory in return for contributions of produce in kind and of service in war. This pattern is virtually certain for the Pylus area. For Greece or the Peloponnese as a whole we have no similar contemporary evidence; but the tradition of at least a war-time allegiance to Mycenae is strong: Menelaus of Sparta is twin brother of Agamemnon; Nestor of Pylus, though of another lineage, is a willing ally, and so with the other heroic principalities. How far friendly relations between them were maintained when no foreign danger or campaign was afoot, we cannot tell. It seems improbable, however, that Mycenae could have exercised any precise centralized control over the more distant parts even of the Peloponnese, since communication cannot have been easy. Built roads can indeed be traced in the

[1] A, 11.   [2] See below, ch. XL.

immediate vicinity of Mycenae,[1] and within the kingdom of
Pylus,[2] and some of the chariotry listed in the Pylus tablets may
have been available for travel as well as for war; but we have so
far scarcely any evidence of built roads over longer distances,
without which communication in Greece must be on foot or by
pack-animal.

V. OVERSEAS CONTACTS

Though slow, communication must have been reasonably frequent, or we should surely find fashions of material culture
diverging more from place to place than they do. The island of
Rhodes, for example, in L.H. III a uses pottery which in the main
is hardly distinguishable from that of Mycenae or of Attica.
Yet there is just enough difference for us to conclude that we
have here a local product, not an import from the mainland.[3] So
far as the evidence goes, most of the Aegean islands seem to have
shared the standard Mycenaean fashions, which by L.H. III b, if
not III a, stretched also to the Ionian islands to the west and into
Thessaly. But Mycenaean pottery also spread by trade far beyond
the areas of Greek population. The eastern Mediterranean
markets already occasionally touched in L.H. II[4] were in L.H. III
more fully exploited. In Egypt the new régime of Akhenaten
favoured foreign traders in Egypt, and the neat little red-
striped Mycenaean stirrup-jars and pilgrim flasks (perhaps filled
with scented oil) were familiar in the new-fangled palace at El-
Amarna[5] during its short life from 1379 to 1362. From the
coasts at Askalon and Tell el-'Ajjūl near Gaza they made their way
to inlands sites in Palestine and even beyond the Jordan.[6] Further
north, in Syria, the port of Ugarit (the modern Ras Shamra) was
an entrepôt favourable to Mycenaeans throughout L.H. III a–b;
and from the mouth of the Orontes their pottery reached Alalakh
(Tell Açana) and occasionally (until the southward advance of
the Hittites), to sites like Qatna and Qadesh, well up the valley
beyond Hama.[7] Occasional finds in the Cilician plain[8] may be
indicative of a more frequent trade there than we yet know of;
more exploration is needed.

Perhaps the most important region of all, in this eastward area,
is Cyprus.[9] The flow of Mycenaean pottery to sites on the south

---

[1] §III, 37, 27, 46 f. See Plate 148 (a).   [2] §IV, 6; A, 12.   [3] §V, 15, ch. II.
[4] See C.A.H. II³, pt. 1, p. 645; A, 8, 135 f.
[5] §V, 15, 90 ff., with references.   [6] §V, 15, 64 ff.; A, 8.
[7] §V, 15, 59–63; A, 8.   [8] §V, 15, 88 f.; §V, 12.
[9] §V, 15, ch. III; §V, 13, 65–73, 205; §V, 6; A, 4, ch. II.

and east coast of the island, which is already substantial by the L.H. III a period, clearly represents a frequent trade, which was probably followed by the permanent establishment of Mycenaean Greeks in these parts. We should envisage them at first as small groups, living as foreigners within the native towns for purposes of trade, rather than establishing their own independent settlements. In Myc. III b, however, we find a growing independence of style in the Mycenaean pottery of Cyprus,[1] and it looks as though there were Greek potters working on the spot, though clay-analyses have raised some doubts about this. Certainly these 'Levanto-Helladic' wares are in this later phase frequently distinguishable among the Mycenaean pottery in Syria and Palestine. This suggests there were Mycenaeans in Cyprus trading on their own account, not merely as agents for mainland Greece; and although their goods did not now penetrate into the Orontes valley they find a wider distribution in the coastal areas further south, from Byblos to the Bay of Acre, areas now restored to greater tranquillity after the settlement between Egyptians and Hittites subsequent to the battle of Qadesh.[2] In the thirteenth century, too, it seems that new openings for Mycenaean traders were developing at Tell Abu Hawwām,[3] outside modern Haifa; for here we find pottery of mainland Greek origin (as opposed to Cypriot Mycenaean), and finds inland seem to hint at a link with caravan routes across the eastward deserts to Mesopotamia.

As we have already suggested, some of these pottery exports perhaps went abroad as containers for oil or perfume, some for their own sake. What Greece imported in return we can only partly deduce. There is no doubt that copper[4] accounts for the Mycenaean interest in Cyprus; it travelled in big ingots,[5] shaped like a dressed ox-hide, such as are known at both Minoan and Mycenaean sites and even as far west as Sardinia; recently some were recovered from the wreck of a Late Bronze Age ship at Cape Gelidonya on the south coast of Turkey.[6] From Egypt may have come gold mined in Nubia; from Syria, ivory, for there is ancient evidence for elephants in those parts, and there was a school of ivory-carving there both in the Bronze Age and later.[7] About other more perishable commodities we can only speculate. The Greek names of various spices and herbs (already current in

---

[1] But cf. A, 3; A, 5; A, 6. Plate 149 (*a*), (*b*).
[2] §v, 15, 71–87, 106 f.; A, 8, 145–7.
[3] §v, 15, 78 ff.; A, 8, 124 f.　　　　　　　[4] Cf. §v, 13, 202; A, 4.
[5] A, 4, ch. xii. See Plate 149 (*c*).　　　　[6] §v, 5; A, 1, esp. 52–83.
[7] §v, 1; §v, 2, especially p. 5. See Plate 106 (*b*).

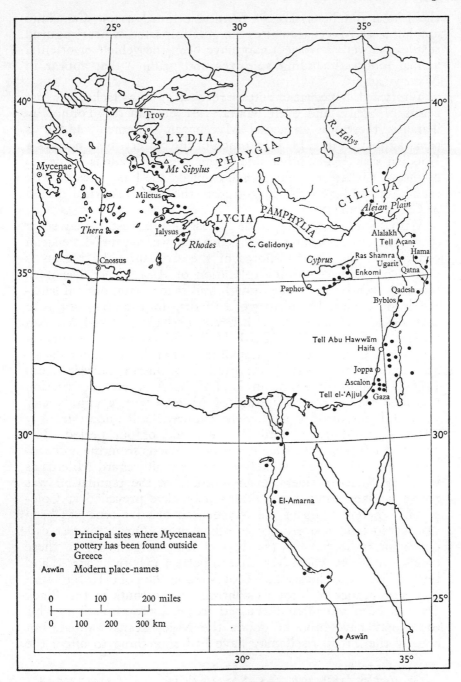

Map 4. The Eastern Mediterranean.

the Linear B tablets) are of Semitic origin;[1] a few Canaanite amphorae at Mycenaean sites suggest imported wines;[2] figured textiles (as well as ivories) may have been the vehicle of oriental animal motifs (including sphinxes and griffins) that appear in Mycenaean art.

Westward, Mycenaean pottery reached as far as Ischia, the east coasts of Sicily, and even Malta.[3] At Scoglio del Tonno, by Taranto, there was an actual Mycenaean settlement, and it is remarkable that in L.H. IIIa much of the pottery there betrays a Rhodian style.[4] The other side to this western trade is harder to divine, but whatever their primary object, the links became well established and were not forgotten in the great historical period of Greek colonization.

With such far-reaching trade to east and to west, it may seem strange that we have not more evidence than we have for Mycenaean contacts on the eastern shores of the Aegean. The reason is partly that archaeological exploration of Asia Minor has until recently been limited; but though still inadequate, our information is increasing. The history of Miletus,[5] for example, begins to take shape. It had trade with Crete, perhaps received Minoan settlers, from M.M. III to L.M. II, but then suffered destruction by fire, somewhere near the time of the fall of the Minoan palaces. Subsequent levels show imported Mycenaean pottery from L.H. IIIa until some time in L.H IIIb. A second destruction was followed by the rebuilding of Miletus with a mighty city wall, and this fortified settlement endured, still under strongly Mycenaean influence, until the very end of our period. The extent of Mycenaean settlement is not obvious from the archaeological evidence, but it is likely that we should regard Miletus as under Mycenaean rulers, even if much of the population was native Carian. Similar conditions may have prevailed at Colophon,[6] where a tomb of the Mycenaean beehive type has been discovered, and conceivably at other sites. Our strongest evidence for trade contacts (as distinct from settlement) on these coasts is at Troy, where Mycenaean pottery is both imported and imitated down to the sack of Troy VIIa in the L.H. IIIb phase.[7] The significance of Troy as controlling the route to the Black Sea has been too often discussed to need recapitulation. This route may have brought goods the Mycenaeans wanted, but equally the Troad itself may have had something to offer: the

[1] §IV, 7, 221–31. [2] §v, 7.
[3] §v, 16, 7–9, 54–78, 79 f. [4] §v, 16, ch. IV. [5] §v, 17 and 18.
[6] §v, 9, 91; §v, 10, 39. [7] §v, 4, vol. IV, 8 f., 23, 46 f.

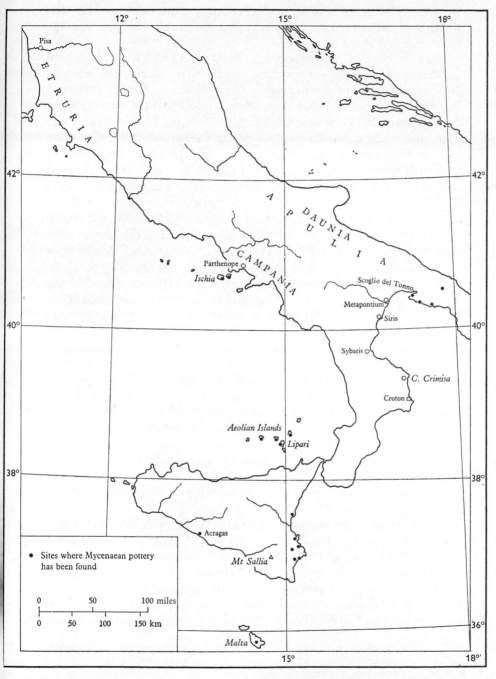

Map 5. South Italy and Sicily.

possibility that Greece imported horses from here, which has already been mentioned, is as valid for L.H. IIIb as for the preceding phases.[1]

But in general the western coasts of Asia Minor have not produced the frequent pottery finds that mark the trail of Mycenaean traders further east. On this kind of evidence alone it might be supposed that Asia Minor itself had little to offer the Mycenaeans, while goods traded from further afield were in any case more accessible by the sea-route to Syrian and Palestinian marts. That may be true; but we can also tell from documentary evidence that the Hittite empire in Asia Minor, even though it did not directly control these coastal areas, must have inhibited any Mycenaean desire for a deeper penetration of the country. It is now generally accepted that the name of *Ahhiyawa* which occurs in Hittite records of the fourteenth and thirteenth centuries refers to the land of Mycenaean Greeks, the *Achaeans* or Ἀχαιϝοί as they were still called in Homer.[2] What is not clear, unfortunately, is whether by this term the Hittites intended the Mycenaean mainland or some other territory, dependent or independent, under Mycenaean rulers; the latter is the more usual view, though there is still debate as to which of several identifications is the right one. Certainly Ahhiyawa was for a time at least regarded by the Hittites as a major power in the near eastern world, ranking with Egypt, Babylon, and Assyria; it was a sea-power, trading with the ports of Syria; and it was closely associated with the city of Millawanda or Millawata, which can be convincingly identified as Miletus. A plausible case can be made that Ahhiyawa is in fact Rhodes,[3] which we have already seen was thoroughly Mycenaean by L.H. IIIa, and moreover was concerned in a remarkably widespread sea trade. The possibility of identification with mainland Greece cannot however be positively ruled out.[4]

In the fourteenth century the relations between Ahhiyawa and the Hittites were cordial; we find the Hittite king choosing Ahhiyawa as a place of banishment for someone who has offended him (perhaps his wife);[5] the gods of Ahhiyawa (as of Lazpa, which may be Lesbos) are invoked when the Hittite monarch is ill;[6] there are allusions that imply that a member of the Ahhiyawan royal house had been sent to the Hittite land to learn chariot-

---

[1] Cf. *C.A.H.* II³, pt. I, p. 645.　　[2] §v, 11, ch. 1; §v, 10; §v, 8, 46–58.
[3] §v, 11, 15–17.　　[4] §v, 10, especially pp. 28 f.
[5] §v, 14, 298–306; §v, 10, 5 f.; §v, 8, 46 f.
[6] §v, 14, 275–94; §v, 10, 5; §v, 8, 47.

driving.[1] The famous Tawagalawas letter,[2] however, datable to
the late fourteenth or early thirteenth century, shows a less friendly
picture. Essentially it is a diplomatic protest by the Hittite king
to the king of Ahhiyawa, asking for the extradition of one Piyama-
radus who had been using Millawanda as a base for hostilities
against the Hittite lands of Lukka (probably equivalent to Lycia).
The same letter refers to the somewhat earlier establishment of
Tawagalawas, a relative of the king of Ahhiyawa, in part of Lukka,
and his claim to be recognized as a vassal of the Hittite king.
It seems to be implied that the authority of Ahhiyawa extends,
at least nominally, over Millawanda, though that city in fact
appears to act with considerable independence. How far the king
of Ahhiyawa was really responsible for these infringements of the
Hittite sphere of influence our evidence does not show. Possibly
we have simply the phenomenon of Mycenaean vassals doing a
little empire-building on their own account. What is clear is that
at this time the Mycenaeans were a power to be reckoned with
and treated with diplomatic respect even by the great Hittite
empire. Greeks had made their début on the stage of world history,
and in a major role.

[1] §v, 8, 49; §v, 14, 59 ff.
[2] §v, 14, 2–194; §v, 10, 1 f., 17; §v, 11, 10 ff.; §v, 8, 47 ff.

CHAPTER XXII (*b*)

CYPRUS IN THE LATE BRONZE AGE

INTRODUCTION

In the five hundred years that the Late Bronze Age lasted in Cyprus the island finally entered into full association with her more developed neighbours. This brought not only a share of their greater cultural sophistication and material prosperity but also of the troubles which beset them and the disasters by which they were eventually overwhelmed. When the end of the period was reached, Cypriot material culture had largely lost its special character, which for better or worse had distinguished it in the preceding phases of the Bronze Age, and had assumed a flavour almost entirely compounded of influences from stronger neighbours.

The Late Cypriot period is divided into three main phases, of which L.C. I occupies the years *c.* 1550–1400 B.C., L.C. II the years 1400–1200 B.C. and L.C. III the final stages from 1200–1050 B.C. These main phases have been divided into a number of subphases, which are not of immediate concern.[1] In many respects, L.C. I is an extension of the Middle Bronze Age, and this is strongly reflected in its material culture. L.C. II coincides with the island's high prosperity in the period of intimate trading ties with the Aegean. Material culture shed its homespun quality. The beginning of L.C. III witnessed major convulsions in neighbouring areas, and the arrival in Cyprus of refugee settlers from Greece whose appearance marked the first major step in the Hellenization of the island, including, it is to be presumed, the introduction of the Arcado-Cypriot version of the Greek tongue. There were few survivors of the last disastrous years of L.C. III to usher in the Early Iron Age.

VI. THE PATTERN OF LATE CYPRIOT SETTLEMENT

The distribution of L.C. sites[2] shows that the period started modestly, even uncertainly. By L.C. II, however, it is clear that

---

* An original version of this chapter was published in fascicle 43 in 1966; the present chapter includes revisions made in 1971.

[1] §VII, 9, 197.   [2] §VI, 1, 142–6.

there had been a great increase in population, which can be deduced from the corresponding increase in the number of occupied settlements and in the overall size of individual sites. In both earlier phases of the Bronze Age, large areas of Cyprus seem not to have been settled; only the Troödos mountains seem to have been shunned in the L.C. period. Comparison of the locations of L.C. sites with their predecessors shows the furtherance of the move to the coast, especially in the area between Cape Pyla and Cape Kiti, which was initiated in M.C. III. The old fears that had concentrated so much settlement inland in the river valleys, on the upland plateaux, and along the foothills of the Kyrenia hills, often under the protection of promontory forts, gave way before an optimistic self-confidence, which encouraged the founding or great expansion of countless sites on or immediately adjoining the coast. Some inland settlements, amongst them Nicosia and Ayios Sozomenos, evidently maintained the importance they had enjoyed in M.C. times, but many of the old centres dwindled to little more than village status, or were abandoned altogether. Thus Dhenia lingered on, a shadow of its former greatness, but the *Vrysis tou Barba* cemetery at Lapithos was deserted. It is very unlikely that even the most prosperous of the inland sites in L.C. could compete in wealth or importance with the coastal settlements. Though north Cyprus seems never to have regained the full importance it had enjoyed in the E.C. period, sites at Vasilia,[1] Lapithos,[2] Kazaphani,[3] Akanthou[4] and Dhavlos[5] suggest that this side of the island must have had some share in the sea traffic. But the richest L.C. sites belong to the south coast. From Palaeopaphos (now Kouklia)[6] in the extreme south-west to Enkomi in Salamis bay on the eastern shore a succession of townships was established on or near the coast. One group merits special mention. This is the concentration that surrounds Larnaka bay;[7] it was based on the sheltered harbours of Citium (mod. Larnaka) and Hala Sultan Tekke. Many of the cemeteries attached to these settlements have been excavated or pillaged;[8] the contents of their graves offer an idea of their material prosperity and the volume of trade goods imported from abroad which their citizens commanded. Only at Enkomi was this level of wealth rivalled.

Insight into the way Cyprus worked in the Late Bronze Age

[1] §vi, 1, 169.   [2] §vi, 1, 165–6.   [3] G, 8 (1964), 335–8.
[4] G, 8 (1962), 374–7; *C.A.H.* ii³, pt. 1, pp. 172, 174 and n. 9.
[5] §vi, 1, 162.
[6] G, 11, 174; §vi, 1, 165; §xi, 7.   [7] §vi, 3.   [8] G, 10; G, 11, 180–8.

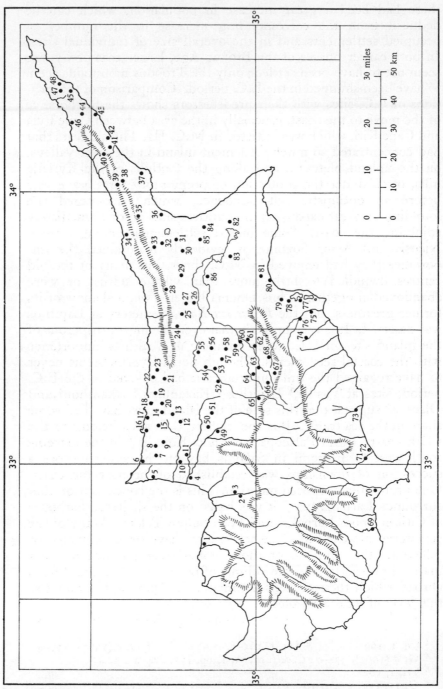

Map 6. Middle Bronze Age Cyprus. (In some cases, several adjacent but separate sites are represented by a single symbol.)

NUMERICAL KEY

1 Kato Pyrghos
2 Linou
3 Katydhata
4 Syrianokhori
5 Ayia Irini
6 Kormakiti
7 Dhiorios
8 Myrtou (Stephania)
9 Myrtou
10 Kapouti (Kapnistos)
11 Kapouti
12 Skylloura
13 Ayios Ermolaos
14 Pileri
15 Larnaka tis Lapithou
16 Vasilia
17 Lapithos
18 Elea

19 Karmi
20 Krini
21 Dhikomo (Onisha)
22 Kyrenia
23 Bellapais (Vounous)
24 Kythrea
25 Bey Keuy
26 Angastina
27 Marathovouno
28 Trypimeni
29 Psilatos
30 Milea
31 Lapathos
32 Ayios Iakovos
33 Ayios Iakovos (Melia)
34 Phlamoudhi
35 Ovgoros
36 Trikomo

37 Ayios Theodhoros
38 Livadhia
39 Komi Kebir
40 Lythrangomi
41 Vasili
42 Neta
43 Korovia (Nitovikla)
44 Galinoporni
45 Galinoporni (Trakhonas)
46 Ayios Thyrsos
47 Rizokarpaso
48 Rizokarpaso (Sylla)
49 Akaki
50 Dhenia
51 Kokkini Trimithia
52 Lakatamia
53 Strovolos
54 Nicosia

55 Kaimakli
56 Leondari Vouno
57 Laxia
58 Yeri
59 Ayios Sozomenos (Nikolidhes)
60 Ayios Sozomenos (Ambelia)
61 Potamia
62 Dhali
63 Kochati
64 Margi
65 Politiko
66 Kataliondas
67 Lythrodhonda
68 Alambra
69 Evdhimou
70 Episkopi

71 Polemidhia
72 Limassol
73 Moni
74 Anglisidhes
75 Arpera
76 Klavidhia
77 Hala Sultan Tekke
78 Larnaka (Laxia tou Riou)
79 Livadhi
80 Pyla (Verghin)
81 Pyla
82 Akhyritou
83 Kalopsidha
84 Enkomi
85 Styllos
86 Sinda

ALPHABETICAL KEY

Akaki 49
Akhyritou 82
Alambra 68
Angastina 26
Anglisidhes 74
Arpera 75
Ayia Irini 5
Ayios Ermolaos 13
Ayios Iakovos 32
Ayios Iakovos (Melia) 33
Ayios Sozomenos (Ambelia) 60
Ayios Sozomenos (Nikolidhes) 59
Ayios Theodhoros 37
Ayios Thyrsos 46
Bellapais (Vounous) 23
Bey Keuy 25

Dhali 62
Dhenia 50
Dhikomo (Onisha) 21
Dhiorios 7
Elea 18
Enkomi 84
Episkopi 70
Evdhimou 69
Galinoporni 44
Galinoporni (Trakhonas) 45
Hala Sultan Tekke 77
Kaimakli 55
Kalopsidha 83
Kapouti 11
Kapouti (Kapnistos) 10
Karmi 19
Kataliondas 66
Kato Pyrgos 1

Katydhata 3
Klavidhia 76
Kokkini Trimithia 51
Komi Kebir 39
Kormakiti 6
Korovia (Nitovikla) 43
Kochati 63
Krini 20
Kyrenia 22
Kythrea 24
Lakatamia 52
Lapathos 31
Lapithos 17
Larnaka (Laxia tou Riou) 78
Larnaka tis Lapithou 15
Laxia 57
Leondari Vouno 56
Limassol 72

Linou 2
Livadhi 79
Livadhia 38
Lythrangomi 40
Lythrodhonda 67
Marathovouno 27
Margi 64
Milea 30
Moni 73
Myrtou 9
Myrtou (Stephania) 8
Neta 42
Nicosia 54
Ovgoros 35
Phlamoudhi 34
Pileri 14
Polemidhia 71

Politiko 65
Potamia 61
Psilatos 29
Pyla 81
Pyla (Verghin) 80
Rizokarpaso 47
Rizokarpaso (Sylla) 48
Sinda 86
Skylloura 12
Strovolos 53
Styllos 85
Syrianokhori 4
Trikomo 36
Trypimeni 28
Vasili 41
Vasilia 16
Yeri 58

may be had from observing the interrelationship of L.C. settlements, even though the means by which internal administration was managed cannot even be guessed at. Behind the prosperity which so distinctively marks the L.C. II period at the coastal towns undoubtedly lay successful management of the commodities sought by foreign merchants, of which none can have been more profitable than copper. A number of L.C. settlements are so located[1] that copper mining and smelting seem likely to have been their *raison d'être*. Into this category may be put the sites at Katydata,[2] Akhera,[3] Lythrodondas[4] and Kalavassos.[5] They were all well placed on lines of communication by which the raw material produced by their energies could be dispatched to the industrial centres at the coast. It is probably significant that the two most prosperous inland sites, Nicosia and Ayios Sozomenos, were situated athwart the routes by which the consignments of ore or smelted copper travelled from the mining centres to the factories. The towns near Larnaka bay, moreover, may have drawn on an extra ore-body at Troulli[6] little more than 10 miles due north of Larnaka, though Late Bronze Age exploitation of this Troulli copper has not been proved.

In addition to these two types of settlement were the old rural sites, many of them in regions inhabited throughout the Bronze Age, depending on agriculture[7] and stock-rearing for their existence. Such agricultural centres continued to be concentrated around the great springs or along the water courses adjoining light and easily cultivable soils, such as those of the Kormakiti peninsula, the Kyrenia foothills, the Karpass peninsula and the river valleys of the western half of the central plain. Settlement not only continued in these areas, it expanded considerably. Possibly this rural expansion resulted from a conscious agrarian policy dictated by the urban centres in response to the needs of their growing populations, more and more of whom, it may be presumed, were absorbed by the urban trades and skills which developed during the L.C. period. If so, the move into the virgin lands of the Kormakiti peninsula[8] was at the behest of the town site at *Toumba tou Skourou*[9] near the sea in the plain north of Morphou, whose wealth and importance may have matched Enkomi's.

It may be inferred that the L.C. period saw the development of

---

1 §VIII, 6, 32.   2 §VI, 1, 164.   3 G, 8 (1960), 245, 248; (1961), 310.
4 §VI, 1, 166.   5 §VI, 1, 164.
6 §VIII, 6, 21; §XIII, 4, 39–40.   7 G, 5.   8 §VI, 1, 142; §VI, 2.
9 G, 8 (1964), 313–14; §VI, 1, 167; *R.D.A.C.* (1936), 115.

a complex internal marketing system, in which the produce of the copper mines was sent to the manufacturing towns, together with surplus agricultural produce from the rural areas. Excavation of the rustic sanctuary at *Pigadhes*, Myrtou,[1] where magazines containing large pithoi were found, suggests that religious centres may have acted as middlemen in such internal trade, and that commercial transactions may have been nominally on behalf of the gods. Return traffic to the inland settlements, both industrial and agricultural, can be seen in the imported trade goods, like Mycenaean pottery, that have been found in their cemeteries; Akhera and Angastina provide clear instances.[2]

There can be no more vivid illustration of the magnitude of the disasters that brought about the end of the Bronze Age than the wholesale desertion of the areas of settlement that took place in the twelfth and eleventh centuries B.C. Even the richest and most powerful sites were not immune from this process. The occupation at Enkomi may have lingered on until the end of the eleventh century;[3] its place was later taken by Salamis. In the coastal area which had been so prosperous only Citium survived of the towns on Larnaka bay. In the long stretch between there and Curium the post-Bronze-Age foundation of Amathus was the only reminder of former prosperity. Only at Palaeopaphos may occupation have continued into historical times without interruption. The same kind of contraction took place inland. The Ayios Sozomenos group of sites was abandoned, though their role and importance were eventually inherited by Idalium (now Dhali) a few miles further up the Yalias valley. The sites at Politiko and Pera survived as did Tamassus, although there was almost certainly an interruption. *Toumba tou Skourou* at Morphou may have survived briefly into the Early Iron Age, but its place was taken by Soli some miles away on the south side of the bay. This change may be explained by a deterioration in the port facilities of the Morphou site due to the silting of the mouths of the Serakhis and Ovgos rivers.

It is difficult to isolate the point at which this calamity took place. But for the flourishing character of material culture at Enkomi, Citium and Palaeopaphos in the twelfth century B.C., a date early in L.C. III would seem probable. Material of this date amongst surface finds from unexcavated L.C. sites is rare, especially in comparison with the mass of sites at which L.C. II material has been collected. Such evidence suggests that the Karpass was deserted by the middle of the twelfth century; so was the

[1] §XII, 12.   [2] §VIII, 22.   [3] §X, 7; §XI; 3.

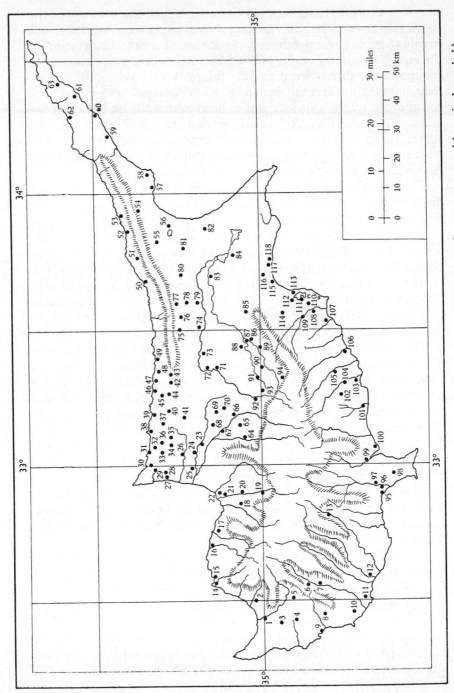

Map 7. Late Bronze Age Cyprus. (In some cases, several adjacent but separate sites are represented by a single symbol.)

2 Magounda
3 Drousha
4 Pano Arodhes
5 Yiolou
6 Milia
7 Ayios Dhimitrianos
8 Tala
9 Maa
10 Yeroskipos
11 Timi
12 Kouklia (Palea Paphos)
13 Omodhos
14 Pomos
15 Pakhyammos
16 Kato Pyrgos
17 Loutros
18 Apliki
19 Kaliana
20 Katydhata
21 Pendayia (Mandres)
22 Pendayia
23 Kyra
24 Khrysiliou

   Skourou)
26 Kapouti
27 Ayia Irini (Palaikastros)
28 Ayia Irini
29 Kormakiti (Ayious)
30 Kormakiti
31 Orga
32 Panagra
33 Dhiorios
34 Karpasha
35 Myrtou
36 Myrtou (Stephania)
37 Larnaka tis Lapithou
38 Vasilia
39 Lapithos
40 Pileri
41 Skylloura
42 Dhikomo (Onisha)
43 Dhikomo
44 Keumurju
45 Karmi
46 Temblos
47 Kyrenia

49 Ayios Epiktitos
50 Akanthou (Moulos)
51 Akanthou
52 Phlamoudhi
53 Dhavlos
54 Kantara
55 Ayios Iakovos (Melia)
56 Trikomo
57 Gastria
58 Ayios Theodhoros
59 Neta
60 Korovia (Nitovikla)
61 Galinoporni (Trakhonas)
62 Ayios Thyrsos
63 Rizokarpaso
64 Kato Moni
65 Akhera
66 Meniko
67 Akaki
68 Dhenia
69 Kokkini Trimithia
70 Paleometokho
71 Strovolos

73 Kaimakli
74 Palekythro
75 Kythrea
76 Bey Keuy
77 Chatos
78 Marathovouno
79 Angastina
80 Psilatos
81 Milea
82 Enkomi
83 Sinda
84 Kalopsidha
85 Athienou
86 Potamia
87 Ayios Sozomenos (Ambelia)
88 Ayios Sozomenos (Nikolidhes)
89 Dhali
90 Kochati
91 Analiondas
92 Politiko
93 Kambia
94 Lythrodhonda

96 Episkopi
97 Erimi
98 Asomatos
99 Polemidhia
100 Limassol
101 Moni
102 Asgata
103 Mari
104 Kalavassos
105 Khirokitia
106 Maroni
107 Kivisil
108 Arpera
109 Klavidhia
110 Dhromolaxia
111 Hala Sultan Tekke
112 Larnaka (Laxia tou Riou)
113 Larnaka (Kition)
114 Aradhippou
115 Pyla (Verghin)
116 Pyla
117 Pyla (Kokkinokremmos)
118 Pyla (Steno)

Phlamoudhi 52
Pileri 40
Polemidhia 99
Polis 1
Politiko 92
Pomos 14
Potamia 86
Psilatos 80
Pyla 116
Pyla (Kokkinokremmos) 117
Pyla (Steno) 118
Pyla (Verghin) 115
Rizokarpaso 63
Sinda 83
Skylloura 41
Strovolos 71
Tala 8
Temblos 46
Timi 11
Trikomo 56
Vasilia 38
Yeroskipos 10
Yiolou 5

ALPHABETICAL KEY

Akaki 67
Akanthou 51
Akanthou (Moulos) 50
Akhera 65
Analiondas 91
Angastina 79
Apliki 18
Aradhippou 114
Arpera 108
Asgata 102
Asomatos 98
Athienou 85
Ayia Irini 28
Ayia Irini (Palaikastros) 27
Ayios Dhimitrianos 7
Ayios Epiktitos 49
Ayios Iakovos (Melia) 55
Ayios Sozomenos (Ambelia) 87
Ayios Sozomenos (Nikolidhes) 88
Ayios Theodhoros 58
Ayios Thyrsos 62
Bey Keuy 76
Chatos 77
Dhali 89

Dhavlos 53
Dhenia 68
Dhikomo (Onisha) 42
Dhiorios 33
Dhromolaxia 110
Drousha 3
Enkomi 82
Episkopi 96
Episkopi (Kaloriziki) 95
Erimi 97
Galinoporni (Trakhonas) 61
Gastria 57
Hala Sultan Tekke 111
Kaimakli 73
Kalavassos 104
Kaliana 19
Kalopsidha 84
Kambia 93
Kantara 54
Kapouti 26
Karmi 45
Karpasha 34
Kato Moni 64

Kato Pyrgos 16
Katydhata 20
Kazaphani 48
Keumurju 44
Khirokitia 105
Khrysiliou 24
Kivisil 107
Klavidhia 109
Kochati 90
Kokkini Trimithia 69
Kormakiti 30
Kormakiti (Ayious) 29
Korovia (Nitovikla) 60
Kouklia (Palea Paphos) 12
Kyra 23
Kyrenia 47
Kythrea 75
Lapithos 39
Larnaka (Kition) 113
Larnaka (Laxia tou Riou) 112
Larnaka tis Lapithou 37
Limassol 100
Loutros 17
Lythrodhonda 94

Maa 9
Magounda 2
Marathovouno 78
Mari 103
Maroni 106
Meriko 66
Milea 81
Milia 6
Moni 101
Morphou (Toumba tou Skourou) 25
Myrtou 35
Myrtou (Stephania) 36
Neta 59
Nicosia 72
Omodhos 13
Orga 31
Pakhyammos 15
Palekythro 74
Paleometokho 70
Panagra 32
Pano Arodhes 4
Pendayia 22
Pendayia (Mandres) 21

Kormakiti peninsula. On the south Kyrenia foothills only Dhikomo and Palekythro provide certain evidence of continued occupation. The onset of the Early Iron Age reveals the full measure of the catastrophe and the nadir of the island's fortunes. By the end of the eleventh century, the known centres of settlement had dwindled to a mere handful of sites,[1] chiefly known from the location of their cemeteries. Lapithos[2] and Karavas[3] represent the occupation of the north coast, Citium,[4] Amathus,[5] Curium[6] and Palaeopaphos[7] the south. In the far west was Marium[8] (now Polis-tis-Krysokhou); Idalium survived in central Cyprus. Cypro-Geometric dawn indeed came on a sombre and desolate scene.

VII. EVENTS IN CYPRUS BEFORE THE AEGEAN CONNEXION

The Late Cypriot period emerged from the confines of the Middle Bronze Age without significant change of population or break in material culture. The process took place in the middle of the sixteenth century B.C., and synchronizes approximately with the expulsion of the Hyksos from Egypt and the establishment of the Eighteenth Dynasty, which was to bring the pacification of the Levantine littoral and the adjoining seas that culminated under Tuthmosis III. The touchstone for the new period is the appearance of a new pottery fabric, Base Ring ware,[9] starting almost exclusively as a class of small jugs (*bilbils*) for unguents etc., later developing larger jugs and cups for common use. White Slip ware[10] came into use almost as soon; both fabrics are handmade. Material culture, however, continued in very much a M.C. mould for many years, so that degenerate versions of the familiar M.C. fabrics—White Painted, Red-on-Black, Black and Red Slip wares—outnumber the new goods. L.C. I metalwork[11] likewise is exclusively a poor reflection of the simple M.C. repertory.

Continuity between M.C. III and L.C. I is to be seen in many ways. At home the rise of the new towns on the east and south coasts continued. At Enkomi[12] to a M.C. III building nucleus

---

[1] §vi, 1, 146.   [2] G, 4(i), 172–265.   [3] *R.D.A.C.* (1964), 114–29.
[4] §xi, 8; §xi, 9; §xi, 10.   [5] G, 4(ii), 1–141.
[6] §xii, 2.   [7] *Liverpool Bulletin*, 2 (1952), 51–2.
[8] G, 4(ii), 181–459.   [9] §vii, 9, 34–43; §vii, 10. See Plate 150(*a*).
[10] *C.A.H.* ii³, pt. 1, pp. 165 f; §vii, 9, 43–50; §vii, 1; §vii, 5; §viii, 12, 39–42. See Plate 150(*b*)
[11] §viii, 6, 299.   [12] §x, 7.

there was added in L.C. I a fortress block on the north side of the town. Though it was destroyed soon after its construction, it was quickly rebuilt, with a modified plan. Part of it was now used for industrial processes connected with copper-working, an industry which was concentrated in the north half of the city almost throughout its history.[1]

At Nitovikla[2] the fortress had been destroyed by fire at the end of M.C. III. It was repaired and recommissioned in L.C. I; it seems to have been demilitarized, but not entirely abandoned, before the end of the period. At Nikolidhes, near Ayios Sozomenos, a very robust building first erected in L.C. I has also been identified as a fortress.[3] It suffered destruction by fire before the end of L.C. I a, was quickly rebuilt, but was abandoned before L.C. I b was over. It is uncertain whether any of the fortified sites above the Aloupos valley or on the south Kyrenia foothills[4] remained in use during L.C. I. It seems probable, however, that the symptoms of insecurity which applied to the M.C. III period continued through much of L.C. I. It is not certain, however, whether the mass-burials which were made in L.C. I a graves at Ayios Iakovos,[5] Pendayia[6] and Myrtou, *Stephania*,[7] are to be attributed to disturbed political conditions or to some natural misfortune.[8]

The Cypriots continued to enjoy and to develop their trade links with the Levant and Egypt throughout L.C. I; this is in sharp contrast with a virtual exclusion from Cilicia (whose local version of Base Ring ware[9] may have been copied from North Syria), for which there must be some political explanation. Conceivably those who enjoyed the protection of the Egyptian fleet[10] did so in return for observing certain economic sanctions. But Cyprus was free to traffic with North Syria, where Alalakh and Ugarit received a high proportion of the trade, Palestine, notably with Gaza (Tell el-'Ajjūl), and Egypt itself, where Base Ring ware *bilbils* were particularly popular.[11] Only a minute number of Cypriot goods travelled to the Aegean in these years; White Slip and Base Ring pottery have occurred in Rhodes,[12] at Phylakopi in Melos,[13] in Thera[14] and at Cnossus.[15] Foreign goods reached Cyprus in some quantity during L.C. I. Especial interest attaches

[1] G, 7, 517.   [2] G, 4(i), 371–407.
[3] *C.A.H.* II³, pt. 1, p. 168; §vii, 19, 11–12.
[4] §vi, 1, 140–1.   [5] G, 4(i), 302–55.
[6] G, 8 (1961), 308–9.   [7] §vi, 2, 52.
[8] §vii, 9, 199.   [9] *C.A.H.* II³, pt. 1, p. 174.
[10] §vi, 2, 51.   [11] §vii, 9, 151–60; §vii, 3.   [12] §vii, 9, 160.
[13] *Ibid.*   [14] *Ibid.*   [15] *C.A.H.* II³, pt. 1, p. 173.

to the highly decorative pottery fabric, often embellished with birds or fish, known as Bichrome wheel-made ware,[1] found on a number of sites in east Cyprus but most particularly at Milia[2] on the north side of the Mesaoria. The ware is probably Palestinian; an important factory was located at Gaza.[3] Of ambiguous origin are the spindle bottles of Red Lustrous ware[4] which first appear in L.C. I a grave groups, many having had *graffiti* incised on their bases before firing. Of the many sources suggested for their manufacture[5] North Syria is perhaps the least improbable. The fabric had a very wide currency in contemporary trade, including the Aegean and Anatolia as well as the Levant and Egypt.

Foreign inspiration must have been responsible for the building at Enkomi in L.C. I a of a small tholos-like tomb[6] within the area of the settlement. The diameter of the chamber, just under 2·50 m., equalled its height. It was partly set into a pit sunk in the bed-rock, but the upper part of the corbelled masonry was probably free-standing, covered by an earth tumulus. Both its diminutive size and the lack of supporting evidence from the Aegean at this date make a relationship with Mycenaean tholoi improbable.[7] A connexion has been suggested with Middle Bronze Age tombs at Megiddo,[8] which may be significant. No other tomb of this type has yet been reported in Cyprus.

The duration of L.C. I may be estimated as a century and a half, between *c.* 1550 B.C. and *c.* 1400 B.C. The atmosphere of insecurity that was mirrored in the material remains at the start of the period gave way to one of prosperous stability that Cyprus owed to and shared with her powerful neighbours. Security in the east Mediterranean for which Egypt was responsible was about to invite the active attentions of the Mycenaean Greeks who, with the destruction of Cnossus accomplished *c.* 1400 B.C., had become masters of the sea routes to the east.

VIII. CYPRUS AND THE AEGEAN AREA

Though there are clear indications in Cyprus of contact with Crete and Greece during the late sixteenth and earlier fifteenth century B.C.,[9] her relationship with the west during almost the whole of L.C. I was insignificant; Syria, Palestine and Egypt

---

[1] §vi, 2, 53; §vii, 2. [2] §vii, 11. [3] §vii, 2.
[4] §vii, 9, 51–4; §vii, 4. [5] §vii, 4, 194–6.
[6] G, 4(i), 570–3; §vii, 9, 18–19; §vii, 12.
[7] Cf. *Antiq.* xxxiv (1960), 166–76.
[8] §vii, 9, 147–50. [9] §viii, 6, 36; §viii, 10, 203–15; §viii, 25, 26–31.

claimed the exclusive attention of her manufacturers and merchants. There had been tenuous links between Cyprus and Crete in E.C. III and M.C. I,[1] but these had lapsed before M.C. III. No L.M. I object has been identified in Cyprus, and L.M. II finds are few and far between.[2] Contemporary Mycenaean pottery has been found in equally small quantities. It is clear that for well over a century after 1550 B.C. the Aegean states were even less interested in Cyprus, or less able to visit her than they had been in the Middle Bronze Age.

A change took place during L.C. Ib (c. 1450–1400 B.C.), when Mycenaean IIb and IIIa I pottery appears in modest, but significant quantities. This material has been found at Milia and Enkomi in east Cyprus,[3] at Nicosia[4] in the centre, and at Maroni, Hala Sultan Tekke and Arpera on the south coast.[5] Its appearance should be associated with similar finds in the Levant and Egypt.[6]

Whatever the historical facts may be that are represented by the sack of Cnossus c. 1400 B.C.,[7] that catastrophe seems to have cleared the way for a great Mycenaean trading expansion into the east Mediterranean, of which Cyprus became the focus. What had been a trickle of Mycenaean trade in the late fifteenth century became a flood during the fourteenth, a flood which was maintained for at least the first half of the thirteenth century. The quantities of Mycenaean IIIa2 and IIIb pottery from the cemeteries of Cyprus are so enormous that some have been persuaded that Greek colonies were established at a number of Cypriot sites early in the fourteenth century[8] and that Greek craftsmen set up their pottery factories in these colonial towns to produce most of the Mycenaean pottery that has been found in Cyprus. Particular attention has been directed to Mycenaean pictorial pottery,[9] more of which has been found in Cyprus than in the rest of Mycenaean world put together. It has been suggested that the style of the pictorial vases found in Cyprus is different from that in which the vases of mainland provenance are decorated. This has led to a fairly widely held belief that the home of the pictorial style was in the ateliers of colonial Cyprus, and that the pictorial work of the mainland came from derivative schools inspired by eastern artists. Any Mycenaean pictorial vase of this

[1] *C.A.H.* ii³, pt. 1, p. 173.
[2] *Ibid.* p. 174 notes 9 and 10; §viii, 10, 205–6.
[3] §viii, 25, 27.   [4] §viii, 6, 36.
[5] §viii, 25, 28–9.   [6] §viii, 25, 56–8.
[7] To adopt the traditional date for this event.
[8] G, 2; G, 3; §vii, 9, 92–7; §viii, 6, 40–4; §viii, 13; §viii, 21; §viii, 25, 25–6.
[9] §viii, nos. 4; 8; 11; 12; 18. See Plate 151 (*a*).

alleged eastern school which appears on the Greek mainland is supposed to be an import from the east. Recent laboratory work suggests[1] that the mass of Mycenaean pottery in Cyprus in L.C. II was imported from the Aegean, almost certainly from the Peloponnese. Some, however, particularly in the later thirteenth century B.C., was made by Cypriot potters in imitation of Mycenaean work. Though Cyprus provided a most appreciative market for the work of the pictorial vase-painters, finds in Greece, particularly at Berbati[2] in the Argolid, have shown that the lack of pictorial vases of the so-called Levanto-Helladic type is more apparent than real. It was the repeated visits of Aegean trading ships during L.C. II, not the presence of Aegean colonies, that was responsible for the proliferation of Mycenaean III a and III b pottery in Cyprus.

The proposal to locate Aegean colonies in Cyprus during the fourteenth and thirteenth centuries B.C. has never surmounted the obstacle of missing evidence.[3] Though Mycenaean pottery is present in such enormous amounts, practically every other characteristic of Mycenaean material culture is missing. An unmistakably Cypriot cultural atmosphere was dominant even at those sites where Aegean pottery has been found in greatest abundance. It is exceptional for a Cypriot tomb group to contain more Mycenaean than Cypriot vases;[4] the tombs themselves are Cypriot in design and burial custom. Fine Mycenaean metalwork in Cyprus is confined to the magnificent silver bowl with inlaid gold and niello bucrania[5] and two other silver vases, all from Enkomi.[6] There is no Mycenaean bronzework in a L.C. II context,[7] while Mycenaean types of stone vases are unknown. No Aegean sealstones have been recorded. Nearly all the characteristic types of Mycenaean jewellery are missing[8] from even the wealthiest Cypriot burials, though the influence of Mycenaean ornament can be seen in some of the work of Cypriot goldsmiths.

Towards the end of the thirteenth century B.C. some kind of recession took place in the trade exchanges between Greece and Cyprus. This happens in the context of the increasing instability on the mainland that is attested by the concentration on military works and by the troubles at Mycenae that resulted in the burning of the houses outside the citadel. This phase is marked in Cyprus

---

[1] §VIII, 5.   [2] §VIII, 1.
[3] §VIII, 6, 35–54; §VIII, 16; §VIII, 19; §VIII, 24.
[4] E.g. G, 4(i), 546–58.   [5] §VII, 8, 379–89. See Plate 146(b).
[6] §VIII, 6, 46; §VIII, 23.   [7] §VIII, 6, 300–1.   [8] §VIII, 6, 45–6.

by an increased output of Cypriot pottery made in the Mycenaean manner, and a corresponding scarcity of the genuine article.[1]

The meaning of the relationship between Cyprus and the Mycenaeans during L.C. II is not difficult to appreciate, particularly if the mass of Mycenaean pottery in Cyprus is accepted as imported. Mycenaean Greece maintained a great demand for Egyptian and Levantine merchandise, and a regular trading association was built up between the two areas. In the process, Aegean merchants learned of the value of the ports of south and east Cyprus both as markets and as bases of operations for their trafficking further afield. The dealings of these Mycenaean merchants can be traced from the 'Amūq plain in north Syria to the Second cataract in Egypt;[2] they are nowhere so much in evidence as in Cyprus. Cyprus proved an appreciative market for their painted pottery and whatever perishable commodities may have been packed in their ubiquitous stirrup jars and pilgrim flasks.[3] The well-to-do evinced an especial liking for the big Mycenaean craters on which processions of chariots or scenes from the bull-ring were depicted.[4] In this they merely foreshadowed the taste for fine Greek pottery shown centuries later by wealthy Etruscans. Though proof is lacking, it can hardly be doubted that copper was bought in Cyprus for Greece. Its importance to the Mycenaean economy is alone sufficient to account for the effort expended on the Cyprus trade.

IX. THE IDENTIFICATION
OF CYPRUS WITH ALASHIYA

The evidence of archaeology proves that intimate terms existed between Cyprus and her more powerful and sophisticated neighbours in the Levant and Egypt during the Late Bronze Age. It is natural therefore to try to identify references to Cyprus in contemporary documents; regrettably, her own few texts are still undeciphered. Both in texts found at Boğazköy[5] and in the archives preserved at el-Amarna[6] are references to a kingdom called Alashiya. Although its location has not been definitely established, it is commonly considered to be Cyprus, whether in part or whole.[7] It is even suggested that Alashiya should be more

---

[1] §VIII, 5; §VIII, 25, 37–44.   [2] §VIII, 25.   [3] §VIII, 21, pls. 20–2; 30.
[4] Bibliography of Mycenaean pictorial pottery in *B.S.A.* 60 (1965), cf. §VIII, 11.
[5] G, 6, 45–7; §IX, 9; §IX, 13.   [6] G, 6, 38–45; §IX, 4; §IX, 14.
[7] G, 6, 36–50, with references, supplemented by *C.A.H.* II[3], pt. 1, p. 174; §IX, 13; §IX, 5.

narrowly identified with Enkomi, and that in the Middle Bronze Age the name belonged to Kalopsidha.[1]

Before the identification is accepted, the evidence of the texts themselves should be considered. In Boğazköy texts of c. 1400 B.C., Alashiya is represented as within the sphere of Hittite political influence.[2] When Tudkhaliash III was assassinated, his brothers were sent into exile in Alashiya. Apparently, Muwatallish, son of Murshilish II (c. 1330–1310 B.C.) confirmed Hittite rule in Alashiya whither, somewhat later, Khattushilish III banished his adversaries.[3] This Hittite suzerainty continued until c. 1200 B.C., according to texts of the time of Arnuwandash III (1245–1220 B.C.). About this time one of the king's vassals, a certain Madduwattash, grew so strong that he eventually emerged as the *de facto* ruler of south-west Anatolia, and elected to attack Hittite territory, including Alashiya. Though the text is mutilated[4] it seems that Madduwattash in company with Attarshiyash of Ahhiyawa and a third ally called 'the man of Piggaia' had invaded Alashiya and taken prisoners. Arnuwandash protests that Alashiya is his territory and demands that Madduwattash should return them. In return, Madduwattash professes ignorance that Alashiya was Hittite territory, and undertakes to return the prisoners. More recently discovered Boğazköy documents[5] refer to an action between the Hittite fleet and the ships of Alashiya, including a Hittite victory that resulted in the burning of the ships of Alashiya, at sea. This engagement took place at the end of the thirteenth century B.C.

In Egyptian sources, there are references to Alashiya in the time of Tuthmosis III,[6] apparently in connexion with towns in the neighbourhood of Aleppo and the Euphrates. But the chief Egyptian contexts are the Amarna letters,[7] which include correspondence that was exchanged between the pharaoh, probably Akhenaten, and the king of Alashiya in the second quarter of the fourteenth century. We note that the king of Alashiya writes to his 'brother', making use of the cuneiform script and the Akkadian tongue. Alashiya complains that his territory is annually raided by the Lukki; they plunder his towns. He exchanges emissaries with Egypt—he sends a present of copper, apologizing for its smallness, but misfortune has befallen the land—Nergal (the Babylonian god of battle and death) has slain all his people.

---

[1] *C.A.H.* ii³, pt. i, pp. 168 and 169 n. 4.
[2] G, 6, 45.　　　　　　　　　　　[3] *Ibid.*
[4] §ix, 3, 9; §ix, 10, 97–102.　　　[5] §ix, 9, 20–3; §ix, 13, 131–4.
[6] §ix, 14, 33.　　　　　　　　　　[7] §ix, 4, nos. 33–40.

In return, Alashiya asks for gifts of silver, oxen and oil. We hear of a citizen of Alashiya who has died in Egypt; his king requests that his property should be sent home for the benefit of his son and widow. There is a puzzling reference to Alashiya in a communication to the pharaoh from Rib-Adda, governor of Byblus, in which he explains that in order to please him he had arranged for an official called Amanmasha to go to Alashiya. Later Egyptian references to Alashiya include mention in an inscription of the eighth year of Ramesses III which deals with his Northern War, where it is associated with Kheta, Qode, Carchemish and, perhaps, Arvad. The last Egyptian mention of Alashiya comes as late as the eleventh century when, c. 1085 B.C., Wenamun, emissary of Hrihor, was sent to Phoenicia to acquire wood from Lebanon. After a number of misadventures, Wenamun was driven off course to Alashiya, where he narrowly escaped death at the hands of the local people. He was brought before Hatiba, the local queen; an interpreter was needed.[1] The document is incomplete, and the sequel is lost.

Egyptian records mention a territory, Asy,[2] that is also considered to be Cyprus, or part of Cyprus. That Asy appears side by side with Alashiya in at least one text[3] would in fact compel identification of the two names as different parts of Cyprus. Asy was subject to Egypt in the time of Tuthmosis III. In the Karnak Annals[4] are references to booty from Asy that included horses, chariots of gold and silver. Tribute levelled on Asy included copper, unrefined and refined, lead and elephants' tusks. Asy is mentioned in the Nineteenth Dynasty geographical lists, under Sethos I and Ramesses II; most of the identifiable names with which it is coupled are on the mainland, towards the north. Since there are no other east Mediterranean islands, however, mention of Cyprus in a topographical list would inevitably place it in juxtaposition with regions which might otherwise be regarded as inappropriate.[5]

There is mention of Alashiya in sources other than Egyptian and Hittite. In the Mari archives of c. 1800 B.C. there is a reference to the export of copper from Alashiya to Mari.[6] Alashiya is also mentioned in eighteenth-century texts from Alalakh, though there is no specific information.[7] Several Ugaritic texts contain details of relations between Alashiya and Ugarit. In one, the king of Ugarit writes to a king who is probably to be identi-

---

[1] G, 6, 44–5.   [2] §IX, 14.   [3] G, 6, 40.
[4] G, 6, 39.   [5] §IX, 14.
[6] C.A.H. II³, pt. 1, p. 174.   [7] §IX, 15, 8.

fied as the king of Alashiya, whom he greets as 'my father', to complain of acts of piracy taking place on his unprotected territory.[1] There is also a letter from Eshuwara, High Steward of Alashiya, to the king of Ugarit confirming the latter's suspicions about some of his subjects who have taken advantage of a call at Alashiya to deliver an entire flotilla to the enemy.[2] Yet another document discusses some individuals who have fled from Alashiya to the Hittite kingdom. They were handed over by Khattushilish III to the king of Carchemish who in turn entrusts them to his son Tili-Sharruma.[3] Of considerable interest is the record of a judgement of Ini-Teshub, king of Carchemish, contemporary of Ammishtamru II of Ugarit. Two royal princes, sons of the lady Ahatmilku (brothers of Ammishtamru), have 'sinned'. The queen mother takes them to Alashiya where, in front of Ishtar, they are made to swear that in future they will not ask anything of the king of Ugarit or his son. This may imply some kind of banishment.[4]

Thus, references to Alashiya extend from the eighteenth century B.C. until the eleventh, as a country with its own king which, at various times, has political and economic relationships with the Hittites, the kingdoms of Syria and with Egypt. If Asy is drawn in as well, it was rich enough by the fifteenth century to pay heavy tribute to Egypt. Near the end of the thirteenth century it was important enough to have its own fleet. Early in the twelfth century it was overrun by the Peoples of the Sea.[5] Were Alashiya and Cyprus one and the same? Though there are undoubtedly good grounds for supporting the identification, it is not as certain as some commentators suppose.[6] Hittite imports are confined to the gold tripod *bulla*, said to have been found at Politiko,[7] and Cypriot objects are extremely rare in the Hittite homelands. Though Cyprus was literate in the Late Bronze Age (see below), no traces of the use of cuneiform can be found, and it is not known what language was current before the introduction of Greek. Yet the Alashiya chancellery was fluent in Akkadian and able to use cuneiform. The copper which Alashiya had to send as tribute has been given undue prominence, not only because there were other sources of copper besides Cyprus, but because the items of tribute cannot necessarily be identified as local produce. There were certainly no elephants in Cyprus, but Alashiya had to contribute elephant tusks.

---

[1] §ix, 8, 165–6.   [2] §ix, 8, 166.   [3] §ix, 6, 144; §ix, 7, 108.
[4] §ix, 6, 144; §ix, 7, 120–2.   [5] G, 6, 44.   [6] §ix, nos. 5; 8; 11; 13.
[7] *C.A.H.* ii³, pt. 1, p. 167.

Not a little weight has been ascribed to the argument that Cyprus *must* be named in contemporary documents, and that Alashiya is the best candidate. It is doubtful, in fact, whether Cyprus had achieved an appropriate degree of importance by the date of the Amarna letters, which were written near the end of L.C. IIa. The much later dedication to Apollo Alasiotas found at Tamassus[1] is not as decisively in favour of the identification as has been argued.[2] 'Apollo of Alashiya' is at least as likely to be a foreign god whose toponym was retained to distinguish him from local deities as to be indigenous. The effect of these and other difficulties is to suggest that the identification should be regarded as unproven until fresh evidence is available.

X. LITERACY IN THE LATE CYPRIOT PERIOD

The proposal that Cyprus was already literate in the Early Bronze Age cannot be seriously entertained, despite the occasional use by E.C. potters of a system of pot-marks.[3] From a date early in the Late Bronze Age, however, there began a much more frequent and systematic use of marks on vases and other objects.[4] The forms of these signs were seen to have a general similarity with the syllabary used in Cyprus,[5] chiefly for writing Greek, in the Archaic and Classical periods. A relationship was also proposed with the syllabic writings used in the Aegean Bronze Age; it came to be known, in fact, as the 'Cypro-Minoan script'.[6] No serious progress could be made with its decipherment while texts of only extreme brevity were available.[7] In 1952, the first fragment of a continuous Cypro-Minoan text was found at Enkomi on a clay tablet;[8] three more have since been found to encourage hope that a library or palace archive will eventually come to light.

The earliest of the four tablets was found in a sealed deposit within the L.C. I fortress on the north side of the town, where it was buried *c.* 1500 B.C. It has three lines of text;[9] it has been said of its syllabary that it has 'many specific similarities...with Cretan linear scripts and in particular linear A'. This must be viewed against what is virtually complete lack of contact between Crete and Cyprus at this date.

The three other tablet fragments from Enkomi are some 200

---

[1] G, 6, 48.   [2] §vii, 8, 1–10.
[3] *C.A.H.* ii³, pt. i, pp. 605 ff.   [4] §x, 3.
[5] §x, 12.   [6] A. J. Evans, *Scripta Minoa*, i, 69.
[7] §x, 15.   [8] §x, nos. 4; 5; 6; 17.   [9] §x, 6; §x, 7. See Plate 152(*a*).

years later and differ somewhat from the earlier one in both form
and script.[1] They were inscribed on both faces, before firing.
The scribe evidently used a carefully prepared bone stylus,
examples of which have been found at Enkomi[2] and at Kouklia.[3]
The largest fragment belonged to a tablet which must originally
have contained a text of about 200 lines; it may have been a
literary text.[4] These tablets are undeciphered; attempts to read
the longest as a Greek text are not convincing.[5]

With these Cypro-Minoan tablets at Enkomi must be linked a
complete tablet and fragments of others found at Ugarit,[6]
written in an almost identical syllabic script. Their context is
within the thirteenth century. The complete tablet has seven lines
of text on each face. These Ugaritic documents must be connected
with Cyprus, either as copies of letters sent to Cyprus, or communications from a Cypriot town to Ugarit. In either event they
were presumably written by Cypriots to be read by Cypriots;
the presence of a Cypriot community at Ugarit has frequently
been suggested.[7]

Although the Cypro-Minoan syllabary suggests the influence
of the Aegean, this influence is not to be seen in the physical
character of the tablets themselves, which are modelled on the
kiln-baked cushion-type familiar in the Near East, not the sun-
dried leaf-shaped Minoan and Mycenaean documents.[8] None of
the Cypriot tablets suggests the ledger-work that comprises the
bulk of their Aegean contemporaries.

While these tablets are unquestionably the most important
evidence for L.C. literacy, mention must also be made of the large
numbers of objects that bear brief inscriptions. Much the largest
class of inscriptions is that on clay vases, in a series from L.C. I
to L.C. III, the latest instance of which,[9] on a pithos in a late
sanctuary at Enkomi, proves the use of the script as late as the
eleventh century B.C. Signs appear either singly or in small
groups on almost any part of a vase. They were most commonly
scratched on after firing.[10] Many have been found on imported
Mycenaean vases,[11] where they are as likely to be painted as
scratched. They were painted after firing, however, and are
quite unlike the painted inscriptions on coarse Mycenaean stirrup

[1] §x, 11, figs. 23–5. [2] §x, 17. [3] Unpublished.
[4] G, 9, pl. xx; §x, 18, 61. See Plate 152(b)
[5] Harv. Stud. Class. Phil., LXV (1961), 39–107.
[6] §IX, 12. [7] C.A.H. II³, pt. I, pp. 174 and 491.
[8] §x, nos. 8; 9; 13; 16. [9] §XI, 3.
[10] G, 1, 98–107; G, 4(iii), 601–18; §x, nos. 1; 2; 3; 11.
[11] G, 12, 120–1; §VIII, 25, 45–52.

jars found on the mainland. As these Cypro-Minoan inscriptions were painted after firing, they cannot be used to prove a Cypriot origin for the vases on which they are painted.[1] Although the significance of the vase inscriptions can only be guessed at, in all likelihood they define the contents or capacity of the container, or they record their owner's identity or they record a dedication.

Similar inscriptions, amounting in some cases to several signs, occur on bronze objects, particularly tools (flat axes, socketed adzes, ploughshares, socketed sickles),[2] vessels[3] and miniature ingots.[4] The marking of the tools almost certainly indicated ownership, and perhaps suggests the existence of a slave or hired labour force to whom valuable tools were only issued with suitable precaution. No satisfactory explanation had yet been advanced to account for the relatively common clay balls, of diminutive size, on which groups of signs were written with a blunt stylus before they were fired. Nearly all these enigmatic objects have been found at Enkomi,[5] but at least one has come from Hala Sultan Tekke.

While it would be misleading to insist on a general literacy in the L.C. period, so many quite humble objects have inscriptions and are distributed so widely that it can surely be inferred that at least a limited degree of literacy was the prerogative of more than the scribal class alone.

XI. THE ACHAEAN COLONIZATION OF CYPRUS

At the end of the thirteenth century B.C. many of the Mycenaean homelands were afflicted by disaster, in the course of which Pylus was overwhelmed, Mycenae grievously afflicted. There took place a considerable diaspora of the mainland population, which resulted in the establishment of refugee settlements at widely separated points from the Ionian islands and Achaea in the west[6] to Chios in the east. At least one substantial group of these people fled to Cyprus, where their establishment at a number of sites was an event of incalculable significance for the future history of the island. The main sources of evidence for this Achaean influx are archaeological, consisting of the abrupt appearance at a relatively small number of sites of Mycenaean material of types that had been entirely missing in the two previous centuries of close commercial contact. In consequence of this Aegean irruption into Cyprus, the early part of the L.C. III

---

[1] §x, 3, 265 f.   [2] §viii, 6, 78–106.   [3] G, 8 (1960), 259; §x, 11, 24c.
[4] §viii, 6, 268–9.   [5] §vii, 8, 397–409; §x, 11, 19–20; §x, 15.   [6] §xi, 4.

period which it inaugurated was a dynamic phase almost without parallel in the island's history. If we may judge from the quality of material objects found in L.C. III contexts, the refugee settlers included many fine craftsmen. So much is clear from the well-known ivories from Enkomi[1] and Kouklia;[2] it is equally applicable to the development of L.C. III bronzework[3] and gem-cutting.[4]

The impact of these Achaean settlers on Cyprus has been most clearly shown by the results of the Enkomi excavations. The L.C. II c period was brought to a close by a major destruction, in which the whole town was affected.[5] It was quickly rebuilt; at the same time it was enclosed with a massive fortification wall. During the rebuilding numbers of large buildings were erected, in which the architects made much use of fine ashlar masonry.[6] Associated with all these activities were large quantities of Mycenaean III c I pottery, whose antecedents belong to the Argolid.[7] Never before had so much Mycenaean pottery been encountered in Enkomi occupation deposits; it virtually ousted native Cypriot painted wares. A very similar set of circumstances has been observed at Citium,[8] including the building of a massive fortification.

Though the cause of the destruction at Enkomi at the end of L.C. II is uncertain, it may have been due to an effort to repel the Greek refugees. It had been a common practice at Enkomi in L.C. II for family vaults to be hewn out of the rock below the courtyards of the town houses. In the rebuilding that was the sequel to the L.C. II c destruction, many of these sepulchres were perforce abandoned as the new constructions encroached on the yards from which they had been entered. This closure applied to one very important tomb in particular, no. 18 of the Swedish excavation,[9] which was last used either shortly before or immediately after the catastrophe. Two of the latest bodies to be buried in this tomb were accompanied the one by a bronze sword,[10] the other by a pair of bronze greaves,[11] the immediate source of both of which can only have been the Mycenaean west. There was no Mycenaean IIIc pottery in the grave, but the IIIb vases in it stand at the very threshold of the transition to the new style. It is tempting to infer from this grave that at least one party of the refugees had arrived before the disaster.

[1] G, 10.   [2] G, 9, pl. xli, 1; §xi, 7.   [3] §viii, 6. See Plate 151 (*b*)
[4] §vii, 8, 72; §viii, 6, 51.   [5] §x, 7, 40.
[6] G, 7, 515–18; §vii, 7; §vii, 8, 239–369; §xii, 5.
[7] §xi, 4, 229.   [8] §xi, 8; §xi, 9; §xi, 10.
[9] G, 4(i), 546–58; §vii, 8, 318–46.   [10] §vii, 8, 337–41; §xi, 2.   [11] §xi, 1.

It is possible that the Greek refugees established themselves on a virgin site in west Cyprus before they moved east into the urban areas. This is the very short-lived fortified settlement at Maa on the coast 5 miles north-west of modern Ktima,[1] where Mycenaean III c i pottery has beeen found. Less certain is a second fortified site at Lara, near Cape Drepanum, a few miles further north.[2] Although Enkomi seems to have been the most important of these Achaean refugee settlements, the presence of the refugees has been recognized at Sinda in the Mesaoria,[3] at Citium[4] and at Kouklia.[5] The Mycenaean III c i pottery that has been found in Nicosia[6] and at Ayios Sozomenos[7] is equivocal, and may represent no more than internal trade.

XII. THE END OF THE BRONZE AGE IN CYPRUS

There is a degree of conflict in the archaeological evidence for the nature of the last century and a half of the LC period. On the one hand, as shown above, there was a terrifying diminution in the population and abandonment of large parts of the island. On the other, at those sites where occupation persisted until the threshold of the Iron Age, there is evidence of reasonable prosperity and a fairly vigorous material culture, in which the native Cypriot elements were heavily overlaid by cultural traits for which the Achaean colonists were responsible. Recent excavation at a number of L.C. III occupation sites has done much to clarify the sequence of events from c. 1200 B.C. until the end of the period c. 1050 B.C.

Enkomi had been replanned and rebuilt after the destruction at the end of the thirteenth century B.C., which coincides with the arrival of Achaean colonists from Greece. It cannot have been long afterwards that a fresh catastrophe afflicted the city; for Mycenaean III c i pottery has been found in the destruction layer that marks this event.[8] Similar destructions at Citium,[9] Sinda[10] and Maa[11] may well be connected with the calamity at Enkomi; all are possibly to be associated with the attempt of the Peoples of the Sea to overrun the east Mediterranean which was finally frustrated by Ramesses III.[12] Though the synchronisms are very tenuous, this was perhaps the occasion for the final abandonment of many of the sites that had continued in occupation into the

---

[1] §xi, 4, 198. [2] *Arch. in Greece* (1954), 54. [3] §xi, 4, 197–200; §xi, 6.
[4] §xi, 10; §xi, 12. [5] G, 8 (1961), 288–90. [6] G, 8 (1959), 354–5.
[7] §viii, 6, 50. [8] §x, 7, 41. [9] §xi, 10, 11.
[10] §xi, 6. [11] §x, 7, 41; §xi, 4, 198. [12] See below, p. 377.

L.C. IIIa period, including the sanctuary at *Pigadhes*,[1] the mining settlement at Apliki[2] and the Ayia Irini sanctuary.[3] It is also possible that this was the occasion for the desertion of Ayios Sozomenos and the complementary founding of Idalium in a more defensible position nearby.

The chief historical problem of these episodes in L.C. IIIa is the part played by the Peoples of the Sea and the relationship of the Achaean colonists with these freebooters. If they were in league, then the destruction at Enkomi and Citium which preceded the period of ashlar construction could be attributed to them. But if they were not associated, then only the second destruction was the work of the Sea Peoples, and a difficulty has been removed by finding agents for an otherwise unaccountable but very widespread catastrophe. The correct solution of this problem is of considerable importance for establishing the date by which Mycenaean IIIc pottery had been developed. The Sea Peoples' onslaught on Cyprus must have taken place before their defeat at the hand of Ramesses III in 1191 B.C.

In the period following the second destruction at Enkomi, when the ashlar buildings were repaired and reoccupied, there are signs of considerable contact with the opposite coast.[4] These signs may mean the arrival in Cyprus of Levantine refugees, however, rather than the continuation of traditional economic ties. The Sea Peoples had been responsible for widespread destruction in the Levant, from which Ugarit, the city most closely tied to Cyprus, did not recover. Almost certainly the survivors of the original bands of Achaean refugees in Cyprus were joined about this time by fugitives from the opposite coast. To the resulting fusion of Aegean and oriental elements in the island is due much of the ambivalent character of L.C. III material culture, perhaps most clearly seen in ivory work and glyptic.

After the second destruction at Enkomi, the buildings on the north side of the town, adjoining the wall, seem not to have been replaced. Elsewhere, occupation continued without interruption until an advanced date in the eleventh century. Well before this date, however, both in Enkomi[5] and at Citium[6] there had appeared new contingents of fugitives from the Aegean, bringing with them painted pottery with the distinctive 'wavy-band' ornament,[7] which at Mycenae was contemporary with the destruction of the Granary and takes its name from it. The date of the destruction

---

[1] §xii, 12.   [2] §xii, 10.   [3] G, 4(ii), 642–74.
[4] §xii, 5.   [5] §vii, 8, 346–50; §x, 7, 43.   [6] §xi, 8; §xi, 10.
[7] §xi, 5; §xi, 8, 570–81.

of the Granary is unlikely to have been earlier than 1150 B.C. Fresh trouble came to Enkomi *c.* 1075 B.C., when the town was destroyed by an earthquake,[1] but life continued on the site, probably on a very reduced scale, almost to the end of the eleventh century, and after the start of the Cypro-Geometric period.[2] The final phases are marked by intensive use of at least two sanctuaries dedicated to a male god, in which a cult associated with bulls was intimately connected.[3] Whether either of the two important bronze figures of men in horned headgear found in the sanctuaries represent the god himself, or should be taken as worshippers, is undetermined.[4]

The stratigraphy at Citium, as already suggested, keeps close pace with Enkomi. During L.C. II family tombs had been constructed within the courtyards of individual houses.[5] These continued in use until near the end of the thirteenth century B.C. The site was then completely rearranged architecturally; the old buildings were demolished and replaced by new, in which the use of ashlar masonry was incorporated. The occupation of these buildings was associated with much Mycenaean III c 1 pottery. Not long afterwards, when Mycenaean III c 1 pottery was still in use, the site was destroyed, perhaps by the Sea Peoples. The next occupation was typified by Granary-style pottery; it was destroyed in the eleventh century by an earthquake, perhaps the same that afflicted Enkomi. The final occupation of Citium can be dated to the beginnings of the Cypro-Geometric period, when most of the houses damaged in the earthquake were levelled and replaced, though others were merely repaired.[6] It was not until the tenth century that the site was finally abandoned.

At the *Bamboula* settlement at Curium[7] four levels of occupation belonged to L.C. III. The evidence for two periods of Achaean settlement is altogether missing, but the pottery shows the site was not abandoned until the end of L.C. III b in the middle of the eleventh century. Achaean influence, however, is clearly to be seen in the nearby *Kaloriziki* cemetery,[8] some of whose tombs show all the characteristics of Mycenaean chamber tombs, notably in the use of long, straight *dromoi*. Others have been recorded in the Kastros cemetery at Lapithos on the opposite side of the island.[9] One *Kaloriziki* tomb was probably a royal sepulchre. It contained the well-known Curium sceptre-head[10]—two gold-

[1] §x, 7, 43. [2] G, 8 (1963), 370–3; §xi, 3.
[3] G, 8 (1964), 353–6; §x, 7. [4] §viii, 6, 256. [5] G, 8 (1964), 350; §xi, 10.
[6] §xi, 10. [7] §xii, 11. [8] §xii, 2; §xii, 8.
[9] G, 4(i), 172–265. [10] G, 9, pl. xl; 1 §xii, 8. See Plate 151 (c).

and-cloisonné hawks perched on a sphere, covered in cloisonné scale ornament—as well as a rich group of bronzes, including weapons, vessels and tripod stands.[1] Notable are the remains of a shield,[2] which may possibly have resembled one of the varieties represented on the warrior vase at Mycenae.[3] The cremated remains of a woman were found in one of the bronze vessels, with a set of fibulae of relatively advanced type.[4] The burial can be dated *c.* 1050 B.C. Many features in it, including the fibulae, the appearance of cremation and some of the details of its proto-White-Painted-pottery suggest that the movements of people from Greece to Cyprus continued even after the stage at which Granary-class pottery was introduced to a date contemporary with the earliest burials in the Ceramicus at Athens, but before the appearance of Protogeometric pottery. It may have been these last comers who introduced the Mycenaean chamber tombs at Curium and Lapithos.

Ten miles west of Enkomi at Sinda in the Mesaoria a small fortified settlement was first occupied *c.* 1300 B.C.[5] It was destroyed by burning at the end of the thirteenth century; its reoccupation immediately afterwards was marked by the same influx of Mycenaean III c 1 pottery already observed at Enkomi and Citium. Not long after there was a second destruction at Sinda, for which the Sea Peoples were perhaps responsible, and there was only a brief and uncertain phase of reoccupation.

Idalium in the Yalias Valley was not founded until L.C. III, yet appears to have stood outside the events in which the Aegean settlers were so heavily involved. The site on the west acropolis[6] was fortified and occupied in L.C. IIIa, and the three Late Cypriot levels continue into L.C. IIIb, but the hill was abandoned before the beginning of the Iron Age. Mycenaean pottery was missing from the occupation.

Though the evidences of the several settlement sites investigated differ in detail, they agree in the broad outline they offer of the L.C. III period. They show the arrival of refugees from the Aegean at the time of the sack of Pylus. The refugees either occupied virgin sites on their first landfall, as at Maa, or fought their way into long-established towns, as at Enkomi and Citium, probably at Palaeopaphos as well. On their arrival at Enkomi and Citium these towns were strongly fortified and largely rebuilt in an architectural style quite novel to Cyprus. Not long

---

[1] §VIII, 6, 193–5.   [2] §VIII, 6, 142–6.   [3] *Crete and Mycenae*, pl. 233.
[4] §XII, 8, 139.   [5] §XI, 4, 196–201; §XI, 6.
[6] G, 4(ii), 460–628; §XII, 11.

afterwards much of the island was involved in a great catastrophe, in which it is reasonable to see the work of the Sea Peoples. Many sites were abandoned for good; but others, perhaps with an injection of new blood from Levantine refugees, picked up the pieces and continued on a somewhat reduced scale. The copper industry remained important. Before the end of the twelfth century fresh groups of emigrants from Greece, bringing Granary pottery with them, were absorbed by Enkomi and Citium. This type of pottery was still to be exercising a profound effect in the Early Iron Age. Some sites, of which Curium is the clearest instance, seem to have remained outside the Aegean sphere until the eleventh century. Yet it was to Curium, and probably also to Lapithos, that a third and final group of Greek refugees made their way at a time when the Mycenaean world in Greece was all but dead, the Early Iron Age about to begin. It fell to Cyprus to shelter the remains of Mycenaean civilization, including its political structure, aspects of its language, traces of its writing and much of its visual art long after its complete disappearance from the Greek mainland. This, then, was the first and most radical step in the Hellenization of Cyprus.

XIII. CYPRUS AND COPPER
IN THE LATE BRONZE AGE

Much of the importance of Cyprus in the L.C. period must have been due to her position, both for commercial and military reasons. Yet her role as a source of copper production must be stressed. If the identification of Cyprus with Alashiya were established (see above), there would be documentary evidence to show that Cypriot copper had at various times been exported to Mesopotamia (Mari), Asia Minor (to the Hittites)[1] and Egypt.

Although the location of many ancient slag-heaps[2] has been noted in the ore-bearing regions of Cyprus, none can be certainly attributed to the L.C. period, nor can mine-workings or other industrial sites. Nevertheless, finds connected either with smelting copper or with the making of copper or bronze objects have occurred on many L.C. sites, including Enkomi, Citium,[3] Hala Sultan Tekke, Klavdhia and Lapithos amongst the most important settlements; Apliki, Ayios Sozomenos, Mathiati and Lythrodondas of the sites of secondary importance.[4] The best documented industrial site is Enkomi, where evidence of copper working

[1] §ix, 9, 14.
[2] §viii, 6, 21.
[3] G, 8 (1964), 350.
[4] §viii, 6, 21.

appears in buildings on the north side of the town as early as
L.C. I; this area continued its industrial activity throughout the
fourteenth and much of the thirteenth centuries. Other parts of
the site show similar activity during the twelfth century.[1] The
volumes of waste material associated with these operations suggest that the ore was only partly processed in the areas where it
was mined, and that the refining was completed in the big industrial towns. There may be political as well as economic
implications in this arrangement. Though tin-bronze was widely
used in Cyprus throughout the L.C. period, the source of the tin
is unknown; it cannot have been produced in the island itself.

During L.C. III, the copper-founders of Enkomi prepared
their raw copper for marketing and transport in the form of
'ox-hide' ingots, several complete and fragmentary examples of
which have been found on the site.[2] Theories that these ingots
were intended to simulate the flayed hide of an ox, and that they
should be interpreted as units of currency echoing an earlier
situation when wealth was expressed in heads of oxen have now
been discarded.[3] Such ingots have been found in widely separated
parts of the Mediterranean,[4] from Sardinia to the bay of Antalya;
they are also represented in several tribute scenes in Egyptian tombs
of the Eighteenth Dynasty.[5] The earliest ingots lack the prominent
carrying handles which distinguish the later examples.[6] This
variety has been found in Crete, both in a great hoard at Hagia
Triada and more recently in the palatial deposits at Zakro;
others come from the sea off Euboea and from the bay of Antalya.
They occur in fifteenth-century tomb paintings in Egypt, sometimes on the shoulders of 'tribute-bearers' of Aegean aspect.[7]
None have been found in Cyprus.

By 1400 B.C. a new type of ingot with a prominent carrying
handle at each corner had been introduced; it appears as an ideogram on Cnossian linear B texts.[8] There are two varieties, with
only a dubious chronological distinction; both have been found in
Cyprus. The most notable find of handled ingots, however,
comes from the cargo of a wrecked ship recently raised from the
sea off Cape Gelidonya in south-west Asia Minor.[9] Some forty
complete or fragmentary ingots were recovered, together with a
large number of bronze artifacts, particularly tools, of types
familiar in Cyprus in L.C. III,[10] and much scrap besides. There

---

[1] §VII, 8, 27-35.   [2] §VIII, 6, 267-72. See Plate 149 (c)   [3] §XIII, 1.
[4] §VIII, 6, 267-72, §IX, 3.   [5] §VIII, 6, 270.   [6] §VII, 8, 30.
[7] §VIII, 10, 227, fig. 24.   [8] §X, 18, 380.   [9] §XIII, 1.
[10] §VIII, 6, 292-4.

is a strong presumption that this ship was on her way to Greece
from some Cypriot port; the voyage should probably be dated in
the first half of the twelfth century B.C.

The Mycenaean colonization of Cyprus at the end of the
thirteenth century B.C. brought a revolution in the working and
management of the metal industry, including the introduction of
the 'ox-hide' ingot as a technical and administrative convenience.
Though the final history of this ingot type belongs to Cyprus,
there is no proof that it originated there.[1] The idea probably was
developed in Crete as an administrative measure in the palaces.
It will then have been adopted by the Mycenaeans (who borrowed
heavily from Minoan metallurgical ideas), who brought it to
Cyprus when they fled there at the beginning of L.C. III.

Bronze-founders' hoards of scrap metal became relatively
common at Enkomi in L.C. III deposits.[2] They can be linked
with somewhat similar hoards in Greece by the cargo of the
Cape Gelidonya ship.[3] The most likely explanation for the
collection of scrap in a copper-producing country is a breakdown
in tin-supplies from abroad, and a consequent enhanced value for
tin-bronzes. This would certainly account for the miscellaneous
rubbish which the Cape Gelidonya ship was taking to Greece.

XIV. THE LATE CYPRIOT PERIOD AND THE FOUNDATION LEGENDS

It is now obvious that there is a broad agreement between the
traditions preserved in Greek literature[4] concerning the foundation of Cypriot towns from Greece and the archaeological
evidence that shows Greek settlers were establishing themselves
in Cyprus from the late thirteenth century B.C. until the end of
the Late Bronze Age. Since there was no comparable movement
in the Iron Age, whatever historical worth these traditions hold
belongs to the Bronze Age. This is where their own context
places most of the traditions, for they refer to men involved in the
Trojan War and the disturbances that followed it. These were the
circumstances which brought Agapenor to Paphos, brought
Teucer to Salamis and led to the arrival of Pheidippus and his
party of Coans.

Nearly every settlement said to have been 'founded' at this
time was in fact long established at the time of which the traditions speak. This applies to Paphos, to the Argive foundation

---

[1] §VIII, 6, 271–2.   [2] §VIII, 6, 278–92.
[3] §VIII, 6, 294–8.   [4] §XIV, 2.

of Curium, Praxandrus at Lapethus and Chytrus at Chytroi. In all likelihood, the Salamis of the Teucer legend must in fact be Enkomi nearby. There is obviously a capricious element in what tradition remembered; for it seems difficult to substantiate the foundation of Chytroi by Chytrus, grandson of Acamas, with an actual Mycenaean IIIc influx, and the same is true at Golgi, said to have been established by Golgus and a party from Sicyon. Yet there are important sites, such as Citium, in whose development the Mycenaean settlers played a dominant role, of which tradition knew nothing.

Some traditions are sufficiently circumstantial to carry conviction, such as that which portrays Agapenor, king of Tegea and leader of the Arcadian contingent at Troy, driven by foul weather to Cyprus after the fall of Troy. He founded Paphos, and established a temple of Aphrodite. Later his daughter Laodice founded a cult of Aphrodite Paphia in Tegea; she also sent a peplos to Tegea as a gift to Athena Alea. There seems to have been a special connexion between Tegea and Cyprus, for Tegea was unique in its cult of Aphrodite Paphia. But if Agapenor founded Paphos, what of Cinyras its king at the time the Trojan expedition was launched? Agapenor cannot be accommodated at Nea Paphos, 10 miles further west, for recent investigation has shown it was not occupied before the classical period.[1] Agapenor and Cinyras must therefore belong to the same town. In one tradition Agamemnon avenged himself upon Cinyras after the Trojan War; such vengeance could be equated with the earliest appearance of Mycenaean IIIc 1 pottery, and Agapenor would then belong to the second colonizing phase, marked by Granary-class Mycenaean pottery.

It is easier to decide that there is a general correspondence between archaeology and the foundation legends than to single out those elements which preserve the true grain of history, those which were retrospective efforts of particular communities to provide themselves with a past that was both politically and emotionally satisfying. But this cannot diminish the importance of the support which archaeology has brought to the traditions.

[1] §xiv, 1, 9–11.

CHAPTER XXIII

EGYPT: FROM THE INCEPTION OF THE NINETEENTH DYNASTY TO THE DEATH OF RAMESSES III

I. THE RISE OF THE NINETEENTH DYNASTY

THE death of Tutankhamun brought about a break in the royal succession; his successors Ay and Horemheb were not of royal blood and neither left an heir of his body. In these circumstances Horemheb appointed his vizier Pramesse[1] to succeed him, so that on the king's death in *c.* 1320 B.C. Pramesse ascended the throne as Ramesses I, thus inaugurating the Nineteenth Dynasty. He was probably well advanced in years when he became king, for no date of his is known higher than Year 2, on a stela from Buhen (Wādi Halfa)[2] which records the dedication and endowment of a temple to Min-Amun. Among the personnel were slaves 'from the captures made by His Majesty'; these 'captures' may well refer to the Asiatic campaign of Year 1 of Sethos I,[3] the son and co-regent of Ramesses who was probably too old for campaigning. The terms of the Abydos stela of Sethos I[4] make it virtually certain that there was in fact a co-regency which may have begun in Ramesses' second year, for duplicating his Buhen stela is another inscription dated in Year 1 of Sethos.[5] Ramesses did not reign long enough to carry out any major building work in Egypt, but a few reliefs from Karnak bear his name.[6] Two stelae of this king at Serābīt el-Khādim[7] testify to activity at the turquoise mines of Sinai, and some faience cartouches of Ramesses were found under the temple of Beth-shan (Beisān),[8] the city which Sethos I had to relieve from hostile attack at the outset of his first campaign. The tomb of Ramesses I, as of all the rest of the dynasty, is in the Valley of the Kings opposite Luxor.[9]

---

* An original version of this chapter was published as fascicle 52 in 1966.

[1] §1, 2.
[2] G, 1, vol. III, sects. 74 ff.
[3] See below, pp. 218 ff.
[4] §1, 4.
[5] G, 1, vol. III, sects. 157 ff.
[6] G, 8, vol. II, 16 (25–6).
[7] G, 5, nos. 244–5.
[8] §II, 6, 24.
[9] §1, 3.

It may perhaps not be out of place here to refer to the era described by Theon of Alexandria as *apo Menophreōs*,[1] which began in 1321–1317 B.C. An attempt has been made to derive the name from *Mry-n-Pth* 'Beloved of Ptah;[2] an epithet regularly attached to the personal name of Sethos I, but it is more plausible to derive the Greek name from Menpehre, the current form of the praenomen of Ramesses I, which is an exact Egyptian counterpart of *Menophrēs*. This identification of *Menophrēs* with Ramesses I is not new,[3] for it held the field until the less convincing alternative was put forward, and it has recently been revived;[4] chronologically there is nothing against it, for the four-year period 1321–1317 B.C. is enough to cover all the known reign of Ramesses I with a couple of years to spare.

II. THE FOREIGN WARS OF SETHOS I

To Sethos I, who succeeded to the throne in 1318 B.C., there fell the task of restoring Egypt to the standing of a Great Power, for her prestige had fallen low during the Amarna episode and its sequel. It is true that the old notion of the total loss of all Egyptian influence in Palestine can no longer be held, for certain fortresses, e.g. Beth-shan, Rehob, and probably Megiddo,[5] were held in the Egyptian interest, but many of the Palestinian city-states were hostile to Egypt, and even engaged in warlike operations against towns which were still loyal. That Sethos did in fact look on himself as dedicated to the restoration of his country's fame is witnessed by his motto 'Repeater-of-Birth', i.e. inaugurator of a renaissance, which he took for his Horus name.

The campaigns of Sethos I are recorded in a series of scenes carved on the east and north walls containing the hypostyle hall of the temple of Amun at Karnak, and these reliefs show actions in the field, the submission of defeated chieftains and the presentation of prisoners-of-war to Amun, the national god.[6] The scenes appear to have been arranged in chronological order, and despite the loss of most of the third or uppermost register, we have records of four campaigns, all of which have been subsumed under the date of Year 1, although four successive wars cannot all have been fought in one year. This kind of single dating to cover several expeditions is known also on the Tumbos stela of Tuthmosis I and on the Armant stela of Tuthmosis III. As

[1] See *C.A.H.* I³, pt. 1, p. 190.
[2] G, 4, 249.
[3] G, 6, 19.
[4] §1, 1.
[5] §11, 1, 36.
[6] G, 9, pls. 34–53; §11, 1.

regards the first campaign of Sethos, information which forms a valuable supplement to the temple record is provided by a stela found at Beth-shan,[1] so that it is possible to reconstruct the course of the war with more detail than usual.

The point of departure from Egypt was the north-eastern frontier town of Tjel, modern Tell Abu Seifa near El-Qantara,[2] the starting-point of the military road from Egypt to Palestine.[3] The distance from Tjel to Raphia (Rafa), the frontier town at the Asiatic end of the road, is 120 miles, and along this distance there were nine fortified wells.[4] The scenes at Karnak depict a battle raging among the wells, so that the fortifications were certainly necessary; clearly the passage of the Egyptian army along the desert road was disputed, the enemy being a force of Shasu[5] probably based on Raphia. This opposition proved unavailing, and first Raphia and soon afterwards 'the town of the Canaan', probably Gaza,[6] fell to the Egyptian army.

On his passage from the Canaanite coastal plain into the plain of Jezreel, Sethos seems to have met with no opposition from the key fortress of Megiddo, commanding the passage of the Carmel ridge, for he does not mention that town, so that it is probable that, like Beth-shan, it was still held for the Egyptians. One of the first tasks which lay before the king when once he had debouched into the central plain of Palestine was to send a column to relieve Beth-shan, which together with the neighbouring town of Rehob, was under attack from an alliance of Hamath and the trans-Jordan town of Pella (Egyptian *Pḥr*). Beth-shan lay about 15 miles south of the Sea of Galilee and 4 miles west of the Jordan; Hamath, not to be confused with the Syrian town of that name, may have lain at the mouth of the Yarmuk valley;[7] and Rehob seems to have been situated a short distance to the south of Beth-shan, where it has been identified with Tell es-Sarem.[8] There was also trouble with the 'Apiru of 'the mountain of Yarmet' and of Tirka-el, who had made common cause against the town of Ruhem.[9] The exact situation of these places is not known, but Tirka-el is named in the Anastasi Papyrus No. 1 in association with Rehob and Beth-shan.[10] In any case, the trouble was effectively dealt with.

To cope with these disturbances, as well as to prosecute his

[1] §II, 6, 24 ff.; pl. 41.
[2] G, 3, vol. II, 202* ff.
[3] §II, 3.
[4] §II, 3, pls. 11–12.
[5] §II, 3, 100, n. 1.
[6] G, 9, pl. 39.
[7] §II, 6, 26, n. 50.
[8] §II, 4, 20; §II, 6, 26, n. 52.
[9] §II, 4, 20.
[10] §II, 2, 24*.

main purpose of advancing northwards, in 'Year 1, 3rd month of Summer, 10th day'[1] Sethos dispatched 'the first army of Amun Mighty-of-Bows' against Hamath, 'the first army of Pre Rich-in-Valour' to Beth-shan, and 'the first army of Sutekh Victorious-of-Bows' against Yenoam, another town of uncertain location which must, however, have been readily accessible from Megiddo, for it is the first-named of the towns which fell to Tuthmosis III after his great victory there.[2] Presumably the relief of Beth-shan automatically brought about the relief of Rehob, since the latter place receives no further mention. We may guess also that it was either the Beth-shan column or the Hamath column which dealt with the trouble at Ruhem. The objectives of this three-pronged operation having been achieved, the army took the sea-ports of Acre and Tyre[3] and advanced into the Lebanon region, taking the town of Qader.[4] Having received the submission of the Lebanese chieftains, on whom he enforced a levy of timber,[5] Sethos returned in triumph to Egypt,[6] having secured the spring-board for his contemplated conquest of Syria. On his return march he crossed the Jordan and chastised Pella[7] for its share in the attack on Beth-shan, and set up a stela at Tell esh-Shihāb in the Haurān.[8]

Of the Karnak record of the second campaign there remains only a fragment showing a scene of the assault on Qadesh with the legend 'The ascent which Pharaoh made to destroy the land of Qadesh and the land of Amurru'.[9] Since the reduction of Qadesh-on-Orontes and the coastal strip of Amurru was the essential next stage in the Egyptian advance, it seems probable that the whole of the lost record referred to this campaign, which presumably took place in Year 2; the names of the Amorite towns Ṣumura and Ullaza on a sphinx from El-Qurna[10] show that part at least of Amurru was overrun. The conquest of the region of Takhsy, recorded on the same sphinx, may have been an event either of this campaign or of the later Hittite war, according to whether Takhsy is to be located south or north of Qadesh.[11]

On the assumption that the sequence of the scenes at Karnak is chronological,[12] it appears that the third campaign was directed

---

[1] §II, 1, 36.
[2] G, 1, vol. II, sect. 436.
[3] G, 1, vol. III, sect. 114.
[4] G, 9, pl. 35.
[5] *Ibid.*
[6] §II, 3, pl. 11.
[7] G, 1, vol. III, sect. 114.
[8] §II, 5.
[9] G, 3, vol. I, 140*.
[10] G, 1, vol. III, §114; G, 7, 17.
[11] G, 3, vol. I, 150* ff.
[12] §II, 1, 35, 38.

not against the Hittites but against the Libyans,[1] showing that the pressure on the western Delta which was to give later kings so much trouble was already beginning to develop. No localities are named where fighting occurred, but the Egyptians were victorious. The fourth and last campaign was against a Hittite army,[2] presumably somewhere north of Qadesh; again no places are mentioned, but a great slaughter of the enemy is claimed and captives were brought back to Egypt. As a result of this success, Sethos seems to have won temporary control of part of Syria, for he claims Qatna and Tunip[3] among his conquests, but there can be no doubt that ultimately he lost the north, though a failure of this kind would certainly not have been placed on public record; Ramesses II would not have had to fight his famous battle at Qadesh if the Egyptians had still held that town. Although the frontier between the Hittite and the Egyptian spheres of influence was not demarcated on the ground, the effective boundary must have run south of Qadesh;[4] beyond that frontier neither Great Power could expect to maintain itself in the face of determined opposition. In recognition of this fact, Sethos concluded a treaty of peace with Muwatallish, the king of Khatti,[5] but even if his Hittite venture had failed, Sethos had to his credit the solid achievement of having restored Egyptian authority over all Palestine and of having made Egypt once more a power to be reckoned with.

III. INTERNAL AFFAIRS UNDER SETHOS I

At home in Egypt it was the task of Sethos I to round off the work set on foot by Horemheb in restoring the ravages of the Amarna episode. Lacking extensive written documentation, the best index to the state of the realm is the amount of building activity undertaken by the pharaohs, and the reign of Sethos was not lacking in this respect, so that it would seem that Egypt was well on the road to recovery. The Ramesside line seems to have sprung from a Delta family with a personal devotion to the god Seth of Avaris (most probably the later Djane, Biblical Zoan, Greek Tanis),[6] formerly the capital of the Hyksos invaders; on account of this association with the ancient enemy and of his legendary role as the murderer of Osiris, Seth was unpopular

---

[1] G, 1, vol. III, sects. 120 ff.; G, 9, pl. 50.
[2] G, 1, vol. III, sects. 142 ff.; G, 9, pls. 45 ff.
[3] §II, 1, 38.   [4] See below, ch. xxiv, sect. 1.
[5] §II, 1, 38; G, 1, vol. III, sect. 377.   [6] G, 3, vol. II, 199* ff. See below, p. 225.

elsewhere. Therefore, despite their family connexions and their preference for residences in the north—the Buhen decree of Ramesses I was issued from Memphis[1] and Sethos I had a palace at Qantīr[2]—the Ramesside kings maintained Thebes as the state and religious capital and Amun as the national god, for his influential priesthood had to be propitiated; the Ramessides were an upstart line of rulers, and it was important for them to have the support of the powerful corporation which served the god of Thebes. In the case of Sethos I, however, we get the impression that will marched with necessity, and that he looked on it as a pious duty to restore the monuments of his predecessors, especially in the matter of replacing the name of Amun where it had been hacked out by the Atenist iconoclasts. In such cases he contented himself with the brief added inscription 'Restoration of the monument which King Sethos made'. That in fact a good deal remained to be done to set the land in order is clear from the stela which Sethos set up[3] in the chapel which he built at Abydos for his father Ramesses I,[4] where the king complains of the utterly neglected state of the sacred necropolis of Abydos.

The principal contribution made by Sethos to the great temple of Amun at Thebes was the building of a considerable part of the famous hypostyle hall.[5] Like every other major construction begun by Sethos, it was unfinished at his death, and the work was completed by his son Ramesses II. On the opposite bank of the Nile at El-Qurna Sethos built his funerary temple, setting aside certain rooms in it for his father's rites.[6] His tomb in the Valley of the Kings is the finest of all; over 300 ft. long, it contains coloured scenes and inscriptions of the highest quality.[7] His greatest work, however, was his splendid temple at Abydos.[8] For centuries this locality had been sacred to Osiris and a place of pilgrimage for the devout, and it was here that Sethos erected a temple with the unusual ground-plan of an inverted L, in which the beauty of the scenes and inscriptions in low relief, often with their original colouring, can challenge comparison with any temple now extant in Egypt. The centre and heart of the building is a row of seven chapels, dedicated respectively to Osiris, Isis, Horus, Amun, Ptah, Re-Harakhte and to Sethos himself in his

---

[1] G, I, vol. III, sect. 77. [2] §III, 8.

[3] §I, 4. [4] §III, 11.

[5] See Plate 154(a). The records of his wars cover the outside of the north wall and part of the east wall, see the plan G, I, vol. III, 39.

[6] G, 8, vol. II, 140 ff. [7] §III, 9.

[8] §III, 3. See Plate 153(a).

capacity of god on earth. It fell to Ramesses II to complete this temple also, and his coarse incised reliefs and hieroglyphs show a marked contrast with the delicate work of his father's craftsmen. A copy of a decree by Sethos describing the endowment of this temple and safeguarding its staff and property from outside interference is inscribed on a rock at Nauri, a short distance north of the Third Cataract.[1]

A characteristic mood of the Nineteenth Dynasty was a harking back to the past and a consciousness of the long history of Egypt, and as an expression of this mood Sethos set up in his temple at Abydos a list of the most illustrious kings of Egypt from Menes of the First Dynasty down to his own reign,[2] and he and his son Ramesses are depicted making offerings to their predecessors. A duplicate list, of which part is in the British Museum,[3] was originally set up in Ramesses II's own temple at Abydos, while a third list was inscribed in a private tomb at Saqqara.[4] Further, in Turin there is the much more extensive but sadly fragmentary chronicle on papyrus known as the Royal Canon,[5] which once contained not only the names of all the ancient kings known to the chronicler, but also the lengths of their reigns and the totals of years of the dynasties. It must have been on documents such as this that Manetho based his division of the kings of Egypt into thirty dynasties, and even today, after a century and a half of Egyptology, these king-lists are not devoid of value.

Behind his great temple at Abydos, Sethos constructed a subterranean building which has no parallel in Egypt. Once known as 'the Osireion', from the belief of the first excavators that it was intended to represent the tomb of the god Osiris, it has in fact been shown to be a cenotaph for Sethos in the holy ground of Abydos.[6] The lay-out of the central hall appears to represent the sacred hill which rose out of the primeval waters at the creation of the world, while the 'tomb-chamber' contains interesting astronomical and dramatic texts. Here also this construction still lacked the finishing touches when Sethos died, but some scenes and inscriptions were added by his second successor Merneptah.

Any buildings erected by Sethos at the other great sites of Egypt have almost entirely vanished, but the base of a votive model of the sun-temple at Heliopolis which bears his name was

[1] §III, 7; §III, 5.   [2] §III, 10, pl. 1, upper. See Plate 26.
[3] §III, 1, 163.   [4] §III, 10, pl. 1, lower.
[5] §III, 6.   [6] §III, 4.

found at Tell el-Yahūdīya,[1] and from Heliopolis itself come an inscribed door-post and an obelisk,[2] showing that he made some additions to the temple there.

IV. SINAI, THE EASTERN DESERT AND NUBIA UNDER SETHOS I

The turquoise mines at Serābīt el-Khādim in Sinai were still being exploited, for there have survived from that site two stelae and some small objects bearing the name of Sethos, as well as another stela in the joint names of Sethos I and Ramesses II, indicating a co-regency.[3] The gold mines in the desert of Edfu were worked on behalf of Sethos' great foundation at Abydos, and owing to the shortage of water on the route to the gold-field Sethos sank a well in the Wādi Miāh, an offshoot of the Wādi Abbād, and also cut in the rock wall of the valley a chapel with a built-up portico;[4] an inscription dated in Year 9 records the construction of the well and the chapel. A second inscription offers thanks to the king for the well, while a third consists of curses on anyone, king or commoner, who shall interfere with the supply of gold to Abydos.

The Egyptian hold on Nubia does not seem to have been seriously weakened by the events of the latter part of the Eighteenth Dynasty, and, as noted above, already in Year 2 of Ramesses I and Year 1 of Sethos I a temple at Buhen was dedicated. We learn from a stela of Ramesses II found in the fortress of Qūbān in Lower Nubia[5] that Sethos also drew gold from the region of the Wādi el-Allāqi, but that an attempt to sink a well on the road thither was a failure, though Ramesses was more successful. In Year 11 Sethos dedicated a hall of columns in the temple of Amun at Napata (Gebel Barkal).[6] Yet even in Nubia Sethos had to enforce the *pax Aegyptiaca* with military action against a tribe named Irem,[7] an event to which allusion in very general terms is made in a rock inscription cut in honour of the king at Qasr Ibrīm.[8] In normal circumstances the government of the Nubian provinces was in the hands of the Viceroys of Nubia, the titular Kings' Sons of Kush, and the pharaoh did not appear in person except on ceremonial or military occasions.

---

[1] §III, 2; G, 1, vol. III, sects. 244 ff.
[2] G, 1, vol. III, sect. 245.
[3] G, 5, nos. 246–50.
[4] §IV, 1; §IV, 5.
[5] G, 1, vol. III, sects. 282 ff.
[6] §IV, 3.
[7] §IV, 4, 168.
[8] §IV, 2.

V. THE FIRST YEARS OF RAMESSES II

The date of the accession of Ramesses II to sole rule was probably 1304 B.C.,[1] but before that date he was co-regent with his father for an uncertain period.[2] The dates on his monuments, however, refer to his sole rule and do not include the years of the co-regency. As has already been remarked,[3] the royal family preferred to reside in the north, the administrative capital as distinct from the state and religious capital at Thebes being probably Memphis. The first recorded act of Ramesses II was to travel south to Thebes for the great festival of Opet, when the god Amun journeyed in state from Karnak to Luxor. When the festival was over, Ramesses halted at Abydos on his return journey northwards, and in the great inscription dated in Year 1 which he caused to be set up in his father's temple[4] he describes how the temple stood unfinished, with its endowments alienated, and how the tombs of former kings were falling into rack and ruin. Summoning his entourage, Ramesses recounted his appointment as his father's co-regent and declared his intention to complete the great temple and to restore its endowments, which in fact he did. The long and verbose inscription of more than a hundred lines of text ends with Ramesses recounting what he has done and praying to his deceased father to intercede with the gods on his behalf; his father is made to give a favourable response. He also appointed a local ecclesiastic, one Nebunenef, to be a high priest of Amun at Thebes,[5] before continuing his northward journey.

The Delta residence of the pharaohs from the reign of Ramesses II on was known as Per-Ramesse 'House of Ramesses', the Biblical Raamses, but its site is still disputed. Its identity with the great city of Tanis seems the more probable, but a case has also been made out for Qantīr,[6] some 11 miles to the south, where both Sethos I[7] and Ramesses II had palaces. The *literati* of the Nineteenth Dynasty at times became quite lyrical in praise of its beauty and luxury.[8] The situation of the Residence in the eastern half of the Delta was certainly more practical for a ruler concerned with affairs in Palestine and Syria than a capital far to the south; when not abroad with an army the kings of the Nineteenth

---

[1] Cf. *C.A.H.* 1³, pt. 1, p. 189.
[2] §v, 4.
[3] See above, p. 222.
[4] G, 1, vol. III, sects. 258 ff.
[5] §v, 5. Cf. below, ch. xxxv, sect. IV.
[6] G, 3, vol. II, 171* ff.; §v, 2.
[7] §III, 8.
[8] §v, 1, 73 ff., 153 f.

Dynasty seem to have spent most of their time in either Per-Ramesse or Memphis.

Another enterprise which Ramesses undertook early in his reign was the securing of an adequate water-supply for the gold convoys to and from the Wādi el-Allāqi. The viceroy of Nubia reported to the pharaoh on the losses from thirst on this route and stated that a well dug by Sethos I had failed to reach water. In Year 5 Ramesses ordered that another well be sunk, and water was struck at one-tenth the depth of the dry well sunk by his father.[1]

A problem which first showed itself in the reign of Amenophis III and which by this time was becoming endemic was the defence of the coast of the Delta against the inroads of Sherden pirates, and already in Year 2 a raid of this kind was driven off.[2] That these raids were of fairly frequent occurrence is suggested by the fact that Sherden prisoners were enlisted in the Egyptian army in sufficient numbers to furnish a contingent of their own, as also were Nubian and Libyan captives.[3]

VI. THE STRUGGLE WITH THE HITTITES

The outstanding feature of the reign of Ramesses II was his long drawn out struggle with the Hittites. Apparently he had to occupy the first three years of his sole reign with setting home affairs in order, for the neglect and corruption that he found ruling at his father's temple at Abydos suggest that during the last years of Sethos I the reins of government had fallen slack. Be this as it may, it was not until Year 4 that we find Ramesses setting up an inscription at the Nahr el-Kalb near Beirut to record his first campaign in Asia.[4] Owing to weathering, except for the date, the inscription is illegible, so we have no information as to the events of this war, though it is possible that some of the names of captured places recorded at Karnak may belong to this first campaign.[5] In year 5 Ramesses used his springboard in northern Palestine and Phoenicia to mount a major attack on the Hittite Empire. No opposition seems to have been met by the Egyptian army during its northward march from Raphia, and at a point on the coast in the south of Amurru Ramesses detached a special task force, presumably to secure the seaport of Ṣumura, whence it was to turn eastward along the Eleutheros valley road to make

[1] G, 1, vol. III, sects. 282 ff.
[2] G, 3, vol. I, 194* ff.; §v, 6.   [3] §v, 3, 476.
[4] Cf. below, ch. xxiv, sect. 1.   [5] G, 9, pls. 54 ff.

junction with the main force at Qadesh,[1] the main Hittite
bastion of defence in the south. Having dispatched this task
force, the Egyptian army, which was organized in four divisions
named respectively after the gods Amun, Pre, Ptah and Sutekh,
turned inland and marched probably by way of the valley of the
river Litani to the valley of the river Orontes, which was crossed
from east to west at the ford of Shabtuna nearly 8 miles south of
Qadesh. Between this ford and Qadesh lay the wood of Robaui,
where once Amenophis II had hunted, and which the army had to
traverse. The division of Amun, under the command of Ramesses
himself, was the first to cross the river. On its northward march
two Hittite spies were taken and questioned. They informed
the Egyptians falsely that the Hittite army was at Aleppo,
and as this news seemed to be confirmed by the inability of the
Egyptian scouts to find any trace of the enemy, Ramesses
pressed on and encamped to the west of Qadesh. At this point two
more Hittites were captured who on being beaten admitted that
the Hittite army, far from being at Aleppo, was concealed
behind the city of Qadesh and was standing on the far bank of
the Orontes. Ramesses at once sent off messengers to hasten the
march of the division of Pre, which was the next in order of
march and which was emerging from the wood of Robaui. But
before any effective action could be taken the Hittite king
launched a heavy chariot charge which took the division of Pre,
still in column of route, in the flank and scattered it. The fugitives
fled to the camp of the division of Amun, hotly pursued by the
Hittites, who broke into the camp. The division of Amun too
was stricken with panic and fled, leaving the pharaoh and a body
of chariotry completely surrounded by the enemy. At this very
opportune moment reinforcements arrived in the shape of the
Amurru task force making its rendezvous with the main army.
Taking the Hittite chariots in the rear, it joined itself to the
hard-pressed band round Ramesses and thus saved the day.
The Hittite king Muwatallish sent off a second force of a thousand chariots, but to no avail; in six successive charges the
Egyptians drove the Hittite chariots into the Orontes, aided in
the last stages of the battle by the van of the newly arrived
division of Ptah. The division of Sutekh was too far in the rear to
take part in the action.

By this time the day must have been far advanced, and further
fighting was impracticable. The Egyptians camped on the

[1] G, 3, vol. i, 188* ff. For the extensive literature of the battle of Qadesh see
below, ch. xxiv, sect. i, Bibliography.

stricken field, Ramesses greeting with bitter reproaches the fugitives who now came filtering back, while the Hittite king, who for some reason made no use of his infantry during the battle, kept his remaining forces on the east bank of the Orontes. One Egyptian account states that on the next day the Hittites asked for an armistice, and this may well be true. The Hittite chariot force had been badly mauled, while a quarter of the Egyptian army, the division of Sutekh, had not been engaged, and thus consisted of fresh troops, including chariotry, so that Muwatallish may well have felt that it would be inadvisable to risk another field action. On the other hand, the morale of one half of the Egyptian army must have been at zero, and Ramesses was no doubt only too glad of an excuse to withdraw without loss of face. Although the actual battle was drawn, strategically the result was a defeat for the Egyptians, and they had to retire homeward with nothing to show for their efforts, though Ramesses did not fail to publicize his admittedly gallant stand against odds. With the retreat of the Egyptians from Qadesh, the Hittites advanced southward to Damascus, which was well on the Egyptian side of the frontier.[1]

The result of the campaign of Year 5 afforded the client states of Palestine the spectacle of an unsuccessful Egyptian army marching home, and the consequent loss of prestige had widespread effects. Many of these petty states took the opportunity to throw off the Egyptian yoke, and the revolt must have spread far south, for in Year 6 or 7 Ramesses had to storm Askalon,[2] while in Year 8 he took a number of places in the Galilee region and the town of Dapur in Amurru.[3] In Year 10 Ramesses was again on the Nahr el-Kalb, where he set up another stela, also illegible,[4] and it may have been in the following year that he broke through the Hittite defences and invaded Syria. Certainly Ramesses must have held Tunip for a period, since there was a statue of himself as overlord in the city; it is mentioned incidentally in the account of a Hittite attack which may have been a surprise assault, since the pharaoh went into battle without his corselet.[5] Qatna also was claimed among his

---

[1] Cf. below, ch. xxiv, sect. i.

[2] G, 1, vol. iii, sects. 353 ff.; G, 9, pl. 58.

[3] G, 1, vol. iii, sects. 356 ff.; G, 3, vol. i, 178* ff., though Gardiner's suggestion that Dapur may have been in the region of Aleppo is surely impossible in view of the military situation prevailing in Year 8.

[4] Cf. below, ch. xxiv, sect. i.

[5] G, 1, vol. iii, sect. 365.

conquests,[1] and further to the north-west he invaded Qode,[2] so that he must have penetrated deeply into Hittite territory. Nevertheless, as Sethos I found, it was impossible for the Egyptians to hold indefinitely territories so far from base against Hittite pressure, and after sixteen years of intermittent hostilities, a treaty of peace was concluded in Year 21 between Egypt and Khatti[3] as between two equal Great Powers, and its provisions were reciprocal. It is clear that a mutual frontier was recognized, but its position is not stated; probably it was not far removed from what it had been before hostilities broke out, so that the long struggle may well have had no other immediate result than to convince the two Powers that neither could overcome the other. The most important provisions of the treaty were a mutual renunciation of further war and a joint defensive pact, while other sections dealt on a similar mutual basis with the extradition and treatment of fugitives from one land or the other.

Once the treaty was concluded and peace restored, relations between Egypt and Khatti became really amicable. Letters on diplomatic matters were regularly exchanged,[4] and a state visit of the Hittite king Khattushilish to Egypt was contemplated, though it is uncertain whether it took place.[5] In Year 34 Ramesses contracted a diplomatic marriage with the eldest daughter of Khattushilish,[6] and there is a possibility that a second daughter of the Hittite king also, at a later date, was married to Ramesses.[7] Clearly the peace and friendship between the two countries now rested on a firm foundation.

VII. THE OTHER WARS OF RAMESSES II

Apart from the years of fighting in Palestine and Syria, Ramesses II had to wage war elsewhere. His undated expeditions against Moab, Edom and Negeb[8] may well have been no more than punitive wars to repress raiders or to punish aid to hostile dynasts in Palestine, but the menace from Libya was more serious. Here the tribes known since ancient times as the Tjemehu[9] and the Tjehenu,[10] and now also their more westerly neighbours the Meshwesh[11] and the Libu,[12] under the pressure of hunger were

[1] G, 1, vol. III, sect. 366.
[2] G, 3, vol. I, 134* ff.; G, 9, pl. 72.
[3] §VI, 3; §VI, 4.
[4] Cf. below, ch. XXIV, sect. III.
[5] G, 1, vol. III, sect. 426; §VI, 1.
[6] §VI, 2.
[7] G, 1, vol. III, sect. 427.
[8] §VII, 3.
[9] G, 3, vol. I, 114* ff.
[10] Ibid. 116* ff.
[11] Ibid. 119* ff.; §VII, 5.
[12] G, 3, vol. I, 121* ff.; §VII, 2.

attempting to invade and settle in the Delta, and the pharaohs from Sethos I onwards had to fight hard to keep them out. Ramesses II has left us a number of general allusions to his Libyan war,[1] but we know no details except that in Year 44 Libyan captives were employed in building the temple of Es-Sebūa in Lower Nubia;[2] it is significant, however, that Ramesses built a string of forts along the western coast road, starting from Rhacotis, the site of the future city of Alexandria, and extending to well beyond El-Alamein,[3] clearly in order to keep the western tribes in check. It has been suggested that the Sherden pirates were making common cause with the Libyans,[4] but this is not certain; the broken inscription in question[5] may be referring to the Libyan war and to a piratical raid by Sherden as separate events, but a Sherden contingent certainly served in the Libyan army in the war of Year 5 of the next reign. Scenes depicting war in Nubia appear in the temples of Abu Simbel, Beit el-Wāli and Ed-Derr, but no details of date or place are recorded, and it is possible that these may be purely conventional depictions without historical value.[6] If there were in fact any fighting, it can have amounted to no more than the driving off of desert raiders or the quelling of local disturbances, for Nubia by now was virtually part of Egypt. Even the undoubted Nubian war of Sethos I was probably only a small-scale affair.[7]

VIII. THE KINGDOM UNDER RAMESSES II

If the building of temples be an index to the prosperity of the realm, then indeed Egypt was flourishing under Ramesses II, for he surely erected more fanes up and down the land than any pharaoh before or since, though it must be admitted that he was apt to be ruthless in dismantling older shrines and re-using the material. Here it is possible to mention only a few of the most important sites where he erected or enlarged temples. The ruins of Tanis are eloquent of his name,[8] but the great temple which he dedicated to Ptah of Memphis has vanished apart from a few remains of statues, though it is mentioned in a stela of Year 35 at Abu Simbel.[9] At Abydos he built a temple near the famous one

---

[1] G, I, vol. III, sects. 457, 464 f., 479; see also Anastasi Papyrus No. II, 3, 4.
[2] §VII, I. [3] §VII, 4, 4.
[4] G, I, vol. III, sect. 448. [5] *Ibid.* sect. 491.
[6] §IV, 170 ff. [7] §IV, 168.
[8] §VIII, 6.
[9] G, I, vol. III, sects. 412 f.

erected by his father;[1] at Karnak he completed the great hypostyle hall[2] and at Luxor he added a pylon and a court,[3] while in
the western necropolis of Thebes stands his great funerary
temple known as the Ramesseum.[4] It is Nubia, however, which
possesses the most astonishing construction of this reign, namely
the well-known rock-cut temple of Abu Simbel, dedicated to
Amun, Re-Harakhte, Ptah and the King as god;[5] near it there was
constructed another rock shrine dedicated to the goddess Hathor
and to Queen Nefertiry.[6] To this lady belonged also a splendid
tomb in the Valley of the Queens at Thebes,[7] the first of a series
of burials of royal ladies in the valley. The reign also abounds in
private stelae and inscriptions of which very few yield any
historical information, but which as a whole suggest a fairly
widespread moderate degree of affluence, at least among the
literate classes.

So far as government was concerned, there was no great
change from the system which had long prevailed, the vizier—
or viziers when there was one for each half of the country—
being the highest official in the land, but a new factor was developing in the increasing influence of the high priests of Amun at
Thebes,[8] who in the Twentieth Dynasty were able to make their
office hereditary and who by the end of that dynasty were on terms
of virtual equality with the monarch.[9] An interesting glimpse of
the administration of law during this reign is afforded by a long
inscription in a tomb at Saqqara, where the course of a lawsuit
heard before the vizier and the Great Court is set out in some
detail.[10] Litigation in respect of a parcel of land amounting to
13 arouras had been going on spasmodically for several generations, forcible ejection and the forging of documents being among
the methods employed by one side to the dispute, and the hearing now recorded was the final one in the case. From the legal
point of view it would appear that men and women were on equal
terms both in regard to the ownership of land and in regard to
the right to plead in the courts.

Beyond the boundaries of Egypt proper, the mining of turquoise at Serābīt el-Khādim in Sinai went on and some fragments
of statuary have been found there.[11] The gold mines of the Wādi

[1] G, 8, vol. vi, 33 ff.   [2] G, 8, vol. ii, 15 ff.
[3] Ibid. 100 ff.   [4] Ibid. 149 ff.
[5] G, 8, vol. vii, 95 ff.   [6] Ibid. 111 ff.
[7] For paintings from this tomb see §viii, 1, pls. 91–3.
[8] §viii, 4.   [9] See below, ch. xxxv, sect. v.
[10] §viii, 3.   [11] G, 5, nos. 263–4.

Miāh in the eastern desert[1] and of the Wādi el-Allāqi in Nubia[2] were exploited. The town-site now known as Amāra West, over 100 miles south of Wādi Halfa, which had been founded in the previous dynasty, was given the name of Per-Ramesse-miamun and endowed with a considerable temple, probably becoming the administrative centre of the province of Kush and the seat of the provincial governor.[3]

During the long reign of 67 years[4] vouchsafed to Ramesses he outlived a considerable part of his family. His first and perhaps favourite consort was Nefertiry, to whose temple at Abu Simbel reference has already been made; she is mentioned in a Boğazköy letter in the form Naptera. Her successor was Isinofre, the mother of four princes, one of whom succeeded Ramesses as King Merneptah. A third queen was Maetnefrure, the Egyptian name given to the eldest daughter of the king of the Hittites when she married Ramesses.[5] It is possible that there was a second Hittite marriage, and Ramesses's daughter Bint-'Anath received the title of Great Consort during her father's lifetime, so that it would seem that she filled the office of queen for a while.[6] The pharaoh also had a considerable harim of which the foundations were laid by Sethos I,[7] and he took pride in his family of well over a hundred children.[8] The original Crown Prince was Amenhiwenmaf, but Ramesses outlived him and eleven of his other sons. The pharaoh celebrated his first jubilee (*Heb-Sed*) in Year 30 and thereafter held others at frequent and somewhat irregular intervals;[9] the organization of these festivals down to the fifth in Year 42 was in the hands of the king's eighth son Khaemuast, high priest of Ptah at Memphis, whose reputation as a sage and magician endured into Graeco-Roman times. In Year 55 he was followed in his office by the king's thirteenth son Merneptah,[10] who at his father's death twelve years later succeeded to the throne.

IX. MERNEPTAH: EGYPT ON THE DEFENSIVE

Merneptah was probably well over fifty years of age when he succeeded to the throne in 1236 B.C., and he inherited a difficult situation, for during his father's old age the vigilance of the

---

[1] §IV, 1, 249.
[2] G, 1, vol. III, sects. 282 ff.
[3] §VIII, 2.
[4] G, 7, 39.
[5] *Ibid.* 34 f., 82 f.
[6] G, 4, 267.
[7] G, 1, vol. III, sect. 267.
[8] G, 7, 35 ff.
[9] *Ibid.* 39; §VIII, 5.
[10] G, 7, 85.

frontier patrols had slackened and the army had fallen into neglect,[1] with the result that, driven by famine in their own land, roving bands of Libyans were raiding into the western Delta[2] and terrorizing the people. With the threat of invasion from the west steadily growing, the first task to which the new king had to set his hand was the reorganization of the army, and the effectiveness of his work was demonstrated when in Year 5 the storm burst.[3] A coalition consisting of Libu, Meshwesh, and Kehek,[4] together with certain 'peoples of the sea',[5] to wit Sherden, Sheklesh,[6] Lukka,[7] Tursha,[8] and Akawasha,[9] led by a prince named Mauroy, overran Tjehenu and advanced on the Delta.[10] These 'Peoples of the Sea' who allied themselves with the invading Libyans seem to have come from the coasts and islands of Asia Minor and the Aegean Sea, and as Gardiner wrote,[11] were 'forerunners of the great migratory movement about to descend on Egypt and Palestine from north and west'. The invaders came with intent to settle in Egypt, for they brought their families and household goods with them.

At the news of this threat Merneptah consulted the oracle of Amun at Thebes. The god expressed his approval of the war, while Ptah of Memphis appeared to the king in a dream, seeming to hand him a scimitar. A fortnight was taken up with the mobilization of the army, which then marched to meet the enemy. Contact was made on the western frontier at an unidentified place named Pi-yer, and after a 6 hour battle the invaders were routed. Over 6000 were killed and many prisoners and much booty were taken. The Libyan prince Mauroy fled alone to his own people, where he was treated with contumely, deposed from his chieftainship, and a brother chosen in his stead.

The principal sources for the Libyan War are a long inscription at Karnak[12] and a stela from Athribis,[13] but there is a third inscription that must be mentioned, the so-called Israel Stela.[14] The information it yields concerning the course of the war adds nothing material to what is known from the other sources, but it expresses at length the intense relief felt by the Egyptians at the defeat of the invaders. A few sentences will be sufficient

[1] G, 1, vol. III, sect. 577.   [2] Ibid. sect. 580.
[3] Ibid. sects. 595, 598.   [4] G, 3, vol. I, 123*.
[5] Ibid. 196*; §IX, 5.   [6] G, 3, vol. I, 196* ff.
[7] Ibid. 127* f.   [8] Ibid. 196* ff.
[9] Perhaps identical with the Ahhiyawa of the Hittite texts.
[10] G, 1, vol. III, sects. 569 ff.   [11] G, 4, 270.
[12] §IX, 2.   [13] §IX, 1.
[14] §IX, 4; see also §V, 3, 376 ff.

to convey the emotion caused by the victory: 'Men come and go with singing, and there is no cry of men in trouble. Towns are populated once again and he who plants his harvest shall eat it. Re has turned himself back to Egypt.'[1] Of even greater interest is a passage which has long been familiar to scholars: 'The chieftains are prostrate, saying "Salaam!", and no one lifts his head among the Nine Bows. Destruction is for Tjehenu, Khatti is at peace, the Canaan is plundered with every evil. Askalon is carried off, Gezer is captured, Yenoam is made non-existent, Israel is waste and has no seed, Khor[2] has become a widow because of Egypt.'[3] In the first place we have here clear evidence of the suppression of a revolt in Palestine, which is confirmed by the epithet 'reducer of Gezer' given to Merneptah in an inscription at Amada.[4] The second point that arises is the mention of Israel, the only instance known from any Egyptian text. Until the discovery of this stela in 1896 the general belief was that Merneptah was the pharaoh of the Exodus, yet here in the middle of his reign we find Israel already settled in Palestine.[5] Discussion of this problem has been endless, but the fact remains that there is no positive evidence relating to the date of the Exodus. A third significant point is the reference to Khatti. Breasted suggested that the Libyan invasion had at least the sympathy, if not the active assistance, of the Hittites, but this seems unlikely. The power of the Hittite kings was diminishing, and Arnuwandash III, the ruler of Khatti contemporary with Merneptah, was too much involved in problems nearer home to wish to embroil himself with Egypt.[6] Against Breasted's suggestion we have the specific statement 'Khatti is at peace', as well as a reference in the great Karnak inscription to the shipping of grain to Khatti at a time of famine.[7] The peace made between Egypt and Khatti half a century before still held.

As might have been expected in his comparatively short reign of ten years,[8] Merneptah did little in the way of erecting new public buildings, though inscriptions of his, including usurpations of older monuments, are not rare.[9] His funerary temple at Thebes, at least partly built of material robbed from the temple of Amenophis III, has been destroyed in its turn, as have his

[1] Ll. 24–5.
[2] G, 3, vol. I, 180* ff. In this context presumably Palestine only is meant.
[3] Ll. 26–8.   [4] G, 4, 273.
[5] G, I, vol. III, sect. 570. See below, ch. xxxiv, sect. III.
[6] See below, ch. xxiv, sect. IV.   [7] G, I, vol. III, sect. 580; §IX, 6.
[8] §v, I, 303.   [9] G, 7, 104 ff.

temple and palace at Memphis; he made additions to the temple of Thoth at Hermopolis,[1] but no notable building still standing dates from his reign. A few fragments from Serābīt el-Khādim[2] show that mining operations in Sinai went on. The remains of a stela in the temple of Amada refer to a rebellion in Wawat (Lower Nubia),[3] but nothing further of interest has come to light from this region. From the north-eastern frontier, however, we have extracts from the journal of a border official which have been included in a papyrus consisting of miscellaneous texts collected for educational purposes. Dated in Year 3, two years before the outbreak of the Libyan war, they record over a period of eleven days a continual coming and going of officials and letter-carriers between Egypt and Palestine, one dispatch being addressed to the prince of Tyre.[4] A copy of a letter from a similar source refers to Edomite tribesmen being allowed to pass a frontier fortress by the pharaoh's permission in order to graze their flocks at 'the pools of Pi-Tum'.[5] A curious text on papyrus which probably dates from this reign purports to be a letter from a scribe Hori to his friend Amenemope in which he points out that Amenemope is a failure in all he undertakes.[6] Among other duties the latter claims to be a *maher*, a scribe accustomed to foreign travel who could be sent on errands abroad, and in exposing his friend's incompetence Hori names a number of places to which such messengers might be sent or through which their route might lie; among many others we may mention Byblos, Tyre, Beth-shan and Qadesh. It seems that, while Egyptian suzerainty in Palestine was maintained, there was constant traffic on the roads between Egypt and the Asian principalities.

X. THE END OF THE NINETEENTH DYNASTY

After the death of Merneptah in 1223 B.C. the Nineteenth Dynasty died out in short reigns and dynastic intrigue, and even the order of succession of its kings is not certain.[7] The names in question are those of Amenmesses, Sethos II, Sekhaenre Ramesses-Siptah,[8] Akhenre-setepenre Merneptah Siptah, and Queen Tewosret. Of these only Sethos II was recognized by Ramesses III as

---

[1] §ix, 3.
[2] G, 5, nos. 266–267A.
[3] G, 1, vol. iii, 259, n. a.
[4] §v, 1, 108 f.
[5] §v, i, 293.
[6] Anastasi Papyrus No. i, cf. §v, 3, 475 ff.
[7] See, for example, §x, 1.
[8] See *C.A.H.* i³, pt. i, p. 190.

a legitimate king,[1] and it is natural to look on him as the immediate successor of his father Merneptah, while it is now fairly generally accepted that there was only one King Siptah who changed his name during his reign.[2] Since two stelae of Amenmesses at El-Qurna were usurped by Siptah,[3] it appears that the latter came after Amenmesses, while Tewosret, the consort of Sethos II, outlived them all to become queen-regnant at the very end of the dynasty. On the face of it, therefore, it would seem that the order of succession was Sethos II, Amenmesses, Siptah and Queen Tewosret, but there is evidence, quoted below, that Siptah directly succeeded Sethos II, and many scholars believe that Amenmesses preceded Sethos. The reason for this belief is that in a papyrus in the British Museum,[4] which contains many serious accusations extending over a considerable period against one Pneb, it is stated that at one stage in his nefarious career he was accused before the vizier Amenmose, who sentenced him to punishment. Pneb then appealed against his sentence to one Mose, who dismissed the vizier from office. Now the only person who could do this was the pharaoh himself, so that Mose was apparently a nickname of the king then ruling, like Sese for Ramesses II. It is assumed that Mose is an abbreviation of Amenmesses, and since there is reason to think that this episode occurred soon after the death of Merneptah,[5] it is believed that Amenmesses preceded Sethos II on the throne. Unfortunately, it is not yet proved that Mose and Amenmesses are identical, for in the Anastasi Papyrus No. 1 (p. 235), which was probably written in the reign of Merneptah,[6] and which is certainly a copy of a work already extant, there is mention of a name Mose which may also be a nickname for the pharaoh,[7] who in this case could hardly be Amenmesses. If at this time Mose was a current designation of any ruling king—perhaps derived from the name of Ramesses, the king *par excellence*—the identification with Amenmesses in particular would fall to the ground. Another fact that raises a doubt about the proposed position of Amenmesses is that it was Siptah and not Sethos who on the Qurna stelae substituted his name for that of Amenmesses, suggesting that it was Siptah who replaced him. Finally, in Liverpool there was a statue base, now destroyed, which is said to have had originally a cartouche of Sethos II which had been usurped by

---

[1] §x, 1, 43; §x, 4, 70, n. 2.
[2] §x, 11.
[3] §x, 5.
[4] §x, 7.
[5] §x, 1.
[6] G, 4, 274.
[7] §11, 2, 20*.

Amenmesses.[1] This, of course, would be conclusive as to the sequence of the two kings, but the reading of the original name as that of Sethos is open to question.[2] The one piece of incontrovertible evidence that we have is an ostracon in the Cairo Museum,[3] which records the death of Sethos II and the accession of Siptah as consecutive events, showing that Amenmesses cannot have intervened at this point. It is clear therefore, that we must either accept Amenmesses as the immediate successor of Merneptah, which seems unlikely, since Sethos was the legitimate heir, or else intercalate him as a temporary usurper into the reigns of either Sethos II or Siptah. It seems not impossible that the unexplained change in the names of Siptah may have had its origin in an interruption by Amenmesses, Siptah assuming a new form of name on regaining his throne; the substitution of Siptah's name for that of Amenmesses on the Qurna stelae would thus be accounted for. In any case Amenmesses's tenure of the throne was probably very short, for we have no date of his, and the only considerable monument is a tomb in the Valley of Kings. His mother Takhaet may have been a child or grandchild of Ramesses II[4] and so have provided a basis for his claim to be king. His consorts were Baktwerel and possibly Tia. It has been suggested that the latter was the mother of Siptah,[5] but this is speculative.

The reign of Sethos II was short, for he died in Year 6, but in that time he was able to carry out a certain amount of building. Apart from his tomb and a funerary temple now destroyed, he built a small temple at Karnak,[6] made additions to the Karnak temple of the goddess Mut of Ishru,[7] and completed the decoration of the temple of Thoth at Hermopolis which had been begun by Ramesses II and of which the fabric had been completed by Merneptah.[8] Some minor remains of his at Serābīt el-Khādim testify to the continuance of turquoise mining in Sinai.[9] As already remarked, he was the only successor of Merneptah who in later years was regarded as legitimate, and his consort was Tewosret,[10] who apparently was the heiress of the royal line. A son Seti-Merneptah[11] and possibly a daughter[12] both predeceased him, so that he left no heir in the direct line, unless indeed Siptah

---

[1] G, 7, 127.
[2] §x, 5.
[3] No. 25515; §x, 6; cf. §x, 1, 44, n. 6; quoted in §x, 9, 190 ff.
[4] §x, 11.
[5] §x, 1.
[6] §x, 8.
[7] G, 8, vol. II, 9.
[8] §IX, 3, 320.
[9] G, 5, no. 268.
[10] §x, 11.
[11] §x, 1; §x, 11.
[12] §x, 2.

was his son. Siptah certainly succeeded him directly,[1] but his parentage is uncertain.[2] What does appear evident is that Siptah was set on the throne while yet a boy[3] by Tewosret and the 'Great Chancellor of the entire land' Bay, who is said to have 'established the king on his father's throne'.[4] On the face of it this designates Siptah as the son of Sethos II, but it is possible that 'father' might refer to royal descent rather than to actual parentage. Even if, as seems likely, Siptah was the direct heir of Sethos, the fact that he was a minor may have made it necessary for Tewosret to seek the support of Bay to set her son in his rightful place, especially if there were an adult rival claimant. In the present state of our knowledge, Amenmesses is the only candidate for the role, and an ostensible ground for such a claim may well have been that the heir was a minor. We do not know why Siptah was not regarded later as a legitimate king; his parentage, if he was not the son of Sethos II, his early age, or even the fact that Tewosret and Bay were his supporters may have been the factors which caused his reign to be disregarded; certainly the memory of Tewosret was not in favour with her successor Sethnakhte, the first king of the Twentieth Dynasty.

To have played the role of king-maker Bay must have been a man of immense influence. He claims to have 'banished falsehood and granted truth', as if he were himself royalty, and in a formal hymn of praise to Siptah he says: 'I placed mine eye on thee alone', which may well be an allusion to his king-making activities.[5] In a relief at Aswān[6] and in another at Gebel es-Silsila[7] he is shown standing behind the king. Most significant of all is the fact that, whether by permission or not, he actually hewed for himself a tomb in the Valley of the Kings. There is a suggestion that he was a foreigner, for from the mid-Ramesside period onwards it became quite usual for men of foreign origin to serve in high office at Court, and, like many such men, Bay adopted an Egyptian pseudonym Ramesse-Khamenteru.[8]

A point which favours the view that Siptah was the legitimate heir of Sethos II is the fact that at Siheil at the First Cataract, at Wādi Halfa and at Abu Simbel there is a series of graffiti of prominent officials from the viceroy of Nubia downwards, all perpetuating the name of Siptah and begging his favour.[9] These

---

[1] Cairo Ostracon No. 25515; see above, p. 237.
[2] Cf. §x, 1, but the conclusions reached are open to question.
[3] §x, 4.   [4] §x, 11.   [5] §x, 11.
[6] G, 1, vol. III, sect. 647.   [7] *Ibid.* sects. 648 f.   [8] §x, 11.
[9] G, 1, vol. III, sects. 642 ff.

graffiti range in date from Year 1 to Year 6, and they show that the Nubian administration supported Siptah's claim to the throne; the graffito of Year 6 is the highest date known of this reign. Siptah's tomb is in the Valley of the Kings, where after his death his cartouches were cut out and later replaced.[1] His funerary temple is destroyed and may never have been finished; Bay's name actually appears beside that of the king in its foundation deposits.[2]

On Siptah's death without issue, Queen Tewosret herself ascended the throne, the fourth queen-regnant in Egypt's long history, the others being Nitocris, Sobkneferu and the illustrious Hatshepsut, and she took the throne-name of Sitre 'Daughter of Re'. The length of her reign is not definitely fixed; the latest date known is Year 8,[3] but she may have included Siptah's six years, since in view of his youth she probably acted as regent during his reign, in which case her sole reign would not have greatly exceeded two years. The latter is more likely, for the vizier and the Nubian viceroy under Siptah were still in office under Ramesses III,[4] with the reigns of Tewosret and of Sethnakhte of the Twentieth Dynasty intervening, not to mention any interregnum there may have been. Unless the officials in question both had an unusually long tenure of office, an interval of four to five years, rather than ten or eleven, is the most that can be allowed between the death of Siptah and the accession of Ramesses III. Queen Tewosret's tomb is in the Valley of the Kings, but it was usurped by Sethnakhte, who evicted its rightful owner.[5] Of her funerary temple nothing has survived except the foundation trenches and some foundation deposits, and it is doubtful whether any considerable part of it was ever built. Some objects with her name were found at Serābīt el-Khādim,[6] but nothing else is known of her reign, and with her the Nineteenth Dynasty came to an end.

XI. THE RISE OF THE TWENTIETH DYNASTY: SETHNAKHTE

The date of the beginning of the new dynasty cannot be fixed with precision, owing in part to the doubt regarding the length of Tewosret's sole reign. Merneptah died in 1223 B.C., and no more

---

[1] G, 4, 278.   [2] §x, 11.
[3] Cairo Ostracon No. 25293, cf. §x, 6.
[4] §x, 12.   [5] §x, 10.
[6] G, 5, no. 270.

than about twenty-three years can be reckoned for the remaining rulers of the Nineteenth Dynasty, even if Tewosret be allowed a total of eight or nine years. There arises also the question of an interregnum following the death of Tewosret before the accession of Sethnakhte, the first king of the Twentieth Dynasty. If there was such an interval it must have been short, perhaps no more than a matter of months; some scholars, probably rightly, do not believe that there was an interregnum,[1] in which case, allowing only two years of sole rule for Tewosret, the accession of Sethnakhte will have taken place in about 1200 B.C.

An important source for the history of the early Twentieth Dynasty is the Great Harris Papyrus in the British Museum.[2] This long and stately document, dated on the day of the death of Ramesses III, represents his claim to enter the company of the gods, and its compilation was ordered by Ramesses IV, who prays that the blessings enjoyed by his father may be vouchsafed to him also. After a brief introduction and a coloured scene of Ramesses III worshipping the Theban triad Amon-Re, Mut and Khons, there comes a detailed list of the benefactions bestowed by the dead king on the temples, which occupies 72 pages, and finally four pages are devoted to the events of his own and his father's reigns,[3] which are almost the only source of information for the reign of Sethnakhte. The first part of this historical summary thus describes the rise of the Twentieth Dynasty:

'The land of Egypt was cast adrift, every man being a law unto himself, and they had had no leader for many years previously until other times when the land of Egypt consisted of magnates and mayors, one man killing his fellow among high and low. Then another time came after it consisting of empty years[4] when Irsu the Asiatic was with them as chief, having put the entire land into subjection before him; each joined with his neighbour in plundering their goods, and they treated the gods as they did men, so that none dedicated offerings in their fanes. But the gods turned themselves to peace so as to put the land in its proper state in accordance with its normal condition, and they established their son who came forth from their flesh as ruler of every land upon their great throne, even Userkhaure-setpenre-meryamun, the Son of Re Sethnakhte-meryre-

[1] §x, 4.
[2] G, 1, vol. IV, sects. 151 ff.; a convenient hieroglyphic transcription in §xi, 2.
[3] §v, 3, 260 ff.
[4] Probably meaning years of famine.

meryamun'. The text then goes on to describe how Sethnakhte set the land in order, appointed the future Ramesses III to be crown prince, and then died and was buried with full rites.

The above quotation is a good example of Egyptian historical writing, but it need not be assumed that conditions in Egypt were quite as chaotic as this passage suggests; it was a convention when describing the advent of a new era to show the preceding state of affairs in as unfavourable a light as possible. On the other hand, it is inherently probable that during the Siptah–Tewosret régime, when there would appear to have been serious dynastic quarrels, the administration of the country may have deteriorated, and it certainly would seem that Sethnakhte, who from his name may have been a scion of the royal family, was at enmity with Tewosret. It is by no means certain who 'Irsu the Asiatic' was. The name, which appears to mean 'the self-made man', may well have been a pejorative pseudonym such as was sometimes given in state papers to offenders in high places; Černý has made the plausible suggestion that the person in question was the Great Chancellor Bay,[1] who was possibly an Asiatic and who was certainly a power in the land. Little else is known of the reign and even its length is uncertain, though lack of public works, as well as the apparently brief interval between the death of Siptah and the accession of Ramesses III, suggests that it was short, possibly no more than two years;[2] apart from a stela at Serābīt el-Khādim on which the date is now effaced,[3] no dated monuments or documents of this reign are known. Sethnakhte's consort Tiy-merenese was the mother of his successor Ramesses III,[4] the last of the great warrior kings of Egypt.

XII. THE WARS OF RAMESSES III

Ramesses III came to the throne in *c.* 1198 B.C. Of the first four years of his reign we lack information, but in the period from Year 5 to Year 11 inclusive there were three major wars for which the main sources are the scenes and inscriptions in Ramesses III's funerary temple at Medīnet Habu.[5] The inscriptions contain but a halfpenny-worth of historical fact to an intolerable deal of turgid adulation of the pharaoh, but combining them with the vivid scenes sculptured on the temple walls and the narrative of the Harris Papyrus, which to some extent supplements the

[1] G, 4, 282. [2] G, 4, 446.
[3] G, 5, no. 271. [4] §XI, 1.
[5] §XII, 1, vols. I and II; §XII, 2.

temple record, we can get a fairly clear picture of the course of events. The war of Year 5 was against the Libyans, who in a coalition of Libya, Meshwesh and an unknown tribe named Seped, were again contemplating a descent into Egypt, having recovered from their defeat by Merneptah. The ostensible cause of the war was interference by Ramesses with the succession to the chieftainship of the Tjemehu when he nominated a child to be chief,[1] but the real cause was the continuing desire of the western tribes to take possession of the rich lands of the Delta. Like Merneptah before him, on receipt of the news Ramesses consulted the oracle of Amun at Thebes, and the god handed him a scimitar with which to destroy the enemy.[2] Where the Egyptians encountered the invaders is not known, but the Libyans were utterly defeated.[3] It is not possible to extract from the somewhat unsatisfactory records[4] the number of slain, but it certainly ran into many thousands, while those taken captive were put to servitude in Egypt.

For two years there was peace, and then in Year 8 Egypt had to face an even more serious danger. All the Levant seems to have been in a turmoil of which the repeated Libyan attacks were a symptom, possibly as a result of pressure by nomad races of the steppes driving to the west, and in the words of the Egyptians: 'The foreign countries made a plot in their islands, and the lands were dislodged and scattered by battle all at one time and no land could stand before their arms, Khatti, Qode, Carchemish, Arzawa and Alashiya.'[5] The confederate peoples consisted of Peleset or Philistines,[6] Tjekker,[7] Sheklesh, Sherden, Weshesh[8] and Denyen,[9] probably the Danaoi of the *Iliad*, and having destroyed the Hittite empire they advanced into Amurru and apparently halted for a while to rest and concentrate their forces. Thereafter the confederates continued their march down the Syrian coast with their women and children in ox-carts, for this was an invasion to occupy and settle in the lands overrun, not merely a raid on a large scale, while offshore a considerable fleet escorted the march. To deal with this threat Ramesses mobilized his garrisons in Palestine with orders to bar the way to the advancing horde and hold them as much as possible while

[1] §xii, 2, 25.
[2] §xii, 1, vol. 1, pl. 13.
[3] *Ibid.* pls. 18–20.
[4] §xii, 2, 14–15.
[5] *Ibid.* 53 ff.
[6] G, 3, vol. 1, 200* ff.
[7] *Ibid.* 199* f.
[8] Otherwise unknown.
[9] G, 3, vol. 1, 124* ff.; on the Sea Peoples as a whole see §ix, 5, and below, ch. xxviii.

he got his main army into action,[1] and in the event the invasion
by land was effectively stopped. Meanwhile the hostile fleet was
trapped by the Egyptian ships in a harbour or an estuary, probably
in one of the mouths of the Nile, and utterly destroyed; the
enemy's ships were capsized or carried by boarding, while any
vessel coming within effective range of the shore was greeted
with a volley of arrows from troops lined up at the water's edge.[2]
The danger from the Peoples of the Sea was thus averted on the
very threshold of Egypt, but at least two of the confederate
peoples remained to settle in Palestine, namely the Peleset or
Philistines and the Tjekker; in the narrative of Wenamun[3]
about a century later the latter people are described as sea-
pirates based on the port of Dor.

This victory was followed by two quiet years and then in
Year 11 the Libyan trouble broke out afresh. The Libu and the
Meshwesh were again the moving spirits, though they were
supported by five other tribes of whom nothing further is known.
From the account in the Harris Papyrus[4] it is clear that they had
achieved some initial success. Peaceful infiltration had apparently
been going on for some years, and that part of the Delta west
of the Canopic branch of the Nile had been occupied from Memphis to the sea; now the western tribes were advancing in force
to overrun the Delta. Ramesses expelled the intruders from
Egyptian soil and met the main shock on the western border
where he had the support of the garrisons of the frontier forts.[5]
Again he achieved a crushing victory; over 2000 were killed and
much booty in prisoners and cattle was taken.[6] Among the captives was Mesher, commander of the Meshwesh, and when his
father Keper came to beg for his release, he was slain together
with his escort.[7]

At Medīnet Habu there are also scenes of Ramesses invading
Syria, Khatti and Amurru,[8] but as political entities these had
ceased to exist; the scenes in question are anachronisms copied
from a building of Ramesses II. Yet there may be a substratum of
fact beneath them. The historical portion of the Harris Papyrus
makes no mention of a war in Syria, but it mentions only one
Libyan war and so cannot be trusted entirely, and it seems not
improbable that after the defeat of the Peoples of the Sea Ramesses may have attempted to follow up his success by pushing on

[1] §xii, 1, vol. i, pls. 82 ff.
[2] *Ibid.* pls. 37–9.
[3] G, 4, 306 ff.
[4] G, 1, vol. iv, sect. 405.
[5] §xii, 1, vol. ii, pls. 70–2.
[6] §xii, 2, 67.
[7] *Ibid.* 91–2.
[8] §xii, 1, vol. ii, pls. 87 ff.

into Syria in an attempt to drive the enemy farther away from Egypt; there are scenes of both Syrian and Libyan wars in the small temple which Ramesses built in the precinct of the temple of Mut at Karnak,[1] and the well-known copy of a Syrian *migdōl* at Medīnet Habu has the look of a war memorial.[2] On the other hand, the scenes of a Nubian war at Medīnet Habu[3] are surely only conventional with no historical reality behind them; Nubia by now was entirely Egyptianized, and it is very unlikely that there was any trouble there[4] apart perhaps from an occasional scuffle with desert raiders. A minor campaign mentioned in the Harris Papyrus was against the Edomites of the Mount Seir region,[5] but it was probably no more than a punitive expedition against raiding nomads. The army with which Ramesses fought was of course mainly Egyptian, but, as under his predecessors, there were also contingents of Sherden and Kehek who apparently had no qualms about fighting against their racial kinsmen.

XIII. THE KINGDOM UNDER RAMESSES III

After the war of Year 11 peace came to Egypt. In the Harris Papyrus the king says: 'I planted the whole land with trees and verdure and I let the people sit in their shade; I caused the woman of Egypt to travel freely to the place where she would, for no foreigner or anyone on the road molested her. I allowed the infantry and the chariotry to settle down in my time, the Sherden and the Kehek lying full-length on their backs in their towns; they had no fear, for there was no destroyer from Nubia or enemy from Palestine, and their bows and their weapons were laid aside in their arsenals.'[6] This idyllic picture was probably largely true for the middle part of the reign, for there seems to have been a good measure of prosperity, though in Ramesses's latter years serious troubles developed. One indication of this prosperity is the temple and palace on the Theban west bank at Medīnet Habu,[7] for such a complex could hardly have been raised by a poverty-stricken people. The palace is ruined, but the temple is by far the best preserved of all the royal funerary temples, with great pylons and columned courts, and its sculptured reliefs are a rich mine for the historian as well as the student of religion. One feature it possesses is unique; in the centre of the eastern side was built a gatehouse which, as already mentioned

---

[1] G, 8, vol. II, 89 ff. [2] See Plate 154(*b*). [3] §XII, 1, vol. I, pls. 9–10.
[4] §IV, 4, 173 ff. [5] G, 1, vol. IV, §404.
[6] Cf. G, 1, vol. IV, sect. 410. [7] §XII, 1.

is a copy of a Syrian fortress (*migdōl*), the upper part forming a resort where Ramesses could relax with the ladies of his harim. Apparently the king spent more time at Thebes than at Per-Ramesse in the Delta, as otherwise he would surely not have permitted the massive infiltration of Libyans which preceded the war of Year 11, but he did occasionally reside in the north.[1]

At Karnak Ramesses built a modest temple to the Theban triad across the south wall of the forecourt of the great temple of Amun, with its entrance within the forecourt.[2] Within the temenos of the great temple he founded a temple to the moon-god Khons which was completed under the later Ramessides,[3] and of his temple in the precinct of Mut we have already spoken. According to the Harris Papyrus a temple of Sutekh was built at Per-Ramesse,[4] but we know of no further building enterprises of importance in this reign.

A great event was the dispatch of an expedition to Punt,[5] probably in the region about Cape Guardafui, to exchange the products of Egypt for tropical produce such as myrrh. The ships were taken overland in sections from Koptos to the Red Sea and there assembled for the voyage, and the cargoes travelled to and from Egypt by the same route. Another mission went to Atike, a region otherwise unknown, but possibly in Sinai, to fetch copper,[6] and yet another went to Serābīt el-Khādim to mine turquoise.[7] Ramesses also sank a great well in 'the country of Ayan';[8] this region has not been identified, but the analogy of the well-sinking activities of Sethos I and Ramesses II suggests that the site may have lain in the goldfields of Nubia or the eastern desert.

One feature of the great Harris Papyrus which makes it of unique interest is the detailed record of the possessions of the temples of Egypt and of the donations made to them during the whole of the reign of Ramesses III,[9] which apart from its intrinsic interest is a testimony to the meticulous keeping of records in the administrative offices of Egypt. As might have been expected, the Theban temples are by far the most wealthy; next in order come those of Heliopolis and Memphis, and after them the smaller fanes to as far south as Koptos; why none of the lesser religious centres south of that point have been included

[1] §XIII, 7.
[2] §XIII, 3.
[3] G, 8, vol. II, 75 ff.
[4] G, I, vol. IV, sect. 362.
[5] *Ibid.* sect. 407.
[6] *Ibid.* sect. 408.
[7] *Ibid.* sect. 409; G, 5, no. 272.
[8] G, I, vol. IV, sect. 406.
[9] *Ibid.* sects. 156 ff.

is a matter for conjecture. What impresses the modern reader is the immense amount of wealth concentrated in the hands of the great religious corporation of Amun; the later history of the dynasty shows the consequences which arose out of it.

The latter part of the reign was beset with troubles arising from administrative incompetence and from active disloyalty. An unnamed vizier was dismissed from his post and expelled from the town of Athribis;[1] in this reign also we hear of the first workmen's strikes on record.[2] On the site now known as Deir el-Medina once stood the village of the necropolis workers whose duty it was to excavate the royal tombs, and as state employees they drew their pay in the form of food from the royal storehouses. In Year 29 these supplies failed and the people of the village were reduced to downright need, so that strikes and rioting ensued. An intervention by the vizier put an end to the disturbances, but even he was able to provide no more than half of what was needed. The source of the trouble in this case was probably less positive misconduct than inefficiency or neglect of duty on the part of those whose business it was to keep the supplies in the storehouses up to date and to issue them to the workmen.

Worst of all, however, was a palace conspiracy to assassinate the pharaoh and to set on the throne one of his sons who was not the rightful heir. We know of this because the conspiracy did not succeed and the conspirators were put on trial, an account of the proceedings having by good fortune been preserved.[3] A secondary wife of Ramesses named Tiy plotted to murder the king and to set her son Pentwere on the throne, and she involved in her plot not only the women of the harim but also the major-domo Paibekkamen, the butler Mesedsure and a number of other officials of the harim and the administration, including the butler Pluka ('the Lycian') and the butler Inini, who was a Libyan. One member of the harim involved her brother Be-yenemwast, who was captain of archers of Nubia, writing to him: 'Stir up the people, make enmity and come to make a rebellion against your lord'; an army-commander Paiis was also involved. Actually we have the names of twenty-eight men among the conspirators as well as an uncertain number of women, none of whom are named except Tiy. Among the names of the accused are examples of the pejorative pseudonyms alluded to above,[4] e.g. Mesedsure 'Re hates him'; Beyenemwast 'Evil in Thebes', though by no means all the conspirators are thus disguised. It

---

[1] *Ibid.* sects. 361.   [2] §XIII, 4, 9.
[3] §XIII, 1. 6.   [4] §XI.

seems also that magical practices were employed, including the making of wax puppets,[1] but the conspiracy was discovered and the offenders arrested. A bench of twelve judges consisting of officials of the Court and officers of the army was appointed to try the accused, two of the judges holding the high Court rank of 'butlers' having foreign names and one at least being obviously Asiatic. Of the seventeen accused in the first list, all were found guilty and sentenced, presumably to death; the actual expression used is: 'they (the judges) caused their punishment to overtake them'. Of the seven persons in the second and third lists of accused, including the prince Pentwere, all were found guilty and were condemned to suicide. It is an eloquent commentary on the standards of conduct then current that five of the bench of twelve judges were arrested for carousing with the accused women and one of the male offenders; of the five, one was condemned to suicide, three had their noses and ears cut off and one was severely reprimanded. There is no reason to think that Ramesses was actually murdered or wounded by the conspirators; his mummy in the Cairo Museum shows no signs of injury, and the documents in the case are not dated, so that the affair may have taken place some time before his death.

Ramesses III died in Year 32;[2] by his consort Queen Ese and the women of the harim he had many sons, four or five of whom predeceased him, but one of them succeeded to his father's throne as Ramesses IV.[3] Seven of the latter's successors took the famous name of Ramesses, but with the death of Ramesses III the glory departed, and Egypt was never again an imperial power.

XIV. RELIGION, ART AND LITERATURE UNDER THE RAMESSIDES

By way of reaction to the Atenist heresy, and under political necessity, the god Amun of Thebes—more fully Amon-Re—attained, as has already been remarked, to greater power than ever before, carrying with him his spouse Mut and his offspring the moon-god Khons, the other members of the Theban triad, so that more and more benefactions were bestowed on the Theban temples until they outstripped in riches all the other sanctuaries of Egypt. Other deities of major rank, though not approaching

[1] I am not convinced by Goedicke's negative argument on this point, §XIII, 6.
[2] G, 1, vol. IV, sect. 182; cf., however, §XIII, 2.
[3] On the family of Ramesses III cf. §XI, 1; §XIII, 8; §XIII, 10.

Amun in wealth, were Re-Harakhte the sun-god of Heliopolis and Ptah the creator-god of Memphis, while Seth of Tanis, patron of the royal family, was of considerable local importance, and in his variant form of the war-god Sutekh had clearly attained more than just local worship; the reigning monarch also was worshipped as god on earth.[1] The possessions of both major and minor deities in the reign of Ramesses III are set out in detail in the Harris Papyrus (see above, pp. 245 f.), and it is certain that the nation was being bled white by so much of its wealth going in one direction.

Other phenomena also were becoming prominent in the world of religion. Long-continued intimate contact with Palestine and Syria had brought with it the worship of foreign deities, and among others we meet with Resheph, often identified with Sutekh, and Ba'al, and with the goddesses Astarte (riding on horseback with shield and mace), 'Anath, Qadesh (standing naked on a lion) and Ishtar.[2] Ramesses II must have had a special attachment to 'Anath, for he named one of his daughters Bint-'Anath 'Daughter of 'Anath' and built a temple to the goddess in Per-Ramesse. But beside the state cults and the worship of exotic deities there grew up among humble folk a very personal relationship to the gods and a consciousness of sin which is something new in Egyptian religion.[3] The deities so worshipped and addressed in humble prayer were Amun, Ptah, Haroeris, Thoth, the Moon, Isis, Meretseger the patroness of the Theban necropolis, and the deified king Amenophis I.[4] Amun, for example, is invoked as 'that beloved god who hearkens to humble entreaties, who stretches out his hand to the humble and who saves the wearied', while of Amenophis it is said, 'whoso enters to thee with troubled heart, he comes forth rejoicing and exulting'. Nothing comparable with this personal relationship between deity and worshipper has been noted during other periods of Egyptian history.

In the royal tombs the greatest part of the wall-space was given up to strange scenes and texts relating to the passage of the sun through the Netherworld during the hours of the night, which were carved not only on the walls of the tombs but also on sarcophagi, and copies on papyrus were made for the non-royal

[1] §III, 3, vol. II, pls. 29 ff.; §XIII, 7; §XIV, 16.
[2] §XIV, 4, 126 ff.; §XIV, 5, 149 ff.
[3] §XIV, 8.
[4] See also §XIV, 4, 73 f.; §XIV, 5, 145 f.; §XIV, 17; statue of Amenophis I carried in procession, §VIII, pl. 85.

dead.[1] Another feature which often occurs in the royal tombs is the cult of the stars, stellar diagrams and tables being found in the cenotaph of Sethos I at Abydos and in the tombs of many Ramesside kings;[2] this stellar cult is of great age, references to it occurring in the Pyramid Texts of the Old Kingdom and stellar diagrams being found in the wooden sarcophagi of the Middle Kingdom, while in the Eighteenth Dynasty there is a very fine diagram in the tomb of Senenmut.

An aspect of religion which developed very extensively during the later part of Egyptian history was the use of oracles to decide not only the policy of kings but also the most mundane affairs, such as appointments to a post, the right decision in disputes over property, or the innocence or guilt of an accused person.[3] The image of the god in a portable bark was brought from the temple on the shoulders of priests, the case was laid before him in writing and he would indicate by a motion of his bark his approval or otherwise of the action proposed; in the case of a decision between two alternatives, both were laid before him in writing and the god indicated the correct choice.

The art of the period under discussion is on the whole a picture of decline. At the beginning of the period it produced a few masterpieces such as the temple of Sethos I at Abydos,[4] where the proportions of the design and the craftsmanship of the delicate low raised relief still preserved on many of the walls are alike admirable, while the statue at Turin of Ramesses II as a young man stands comparison with any of Egypt's celebrated portrait statues.[5] Yet even here, despite their grace and beauty there is, especially in the wall-reliefs, a certain languor, a lack of the vigour that characterizes much of the work of the earlier Eighteenth Dynasty; the sculptors seem to have inherited something of the 'softness' of the immediately pre-Amarna work as found, for example, in the Theban tomb of Ramose. On the grand scale, the façade of the great temple at Abu Simbel is an astonishing achievement, but most of the colossal statues of Ramesses II at Thebes and Memphis have survived only in fragments. In architecture generally, the Abydos temple apart, the surviving temple remains are impressive rather than beautiful; the great hypostyle hall at Karnak is an architectural *tour de force*,[6] but it impresses by mass rather than by proportion, and the columned courts at Medīnet Habu can hardly be described as graceful. The scenes of battle and the chase carved in sunk

---

[1] §III, 9; §XIV, 2; §XIV, 10; §XIV, 15.   [2] §XIV, 13.
[3] §XIV, 1.   [4] See Plate 153(*a*).   [5] See Plate 153(*b*).   [6] See Plate 154(*a*).

relief on temple walls and pylons are often striking in their portrayal of vigorous action, but the coarse and often ill-proportioned hieroglyphs in the temple inscriptions are a sad decline from the grace of earlier work. The mural painting which has survived on temple walls from Abydos to Nubia, while it is skilfully executed and is pleasing to the eye, deals with entirely stereotyped subjects of battle and ritual; for painting as an art it is necessary to turn to the walls of tombs. There is some beautiful work in the tomb of Queen Nefertiry,[1] and in the tomb of the high priest of Amun named Userhet we find good drawing and a wider range of colours than in earlier times,[2] while in the tomb of Nakhtamun there is a pleasing portrait of Ramesses II.[3] In the private tombs the scenes from daily life persist and are often lively and humorous,[4] but the tombs of the sons of Ramesses III in the Valley of the Queens show a sad decline; there is an overall effect of gaudiness in the painting and the hieroglyphs in the inscriptions are not well formed.[5] On the other hand, a meed of praise cannot be witheld from the painted illuminations accompanying the texts in the more elaborate copies of the Book of the Dead.

In contrast with the artistic decline, the period here dealt with showed great activity in the literary field. The masterpieces of the Middle Kingdom were still being copied and read, but there was no lack of new composition. Especially was this the case in the realm of fiction. Here we have historical tales, 'Seqenenre and Apophis',[6] 'The Capture of Joppa';[7] stories with a religious background, 'The Tale of the Two Brothers',[8] 'The Contendings of Horus and Seth', an entertaining burlesque of the dispute between Horus and Seth for the kingship of Egypt as tried before the tribunal of the Heliopolitan Ennead;[9] an allegorical story, 'The Blinding of Truth by Falsehood';[10] a folk-tale, 'The Doomed Prince',[11] and a number of other stories of which only fragments remain. Of more serious works, intended for the instruction of boys and young men with regard to conduct, the writing of letters, the learning of geography, the adoption of the profession of scribe and so forth, we have 'The Teaching of

---

[1] §viii, 1, pls. 91 ff.; §xiv, 11, 140, 142–3. See Plate 155 (a).
[2] §viii, 1, pls. 87 ff.; xiv, 11, 132, 135 ff.
[3] §viii, 1, pl. 100.
[4] §viii, 1, pls. 96 ff.; §xiv, 11, 145 ff.
[5] §viii, 1, pl. 103.
[6] §xiv, 9.
[7] §xiv, 14.
[8] §xiv, 6, 150 ff.
[9] §xiv, 7, 8 ff.
[10] §xiv, 3, vol. 1, 2 ff.
[11] §xiv, 14.

Anii',[1] the letter of Hori to Amenemope,[2] and the curious medley known today as 'Late Egyptian Miscellanies'.[3] There are many magical or medico-magical compilations, and a work on the interpretation of dreams,[4] while poetry, apart from stereotyped hymns to the gods, is represented by some charming love-songs;[5] also, despite a recent objection, the inscription on the Battle of Qadesh hitherto known as the Poem surely has a right to that title.

[1] §xiv, 6, 234 ff.

[2] §ii, 2.

[3] §v, 1.

[4] §xiv, 3, vol. i, 9 ff.

[5] §xiv, 7, 27 ff.; §xiv, 12.

CHAPTER XXIV

THE HITTITES AND SYRIA
(1300–1200 B.C.)

I. THE LATER REIGN OF MUWATALLISH

SINCE the conquest of Shuppiluliumash the Hittites had considered Kinza (Qadesh on the Orontes) and Amurru their southernmost possessions. With the rise of the Nineteenth Dynasty, the Egyptians sought to recover their former Syrian dependencies, in other words to dislodge the Hittites and to drive them as far north as possible. The issue then, seen from the Hittite point of view, was this: which of the two rivals was to dominate Syria and, more specifically, which of them was to control Kinza and Amurru?

The latent rivalry between the Egyptians and the Hittites erupted into open warfare as soon as Amurru, as an immediate result of the successful Syrian campaign of Sethos I (1318–1304) which had brought the pharaoh at least as far north as Kinza (Kidsa, Qadesh),[1] was compelled to abrogate the treaty which bound it to the Hittite king. This was done in a formal way which must have made it clear to the Hittite that Bente-shina, then king of Amurru, had no other alternative.[2] Kinza had likewise been drawn into the Egyptian orbit, the rest of Syria, however, remained in Hittite hands. At that time Muwatallish had ruled over the Khatti Land for only a short time. Conditions induced him to acquiesce temporarily. He doubtless sent the customary message to Ramesses II (1304–1237) upon his accession to the throne of the pharaohs; but he definitely did not consider himself, as Egyptian sources will have it, a subject of the pharaoh.[3] On the contrary, it is obvious that he prepared feverishly for the inevitable trial of strength. It was close at hand when Ramesses in the campaign of his fourth year (1301), reached Beruta and Byblos.[4]

Muwatallish, now fully prepared, accepted the challenge. Lists

---

* An original version of this chapter was published in fascicle 37 in 1965.
[1] §1, 8; §1, 15, 200 ff.; §1, 20, pl. 28 and pp. 19 ff.
[2] G, 6, xxiii, 1, i, 28 ff.; §iv, 12, 114 ff.
[3] Pap. Anastasi, 2, 1 ff. (§iii, 16 col., 1878 f.).
[4] §1, 19; G, 9, pl. 9 and pp. 19 ff.

of the contingents composing the Hittite army which he assembled for the impending war have come down to us in Egyptian sources.[1] First of all, these lists state that Muwatallish 'had gathered together all countries from the ends of the sea to the land of Kheta'. Secondly—and this is of particular value—they specifically enumerate these countries; most of them recur in the Hittite texts. Their geographical range gives us a fair idea of the empire of Muwatallish. The first place after Khatti itself is occupied by *Nhrn* and *'Irṯw*, i.e. Mitanni and Arzawa; these two are called '*kuirwana* countries' by the Hittites, a term which signifies a preferred status in the Hittite confederacy.[2] Then a group of Anatolian countries follows: *Drdny, Ms, Pds, 'Irwn, Ḳrḳš, Lk*. Only the first mentioned remains obscure; the others, in Hittite terms *Maša, Pitašša, Arawanna, Karkiša*, and *Lukka*, can all of them with certainty be localized in the central and western parts of Anatolia. The list concludes with the enumeration of south-eastern and Syrian territories: *Ḳḏwdn, Krkmš, 'Ikrṯ, Ḳd, Nwgs, Mwšꜣnt*, and *Ḳdš*. In Hittite they correspond with *Kizzuwadna, Karkamiš, Ugarit*, (probably) *Ḫalba, Nuḫaš*, and *Kinza*; *Mwšꜣnt* is not identified. It is no accident that Amurru is missing; that country had temporarily been taken over by the Egyptians. It goes without saying that the Hittite provinces furnished contingents; we know from other sources that Khattushilish, the king's brother, took part in the campaign as commander of the contingent raised in the provinces under his administration.[3]

Muwatallish assembled his army near Qadesh on the Orontes where the decisive battle was fought.[4] It is better known than most other battles of antiquity, for Ramesses has described it for posterity in wordy compositions and pictured it on the walls of temples which he built.[5] This documentation naturally gives the Egyptian point of view and must be used with caution by the historian.

The Hittite king had chosen his position well. It could be foreseen that the Egyptian army, approaching from the south, had either to use the coastal road or the inland road through Amqa. In either case it would have to strike out for the Orontes valley where the fortified city of Qadesh blocked its advance. Ramesses left the Delta in the spring of his fifth year (1300) and probably followed

---

[1] G, 3, vol. III, sects. 306, 309; §1, 15, 204 ff.   [2] §v, 4, 98 f.
[3] §1, 12, ii, 69 ff.   [4] See generally Bibliography, §1.
[5] G, 10, pls. 16–25 (Abydos); pls. 63–64 (Luxor); pls. 92–95 (Ramesseum 1st courtyard); pls. 96–99 (Ramesseum 1st pylon); pls. 100–106 (Ramesseum 2nd pylon); pls. 169–178 (Abu Simbel).

the coast right to the northern end of the Lebanon mountains. Advancing north-eastward he then marched toward Qadesh. His troops were organized in four divisions. Without precise information as to the whereabouts of the enemy he allowed his columns to stretch out over a long distance. When the advance division, with which the king himself was, had already reached the heights west of Qadesh, where it prepared to pitch camp, the others had fallen behind several miles, the rear division still being on Amurrite territory. In this dangerous situation Ramesses was caught by a surprise attack of the Hittites who had shifted their chariotry from the north to the south of Qadesh. Fording the Orontes they fell upon Ramesses's second division and shattered it. The first was attacked immediately afterwards, while encamping, and was severely mauled. Fierce fighting ensued in which the Egyptians were able to hang on until the third division could be brought up. This took the Hittite charioteers in the rear and threw them back on to and into the river. Ramesses was able to extricate himself from impending disaster and to reconstitute his forces. However, he recognized that further advance was impossible and decided on retreat. The Hittites remained masters of the battle-field.

There is no doubt that they were quite satisfied with the outcome of the campaign. They pursued the retreating Egyptians and were able to penetrate as far south as Apa (= Apina, Upi, i.e. Damascus),[1] that is to say a considerable distance beyond the border as it had existed before the outbreak of the war. That line was fully held. Kinza, which had temporarily fallen into Egyptian hands, remained a Hittite possession; and Amurru, the chief objective of the fighting, had to surrender to the Hittites. Bente-shina, its prince, was deposed by Muwatallish. But the mild treatment that he accorded to the prince of Amurru was a recognition of the fact that the latter could hardly have acted otherwise. Bente-shina was to live in Khakpish for a while under the eyes of Khattushilish; he was later to play his role in the conflict between that prince and his nephew Urkhi-Teshub. For the time being, he was replaced in Amurru by a certain Shapilish.[2]

No Hittite text, either of Muwatallish or of his successors, suggests in any way that the control over Amurru was lost again by the kings of Khatti. On the contrary, the sources leave no doubt that nothing of the kind happened. This means that not even Ramesses II can have had enduring military successes of any

[1] §1, 14, col. 837; §1, 6, 212.
[2] §1, 23, 124 ff. (obv. 11 ff.); G, 6, xxiii, 1, i, 28 ff. (see §iv, 13).

significance in Syria after the battle of Qadesh. His 'war' in Amurru in his eighth year during which *Dpr*—probably in the vicinity of Qadesh—was captured,[1] his raid up to Tunip[2] and his second visit, in his tenth year, to the Dog-River[3] remained episodes.

Muwatallish, in the meantime, renewed the treaty which Murshilish had concluded with Talmi-sharruma, the king of Aleppo.[4] A witness to the treaty was, among others, Shakhurunuwash, the king of Carchemish. As stated before (p. 224), this younger son of Sharre-Kushukh had served since the preceding reign as something like a Hittite vicegerent in Syria, and Syrian kings, such as that of Ugarit, were made responsible to him.

The Syrian War did not pass for the Hittites without serious loss. The Assyrians did not let the preoccupation of Muwatallish in Amurru and Kinza pass without exploiting the opportunities it offered them. Adad-nīrāri, after having been king of Assyria for a comparatively short time, defeated Shattuara, the king of 'Khanigalbat', who must have been one of Kurtiwaza's descendants and successors. He was taken prisoner, carried off to Ashur, but released after having taken an oath of allegiance to Adad-nīrāri.[5] This meant that the Hittite and the Assyrian zones of influence now touched each other at the Euphrates.[6]

On the northern frontier, in Asia Minor, the situation had also markedly deteriorated. The Kaska people had taken advantage of the absence of Khattushilish with the greater part of his forces and had renewed their frontier raids. Even Khakpish, where the governor was exercising the power of a 'king', had been lost and had to be recovered when he returned from the Egyptian war.[7] Furthermore, the absence of the Great King as well as his brother gave personal enemies of Khattushilish an opportunity to work and plot against him. We are told that Arma-Tattash, who years back had been relieved of the governorship of the Upper Land in favour of Khattushilish, employed black magic against his rival. His efforts failed, and the Great King turned the plotter over to his brother; he was sent with his family into exile to Alashiya; only his son, Shippa-zitish, escaped.[8] The incident is of no great importance, but it seems to demonstrate the king's unwavering confidence in his brother's loyalty and good faith. Muwatallish died soon afterwards.

[1] G, 3, vol. III, sects. 356 ff.; §1, 15, 223.
[2] G, 3, vol. III, sects. 364 f.   [3] G, 9.
[4] §1, 23, 80 ff.   [5] §1, 24 (obv. 7 ff.).
[6] G, 4, 58 ff. (ll. 8–14).   [7] §1, 12, iii, 9 ff.
[8] §1, 12 and 13, ii, 74 ff., iii, 14 ff.

The chronology of this reign is dependent on Egyptian synchronisms. The end of the preceding reign, and therefore also the accession of Muwatallish, has been put above at (p. 127) about 1320 or a few years earlier. The main event of the later years of Muwatallish is the battle of Qadesh, which falls in the fifth year of Ramesses II, i.e. 1300 B.C. As we shall see presently, the war between the Egyptians and the Hittites was officially concluded by the peace treaty of the twenty-first year of Ramesses, i.e. 1284. Khattushilish had then been king of the Khatti Land for some time, and before him his nephew Urkhi-Teshub had reigned at least seven years. This places the death of Muwatallish at about 1294 or a few years earlier.

II. URKHI-TESHUB AND KHATTUSHILISH

Muwatallish died without leaving a legitimate son to succeed him. Hence it was necessary to invoke the 'constitution' of Telepinush which provided that in such a case the eldest son of a royal concubine should be made king. In this manner Urkhi-Teshub was proclaimed king. Khattushilish supported his claims; in his 'apology', our main source for this development, he makes much of it and insists that his attitude toward his nephew is proof of his loyalty and generosity.[1] The internal strife that was to follow, he insists, was exclusively the fault of the young king, who obviously mistrusted him.

Urkhi-Teshub, as Hittite king, assumed the name of Murshilish (III). We know that from his official seal which was found at Ras Shamra.[2] Khattushilish—obviously writing *post factum* and under the influence of the conflict with his nephew—always calls him only Urkhi-Teshub, certainly a sign of contempt.

Khattushilish in the meantime had further increased both his prestige and the territory over which he ruled. Above all, he had succeeded in liberating the holy city of Nerik, which for long years had been in the hands of the Kaska people, who had prevented the important cults of that city from being properly attended to. From then on, Khattushilish was known as the king of Khakpish and Nerik.[3] Urkhi-Teshub may have had valid reason for distrusting his uncle. There are definite indications that, at least since early in his nephew's reign if not before, he had ambitious plans of his own. What else could possibly have been the purpose of seeking the friendship of those who had had quarrels with

---

[1] §1, 12 and 13, iii, 38 ff.   [2] §11, 1; §11, 3.
[3] §1, 12 and 13, iii, 45; see *Bull. A.S.O.R.* 122, 22.

Muwatallish or Urkhi-Teshub? Bente-shina of Amurru is an example of which we have accidentally some knowledge.[1] Another case in point is that of the physician Mitannamuwash.[2] There were probably more like these. Urkhi-Teshub obviously suspected that his uncle might prepare an armed coup, and decided to take anticipatory action. He revoked his uncle's appointment as the governor of the Upper Land, a territory to which Khattushilish had greatly added by his military successes, but allowed him to keep for the time being his 'kingdom' in Khakpish and Nerik. When he took this too away, Khattushilish revolted. An uprising ensued in which the Hittite nobility, dissatisfied with the young king and quite possibly contemptuous of his illegitimate birth, took the uncle's side. Urkhi-Teshub was defeated, finally besieged in Shamukha and taken prisoner. Khattushilish assumed the kingship himself. He sent his nephew into exile, first to northern Syria and later, when there were indications that he might try to escape to Babylonia (or to Egypt), 'across the sea', i.e. to Alashiya (Cyprus).[3]

III. KHATTUSHILISH AS GREAT KING

The sources for this reign are by no means ample, at least as far as actual historical documents are concerned. In his 'apology' (a kind of autobiography) Khattushilish himself states with considerable pride about his reign:

Those who had been well disposed towards the kings, my predecessors, became well disposed toward me. They kept sending envoys and they kept sending me presents as well. Such presents as they kept sending me they had not sent to any of my fathers and forefathers. Whatever king owed me homage did pay homage to me. The lands that were hostile to me I conquered; I added district after district to the Khatti Lands. Those who had been hostile in the time of my fathers and my forefathers made peace with me.[4]

Whatever the events may have been in detail, it is certain that Khattushilish preserved the power of the empire which he had inherited.

When he became 'Great King' the relationship with Egypt was still tense, although diplomatic relations had probably been resumed. Ramesses seems to have written to the new king a somewhat cool letter on the occasion of his accession to the throne, and Khattushilish replied in an equally cool manner.[5] Be this as it may, Syria certainly required the new king's full attention. The suc-

[1] §I, 23, 124 ff. (obv. 11 ff.). [2] G, 5, IV, 12 (see §I, 12, 40 ff.).
[3] §I, 12, iv, 32 ff.; §II, 2. See above, pp. 201 ff.
[4] §I, 12, iv, 50 ff. (pp. 36 f.). [5] §III, 9.

cesses which Ramesses had won in Palestine[1] may have contributed to making the situation appear more menacing. The fact that the king of Mira corresponded with the pharaoh[2] is another indication of the tensions that had arisen; if the king of Mira was a Hittite vassal he certainly violated his oath of loyalty by writing to Egypt. Moreover, Khattushilish could never be certain that the Assyrians would not utilize a fresh outbreak of the Hittite–Egyptian war for a simultaneous attack upon the Euphrates frontier.

A revolt of Wasashatta of Mitanni, Shattuara's son, had given Adad-nīrāri I, then king of Ashur, the welcome pretext to incorporate the former Mitannian territory into Assyria.[3] After this victory he had claimed the title of a 'Great King'. The ensuing anger of Khattushilish is plainly evident in a letter rejecting such claims. He writes rather contemptuously:

With respect to brotherhood, . . . about which you speak—what does brotherhood mean? . . . With what justification do you write about brotherhood. . . ? Are not friends those who write to each other about brotherhood? And for what reason should I write to you about brotherhood? Were perhaps you and I born of the same mother? As my [father] and my grandfather did not write to the king of Ashur [about brotherhood], even so must you not write [about brotherhood and] Great-kingship to me.[4]

Such words are not indicative of much love lost; on the contrary, they are suggestive of the apprehension with which Khattushilish watched the Assyrian.

In this situation the Hittite king sought the friendship of the Babylonian king. He concluded a formal treaty of friendship and mutual assistance with the Kassite Kadashman-Turgu. It was the purpose of this treaty to threaten the Assyrian with a retaliatory attack from the south, should he ever think of attacking Syria. The scheme served its purpose for a while and helped to maintain the balance of power. But it did not survive Kadashman-Turgu's death for long. His son and successor Kadashman-Enlil, was still a minor when he ascended the throne, and royal power was actually exercised by his vizier Itti-Marduk-balāṭu. He refused to make the interests of a foreign state the guiding principle of his external policy.[5]

But this setback no longer mattered, for Khattushilish had in the meantime come to terms with Ramesses. In the latter's twenty-first year (i.e. 1284), sixteen years after the battle of Qadesh, the two kings concluded a treaty in which they mutually acknowledged

---

[1] G, 3, vol. III, sects. 356, 366. [2] G, 5, 1, 24; §III, 1; §III, 12, 43 f.
[3] §1, 24 (obv. 18 ff.); §1, 25; G, 2, 36 ff.
[4] G, 6, XXIII, 102; §III, 7, vol. I/2, 246 f. [5] §III, 8, 24 ff.; §III, 14; §III, 5.

their equal status. Thus the rivalry between the two great opponents came to an end and the frontier between the Egyptian and
the Hittite spheres of influence was stabilized. The treaty, of
which we possess both the Egyptian and the cuneiform versions,[1]
makes no mention at all of territorial claims. This means that the
border remained on the line which the conqueror Shuppiluliumash
had established and which his successors had successfully defended. It implies the final renunciation of the traditional Egyptian claims to Syria. The conclusion of the treaty was accompanied
by a cordial exchange of messages not only between the kings, but
also between the queens;[2] the Egyptian crown prince also joined
in the greetings.[3] Abroad, the event was hailed as one of the
greatest importance. The peace of the world seemed assured for a
long time to come.

During the following years a plan seems to have been conceived to arrange for a personal meeting between Khattushilish
and Ramesses. One talked about a possible journey of the Hittite
king to Palestine.[4] Whether the plan was realized or not, it
certainly testifies to a stability in the political situation such as had
not existed for a long time.

That it was a reality can be shown by the example of Amurru.
The geographic position of that country between the two con-
testants furnishes us with an excellent measuring stick. Khattushilish reinstalled Bente-shina as local king, the same man whom
Muwatallish had deposed; he also made him his son-in-law.[5] We
possess the explicit statement that Bente-shina proved himself
worthy of the confidence lodged in him and remained loyal to the
Khatti Land throughout his lifetime.[6] In other words, Ramesses II
was never again able to encroach upon his territory.

If the Egyptian sources try to give the impression that the
pharaoh later won successes against the Hittites, it has no basis
in fact. It is true that Khattushilish gave his daughter in marriage
to Ramesses, an event which falls into the pharaoh's thirty-fourth
year (c. 1271), i.e. thirty years after the battle of Qadesh.[7] But
this must not be construed as consequence of a new, revised peace
forced upon Khattushilish after defeat. It only testifies to enduring good relations between the two powers; it was one of the
numerous dynastic marriages that were frequently concluded—
certainly for political reasons—during this period.

[1] §1, 23, 112 ff.; §III, 13; §III, 15; G, 8, 199 ff.
[2] G, 5, 1, 29; §III, 12, 59; §III, 8, 23.
[3] G, 6, III, 70.   [4] §III, 6.   [5] §1, 23, 124 ff. (obv. 19 f.).
[6] G, 6, XXIII, 1, ii, 45 ff.; §IV, 13.   [7] §III, 3 and 4; §III, 11.

We are ill-informed about the affairs of Asia Minor during this reign. In view of the almost normal restiveness of the Kaska people it is not surprising to hear of continuing conflicts with these mountaineers. Khattushilish, we are told, fought with them for fifteen years, and his son, as major-domo, for at least twelve years more.[1] Perhaps it was at that time when the treaty with the town Tiliura, of which we possess a fragment,[2] was concluded.

In Arzawa Mashturish, the prince of the Shekha-River Land, became one of the king's staunchest partisans.[3] A peculiar light is thrown upon the situation in the other western countries by the fact that the prince of Mira, shortly before the official peace with Egypt, could have asked the pharaoh to intervene in favour of Urkhi-Teshub.[4] It is not known whether and how Khattushilish reacted to this endeavour which, from his point of view, could not have been regarded otherwise than as treasonable; but we have no reason to doubt that he knew how to deal with it. His claim that he maintained the power of his predecessors must be taken as substantially true.

Warfare in the Lukka lands is indicated by the miserable remnants of the annals of this reign.[5] In Tattashsha, situated in the southern mountains, which during the Egyptian war of Muwatallish had served as an alternative capital, Khattushilish established a new 'small' kingdom; Inarash, a member of the royal family, was installed as its ruler.[6] Upon his death it was transferred to Ulmi-Teshub and the treaty renewed with him.[7]

During the whole reign of Khattushilish, his consort Pudu-Kheba, whom he had married as prince when returning from the campaign against Egypt, played a prominent role in all important affairs, more so than any queen before her. Documents of state were usually made out in the name of both the king and the queen. Letters to Egypt, for instance, were written out in two copies, one to the pharaoh in the king's name, the other to the pharaoh's consort in that of the queen.[8] There must be some legal reason for this complicated procedure. That no documentation of the same kind exists for other queens is possibly due to an accident.

The chronology of Khattushilish, like that of Muwatallish, depends mainly on Egyptian synchronisms. The peace treaty with Ramesses falls in the latter's twenty-first year (i.e. 1284); thirteen years later (i.e. 1271) Khattushilish sent his daughter to the Egyptian court. He himself had reigned for some years when he

---

[1] G, 6, xix, 8, iii, 21 ff. [2] G, 6, xxi, 29 (untranslated).
[3] G, 6, xxiii, ii, 20 ff.; §iv, 13. [4] G, 5, 1, 24; §iii, 12, 44.
[5] G, 6, xxi, 6 and 6a; §iii, 7, fasc. 1/1, 6 ff.; G, 6, xxxi, 19.
[6] §i, 12 and 13, iv, 62 ff. [7] G, 5, iv, 10; §iii, 10. [8] §iii, 2.

succeeded in concluding the peace treaty; his reign—it was estimated above—had begun about 1286. At that time he would have been at least forty years old, for his mother, the wife of Murshilish, had died in that king's ninth year, i.e. about 1326. Both Khattushilish and his son Tudkhaliash were contemporaries of Kadashman-Enlil of Babylon, to whom fifteen years are ascribed. The son, still reigning when Tukulti-Ninurta became king in Ashur, cannot have assumed kingship over Khatti much later than Shalmaneser I did in Assyria. When he ascended the throne he had been an army leader for at least twelve years, i.e. he was then at least thirty years old. Being the son of Pudu-Kheba he might have been born in 1299 (the year after Qadesh) at the earliest. Considering all circumstances 1265 B.C. seems a reasonable estimate for the death of Khattushilish.

IV. THE LAST KINGS OF THE KHATTI LAND

Tudkhaliash (IV), the son of Khattushilish and Pudu-Kheba, like his father, had begun his career as a 'priest'[1]—in his case of the 'Ishtar' (i.e. Shaushga) of Shamukha, his father's patroness. It seems that before becoming king he was known under the name of Khishmi-Sharruma.[2]

The new king had to strain the resources of the empire to the utmost. Relations with Egypt were, as far as we can see, friendly during his lifetime. But the renascent Assyria caused new troubles to the Hittites. And in the west there was Ahhiyawa which was intent upon taking advantage of any sign of weakness on the part of the central power. The political problems of the times can be sensed when we consider the list of contemporaneous powers which is contained in a treaty made at this time with Amurru. It includes the names of Egypt, Ashur, Karduniash (i.e. Kassite Babylonia), and—erased again in the draft which is preserved—Ahhiyawa.[3]

In the east, in Syria, Carchemish continued its role as the main Hittite centre. It was now Ini-Teshub, the son of Shakhurunuwash, who represented the Great King here and acted in his name in all Syrian affairs. The sources at our disposal show him dealing with matters concerning Ugarit and Amurru, both vassals of Khatti. In Ugarit the former[4] decision to separate Shiyanni from Ugarit was confirmed by Tudkhaliash.[5]

Ini-Teshub was instrumental in keeping interior peace when

---

[1] §1, 12, iv, 67 ff. [2] §v, 8, 387 f.; §v, 12, 118 f.
[3] G, 6, xxiii, 1, iv, 1 ff.; §iv, 13; §iv, 12, 320 ff.
[4] See above, p. 125. [5] G, 7, 290 f.

two brothers revolted against Ammishtamru, the new king. They received the shares in their mother's inheritance to which they were entitled and were sent (as refugees) to Alashiya (Cyprus).[1] Also marital complications among the vassals kept Ini-Teshub busy. There is above all the case of the Amurru princess, daughter of Bente-shina and married to Ammishtamru, who committed adultery, fled to her homeland, but finally on Hittite request had to be extradited, which might have meant death for her.[2]

Amurru was likewise under the supervision of Ini-Teshub. But, of course, the treaty by which Shaushga-muwash (*IŠTAR-muwaš*) was recognized as king of the country was concluded in the name of Tudkhaliash himself.[3] The fact alone that Amurru remained a Hittite vassal in spite of the international situation is worthy of note. The treaty of course envisaged the possibility of war against Egypt, and also against Ashur, but that was theoretical rather than real.

With Ashur the relations of Tudkhaliash must indeed have been tense, to say the least. Although he was still alive under Tukulti-Ninurta I (1244–1208),[4] most of his reign must be assumed to be contemporary with that of Shalmaneser (1274–1245). The latter, like his father Adad-nīrāri, had become heavily engaged in Upper Mesopotamia. Apparently, domination over 'Khanigalbat'—this is what they called the revived Mitanni state—almost assured when Wasashatta had been defeated,[5] had again slipped away from the Assyrians. The local king, another Shattuara, had to be vanquished anew by Shalmaneser and after his downfall the war was carried to the banks of the Euphrates.[6] Ini-Teshub of Carchemish had part in it.[7] It is not by chance either that the treaty with Amurru contains an interesting clause— not duplicated anywhere else—which prohibited commercial relations between Amurru and Ashur.[8] Its purpose patently was to cut off Ashur from the Mediterranean coast and thereby from access to world trade. The success of his defence of Upper Mesopotamia is attested by the fact that Tudkhaliash himself— certainly in defiance of Assyrian claims—adopted the title 'king of the world' (*šar kiššati*).[9]

It has been remarked above that in the Amurru treaty of Tudkhaliash the name of the country Ahhiyawa had been secon-

[1] G, 7, 120 ff.   [2] G, 7, 125 ff.; §IV, 6; §IV, 15. See above, pp. 142 f.
[3] G, 6, XXIII, 1; §IV, 13.   [4] G, 6, III, 74; §IV, 9, 65.
[5] See above, p. 258.   [6] G, 4, 116 ff.
[7] G, 7, 150 f.   [8] G, 6, XXIII, 1, iv, 14 ff.; §IV, 13.
[9] §IV, 8, 74.

darily struck from the list of the great nations of the period. This indicates that Ahhiyawa did not properly belong to them. Nevertheless, it remains remarkable that a court historiographer, if only momentarily, could have thought of the king of Ahhiyawa as equal to the other Great Kings. Hittite kings and the military must have had reason to fear the man of Ahhiyawa. Indeed, he is mentioned as an enemy in the annals of Tudkhaliash.[1] His home was obviously in western Anatolia. The available evidence, fragmentary as it is, allows the observation that at this time the interest of the Hittite kings in the affairs of Anatolia is clearly on the increase.

In this connexion the raids of the Kaska people,[2] eternally repeated routine, do not mean much. But great interest must be attached to the Arzawa war of Tudkhaliash. Its immediate cause was the defection of Kupanta-Inarash, the local king. The sources are rather fragmentary, but there is reason to suspect that once more the king of Ahhiyawa stands behind the revolt.[3] Tudkhaliash gives a long list of Arzawa districts which he says he vanquished,[4] he adds a still longer list of towns in Assuwa.[5] Only in exceptional cases are they mentioned in other Hittite sources. This suggests that Tudkhaliash penetrated westward into regions which earlier kings had not reached. Did he do so in order to ferret out the king of Ahhiyawa?

Another important event may be connected with this trend. As a continental power the Hittite Empire had never shown much concern about Alashiya (Cyprus), the island lying offshore in the north-eastern corner of the Mediterranean. But changes had come about which had enhanced the importance of the island significantly. Not only had it become the foremost source of copper, the metal basic for the civilizations of the Bronze Age; it had also developed into a focal point of civilization through which, by-passing the Hittites, ran the communications between the east and the west, from Egypt and Syria to the Aegean world. As long as this was only a trade route, the Hittites might have acquiesced. But as soon as it assumed political importance—and sooner or later this was inevitable—the Hittites had to intervene; otherwise they were in danger of being cut off from Syria. This stage was reached under Tudkhaliash. He therefore invaded

---

[1] G, 6, xxiii, 13, obv. 5; §iv, 11, 52; §iv, 12, 314 f.
[2] G, 6, xxiii, 11, iii, 9 ff.; §iv, 11, 58 ff.
[3] G, 6, xxiii, 21, ii, 12 ff.; §iv, 2, 156 ff.
[4] G, 6, xxiii, 11, ii, 2 ff.; §iv, 11, 53 f.
[5] G, 6, xxiii, 11, ii, 16 ff.; §iv, 1, 27 ff.; §iv, 11, 54 ff.

Alashiya—probably with the help of his Syrian vassals—and subjected the island by military victory to Hittite domination.[1]

The fateful role played by the king of Ahhiyawa in the further development becomes abundantly clear through the so-called Madduwattash text.[2] This is the bill of indictment in which Madduwattash, prince of Zippashla-Khariyata (in north-western Anatolia), was accused of conspiracy with Attarshiyash, king of Ahhiyā (Ahhiyawa) and of acts hostile to the Great King. The events recorded in the text begin in the reign of Tudkhaliash and continue into that of his son and successor Arnuwandash. Seen in the context of Hittite history it draws a vivid picture of the rise in the west of Anatolia of a strong anti-Hittite coalition. This coalition proceeded step by step to undermine Hittite authority. Slowly advancing toward the south-east it threatened the Empire with slow disintegration.

Madduwattash had been driven from his country by Attarshiyash of Ahhiyā; he had taken refuge with Tudkhaliash and had been reinstated by him. Later Madduwattash had tried to bring the Arzawa Land under his rule, but the local prince, Kupanta-Inarash, had thwarted such efforts. Again it had been the Great King's intervention which saved him, and also provided aid against renewed attacks on the part of Attarshiyash. Madduwattash, nevertheless, persisted in his independent policies. It was clearly his aim to unite the states of western Anatolia and to build up an alliance strong enough to defy the Great King. It may well be that the latter's campaign against Kupanta-Inarash of Arzawa[3] was intended to break up the dangerous coalition in the making. If so, it had the opposite effect; it brought about the reconciliation of the two enemies. From now on they acted in unison.

This was the state of affairs when Arnuwandash succeeded his father as Great King. The increasing tenseness of the situation becomes noticeable in the Syrian sources. Ibiranu of Ugarit, who had just ascended the throne of his father Ammishtamru, had to be reminded by the Hittite—probably Arnuwandash—that he was supposed to appear before his suzerain or at least to send an ambassador.[4] Apparently he was in no great hurry either to fulfil the military obligations of a vassal.[5] These are symptoms of beginning contempt for the overlord.

The position of Arnuwandash soon grew worse. In his days the western alliance of Madduwattash with Ahhiyā and Arzawa took over Khapalla and finally Pitashsha; it was even able to ravage

[1] G, 5, XII, 38, i; §IV, 10, 13.   [2] §IV, 2.
[3] See preceding page.   [4] G, 7, 191.   [5] G, 7, 192.

Alashiya. A climax was reached when Madduwattash came to terms with Attarshiyash of Ahhiyā, his former adversary. Thus the whole west was now united against the central power.

King of Assyria at that time was Tukulti-Ninurta I (1244–1208), who naturally took advantage of the Hittite plight. Once more the Assyrians advanced to the Euphrates, and when Tukulti-Ninurta boasts[1] that he captured and deported thousands of 'Hittites' from across the Euphrates to Assyria this is substantially true although he may have exaggerated their number.

The Egyptian contemporary of Arnuwandash was Merneptah (1236–1223). The two sovereigns remained on good terms with each other. Even Egypt felt in these days an increasing pressure from the north-west. Therefore, it had an interest in keeping the Hittites, who formed a bulwark against the new enemies, as strong as possible. This seems the motivation behind his 'generosity' when, in his second year, he sent grain to the Hittites to alleviate a famine which plagued their land.[2]

Arnuwandash died without offspring[3] after a reign which cannot have been very long. His younger brother *Šuppiluliamaš* (Shuppiluliumash II)[4] took over as the next in line.[5] His name alone, harking back to the days when the Empire was founded, contained a programme. Certainly the new king must have bent every effort to master the menacing situation which he had to face.

In Syria he was, as it had become a tradition, supported by the king of Carchemish. There exist fragments of a treaty which he concluded with Talmi-Teshub, the son of Ini-Teshub.[6] Ugarit remained a vassal of the Hittites until the very end. Talmi-Teshub corresponds in an official capacity with 'Ammurapi of Ugarit, the last king of that town of whom we have records.[7]

Ugarit was probably the home port of the ships with which Shuppiluliumash conducted naval warfare off Alashiya. Either the people of Alashiya had rebelled or they had been themselves overwhelmed by invaders who had come over the sea. However this may be, Shuppiluliumash was able to sink the Alashiyan fleet and to land on hostile soil. At any rate Alashiya remained in Hittite possession.[8]

The Hittite king even seems to have undertaken a campaign in

[1] §iv, 14, no. 16; G, 2, 82.
[2] G, 3, vol. iii, sect. 580.   [3] G, 6, xxvi, 33, ii, 6 ff.
[4] G, 6, xxvi, 32+xxiii, 44+xxxi, 106; §iv, 3.
[5] G, 1, 56; G, 5, xii, 38 and 41; §iv, 3. All other reconstructions are disproved.
[6] G, 5, xii, 41 (and Bo. 4839 unpublished); §iv, 16, 17.
[7] G, 7, 205 ff.
[8] G, 5, xii, 38; §iv, 16, 13 ff.; §iv, 7, 166.

Upper Mesopotamia,[1] perhaps to forestall Assyrian action. It is quite possible that Tukulti-Ninurta was still alive. His downfall came too late. The Hittites hardly profited by his murder and the ensuing period of Assyrian weakness. Shuppiluliumash seems not to have been very successful either. Turbulent times lay ahead.

The written sources peter out at this point and finally cease altogether. The archaeological evidence proves that a catastrophe overtook Anatolia and Syria. Wherever excavations have been made they indicate that the Hittite country was ravaged, its cities burned down. When civilization slowly rises again from the ruins, it is no longer Hittite and clearly bears new characteristics.

The catastrophe can be dated to about 1200 B.C. The main fact cannot be denied, but all details are shrouded in mystery. Did Madduwattash and Attarshiyash contribute to the destruction of the mighty Empire which for the last two centuries had dominated the Near East? Were they themselves swept away in the disaster? A firm answer cannot be given to these questions. But certainly the change was brought about, directly or indirectly, by the migrations which engulfed at that time the Aegean world and the eastern Mediterranean; they were stopped, with considerable difficulty at the very gates of Egypt. What the Egyptian chronicler says about the countries attacked by these 'Peoples of the Sea', as he calls them, is true: 'Not one stood before their hands from Khatti on. Qode, Carchemish, Arzawa and Alashiya were crushed.'[2] It was the end of an epoch.

V. HITTITE CIVILIZATION IN THE EMPIRE PERIOD

The Empire period, from Shuppiluliumash to the catastrophe around 1200 B.C., saw the Hittites at the height of their political power. They ruled supreme over the Anatolian plateau from the western valleys to the headwaters of the Euphrates, and had expanded their domain to include Cilicia and Syria from the Taurus to the Lebanon. It is only natural that over all this territory a unified civilization developed which we call 'Hittite'. The term[3] has often been used in a loose way; it should be limited to the cultural phenomena of the period in question and its preliminary stages which reach back into the early centuries of the second millennium.[4] Specifically, it should not be extended without careful qualifications to the beginning of the first millennium. The

---

[1] G, 5, IV, 14; §IV, 16, 5 f.   [2] G, 3, vol. IV, sect. 64.
[3] §V, 9.   [4] C.A.H. II³, pt. 1, pp. 232 ff.

name 'Hittites' lingers on in northern Syria; however, the civilization of this late period, even though it contains some genuinely
Hittite elements, should be kept apart.

In this place no detailed description of Hittite civilization can
be given. Only its most striking characteristics can be sketched.
When doing so, it must be particularly emphasized that the
Hittite civilization (applying the term in the restricted sense just
defined) is the result of complicated historical processes. Its
foundations are heterogeneous and are only now becoming gradually clearer.[1] The 'Khattians', an eastern people of whose language
we know a little, are only one element of many in this mixture.
There may have been others in the east, and certainly also in the
west and north-west of whom not even the names are known.
Only archaeology bears witness of their existence.

Over these 'Asianic' elements in the course of history a younger
population was deposited, and it is they who appear to us as the
real creators of the 'Hittites'. They spoke languages that are
either outright Indo-European or at least related to that linguistic
group. We know from the epichorial texts 'Palaic', 'Luwian', and
'Neshian' (which is the language customarily called 'Hittite').

Finally, there are the Hurrians. Originally a people *sui generis*
at home in easternmost Anatolia they had spread to Upper Mesopotamia where they had been influenced by the variant of Sumero-
Akkadian civilization at home there. At the beginning of the
Empire period they expanded into Anatolia[2] and contributed to
its civilization. They imparted to it much of that flavour which
makes it particularly 'Hittite'.

He who compares the Empire with the preceding periods
realizes at once that significant changes have taken place in the
meantime. They go deep and concern essential points. Above all
the concepts of kingship and state[3] have assumed new aspects.
The king is no longer the patriarch he had been in the old days.
While he called himself just 'king', he now styles himself 'my
Sun'. The new title expresses a change in the king's relationship
to the divine world; he is on his way to being translated thither.
The texts make him the deputy of the Storm-god, the country's
highest god; it is in his stead that he administers the Hittite realm.
One has the impression that kingship has gathered into itself
divine qualities on every side. Being the mediator between the
gods and men, the one who has to see to it that the gods remain on
the side of his people, the king is now subject to strict rules designed to assure his ritual purity.[4] He also has become more of an

[1] §v, 4, 45 ff.   [2] §v, 8.   [3] §v, 4, 85 ff.; §v, 6; §v, 18.   [4] §v, 4, 89 ff.

absolute monarch; it is taken for granted that his office is inherited by his descendants. In fact the idea of the royal dynasty gains central importance.

When the king dies he himself 'becomes god'; images are erected for him and he becomes the subject of a cult with sacrifices offered daily and festivals regularly celebrated. It is strange to observe that the role of the queen, although sacrifices are likewise due to her after death, preserves more archaic features. Queenship is still an office of its own with functions paralleling those of the king. It is inherited independently of kingship.

As far as political organization[1] is concerned, the Hittite Empire has the appearance of a confederacy. Its structure is feudalistic throughout, and the principles of feudalism are applied at every level. Already during the Old Kingdom tendencies leading toward feudalism were observable. These tendencies were strengthened by the developments in the technique of warfare[2] which mark the middle of the millennium. The horse had been trained to draw a light chariot; horse and chariot together had a revolutionizing effect. Horses capable of drawing chariots had to be bred and trained, the training had to be continued so as to maintain efficiency. This is also valid for the men. A military caste developed, a veritable class of knights, which had to be made economically independent so that it could devote itself to its vocation. The crown (or state) achieved this by placing at their disposal sufficient tracts of land in the form of fiefs. The relationship between the king and those feoffed by him, their obligation to 'protect' him and his descendants (*paḫš-*), becomes a feature of growing concern. The security of the dynasty and the permanence of the state, its ability to withstand its foes depended on this system.

Feudalism soon determined the relationship of the king not only to the military, but also to his civilian officials, it became an instrument of politics. The governors of the provinces, by now 'small' local kings, swore oaths of allegiance and did homage to their overlord at regularly repeated times. Still further out, on the periphery of the Empire, there were the vassals who were bound to the Great King by treaties describing their duties: to send help in times of war, to pay tribute each year, to extradite refugees and fugitives and above all to renounce the right to conduct their own external policy. The Great King acted in their stead. Thus the concept of the *išḫiul* 'bond, obligation, treaty' gains all-embracing significance for the structure of state and society.

The changes described were forced upon the Hittites by the

---

[1] §v, 4, 109.   [2] §v, 5.

progress of the times, ultimately by technical achievements which nobody could neglect, least of all those who aspired to a leading political role. Otherwise, conservatism is a most characteristic feature of Hittite civilization. Nowhere can it be better observed than in the religion.[1] Here it went so far that cults of the various ethnic layers amalgamated to form the 'Hittite' people were to be conducted in the time-honoured manner, including the use of the original and already half-forgotten languages. In spite of multifarious origins syncretism is avoided; the old gods inherited from preceding periods are carefully kept apart, similar to one another as they may be. One can still recognize that animal worship lay behind certain gods who otherwise had long since acquired human appearance. The Storm-god was originally conceived in the form of a bull, and this idea still lives on in the 'god on the bull' in Roman times. There was a stag god, and a god of the hunt, to whom eagle and hare were sacred.

The exception to this aversion from syncretism is the official cult of the Imperial dynasty as exemplified by the rock sanctuary of Yazilikaya, near the capital Khattusha (Boğazköy), and its reliefs. This requires a special explanation;[2] it is provided by the (very likely) hypothesis that this dynasty was of Hurrian origin and inserted itself into Hittite history in a way the details of which are still unknown. The rocks of Yazilikaya form the open-air courtyard of a sanctuary; on its walls one sees a procession of deities, the goddesses coming from the right, the gods from the left. In the middle where both meet one recognizes the main gods of the Empire, the great Storm-god, the Sun-goddess (of Arinna) and their circle. The astonishing fact here to be stressed is this: to each figure its name is ascribed in so-called 'Hittite' hieroglyphs, and the names so written are linguistically Hurrian names. The mixture well symbolizes the elements which, in the Empire period, had fused into what we call 'Hittite'.

It is interesting to observe that the advanced stage of fusion represented at Yazilikaya is in striking disagreement with the state religion as visible in the great number of surviving texts. Yazilikaya is far ahead of them. Ordinarily the capital united in its temples the cults brought together from the various regions of Asia Minor and Syria. The gods resided there not only in the spirit, but we assume also in the body, namely in the form of images. Many of them had been brought home by conquering kings. Native gods and the new conquered gods were worshipped in the capital according to their accustomed ritual which left nothing to chance.

[1] §v, 4, 130 ff.; §v, 10.　　　　　　　[2] §v, 11.

Ceremonialism and ritualism are the basic religious attitudes; they deserve some additional remarks. At the back of them stands the fundamental notion of cultic purity. It has been observed before that such is essential in the relation of the king to the divine world. Violations of the canon of purity by contamination of any kind, corporeal as uncleanliness or spiritual as 'sin', were believed to cause the wrath of the gods, and thus were the reason for all human misery and suffering. It was the purpose of all cultic actions, for which the king was chiefly responsible, to keep the gods favourably inclined. On their regular and correct observance depended the well-being of state, king and common people.

Unfavourable situations could be prevented from arising by divination. Portents had to be interpreted by experts, and *omina* consulted to recognize dangers that lay ahead. When the gods struck, *omina* made it possible to find out by systematic questioning what was the reason for divine anger, what god was angry and how he could be pacified.

Unfavourable situations when they did arise despite all caution and forbearance could be eliminated by magical means. Man could intervene by staging a magic 'ritual', and thus restore the purity required by the gods. The expert also knew how to foil malicious sorcery performed with the intention to do harm.

Thus magic had a very wide range—so wide that even legislators had to deal with it. White magic, beneficial to him who performs it or has it performed for himself, is the business of an authorized expert, a priest or physician. Black magic which inflicts harm on an enemy is no better than murder and must be punished accordingly.

During the Empire period all regions of the Near East formed part of a power-system that embraced their world. This was first of all a political phenomenon. But the longer it lasted, and the more intimately it operated, the more it was bound to produce parallel intellectual phenomena. In the end these effects appear to the observing historian as more characteristic for these centuries of vivid cultural exchange than the resulting political balance. Within the limited world of those days an international consciousness developed which, despite armed conflict, united its parts, whether they were Mesopotamian, Egyptian or Hittite.

To a large degree the cuneiform system of writing[1] and the clay tablet on which it was inscribed served as a vehicle of this internationalism. Mesopotamia had been its original home. With the

[1] §v, 4, 171 ff.; §v, 17.

expansion of Sumero-Akkadian civilization it spread up to Syria and it is there that the ancestors of the Hittites must have picked it up. The reception of cuneiform must go back to a rather early period; it is certain that in the Old Kingdom Hittite scribes already employed the art of writing. If most of the preserved tablets have been copied or produced during the Empire period, it is a mere accident. Even Egypt had learned scribes who could read and, if need be, write cuneiform and thereby communicate with their contemporaries in the north.

Besides the cuneiform script borrowed from outside, the Hittites also possessed a native 'hieroglyphic' script.[1] It has a long history too but does not play the international role which cuneiform played. A few monumental inscriptions of the Empire age, not sufficiently understood as yet, have come down to us from Anatolia; it was perhaps more widely used for writing documents of daily life on wood. It lived on in the stone inscriptions of post-Empire times, most of them found in the Taurus regions and in northern Syria.

Their familiarity with cuneiform writing and the continuous connexions of scribal schools with Mesopotamian centres of learning enabled the Hittites to take part in the intellectual life of the times. To an appreciable degree the Hurrians of Upper Mesopotamia were the intermediators. In this way, for example, the Gilgamesh Epic became known in Anatolia. We possess not only Hittite but also Hurrian fragments of this literary work which can justly be called the greatest of the Ancient Near East. The Hurrian source of the epic dealing with the generations of gods who succeeded each other in the domination of the world, and of the Kumarbi Epic, is obvious. Both these cycles of mythic tales are at home in a Hurrian milieu.

Of greater importance for our evaluation of Hittite civilization under the Empire are those texts that are not borrowed, but rooted in a genuinely Hittite thought. The practices of religious life gave rise to a great number of ritual and ceremonial texts, not to forget the *omina*; the political customs produced rules and regulations, oaths and treaties. Most characteristic for the Empire are the annals of the kings. These too have their foundation in religious life: the kings had to report their achievements to the gods whom they represented on earth. These reports grew out of the annals of the Old Kingdom, but they assumed a definite literary style only under the Empire. The annals of the Empire can justly be claimed as the oldest examples of true historiography that

[1] §v, 13; §v, 14.

we possess. Events were here reported objectively for their own sake; but at the same time situations resulting from the inter-dependence of various individual facts were artfully described. The author, so to speak, views them in a higher perspective from outside. Fateful complications were followed up to their final dénouement with a definite feeling for the dramatic. A historical style was here created which was later continued and developed by the Assyrians. But there are essential differences: Hittite annals have a quality of realism which is lost in Assyrian historical writing. They impress us by their unspoiled vitality, which tends to petrify into patterns and clichés later on.

The political greatness of the Hittites, who after all in the Empire period were world leaders for two centuries, must, one should suspect, have its counterpart in the field of art. Their in-dividuality and originality in architecture[1] is apparent in all the remnants that have survived. Hittite temples and Hittite palaces would plainly be impossible in any other part of the ancient world; they exhibit characteristics which are specifically Hittite. The foundations of their walls are formed by gigantic blocks which are sometimes adorned with reliefs. Large windows in the outer walls, beginning immediately above the foundations blocks, are particu-larly striking. They open up the buildings toward the outside so that the inner courtyard does not play the centralizing role which it plays in other provinces of the Near East. It now keeps loosely together various groups of rooms which surround it. The house does not have the castle-like aspects it has elsewhere.

The acropolis of Boğazköy (Büyükkale) as it existed during the Empire was a rather impressive group of buildings within the protective ring of fortifications which made skilful use of the natural strength of the location. From the gate a road led upward across open spaces toward and into the public buildings and the residence of the Great King. Behind it and in its substructures were hidden the storerooms and magazines without which the administration of a great empire cannot function.

What is left of the representative art of the Hittites[2] is inti-mately connected with architecture. There are the sculptures still to be seen on the gates of Boğazköy and Hüyük. There is the sanctuary of Iflatun-Pinar. Among the so-called 'rock-sculptures', some like those of Gavur-kalesi belonged to a fortress; those, for example, of Yazilikaya near Boğazköy to a sanctuary. It would be rash, however, to generalize thus. Let us not forget that—to judge by the texts—many works of art, especially the movable ones,

---

[1] §v, 16. [2] §v, 15; §v, 3; §v, 1; §v, 2.

must have perished. Only few examples, like statuettes,[1] seals[2] and other small pieces escaped destruction. The remnants left give a very inadequate idea of Hittite art, but they justify the statement that it indeed had an individual quality which was worthy of a great nation.

The reliefs which have been recovered excel by soft round modelling, in many cases they become half plastic. They display a forceful monumental style which does not have its equal elsewhere in the Ancient Near East.

In the discussion of Hittite art the problem of its origins has been too much in the foreground of interest. Admittedly this is important, but it should not be allowed, by over-emphasis on terminology, to deny the existence of a genuine Hittite art commensurate with the grandeur of the Empire. We may say that a great art was here in the making, that it did not reach the limits of its potentialities, that its growth was broken off before it became fully mature. Fate interrupted a development full of promise when the catastrophe of 1200 swept the Hittites and their Empire away.

[1] See, for example, Bittel, K., *Boğazköy*, III (1957), pls. 23 ff.; Alp, Sedat, in *Anatolia*, 6 (1961/2), 217 ff.

[2] §v, 7; §v, 11; also Beran, Th. and Otten, H., in *M.D.O.G.* 86 (1953), 87 (1955), 89 (1957), 91 (1958), 93 (1962), *passim*.

CHAPTER XXV

ASSYRIAN MILITARY POWER

1300–1200 B.C.

I. THE CAMPAIGNS OF ADAD-NĪRĀRI I

THE reign of Adad-nīrāri I (1307–1275), the son of Arik-dēn-ili, inaugurated a period of rapid expansion. Under his able leadership and that of his immediate successors, Shalmaneser I (1274–1245) and Tukulti-Ninurta I (1244–1208), Assyria in the course of some eighty years greatly extended its territories and eventually emerged as one of the most powerful states of the Near East. Its success must in large part be attributed to its growing economic and military strength, to its political stability, and to the vigorous personalities of its kings, but it was also favoured by the international situation, for the Hittite Empire, faced by more urgent problems, both internal and external, was not in a position to offer a sustained resistance to Assyrian expansion in upper Mesopotamia. The conquests of Assyria, however, outran its capacity to hold and govern all that had been gained and its political decline was as meteoric as its rise. Nevertheless, the empire of the thirteenth century, although ephemeral, laid the foundations of future Assyrian greatness, not only in the political sphere but also in literature and in art.

In the introduction to a number of building inscriptions, Adad-nīrāri boasts that he smote the armies of the Kassites, Quti, Lullume and Shubari, smashed all enemies above and below and harried (lit. 'threshed') their lands from the towns of Lubdu and Rapiqu in northern Babylonia to Elukhat in upper Mesopotamia.[1]

More precise information on the war with Babylonia is given by the Synchronistic History.[2] He defeated Nazimaruttash (1323–1298) at the town of Kār-Ishtar in the land of Ugarsallu,

---

* An original version of this chapter was published as fascicle 49 in 1967; the present chapter includes revisions made in 1973.

[1] G, 2, 57; G, 11, 27. Lubdu lay south of Arrapkha, perhaps near modern Tāūq (Dāqūq), for literature see A, 2, 178 f., n. 1096; Rapiqu was on the middle Euphrates, probably near modern Ramādi, *ibid.* 127, n. 748; Elukhat west of the Ṭūr 'Abdīn, §1, 3, 9 f.

[2] Col. 1, 24–31; G, 14, 60.

plundered his camp and carried off his royal standards.[1] The Assyro-Babylonian frontier was then realigned to run from Pilasqi, on the east side of the Tigris,[2] through Arman in Ugarsallu, a city which lay between the Lesser Zab and the Shaṭṭ el-'Adhaim,[3] to the border of the land of the Lullume (Lullubi). Although the boundary change was probably of a minor nature, the Assyrians considered that they had avenged the reverses suffered by Arik-dēn-ili at Kassite hands and a long epic was composed to celebrate the exploit.[4] In default of a Babylonian account, it is not certain that it was as decisive as the Assyrians claimed.[5] It did, however, restore the state of uneasy equilibrium which had existed between the two countries in the time of Enlil-nīrāri and Kurigalzu.[6] Indeed, the advantage appears to have shifted from Babylonia to Assyria. Whereas Kurigalzu met the Assyrian army at Sugagu, only a day's journey south of Ashur,[7] and at Kilizi, near Erbil, Adad-nīrāri fought and plundered in the northern borderland of Babylonia. When he raided Lubdu and Rapiqu is uncertain. There is no record that he was involved in hostilities with Kadashman-Turgu (1297–1280) and Kadashman-Enlil II (1279–1265).

No details are known of his expeditions against the Lullume and Qutu. Any permanent pacification of these turbulent Zagros peoples was as yet out of the question, but by punitive action he may temporarily have secured a cessation of raids on Assyrian territory and plundering of caravan traffic at the western end of the routes to Iran. When giving his genealogy, he records the defeat by Arik-dēn-ili of Turukku and Nigimṭi, from which it may be inferred that he retained control of both these eastern districts. In Katmukhi, in the Tigris valley west of the Judi Dağ, he probably suffered a reverse, for his reference to the subjection of this land by his father is omitted from a number of his inscriptions. There is no record that he campaigned against the other

---

[1] According to the dates adopted for Nazimaruttash in the chronological scheme of this *History*, the war must have occurred in the earlier part of the reign of Adad-nīrāri. A wider margin of variation downward for the last Kassite rulers is proposed in A, 5, 305 f.

[2] Location unknown, cf. A, 5, 309, n. 96.

[3] For Arman in general, A, 2, 195, n. 1195.

[4] §IV, 20, 113 f. In the epic, Adad-nīrāri says of Arik-dēn-ili: 'My father could not rectify the calamities inflicted by the army of the king of the Kassite land.' The war between Adad-nīrāri and Nazimaruttash is also mentioned briefly in the Tukulti-Ninurta Epic, §IV, 5, col. v, 11. 31–2, corrected to col. II in §IV, 7, 40.

[5] Babylonian Chronicle P, G, 1, 45, 11. 23 f., which may have recorded these events, breaks off after a reference to Nazimaruttash and an Assyrian king.

[6] See above, pp. 31 f.

[7] A, 5, 313 f.

small states of the upper Tigris valley. Although this area formed part of the land of the Shubari or Subarians, his claim to have defeated these people must refer to his conquest of Mitanni-Khanigalbat.[1]

His main territorial gains were made at the expense of Khanigalbat, which at this period extended from the Ṭūr 'Abdīn westwards across the upper reaches of the Khabur and Balīkh to the Euphrates. For Adad-nīrāri it was both a traditional enemy and a present threat to the security of his country. The earlier subjection of Assyria by the kings of Mitanni and the subsequent attempt of Ashur-uballiṭ to seize control over the land of Mitanni had certainly left a legacy of mutual hatred. Behind it, moreover, lay the power of the Hittite Empire, which, since the time of Shuppiluliumash, had sought to maintain it as a buffer state against Assyria. Hittite influence, lost at the death of Shuppiluliumash, had been re-established, presumably by Murshilish II, since a contingent from Naharain, i.e. Mitanni-Khanigalbat, was among the forces of Muwatallish at the battle of Qadesh. Although the ruler of Khanigalbat was recognized by Muwatallish as an equal[2] there is little doubt that, as in the case of Kurtiwaza of Mitanni, he was a *kuirwana* vassal, accorded a semblance of independence but in fact acknowledging Hittite 'protection'.

According to Adad-nīrāri, his first war with Khanigalbat was caused by the attack of its king, Shattuara I.[3] If the Hurrian was indeed the aggressor, he may have feared that the growing power of Assyria would lead Adad-nīrāri to renew the attempt to overrun his country and so have taken the offensive in the hope of forestalling such a move. Whatever his motives, he had fatally misjudged the strength and temper of his adversary. He was captured and taken to Ashur, but on swearing an oath of allegiance was permitted to retain his kingdom as an Assyrian vassal. He remained loyal to Adad-nīrāri for the rest of his life, sending him tribute year by year.[4]

The war against Shattuara I must be dated after the battle of

---

[1] For the Assyrian use of the term Khanigalbat for Mitanni, see A, 26, 526 f.
[2] §1, 5, 68, col. III, 10 f.   [3] §1, 14.
[4] Weidner suggests that Adad-nīrāri annexed most of Khanigalbat so that Shattuara returned to a diminished kingdom. In consequence he was known, not as king of Khanigalbat, but as king of Shubria (Subartu), A, 26, 523 ff. The text cited, a letter from an Assyrian vassal found in the Boğazköy archive, is difficult to interpret because of its damaged condition. According to the best preserved passage, the king of Shubria had seized the throne of an unidentified land, perhaps that of the writer, and had also secured the return of people who had fled from Khanigalbat during a war with Adad-nīrāri: G, 8, 1, 20; G, 6, 258 f.

Qadesh in the fifth year of Ramesses II (1300), in which Khani-galbat fought as a Hittite ally. That it preceded the accession of Khattushilish III is suggested by a letter from the Hittite to another king, almost certainly Adad-nīrāri.[1] Writing soon after he came to the throne, Khattushilish requested the Assyrian to stop the people of the frontier town of Turira from raiding Carchemish. Since the king of Khanigalbat was claiming Turira it may be inferred that the Hittite was asking Adad-nīrāri to intervene in his capacity as overlord of the Hurrian ruler. As Shattuara apparently received no Hittite assistance, it is a reason-able assumption that his defeat occurred during the troubled years of Urkhi-Teshub.

The advance of Assyrian influence to the Euphrates repre-sented the collapse of the Hittite attempt to maintain Khanigalbat as a buffer state and constituted a potential threat to their control of Syria. It did not, however, lead to an open breach of relations between the two countries. Khattushilish refers in his letter to regular diplomatic exchanges between Adad-nīrāri, Urkhi-Teshub and another Hittite king who must be Muwatallish. He himself appears anxious to placate the Assyrian who had failed to send him the customary gifts of a royal garment and oil at his accession. In neglecting this courtesy, Adad-nīrāri may have wished to mark his displeasure at the treatment of his messengers who, as Khattushilish admits, had had 'sad experiences' in the time of Urkhi-Teshub. Khattushilish also excuses himself for not sending the supplies of iron and iron weapons for which Adad-nīrāri had asked. His conciliatory tone may be explained by his wish to secure Assyrian neutrality in the event of an attack by Ramesses II, a danger which at the time seemed imminent. To strengthen his position against both Egypt and Assyria, Khattushilish entered into a defensive alliance with Kadashman-Turgu of Babylonia who, in fulfilment of its terms, broke off diplomatic relations with Ramesses and promised military aid.[2]

In the event, war with Egypt was avoided but, perhaps while the situation was still critical for the Hittites, developments in Khanigalbat led to a strengthening of the Assyrian position.

---

[1] G, 8, 1, 14; §1, 7, 27 ff.; §1, 10, 3 ff.; C.A.H. I³, pt. 1, p. 216.

[2] G, 8, 1, 10; §1, 2; §1, 11, 16 ff.; for a fragmentary letter from Kadashman-Turgu to Khattushilish III, see G, 9, III, 71. If a passage in a letter from Khattu-shilish to Kadashman-Enlil has been correctly restored, the former did not place much reliance on the promises of Kadashman-Turgu: 'They used to call [your father] a king who prepares for war but then stays at home.' See A, 20, 146.

Wasashatta, son of Shattuara I, rebelled and went to Khatti to solicit support.[1] The Hittites accepted his presents but, presumably because of their preoccupation with Egypt, failed to send aid when Adad-nīrāri attacked. Forced westward by the Assyrian advance, Wasashatta made his final stand at Irrite, between Carchemish and Harran, probably the modern town of Ordi. Here he was captured and, together with his palace women, his sons, his daughters and his people, taken in chains to Ashur, where his royal standard was triumphantly set up in the temple of Ishtar. It is probable that Adad-nīrāri abandoned the attempt to rule Khanigalbat through a vassal and annexed it to Assyria. Although this campaign is more fully reported than the earlier war against Shattuara I, there is no reference to the installation of a ruler, and at Taidi, the royal city of Wasashatta between Cizre and Diyārbakr,[2] he rebuilt the palace, doubtless as the residence of an Assyrian governor. In addition to Irrite and Taidi, he captured and looted the towns of (A)masaki, Kakhat, Shuri, Nabula, Khurra, Shudukhu and Ushukanni (Washshuganni). All seven lay in the area of the Khabur triangle but the only one to be certainly located is Kakhat, modern Tell Barrī on the River Jaghjagha.[3] He defines the conquered area as extending from Taidi in the east to Irrite; it included 'Elukhat and the Kashiari mountain (Ṭūr 'Abdīn) in its entirety, and the fortified districts of Suda and Harran up to the bank of the Euphrates'. To celebrate this conquest of upper Mesopotamia he revived the royal title 'king of the totality' (šar kiššati), previously held by Shamsi-Adad I.[4]

He now felt able to treat on equal terms with the Hittites. He informed Khattushilish of his defeat of Wasashatta, claimed the status of 'great king', wrote of 'brotherhood' and proposed himself for a visit to Mount Ammana, the Amanus.[5] While admitting that he was entitled to recognition as a great king, Khattushilish furiously rejected his other demands. 'What is this talk of brotherhood and visiting the Ammana mountain?... Why should I write to you concerning brotherhood? You and I, were we born of one mother?'[6] The request to visit the Amanus has been interpreted as a veiled threat of aggression or a territorial claim, but a more

---

[1] §1, 14; §1, 15; §1, 16.   [2] §1, 9, 59.

[3] On the left bank of the river, 12 km. upstream from Tell Brak, §1, 1. For Elukhat, Khurra, Irrite, Suda and Washshuganni, cf. §1, 3.

[4] The title was accorded to Ashur-uballiṭ by a scribe but is not attested in his official titulary. Cf. A, 24, 308.

[5] G, 9, xxiii, 102; G, 6, 262 f.; §1, 15, 21 f.; §iii, 12, 67.   [6] See above, p. 258.

plausible explanation is that Adad-nīrāri had asked for an agreement for Assyrian trade in Amanus timber, hence his 'talk of brotherhood' or a treaty relationship. The violent reaction of Khattushilish is a measure of his fear of Assyrian designs on Syria, a fear which in all probability drove him to compose his quarrel with Egypt and negotiate the treaty with Ramesses II in the latter's twenty-first year (1284). He may have had immediate cause for anxiety. In certain texts Adad-nīrāri claims to have conquered 'as far as Carchemish on the bank of the Euphrates'. While this probably represents no more than the desire of the Assyrian scribe to give precise definition to the Euphrates frontier, the possibility exists that it refers to an Assyrian attack against the city or at least the territory of Carchemish which, since it guarded the principal crossing of the Middle Euphrates, was one of the most strongly held Hittite positions in Syria.

There can, however, be little doubt that Hittite support was in large measure responsible for the success of the rebellion which broke out in Khanigalbat, either late in the reign of Adad-nīrāri or early in that of Shalmaneser. If Muṣri lay south of the Taurus in the plain of Harran,[1] the fact that Adad-nīrāri does not refer to its conquest by Ashur-uballiṭ in all his inscriptions would strongly suggest that at least the western part of Khanigalbat had been lost to Assyria before his death. Less significant is the omission from certain texts of the list of captured towns of Khanigalbat. It could have been left out for the sake of brevity.

II. SHALMANESER I AND THE CONQUEST OF KHANIGALBAT

Immediately Shalmaneser I succeeded his father he was attacked by Uruaṭri (variant Uraṭri), the later Urarṭu, one of a large number of Hurrian principalities in the mountainous regions round Lake Vān and Lake Urmia, known to the Assyrians from the time of Tukulti-Ninurta I as the Nairi lands.[2] Their territory corresponded, at least in part, to that of the Khurri land ruled in the fourteenth century by Artatama, but was now split up into a loose confederation of small political units. Shalmaneser names eight districts of Uruaṭri which may have been situated on the middle or higher reaches of the Greater Zab.[3] Whether it also included the area of Lake Vān, the centre of the later state of Urarṭu, is uncertain. Information on the civilization of the Nairi

---

[1] See above, p. 28 and below, p. 460 and n. 2.
[2] §ii, 6, 190 ff.; §ii, 8, 13 ff., 150 ff.   [3] §ii, 8, 150 ff.

lands is at present derived mainly from textual and archaeological evidence of the ninth to seventh centuries when they had been united in the kingdom of Urarṭu.[1] That their population was Hurrian is evident from personal and place names and the Urarṭian language known from texts of this period, which was a later dialect of the Hurrian spoken in Mitanni in the second millennium.[2] With its rich mountain pastures the country was especially suitable for stockbreeding, and cattle, sheep, goats and pigs were kept in large numbers. Certain areas, notably the Urmia plain, were also important centres of horse breeding. The principal crops were wheat, barley, rye, millet, sesame and flax; and vines were grown extensively for wine. The country also possessed important resources of copper, iron and lead, and the metal industry was, in consequence, highly developed. In warfare the inhabitants were redoubtable fighters, putting into the field armies that were well equipped and strong in chariotry and, at this later date, cavalry. The towns, many of large size, were strongly defended by walls of cyclopean masonry.[3]

Although there is no reference to Uruaṭri in the extant records of his predecessors, Shalmaneser accuses it of rebellion. He conquered its eight lands and their forces, sacked fifty-one (variant forty-one) towns, imposed tribute on the inhabitants and carried off young men to Ashur as hostages. He boasts that he brought the whole land of Uruaṭri into submission at the feet of the god Ashur in three days. Although the eight districts overrun were certainly small and the sack of some fifty towns and villages could have been carried out by a number of columns operating simultaneously, it is difficult to believe that the whole campaign was concluded in so short a time. If his claim is to be taken seriously and not dismissed as a flight of literary fancy,[4] and if, as seems most likely, it refers to the actual fighting, it can only relate to the decisive battles and not to the subsequent reduction and pillage of individual settlements.

His next attack was directed against the strongly defended city of Arini in Musri, which he accused of rebellion. It was sacked and razed to the ground, earth from its ruins being taken to Ashur and symbolically scattered in the city gate. The subjection of the whole of Muṣri followed. If this land lay to the west rather than to the east of Assyria, then this expedition must be interpreted as a preliminary move against Khanigalbat, the reconquest of which was achieved in his next campaign.

[1] §ii, 5, 70 ff.; §ii, 6, 195 ff.; §ii, 9, 131 ff.   [2] §ii, 2; §ii, 6, 193.
[3] §ii, 1.   [4] §iv, 2, 56.

In Khanigalbat he was opposed not only by its ruler, Shattuara II, but by a Hittite army which, since it included a contingent of the Akhlamu tribe of the Syrian desert, may have been raised and commanded by the ruler of Carchemish. Well-organized measures had been taken to resist his advance. The passes and watering places on the line of his march had been occupied and in consequence his troops suffered severely from exhaustion and thirst. Nevertheless, there was no wavering in their discipline and morale, and when the opposing forces met in pitched battle Shalmaneser inflicted a crushing defeat on the Hurrians and their allies. Shattuara himself escaped from the field and fled westward but Shalmaneser took 14,400 prisoners, whom he blinded, probably partially, as a reprisal for their rebellion. The reduction of all Khanigalbat followed, nine fortified towns, the royal city of Shattuara II and 180 other places being laid waste. He defines the conquered area in terms similar to those of Adad-nīrāri and like his father gives Carchemish as the western limit.[1]

There is no doubt that on this occasion Khanigalbat was annexed to Assyria. To the reigns of Shalmaneser and Tukulti-Ninurta I belong texts from Ashur mentioning governors of several of its cities[2] and a few legal documents from Tell Fakhari-yah, south of Ras el-'Ain, which are dated by Assyrian eponyms and the Old Assyrian months. All the personal names in the Fakhariyah texts are Assyrian but, since there is no indication of the profession or title of the persons mentioned, it is not possible to say whether they were members of the administration, garrison troops or colonists.[3] One of the urgent problems facing the newly appointed Assyrian officials was the maintenance of those who had fled or been forcibly removed from their homes. Issues of royal grain collected from Amasaki were made to the 'uprooted' people of Shudukhu and Nakhur.[4]

The victory over Shattuara II was the most significant of the thirteenth century. It brought to an end over three hundred years of Hurrian rule in upper Mesopotamia and finally decided the century-old struggle of Assyrian and Hittite for control of the area. It gave Assyria undisputed command of trade-routes leading to Syria and Anatolia, added rich agricultural land and prosperous cities to its territory and placed at the disposal of its military command a large population with long experience in the art of

---

[1] For a letter from a ruler of Khanigalbat to a Hittite king, see §11, 7, where the writer is identified as Shattuara II. A, 26, 253 prefers Wasashatta or, less probably, Shattuara I.

[2] G, 6, 266.   [3] §v, 14, 86 ff.; see now A, 23.   [4] G, 5, 44, n. 8.

war. That the Assyrian skill in chariot fighting owed much to Hurrian example is shown by the Middle Assyrian version of a Hurrian treatise on the breaking in and training of horses for team work.[1] The Assyrian onomasticon of the thirteenth century also shows a marked increase in Hurrian names, which are borne by persons in all walks of life. Some held high offices of state, two indeed being *līmu* officials.[2] For Assyria, limited as it was in area, population and economic resources, the conquest of Khanigalbat was an indispensable condition of its rise to the stature of a major power.

Shalmaneser also had to deal with renewed revolts in Qutium and Lullume. The Qutu were attacking in the north, between the Uruatrian frontier and Katmukhi. Since a call-up of the general levy would have involved a dangerous delay he decided, after obtaining a favourable omen, to hasten north with a third of his chariotry. The enemy, caught unawares by his swift action, suffered considerable punishment and their attack was repelled, but significantly he does not claim to have brought Qutium into submission. Developments on the north-western frontier are obscure but it is possible that Shalmaneser reimposed Assyrian suzerainty on Katmukhi and other Shubari lands in the upper Tigris area only to lose it again later in his reign, for according to Tukulti-Ninurta they rebelled against him.

There is no reference in his extant inscriptions to his relations with his Babylonian contemporaries, Kadashman-Enlil II (1279–1265), Kudur-Enlil (1263–1255) and Shagarakti-Shuriash (1255–1243), and such information as is available from other sources throws only a partial light on their nature. Babylonia was now less of a danger to Assyria, for the recovery of Elam from its defeat by Kurigalzu II threatened the security of its eastern border.[3] Probably in the time of Kadashman-Turgu, Attar-kittakh regained Susa, earlier subjected by Kurigalzu, and his son, Khumban-numena, further extended the kingdom. If a broken word in a statue inscription originally read [Ṭup]liash, then his successor, ·Untash-(*d*)*GAL*, raided across the Babylonian border, west of the river Kerkhah.

By the end of Adad-nīrāri's reign the close alliance of Babylonia and Khatti had also come to an end. Since Kadashman-Enlil II, son of Kadashman-Turgu, was a minor at his accession the conduct of state affairs was for some years in the hands of the vizier, Itti-Marduk-balāṭu. He strongly opposed the Hittite connexion, believing that Khattushilish was attempting to use Babylonia as

[1] §II, 3.   [2] G, 5, 103 f.   [3] See below, pp. 383 ff.

a tool for the furtherance of his own policies and, in particular, seeking to embroil it in his struggle with Assyria. In view of the expansionist activities of Khumban-numena of Elam, it may be surmised that Itti-Marduk-balātu considered that the interests of his country would be better served by the adoption of a con-ciliatory policy towards its northern neighbour. Khattushilish, in fulfilment of his treaty with Kadashman-Turgu, wrote on the latter's death to the Babylonian notables, promising aid should any power attack Babylonia but threatening war if they refused to recognize Kadashman-Enlil as king. Itti-Marduk-balātu chose to regard this as a sinister attempt to interfere in the affairs of Babylonia and in his reply accused the Hittite of treating it as his vassal. Later, Kadashman-Enlil complained of Hittite opposi-tion to his resumption of diplomatic relations with Egypt, which had been broken off by his father at the time of the crisis between Ramesses II and Khattushilish. Babylonian messengers were no longer sent regularly to the Hittite court on the pretext that the nomadic Akhlamu were interrupting communications north of Hīt and that Assyria refused them passage through its territory. Writing to Kadashman-Enlil after he attained his majority, Khat-tushilish was at pains to refute the Babylonian charges made against him and bitterly attacked Itti-Marduk-balātu for mis-representing his actions.[1] His anxiety to placate the Babylonian king and secure him as an ally against Assyria leaps to the eye. Appealing to his pride, he assured him that Assyria was too weak to threaten Babylonia and that as a great king he could compel it to allow his messengers to pass. In another passage, which can only refer to Assyria, he urged him to attack the enemy land. As further evidence of his good will, he promised the settlement of Babylonian claims against two of his Syrian vassals. One con-cerned the murder of certain Babylonian merchants while on a journey to Amurru and Ugarit. The other involved Bente-shina of Amurru whom Kadashman-Enlil had accused of disturbing his land. Khattushilish reported that when taxed with this offence Bente-shina had advanced a counter-claim for thirty talents of silver against the inhabitants of Akkad. He advised Kadashman-Enlil that he should prosecute his claim; Bente-shina should defend himself in the presence of the Babylonian ambassador; and if Kadashman-Enlil could not conduct the action in person he should send a representative with knowledge of the affair. Bente-shina, concluded Khattushilish, 'is (my) vassal. If he troubles my brother, does he not trouble me?'

[1] G, 8, 1, 10; §1, 2; §1, 4, 24 ff.; §1, 11, 16 ff.; §1, 13, 74 f.; A, 20, 139 ff.

It is not known whether Kadashman-Enlil was persuaded by these blandishments to reverse the policy of his vizier and resume intimate relations with Khatti. That Shalmaneser had trouble with one of his Babylonian contemporaries is, however, suggested by a passage in the Epic of Tukulti-Ninurta, which deals with past conflicts between Assyria and Babylonia. The much damaged passage relating to Shalmaneser describes his defeat of the Shubari[1] and, in a broken context, names the Hittites. The Babylonians do not appear in the extant text but, in view of the subject matter of the section, were presumably involved in some way. It is tempting to connect the war against the Shubari with the defeat of Shattuara II, but so much of the text is lost that speculation as to its date and circumstances can hardly be profitable.

III. TUKULTI-NINURTA I AND THE CONQUEST OF BABYLONIA

The conquests made by Shalmaneser's son, Tukulti-Ninurta I, during the early part of his reign consolidated and greatly extended those of his predecessors. For much of his first decade his energies were directed to establishing a firmer control over the lands to the east and north than had been achieved by his predecessors. In his accession year he marched against the Qutu, concentrating his attack on the land Uqumeni. Despite the fierce resistance of the inhabitants it was forced into submission, its settlements being laid waste and the corpses of the slain piled up at the gate of the principal city. Its king, Abuli, and his nobles were taken in chains to Ashur but on swearing an oath of allegiance were returned to their land. Control of the Zagros districts through vassal princes, although unsatisfactory, was enforced by the nature of the country. The isolation of the settled valleys, the poor lines of communication and the opportunities for resistance afforded by mountain and forest have throughout history made the administration of this area a task of peculiar difficulty. Direct rule by Assyria would have necessitated the permanent deployment of a large occupying force, the burden of which on the national resources would have been out of all proportion to the advantages gained. The subjugation of the country was more economically attained by the regular dispatch of punitive expeditions and the establishment of military bases at strategic points. Rebellion was endemic, but by the determined prosecution of such measures it could be controlled. Cowed by the defeat and savage treatment

---

[1] §IV, 5, 20 f., col. v, 33–41.

of Uqumeni, the inhabitants of Elkhunia submitted without resistance. Nor was opposition apparently encountered when, either
in the same or the following year, the Assyrian army appeared in
Sharnida and Mekhru. In the latter district Tukulti-Ninurta
employed Qutian troops to cut supplies of its much prized timber
for the construction of a palace at Ashur. His reduction of the
Qutian lands although brutal was effective and for many years
they sent tribute regularly to Ashur.

Other campaigns were directed to the restoration of Assyrian
authority over the small Hurrian states of the upper Tigris area
which he refers to collectively as the land of the Shubari. They
are listed as the land of the Papkhi, Katmukhi, Bushe, Mumme,
Alzi, (A)madani, Nikhani, Alaya, Tepurzi and Purukuzzi.[1] According to the fullest account of these wars,[2] his first attack, in
the same year as the expedition to Mekhru, fell on Katmukhi,
which had been plundering Assyrian territory and carrying off
the inhabitants. Five of its main strongholds were attacked and
captured and their people and property taken to Ashur. Returning to the Kashiari mountain, he advanced against the other
Shubari lands which, alerted by the fate of Katmukhi, had formed
a coalition to oppose him, probably under the leadership of Ekhli-
Teshub of Alzi. After seizing the capital of Purukuzzi, he overpowered four towns in Alzi and six in Amadani, the Diyārbakr
district. Ekhli-Teshub thereupon panicked and fled to Nairi with
members of his family and court while his leaderless troops took
to the hills to save their lives. The resistance of Alzi having
collapsed, Tukulti-Ninurta proceeded to devastate it, sacking 180
towns. Certain texts also mention that the land of the Papkhi
resisted and had to be crushed by force.[3] The reduction of the
Shubari lands brought Assyria important economic and strategic
gains, notably access to the rich and easily workable copper deposits at Ergani Maden, and command of the routes leading
across the Euphrates and Murad Su into central and eastern
Anatolia. In a triumphant summing up of these early campaigns,
Tukulti-Ninurta enumerated the conquered territories in approximately geographical order, beginning in the south-east with lands
on the further bank of the Lesser Zab and ending in the north-
west with the land of the Shubari 'as far as the frontier district
of Nairi and the frontier district of Makan to the Euphrates'.
The reference to Makan shows the confused ideas of the Assyrians about countries beyond their immediate ken. The scribes,
having heard of Magan on the Gulf of Oman as a distant land,

[1] §III, 12, Text 5.   [2] §III, 12, Text 1.   [3] §III, 12, Texts 6, 16, 17.

located it in the unknown territory to the west of Nairi.[1] That subsequently they realized their error is suggested by the fact that in later texts of Tukulti-Ninurta the non-committal phrase 'the frontier district of the totality' is substituted for this passage.

The northern frontier had been re-established and strengthened but beyond it lay the Nairi lands which by border raiding or intrigue with dissident elements could imperil its security. Their rich supplies of metal, cattle and horses were an added incentive to conquest. Their subjection led Tukulti-Ninurta into territory unknown to his predecessors, the mountainous nature of which represented a formidable challenge to the military engineers charged with the task of preparing a passage for troops and chariotry. 'Mighty mountains, a narrow *massif*, whose paths no king had known, I traversed in the triumph of my transcendent might, their highlands I widened(?) with bronze axes, their untrodden paths I made broad.' He claims that his conquests extended as far as the shore of the Upper Sea, either Lake Vān or Lake Urmia. Forty Nairi kings who opposed him in battle were heavily defeated and taken to Ashur with copper chains round their necks but were subsequently released to their lands as tributary vassals. In his titulary Tukulti-Ninurta calls himself 'king of the Nairi lands', but neither he nor his successors ever achieved the permanent subjection of these mountain peoples and in the course of the following centuries repeated Assyrian attacks led to their unification in the kingdom of Urarṭu. In certain texts the account of the Nairi war is followed by the statement that he made Azalzi and Shepardi his frontier, but whether these districts lay in Nairi or elsewhere is unknown.

The Nairi war was followed by the greatest military triumph of Tukulti-Ninurta's career, the defeat and occupation of Babylonia. By the time Kashtiliash IV (1242–1235) succeeded his father, Shagarakti-Shuriash, there had been a change of dynasty in Elam and the danger of invasion from this quarter had receded.[2] Possibly while Tukulti-Ninurta was occupied in the distant north against the Nairi lands, Kashtiliash judged the moment opportune to attack Assyria. The war provoked by this ill-advised action and its disastrous consequences for Babylonia are described by Tukulti-Ninurta,[3] Chronicle P,[4] and an Assyrian epic composed soon after the event.[5] According to the first two sources, Tukulti-Ninurta captured Kashtiliash in battle and took him in chains to Ashur.

[1] §III, 11, 9.
[2] See below, pp. 383 ff.
[3] §III, 12, Texts 5, 6, 15, 16, 17.
[4] §III, 12, Text 37.
[5] §IV, 5; §IV, 7; §IV, 15, 116 ff.; §IV, 16, 131 ff.

The Chronicle then states that he returned to Babylon, demolished its fortifications, put the inhabitants to the sword, looted
Babylon and the temple E-sagila and carried off the statue of Marduk to Assyria. The epic gives a vivid and more detailed account
of the war. Responsibility for its outbreak is firmly placed on the
Kassite, who by invading Assyrian territory had broken his treaty
with Assyria. Before marching against him, Tukulti-Ninurta read
out its terms before Shamash, god of the oath, in order to pin the
guilt on his adversary and secure divine sanction and support for
his counter-attack. Kashtiliash, having failed to obtain a clear
omen, realized that the gods had condemned and abandoned him.
Urged on by his troops he nevertheless gave battle, only to turn
and flee at the first clash of arms. He withdrew to a distant place
but eventually stood to fight, after Tukulti-Ninurta had taunted
him with cowardice and boasted of his capture and spoliation of
Babylonian cities. A great battle ensued in which Kashtiliash was
captured. The epic goes on to describe how Tukulti-Ninurta
carried off the treasures of the Kassite king, using them to enrich
and embellish the temples of his gods.[1] According to this contemporary or near contemporary account, therefore, the final
defeat of Kashtiliash in 1235 was accomplished only after considerable fighting and after Tukulti-Ninurta had seized part of
Babylonia. It may also be inferred from the Chronicle that the
strongly defended city of Babylon either continued to resist after
the capture of Kashtiliash or rebelled later, so that a further campaign was needed for its reduction. The subjection of the whole
country as far as the Persian Gulf was then completed and its
citizens were deported to Assyria in considerable numbers.[2]
He removed from the control of Babylonia 38 districts which were
of particular strategic and commerical value to Assyria. They included Mari, Khana, Rapiqu and the hill of the Akhlamu, which
gave him command of the middle Euphrates, and Arrapkha, ter-
minal of the trade route leading through Sulaimaniyah to Iran.
Sikkuri and Sapani lay in the mountains south-east of Assyria,
while Turna-suma and Ulaiash were on the Babylonian–Elamite
border. The location of the remainder is unknown.

Having occupied Babylonia, Tukulti-Ninurta assumed its royal
titulary, styling himself 'king of Karduniash, king of Sumer
and Akkad, king of Sippar and Babylon, king of Tilmun and

[1] They included a seal of Shagarakti-Shuriash which was later returned to
Babylon, only to be carried off once again by Sennacherib, §III, 12, Text 29. For
a list of booty from Babylonia see §III, 10, 123 f.
[2] §III, 10, 121 f.

Meluhha'.[1] Because of ambiguities in the historical sources, however, there is considerable uncertainty as to the duration and character of his administration. According to the Chronicle, he appointed governors and ruled the country for seven years. Afterwards the Akkadian nobles of Babylonia rebelled and placed on the throne Adad-shuma-uṣur,[2] a son of Kashtiliash.[3] However, the name of Tukulti-Ninurta does not appear in the Babylonian King List A, which between Kashtiliash and Adad-shuma-uṣur gives Enlil-nādin-shumi and Kadashman-Kharbe II, both of whom ruled for 'one year six months', and Adad-shuma-iddina, who reigned six years. Thus it appears to assign a total of nine, not seven, years to the interval between Kashtiliash and Adad-shuma-uṣur. Furthermore, the three successors of Kashtiliash can hardly be identified with the governors (*šaknūtu*) of the Chronicle since it is unlikely that kings would have been so designated, and that they actually exercised the kingship is confirmed by documents from Ur dated by the accession years of Kadashman-Kharbe and Adad-shuma-iddina.[4]

This evidence has been interpreted to mean either that the seven-year period of Assyrian rule is omitted from the King List or that it is represented by the three successors of Kashtiliash. According to the first solution, which is that adopted in the chronological scheme of this *History*, Tukulti-Ninurta administered the whole of Babylonia directly through governors for seven years (1234–1228).[5] At the end of this period Enlil-nādin-shumi rebelled and seized the southern part of the country including Nippur, possession of which entitled him to recognition in the royal canon. The Assyrians, however, retained Babylon and the north until they were driven out by the revolt which brought Adad-shuma-uṣur (1218–1189) to power. Therefore their rule, although it weakened and contracted, lasted not seven but sixteen years. Against this reconstruction it may be pointed out that Enlil-nādin-shumi, far from being kept out of Babylon by the Assyrians, is attested there by tablets dated during his reign. Also there is no evidence in the Kassite period or later that possession of Nippur secured recognition in the royal canon.[6] According to the alternative solution, Tukulti-Ninurta governed Babylonia indirectly through vassal rulers who appear in the King List instead of their overlord, presumably because they had been duly invested

---

[1] For Babylonian contacts with Bahrein and Failaka in the Kassite period, see A, 1, *passim*; A, 9.
[2] For the reading of the name, see A, 3, 233 ff.   [3] §III, 1, 151.   [4] §I, 11, 19.
[5] *C.A.H.* I³, pt. 1, p. 199; §I, 11, 18 ff.   [6] A, 5, 311, n. 125; 313.

with the kingship. It has to be assumed on this interpretation that the governors of the Chronicle were Assyrian officials appointed by Tukulti-Ninurta to supervise and control these puppets. Numerous attempts have been made to resolve the difficulty presented by the apparent discrepancy between the Chronicle and the Canon as to the duration of Assyrian rule. If the reigns of the three immediate successors of Kashtiliash were consecutive, so that they covered a period of nine years, then it is possible that the Chronicle reckoned the seven years of Assyrian rule not from the defeat of Kashtiliash but from the occupation of Babylon. The eighteen-month reign of Enlil-nādin-shumi and the first six months of that of Kadashman-Kharbe would then fall in the interval between these two events and the latter king, who remained on the throne after the conquest of Babylon, and also Adad-shuma-iddina were Assyrian vassals.[1] However, this may be a case in which reigns listed as consecutive in the royal canon in fact overlapped and the seven years of the Chronicle may therefore be a correct figure for the period between Kashtiliash and Adad-shuma-uṣur.[2] If so, one possible reconstruction is that Enlil-nādin-shumi was recognized by Tukulti-Ninurta as his vassal immediately after the defeat of Kashtiliash. The Kassite, Kadashman-Kharbe, however, continued to resist in the south, being recognized at Ur, and, when Enlil-nādin-shumi was defeated by Kidin-Khutran of Elam, instigated a revolt in Babylon. Tukulti-Ninurta thereupon returned to Babylonia, sacked the capital, brought the southern districts under his control and installed Adad-shuma-iddina in the kingship.[3]

Another suggestion is that the 'one year six months' of the King List is not to be taken literally as 'eighteen months' but is rather to be understood as 'one year (that is) six months'. If this meant that the combined reigns of Enlil-nādin-shumi and Kadashman-Kharbe amounted to no more than a year, then the King List and the Chronicle would be in agreement. However, one would expect the King List to reckon in official regnal years, and this would extend the period between Kashtiliash and Adad-shuma-uṣur to eight years. A further difficulty is that economic texts from Ur indicate that Kadashman-Kharbe ruled for at least fourteen months. In fact, since his reign extended into two Nisans, the King List should have credited him with two regnal years. It could be that it was defective or that its calculations were confused by the Elamite removal of Enlil-nādin-shumi or by a

---

[1] §III, 12, 41; §III, 6, 41 f.   [2] §III, 8, 286 f., 356.
[3] For a further discussion of the problem see below, pp. 387 ff.

struggle for the throne between Enlil-nādin-shumi and Kadash-man-Kharbe.[1]

Whatever the status of Enlil-nādin-shumi and his two successors, their reigns represent a period of Babylonian weakness of which the Elamites were able to take advantage. Kidin-Khutran raided Nippur and Dēr, massacring or deporting the inhabitants, drove away Enlil-nādin-shumi and ended his rule. Later, in the time of Adad-shuma-iddina, he captured Isin and advanced as far as Marad, west of Nippur.

The defeat of Kashtiliash established Tukulti-Ninurta as the outstanding military leader of the thirteenth century. Ability on the battlefield, however, is not necessarily matched by political vision or personal courage by the strength of character to withstand the lure of victory and power. In retrospect his occupation of Babylonia must be judged to have been against the real interests of his country. Admittedly the temptation was great. For over a century the Babylonians had contested the establishment of Assyrian control over the Zagros area. That, so long as they remained independent, they would continue to do so was inevitable. From the earliest historical period the eastern hills had been their main source of supply for the metal, stone and building timber which they themselves lacked. Assyria, by diverting the trade of this area to its own markets, was striking at the basis of their economy and threatening their existence as a political force of any consequence. This was a situation no Babylonian king could accept. Nevertheless, Tukulti-Ninurta would have been better advised to continue the policy of his predecessors who had held the Babylonians in check by limited campaigns and the establishment of a favourable southern frontier. The main economic motive underlying Assyrian expansion and determining its direction was the quest for raw materials. These Babylonia could not provide and the heavy and continuous military effort required for its occupation diverted Assyrian energies and resources from the task of securing them elsewhere. Weakened by over-extension of its forces, Assyria lost Babylonia, suffered reverses on other fronts, and fell into a condition of internal disorder.

Between Tukulti-Ninurta and Tudkhaliash IV of Khatti relations were tense and at times deteriorated into open hostility. The customary letter of congratulation sent by Tudkhaliash to Tukulti-Ninurta at his accession was conciliatory in tone.[2] After paying tribute to Shalmaneser, who had become a great king

---

[1] A, 2, 63 ff.   [2] G, 9, XXIII, 92, XXIII, 103; §III, 5.

and defeated great kings, he exhorted him to protect his father's
frontiers and offered assistance should any of his subjects rise
in rebellion. At the same time he addressed letters to two high
Assyrian officials, one being the chancellor, Baba-akha-iddina,
who had previously held office under Adad-nīrāri and Shalmaneser.[1] He assured them of his friendship for Tukulti-Ninurta
and called on them to protect their lord. News had, however,
reached him that Tukulti-Ninurta was planning to attack Papan-
khi, the land of the Papkhi of the Assyrian records, and he warned
the chancellor of the dangers and hazards of an expedition into
this mountainous country. This concern for the safety and reputation of the young prince can hardly be taken at its face value but
must rather be understood as a polite intimation that Khatti
maintained its interest in Papkhi and other lands of the Shubari
and that an Assyrian attack in this quarter would be regarded as
an unfriendly act.

Not only did Tukulti-Ninurta disregard this warning, since he
subdued the lands of the Shubari, including Papkhi; he also
crossed the Euphrates and, according to his account, carried off
eight *sar* (28,800) Hittite subjects. This raid heads the list of
expeditions undertaken in his accession and first regnal years but
their order is not necessarily chronological. Even though the
number of captives was certainly greatly exaggerated, it appears,
as reported, to have been a major operation. However, if this
was indeed the case, it is strange that it is mentioned only in
inscriptions composed after the conquest of Babylonia, more than
a decade after the event. There is no reference to it in the detailed
report of the early campaigns. It is possible, therefore, that
Tukulti-Ninurta, triumphant and self-confident after his Babylonian victory and infuriated at the hostile actions of the Hittites,
of which an example is cited below, for his own self-glorification
and the belittlement of his rivals, magnified what had been a
relatively minor incident into a major victory. It may well be
referred to in a document from Ras Shamra.[2] In this Tudkhaliash absolved Ammishtamru of Ugarit from the obligation
to provide soldiers and chariots for a war with Assyria then in
progress. This exemption would not have been given if it had
been a major conflict and, since Ini-Teshub of Carchemish conveyed the decision of Tudkhaliash to Ammishtamru, it may be
inferred that it was a localized frontier clash affecting his territory.
Possibly it was provoked by border raiding, a case of which was

---

[1] G, 5, 75 f.; §III, 2, 3 ff.; §III, 13.
[2] §III, 4, 149 ff., see above, p. 144.

the occasion of a letter probably sent by Tukulti-Ninurta to Tud-khaliash.[1] Replying to a complaint by the Hittite that Assyrian subjects were continuously raiding his land, he strenuously denied the charge, asserting that not so much as a length of timber had been removed from Hittite territory. Whether Tudkhaliash was goaded into retaliation by this war, the reconquest of the lands of the Shubari or some other action on the part of Assyria cannot be said, but he determined on a measure which was an open declaration of his hostile intent and a defiance of Assyrian designs on Syria. In a treaty with his vassal, Shaushga-muwash of Amurru, the Syrian was not only called on to furnish aid in the event of an Assyrian attack, but was obliged to institute a trade blockade against Assyria: 'As the king of Assyria is the enemy of My Sun, so may he also be your enemy. Your merchants shall not go to Assyria, you shall not allow his merchants in your land, neither shall they pass through your land. If, however, one of them comes into your land then seize him and send him to My Sun. As soon as the king of Assyria begins war, if then My Sun calls up troops and chariots...so do you call up your troops and chariots and despatch them.'[2] Although direct evidence for Assyrian trade with Syria at this period is slight,[3] access to its commercial centres was certainly of considerable importance and such economic sanctions, if widely applied, must have hit Assyria hard. Since, in another section of the treaty, Tudkhaliash refers to the king of Babylonia as his equal, the treaty was concluded before the defeat and deposition of Kashtiliash.[4]

After the capture of Babylonia an Assyrian bid for control of Syria must have seemed imminent, and the interests most plainly challenged, if that had occurred, would have been those of the Hittite monarch. However, the threat never materialized. Years of strenuous campaigning followed by the occupation of Babylonia had so overtaxed the resources of Assyria that it was incapable of the sustained effort necessary to hold its conquests. The Babylonian wars are the last to be recorded by Tukulti-Ninurta. After he had reigned for another twenty-five years or so, 'Ashur-nāṣir-apli, his son, and the nobles of Assyria, rebelled against him and tore him from his throne. In Kār-Tukulti-Ninurta in a house they shut him up and slew him with the sword.'[5] That military defeats and territorial losses were a

---

[1] G, 9, III, 73; §III, 12, Text 36.
[2] G, 9, XXIII, 1; G, 6, 272 f.; §III, 9, 320 ff.   [3] §III, 13, 38.
[4] For a dating of this treaty to the time of Shalmaneser I, see above ch. XXIV, sect. IV.   [5] §III, 12, Text 37; see below, ch. XXXI, sect. III.

chief cause of this violent deed is certain. Although the only countries known to have seceded are Babylonia and the small states of Sikkuri and Sappani in the eastern hills,[1] a prayer of Tukulti-Ninurta to the god Ashur suggests that revolt was widespread.[2] In it he speaks of the ring of evil with which all the lands surrounded his city Ashur. Those whom he had helped and protected threatened Assyria, and his enemies plotted its destruction. It may be assumed that the peoples of the eastern and northern hills were among the rebels, while one of the enemies may have been the Hittite, Shuppiluliumash II, who, perhaps when Tukulti-Ninurta was still alive, seems to have made an unsuccessful attempt to regain Upper Mesopotamia.[3] It can hardly be believed that Tukulti-Ninurta abandoned his conquests without a struggle, and the absence of royal records must be interpreted as a sign not of inactivity but of military defeat.

Nevertheless, in view of his long reign of thirty-seven years, age may in time have diminished his energy and impaired his power of decision, and the hope that under a younger man the fortunes of Assyria could be retrieved doubtless furnished an additional motive for his murder. To what extent this was also prompted by discontent with his internal policy must, in the absence of positive evidence, remain a matter of speculation. It may well be that the economic burdens placed on the Assyrian people had become intolerable. Not only had the needs of the army to be met; men and materials were also deflected from productive uses for the grandiose building schemes of the king which culminated after the defeat of Kashtiliash in the foundation of a new royal city at Kār-Tukulti-Ninurta, about 3 km. upstream from Ashur on the left bank of the Tigris. While prisoners of war certainly provided much of the immense labour force required for these projects and booty and tribute supplied many of the materials, a heavy contribution was undoubtedly exacted from the Assyrians themselves.[4] The economic situation must also have been adversely affected by the political and military reverses. The Syrian markets had

---

[1] §III, 12, Text 38c.   [2] §IV, 4.

[3] G, 8, IV, 14; §III, 6, 5 f.; the Middle Assyrian occupation at Tell er-Rimah, 13 km. south of Tell 'Afar, may have ended about this time; the latest eponyms attested in the economic texts belong to the early part of the reign of Tukulti-Ninurta. Since it lay on the edge of the cultivated zone it may have been deserted because of the inability of the government to provide security against the Bedawin, as happened in this area under the Ottoman régime. See A, 14, 66, 75; A, 15, 130; A, 16, 71, 91.

[4] After the Babylonian war building work was in progress at Kār-Tukulti-Ninurta and on the defences of Ashur, the New Palace and the Shalmaneser Palace. For texts recording large deliveries of bricks see §III, 8, 112.

been closed by Tudkhaliash and if, as seems likely, Tukulti-Ninurta in his later years lost control of the Zagros districts and those on the northern frontier, Assyria was cut off from important sources of raw materials.[1] The further suggestion has been made that, fascinated by the superior civilization of Babylonia, he introduced some of its cult practices into Assyria, gave increased importance to Marduk, and raised Babylonians and Kassites to important state positions, so falling foul of the Assyrian nobility and priesthood.[2] More recent research has indicated that by the fourteenth and thirteenth centuries, Assyria had assimilated many Babylonian cultic elements. There is, however, very little source material for the Middle Assyrian period, and it is therefore difficult to assess the extent to which this trend was intensified by the conquest of the south. The statue of Marduk carried off from Babylon by Tukulti-Ninurta, which had political as well as religious significance, played a central rôle in certain ritual processions in Ashur.[3] The assumption that its possession led to an increase in the importance of the existing local cult of Marduk has, however, been queried on the grounds that an analysis of theophorous names does not show any significant increase in the element 'Marduk' until the twelfth century.[4] It is indeed possible that, in the thirteenth century, the cult of Enlil of Nippur exercised more influence than that of Marduk of Babylon. This is suggested by the fact that in inscriptions referring to his rebuilding of the Ashur temple, many of the names used for the building by Shalmaneser allude to the shrine of Enlil at Nippur.[5] The evidence for the employment of Babylonians in the administration at present rests mainly on a Middle Assyrian eponymous official who bore the Kassite name Kashtiliash.

Whatever hopes for a speedy recovery of national fortunes lay behind the assassination of Tukulti-Ninurta they were not realized, for, although Assyria retained control of Khanigalbat and the districts immediately adjoining the eastern frontier, the decline of its political and military power continued under his immediate successors.

---

[1] For evidence of trade in tin from Nairi in the latter part of the reign of Shalmaneser and early in that of Tukulti-Ninurta, see A, 21; A, 27.
[2] §III, 10, 109 f.
[3] A, 25, 52 ff.
[4] G, 5, 98 ff.
[5] A, 25, 35, n. 13, 151 f.

IV. LITERATURE

The military triumphs of the fourteenth and thirteenth centuries acted as a powerful stimulus to Assyrian literary activity. The desire to record and perpetuate the memory of victory and conquest led to the elaboration of campaign reports in the royal inscriptions and to the composition of epics and also, perhaps, of chronicles. At the same time, closer contact with countries with a developed literary tradition, in particular Babylonia, greatly enriched the resources of literature and learning at the command of the Assyrian scribes.

The official inscriptions with historical content revived and developed a literary form which had arisen in north Mesopotamia some five centuries earlier. Its basic scheme was that of the traditional Babylonian building inscription, the chief elements of which consisted of the royal name, titulary and epithets, an account of the building operation, sometimes accompanied by a brief reference to the historical circumstances of the dedication, and finally curses against those who damaged the foundation document. In the nineteenth century this scheme was adapted to include a narrative of military events. In a text of Iakhdunlim of Mari, recording the foundation of a temple to Shamash, the circumstances of the dedication were expanded into a lengthy description of his expedition to the Mediterranean.[1] Although formally part of the introduction to the building report, it constituted the principal feature of the inscription. Whether this type of historical writing first arose in Mari cannot be said, but that it was practised in Assyria is shown by a text of Shamshi-Adad I (1813–1781).[2] Admittedly this is markedly inferior in construction and literary style to that of Iakhdunlim but it may not represent the best of which the Assyrian scribes were capable. Shamshi-Adad, as ruler of Mari after the murder of Iakhdunlim, was certainly acquainted with the achievements of its scribal school and if they were indeed superior to those of Assyria would, one imagines, have sought to emulate them. No historical texts of this type are known for the period between Shamshi-Adad and Enlil-nīrāri (1329–1320). This is hardly surprising since, during the period of Assyrian political decline after Shamshi-Adad, occasions for their composition must have been rare. Nevertheless, the reappearance of this distinctive type of historical writing in the fourteenth century indicates continuity of tradition. If it had indeed died out in the preceding centuries, then the Middle Assyrian kings may have gone back

[1] §IV, 3.   [2] G, 2, 23 ff.; G, 11, 16 f.

for their models to the earlier period of Assyrian greatness under Shamshi-Adad.

In their inscriptions the historical report takes two forms. In the first, which is not attested earlier, the royal epithets are elaborated to describe the king as conqueror of specific peoples, lands or cities, a device which enabled the scribe to summarize, sometimes at considerable length, the results achieved by war. It did not, however, permit a detailed narrative account of campaigns. This required treatment in a separate section, the position of which within the body of the text was still the subject of some experimentation. Whereas Adad-nīrāri, like Iakhdunlim, placed the narrative of his wars against Khanigalbat immediately before the building report,[1] Shalmaneser inserted his historical passage as a parenthesis in the collection of royal epithets.[2] The latter solution, however, was obviously unsatisfactory, for the clear construction of the inscription was lost, and Tukulti-Ninurta reverted to the more logical scheme of his grandfather.

When conquests are summarized in the royal epithets, their order usually appears to be geographical rather than chronological, but in the narrative passages campaigns of different years seem normally to be listed in temporal sequence, although the expeditions of any one year may be given in variant order in different editions. However, at this period no clear distinction was made between the annual campaigns, and precise dating was given only in the case of wars of the accession year or accession and first regnal years.[3] Others which were certainly later in date either follow these directly without any temporal indication or are introduced by vague phrases such as 'afterwards' or 'in those days'. A clear annalistic form was not achieved until the time of Tiglath-pileser I (1115–1077) when, although annual campaigns were not numbered or dated, they were separated by lyrical passages in praise of the king. A fragmentary text listing the wars of Arik-dēn-ili, thought to be the earliest example of an annalistic royal inscription, can now be identified as a chronicle.[4] It is similar in construction to, and perhaps of the same date as, chronicle fragments dealing with the reigns of Enlil-nīrāri and Tiglath-pileser I, which were probably composed shortly after the latter's death.[5] In this type of document the narrative is in the third person and the events recorded are divided by lines into sections which presumably correspond to regnal years. In compiling the record of previous

[1] §1, 14. [2] G, 2, 110 ff.; G, 11, 25 f.; §IV, 2, 57 f.
[3] §IV, 13, 26 ff. [4] G, 2, 51 ff.; G, 11, 25 f.; §IV, 11.
[5] §IV, 14, 133 f.; §IV, 19; §IV, 20, 115.

reigns, however, the eleventh-century chronicler must have had earlier historical sources at his disposal and it is therefore possible that chronicles were already being composed in the fourteenth and thirteenth centuries. In view of the discovery of the Iakhdun-lim inscription and the identification of the Arik-dēn-ili text as a chronicle, it may be doubted whether the historical literature of the Hittites exercised any significant influence on that of Assyria. The inclusion of campaign reports in the building inscription represents a revival of an earlier, north Mesopotamian tradition and the origin of the annalistic form may be seen in the tentative attempts of the thirteenth-century scribes to arrange events in temporal sequence.

Considerable progress was made during the thirteenth century towards the development of an appropriate literary style for official inscriptions. Particularly in the adulatory phrases applied to the king and in the narrative passages, the prose was increasingly enriched by the introduction of new expressions and formulae and the use of metaphor and simile. From the time of Shalmaneser the recital of military events was enlivened by descriptive detail of the difficulties encountered and overcome by the army. Other elements, which subsequently became standard in Assyrian royal texts, are found in his reign, notably the emphasis on the religious character of wars, which were undertaken at the command of the gods and won with their aid, and the description of the fearful punishments meted out to those who by rebelling had sinned against the gods. In the royal titulary, increasing emphasis is placed on the monarchical and more secular aspects of kingship. In the Old and Middle Assyrian periods, the formal title most commonly employed was 'vicar of the god Ashur' (*iššiʾ(i)ak ᵈAššur*); only Shamshi-Adad I deviated from the norm by styling himself 'king of the totality'. In the fourteenth century, however, Arik-dēn-ili assumed the titles 'king of Assyria' and 'mighty king'. To these Adad-nīrāri added 'king of the totality'. Military epithets were also introduced during his reign, as was that of 'city founder'. The lauding of the king as conqueror reached its climax under Tukulti-Ninurta. In addition to the titles which refer specifically to his rule over Babylonia, there are numerous more general and grandiose epithets, such as 'king of the four quarters', 'king of kings', 'lord of lords', 'prince of princes', 'sun of all the peoples'. The new developments in the royal titulary during the fourteenth and thirteenth centuries reflect not only the recovery and expansion of Assyrian military power but also a fundamental change in political concepts. The stress is now on the whole land of Ashur, rather than the city. To this period must be attributed the growth of a national consciousness which Assyria was to retain, even during periods of decline, until its destruction in 612 B.C.[1]

A branch of Sumero-Akkadian literature attested for the first time in Assyria is the epic, of which two examples are known, both inspired by wars against Babylonia. The first, of which little survives, celebrated the victory of Adad-nirāri over Nazimaruttash.[2] The second commemorated the defeat of Kashtiliash IV by Tukulti-Ninurta, by whom it may have been commissioned.[3] When complete it must have consisted of not less than seven hundred lines. It describes in detail the events which led up to the outbreak of hostilities, the course of the struggle and the ultimate triumph of Tukulti-Ninurta. Its central motif is the king as hero. His praises are sung in hymnal passages and his courage, his might and his righteous behaviour are extolled and contrasted with the cowardice and perfidy of his opponent. In the treatment of this heroic theme, the Assyrian scribe shows a sure command of poetic form and narrative style. The attention of the listener is held by a wealth of striking imagery and by variation in the character and pace of the story, lyrical passages, direct speech and graphic accounts of action being skilfully alternated. This composition, as also the prayer of Tukulti-Ninurta, which is bilingual in Akkadian and dialectal Sumerian,[4] attests the growth of a native literature which, although inspired by Babylonian prototypes, was distinctively Assyrian in outlook and style.

According to the epic, Tukulti-Ninurta, like Ashurbanipal, looted the libraries of Babylonia and carried off their tablet collections to enrich those of Assyria, which prior to his reign were probably limited in extent. His booty included incantations, prayers, omens and medical texts, some of which are doubtless among the Babylonian tablets found in the remains of the library of Tiglath-pileser I.[5]

V. ARCHITECTURE AND THE ARTS

The prosperity of Assyria in the thirteenth century is shown by the greatly increased building activity. New towns were founded at Kalkhu and Kār-Tukulti-Ninurta, and at Ashur there was an impressive amount of new building in addition to the routine

---

[1] §IV, 2, 26 ff.; A, 24; A, 5, 303 ff.
[2] §IV, 20.   [3] §IV, 5; §IV, 7; §IV, 15, 116 ff.; §IV, 16, 131 ff.; §IV, 17.
[4] §IV, 4, 40 ff.   [5] §IV, 18, 200; see below, pp. 477 f.

maintenance of existing structures. Although excavation has revealed no major architectural innovation there was an interest in building methods employed outside Assyria, for Adad-nīrāri removed the wooden columns of the palace of Nakhur in Khanigalbat to his own residence at Ashur, whence they were later transferred first to the 'New Palace' and then to Kār-Tukulti-Ninurta by his grandson.[1]

The construction of new temples, palaces and defence works at Ashur is recorded in the royal inscriptions and attested by excavation, although in almost every case the walls had been demolished to the foundations by later builders. Both Adad-nīrāri and Tukulti-Ninurta repaired and strengthened the fortifications.[2] On the vulnerable western side of the town, Tukulti-Ninurta excavated a dry ditch beyond the outer wall, making it 20 m. in width and 15 m. in depth, with almost vertical sides. It extended from the Tabira gate at least as far as the beginning of the New Town,[3] and was crossed by ramps leading to the Tabira and west gates. Commanded by the battlements of the outer wall and too wide to be easily spanned by storming ladders, it presented a formidable obstacle to attack. To protect the river bank against erosion, Adad-nīrāri reconstructed the quay wall along the Tigris with massive limestone blocks set in bitumen mortar and faced with baked brick.[4]

The temple of Ashur, rebuilt by Shamshi-Adad I and kept in repair by later kings, including Adad-nīrāri, was destroyed by fire in the time of Shalmaneser. In rebuilding it, he adhered faithfully to the original lay-out but added the south-west court and also made certain alterations in the cult room and elsewhere.[5] A rebuilding of the Sin-Shamash temple is probably to be attributed to Tukulti-Ninurta and here also the earlier shrine was reproduced.[6] However, in a new temple for Ishtar, now called *Aššurītu*, Ishtar of Ashur, Tukulti-Ninurta not only departed from the plan of the archaic sanctuary, which he demolished, but resited it slightly to the south-west.[7] The chief innovation was the addition of a subordinate, single-roomed sanctuary dedicated to the goddess Dinītu (= Ishtar). Although joined structurally, there was no communication between the two shrines, each having its own towered entrance and paved processional way. The re-

---

[1] §v, 26; A, 12, 534 f.   [2] §v, 1; §v, 5, 119 ff.; A, 10.
[3] §v, 1, 124 ff.; §v, 5, 120; §iii, 12, commentary on Text 18.
[4] §v, 1, 149 ff.; §v, 5, 119 f.   [5] §v, 11, 37 ff.; §v, 5, 118 f.; A, 25, 15 f.
[6] §v, 11, 82 ff.
[7] §v, 4, 15 ff.; §v, 5, 108 ff.; §iii, 12, Texts 7, 8, 9 and commentary.

mains of this double temple were exceptionally well preserved, the mud brick superstructure standing in places to a height of over 2 m. It provides welcome information on the appearance and cult arrangements of religious buildings of the thirteenth century. The exterior wall faces were ornamented in Babylonian style with groups of pilasters and stepped niches and on the evidence of Middle Assyrian seal designs it may be assumed that they terminated in crenelations. The cult room of the Ishtar shrine, entered through a large chamber, was of imposing dimensions (32·50 m. × 8·70 m.). Almost half was occupied by a high platform, set against the short end, with an alcove for the cult statue and an approach stairway with stepped balustrades. Five limestone slabs set into the floor in front of the entrance may have supported a cult emblem and the posts of a baldachin. The numerous intact foundation deposits from the temple, which include inscribed tablets of Tukulti-Ninurta, of limestone, lead, gold and silver, provide valuable information on the ceremony of deposition, to which allusion is made by Shalmaneser.[1] Tukulti-Ninurta also completed the temple of (An)nunaittu, begun by his father, but its location is unknown. At Nineveh the temple of Ishtar, which had been damaged by an earthquake, was restored by Shalmaneser and later renovated by Tukulti-Ninurta.

Repairs were effected by all three kings to the 'Old Palace' of Ashur between the Anu-Adad temple and the great zikkurrat,[2] but perhaps because it had proved inadequate as the administrative centre of the enlarged kingdom Tukulti-Ninurta early in his reign began the construction of a royal residence between the Tabira gate and the Anu-Adad temple.[3] Of this 'New Palace' only part of the mud-brick terrace and a few foundation walls remain but its scale may be judged from the fact that the area cleared and levelled for the platform was c. 40,000 sq. m. in extent. Between the zikkurrat and the Ashur temple Shalmaneser built another palace, which was renovated by his son. It is probably represented by the remains of a monumental building with inscribed paving bricks of both rulers.[4] Its dimensions could not be determined but in view of the limited area available it must have been considerably smaller than the 'Old Palace'.[5]

[1] G, 2, 123; G, 11, 41.   [2] §v, 23, 13 f.; §v, 5, 108.
[3] §v, 23, 30 ff.; §v, 5, 115 ff.; §III, 12, 6, commentary on Text 1.
[4] §v, 23, 28 f.; §III, 12, 14, commentary on Text 6; A, 25, 13 f.
[5] There was the same close connexion of palace and temple in other Assyrian cities, e.g., Khorsabad. Annual visits by the gods to the royal palace are mentioned by Adad-nīrāri and Tukulti-Ninurta; see A, 25, 14, 165.

Adad-nīrāri describes himself as a 'city founder' but it is not known to which town he refers. According to Ashurnaṣirpal II, Kalkhu (O.T. Calah, modern Nimrūd), on the left bank of the Tigris 22 miles south of Nineveh, was founded by Shalmaneser. His choice of site must have been determined by the need for an administrative and possibly also a military base between Ashur and Nineveh but of its character and function at this period nothing is known. There is no reference to it in his extant inscriptions and because of the overburden of the Late Assyrian city it remains virtually unexcavated. Since in the time of Tukulti-Ninurta an official of Kalkhu had command of 350 Kassites deported from Babylonia, building may have continued here after the death of Shalmaneser.[1] Following the victory over Babylonia, however, the interests and energies of his son were undoubtedly concentrated on the construction of Kār-Tukulti-Ninurta. Here he laid out a new town defended by stout mud brick fortifications and dominated by a zikkurrat and temple of Ashur and a royal palace.[2] A canal was dug to bring water to the town, taxes on the use of which provided for the sacrifices in the temple. He describes it as 'a great cult city (maḫāzu rabû), the dwelling of my majesty' but the reasons which prompted him to move his residence from Ashur must remain a matter of speculation. Was it simply the desire to give concrete form to his enhanced prestige as king of both Assyria and Babylonia or, in view of the fact that he had already founded a new palace at Ashur, work on which was still in progress, should some additional motive be sought? Had he indeed become 'an incalculable despot, afraid for the safety of his person', and was he driven to leave Ashur because of the hostility of its citizens?[3] That opposition developed in the latter part of his reign is obvious from his assassination, but whether one is justified in assuming that it existed and had assumed dangerous proportions at the time Kār-Tukulti-Ninurta was founded is questionable. To judge from the historical information given in the building inscriptions, work on the town seems to have begun after the defeat of Kashtiliash but before the subjection of the borderlands of Babylonia and possibly even prior to the capture of Babylon, that is to say at a moment when one would expect the prestige, authority and popularity of the king to have stood high. Of earlier unrest there is no evidence.

Although Kār-Tukulti-Ninurta was still inhabited in the eighth century B.C. it lost its importance after the murder of its founder.[4]

[1] §III, 10, 122.   [2] §v, 5, 122 ff.; §III, 12, 24, commentary on Text 15.
[3] §III, 10, 109 ff.   [4] §v, 26, 160, n. 3.

By the time of Tiglath-pileser I its gods had been moved to Ashur and it may be doubted whether any attempt was made to keep its public buildings in repair. Of the royal palace, which stood on a high mud-brick platform near the Tigris, little has survived, but fragments of painted wall plaster show that its interior decoration was elaborate and colourful.[1] The designs, which began at eye level above a bitumen dado and a band of plain red, were composed of rectangular compartments of varying size and shape, containing such motives as gazelles or griffins flanking a stylized tree, a device popular on contemporary seals, the sacred tree, rosettes, palmettes and flowers. The division of the design into compartments, each with a self-contained motive, is similar to that of the wall paintings of the fifteenth-century palace at Nuzi,[2] but although this points to continuity of tradition there is a complete change in the colour scheme: instead of the muted pink, red and grey tones of Nuzi, the predominant colours at Kār-Tukulti-Ninurta were the clear red and blue which remained characteristic of Assyrian mural art. It is possible, as suggested by Andrae,[3] that the designs represented or were inspired by woven wall hangings made up of patterned rectangles, like carpets sculptured in stone at Nineveh and Khorsabad which also have a fringe of buds and flowers, very similar to the border of one of the Kār-Tukulti-Ninurta wall paintings.[4] In this connexion it is of interest that an inventory from Kār-Tukulti-Ninurta describes two woven carpets, on one of which the design included a pomegranate tree and bouquetin, while the other has scenes representing respectively men and animals, towns and towers, and apparently three figures of the king.[5] The design of the first suggests a central panel. On the second the motives could have filled rectangles, as on the tapestry of the fifth century from Pazyryk, or been disposed in borders, as on a carpet from the same site.[6] As in the Anu-Adad temple at Ashur, the zikkurrat and temple of Ashur formed a single complex. The temple lay directly against the eastern face of the tower, into the brickwork of which was set the deep cult niche, so that Ashur in his epiphany issued directly from the mountain. Symbols of the other seven great gods associated with the temple may have stood in wall niches in one of the larger

---

[1] §v, 2, 11 ff. [2] §v, 25, pls. 128, 129. [3] §v, 2, 16.
[4] A. H. Layard, *Monuments of Nineveh*, 2nd series, pl. 184; G. Loud and C. B. Altman, *Khorsabad*, II (*O.I.P.* 40), pl. 48.
[5] §v, 12, 307, col. III, 27–38.
[6] R. D. Barnett, 'The World's Oldest Persian Carpet.' In *Ill. Ldn. News*, 14 July 1953, 69 ff., figs. 4, 10.

subsidiary chambers. Whether the statue of Marduk carried off from Babylon was placed in this temple is unknown. As there were no traces of stairs or ramps giving access to the tower it may have been approached by a bridge thrown across from a small structure of curious plan opposite the western face or more prob- ably from the roof of the temple. The number of stages could not be determined but zikkurrats depicted on Middle Assyrian seals have four or five.

The royal palaces and temples were certainly lavishly furnished with the finest and most costly objects which the workshops of Assyria could produce, but of their contents little has survived. The only branch of art adequately represented is the glyptic, known mainly from seal impressions on tablets from Ashur and Tell Fakhariyah in Khanigalbat belonging to the reigns of Shalmaneser and Tukulti-Ninurta.[1] The seal designs show a further development of the specifically Assyrian style which arose at the end of the fifteenth century, and at Ashur, although not at Fakhariyah, Mitannian seals disappear, except for a few re-used earlier pieces. With the possible exception of a ploughing scene, no new themes were introduced but the mythical contest of heroes, animals and demons now predominates. It is depicted either in the old, static heraldic group or in a free spacious composition, the finest examples of which rank among the masterpieces of Assyrian art. This free design, which is also characterized by the introduction of landscape and a realistic treatment of human and animal forms, appears in both Assyria and Babylonia in the fourteenth century and is curiously reminiscent of Akkadian art of the third millennium.

Since no Assyrian seal impressions can be certainly dated to the half century between Ashur-uballit I and Shalmaneser I, it is not possible to say how much progress was made during this period. Babylonian seal designs belonging to the reigns of Kurigalzu II and Nazimaruttash are, however, markedly superior in quality and vitality to those of Ashur-uballit and there may well have been a parallel development in Assyria. As compared to the seals of Ashur-uballit those from the reigns of Shalmaneser and his son show a striking advance in execution and artistic concepts. There is a much surer feeling for balance in design and the basic contest theme is enriched by the introduction of new participants, both actual and imaginary: the horse and winged horse, the ostrich and the winged, human-headed ibex. The hero appears as a hunter, armed with bow, spear, axe or dagger, stalking his quarry, usually

[1] §v, 15; §v, 14, 69 ff.

a cervoid, or fighting lions, griffins and griffin demons, sometimes in defence of their prey. He may be naked but more often is clad in a kilt with pendent tassels, over which he may wear a long robe. Other scenes depict demons and animals engaged in single combat, the predator and his victim, the latter sometimes endeavouring to protect its young or some smaller weaker creature. These contests are set in the open; birds of prey hover in the air and natural surroundings are indicated by the scale-pattern mountain, plants and trees, a bush with a globular crown and crooked trunk being especially characteristic.

In the portrayal of men and animals there is a strong tendency towards realism. Anatomical details, in particular musculature, are finely observed and rendered and the characterization of each animal is both sensitive and forceful. The fighting mare rears up with flaring nostrils and starting eyes, and the whole attitude of the attacking lion, the gaping jaws, spread claws and lashing tail, directly conveys the power and ferocity of the beast. The spacious treatment and realism which distinguish these contests are also found in the attractive designs of single animals moving in a wooded landscape.[1] Here and in the combat scenes the seal-cutter was able to give full play to his imaginative and creative talents. Full of vitality and infused with the excitement of a new and fresh form of artistic expression, they contrast sharply with the formal, traditional compositions of the cult scenes and the antithetical groups of hero and animals or the sacred tree flanked by animals or demons. In view of the rarity of stamp seals in Mesopotamia during the second millennium, an impression from Fakhariyah with a typically Middle Assyrian motive of a pomegranate tree has a particular interest.[2] It proves that such seals were being made in the thirteenth century and that there was therefore an Assyrian precedent for their extensive use in Late Assyrian times.

Other minor arts, in particular jewellery, are represented in a remarkable burial at Ashur, dated approximately to the period of Tukulti-Ninurta.[3] The vaulted brick tomb, which had been in use for a considerable period, contained as its final occupants two bodies, which may have been interred simultaneously. Both wore elaborate and finely wrought jewellery of gold, silver and semi-precious stones: hair ornaments, earrings, multiple necklaces and pendants. Accompanying them were further pieces of jewellery and fine alabaster and ivory vessels. Because of the poor state of preservation of the skeletons their sex could not be determined

---

[1] See Plate 156 (a)–(c).   [2] §v, 14, 81 f., pl. 80, LIII.
[3] §v, 10, 123 ff.

with certainty. One had less jewellery than the other but it is doubtful whether this implies a difference of sex. The richness of the furnishings and the fact that the tomb was in the vicinity of the temple of Ishtar suggest that its occupants may have held some special position in the service of the goddess. It has been thought that they may have acted as substitutes for the king in the sacred marriage and thereafter been put to death, but in view of doubts as to their sex and the fate of such royal substitutes this can only be speculation.

In technique and design the jewellery attests both the high standard of skill and artistry of the thirteenth-century craftsmen and the continuation of a tradition which goes back to the Royal Tombs at Ur of the third millennium.[1] Two of the most popular motives here and in Middle Assyrian graves at Mari[2] were the pomegranate and the double spiral, both ancient fertility symbols. The existence of a native school of ivory carving is shown by a pyxis and a comb from the Ashur tomb engraved in linear style with typical Assyrian scenes.[3] Fragments of ivory inlay found at the foot of the 'New Palace' terrace[4] may, however, be Babylonian rather than Assyrian work, for the frieze includes the mountain god associated with the flowing vase, a theme characteristic of Kassite art but otherwise attested in Assyria only on a relief sculpture which may also be an import from the south.[5] A completely different style of ivory carving is represented by fragments of ornamental inlays of furniture or boxes from Tell Fakhariyah.[6] The themes, stylistic details and execution of these ivories are strikingly paralleled by the Megiddo hoard of the thirteenth century, although their workmanship is inferior. Their iconography also has close connexions with other products of the Canaanite school of art, characteristic of Palestine and Syria in the Late Bronze Age. The co-existence at Tell Fakhariyah of Canaanite ivories and a glyptic art which is typically Assyrian demonstrates the cultural cross-currents affecting north Mesopotamia and the importance of this area as an intermediary between the civilizations of Assyria and the West.

The only examples of Assyrian sculpture securely dated to the thirteenth century are two symbol bases carved in low relief with representations of the king worshipping divine emblems.[7] On one he stands between two men holding sun standards while in

[1] §v, 13, 107.
[2] §v, 18, 83 f.
[3] §v, 10, 135 ff.
[4] §v, 23, 30 f.; §v, 5, 116 f.
[5] §v, 3.
[6] §v, 14, 57 ff.
[7] §v, 4, 57 ff.; §v, 5, 112 f.; §v, 16; see Plate 155 (*b*)–(*c*).

a narrow register on the plinth men and horses clamber over mountains, a scene which foreshadows the war reliefs of the ninth century. On the other, which was dedicated by Tukulti-Ninurta to the god Nusku, the king appears twice, standing and kneeling, before divine symbols on a base. Since the kneeling posture was prescribed for the Kassite *šigū* prayers it may have been introduced into Assyria from Babylonia.[1] Although the old intimate meeting of worshipper and seated deity continues as a theme of glyptic art, the representation of à god by his symbols, instead of in person, was becoming more common. This tendency, which, as is shown by the *kudurru* sculptures, was shared by the Babylonians, must express a change in theological concepts. The gods were becoming more remote and withdrawn from mankind.

That faience was employed for large-scale statuary is shown by parts of the human body from the Ishtar temple at Ashur. This material was also extensively used for human and animal figurines, human masks, amulets, vases and beads.[2] Small reliefs and roundels of lead occurred in large numbers in the Ishtar temple and on the site of the New Palace.[3] Many of the designs can be paralleled on the cylinder seals and wall paintings, elaborate rosettes being the most common. Their provenance and motives prove that they were connected with the cult of Ishtar. Their function, however, remains uncertain, although the suggestion has been made that the roundels were used as currency.[4]

[1] §v, 17, 475 f.
[2] §v, 4, 76 ff.; §v, 18, 83 f.; A, 7, 49 ff.; A, 14, 74; A, 15, 125.
[3] §v, 4, 102 ff.; §v, 23, 30.   [4] §v, 24.

CHAPTER XXVI

PALESTINE IN THE TIME OF THE NINETEENTH DYNASTY

(a) THE EXODUS AND WANDERINGS

I. THE LITERARY CHARACTER OF THE PENTATEUCH

THE only historical sources at our disposal recording the settlement of the Israelite patriarchs in Canaan, their stay there, Israel's sojourn in Egypt, the exodus and the wanderings in the Sinai peninsula and east of the 'Arabah and the Dead Sea are the narratives in the Pentateuch. There are isolated and scattered pieces of information from sources outside the Bible—the texts from Mari, which shed new light upon the 'Amorites';[1] the Egyptian evidence as to the Hyksos;[2] the statements of writers of the Hellenistic and Roman periods concerning the connexion of Israel's sojourn in Egypt with the episode of the Hyksos, which are preserved by Josephus;[3] Akkadian and Hittite texts of the first half of the second millennium, thought to refer to military events recorded in Genesis xiv;[4] documents from Nuzi mentioning legal customs which are, or appear, similar to those presupposed in the stories of the patriarchs;[5] the mention of Ḥabiru or Ḥapiru[6] in the Amarna letters[7] and the other texts of the same period containing this and similar names. But these are so ambiguous in interpretation that they can be adduced only as supplementing the story to be obtained from the Pentateuch narratives; they should not be used as a guide in any attempt to answer the complex questions posed by the biblical account.

The Pentateuch constitutes a combination of several distinct narrative works dealing with the same general subject. These start with the Creation, in the case of L also called J¹, J also called J², and P, or with the first mention of Abraham, as does E, or with the Theophany on Mount Sinai, as does D; in the Pentateuch they are used until the death of Moses in Trans-Jordan, in the sight of

---

* An original version of sections I–VI was published as fascicle 31 in 1965.

[1] See below, pp. 312 f.   [2] See p. 312.   [3] See p. 312.
[4] See p. 313.   [5] See p. 313.   [6] See p. 314.
[7] See p. 314.

the Holy Land, but originally continued to the death of Joshua and perhaps even later. They all arose in the centuries between 1000 and 500 B.C., and manifest divers incongruities in their conceptions of the course of events. But one thing they all have in common: except when the narrative consists of folk-tales or romantic stories which dispense with considerations of time and space, and are therefore useless for historical purposes, the different forms contain correct, historically useful reminiscences of the time they claim to record, while at the same time they reflect back into the older period circumstances and ideas which cannot in reality belong to it, but date from the time at which that form of the narrative was composed.

All the narrative works, even the oldest, share the view that the entity Israel, with its twelve tribes, existed in a germinative stage from the time of Abraham onwards. Consequently, the narratives concerning the period before David always have this entity, Israel, in view. This is an anachronism, with consequences which are not historical. The entity Israel, though probably prepared by a much older national-religious team-spirit of some tribes or tribal groups[1] which later merged into 'Israel', was first created by David, and thereafter continued to exist at least as an ideal, an object of desire for which man strove. In view of this idea, 'all Israel', all those groups and individual personalities of the time before Moses who were remembered thereafter were given enlarged dimensions, quite as a matter of course. They were treated as precursors of the Israel which David created, not simply of particular parts of it. This had widespread effects, one of which was that it became necessary to place these personalities in a genealogical succession. For as each of them represented the entity of Israel, or at any rate the kernel of all Israel as it existed later, they could be thought of only as succeeding one another. In the case of the patriarchs, this results in Abraham, Isaac and Jacob appearing as grandfather, father and son. In other cases the same interpretation of older traditions, as referring to all Israel, forced on the story the arrangement of events as occurring in an itinerary; stories which, in their original form, were intimately connected with a particular district, and confined in their significance to its immediate surroundings and inhabitants, could be made to fit the entity, Israel, only by representing this same united Israel as visiting these districts in its wanderings. This is what happened in the stories about Israel's wanderings in the desert.

The conclusion, then, is that the arrangement of the stories in

[1] See below, pp. 319, 324.

the Pentateuch based on a genealogical order that appears chronological, or in the form of itineraries, has no claim to be in itself truly
historical. On the contrary, each narrative should be examined by
itself and in isolation, to see to which period or which area its
subject belongs.

II. THE TRADITIONS OF THE PATRIARCHS
AND MODERN CRITICISM

Among those who study closely the stories of the Genesis (Abraham's journey from Ur Kasdim by way of Harran to Canaan; the
attribution to him of Ishmael and Isaac as sons, to Isaac of Esau
and Jacob, and to Jacob of his twelve sons; the sale of Jacob's last
son but one, Joseph, to Egypt by his jealous brethren; the subsequent descent of Jacob and the brethren into Egypt during a
famine) there is complete unanimity on one point: these accounts
can be used for historical purposes only after critical examination.
But opinions differ widely as to what can be accepted as reliable
statements in the detail of these stories.

The first cause for disagreement lies in the question whether
the three patriarchs and the twelve sons of Jacob, or at least Joseph,
are to be considered as individuals, or as personifications of tribes,
or as groups and sections of tribes. It is clear that in Israelite
thought the personification of communities was quite common,
and it is practically certain that the twelve sons of Jacob (including
Joseph) are to be so regarded. The patriarchs might be interpreted
in the same way, and many scholars do so. Others, however, see
in the patriarchs and in Joseph real individuals belonging to the
prehistory of Israel. Still others explain the three patriarchs as
former gods of Canaanite origin, bereft of their divine aspects. In
addition to this difference, there is another question still unsettled:
to what period do the patriarchs, whatever their character may be,
belong? Did they actually exist in the time before Moses, as the
tradition affirms, or do they really belong to a later period, simply
having been transferred to an earlier date? Stade[1] and Well-
hausen,[2] for example, were inclined to the second assumption,
and thought it difficult to accept anything derived from statements
in the stories of the patriarchs as valid for the period before Moses.
R. Kittel,[3] Th. H. Robinson,[4] A. Alt,[5] W. F. Albright,[6] J. Bright,[7]
A. Parrot[8] and others consider that the patriarchs really belong to

[1] G, 26, 9f.   [2] G, 27, 11f.   [3] G, 10, 270ff.
[4] G, 20, vol. 1, 45ff.   [5] §II, 5, 45ff.
[6] G, 1, 150ff.; G, 2, 350; §II, 1; 2; 3.   [7] G, 4, 60ff.   [8] §II, 50.

the early period before Moses. Eduard Meyer,[1] G. Hölscher[2] and C. A. Simpson[3] derive them from the Canaanite pantheon (or panherôon) and thereby admit their great antiquity.

As to the question whether these figures are individuals or personifications, the individuality of Abraham is the most strongly marked of the three, so that he must be considered a historical personality, while in the cases of Isaac and Jacob it looks rather as if we have to deal with personifications of tribes or tribal groups or sections. This impression finds confirmation in the fact that 'Abraham' is never used as the name of a people, while 'Isaac' can be (Amos vii. 9, 16), and 'Jacob' constantly is (Num. xxiii. 7, 10, 21, 23; xxiv. 5, 17, 19; Exod. xix. 3, etc.). As to the period to which it may be claimed the patriarchs belong, it must be admitted that many of the statements made about Abraham, Isaac and Jacob clearly reflect conditions at the time after the settlement or under the kings of Israel. Isaac's treaty with the king of the Philistines, Abimelech of Gerar, probably belongs here. According to all we know from other sources about the appearance of the Philistines in Palestine they invaded the country only after the settlement of the Israelites,[4] and it seems artificial to suppose that before the invasion by the main body of the Philistines smaller pioneer groups of them had come into the country, enabling Isaac at the time attributed to him—about the sixteenth century B.C.— to negotiate with one of their representatives. The attribution to Abraham (Gen. xii. 16; xxiv. 10) and Jacob (Gen. xxx. 43; xxxii. 8) of camels as transport and riding animals may be looked upon as an anachronism. At the time assumed for these patriarchs, that is the first half of the second millennium B.C., there seem to have been no domesticated camels in Western Asia and Egypt.[5] But we must leave open the possibility that the camel, that is the dromedary (with one hump), was in fact already domesticated about the middle of the second millennium B.C. in Palestine. But the account of Genesis xxvii where Jacob surreptitiously obtains the blessing as the first-born, and makes his father promise that Jacob would become the master of his brothers and that Esau would serve him, almost certainly presupposes the subjection of Edom by David as told in II Samuel viii. 13–14, and in other places. It must also be admitted, in general, that often no sharp line is drawn in the narratives between the final, decisive invasion of Canaan by Israel, almost certainly in the thirteenth century, and the previous stay of individual Israelite heroes or groups in the Holy Land

[1] G, 16, 249 ff.   [2] §1, 7, 60 ff.   [3] §1, 16, 455 ff.
[4] G, 4, 73.   [5] §11, nos. 15; 39; 44; 58.

that is claimed in the tradition.[1] Episodes in the land settlement, that is, events of the later period, are attributed to the patriarchs, that is to the earlier time.

Yet it is difficult to suppose that no correct recollections of the period before Moses were current in Israel at all, and that events and persons were simply invented, either through complete self-delusion, or consciously. Some have interpreted the patriarchs as Canaanite gods or heroes adopted as their own by the Israelites and then turned into men. Improbable as this is in view of the sharp opposition to all things Canaanite which is so apparent everywhere else in the Old Testament, it is obviously due to the impression that we have to deal, in these figures, with things really ancient. Some account, then, must be taken of the probability that, before the final settlement of Israel (linked with the names of Moses and Joshua), individual Israelites like Abraham, and tribal groups like Isaac and Jacob, did live for a longer or shorter time in Canaan, especially in those districts with which the tradition brings them into close connexion.

The stories say that Abraham stayed in and around Hebron, Isaac further south at Beersheba and Beerlahairoi, Jacob partly east of Jordan, partly in the neighbourhood of Shechem and Bethel. This connexion of Abraham, Isaac, and Jacob with certain Canaanite places was first of all, according to our tradition, influenced by worship, the patriarchs worshipping the deities living in these places. Abraham gives the tithe to El 'Elyon of Jerusalem and receives the blessing of Melchizedek, high priest of this god (Gen. xiv). Also he worships El Shaddai of Hebron (Gen. xvii. 1) and El 'Olam of Beersheba (Gen. xxi. 33). Hagar, mother of Abraham's son Ishmael, is related to El Roi of Beerlahairoi (Gen. xvi. 14), and this also applies to Isaac (Gen. xxiv. 62). Jacob experiences in Bethel a revelation of El Bethel (Gen. xxviii. 10–22) and erects in Shechem a *maṣṣēḇāh* or an altar for El, god of Israel (Gen. xxxiii. 20). Everywhere we have hypostases of the Canaanite god El.[2] The ancestors of later Israel who, in pre-Mosaic times, stayed in the country of Canaan evidently joined this cult. In most cases this surely meant a renunciation of gods they had brought to Canaan, the 'gods of the fathers' (Gen. xxxv. 4; Joshua xxiv. 2, 14–15).

The various attempts to arrive at a more exact dating of the patriarchs based on chronological dates in the Old Testament itself, and facts known from sources outside the Bible which are of doubtful relevance, must be regarded with extreme caution.

[1] §II, nos. 4; 5; 6.   [1] §II, 17, 73 ff.; §II, 24; §II, 25; §II, 52.

The statements in the Old Testament are self-contradictory. According to I Kings vi. 1[1] the exodus of Israel from Egypt took place 480 years before the commencement of the building of the temple, which may have been about 970 B.C. The exodus then fell about 1450 B.C. In Exodus xii. 40,[2] the length of Israel's sojourn in Egypt is given as 430 years. Israel's movement from Palestine into Egypt would then fall about 1900 B.C., and thus the period of the patriarchs would have to be reckoned as covering the end of the third millennium and the beginning of the second. But the patriarchs are brought much nearer to the exodus from Egypt by another reckoning. Abraham, Isaac, Jacob and Joseph are thought of as four generations in direct descent, averaging about forty years each. According to Exodus i. 8, the oppression of the Israelites by a new pharaoh, which led to their migration from Egypt, began immediately after the death of the pharaoh who befriended Joseph. On this reckoning, if we date the exodus in the thirteenth century B.C., for reasons still to be given, then the time of the patriarchs would seem to be the fourteenth century.

Among the efforts to determine this period with the help of information from sources outside the Bible, the first to demand attention is the attempt to connect the patriarchs with a people attested in the first centuries of the second millennium B.C. in Mesopotamia, Northern Syria, and in other places. These people are called Amorites, Eastern Canaanites, Proto-Aramaeans, or more generally, Western Semites.[3] The personal names of these people greatly resemble the oldest names occurring in the Old Testament; and in sociological and juridical conceptions and customs as well as religion the Old Testament has much in common with this group. Efforts were therefore made to connect the patriarchs with this group and to place them in the first centuries of the second millennium B.C.; consequently the entry of the Israelites into Egypt was considered as part of the conquest of that country by the Hyksos about 1700 B.C.[4] Thus the exodus was connected with the expulsion of the Hyksos about 1570 B.C., so that the statements of certain writers of the Hellenistic and Roman periods[5] were given new currency. But even if we abstain completely from the different nominations of the 'Amorites' which make it difficult to determine them sufficiently, the traits this group and the patriarchs have in common are much too open to

---

[1] G, 24, 57 ff. [2] *Ibid.*
[3] §II, nos. 8; 19; 27; 37; 42; 43; 47; 48; 49.
[4] §II, 7; §II, 36, 15 ff.; §II, 45; §II, 53.
[5] Cf. Josephus, *Contra Apionem*, I, 26 f. = §§ 227 ff.

various interpretations to allow a clear placing of the patriarchs in it. There is a similar situation with regard to the Nuzi texts,[1] which belong to the middle of the second millennium B.C. These texts contain some ideas and customs presupposed in certain stories of the patriarchs. The Old Testament, that is Genesis, continues to be the chief source for the assignment of the patriarchs, and for determining their characters. This authority connects Abraham with the Mesopotamian Harran and tells us about connexions of Isaac and Jacob with the same place. This may be a genuine memory, though it is also possible that the account is merely expressing the theory that Mesopotamia was the native place of all Semites. Similarly, in Genesis xi. 28–31, Terah, Abraham's father, is connected with Ur-Kasdim.[2] One conjecture which must be considered valid even today is that Terah's wandering from Ur-Kasdim is not a folk-memory of an actual event but reflects the close relationship between the two cult-places of the moon god, at Ur and Harran. On the other hand it is possible that a nomadic or semi-nomadic group which may be placed among the forefathers of Israel came to Ur-Kasdim in their wanderings, and went on to Harran. The question is further complicated by the fact that the Septuagint translates Ur-Kasdim as 'Land of the Chaldeans', and it is not certain that the accepted identification of Ur-Kasdim with the South-Babylonian El-Muqayyar is in fact correct; we ought perhaps to look for Ur-Kasdim in the area around Harran.

It has proved a delusion to think that the story of the struggle of Amraphel king of Shinar, Arioch king of Ellasar, Chedorlaomer king of Elam, and Tid'al king of the 'nations' or of the land Gōyīm, against five petty kings in the region of the Dead Sea might be a basis for a fixed date for Abraham and therefore for the other patriarchs.[3] Even if it were possible to agree upon the identity of the eastern kings named, it would remain questionable whether the contemporaneity of Abraham with them has any real claim to credibility, owing to the peculiar character of the narrative in Genesis xiv in which Abraham is represented as connected with them. So we must be satisfied with the following facts: the account of Genesis xiv contains genuine folk-memories of historical events as well as of religious conditions (Melchizedek, priest of El 'Elyon[4]) but the details remain obscure.

Finally it was hoped that the Amarna letters of the fourteenth century B.C.[5] would support the historical character of certain

---

[1] §II, nos. 26; 28; 30; 31; 55.   [2] §II, 32; §II, 50, 14 ff.; §II, 54.
[3] §II, 10; §II, 11; §II, 12, 43 ff.   [4] §II, nos. 24; 25; 52.   [5] See above, pp. 98 ff.

features and figures of the biblical narratives. The *Ḥabiru*, who appear very often in these letters and in other documents from the second millennium B.C., have been compared with the *'Ibrīm* of the Old Testament;[1] and attempts have been made to identify Joseph with Iankhamu, an Egyptian ambassador to Syria and Palestine often named in the Amarna letters.[2] But these attempts have in general failed.[3]

So the patriarchs remain figures enshrouded in mists and shadows, and historical conclusions as to their character are hard to reach. No date assigned to them is indisputable. The point of importance for the tradition through which we know them was not their own careers but the future promised them for Israel in the land of Canaan.

The nature of the evidence, with its emphasis on the future of Israel rather than on personal details concerning the patriarchs, does not allow us to draw conclusions about the history of individuals, or about the period in which they lived. Nevertheless we may say that the narratives concerning them point more probably to the two centuries immediately preceding the final land settlement of Israel than to the first half, or rather the first third, of the second millennium or to yet older times. This earlier dating depends, as we have seen, on the figures given in Exodus xii. 40 and I Kings vi. 1, and these are clearly secondary.

III. THE ISRAELITE SETTLEMENTS BEFORE THE DESCENT INTO EGYPT

Conditions in the North Arabian steppe, arising from its geographical position and climate, permit its inhabitants to maintain their cattle, the basic means of existence, only in the winter during the rainy season. In summer, when the sparse vegetation of the desert dies off, the inhabitants are compelled to move into the neighbouring lands surrounding the desert on the east, north or west. The result has been that Palestine, from the most ancient periods down to the present, has had to accept the presence of tribes from the desert in search of pasture. Nowadays it is generally the nomadic tribes which go there with their herds of camels in summer, and these have their own pasture-areas and watering-places exactly defined. At the end of the second millennium, when the camel was still not used in these parts, there were

---

[1] §II, nos. 13; 14; 33; 35; 40; 41.
[2] G, 10, 303; G, 21, 162ff., 167, 173, 188f., 191f.
[3] But see below, p. 317, nn. 1, 2.

semi-nomads with their asses, sheep and goats who did the same thing.[1] There are several indications that the patriarchs' sojourn in Canaan was due to the same factor in the mode of living, though it is concealed in the narratives by the religious conception, arising from theology, that Abraham went to Canaan by God's direct command, and that he, Isaac, and Jacob stayed there for a considerable time as recipients of the promise given to Israel for its future in Palestine.

Certain features of the narratives disclose this factor of social economy. There is the dispute between the shepherds of Abraham and Lot as to the pasture and watering-places they were entitled to (Gen. xiii), or that between the shepherds of Abimelech and those of Abraham or Isaac as to the wells belonging to them (Gen. xxi. 22–33 and xxvi. 12–33). It will be shown in detail that actually this necessity for change of pasture plays a considerable part in the entry of Israelite groups into Egypt too, and also in the final land settlement, though the latter now appears in the narratives as a military enterprise of the entity Israel under a unified command. This means that the three periods, the time of the patriarchs, the sojourn in Egypt, and the final land settlement, though they seem separated from one another by clear intervals, belong together as phenomena arising from a single cause. Individual events divided between the three periods are to be treated as constituent parts of a coherent, much larger movement. These events were no doubt spread over a considerable period of time, and their sequence is probably, at any rate speaking generally of the whole story, correctly maintained by the tradition. Nevertheless they must all be much more closely related than the conception to which the extant narratives have been accommodated makes apparent. The stay of the patriarchs in Canaan and the later conquest of the land by an Israel which, according to the tradition, consisted of twelve tribes, are plainly distinguished. In the first case the patriarchs were clearly guests, and no direct consequences were entailed, while in the second the invasion led to permanent supremacy over Canaan. There is this further distinction that, in the case of the patriarchs, disputes with the Canaanites led to fighting only in exceptional cases, whereas the invasion had to be carried through to a large extent by force of arms. That the interval between the two is not so clear-cut can be shown by two or three examples.

The account of Reuben's conduct with his father's concubine Bilhah (Gen. xxxv. 21–2a) at first probably preceded the story

[1] See below, pp. 319, 320.

about Simeon's and Levi's treacherous and violent assault on Shechem[1] the son of Hamor (Gen. xxxiv). It is in all probability one of local origin, connected with a place, perhaps east of Jordan, called Migdal-Edar, while the story about Simeon's and Levi's misdeed is connected with the neighbourhood of Shechem. It is quite conceivable that these stories, like that of the shameless behaviour of 'Ham the father of Canaan', or—since 'Ham the father of' is a later addition to the original story—of Canaan himself to his father, Noah (Gen. ix. 20–7), are to be explained as literary inventions, poetic symbolizations, to account for the fall of those tribes from their former importance into weakness and dissolution as due to misdeeds of the three eponymous ancestors of the tribes. But if that is not so, we probably ought to consider the Genesis stories of Reuben, and of Simeon and Levi, as preceding by a considerable period the land settlement linked with the names of Moses and Joshua. The position in Genesis xxxviii is much the same. The point of the story is to explain the origin of two sections of the tribe of Judah,[2] which was obviously thought of as already settled finally in the area it occupied later.

It may be that the division of the twelve sons of Jacob between two recognized wives and two concubines or slaves[3] is simply poetic invention serving to enliven the narrative. The assumption that the division reflects, at any rate to some extent, the historical facts, is not necessarily correct. If it is, the facts reflected in the stories of Reuben, Simeon, Levi, Judah, Zebulun and Issachar, would concern the common fortunes of these six tribes, that is, presumably, their joint entry into Canaan from the south, from the Sinai peninsula, at a time earlier than the final conquest. In that case the attribution of Reuben, Simeon, Levi and Judah, with Zebulun and Issachar, to the same mother, Leah, would lead to the inference that these tribes were in Palestine for a fairly long time before the final land settlement of Israel. The statements in Numbers xiv. 39–45; xxi. 1–3; Joshua xiv. 6–15; xv. 13–19; Judges i. 1–21, should be considered in this connexion. In their present context these passages form a part of the narrative of the enterprise of the entity Israel, under the command of Moses and Joshua, with the object of gaining possession of Canaan. But in themselves they, or some of them, may refer to the individual fortunes of Simeon, Judah and other groups; that is to their entry into Palestine from the south, from the neighbourhood of Qadesh. But in their present form these narratives link the entry of these six tribes closely in time with the final land settlement.

[1] §III, 4; §III, 7. [2] §III, 9; §III, 10. [3] G, 25, 71 ff.; §III, 5.

However, this dating of the events was a necessary consequence of the inclusion of the separate enterprises of these tribes and groups in the general, united attack of the entity Israel under a unified command, the conception embodied in the form of the tradition extant. The impression arising from the narratives in Genesis is to be preferred; the fortunes of the Leah tribes as told in those narratives should be regarded as considerably earlier than the events which, as will be seen in what follows, finally secured Israel's possession of Palestine. But many details, of course, remain hazy and uncertain. It is no longer possible to decide when and how the tribe of Reuben arrived in its habitations east of Jordan where the tribe is found later; the first mention of it there is almost certainly in the song of Deborah, that is about the middle of the twelfth century. We may proceed to assume, recognizing that it is only an assumption, that Simeon and Levi, after incurring heavy losses in the struggle with the city state Shechem, of which Genesis xxxiv and xlix. 5–7 give some hint, returned to the places in the south from which they started, Simeon to the Negeb and Levi still farther south to the neighbourhood of Qadesh. It would appear, however, that Zebulun and Issachar, the Leah tribes which pushed farthest north, to southern Galilee, were able to maintain themselves there for good. It is possible also to derive from the story of Issachar a date, which will serve as a hypothesis, for the occupation of settlements in Palestine by the Leah tribes, which preceded the final land-settlement of Israel. In the first half of the fourteenth century a certain Labaya destroyed the city-state Shunama,[1] the Shunem of Joshua xix. 18; I Samuel xxviii. 4; II Kings iv. 8. It has been shown[2] that there is reason to connect with this event the settlement of the tribe Issachar in the plain of Jezreel, at the sacrifice of its political independence, and therefore to date Issachar's settlement shortly after Labaya's conquest.

This is all that can be said with any degree of probability about the abode of Israelite tribes in Canaan at a time before the descent into, and sojourn in, Egypt. It must therefore remain an unsolved problem, whether the name 'Israel' was (as Gen. xxxii. 29; xxxiii. 20; xxxv. 10, make probable) already applied at that time to these groups or to some particular part of them or whether this first arose as an appellation of their descendants, either in the period between the exodus and the final land settlement, or in the period after that settlement, when the twelve tribes founded an amphictyonic community whose centre, as many think, was

[1] EA 250, 43 ff. See above, pp. 100 f., 114 ff.   [2] §III, 1.

Shechem.[1] There is the story about the change of Jacob's name to Israel, which occurred at Penuel or Bethel (Gen. xxxii. 29; xxxv. 10), and another story that he gave the name 'El, god of Israel' to an altar erected at Shechem (or rather a sacred stone, *maṣṣēbāh*, as the text, Gen. xxxiii. 20, is perhaps to be corrected). These stories suggest as probable inferences that the name Israel was a local one in Canaan and indigenous there, and was only transferred to the newcomers secondarily. But there can be no certainty about this, for it is also possible that (as Gen. xxxii. 29; xxxiii. 20, seem to show) the name Israel was accepted by the Jacob group in connexion with the acceptance of the worship of El. Unfortunately, even the supposed earliest mention of the name Israel in the triumphal hymn of Merneptah composed about 1230 B.C. does not provide any unambiguous answer to this question.

The Egyptian sojourn was followed by the completion of the conquest, and the land settlement. This conquest, in the revised form that is the tradition, was presented as an enterprise of the entity 'all Israel', consisting of twelve tribes. We shall see that the house of Joseph led this undertaking, and that it included perhaps other tribes as well as those descended from Leah, or at any rate parts of other tribes. It is certain that Manasseh and Ephraim originated through splitting off from the house of Joseph. This is very probably true of Benjamin,[2] though some scholars would trace a connexion between the biblical tribe of Benjamin and the Mesopotamian Benē-Iamina as testified in the Mari texts for the eighteenth century B.C.[3] They suppose that a sub-group of these Benē-Iamina, called Iarikhu, wandered to Canaan, settled in the area of the later tribe of Benjamin, and changed the older name— which we do not know—of its most important town into Jericho, after their own name. As for Dan and Naphtali it is also probable or at least possible that they separated from the 'House of Joseph'. At any rate the tradition which calls their eponymous ancestors sons of Bilhah, slave of Rachel, mother of Joseph, could be understood in this way. On the other hand, as the ancestors of Gad and Asher were regarded as sons of Leah's slave Zilpah, it is at least a matter for consideration whether these tribes did not force their way into Palestine from the south, together with the Leah tribes, and so were already settled there before the advance of the house of Joseph. However, conclusions about the period and manner

---

[1] G, 25, 10ff.; §III, 8.
[2] §III, 3.
[3] §III, 2; 6; 11. [The 'Benē-Iamina' have now disappeared from the Mari Texts: see *C.A.H.* II[3], pt. 1, p. 25, no. 1. (Ed.)]

of the settlement of these tribes should not be based with much confidence on the attribution of Gad and Asher to one mother, the slave of Leah, and of Dan and Naphtali to another, the slave of Rachel, for this reason. In later times Dan and Naphtali were neighbours, owing to the migration of the tribe Dan to the north.[1] It may be that this later position is the real cause of the ancestors of these two tribes being classed together. At the time of the song of Deborah and thereafter Gad and Asher were not connected by their geographical situation at all. Their abodes were pretty well at the extreme opposite ends of the Israelite settlements, one in the north-west, the other in the south-east. The story of the birth of the sons of Jacob may conceivably have assigned one and the same mother to the eponymous ancestors of these two tribes because their names suggested a similar interpretation, something like 'Good luck'.[2]

The conception that governs the tradition as we have it is that before the sojourn in Egypt, and before the final land settlement of Israel which followed it, the twelve tribes, or at any rate their eponymous ancestors, had already been in Palestine. This cannot, in any circumstances, be correct, but must be revised in the sense that only some of these tribes had forced their way into Palestine from the south in the course of seeking new pastures. Most of the tribes that did so were those which played no conspicuous part later, and some of them maintained themselves in Palestine only for a time that varied in length for each, while others stayed for good. It is unfortunately no longer possible to judge whether tribes already worshipped Yahweh, and if so, in what sense he was their God. It would seem that his cult was not unknown to them, a point still to be discussed,[3] but it also seems clear that Yahweh did not occupy the exceptional position he held later. So far as we can discern the truth, the worship of Yahweh by the tribes already settled in Palestine was first kindled into flame by the advance of the house of Joseph into the land, undertaken as the result, and proof, of the worship of this god.

IV. THE NATURE OF THE DESCENT INTO EGYPT

The tradition represents the entry of Jacob and his sons with their families into Egypt from Canaan as resulting from a famine arising in Canaan. Thus the impression is created that this was an

[1] See below, p. 547 and Map 11 (p. 542).
[2] See *J. Bibl. Lit.* 82 (1963), 195 ff.　　　[3] See below, p. 324.

isolated event of a special kind. But there is no lack of indications that immigrations of individuals and of groups from the eastern lands neighbouring on the Nile valley owing to this cause were fairly frequent. Abraham and Isaac are said to have journeyed to Egypt with their wives Sara and Rebecca because a famine made it necessary to do so (Gen. xii. 10; xxvi. 1). A report of Egyptian boundary officers, belonging to the end of the thirteenth century B.C., mentions the fact that bedawin or half-settled nomads had been allowed to cross the border and proceed to the marshes round the city of Pithom, to save their own lives and their herds.[1] This should tend to show that the entry of Israelites into Egypt is to be understood as due to a change of pasture, just like the advance of Israelite tribes from the Sinai peninsula into southern, and then into central and northern Palestine which has been discussed. It is not necessary to assume that there was a clear-cut interval between the first and the second movement. It is possible that the sequence of the two movements claimed in the tradition should be rejected in favour of the view that both were contemporary. While one part of the Israelite tribes which pitched their tents in the Sinai peninsula looked for a change of pasture in Palestine and remained there, another section preferred to take its herds to Egypt during the summer drought, and settled there for a time.

The reason for differing from the traditional view is that the arrangement of the two processes, the movement into Egypt and then into Palestine, is due to the conception that the entity 'all Israel' played a part in both. That this conception is erroneous can be shown by the general considerations already stated. This is confirmed by an analysis of the sagas relating to the entry into Egypt and to the exodus. In these, the importance of the part played by Joseph, the eponymous hero of the tribe, and of the house of Joseph, is so clearly emphasized that a historical interpretation of this characteristic feature of the story is forced on us. Thus there is much reason to believe that it was, in fact, the tribe of Joseph, or perhaps only a part of it, which emigrated to Egypt.

A question that arises is whether we must take account of a stay of individual members of the tribe of Levi in Egypt. According to the tradition it was in fact Moses,[2] born in Egypt of parents belonging to the tribe of Levi,[3] who at the command of Yahweh encouraged Israel to break out of bondage in Egypt and then successfully executed that enterprise. It is conceivable that

---

[1] G, 22, 259; on Pithom see below, pp. 321 f.
[2] §v, nos. 2; 6; 13.   [3] §v, 9.

the tradition misrepresents the historical facts. It may be that a member of the tribe of Levi, which was settled or had pitched its tents in and around Qadesh, has been wrongly represented as being in Egypt, so that the decisive part in freeing the Israelites from the bondage there could be attributed to him. The purpose of the narrative would be to assign the same importance to the tribe of Levi in earlier times that it unquestionably had for the group which made its way out of Egypt later. But there are really no decisive reasons against believing the tradition that the Levite Moses inspired the movement out of Egypt by his preaching, which invoked a direct order of God, Yahweh. The feature in the tradition which may be unhistorical is that Moses proposed the Holy Land, Palestine, as the goal for the march. In all probability a much nearer and more modest objective would have been sought, at least as a provisional goal, namely reunion with the related tribes staying in and around Qadesh. Perhaps there was also the idea of a pilgrimage to Mount Sinai, the principal abode of the God, Yahweh, who sanctioned or ordered the exodus.

V. THE HISTORICAL EVIDENCE FOR THE EXODUS

There is no evidence outside the Old Testament for the sojourn of Israel in Egypt or for the exodus. But the statements therein that have to be considered are, in spite of their character as sagas, sufficient warrant for treating what is told as referring to actual events. It is quite inconceivable that a people could have obstinately preserved traditions about a dishonourable bondage of its ancestors in a foreign land, and passed them on from generation to generation, unless it had actually passed through such an experience. Moreover the narratives of the forced labour imposed on the Israelites in Egypt contain features which not only indicate that the Egyptian settlement is historical, but actually correspond quite well with the circumstances prevailing in Egypt at the time to which the Egyptian bondage is to be dated, i.e. the end of the fourteenth and beginning of the thirteenth century B.C. The tradition relates that, after the Israelites had spent a few decades in Egypt, they were compelled by the new pharaoh to do forced labour on the building of the cities Pithom and Ramses which he had ordered. The implication that there was some specially energetic activity in building leads to the assumption that the pharaoh who displayed it was Ramesses II (1304–1237 B.C.), pre-eminent among the rulers of Egypt for his building activities. The mention of the cities Pithom and Ramses makes the conclusion a practical certainty. It is known that Ramesses II undertook very considerable renovations and alterations in building at Pithom, the modern Tell er-Ratāba in the Wādi Tummilāt, and in Ramses, Pi Ramessu, which is the modern Sān el-Hagar on the Tanitic arm of the Nile[1] or perhaps Qantīr[2] fifteen miles to the south. This was soon after his accession, at the beginning of the thirteenth century. If the inclusion of the Israelites among those compelled to do forced labour is to be assigned to the decade 1300–1290 B.C., or thereabouts, then their entry into Egypt must be dated to about the end of the fourteenth century. The exodus will then fall in the second half of the thirteenth century, for the tradition gives the impression that both phases of the Egyptian episode (first the favourable reception by the pharaoh then ruling, and afterwards the forced labour on new building imposed by his successor) lasted only a few decades. General considerations make it possible that this was in fact the course of events.

The tradition of the sojourn of Israelites in Egypt can be corroborated by an argument from the history of their religion. The Israelites, when reflecting on the earliest stages of their worship of God, maintained so firmly that it was connected with a miraculous act by which God saved his people, an act experienced by their ancestors in Egypt, that one is forced to regard their tradition as deserving belief. For this reason it is likely to be true that the Israelites enslaved in Egypt came to choose Yahweh as their God through the agency of Moses. They probably did not know of him, or hardly knew of him, before, though the Midianites and Kenites and some tribes quite closely related to the Israelites sojourning in Egypt had long done so. It was in confident reliance on this God that they ventured the march out of Egypt. When, in doing so, they were saved from a dangerous situation, they could only explain their salvation as due to direct intervention by their God. For that reason they retained the grateful memory of that experience as an indisputable proof of their election to be his people by this God whom they had recently chosen to worship.

The exact course of this historical event, the exodus and the miraculous act of Yahweh, can unfortunately no longer be discerned. In particular, the question of where Yahweh's intervention took place will probably never be answered with certainty.[3] The statements which have to be considered in determining the

---

[1] G, 14, 58; §vi, 2, 15. [2] §v, 3; §v, 8.
[3] §v, nos. 1; 5; 10.

scene of the event are ambiguous, including the description 'at the sea of reeds' or 'at the sea'. It remains doubtful whether the northern end of the Gulf of Suez, or one of the salt lakes, or the Gulf of 'Aqaba, or the Serbonian Sea is meant. The doubt is the greater because the Old Testament tradition is self-contradictory on this point, and seems to have admitted at least two of these possibilities, namely the salt lakes or the Serbonian Sea. But this uncertainty does not in the least affect the credibility of the tradition in the main, namely that Israelites in flight were saved from destruction on the Egyptian border, and that they attributed this to Yahweh's aid. The position is rather that the tradition on these points is so firmly established that it makes a historical core to the sagas a practical certainty.

As to the nature and size of the group which was in Egypt and took part in the exodus from that land, it has already been said that except for individual members of the house of Levi (including Moses) it consisted probably only of the 'house' of Joseph, and perhaps merely a part of it. An indication of the date of the miracle of the parting of the waters has already been mentioned; it points to the event having taken place in the second third of the thirteenth century B.C.[1]

VI. THE WANDERINGS

In the narratives of Israel's wanderings in the period between the exodus from Egypt (Exod. xiii) and the death of Moses in sight of the Holy Land (Deut. xxxiv), large sections dealing with laws of later origin have been inserted. Even apart from these, the narratives belong to several different types. There are aetiological sagas and legends intended to explain why certain geographical areas have a peculiar nature, and why places received certain names, or to account for the origin of customs and institutions and religious practices. These are, as such, not of one single period, but of many. Other stories, though they take the form of legends or sagas, clearly retain memories of the period we are here considering, on which reliance can be placed. The latter class, as is immediately evident on closer examination, centres about three geographical points, Qadesh,[2] the modern 'Ain Qadais or 'Ain el-Qudairat, between six and seven miles north-west of 'Ain Qadais, in the Sinai peninsula; Sinai itself,[3] the position of which will have to be discussed; and Trans-Jordan.[4] These groups of narratives

---

[1] §v, nos. 8; 11; 12.   [2] See below, pp. 325f.
[3] See below, pp. 324f.   [4] See below, p. 329.

must be examined to see what their historical content is. For this purpose, no value must be accorded to the position which the stories now have in the account of an itinerary. It is essential to bear in mind that the position in the itinerary must have been a consequence of the conception in which the narratives are enwrapped, since the narratives refer to the entity 'all Israel'.

The Sinai and Qadesh narratives are dovetailed into one another in various ways. The material that relates to Sinai exceeds that connected with Qadesh by a good deal. But on close examination the historically useful results of the Sinai narratives in Exodus xix–Numbers x are reduced to a very small content. The principal portions of the material contained in these chapters are demonstrably laws which are for the most part, at any rate as they stand now, of late date. They originated in the periods just before, during, and just after the Exile, and have, of themselves, nothing to do with Sinai.

That leaves only the account of a march of Israel to the mountain of God, of which the central point is the experience of Yahweh's epiphany, the confirmation of his bond with Israel, and the promise of the land Canaan.[1] What Israelites took part in this march to Sinai cannot be said. If it was only the tribe of Joseph, or merely a part of that tribe, which had ventured to leave Egypt because it trusted the God it had hardly known before, and had formed the belief that it had been saved during the flight by Yahweh's aid, then it is permissible to assume that the horde rescued by a miracle went immediately to the pre-eminent abode and oracle of this God, to Sinai. They wished to manifest the worship and gratitude felt for him, and to assure themselves of his protection and assistance for ever. But there is another conceivable explanation. The worship of Yahweh had long flourished among the Midianites and other tribes, including some like the Levites with whom the people leaving Egypt recognized a close relationship. These worshippers of Yahweh had almost certainly striven to maintain the connexion with the principal abode of their God, Sinai, by regular pilgrimage to it. It would be possible to explain the Sinai narratives as arising from a recollection of this kind of pilgrimage.

The position of Sinai or Horeb,[2] as the mountain of God is called in some narratives, is still disputed. There is a tradition of the Church which can be proved to go back to the fourth century A.D., and is certainly at least two centuries older than that.[3] Ac-

---

[1] G, 24, 79 ff.; §vi, nos. 5; 7; 8; 19. [2] §vi, nos. 1; 2; 14; 22.
[3] §vi, 11; §vi, 22.

cording to this Sinai is one of the mountains in the southern part of the Sinai peninsula, which rise to a height of 7500 feet or more; the heights mentioned in identifications are Jebel Sirbal, Jebel Mūsa, Jebel Qaterin, and others. Some modern discussions start from the incorrect assumption that the narratives render it necessary to locate Sinai near Qadesh, and would accordingly identify it with one of the mountains in the neighbourhood of Qadesh,[1] say Jebel 'Ara'if. The accounts of Yahweh's epiphany on Sinai make probable a natural explanation of the phenomenon, a volcanic eruption. The scanty notices of the position of this mountain available in the Old Testament seem to locate it in the Midianite area, and the Midianites had their tribal settlements east of the Gulf of 'Aqaba and, generally speaking, east of the northern end of the Red Sea.[2] At the time with which we are dealing, the middle of the thirteenth century B.C., volcanic eruptions did still occur there. Sinai ought then to be this district. We may therefore believe that the pilgrimage of those who fled from Egypt had as its objective a volcano on the eastern side of the Gulf of 'Aqaba, or at the northern end of the Red Sea.

It seems that when Israel settled in Canaan, it kept up at first the connexion with this mountain of God. A phrase in the song of Deborah (Judges v. 4–5) shows that about the middle of the twelfth century B.C. Yahweh was still thought of as enthroned there, and hastening from there to aid his people, as they were still fighting in Canaan. An incident in the story of Elijah (I Kings xix. 8–18) proves that, if God was really to be approached in close communion, a pilgrimage to Horeb must still be undertaken even in Elijah's time, about the middle of the ninth century B.C. But the more firmly Israel, and therefore not only Israel, but Israel's God Yahweh, was associated exclusively with the land of Canaan, and the places of worship there, the more vague became the association with Sinai. The pilgrimages thither ceased, and all knowledge of the position of the mountain was lost. The identification of Sinai with one of the mountain peaks on the Sinai peninsula (which is thus incorrectly so named) was first made a thousand years later and has remained so till the present day.

While the historical content of the Sinai stories amounts to no more than a pilgrimage of Israel to the outstanding abode of Israel's God, Sinai, much more results from the Qadesh narratives. These include, besides Numbers xi. 1–xx. 21, the sagas connected with other localities in the text as we have it, Exodus xv. 22–xviii. 27. The neighbourhood of Qadesh is well-watered, for it includes not

[1] G, 10, 346 ff.   [2] §vi, nos. 22; 26; 27; 28.

only the water at 'Ain Qadais, which lies about ninety miles or so south of Jerusalem, but also the neighbouring water-sources at 'Ain el-Qudairat and 'Ain Qusaimah.[1] The impression given by the narratives is that the horde which left Egypt conquered the owners of this land, the Amalekites (Exod. xvii. 8–13), took their place, stayed in that neighbourhood a fairly long time, and came into touch there with related tribes which had previously pitched their tents there. The most important of these was that of the Levites, to which Moses belonged. This impression seems to be correct, for it is specifically stated in Deuteronomy i. 46—admittedly contradicting ii. 14—that the Israelites camped at Qadesh 'many days'. The hypothesis is clearly justified by the importance of this period in the formation of the religious, moral and legal standards accepted in Israel, and the part played in that process by Moses and his tribal brethren, the Levites, whose special duty was the maintenance of the cult of Yahweh.

The formation of such standards of conduct must have been in the first place, and principally, to the advantage of the horde which left Egypt and regarded Qadesh as the next objective of their flight.[2] But it is hardly possible to suppose that all the stories relating to Qadesh affect only the tribe of Joseph, the people who came thither from Egypt. Even apart from the Levites, there were still other related tribes settled in that neighbourhood who had to do with the holy place of Yahweh at Qadesh. Among these must be reckoned, at any rate partially, those tribes which, as previously explained, had advanced into southern, central and even northern Palestine in search of change of pasture from the Sinai peninsula, and had remained in the new area for a considerable time or even permanently, without breaking the link with Qadesh and the fractions of their groups which stayed there. The tribes dwelling round Qadesh and those which had emigrated thence retained a bond of union with the holy place there, though we have not the means to determine the nature and strength of that bond.[3]

The subsequent course of Israelite history presupposes the existence of a feeling that these and other tribes belonged together. This is exemplified in the combination of several tribes when Israel was threatened by Jabin of Hazor and Sisera of Harosheth ha-Gōyīm, the subject of the narrative (Judges iv) and of the song of Deborah (Judges v).[4] Even the tribes which failed to join the combination should have done so, according to the conception of the song, and are sharply reproached for their failure. It is not

---

[1] §VI, 1, 295 f.; §VI, 22; §VI, 30. [2] Cf. pp. 17, 25.
[3] G, 25, 10 ff. [4] See below, ch. XXXIV, sect. v.

enough to suppose that the tribe of Joseph, the last to force its way into Palestine, imposed its enthusiastic, but quite recent—and so the more zealous—acceptance of the worship of Yahweh on tribes long settled in Palestine, and thus laid the foundation for the development of Israelite national sentiment, conditioned as it were by religion. The basis for this feeling of unity must have existed at a much earlier period than the political union.[1] The twelve tribes which constituted the later Israelite state recognized that they were related to other tribes like Cain and Jerachmeel, and that they were united with them by a common bond of worship. But Cain and Jerachmeel did not become members of the Israelite state, and parts of them were never settled in Palestine.

The feeling of national unity among the Israelite tribes, based on religion, which made it possible for them to combine first into a coalition, and then into a state, can thus be said to have its original basis in the common relations of the tribes with the holy place at Qadesh and its God, Yahweh, and with his mountain Sinai or Horeb. The proper place for the epiphany of the God worshipped at Qadesh was on Sinai, and pilgrimages thither constituted a substantial part in the cult. To that extent interconnexion of the tribes which had dwelt in and around Qadesh with Sinai can be regarded as the source of the feeling for unity. Perhaps it can even be described as a union of comrades bound by an oath of fidelity to Sinai. But a reservation must be made, for Sinai and its God were holy not merely to those tribes which came to form the entity Israel because of their relations with Qadesh, but also to other tribes. These were the Midianites, who never joined the political unity and at any rate in later periods were actually reckoned as Israel's enemies, and perhaps also the Amalekites who were—as we have seen[2]—expelled from the area of Qadesh by the Israelites. It will therefore be better to abandon the description of the Israelite tribes as a union of comrades bound by an oath of fidelity to Sinai, and to be satisfied with the conclusion that the sense of national unity based on religion was deeply rooted in the connexions of the Israelite tribes with Qadesh and Sinai.

Among the sagas connected with Qadesh is the story in Numbers xiii–xiv of the despatch of agents to Palestine to collect information. Their discouraging report caused the Israelites' refusal to risk a dangerous undertaking, the invasion of the land; they were for that reason condemned to wander for forty years in the wilderness. The result was the advance northwards, undertaken in opposition to Yahweh's command, leading to their dispersal as far north as

[1] G, 25, 10ff.; G, 27, 23.   [2] See above, pp. 325f.

Hormah (Numbers xiv. 40–5). In Numbers xxi. 1–3, there is an account of a victory of Israel over the Canaanites at Hormah. The idea underlying the narratives, that there were enterprises undertaken by the entity 'all Israel', under a single command, is in any case unhistorical; but it would seem that there is reflected in them a memory of actual events about a century or two earlier than the advance of the 'house' of Joseph and the final land settlement by Israel. This hypothesis is supported by the part played in the story, Numbers xiii–xiv, by Caleb the Kenizzite.[1] There are several indications that the Kenizzites, to whom the tribe or clan Caleb belonged (Joshua xiv. 6–15; xv. 15–19; Judges i. 12–15), may have found their way into Palestine with the Leah tribes. There are however arguments that can be urged against so early a date for the narratives of Numbers xiv. 40–5; xxi. 1–3. Judges i. 17, reports that Judah and Simeon, marching southward from the permanent camp at Gilgal, used in common by the Israelites, 'slew the Canaanites who inhabited Zephat and utterly destroyed it; and the city was renamed Hormah'. As we see, the defeat of the Canaanites near Hormah is linked here with the *Landnahme* of the Israelites under the leadership of Joshua. But it is possible that the place of Hormah in Numbers xiv. 40–5; xxi. 1–3 may not be identified with that of Judges i. 17, but is to be sought further in the south, so that the event reported in Numbers xiv. 40–5; xxi. 1–3, and that of Judges i. 17 belong to different times: the event of Numbers xiv. 40–5; xxi. 1–3, to the fourteenth, and that of Judges i. 17 to the thirteenth century B.C.

It remains possible, then, to see in the narratives of the defeat or the victory at Hormah in Numbers xiv. 40–5; xxi. 1–3, a reminiscence of the entry of the Leah tribes into Palestine. On the other hand, the idea that the 'house' of Joseph actually made an effort to force its way from the south before deciding on the advance into Palestine from the east should not be summarily rejected. The allusion to the ark of the covenant,[2] which was in the possession of the Joseph tribe, in Numbers xiv. 44, is perhaps an argument for this thesis. The distinction between the advance of the tribe of Joseph and that of the tribes settled in Palestine before Joseph seems to be that the tribe of Joseph used force, or was at least prepared to use force, from the start, while the Leah tribes reached their areas in the course of a peaceful process, the search for a change of pasture. It was an exception for the Leah tribes to be involved in disputes leading to war, as happened in the case of Simeon and Levi (Gen. xxxiv).

[1] §vi, 10.   [2] G, 25, 56 ff.; §vi, nos. 4; 6; 13; 18; 20.

If the 'house' of Joseph did, in accordance with this hypothesis, advance into Palestine at first from the south, then the attempt in any event failed. In the case of this group, that did not at all mean giving up the objective aimed at; another way soon seemed to be opened up for them, namely the way through Trans-Jordan. The statements about the march of the Israelites from Qadesh to Shittim, which lay east of Jordan opposite Jericho (Num. xx. 22–xxv. I and xxxiii. 36–49) have little claim to credibility in detail, and the narratives dealing with the fortunes and deeds of Israel in Trans-Jordan in Numbers xxi. 10–xxxii. 42, are, in type, sagas.[1] Yet there is a good deal to be said for believing that an Israelite horde, the tribe of Joseph, started forcing its way into Palestine from the east, across Jordan, and made its way thither through Trans-Jordan.[2]

It may be that some information reached Qadesh that one of the political units existing in Trans-Jordan was so weak that it would fall before an attack, and thus gave the first impulse to this undertaking. In Judges xvii–xviii something of the sort happened when Laish-Dan fell into the hands of the tribe Dan after such a report. Neither Edom nor Moab can have been the weak element. Archaeological investigations and isolated Egyptian reports are sufficient to prove that both were strongly organized, flourishing states in the thirteenth century B.C.[3] The tradition (Num. xx. 14–21; xxi. 4; Deut. ii; Judges xi. 17–18) implies that Israel treated these states with respect and raised no claims of any kind to their territory; much less, then, did Israel make any move to attack them. But the tradition was able to record Israel's victorious struggle against the Amorite king Sihon of Heshbon and his territory north of Moab, between the Arnon and the Jabbok, against the city state of Jaazer (Khirbet Jazzir) about twenty miles north of Heshbon, and against Og of Bashan, whose kingdom stretched from the Jabbok far to the north-east; and the tradition added that Moses divided these territories between Reuben, Gad and half Manasseh (Num. xxi. 21–35; xxxii; Deut. ii. 26–iii. 22; Joshua xiii. 8–33).

Now there can be no possible doubt that the true explanations of these stories is that, to a great extent, they reflect later events and conditions back into an earlier period. The settlement of Israelites east of Jordan for the most part at least followed the settlement in the west and did not precede it. Thus sections of the tribe Manasseh went into Trans-Jordan from their abodes in the parts west of Jordan (Joshua xvii. 14–15). Further, the twilight

[1] §vi, 24.   [2] §vi, nos. 3; 9; 12; 16; 17; 25.
[3] G, 4, 109f.

of myth plays round the figure of Og, as is shown by the remark in Deuteronomy ii. 11: the king belonged to the Rephaim, and his coffin, of superhuman proportions, was kept in the Canaanite city Rabbath. No historical affirmation can be made about such a figure. The case of the Amorite Sihon of Heshbon is different. Serious arguments have been advanced in an attempt to show[1] that the narrative about him in Numbers xxi. 21–30, is in reality an account of a victory over a king of Moab called Sihon won by Israel in the ninth century B.C. The poem attached to the narrative Numbers xxi. 27–30 (the text of which is unfortunately greatly damaged and therefore often interpreted differently) refers in fact, by its nature, to a later Israelite invasion of territory possessed, at the time the poem was written, by Moab, but in the earlier period ruled by the Amorite king Sihon. But it does not follow at all that the narrative itself cannot have preserved a reliable recollection of an event belonging to the time of the land settlement by Israel. On the contrary it is quite possible that a city state surviving from the earlier time, corresponding with the city-states of the pre-Israelite period west of Jordan, maintained itself among the national states that arose during the thirteenth century in the 'Arabah, east of it, and in parts east of Jordan, that is side by side with Edom, Moab and Ammon. The emphatic way in which Sihon is called a king of the Amorites favours this view. Such a state might not be strong enough to resist the attack of the Israelite horde in its fresh enthusiasm.

The victory over Sihon of Heshbon, and therewith the creation of a corridor that made it possible to march from the desert of Trans-Jordan through to the Jordan can, then, be attributed to the horde which left Qadesh, the tribe of Joseph. But another possibility must be reckoned with. The tradition may have attributed a success won by one of the tribes settled in the neighbourhood of Heshbon, that is by Reuben or Gad, either earlier or later than the land settlement, to the advance of the tribe Joseph through Trans-Jordan towards its goal, the land west of Jordan. This would be a use of the narrative meant to lend credibility and colour to the account of Joseph's advance, and would therefore be unhistorical. Even so, this advance of the 'house' of Joseph would still retain its historical credibility for the decisive reason that it is the necessary presupposition for the crossing of the Jordan by this group. That crossing was part of a process that will have to considered at length later.

---

[1] G, 16, 530.

(b) ARCHAEOLOGICAL EVIDENCE

VII. PROBLEMS: THE NATURE OF
THE EVIDENCE

IN this part of this chapter an attempt is made to answer the question: what is the archaeological contribution towards an elucidation surrounding the origins of the Israelite tribes in Palestine?

The nineteenth Egyptian dynasty covers a period of time which in Palestine may be equated with the Dark Ages following the collapse of the Mycenaean world in Greece. The period 1320–1200 B.C. involves some of the most thorny and complicated problems in the whole of Palestinian history, comprising as it does the date and nature of the Hebrew conquest and settlement; the cultural interrelationship of Canaanite and Hebrew tribes and their place in the Near East as a whole: the historicity of such Old Testament heroes as Joshua and Baraq; the sifting of historical events from folk tales, religious propaganda and certain editorial practices.

Owing to the peculiar position which Palestine holds in respect to three world religions, the reason for and the evolution of excavations in her soil have been somewhat different from those in other parts of the world. The impetus to dig for history in classical lands was stimulated by a combination of romanticism and a familiarity with the literature, philosophy and art of the Greeks and Romans which was shared by all educated people of the Western world. Something of the same romanticism, added to the excitement of discovering that the history of the world was far older than had been supposed, spurred on excavation in Mesopotamia. The discovery of the Assyrian cities and Babylon in turn gave the first firm link with the world of the Old Testament. However, almost from the start, excavations in Palestine took on a slightly different hue from those being made in neighbouring countries. The driving force behind excavations in Palestine may, in the main, have been a desire to write history where none was written, but often subconsciously, and on occasion quite outspokenly, the *raison d'être* of these excavations was to support the biblical text. This is easy to understand and even to condone when it is seen in the context of the late nineteenth century con-

---

* An original version of sections VII–VIII was published as fascicle 67 in 1968.

troversies concerning the unique position of the Bible, brought to a head by Darwinism and liberal German exegesis. There was a great urgency in many circles to put something weighty in the balance against scientific free-thinking, and because archaeology of necessity deals in physical, tangible objects, the results of excavations in Palestine tended to gain an exaggerated significance in the popular public mind. One must not forget that the interpretation of these finds has been and still is largely dependent on the school of biblical exegesis to which the excavator adheres. It is, unfortunately, an inherent characteristic of archaeological evidence that, with the best objective will in mind, it is only too easy to distort it by stressing one aspect of the finds more than another—finds which have come to light not as a controlled scientific experiment, but subject to many different aspects of chance (method of excavation, chemical properties of the soil, climate etc).

With this in mind it seems that for the time being Eggers's *archaeologische These, literarische Antithese*, in which he acknowledged archaeology in its own right, will in Palestinian archaeology of this period have to be changed to *literarische These, archaeologische Antithese*.[1] The literary thesis has been demonstrated in the first part of this chapter, and without this no archaeologist would have had any reason to suppose that the thirteenth century B.C. in Palestine saw the birth of a new nation which came to its fullest development about the end of the eleventh century B.C. With one exception[2] there is no evidence, in the proper sense of the word, that a new ethnic group was taking over power in the land at this time. It is impossible for archaeology, in its present state, to detect new ethnic elements in, or replacing, the population of an area unless, at the time of its arrival, it deposited cultural artifacts of an indestructible nature which differ markedly from those of the established group.

Various distinguishing features of the beginning of the Iron Age, such as the introduction of iron to replace bronze for tools and weapons, and the invention of non-porous plaster for the lining of cisterns, which made settlement less dependent on springs,[3] cannot be attributed to the earliest Israelites in Palestine. Nor, on the whole, can the changing shapes of the pottery repertoire. Albright has suggested[4] that a certain type of storage jar was distinctive for the earliest Israelites but even this 'fossil type' collared rim has been found in Canaanite contexts,[5] and thus

---

[1] §vii, 6.   [2] See below, p. 335.   [3] §vii, 3, 113.
[4] §vii, 4, 548.   [5] §vii, 12, 16.

loses its diagnostic value. However, Aharoni has pointed to a cooking-pot with a high rim as distinctive early Israelite ware, and this may prove a fixed point in the search, though it may well prove to be a valid point of recognition for only some of the Hebrew tribes.[1]

A very poor building tradition is frequently taken as an indication of new settlers and on the whole it is assumed that the newcomers largely took over the material culture of the groups which they eventually displaced.[2] However, shabby rebuilding of a flourishing Late Bronze town cannot be taken as proof of the presence of Hebrews. If the population of a town is practically decimated during a destruction (and the cause of this may be accidental fire, earthquake, a local attack from a hostile neighbouring city-state, or a band of marauders or an Egyptian raid), it may take more than one generation before the survivors have even rebuilt their defences.[3] Unless the identity and date of the attackers and destruction can be fixed, the mere destruction of cities cannot be taken as sound archaeological evidence of the arrival of a new ethnic group.

The essential elements for tracing a slow process of penetration of a semi-nomadic folk into urban and agricultural Canaanite populations such as is described as having taken place in Palestine in the first part of this chapter are still lacking, though a beginning has now been made.[4]

The newcomers, being semi-nomadic pastoralists, were unlikely either to have been able or to have wished to build towns for themselves in the pattern of the Canaanite Late Bronze Age inhabitants. Almost all the available archaeological material comes from urban areas, with the exception of some village settlements in Galilee[5] and the temple mound at Deir 'Allā. As it is most likely that the penetrating Hebrew tribes established themselves first of all in the uncultivated areas before attempting either to intermingle peacefully with the established Canaanite population or to take a town by force, it is to be expected that some of their property may be found mixed with Canaanite sherds in the occupation level before the destruction of a town. In order to be able to recognize this material, far more archaeological work will have to be done outside the great tells. Lack of fossil types makes it apparently superfluous to attempt to locate one or other Hebrew tribe outside the borders of Canaan in the period immediately preceding the Settlement. Up till now there

---

[1] §vii, 2, 220.   [2] §vii, 10, 209.
[3] §vii, 7.   [4] See below, p. 335.   [5] §vii, 1.

is no indication, for instance, that any of these tribes had lived for any period in Egypt. The origin of newcomers in any area can be determined only by comparison of their material culture in their new homes with that found outside the new dwelling area.

Those tribes which never left Palestine and were already completely assimilated to Canaanite culture, as, for example, at Shechem, are virtually untraceable archaeologically, when they became part of the Israelite confederation. That it is possible to trace and distinguish nomadic cultures has been demonstrated by Miss Kenyon's work on the E.B.–M.B. tomb groups in Jericho.[1]

The one distinctive element of the culture of the Hebrew tribes of which one may speak with any certainty is their religion, the nature of which was such that during the period in question it remains, archaeologically speaking, an invisible attribute. The culture of the Philistines can be distinguished from the Canaanite not only by its pottery repertoire but by its distinctive burial customs.[2] This is not the case, so far as is yet known, with the incoming Israelites, though the situation may change if more burial grounds of the period are found and excavated.

VIII. RESULTS

The following are sites where excavation has revealed a destruction which could have been caused by the incoming Hebrew tribes.

Bethel[3] was destroyed in the thirteenth century, but the resettlement did not follow immediately. Tell Beit Mirsim (possibly Debir or Kirjath Sepher) was destroyed c. 1240 B.C., either by Israel[4] or by Merneptah.[5] Tell ed-Duweir (possibly Lachish) was destroyed c. 1230[6] or slightly later, by the Israelites, Merneptah, or the Peoples of the Sea.[7] Of the destruction of the Late Bronze Age cities of Megiddo,[8] c. 1050, Beisan (Beth-shan), c. 1150, Tell Qedah (Hazor),[9] only the last is attributed to the Israelites.

Tell el-Jib (identified by the excavator as Gibeon) has not revealed its origin as an Israelite town, and Tell el-Fūl (Gibeah) apparently developed from its beginning before 1100 B.C., but was, at least in its later stages, in Hellenistic times, an Israelite village.

---

[1] §VII, 8; §VII, 9; §VII, 11.
[2] §VII, 5, 151 ff.
[3] §VIII, 4, 11 ff.
[4] §VIII, 1, 38; §VIII, 2, 15 f.
[5] §VIII, 20, 100; §VIII, 22, 215.
[6] §VIII, 21, 51 f.
[7] §VII, 10, 209; §VIII, 22, 302.
[8] Ibid.; §VIII, 22, 321.
[9] §VIII, 11, 39; §VIII, 22, 254, 260.

Key sites for the later history of the Israelite kingdom, such as Jerusalem, Tell Balāṭa (Shechem) and Samaria,[1] throw no light on our problem for various reasons. Jerusalem remained a non-Israelite city until the time of David; Shechem, so far as is known, was never taken by the Israelites; and on the hill of Samaria no traces of settlement have been found which precede the kings of the house of Omri. From other key sites, such as Hebron, Beersheba and Qadesh Barnea, no archaeological evidence is known at all. Jericho seems to have had a slight fourteenth-century occupation but none in the twelfth century,[2] and no site in the Ghor of Jericho stemming from the second half of the Late Bronze Age has been found. Sites once identified with Gilgal bear no traces of occupation earlier than the seventh century B.C.[3] However, an early thirteenth-century occupation was found on the ruins of Et-Tell ('Ai).[4] Aharoni found a 'continuous chain of small settlements' in the southern part of Upper Galilee, which he dates to the beginning of the Iron Age and which seem to be distinctive of a new group of settlers.[5] Although their identity cannot yet be fixed on internal evidence, there seems at least to be no alternative rival identification to that of the Hebrew tribes.

From surface explorations by Nelson Glueck[6] and, more recently, B. Rothenberg,[7] it is argued that the southern and eastern borderlands of Palestine did not have a settled population during the greater part of the Late Bronze Period. The temple at 'Ammān and work at Dhiban have done nothing to upset this picture,[8] though so little has been done on any scale in these border lands that it is too early to draw any firm conclusions on this point. The history of these areas plays an important part in the reconstruction of the arrival of the Hebrew tribes and, in particular, in detecting the closer dating of successive waves of penetration.

An Israelite invasion supposes a settled population and kingdoms. So far, however, there is no archaeological indication of the movement of tribes through these regions, and the fact that some place-names can be identified with certain geographic locations cannot be taken as archaeological evidence.[9] Until such sites are excavated and the archaeological context is seen to fit with a reasonable measure of certainty into the wider geographical context, the traditional identification can only be taken

---

[1] §VIII, 5.
[2] §VIII, 14, ch. XI.
[3] §VIII, 23, 57 ff.
[4] §VIII, 15.
[5] §VII, 1 and 2.
[6] §VIII, 10.
[7] §VIII, 19.
[8] §VIII, 12, 155 ff.
[9] §VIII, 7, 100.

as an indication. One site in Transjordan—Deir ʿAlla—, traditionally taken to be ancient Succoth, has been excavated and can now with some certainty be proved not to be Succoth. This tell has turned out to be an undefended temple mound, without any village occupation throughout the Late Bronze age from *c.* the sixteenth century to the twelfth century B.C.[1] It remained a holy place during the Iron Age until well into the Persian period. One must look for another biblical identification for this important site, and Joshua xxii. 10, 11 may perhaps prove a link here, or one may suppose that a tradition that Jacob founded this sanctuary, which indeed remained independent of Jerusalem right through the history of the Kingdoms and even after the Exile, was suppressed by later biblical redactors. There is no definite proof for either of these suggestions.

Of far greater archaeological importance is the bearing which the Deir ʿAlla excavations have on the problems of recognizing the arrival of new population groups. This has been derived from a technical analysis of the pottery; that is to say, from a study of the sherds and vessels based on the way they were made and not only on a typology of form.[2] It can now be proved that the Early Iron Age cooking-pot cannot be a straight descendant of the Late Bronze cooking-pot, as is generally assumed. It is made by potters with a different tradition, not indigenous to Palestine. Occasionally examples of this cooking-pot are found in sites at an earlier date, which indicates contact with a group or groups of nomadic people who had their main centre of activity elsewhere. At Deir ʿAlla, at some time in the second half of the thirteenth century B.C., a pottery, totally different technically from the foregoing and generally known Late Bronze repertoire, appears. This can only be taken as an indication that a different population took over the sanctuary. In the first quarter of the twelfth century B.C. the sanctuary was destroyed by earthquake, after which the site was occupied by yet another group or clan, whose pottery once again differs markedly from a technical point of view from the pre-earthquake repertoire, although the shapes of the vessels remain very much the same. Some pottery of Philistine type has been found together with this pottery.

The Deir ʿAlla clay tablets do not belong to this period but to the previous one.[3] This phase is followed in the second half of the twelfth century by the building of a village, presumably attached to the sanctuary. This village again exhibits a different pottery

---

[1] §VIII, 9, *passim*.   [2] *Ibid.*
[3] See below, p. 510.

tradition. To sum up: there is evidence for Late Bronze Age semi-nomads living in Trans-Jordan with their religious centre at Deir 'Allā. They are followed by a similar group of nomads who apparently peacefully ousted the earlier group from their place of worship and, by analogy, from the rich grazing grounds in the area of the Jordan valley in which Deir 'Allā is situated. Shortly after 1200 B.C. they in turn move on to make place for a clan of metal-workers who were regular winter and spring visitors at the site, as can be seen archaeologically by the annual deposits in the soil. After another earthquake disaster this group is replaced by a tribe whose cultural orientation is quite definitely eastwards and atypical for the west side of the Jordan. There is as yet nothing by which these ethnic groups can be identified, and although their arrivals and departures can clearly be traced at Deir 'Allā it is still impossible to say where they came from or where they went. A new comprehensive surface survey published in distribution maps might do something to help elucidate this problem, though chance plays a weighty role in such surveys.

As has already been said, the archaeologists would be totally unaware of any important ethnic changes at the end of the Late Bronze Age were it not for the biblical traditions. An analysis of these traditions which in itself tries to conjure up an historically more reliable reconstruction of events can be the only true incentive for the archaeologist to attempt to find relevant traces in the soil. This frequently makes the matter of interpretation even more difficult than when the traditional stories are taken at their face value. Two heavy handicaps rest on the archaeologist of this period: the uncertainty as to the location of territorial boundaries between the tribes and the absence of evidence of close dating. Neither the literary nor the archaeological evidence can be hung on to a firmly fixed chronological peg; both archaeologist and exegete have to deal with the question of whether there ever was a nomadic Israelite invasion and whether this element left the region again after a certain period only to return once more after an unknown period of time. Did the earlier waves of arrivals carry some distinguishing feature which the latter ones did not? And so on. Even inscriptional material lacks the required precision, as can be seen from the Merneptah stele.[1] It is the nature of the archaeological evidence and the almost entire lack of inscriptional material which classify this period as proto-historical. As such it demands a different archaeological approach from that which is generally given to it.

[1] §VIII, 17, 278.

CHAPTER XXVII

THE RECESSION OF MYCENAEAN CIVILIZATION

I. DISTURBANCES IN THE EASTERN MEDITERRANEAN

THE expansion of Mycenaean civilization had been bound up with a vigorous trading activity in the eastern Mediterranean, and for the archaeologist the recession of that trade is one of the most obvious symptoms of the Mycenaean decline. But this generalization will not get us far in the reconstruction of the history of the period. Cultural and political history are not the same thing; and in the L.H. IIIb phase, when pottery of Mycenaean style found its widest distribution in the east Mediterranean lands, the political decline of the Mycenaean world may already have begun. We have already noted[1] that at this time the Mycenaean potters of Cyprus were showing a greater independence of the style of mainland Greece, and that their wares seem to have captured most of the eastern market, for nearly all the Mycenaean pottery of L.H. IIIb style that turns up in Syrian and Palestinian sites shows Cypriot peculiarities. Cities such as Alalakh (Tell Açana) and Ugarit (Ras Shamra) continued to import Mycenaean-style pottery[2] until their destruction in the early twelfth century,[3] but that pottery came in the main from Cyprus. At the least this must imply that direct trade from the Aegean was now less frequent, and it is difficult to see why. Either, one would suppose, something had undermined the commercial vitality of Greece at home, or else the political conditions in the east Mediterranean had become less favourable to trade. It may be partly that Mycenaean traders in Cyprus were better placed, and had therefore become rivals to their homeland; on these lines we might explain the curious situation at Tell Abu Hawwām near Haifa, where, quite exceptionally, the Mycenaean imports at this time do include pots which must have come from mainland Greece.[4] Perhaps there was here an attempt to by-pass

* An original version of this chapter was published as fascicle 39 in 1965; the present chapter includes revisions made in 1970.   [1] See above, pp. 182 ff.
[2] §1, 8, 71 ff., 87; §1, 10, 162.   [3] See below, p. 340.   [4] See above, p. 182 with refs.

Cyprus in the route to the east, though it is difficult to believe that Mycenaean shipping could have reached that far without using some intermediate port of call after leaving the Aegean. In Egypt too it seems likely that a majority of the L.H. IIIb pottery imports were of Cypriot origin;[1] but in any case the quantity of Mycenaean pottery reaching Egypt was comparatively small after the brief Amarna period. Mycenaean merchants from whatever quarter probably met with little encouragement there.

Though archaeology fails to explain the recession of Mycenaean intercourse with the east, one can in this period glean at least some hints of what was going on from the historical records of the Egyptians and the Hittites. It is clear that conditions were becoming less and less favourable to peaceful commerce. In the fifth year of Merneptah (1236–1223 B.C.) Egypt met and successfully repelled an attack by the people of Libya, who were supported by a number of allies from overseas, named as Akawasha, Tursha, Lukka, Sherden, and Sheklesh, 'northerners coming from all lands'.[2] In the debate which has long continued over the identity of these peoples it has often been held that the *Akawasha* 'of the countries of the sea' are Ἀχαιϝοί, Achaeans, or Mycenaean Greeks; but some of the relevant records seem to indicate that the Akawasha warriors were circumcised, which is something not otherwise known of Achaeans.[3] If the Akawasha really were Mycenaeans, we still have no evidence of where they came from, whether from Greece itself, or from, say, Rhodes or some other Mycenaean principality. They need be no more than a band of mercenaries or adventurers. Whether they included Achaeans or not, this wide coalition of presumably maritime allies who assisted the King of Libya is indicative of seriously disturbed conditions in the eastern half of the Mediterranean; and though Merneptah was at this time successful in repelling them the disturbances were to recur in the reign of Ramesses III (1198–1166 B.C.). This time Egypt had to face not only the Libyans, assisted from without as before, but also, a few years later, a combined land and sea invasion by a number of different peoples including Peleset, Tjekker, Sheklesh, Denyen, and Weshesh.[4] Again their identifications are not all clear; but it is agreed that the Peleset are the Philistines, later to settle in Palestine,[5] and the name Denyen may

---

[1] §1, 8, 100 f.   [2] §1, 1, vol. III, sects. 569 ff. See above, pp. 233 f.

[3] §1, 6, 21, n. 1, with review in *Class. Rev.* II (1961), 9 f.

[4] §1, 1, vol. IV, sects. 35–135, esp. 59 ff.; §II, 3, 80 ff.; §1, 2, 237 f. See above, p. 242 n. 8.

[5] See below, p. 372.

perhaps be equivalent to Δαναοί. If so, it appears that Mycenaean Greeks were again involved; and even apart from the name there is evidence that some of the marauders were of maritime origin and that they had been operating against the Hittite land of Arzawa and against Alashiya (probably Cyprus) before they joined the other forces in Syria. Thence the allies made their way south, destroying many cities (including Alalakh, Ugarit, and Tell Abu Hawam, already mentioned) before they were defeated, in 1191 B.C., on the borders of Egypt.

Such far-reaching operations through territories formerly controlled by the Hittites obviously imply an advanced decay of the Hittite power; and we can in fact trace darkly in the Hittite records something of the way events had been turning in the preceding half-century. Millawanda (Miletus), which had in the early thirteenth century been at least nominally under the control of Ahhiyawa, appears in the records later in the century as a vassal of the Hittites.[1] Archaeology shows that the city was destroyed some time in the L.H. IIIb period, and rebuilt with massive fortifications;[2] and there can be little doubt that it was fortified with Hittite approval, against Ahhiyawa. Mycenaean–Hittite relations had deteriorated from friendliness and respect to open hostility, and in the text of a treaty made between the Hittite Tudkhaliyash IV (c. 1265–1240) and the King of Amurru (in northern Syria) the name of the King of Ahhiyawa is found deliberately deleted (though still legible) from a list of kings reckoned of equal rank to the Hittite emperor. The same text, if correctly restored, shows it was Hittite policy to prevent ships of Ahhiyawa trafficking with Syria.[3] Though the Hittites were thus unwilling to recognize the power of Ahhiyawa, and though their hostility must have contributed to the decline of Mycenaean trade eastwards, it is clear that they were not having it all their own way. For another fragmentary text, probably of the same reign, mentions the King of Ahhiyawa as campaigning in person with both chariotry and infantry in Asia Minor;[4] and it was also during the reign of Tudkhaliyash IV that there began the hostilities referred to in a long text of the succeeding king, Arnuwandash III (c. 1240–1230), which details the acts of a former Hittite vassal named Madduwattash.[5] This Madduwattash first appears as seeking

---

[1] § 1, 7, 198–240; § 1, 4, 50; § 1, 5, 2 f. (no. 3).
[2] § 1, 10, 187, corrected in § 1, 9(b).
[3] § 1, 7, 320–7; § 1, 5, 8 (no. 17); § 1, 8, 110; § 1, 4, 50f.
[4] § 1, 7, 314–19; § 1, 5, 7 (no. 16); § 1, 4, 51.
[5] § 1, 7, 329–49; § 1, 5, 9 (no. 19); § 1, 3; § 1, 6, 97 ff. See above, pp. 264 f.

Hittite protection from the attacks of a 'man of Ahhiyā' named Attarshiyash. (The name has, notoriously, been equated with *Atreus*; but the phonetic equation is uncertain, and in any case Attarshiyash is not referred to as the *King* of Ahhiyawa.) Later, Madduwattash throws off all pretence of allegiance to the Hittite empire, seizing for his own the land of Arzawa, formerly a vassal-state of the Hittites, through which they had dominated all the south-west of Asia Minor. Moreover we find him actually in league with Attarshiyash, engaged in raids on Alashiya (most probably to be identified with Cyprus, or a city of Cyprus) which the Hittite emperor claims as his own territory. Such activity by Attarshiyash suggests that he too was endeavouring to profit by the folding up of Hittite power in the south-west.

But this was not the only area of Asia Minor where the recession of the Hittite control was tempting local powers to aggrandisement. Another text[1] tells of rebellion and hostilities against the empire, in the reign of Tudkhaliyash IV, by a league of states headed by the land of Assuwa, which must be located somewhere between Miletus and the Troad. (The name may indeed be the original of *Asia*, which in Roman times was applied to the province in just that area.) As many as twenty-two places are listed as taking part in the rebellion, from Lukka in the south to Taruisa and Wilusa in the north, the names of which have been tentatively identified with the Greek Τροία and Ϝίλιος, though there are some philological difficulties.

In any case these documents are of importance when we consider the story, preserved on the Greek side, of the great Trojan War which marks the beginning of the end of the second heroic age. Here in these undoubtedly historical Hittite texts we find a setting in which that war could well have taken place. Earlier, any major activity in the lands east of the Aegean would have provoked a powerful reaction by the Hittites, as indeed happened in the Miletus area. In the regions between Miletus and Troy there is extremely little evidence of Mycenaean trade, and if this is not due to accidental limitations of archaeological knowledge it may have been the power of Assuwa, backed by the Hittites, that blocked Mycenaean entry. In Troy, however, the Mycenaeans had at least found commercial opportunities, though never any possibility of settlement. Now, in the latter part of the thirteenth century, the changing situation in the hinterland might prompt a more active Mycenaean approach. The Hittite Empire was crumbling; the states to the west which had been a buffer between

---

[1] § 1, 6, 102 ff.; cf. § 1, 5, 32 ff.

Mycenaeans and Hittites were asserting themselves; and it was almost inevitable that the Greeks should become involved against them, whether as competitors for their territory, now left clear of Hittite influence, and for new trading opportunities, or merely to forestall the dangers that might beset them with fully independent neighbours in western Asia Minor. The Hittite records of the aggrandisement of Madduwattash and the rebellion of Assuwa and its allies show that even now the south-west and west offered no easy field for any Mycenaean aggression. But in the north-west the Troad, where they already had trading access, may have seemed a more practicable approach. Even so they would have to reckon with the other powers of western Asia Minor as allies of Troy.

II. THE TROJAN WAR

For later Greeks the Trojan War was the best remembered event of the Mycenaean age: it is the central fact of history behind the *Iliad* and *Odyssey*;[1] and it was constantly present to the Greek mind as a turning-point of the heroic age. The two greatest Greek historians both refer to it in the opening chapters of their work: Herodotus recalls it[2] as an earlier conflict of east and west, analogous to that of the Persian Wars; Thucydides speaks of it[3] as the first united foreign enterprise of the Greeks. That it was a united Greek enterprise is a point of some importance. The fame and glory of it were a joint inheritance of all the Greeks, just as the Homeric epics were. But we should be wrong to suggest that it was the Homeric epic that made it so, or that the epic was the sole source of knowledge of the war. It is true that a considered reading of the *Iliad* and the *Odyssey* will give one the outline— that Agamemnon mustered a force of men and ships from all Greece to sail against Troy to avenge the abduction of Helen, wife of his brother Menelaus of Sparta, and that Troy was eventually sacked after a long-drawn-out siege. But Homer does not actually recount these events; rather they are alluded to as though known already, and so no doubt they were. For Homer's poems are nowadays recognized as not the beginnings but the climax of a tradition of epic, in which earlier poems may indeed have been more concerned with the annals of history. But Homer's purpose was to tell a tale of human experience of universal application; and his narratives have the Trojan War for their backcloth because the period of that war and its aftermath was

---

[1] On the Homeric poems as history see below, pp. 820 ff.
[2] Hdt. 1, 3.   [3] Thuc. 1, 3.

the most momentous in the then remembered past of the Greeks, and was universally recognized as such. Indeed the fact that the Trojan War was accepted as historical by all the ancient Greek world, and that no writer in all that nation of sceptics ever questioned its historicity, is the most compelling evidence that it really did take place.

But though the *Iliad* does not pretend itself to be history, there is incorporated within it what may almost be described as a Mycenaean historical document, the *Catalogue of Ships*[1] in Book II. This list of the contingents (with their leaders and their places of origin) that composed the force attacking Troy represents a political geography quite unlike that of historical Greece.[2] It is not simply that the post-Mycenaean Dorian occupation of Greece is ignored. The cities are grouped in kingdoms with centres such as Mycenae, Tiryns, and Pylus, which are known to have been the focal points of the Mycenaean civilization though unimportant in historical times. Thebes, on the other hand, prominent in early Mycenaean times, is not mentioned; and this too is appropriate, since, as we have seen, the power of Thebes was eclipsed in L.H. III b.[3] This correspondence of the *Catalogue* with the Mycenaean reality extends to more detail. Of nearly 170 places named, over 90 can be pretty certainly identified; and of these a good half can be shown to have been occupied in Mycenaean times, while none of them is known to have been founded later than the Dorian invasion. Further corroboration of the *Catalogue*'s Mycenaean date is to be seen in its inclusion of at least forty places whose very location was no longer identifiable by the classical Greeks.[4]

In view of the good case that can on such grounds as these be made for the authenticity of the *Catalogue*, it will be worth while noting both its general content and, in particular, a few points which, though unexpected and not always corroborated by archaeology, may none the less be historically sound. While Agamemnon, the commander-in-chief, is elsewhere in the *Iliad* (II, 108) spoken of as ruler of 'many islands and of all Argos' (whether *Argos* means the city, the Argolid, or some larger area of Greece), the *Catalogue* defines more narrowly his personal kingdom. This, with its capital at Mycenae, includes only the northern end of Argolis, together with Corinthia and the country between Arcadia and the Corinthian Gulf.[5] The rest of the Argive plain, including the great fortress of Tiryns, is under Diomede, who also rules the

---

[1] Further discussed below, pp. 836 f. [2] § 11, 1; § 11, 2; § 11, 7, ch. IV.
[3] See above, pp. 168 f. [4] § 11, 7, 121 f. [5] *Iliad*, 11, 569–80.

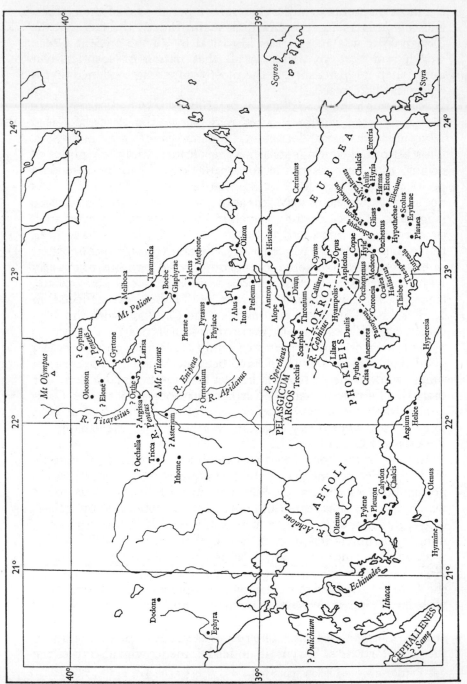

Map 8. Homeric geography, I. (Based on Allen and Burr.)

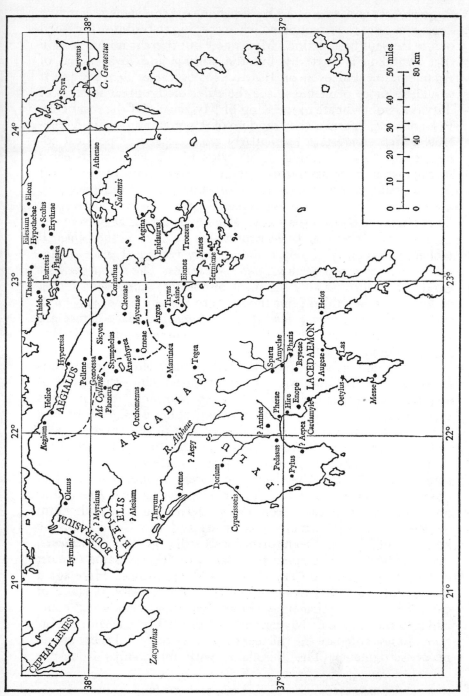

Map 9. Homeric geography, 2. (Based on Allen and Burr.)

Argolic Acte and Aegina.[1] This division of Argolis may seem like a recurrence of the situation which according to tradition obtained before Perseus first fortified Mycenae;[2] but there is no suggestion that Diomede is anything but the willing and loyal vassal of Agamemnon, and even on the archaeological evidence alone it would be more plausible to see the ruler of the great fortress of Tiryns as subordinate to the King of Mycenae. Of the rest of the Peloponnese, Sparta is the kingdom of Agamemnon's twin Menelaus, which suggests a particularly close degree of political co-operation. Nestor's kingdom of Pylus in the south-west seems in somewhat freer association; it had never come under direct Pelopid rule, and its longer traditions and greater independence are reflected in the picture of Nestor's great age and the respect he is always shown in the story. The Pylus area is at present the only part of Mycenaean Greece for which we have (in the Linear B tablets) some fairly closely contemporary record of place-names with which to compare the *Catalogue* entries. The *Catalogue* lists eight towns (presumably the most important) along with Pylus, and so do some tablets; but the lists are not the same, and in all the Pylus tablets only a few of these *Catalogue* place-names are even tentatively traceable. The lack of correspondence is disappointing and puzzling.[3]

Arcadia and Elis complete the list of the Peloponnesian contingents. The Arcadian warriors, transported (since they were no seafarers) in sixty ships provided by Agamemnon, seem perhaps more numerous than present archaeological knowledge of the area would lead us to expect. The chief interest of the entry for Elis is that the territory is defined rather by names of physical features than by names of towns, which suggests a sparser population; and similarly the fact that they had four leaders implies that they had a looser political organization. Their collective name is *Epeioi*, and others of this name came from the western islands of Dulichium (which cannot be certainly identified) and the Echinades, the kingdom of Meges. From further west still came the *Kephallenes*, under Odysseus, who ruled the islands of Ithaca, Same (almost certainly equivalent to Cephallenia), and Zacynthos. Here again the use of the tribal name suggests a less developed stage of civilization; and archaeology shows that these islands had come late into the sphere of Mycenaean culture.[4] Mycenaean remains there do not antedate the thirteenth century B.C., and there are no major settlements. The Aetolians, with forty ships from five

---

[1] *Iliad*, ii, 559–67. [2] See *C.A.H.* ii³, pt. 1, p. 650.
[3] § ii, 8, 141 ff. [4] § ii, 9, ch. xiii (iii).

towns, represent a rather different situation; the fame of the earlier heroes Tydeus and Meleager and the legend of the siege of Calydon[1] imply that Aetolia had once been an important Mycenaean centre, but to judge from the *Catalogue* it had much declined. It is indeed on the fringe of the Mycenaean world, so far as material remains yet tell; and the *Catalogue* equally has nothing to say of the areas to the north-west of it, either the islands of Leucas and Corcyra or the mainland areas of Acarnania, Thesprotia and Epirus. These were peopled, if by Greeks, by rougher, un-Mycenaean Greeks, whose hour had not yet come.

The peoples of central Greece are given by their tribal names, Phokeeis, Lokroi, and Abantes from Euboea, which again is probably indicative of a less advanced political organization than in the Peloponnese.[2] The same probably holds good for Boeotia; for the power of Thebes, which might have led a well-knit state, is a thing of the past, as we have seen, and the Boiotoi are probably newcomers to the Boeotian plain.[3] No less than thirty towns are listed, but their leadership is divided among five commanders. Why the Boeotians should have been given pride of place in the list is now no longer clear; possibly the *Catalogue* was originally composed in Boeotia.[4] Further north also we can recognize a diversity of political development. The people of Achilles, from Pelasgic Argos (probably the Spercheus Valley), from Hellas and from Phthia, go under the names of *Myrmidones* and *Hellenes* and *Achaioi*. *Hellenes* here is still a tribal name, like *Myrmidones*, and like *Hellas* has only a narrow local connotation, though we cannot clearly define it. *Phthia* is still more obscure; nor is it clear in what particular sense this contingent especially are called Achaeans. Only three towns are mentioned, though the contingent comprised fifty ships; but there is nothing incongruous in somewhat undeveloped hill-country producing some of the toughest fighting men in the army. The rich plain of Thessaly is represented in the *Catalogue* by eight small kingdoms with some twenty-five towns between them. This implies a degree of civilization for Thessaly which is only now becoming archaeologically apparent.

Coming south again we are in the area of fullest Mycenaean culture. Finds in Attica have shown that it was as prosperous and populous in L.H. IIIb as any part of Greece; in the *Catalogue* it has fifty ships, yet only the one city, Athens, is mentioned, and the people are named after it, 'Αθηναῖοι. Have we not here further evidence that the political union of Attica was achieved

---

[1] See *C.A.H.* II³, pt. 1, pp. 647 f.   [2] § 11, 4, 65 f.
[3] See Thuc. I, 12.   [4] § 11, 7, 152.

before the Trojan War?[1] Some ancient critics held that the next *Catalogue* entry, referring to Salamis, had been tampered with in the interests of Athenian propaganda; but even so Salamis appears as an independent unit, contributing a dozen ships under the great Ajax.[2]

Crete in the *Catalogue* still bears the epithet ἑκατόμπολις, '(isle of) a hundred cities', which might better have fitted the Minoan than the L.H. III situation; but only seven cities are named, contributing a force of eighty ships under Idomeneus, the grandson of Minos. Cnossus comes first, presumably as the capital, though archaeology shows it never recovered the splendours of the palace period. Phaestus, where too the remains show the palace site reoccupied only on a minor scale, has no distinctive position or comment in the list. Of the other five we can say little enough, except that Gortyn, described as τειχιόεσσα, is not known ever to have merited this epithet in the way that Tiryns did.[3] If the epic tradition is in this particular less soundly based than in some parts of the *Catalogue*, could this be because Crete was, as mentioned earlier,[4] more detached from full Mycenaean culture than most of Greece? That detachment need not have prevented Crete from taking part in the war.

Rhodes is represented by nine ships under Tlepolemus, Syme by three under Nireus and the other islands of the southern Sporades by thirty, led by Pheidippus and Antiphus. Tlepolemus as the *Catalogue* reminds us was a son, and Pheidippus and Antiphus were grandsons, of Heracles—a genealogy which probably reflects the already long-standing traditions of these islands, settled by Mycenaeans as early as L.H. II.[5]

The Cyclades and the northern Sporades find no mention in the list. This is unexpected, since we know that these islands shared the Mycenaean way of life. Probably the simplest explanation is that they did in fact remain neutral in the war. Lesbos and Lemnos in the north-east Aegean were non-Greek, and Lesbos is mentioned elsewhere in Homer[6] as having been conquered by the Achaeans—perhaps as a strategic prelude to the siege of Troy? Excavation has shown that Thermi in Lesbos was actually destroyed at a date which on the evidence of imported Mycenaean pottery must be near that of the fall of Troy.[7]

Agamemnon, king of Mycenae, is throughout the epic recognized as the commander-in-chief of the whole Greek host; but

---

[1] § ii, 7, 145 and notes. See above, p. 169.
[2] Strabo, 394.   [3] See above, p. 173.   [4] See above p. 166.
[5] See *C.A.H.* ii³, pt. i, p 654.   [6] *Iliad*, ix, 129f.   [7] § ii, 6, 72, 213.

there is no special emphasis on his overall kingship in the *Catalogue*, and we are left on the whole with a picture of a temporary union, for the purposes of the war, of a number of diverse and independent kingdoms, rather than of a close-knit Mycenaean Empire. Possibly the ties of political unity were already loosening; or perhaps they had never existed to the degree we tend to imply in talking of 'empire'. Our consideration of the Hittite documents has shown that Mycenaean princes may well have engaged in hostilities abroad without reference to a suzerain in mainland Greece; and even in peace we may suppose that Bronze Age communications would necessitate a fair degree of decentralization in government, and a corresponding independence of local princes. For the Trojan War, however, there is no reason to doubt that the Greeks showed a united front.

The list of Trojan allies[1] in *Iliad* 11 is but sketchy compared with the Greek catalogue; and this strengthens our belief in its Mycenaean date. It covers western Asia Minor from the Propontis and the Troad down to Miletus and Lycia, but without detail. It includes only such knowledge of these lands as would have been available in Mycenaean times, and has not been elaborated during the later history of the epic, when Asia Minor was quite familiar to Greeks. It is significant in this connexion that the one coastal city south of the Troad which is named is Miletus, the chief city of the Carians, who are characterized as of foreign speech ($\beta\alpha\rho\beta\alpha\rho\delta\phi\omega\nu\omicron\iota$). This is precisely the area which archaeology and the Hittite texts show to have been long familiar to the Mycenaeans, and perhaps even, for a time, under Mycenaean rule.[2] Now, however, it is ranged on the enemy side. Furthermore, the Trojan *Catalogue*, like the Greek, mentions some places which were not identifiable by the later Greeks, a sure sign that such references go back to a time before the Ionians settled in Asia Minor.[3]

This Homeric account of the allies of Troy naturally invites comparison with the Assuwan alliance in western Asia Minor which rebelled against the Hittite emperor Tudkhaliyash IV.[4] A certain difference between them is that the Homeric *Catalogue* includes allies of Troy on the European side of the Hellespont—Thracians, Cicones and Paeonians—who are not mentioned in the Assuwan league. On the Asiatic side the difficulty of identification of the names in the Hittite document hampers the inquiry; but we can be fairly sure that *Lukka* and *Karkisha* are the same as

[1] Cf. §11, 7, 137 ff. [2] See sect. 1 above and p. 184 above.
[3] §11, 7, 140 ff. [4] §11, 5, 34–7. See above, p. 164.

the Lycians and Carians of the epic. The Assuwan league was defeated, according to the Hittite records, but it nevertheless seems that Hittites did not thereafter intervene in western Asia Minor, and the same or another grouping of states may have recovered and even enlarged itself to meet the Mycenaean aggression. In the present state of knowledge, however, we are reduced to conjecture.

From Troy itself[1] there is good archaeological evidence that the city known as Troy VIIa was in fact destroyed by an enemy, after a siege, at a date when L.H. IIIb pottery was still being used; and there can be no reasonable doubt that this was the event which has echoed through the world's literature ever since. It is the only archaeologically recognizable sack of Troy at all near the period assigned by tradition. But when we inquire more closely after the date of this event,[2] there are difficulties on both sides. Tradition was not unanimous as to an 'absolute' date, though it was agreed[3] that Troy fell from sixty to eighty years (or two generations) before the Return of the Heraclidae, the dynasty ousted from the Peloponnese by the Pelopids. The Return itself was dated through the Spartan royal pedigrees which could be traced back to it. By such rough calculation various dates were arrived at, with the mean at 1203 B.C., in our terminology.[4] Archaeology, in turn, cannot yet date L.H. IIIb pottery with sufficient precision for us to do any better than place the fall of Troy 'c. 1200 B.C.'. Nor can we place it with any real precision in relation to Hittite chronology, though this has been attempted.[5] It is probably safe to assume that it was later than the texts of the reign of Tudkhaliyash IV referring to the Assuwan alliance, but how much later is by no means certain. There are difficulties, too, in establishing the chronological relation of the sack of Troy to events in Greece itself, attested by archaeology, which must now be considered.

III. DISTURBANCES WITHIN GREECE: INVASION AND EMIGRATION

The general evidence of the history of Mycenaean settlements, as observed by the archaeologist, shows clearly enough the expansion that took place in the L.H. IIIb phase. Whereas L.H. IIIa is represented at some ninety sites, L.H. IIIb is represented at 143. These figures disregard sites known to have been occupied in

---

[1] See above, pp. 161 ff.
[2] Cf. *C.A.H.* I³, pt. 1, pp. 246 f., and bibliography thereto.
[3] Cf. Strabo 582, 3; Thuc. I, 12, 3.   [4] §II, 3, ch. IV.   [5] §II, 5, 30–6.

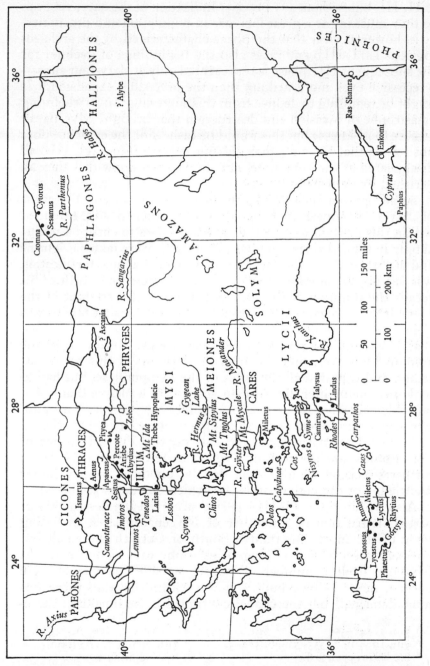

Map 10. Homeric geography, 3. (Based on Allen and Burr.)

L.H. III, but without any preciser indication of the date; yet even so they must imply a great increase in population and prosperity. It is, however, clear that the phase characterized by the archaeologist as L.H. IIIb embraces also the beginnings of decline; for the subsequent IIIc phase is represented only at sixty-four sites— a recession even more striking than the preceding expansion.[1] It might be tempting to deduce from this some single overwhelming catastrophe of invasion and destruction that brought Mycenaean Greece to its knees; but this would be rash. For the evidence does not tell us that the sites that did not survive into L.H. IIIc all disappeared at the same time, nor do we even know that they all perished by sword and pillage.

Some signs of such perils can, however, be traced. The walls of Mycenae appear to have been strengthened and extended within this period,[2] and special care was taken to ensure a water-supply in time of siege. Similar precautions were taken at Tiryns and at Athens.[3] At the Isthmus of Corinth[4] a new fortification was set up, apparently to check invasion from the north. This recalls the tradition of the first and unsuccessful attempt of the Heraclidae[5] to regain their kingdom, when their leader Hyllus was slain in single combat at the Isthmus, and an agreement reached that they should not return for two generations. According to one account,[6] however, they did pass the Isthmus at this earlier attempt, and captured all the cities of the Peloponnese, but had to withdraw again after one year on account of a plague that broke out. This abortive attack occurred before the Trojan War; Pausanias is specific about this, rejecting a view he had held earlier in his work.[7] The archaeologist can only say that the fortification of the Isthmus and the sack of Troy both fell within L.H. IIIb; further precision should some day be obtained from a better knowledge of the pottery styles on which our dates are based.

Also within the L.H. IIIb period occurred the destruction or partial destruction of a number of Mycenaean sites, including some of the most important.[8] South of Corinth the small but prosperous settlement of Zygouries[9] came to a violent end. At Mycenae itself a number of houses outside the citadel were burned, never to be rebuilt.[10] Even within the walls there was some damage,[11] but the citadel continued to be inhabited there-

---

[1] §III, 1, 148–50. [2] §III, 16, 1959, 93 ff.; §III, 15, 206; A, 2, 31 f.

[3] §III, 19; §III, 8, 355; §III, 6, 422–5. [4] §III, 9; §III, 7, 299 (plan).

[5] See below, pp. 686 ff. [6] Apollod. II, 8, 2.

[7] Paus. VIII, 5, and I, 41. [8] §III, 1, 149.

[9] §III, 5. [10] §III, 21; §III, 10. [11] §III, 12; A, 3, 260, with refs.

after. Tiryns too seems to have been attacked; there is considerable
evidence of destruction by fire;[1] but here again the citadel did
survive. In Laconia, the settlement at the Menelaion[2] was destroyed; in Messenia, the great palace of Nestor at Pylus.[3]
Neither was rebuilt. Blegen, the excavator of both Pylus and
Troy, can assure us that Pylus was destroyed after Troy,[4] but we
do not know just how long after. The sequence of the events at
the other sites is less certain. But sites in central Greece tell a
similar tale. The huge island fortress of Gla in Boeotia did not
outlive L.H. III b, but little detail is yet available for this site;[5]
its previous history is virtually unknown, but it is possible that its
whole existence was short. If so, the very construction of so great
a fortification (enclosing ten times the area of Tiryns or Troy) is
a symptom of the dangers that now beset Mycenaean Greece.
Crisa in Phocis is another site that seems to have come to a violent
end at this time.[6] Further north, the final destruction of the
palace at Iolcus[7] is obviously another serious disaster for Mycenaean civilization about which the evidence of further excavation
will be particularly welcome; it is believed to have occurred at the
very end of L.H. III b.

What archaeology at present fails to tell us is the order of
sequence of these events, and whether they occurred after the
Trojan War or not. The traditional history would lead us to
expect that they did; for otherwise it would have been a sadly
weakened and depopulated Greece that put up the expedition
against Troy. Could it indeed have launched its thousand ships?
It seems improbable. As events of the post-war period they raise
no such question, but rather accord with the traditional picture, in
which the nominal success of the taking of Troy is followed by no
occupation of the foreign territory, no resultant access of prosperity at home. Honour had been satisfied; and if we believe
tradition alone, that was the sole purpose of the expedition. But
the historian, however willing to *chercher la femme*, looks for
profounder and more substantial interpretations, which at present
elude us. The tradition of the Trojan War implies a powerful
Greece. The fact of the destruction of sites—and even though the
sites are at present few, they are widespread—implies that the
Mycenaean glory was departed. We should be perverse not to

---

[1] §III, 19; §III, 1, 35 f.   [2] §III, 22, 72.
[3] §III, 4, vol. 64, 159; A, 1, 419–22.
[4] §III, 4, vol. 61, 133; A, 1, 422–3.
[5] §III, 16, 1957, 29; 1960, 37 f.; §III, 1, 122 f.
[6] §III, 13; §III, 1, 130 f.   [7] §III, 16, 1956, 49; 1960, 57; §III, 1, 143.

recognize the strong probability that the destructions are to be linked with the Dorian invasion, of which clear and irrefutable accounts have come down to us.[1]

The Dorian invasion and the final break-up of Mycenaean Greece are discussed below, chapter XXXVI; but the Greeks had traditions of events more immediately following upon the Trojan War which also deserve the historian's attention. The heroes had sacked Troy; they shared out the loot and the captives and pointed their ships homeward; but a hard coming they had of it. From Homer onwards the period of the 'homecomings', the *Nostoi*, is a tale of shipwreck and wandering off course, of enforced settlement in distant lands, of return to broken homes and family strife, of consequent emigration to build life afresh in new lands. The story of the *Odyssey* is typical in the picture of difficulties encountered, though not in the hero's ultimate attainment of home and happiness (and even Odysseus, we may recall, was destined to further wandering).[2] Other homeward journeys of heroes presented in the course of the poem have a special interest, in that they are there as background to the main tale, and are therefore presumably intended as a picture of the typical post-war situation. Menelaus, before he reached Sparta, had visited Cyprus, 'Phoinike' (Syria or Palestine) and Egypt; in Egypt he had stayed a considerable time, and accumulated valuable possessions which he brought home with him.[3] Odysseus himself puts over a story of similar wanderings, on occasions when he is at pains to conceal his identity. He claims that after taking part in the Trojan War he had travelled to Egypt, 'Phoinike', and Libya; and more particularly he states in one place that his visit to Egypt was in company with roving pirates—ἅμα ληϊστῆρσι πολυπλάγκτοισι—who got into considerable trouble with the Egyptian forces.[4] These adventures are fiction, even within the framework of the story; but the story demands that they be plausible, the kind of adventures which were typical of the period; and as such both they and Menelaus's wanderings invite comparison with the land and sea raids in the first decade of the twelfth century which we have already noted in the records of Ramesses III. It is not fanciful to see here the poetic record, from the other side, of the same events.

There were current in historical Greece many more such stories, some of them crystallized in the epic *Nostoi* (of which we have now but fragmentary knowledge), others remembered as part of the

[1] Discussed below, pp. 694 ff. [2] *Od.* XI, 128.
[3] *Od.* IV, 81ff., 128 ff. [4] *Od.* XVII, 425ff.

traditional history of individual cities. What survives today is in late authors, but it is clear that they depended on much older sources. The general picture is of Greek heroes emigrating, either direct from Troy, or after a brief return home, to almost every part of the Mediterranean: Apollodorus, for example, mentions Asia Minor, Libya, Italy and Sicily, and even the islands near Iberia.[1] The individual instances which may be collected from the literature are almost innumerable, and a selection must suffice here for illustration.

Teucer, for example, was banished from his home in Salamis and went to found a new Salamis in Cyprus.[2] Agapenor, the Arcadian leader, forced off course on his way from Troy, founded or re-founded Paphus, with its famous temple of Aphrodite.[3] Pheidippus, again, the leader of the Coans, was reputed to have found his way to Cyprus and settled there.[4] For such settlements there is at least some archaeological corroboration. Enkomi, the Bronze Age predecessor of the Cypriot Salamis, had been destroyed at the end of L.H. IIIb, and the people who rebuilt it used L.H. IIIc pottery of a style which is clearly not developed from local antecedents, but from mainland Greek wares.[5] The history of Paphus is less well known at present; but some connexion of the cult there with Arcadia is attested by the fact that in Greece itself the *Paphian* Aphrodite was worshipped only at Tegea.[6]

Equally remarkable is the story of the colonization of Pamphylia and Cilicia by Greeks who left Troy under the leadership of Amphilochus, accompanied by the prophet Calchas. This is mentioned by Herodotus,[7] and Strabo in his several references to it cites Callinus and Hesiod as sources, and indicates that it was known to Sophocles. The migrants apparently proceeded by a coastal route, for Clarus near Colophon is the scene of a picturesque incident between Calchas and another seer, Mopsus, who replaces him and eventually assists in the founding of Mallus in Cilicia. Subsequently, Amphilochus revisited his native Argos, and on returning to Mallus was hostilely received by Mopsus; but despite the tradition that the two killed each other in single combat the names of both were closely associated with the local oracle in later times. The particular interest of this tradition lies in the fact

---

[1] Apollod. epitome, VI, 15.
[2] Schol. on Pindar, *Nem.* IV, 75.   [3] Lycophron, 479 ff.; Strabo, 683.
[4] Schol. on Lycophron, 911. Further examples in §III, 11.
[5] See below, p. 660.   [6] Paus. VIII, 5, 2.
[7] Hdt. VII, 91; Strabo, 642, 668, 675–6; Paus. VII, 2, 1.

that Mopsus may plausibly be identified with one Mukshush whom late Hittite kings of this area in the eighth century B.C. claimed as the first of their line.[1] Finds of pottery show that Cilicia had for some time before this (perhaps from L.H. IIIa) been in touch with the Mycenaeans, and the pottery evidence continues into the L.H. IIIc period;[2] but without further excavation of settlements we are not yet able to corroborate by this means the story of the settlement of Amphilochus. For Pamphylia (where some of the migrants made their new home) there is as yet even less archaeological evidence; philological data suggest that Greek settlements there were established at least as early as in Cyprus,[3] but this is not precise enough for our purposes. Certainly the traditions must not be lightly dismissed as unhistorical, especially if we observe how far the tale of this migration through Asia Minor, and of the settlements in Cyprus, seems to echo what the Egyptian records have to say of the movement of peoples in just these areas in the reign of Ramesses III.[4]

For regions to the west of Greece, tradition presents us with a similar picture.[5] The Pylians who sailed away from Troy with Nestor are credited with the foundation of Metapontum on the Gulf of Taranto, and even of Pisa in distant Etruria;[6] Crimisa is said to have been founded by Philoctetes, and the same hero is later associated with the foundation of the more famous colonies of Croton and Sybaris in the same area;[7] Diomede settled in the region of Apulia called Daunia.[8] Most remarkable of all, perhaps, the Rhodians are said to have founded colonies as far off as Spain and the Balearic Islands, besides others on the Italian coasts—at Parthenope in Campania, at Elpia in Daunia (this in conjunction with the Coans), and in the vicinities of Siris and Sybaris on the Gulf of Taranto.[9]

The coasts of southern Italy and Sicily were not of course unknown to the Mycenaeans before this date: pottery and other evidence proves at least trading contact in these parts from L.H. II onwards; and settlement there in the disturbed twelfth century would conform to the same pattern as the migrations to the eastern Mediterranean, which nowhere seem to have opened up wholly new lands or routes. Archaeological support for the traditions is not impressive in either quantity or detail, but it is not

[1] §III, 2. See below, pp. 363 ff.   [2] §I, 8, 88f.; §III, 17, 134.
[3] §III, 14.   [4] See above, pp. 339.
[5] §III, 3, ch. IX.   [6] Strabo, 264, 222.
[7] Strabo, 254.   [8] Strabo, 283 f.
[9] Strabo, 654, 264; cf. §III, 3, 61 f. and 348.

wholly wanting. As in the east, there is a falling-off in the pottery evidence at the end of L.H. IIIb. In Sicily no IIIc imports have been discovered, though there are suggestions of IIIc influence in local wares: in the Aeolian Islands it is only at Lipari that IIIc wares appear.[1] But at Scoglio del Tonno, by Taranto, the Mycenaean pottery sequence runs right through into L.H. IIIc; and in Apulia there are local wares which show marked signs of IIIc influence.[2] There is at present no trace of Mycenaeans in Campania or Etruria; but there is nothing unreasonable in the tradition, especially if we recall that Mycenaean sherds of earlier date have been found as far north as Ischia.[3] That Pylus should colonize in the central Mediterranean is likely enough, since it lies on the coasting route up through the Ionian Sea, and there is a further reminder that this was a natural course for shipping in the identification of features in the IIIc pottery from Scoglio del Tonno which derive from Cephallenia.[4] Cephallenia itself seems to have had a fresh access of population in L.H. IIIc;[5] but this movement did not extend northwards to Leucas or Corcyra, which still remained strangely isolated from Mycenaean culture. The superficially improbable tradition of colonization from far-off Rhodes is on examination of the archaeological evidence perhaps the most plausible. Rhodes had been a flourishing corner of the Mycenaean world from L.H. II onwards, and seems not to have suffered as mainland Greece did from the troubles of the IIIb period, but with some others of the Aegean islands continued to enjoy comparative prosperity in IIIc.[6] Moreover, it is clear that Rhodes was a chief participant in the activities of the Mycenaean trading station at Scoglio del Tonno.[7] It would be natural, therefore, that the Rhodians should be foremost in any colonizing that went on in the Gulf of Taranto after the Trojan War. That they went so far as Spain or the Balearics there is as yet no proof; but we shall do well to restrain ourselves from the felicity of incredulity.

The flight from mainland Greece that is represented by all these eastward and westward migrations is not easily explained; and as so often in history, causes and effects seem inextricably tangled. Clearly, conditions at home must have been unsatisfactory, and it is easy to blame the Dorian invasion; but why was Mycenaean Greece unable to resist invasion? Possibly resources had been squandered in the Trojan campaign. But why was the

---

[1] §III, 18, 74 and 47.   [2] §III, 18, 128 ff. and 138 ff.
[3] §III, 18, 7 f.   [4] §III, 18, 132.
[5] See below, pp. 659 f.   [6] See below, p. 663.   [7] §III, 18, 128 ff.

war undertaken? There seems to have been good warning of dangers at home before it began; it was not a moment for aggression in the opposite direction. Perhaps the weakening of the Hittite Empire and the consequent difficulties in east Mediterranean trade had a graver effect on the Mycenaean economy than we can now discern, and the Trojan campaign was a desperate attempt to gain a new opening. Perhaps Greece had burned up her home resources—almost literally, for the consumption of timber in Mycenaean times for building as well as for fuel in the metal and pottery industries must have been enormous. It is not impossible that the first disastrous steps in deforestation, with the inevitable impoverishment that it brings, were taken in Mycenaean times. When the Dorian pirates hove in sight the Mycenaean ship had fought its last fight and was already sinking. There was nothing to do but to take to the boats and row manfully out of reach.

CHAPTER XXVIII

THE SEA PEOPLES

I. ANATOLIANS AT THE BATTLE OF QADESH

The thirteenth century B.C. was an age of increasing turmoil, confusion and obscurity, after which it is largely clear that the civilization of the Age of Bronze in the Levant really tottered to its end. If we wish to obtain a picture of this period of sudden decline and collapse, we have to be content to pick our way through a bewildering tangle of evidence, much of it highly fragmentary, much of it highly conjectural and insecure. The former class is based, it is true, on more or less historically authentic records, partly in cuneiform (but these are sparse), partly in Egyptian hieroglyphic documents (but these suffer greatly in value from the imperfect system of vocalization used in them in transcribing foreign names). In the second group of data, we are driven to fall back on the evidence of Greek legendary traditions. These, though precarious, are clearly not to be ignored. The resultant picture is naturally far from clear, and such objectivity as it may possess has been sometimes brought into doubt by too passionate partisanship on the part of individuals who have sought to win conviction for their possibly justifiable theories by massive over-accumulation of uncertain arguments.[1] The picture drawn here is further incomplete in so far as the publication of several important excavations in Lycia,[2] Syria,[3] Cyprus,[4] and Israel,[5] which, it is to be hoped, may soon throw much light on different aspects, is still awaited.

In the year 1300 B.C., the great clash took place at Qadesh in Syria (modern Tell Nebi Mind on the upper Orontes river) between the young Ramesses II and Muwatallish, the Great King of the Hittites.[6] The list of the Hittites' allies, recorded by the Egyptian scribes,[7] includes a number of peoples of Anatolia and

---

* An original version of this chapter was published as fascicle 68 in 1969; the present chapter includes revisions made in 1973.

[1] §1, 2; §IV, 19; §IV, 20; §IV, 21; §IV, 22.   [2] §IV, 17.   [3] §VI, 5.

[4] That of Enkomi by Schaeffer and Dikaios is of particular importance. See now §VI, 2 for a brief account.

[5] See A. Biran and O. Negbi, 'The Stratigraphical Sequence at Tel Sippor', in *I.E.J.* 16 (1966), 160 ff.

[6] §1, 4, vol. III, 125 ff.; §1, 6.   [7] See above, p. 253.

Syria. This list is of particular importance to us, since it mentions several peoples who all, save the first (*Drdny*), are hitherto already familiar and recognizable from the Hittite imperial records as being the names of peoples of Western and Central Anatolia. The identifications of the remaining names, though necessarily tentative, have been fairly generally accepted among scholars for many years. The list mentions after *Nhrn* (i.e. Mitanni) and *'Irtyn* (Arzawa, the Western Anatolian kingdom[1]), the following apparently Western Anatolian names:

Drdny	usually taken as Δάρδανοι, a Homeric Greek name for Trojans.
Ms	usually taken as equivalent to *Maša*.
Pds	usually taken as equivalent to *Pitašša*.
'Irwn	usually taken as equivalent to *Arawanna*.[2]
Krkš (or *Klkš*?)	usually taken as equivalent to *Karkiša*.
Rk (or *Lk*)	usually taken as equivalent to *Lukka*.

The Egyptians were on their side aided by *Šrdn* (Sherden)[3] mercenaries, otherwise only once previously mentioned in an Amarna letter *c.* 1375 B.C.[4] The Maša are identified by some with the Μηίονες, or *Μαίονες, an ancient name of the Lydians, but this identification presents difficulties, since, according to some authorities, the Μηίονες invaded Lydia only in the early Iron Age. The mention of *Pds* (*Pitašša*) is of some importance in a later connexion. We do not know exactly where this was, though a place of that name in Western Anatolia was known to the Hittites: in classical times there was a Pedasa near Miletus, and Homer knew very well a Pedasos on the River Satnioeis in the Troad (*Iliad* VI, 35, XX, 92, XXI, 87). Strabo (XIII, 584 and 605) speaks of Pedasos as a city of the Leleges opposite Lesbos. In his second year (1235 B.C.), the pharaoh Merneptah sent a huge gift of corn via Mukish in North Syria through Ura[5] in Western Cilicia to alleviate a severe famine in *Pds* which had formerly fought against Egypt.[6] It is perhaps permissible, with due hesitation, to connect this historical event with legend, and to see in this

---

[1] §IV, 8, 83 ff.; on the correct location of Arzawa, see H. Otten in *J.C.S.* 11 (1961), 112 f.   [2] See above, p. 253.   [3] §I, 6, vol. I, 194 ff.

[4] §I, 10, I, nos. 81, 122, 123 (*še-ir-da-ni*, *ši-ir-da-nu*), II, pp. 1166 f., 1521 for reference. Cf. W. F. Albright in §VII, 2, 167, who argues that this word is merely a form of a noun *šerdu*, 'servitor'.

[5] See §I, 2, 21, n. 4, on its location (see again below, p. 376). Another Ura in Anatolia is known on the frontiers of Azzi-Khayasha.

[6] §I, 4, vol. III, 244; §IV, 1, 143. A second grave famine in Anatolia occurred some thirty years later; see below, p. 369.

famine, so sore as to become known across the width of the Mediterranean Sea, the grim tribulation which is said by Herodotus[1] to have afflicted Lydia for eighteen years, and finally forced the Etruscans to emigrate from that country. This event is recorded by Herodotus as the Lydians' own version,[2] and is clearly ascribed to a remote antiquity. If it happened at all, it must have taken place before 1000 B.C., for the Etruscans are said to have embarked from the Gulf of Smyrna and they could hardly have done this later without coming into conflict with the Aeolic Greeks who settled, as excavations show,[3] at the head of the bay about this time. It may be noted that an Anatolian origin for the Etruscans was evidently accepted by the Hebrews (or their sources) in the early *mappa mundi* presented in Genesis x, which places Tiras (connected by some with Τυρσηνοί) as a brother of Meshech and Tubal, namely in Phrygia.

The *Arawanna* have sometimes been identified with the Hittite city Arinna[4] and *Karkiša* with Caria.[5] The mention of *Lukka* is of importance since it first raises the question where their home was. According to the Egyptians, they are brigaded closely with the *Krķš*, and it may be no coincidence that in the Hittite treaty of Muwatallish with Alakshandush of Wilusa, Lukka is placed next to *Karkiša* and *Maša* among Wilusa's allies. The Lukka-lands are often mentioned in Hittite annals as a restless and turbulent area in the west of Anatolia, but we meet some difficulties if, as is often done, we identify the *Lk* mentioned in Egyptian records with the later Lycia—an identification first put forward by de Rougé[6] in 1861—even if we combine the Hittites' *Lukka* with Lycia and even with Lycaonia.

Here archaeology is, for the present, of little help, because no remains of the Late Bronze Age have so far been found or excavated on the Lycian coast, though there are signs that this apparent absence may turn out not to apply to the interior.[7] Perhaps the existence of a common stem *Lu-* in the names of several Anatolian peoples (Lycians, Lydians, Lycaonians, Lulahhi, Luwians) may suggest a common origin. A tribe of 'Inner Lycaones' lived even in Central Phrygia near Pisidian Antioch in Roman times,[8] but the *Lukka* appear to have been a people living on and by the sea, being mentioned in 1375 B.C. as pirates in another Amarna

---

[1] Book I, 94. [2] *Ibid.*
[3] E. Akurgal, 'Bayrakli Kazisi on Rapor.' In *Ankara Üniversitesi Dil ve Tarih-Coğrafya Fakültesi Dergisi*, 7 (1950).
[4] §IV, 8, 20. [5] §IV, 6. [6] §I, 8, 303 ff. [7] §IV, 17.
[8] A. H. M. Jones, *The Cities of the Eastern Roman Provinces* (1937), 38, 66, 93.

letter.[1] (It has been claimed that the Lukka or *Lk* were present in
the Levant from at least the Egyptian Middle Kingdom, on the
basis of a reference to a member of that people in an Egyptian
hieroglyphic inscription found at Byblos, but this evidence has
now been disputed.[2]) The Lycians in later times spoke a dialect
descended from Luwian and closely related to Hittite,[3] and preserved it tenaciously into Hellenistic times. It would seem not
unreasonable that their historical origins should be traced back to
the *Lukka*. According to Greek traditions the Lycians, led by
Sarpedon, in the Homeric poem formed part of the allies of Troy.[4]
A slight difficulty remains in that we are told that the true name of
the Lycians was Termili[5] (Lycian *trm̃ml*), while Lukka was, to the
Hittites at least, only a geographical, not a tribal or racial, appellation. Whatever the explanation may be, in the deteriorating
state of affairs of the fourteenth to thirteenth centuries B.C. the
Lukka certainly played a part, if only that of an irritant.

What was going on in the cultural world of the coast of
Western Asia Minor at this time is still largely wrapped in
mystery, except for the fitful disclosures of excavation. If Troy
and Ilios are correctly identified with *Taruiša* and *Wiluŝiya*, then
Troy formed part of the Hittite Empire,[6] and if Assuwa was Asia[7]
we have in this treaty to which we have referred a picture of the
Assuwan league in the thirteenth century B.C. Miletus is widely
thought to be the Millawanda of the Hittites.[8] At Miletus, though
it was a Carian country, a powerful Mycenaean or pro-Myce-
naean colony was evidently established from the fifteenth century
B.C.[9] At Old Smyrna was a pre-Greek, non-Greek city, but unfortunately the details are largely unpublished.[10] The coastal darkness is only deepened by an occasional discovery such as that at
Phaestus in Crete, in a Middle Minoan context *c.* 1500 B.C., of an
extraordinary clay disk bearing a spirally written inscription[11] in a
strange form of pictographs impressed with movable stamps into
the clay while yet soft—a primitive but undeniable anticipation
of printing; an invention which remained as far as we know
unique in antiquity, and still-born. The forty-five signs used include designs which may represent a ship with a high prow, a
house or hut possibly of Lycian type and, most notably, a war-

---

[1] §I, 10, no. 38, 10—*amēlūtu ša (māt)lu-uk-ki*, 'people of Lukki'.
[2] §I, I.   [3] §IV, 12.   [4] *Iliad*, II, 876; V, 479, etc.
[5] Herodotus, VII, 92.   [6] See *C.A.H.* II³, pt, I, p. 677.
[7] §IV, 2.   [8] §IV, 8, 80 ff.
[9] See above, pp. 340 f.   [10] See above, p. 361, n. 3.
[11] A. Evans, *The Palace of Minos*, fig. 482. See *C.A.H.* II³, pt. I, pp. 595 ff.

rior's head crowned with what appear to be feathers. The discovery in Crete of two allegedly similar, but incised and shorter texts[1] now gives some scholars to think that the Phaestus disk is Cretan, but it may well have some Anatolian affinities or describe some Anatolian business.[2] Does the disk refer, or belong, to some other kindred people? Is it about Lycians?—or are these the σήματα λυγρά carried by Bellerophon to Lycia?[3] Herodotus (VII, 92) mentions that in his day the Lycian sailors wore a 'cap set about with feathers', but we have as yet no illustration of this headgear to compare it with that on the disc and to cause us safely to accept its evidence for a continuity of tribal fashions lasting until a thousand years later. Nor can either of these feather headdresses, whether that of Phaestus, or of the Lycians, even if mutually connected in our view, safely be connected with that of the Philistines to be described below.[4]

II. MOPSUS AND THE *DNNYM*

The impression of deepening distress and disturbance in Western Anatolia in the thirteenth century B.C., possibly due to climatic changes and famine,[5] amply reflected in Greek legends and the Hittite records, is conveyed more clearly by the affair of the prince of Zippashla, Madduwattash[6] (bearer of a name seemingly of later Lydian type similar to such as Sadyattes or Alyattes) who, in conspiracy with the king of Ahhiyawa, eventually united the western kingdoms of Anatolia against their lawful liege lord, the king of Khatti, and even swallowed up Pitashsha (= *Pds* of the Egyptians?). In his train came a freebooter named Mukshush, who followed him in some capacity which is left unclear by the fragmentary nature of the text, in which Mukshush is mentioned

[1] W. F. Brice, *Inscriptions in the Linear A Script*, 2.

[2] The hut sign (no. 24) has a strange and apparently identical precursor on a sign incised on an Early Bronze Age potsherd found in 1963, suggesting a direct continuity both of the script and of the timber architecture of Lycia. (Machteld J. Mellink, 'Lycian Wooden Huts and Sign 24 of the Phaistos Disk', *Kadmos*, 3, 1, 1964.)

[3] *Iliad*, VI, 168.   [4] See below, p. 372.

[5] The theory that the collapse of the Late Bronze Age world in both Greece and Anatolia alike was due to a vast cyclic climatic change, producing drought and universal famine conditions leading to mass migrations, is powerfully argued in §1, 5. Another theory would attribute it in large part to the great volcanic explosion of Thera and consequent tidal wave, which is ascribed to 1200 B.C. instead of, as hitherto, *c.* 1500 B.C. See Leon Pomerance, *The Final Collapse of Santorini (Thera)* (Studies in Mediterranean Archaeology, vol. XXVI, Göteborg, 1970).

[6] §IV, 9; see also above, pp. 264 f.

only once.[1] The significance of his name was not apparent until Bossert's brilliant discovery at Karatepe of the bilingual text where the name of Mukshush is rendered in the Hittite hieroglyphic (i.e. Luwian) version as Muk(a)sas, but in Phoenician as *Mpš*.[2] It is now accepted that Mukshush, the companion of Madduwattash, is identical in name with Mopsus, a strange figure of Greek legend, a seer and prince of Colophon, a city where a Mycenaean settlement certainly existed, as shown by excavations.[3] Mopsus, son of Rhakius of Clarus and Manto, daughter of Teiresias, was reputed to have engaged in a contest of divination with another seer, Calchas, at Clarus and to have founded the famous sanctuary of Apollo there.[4] Another version calls him a Lydian, son of Lydus, and brother of Torrhebus. In Lydian traditions, Mopsus' name seems to be recorded as Moxus,[5] a name also met in Greek Linear B tablets as *mo-qo-so*.[6] A year before the end of the Trojan war (so legend tells) Mopsus set out southwards with a band of followers, accompanied by Amphilochus and two Lapiths named Leonteus and Polypoetes.[7] Moving into Pamphylia, Mopsus founded its most notable cities, Aspendus and Phaselis; then, entering Cilicia, he built the half-Greek cities of *Mopsou-hestia*, 'Mopsus' hearth' (where there was later a famous oracle of the hero, clearly in recollection of his prowess in life as a soothsayer himself), and Mallus, the latter founded jointly with Amphilochus. Mopsus' name was also commemorated in Cilicia at *Mopsou-krene* ('Mopsus' spring'). Less factually perhaps, but significantly, he is said to have married Pamphyle, daughter of Kabderus (a name obviously derived from Caphtor[8]), an aetiological myth evidently designed to explain how the mixed population of Aspendus and Phaselis resulted from intermarriage of Greeks (or half-Greeks) with natives. Whoever those were, it was agreed by the Greeks that the Pamphylians were a racial hotch-potch, as their name suggested. From Cilicia Mopsus, according to the Lydian historian Xanthus,[9] moved on to Askalon, where he threw the statue of the goddess Astarte into her own lake, and finally died there.

H. Bossert's discovery in 1946[10] of the bilingual inscriptions at Karatepe in the Ceyhan valley of Cilicia in Southern Turkey, written in the Phoenician alphabet and in Hittite hieroglyphs (i.e. Luwian), described above, not only finally solved the riddle

---

[1] §1, 2, 61 ff.   [2] §IV, 1, 142.   [3] See above, p. 184.
[4] §IV, 2, 54.   [5] §1, 2, 56 ff.
[6] §v, 6, tablets KN X 1497 and PY Sa 774.   [7] See above, pp. 355 f.
[8] See below, p. 374.   [9] §IV, 25.   [10] §IV, 4; §IV, 5.

of the reading of the hieroglyphs, but made a historical contribution of unusual importance by transforming for the first time a figure of Greek legend, Mopsus, into an undeniable historical personality.[1] In this inscription, King Azitawatas, author of the Karatepe texts, discloses himself as a lesser chieftain of the Danuniyim (the exact vocalization of the name is uncertain; these people of the ninth century B.C. are clearly the same as the Danuna mentioned in the fourteenth century B.C. in an Amarna letter[2]) who seem to have formed an important kingdom[3] in the fourteenth century B.C., but whose chief city was probably Pakhri, mentioned by Shalmaneser III[4] and identifiable with Pagrai in the Amanus mountains. It is of importance that, where the Hittite hieroglyphic, i.e. Luwian, text describes Azitawatas's overlord Awarkus[5] (identified usually with a king of Que or Cilicia mentioned in the Assyrian records of Tiglath-pileser III under the name of Urikki), as 'king of the city of Adana', the Phoenician text describes him as 'king of the Danuniyim'. The names are thus virtually identical, the prefixed 'A' of Adana having some unexplained implication.[6] Further, a connexion is perhaps to be seen with Greece in the likely identification of Danuniyim–Danuna with the Greek Danaoi and the family of Danaos, who is credited in Greek legends with an oriental origin.[7] Possibly these *Dnnym* may be also the hitherto elusive Hypachaioi, or 'sub-Achaeans' of Cilicia, mentioned by Herodotus (VII, 91) as a former name of the Cilicians.[8] Some scholars have seen, somewhat dubiously, a survival of the name of Achaeans ('Αχαιοί) in the Assyrian name Que (= *Qawa?) for Eastern Cilicia.[9] More important, Azitawatas states in his inscription that he is of the house of *Mpš*, or Mopsus, whose name, as we have said, is rendered in the Luwian version as Muksas by a $p > k$ change for which

---

[1] See below, pp. 679 ff. Since 1969, however, it has been powerfully argued by Otten (A, 12) and others, on both philological and historical grounds, that the Madduwattash episode and consequently Mopsus' date have to be put back to the early fourteenth century B.C. As stated in *C.A.H.* II³, pt. 1, p. 677, the present *History* cannot take full cognizance of this development and treats these texts in the traditional way.

[2] §1, 10. The value of the Mopsus legend in history is well discussed in §1, 2, 53 ff.

[3] The considerable extent of their kingdom as far as the Amanus is discussed by §1, 2.

[4] §1, 2, 2 n. 4.   [5] '*Wrk* in the Phoenician version.

[6] Since, according to Stephanus, the founder of Adana was called Adanos, M. C. Astour believes that Adana is derived from a personal name (Adan = lord), §1, 2, 39; §1, 2, 2.

[7] §1, 2, ch. 1.

[8] §IV, 13; §IV, 14.   [9] §IV, 13.

Lydian gives illustrations.[1] This form of his name (Moxus), which is recorded by Xanthus, adds a city, Moxoupolis, in Southern Phrygia to his list of foundations and connects with him a tribe of Moxianoi in Western Phrygia.

III. THE CLASH OF SEA AND LAND RAIDERS WITH EGYPT

The *razzia* of Mopsus may be reasonably regarded[2] as part of the downward thrust of the horde of assailants whom the Egyptians called collectively the 'Peoples of the Sea'—who first massed against Egypt from the West via Libya in the reign of the pharaoh Merneptah about 1232 B.C., but were then repulsed and withdrew.[3] These events were known to us largely from the Egyptian accounts, but a casual reference in the Bible to the bloody repulse by Shamgar Ben-Anath of a force of six hundred invading Philistines (Judges iii. 31) may refer to this phase of preliminary probings, and there are some archaeological reasons to think that some settlement by Philistines or other closely related 'Sea Peoples' in Palestine, e.g. at Beth-shan and Tell el-Fār'ah, may start in this period[4] before 1200 B.C. Soon, gathering full strength and benefiting from the overthrow of the Hittite Empire in about 1200 B.C., the Sea Peoples surged down again like a flood through Syria and Palestine, carrying all before them, until they were stayed only at the north-eastern gates of Egypt.

Let us take the earlier onslaught first. In his records at Karnak and Athribis[5] Merneptah (1236–1223 B.C.) boasts that he won his great victory in Libya in his fifth year (1232 B.C.) against an army of Libyans and Meshwesh (the later 'Maxyes'), who were supported by an alliance of northern sea-borne forces. Their names are given as *'Ikwš* (vocalized variously as Akawasha, Akaiwasha, or Ekwesh), *Trš* (Teresh or Tursha), *Lk* (Lukku or Lukka), *Šrdn* (Sherden or Shardana), *Škrš* (Sheklesh or Shakalsha), 'northerners coming from all lands'. These names

---

[1] §1, 2, 62: as stated above, p. 364 and n.6, the *q* is preserved in Mycenaean Greek, i.e. Linear B versions of his name, but paradoxically it is the Phoenician version in the Karatepe text which has followed a Western Anatolian tendency to change *q* to *p*.

[2] See now, however, above, p. 365, n. 1.

[3] §1, 4, vol. III, 238 ff.; see also above, p. 233.

[4] §VII, 25; §VII, 27. At Tell el-Fār'ah, five tombs with multiple burials in the '900' cemetery have been recognized as strongly Mycenaean in type, containing LM IIIb ware, yet otherwise Philistine in their content.

[5] §1, 4, vol. III, 240 ff; see also above, pp. 233 f.

include only two which were previously known, namely Lukka and Sherden.[1] The numbers of prisoners recorded by the pharaoh's scribes as captured are given as: Sheklesh, 222; Teresh, 742; Akawasha, 2,201. These figures, though we need not trust them too blindly, might well imply that the Akawasha were the strongest element and very probably to some extent the ringleaders, but the Athribis stela gives the figure of 2,200 as Teresh, thereby injecting some doubts into our minds about its accuracy. All these peoples are described as 'of the Sea'.[2] The ending of their names in -*sha* has suggested since Maspero (1897) an Asia Minor ethnic ending; today we might see it as an Indo-European nominative. Illustrations of several of these peoples occur in various Egyptian triumphal scenes,[3] and aid us in identifying them. No illustration exists of Lukka or Aka-washa, but we learn with surprise that the Akawasha were cir-cumcised Merneptah, in his victory inscriptions at Karnak and Athribis,[4] records the number of slain Akawasha, mentioning that their hands were cut off instead of their genital members as was done in the case of uncircumcised victims. Since de Rougé's time, too, Akawasha have been identified with 'Αχαιοί, the Mycenaean Greeks and, since the recovery of the Hittite records, by most with the Ahhiyawa.[5] If this is so, it is absolutely out of keeping with everything that we know about the Greeks, and therefore about the Akawasha, that they should have been circumcised, though it was a practice common to both Egyptians and Semites. The matter remains inexplicable.[6]

The Tursha (or Teresh) and Sheklesh–Shakalsha are shown bearded alike, the Sheklesh wearing a high headcloth, the Tursha a smaller type; both sport a pointed kilt with tassels and many hang a medallion on a cord or thong round their necks—a custom common in Syria and Anatolia, even in Iran.[7] Their armament consists of a pair of spears or a *khepesh* (scimitar); their chests are protected by bandaging with strips perhaps of linen or leather. These two races have been identified since Champollion and de Rougé,[8] though, admittedly, only speculatively, with the Etrus-cans (the Tyrsenoi of Lydia who bear the ethnic ending in -ēnos, common in Anatolia) and the Sicels, who are supposed by the

---

[1] See above, pp. 360 f. also p. 233 and below p. 508.
[2] §1, 8, 305 and 318.
[3] §1, 19, pl. 160A and 160B; §1, 19, plate on p. 342.
[4] See above, p. 366 n. 5.   [5] §1, 8.
[6] But see §1, 2, 355 ff.
[7] §III, 3, 83 ff. and reference therein; §III, 2.
[8] §1, 8.

advocates of this view to have been on their way westwards to their ultimate Mediterranean home in Sicily.[1] In fact, new-comers are said to appear at this time in Sicily bringing with them a new type of lugged axe; the archaeological evidence in Italy, however, for the arrival of the Etruscans so early is still wanting.

The Sherden, who as mercenaries are known in Egyptian records from the time of Amenophis III, are shown in Egyptian reliefs as beardless and wearing a very distinctive helmet (some-times held under the chin with a chinstrap) with a large knob or disc at its apex, and ornamented with enormous projecting bull's horns.[2] They are armed with a round shield with a handle, and brandish a huge two-edged sword of distinctive type, suitable either for slashing or thrusting. A unique example of it, now in the British Museum, was obtained in 1911 at Beit Dāgān, a Pales-tinian village near the town of Jaffa (it was not from Gaza, as often misstated).[3] The Sherden have been very plausibly identified with the bronze-working population of the Sardinian stone-built towers or *nuraghi*, a race whose remarkably vigorous bronze statuettes (though hitherto known from examples not earlier than the ninth century B.C.) often show them as warriors armed with round shields and wearing horned helmets resembling the Sherden type, but without the central knob or disc very characteristic of Sherden.[4] A further connexion between Corsica and the Sherden is strongly suggested by R. Grosjean's[5] recent observation that menhir-like tombstones still stand in Corsica showing male warriors wearing banded corselets, daggers and formerly horned helmets, the horns having been separately inserted into holes in the stone, but now having long disappeared. That the Sherden were seafarers and pirates is more than likely. It fits the evidence fairly well that the builders of the *nuraghi* appear suddenly in Sardinia between about 1400 and 1200 B.C., though we have no positive indication as |to whence they came.[6]. It is likely enough that they immigrated into Sardinia from Cyprus,[7] where they may well have been a native

---

[1] See below, ch. XXXVII, sect. II.   [2] E.g. §1, 19, pl. 160 B.

[3] See R. D. Barnett, *Illustrations of Old Testament History* (London, 1966), 29 and fig. 16. Near Beit Dāgān is the ancient site of Azor, now under excavation, where plentiful Philistine material occurs.

[4] §II, 1, 187 ff.   [5] §II, 2.   [6] §II, 1, 111 and 187 ff.

[7] A significant pointer to contacts between Cyprus and Sardinia in this period is to be seen in the occurrence in Sardinia of copper ingots of the characteristic 4-handled Cypriot shape, derived from a leather hide, now well known from the Cape Gelidonya wreck. (See above, pp. 214 f.; and G. Bass, 'The Cape Gelidonya Wreck' in *A.J.A.* 65 (1961), 267 ff.)

copper-working people. In the earliest Phoenician inscription found in Sardinia, that from Nora, probably of the ninth century B.C., although it is incomplete, the name of the island appears as Shardan (*be-shardan*), and thus the identification of Sardinia with the Sherden seems much strengthened.[1] Another pointer in Sardinia to the former presence of the Sea Peoples lies in the representation in a bronze figure and on the island's coins in Roman times of the eponymous divine ancestor Sardus Pater as a bearded man wearing a stiffly erect headdress,[2] resembling that favoured by Sea Peoples, particularly the Philistines, to be described below.

As we have said, the final assault on Egypt came after the turn of the thirteenth century B.C. The gathering clouds are reflected in the last documents found at Khattusha and Ugarit. Among the tablets from the archives of Rap'anu found at Ras Shamra (Ugarit) during the 20th and 26th seasons of excavations were three letters mentioning a famine in Anatolia (Khatti). Ugarit is asked to send 2,000 measures of grain from Mukish to Ura in Cilicia.[3] In another letter from Ras Shamra[4] the king of Ugarit appeals for help to the king of Alashiya (almost certainly Cyprus), whom he calls 'my father'. A reply (?) found in the oven from one *Ydn* urges him to arm a considerable fleet of 150 ships to resist the enemy. Meanwhile, the king of Ugarit writes: 'Does not my father know that all my forces and chariots are stationed in Khatti Land, and all my ships are in Lukka Land?' [which is thus identifiable as coastal] 'Thus the country is abandoned to itself. . . seven enemy ships have appeared and inflicted much damage upon us.'[5] Clearly, the combined fleets are massing off Lycia, while the armies are joining up in the West. By the end of the reign of Shuppiluliumash II, the last Hittite king, we find from Hittite sources that Alashiya has changed sides, and its ships are fighting against the Hittites. Finally, a tablet found at Boğazköy in 1961 reports the defeat of the Alashiyan navy.[6] 'I called up arms and soon reached the sea, I, Shuppiluliumash, the Great

---

[1] *C.I.S. I*, no. 144, on p. 191; see also W. F. Albright below, ch. XXXIII and *Bull. A.S.O.R.* 83 (1941), 14 ff.

[2] G. Perrot and C. Chipiez, *Histoire de l'Art dans l'Antiquité* (Paris, 1887), vol. IV, fig. 7 on p. 21. He seems however to have been also identified with the Phoenician god of Hunting, Sid; see U. Bianchi, 'Sardus Pater' in *Rendiconti dell'Accademia Nazionale dei Lincei*, ser. VIII, 18 (1963), 97 ff. and S. Moscati, 'Antas: a new Punic site in Sardinia', in *Bull. A.S.O.R.* 196 (Dec. 1964), 23 ff.

[3] J. Nougayrol, *Ugaritica* v (1968), texts 33, 44 and 171. See also §1, 3, 253 ff.

[4] §1, 3, 255.   [5] §IV, 18, 20 ff.

[6] See above, p. 265; §IV, 18.

King, and with me the ships of Alashiya joined battle in the midst of the sea. I destroyed them, catching them and burning them down at sea.' Meanwhile, at Boğazköy, in the royal palace of Büyükkale all the walls were demolished and the flood of invaders poured onwards in a southerly direction perhaps joining hands with the coastal force led by Mopsus and his allies. At about this time the late Mycenaean settlement at Miletus in Caria was burnt. In Cilicia Mersin,[1] with its late Hittite palace, fell, as did Tarsus.[2] So, too, fell Carchemish, the great capital city controlling the crossing of the Euphrates, from which the Hittite Great King's Viceroy had long ruled over the cities of North Syria.[3] Ras Shamra–Ugarit and Tell Sūkās[4] on the Syrian coast were sacked; the former never recovered. Hamath was captured and occupied by the newcomers, who, it seems, after the resettlement were responsible for introducing the rite of cremation burial,[5] as happened at Carchemish,[6] Tell Sūkās,[7] and Açana.[8] This suggests that the Sea Peoples brought it with them. Sidon, too, was destroyed, according to tradition, while its inhabitants fled to Tyre.[9] Tell Abu Hawwām (identified by Mazar with Salmon, a Tyrian colony), a vast site on the Palestinian coast near Haifa, likewise fell.[10] With several of these destructions is associated the discovery of LH III c 1 a pottery, a circumstance which may well indicate the presence or passage of the Akawasha–Achaeans mentioned by Merneptah. The story in Cyprus is similar. Excavations at Kition (Larnaca) since 1962, until then supposed to have been a purely Phoenician foundation of the Iron Age, show that it was a wealthy city in the Bronze Age, comparable with Enkomi,[11] but there are traces of a great catastrophe at the end of the thirteenth century B.C., followed by fresh settlers. These were evidently the first Greek settlers, who built themselves large houses of ashlar masonry, and used LH III c 1 pottery. This settlement was short-lived, being destroyed by the same movement of the Sea Peoples as Enkomi. It was reconstructed before the period of LH III c 2 or 'Granary Style' pottery which was used there in the eleventh century. It was finally abandoned c. 1075 B.C. after a catastrophe, probably an earth-

---

[1] §IV, 7. [2] §IV, 10.

[3] See E. Laroche, 'Matériaux pour l'étude des relations entre Ugarit et le Hatti', *Ugaritica*, 3, 1956 (ed. C. F. A. Schaeffer).

[4] §I, 15

[5] §I, 16; W. F. Albright in *Bull. A.S.O.R.* 83 (1941), 14 ff.

[6] C. L. Woolley and R. D. Barnett, *Carchemish*, vol. III (London, 1952).

[7] §I, 15. [8] §I, 18.

[9] Justin, XVIII, 3, 5; cf. Josephus, *Ant. Jud.* VIII, 62.

[10] §VII, 20. [11] §VI, 3; A, 9.

quake, only later to be recolonized by the Phoenicians. Similarly, at Enkomi[1] in the early twelfth century the 'Close Style' appears, perhaps emanating from Rhodes, which was by now under control of the Achaeans, possibly those known to the Hittites as Ahhiyawa. (This is the point at which the Hittite king Arnuwandash III is complaining to Madduwattash that he has supported Attarshiyash and Piggaya in seizing Cyprus.[2]) The 'aristocratic' quarter on the west side of the city was burnt, probably by Sea Peoples, at the beginning of the twelfth century B.C., but industrial life continued, using debased Levanto-Helladic ware in Levels IV–II. 'Granary Style' then appears in Levels III–II, finally dominating by the time of Level I, together with Cypriot Iron Age I pottery.[3] At Paphos, the city and shrine of Aphrodite was traditionally founded (or refounded) by an Arcadian, Agapenor.[4]

IV. THE PHILISTINES

In his fifth year (1194 B.C.), Ramesses III found himself involved in a fresh war with the Libyans on his western border, and reports in his triumphal record at Medīnet Habu that already[5] 'the northern countries quivered in their bodies, namely the Peleset, Tjekk[er]... They were cut off [from] their land, coming, their spirit broken. They were *thr*[6]-warriors on land; another [group] was on the sea...' Three years later, he graphically pictures the collapsing world of the Levant as far as the farthest horizon: 'As for the foreign countries, they made a conspiracy in their isles. Removed and scattered in the fray were the lands at one time. No land could stand before their arms, from Khatti, Qode [= Cilicia], Carchemish, Yereth [= Arzawa], and Yeres [Alashiya] on, [but they were] cut off at [one time]. A camp [was set up] in one place in Amor [Amurru]. They desolated its people, and its land was like that which has never come into being. They were coming, while the flame was prepared before them, forward toward Egypt. Their confederation was the Peleset, Tjekker, Sheklesh, Denye[n] and Weshesh lands united.'[7] From

---

[1] §vi, 2; §vi, 4; §vi, 6.
[2] §iv, 9, 157 ff.; §vi, 3; see above, ch. xxiv, sect. iv; but see above, p. 365, n. 1.
[3] §vi, 3.
[4] Strabo, xiv, 6, 3.
[5] §i, 4, vol. iv, 18–26; W. F. Edgerton and J. A. Wilson, *Historical Records of Ramses III*, pp. 30 f.; see below, pp. 507 ff.; above, pp. 241 ff.
[6] A foreign word for chariot-warriors, see §i, 13, 239, n. 3; §i, 7, 40.
[7] Edgerton and Wilson, *op. cit.* p. 53.

the above account it is deducible (though not by any means proved) that the clash took the form of two battles:[1] the first in Syria (Amurru or Zahi) against the Land Raiders, perhaps taking the form of a rearguard action; the second real fight, against the Sea Raiders, taking place in the Delta at the entrance to Egypt itself, though Schaeffer[2] believes that this battle too occurred far north of the frontier, near Arvad. This sea battle is depicted in the sculptures of the exquisite temple at Medīnet Habu with great realism.[3] The Egyptians are aided by Sherden mercenaries. The Peleset are clean-shaven, wearing a very distinctive head-gear made of what seems to be a circle of upright reeds (or possibly leather strips or horsehair not, as often said, feathers) mounted on a close-fitting cap with a horizontal, variously decorated band round the wearer's brow.[4] The whole head-dress was held in place by a chin-strap tied under the chin. On their bodies the Peleset or Philistines, for such they are, wear a panelled kilt, falling in front to a point, usually decorated with tassels (such a tasselled kilt is worn by a Southern Anatolian god on a stele from near Çağdin[5]) and their chests are protected by bandaging with horizontal strips, perhaps of linen, or a ribbed corselet. They carry a pair of spears, sometimes a full-size rapier sword (which, it has been argued, has Caucasian affinities[6]), and a circular shield with a handle like those of the Sherden. On land, they fight in the Hittite manner from a chariot with crews of three, consisting of two warriors and a driver, while their families follow, partially guarded in wooden ox-drawn peasant carts usually of Anatolian type with solid wheels, like those used by the Hittites at the Battle of Qadesh. The draught animals are humped oxen, a breed bred in Anatolia, but not used in the Aegean or Palestine.[7] It is universally agreed that the Peleset are the Philistines of the Bible, of whom these Egyptian records thus form the first explicit historical mention. This people clearly in some respects has a strong connexion with Anatolia—a point supported by their monopoly and expert mastery of metal-working (cf. I Sam. xiii. 19–22 often interpreted as reference to

[1] This is suggested in §1, 13, 260, n. 4.

[2] §vi, 4, 60.

[3] §1, 20, 334–8, 340.

[4] T. Dothan suggests that this decorated band, bearing knobs, zigzag patterns or vertical fluting indicates differences of rank or class (A, 5). It is also worn in this battle by Tjekker and Denyen.

[5] H. T. Bossert, *Altanatolien*, fig. 567.

[6] R. Maxwell-Hyslop, 'Daggers and Swords in Western Asia', in *Iraq*, 8 (1946), 59 f. (type 53).

[7] §1, 10, 338 f.

ironworking) of which the Hittite kings boasted some skill, and which is attested by the actual discovery of increasing amount of artifacts of iron at the Philistine sites in Palestine of 'Ain Shems, Tell Jemmeh, Fā'rah, Azor and Ashdod.[1] Other indications equally, or even more clearly, point to very close connexions with the Mycenaean Greeks (who as Akawasha are in fact quoted by the Egyptians as serving with the Philistines against Egypt in year 5 of Ramesses III). That the Philistines traditionally had a connexion of some kind with Crete is upheld by the fact that part of the Philistine coast was called the 'Cretan' South or *negeb* (I Sam. xxx. 14), and Cretans are sometimes described with Philistines in the Bible (Ezekiel xxv. 16, Zeph. ii. 5).[2] The ships in which the Philistines are shown fighting against the Egyptians in the sea battle are of a most unusual type, powered by sail only, not by oars, with a central mast bearing a crow's nest, a curved keel, a high stern and prow ending in a duck's head; yet such a ship is depicted on a late Helladic III vase[3] from Skyros, and on a Levanto-Helladic Pictorial Style vase from Enkomi.[4] Some scholars have seen significance in two Philistine words preserved in the Hebrew Bible: *kōba'* (I Sam. xvii. 5), for Goliath's helmet, apparently to be derived from the Anatolian word *kupaḫḫi* (helmet); and the Philistines' word for chieftain, preserved in Hebrew as *seren*, which may be connected with the word τύραννος 'lord', itself borrowed by the Greeks from Lydia.[5] Others see in the challenge to single combat between David and the Philistine champion Goliath a typically European, Hellenic idea. An important index is naturally the Philistines' very distinctive pottery (including a rapidly growing group of distinctive cult vessels and figurines),[6] partly Mycenaean in shape, yet unlike Mycenaean ware in being not varnish-painted but matt-painted bichrome ware, decorated in metopes, often with volutes, a common design being a swan with turned-back head. It is connected with LH III c 1 b ware of Greece and Rhodes (the so-called 'Close Style'). This Philistine pottery is not merely found at the sites in Palestine associated with the Philistine invasion, at Megiddo in Levels VII A, VI B and A and in Beth Shemesh in Level III, but also closely

---

[1] §vii, 1; §vii, 6. R. de Vaux considers that the Sea Peoples' ships, apart from prow and poop, basically do not differ from Syrian merchant-ships depicted on Egyptian reliefs (A, 13).

[2] A group of Cretan seals was found near Gaza: V. Kenna, *Cretan Seals* (Oxford, 1960), 65, 78, 151 f.

[3] §v, 7, figs. 43 f. on p. 259.

[4] §vi, 7, fig. 10 (from Tomb 3, no. 2620).

[5] See below, p. 516 and n. 3.   [6] §vii, 5; §vii, 15; §vii, 16.

resembles LH III 1b ware found at Enkomi and Sinda[1] in Cyprus.

We might perhaps hope to find some clues to the Philistines' origins in their religion, but of the Philistines' religion we know almost nothing, since their gods of later times—Dagon, Ashtoreth and Ba'al-z°būb—are clearly either Canaanite or adaptations to Canaanite cults. B. Mazar sees in the introduction and spread of the cult of Ba'al-shamem, god of the sky, Philistine influence inspired by the Greek Olympian Zeus.[2] H. Margulies[3] sees in the reference to flies and bees in Philistine cults and legends such as that of Samson allusions to bee-cults and other worships and beliefs of the Greek and Minoan world. Early terracotta figurines illustrating a seated female deity of Mycenaean style have been found in excavations at Ashdod which point clearly to a Mycenaean origin.[4] Philistine burial customs take various forms, including Mycenaean-type chambers with *dromoi* and anthropoid clay coffins at Tellel-Fār'ah[5] (probably to be identified with Sharuhen) in the twelfth and early eleventh centuries B.C. and cremations at 'Azor (like those of Hamath) in the eleventh. At Beth-shan in the thirteenth century begin these clay slipper-type sarcophagi with heads crudely modelled in relief.[6] Some of the heads on these sarcophagus lids have the decorated headbands characteristic of the Philistines and in one case a row of vertical strokes indicating the common Sea Peoples' war headdress. Over the dead man's mouth a plate of gold foil was occasionally tied, a custom reminiscent of burials at Mycenae, but also met surviving into the tenth century[7] at Tell Halaf (Gozan), a half-Aramaean city of North Syria, suggesting a remote echo of the passage of the Peoples of the Sea.[8] Hebrew traditions about the origins of the Philistines unanimously agree on their connexion with the Aegean world. In Genesis x. 14 (cf. I Chron. i. 12) they are said to be derived from Caphtor, son of Miṣraim (= Egypt) brother of Ludim (i.e. the Lydians) and various Egyptian and North African races —a highly possible allusion to the participation of the Peleset in

---

[1] §vii, 5, 154. Recent discoveries at Ashdod in the earliest Philistine levels have disclosed two things: first, its LH III 1c pottery can be in fact demonstrated by analysis of the clay to have been locally made (A, 4). Next, it is accompanied by the earliest form of Philistine ware, a white wash and bichrome pottery in which several later characteristic Philistine shapes are represented.   [2] §vii, 20.

[3] In an unpublished MS, to which the author kindly allowed me to refer.

[4] §vii, 5.   [5] §vii, 27; see also above p. 366, n. 4.

[6] §vii, 5; see below, pp. 510 f. I am indebted to Mr E. Oren, who will shortly publish the Beth-shan cemetery, for this information and for his comments.   [7] §vii, 23.   [8] *Ibid.*

the Egyptian wars. But according to Amos (ix. 7), Deut. (ii. 23) and Jeremiah (xlvii. 4) their home was Caphtor, 'an island in the sea', certainly identifiable with the land *Kapturi* or *Kaptara* known from cuneiform texts,[1] and probably correctly identified with Crete, for Egyptians the home of the Keftiu,[2] an Aegean people often depicted in Eighteenth Dynasty tombs as foreigners bearing tribute. It is, however, conceivable, as argued by Wain-wright, that Caphtor and the land of the Keftiu were Cilicia;[3] yet if so, how is it that Caphtor–Keftiu is never mentioned by the Hittites? Probably in Egypt and the Levant during the Eighteenth Dynasty Kaphtor became used as a generalized term for the Cretan–Mycenaean world. The word then seems to have gone largely out of use after the fall of Cnossus. The word *kaptōr* remains in Hebrew as a curious vestige that by the time of Exodus (xxv. 31–6, cf. Amos ix. 1) had come to mean for the Hebrews, doubtless borrowing it from the Phoenicians, an ornament perhaps in the form of a lily-flower or palmette, presumably originally of Aegean (Minoan) origin. Other origins, however, have been proposed for the Philistines:[4] Albright[5] returns to the old identification of them with the mysterious pre-Greek population called by the Greeks Pelasgians, assuming this name to be equated somehow with Peleset.

Archaeological finds, on the other hand, suggest that the immigration of the Philistines into Palestine was effected in two or even three stages. First come some settlements represented by tombs at Deir-el-Balaḥ and Beth-shan.[6] Then, about 1200 B.C., comes a period of invasions and burnings, e.g. at Megiddo and Ashdod. To about 1200 B.C. is to be dated the find in a sanctuary at Deir 'Allā of clay tablets bearing inscriptions in an unknown script of very Aegean appearance.[7] (This date is given by a broken faience vase found in the sanctuary bearing the cartouche of Queen Tawosret of Egypt.) After this comes the third stage: the Land and Sea Battles, followed by final Philistine settlements in Palestine to be described. There also seem to be increasing indications of Philistine connexions with some part of Cyprus. In

---

[1] E.g. §1, 12, vol. IV, 107, text 16238, 10. Kaphtor is also known in the Ras Shamra Texts, where it is called the residence of the artificer god, *Ktr-w-Ḥss* (§1, 2, 110). [2] §1, 17, 110 f.

[3] §IV, 19; §IV, 10; §IV, 21; §IV, 22; §IV, 23.

[4] E.g. by M. Müller, §VII, 22. [5] See below, pp. 512 f.

[6] Bronze figures of men wearing feather head-dresses from sites in Syria and Phoenicia, e.g. H. T. Bossert, *Altsyrien* (1951), fig. 584, have been used in discussion of the Sea Peoples but evidently are unconnected with them.

[7] §VII, 11. See below, p. 510; above, p. 336.

the first place we have connexions indicated by the origin of Philistine ware, described above. Above this level were traces of Philistine 'squatters'. Ramesses III (1198–1166 B.C.) mentions among a list of his enemies several towns of Cyprus, *Srmsk* (Salamis), *Ktn* (Kition), *'Imr* (Marion?), *Sr* (Soli), *Rtr* (Idalion). Ramesses III claims to have repulsed the *tk(k)r* (Tjekker),[1] a group identified on Egyptian reliefs as wearing a head-dress of a type described above,[2] commonly accepted as Philistine. One branch of this people certainly settled in strength at points on the coast of Phoenicia and Palestine, at Byblos and Dor, as is shown by the Tale of Wenamun, the Egyptian emissary from Thebes in the time of Smendes (early eleventh century B.C.), who is sent to buy cedar logs but brings back a long tale of woe.[3] But to connect the Tjekker with the Greek hero Teucros or Teucer of Salamis is very tempting. To Teucer is traditionally ascribed the foundation of Olba (Ura?) in Cilicia and Salamis in Cyprus. Tjekker appear to be already present in Enkomi (Salamis) even before its destruction at the turn of the thirteenth to twelfth century B.C., for late thirteenth-century vases from Enkomi Tomb 3 show men wearing what is apparently a headdress of 'Philistine' type, walking or riding in chariots.[4] The ivory gaming-box from Enkomi in the British Museum decorated in Mycenaean style shows a charioteering nobleman or king of Syrian type followed by a bearded Tjekker servant with 'Philistine' head-dress holding an axe.[5] In the ruins of the city of Enkomi of the twelfth century B.C., afterwards rebuilt, was found a stone seal engraved with figure of a warrior holding a large shield and again wearing the familiar 'Philistine' head-dress.[6] It may very well be that the Teucrians–Tjekker destroyed, rebuilt and ruled over the new Salamis. Thereafter, we find that in Cyprus the Philistine type of boat, ending in a duck's head, continued in use there till the seventh or sixth century, as depicted on a vase.[7]

The Tjekker were, it would seem, not the only group of Sea Peoples to live, or to gain a foothold, in Cyprus. A splendid bronze statuette of a god wearing a felt or fur helmet with huge horns somewhat resembling the Sherden type was discovered at Enkomi by Dikaios in 1952.[8] In 1963 other statuettes with horned helmets were discovered, one holding a spear and round

---

[1] §1, 4, vol. IV, 24–5 and 75–6. [2] §VI, 8; §III, 3. See above, pp. 372 f.
[3] §1, 13, 25 ff. [4] §VI, 7, fig. 19 and fig. 10.
[5] A. S. Murray, A. H. Smith and H. B. Walters, *Excavations in Cyprus* (1900), pl. 1. [6] §VI, 2, fig. 11.
[7] Unpublished, in National Museum, Cyprus. [8] §VI, 2; A, 1.

shield standing on a model of an ingot.[1] Such figures tempt us to suggest not only that the Sherden came to Egypt from Cyprus, but that there were other Sea Peoples there too. In the Great Harris Papyrus, Ramesses III declares:[2] 'I extended all the frontiers of Egypt and overthrew those who had attacked them from their lands. I slew the Denyen [who are] in their islands, while the Tjekker and the Peleset were made ashes. The Sherden and the Weshesh of the Sea were made non-existent, taken captive all together and brought in captivity to Egypt like the sands of the shore. I settled them in strongholds bound in my name. The military classes were as numerous as hundred-thousands. I assigned portions for them all with clothing and provisions from the treasuries and granaries every year.' As for the 'Weshesh of the Sea', there is little to be said. Axos in Crete (spelt *Waxos* on its coinage) and Iasus or Iassos (also spelt Ouassos in inscriptions) in S.W. Caria have been suggested.[3] But this proclamation gives us an explicit clue that the invading Denyen—Danuniyim at least came through the Aegean islands; possibly also through Cyprus, and evidence may be plausibly seen in the Assyrian name for Cyprus in the eighth century B.C.,[4] Yadnana, to be interpreted as 'ia-danana, 'Isle (or Coast) of the Danana', though no archaeological proof of Danuna settlement in Cyprus has so far been found. Very possibly Aspendus in Pamphylia was an outlying settlement of theirs, since its native name as given on its coins was *Estwedi*, apparently identical with the name of *Azitawata*, king of the city at Karatepe. In Eastern Cilicia, however, their old home, the Denyen lived on, as we have seen, into the ninth century B.C., strong enough to cause alarm to their neighbour across the Amanus, Kalamu of Sam'al,[5] and to be a thorn in his flesh. Whatever their original racial affinities, both groups were by then alike Semitized in speech though largely Anatolian in culture.

The outcome of the war between Egypt and the Sea Raiders is well known. Ramesses III claims to have utterly defeated them and suggestions that he and his successors settled groups of Peleset (Philistine) mercenary garrisons in Beth-shan in Palestine are demonstrated by the finds there of 'Sea People' burials. Others are found at Tell el-Fār'ah. He further seems to have given over to their care the four Canaanite cities of Gaza, Askalon, Ashdod and Dor, occupied by the Tjekker, as is made clear by Wenamon's

---

[1] §vi, 5.   [2] §i, 13, 262.   [3] See §iii, 3, 71, n. 3.
[4] D. D. Luckenbill, *Ancient Records of Assyria and Babylonia*, §§ 54, 70, 80, 82, 92, 96–9, 102, 186, 188 (Sargon II); §690, 709–10 (Esarhaddon).
[5] §iv, 15.

report. (Two more cities, Gath and Ekron in the plain to the east, were occupied by them and formed with Gaza, Askalon and Ashdod a league of five cities ruled by *seranim*.)[1] One may perhaps wonder if the pharaoh's victory was as crushing as he suggests or whether, as was his wont, he is protesting too much; whether in fact it was not a Pyrrhic victory. The Peleset hordes were indeed prevented from entering Egypt, if such was their intention, but whether by treaty or tacit consent of the pharaoh were able to settle unhindered in the fertile Shephelah or coastal plain of Palestine,[2] to which they have given their name ever since, commanding the 'going out from Egypt', the *Via Maris*, and forcing the pharaohs to abandon their claims—maintained since the Eighteenth Dynasty—to sovereignty over Palestine. Egypt thereupon withdrew upon herself and a new phase of the history of the Near East was begun.

[1] The Egyptian *Onomasticon* of Amenemope, *c.* 1100 B.C. (see §1, 6)—a kind of gazetteer—mentions Shardana, Tjekker and Philistines after naming the cities of Askalon, Ashdod and Gaza.

[2] §7, 26. See also W. F. Albright, 'An Anthropoid Clay Coffin from Sahab in Trans-Jordan', in *A.J.A.* 36 (1932), 295 ff.

CHAPTER XXIX

ELAM *c.* 1600–1200 B.C.

I. REIGNS AND EVENTS

I T is generally admitted that after the end of the First Dynasty in Babylon, and following upon the death of Shamshi-Adad I in Assyria, there begins a period of great obscurity. The former abundance of documents ceases as though some catastrophe had paralysed the ordinary life of these countries. No text reveals the true causes of this overthrow, but we know that, with the beginning of this sterile period, there came a fresh and powerful advance towards Mesopotamia of the mountain peoples which had harassed it so long. By this time the Hurrians had settled about the upper reaches of the Tigris, and Kassites from the Zagros had drifted into the Mesopotamian plain as workers.

Tribal groups of these peoples who dwelt on the mountain border were now driven from behind by a new Indo-European influx coming, this time, from the north and north-east. The Hurrians, mingled with Aryans, spread over the area between the bend of the Euphrates and the district of Nuzi, to the east of Assyria, and advanced southwards into Palestine. At the same time the Kassites descended in force and made themselves masters of Babylonia, carrying with them isolated groups of Hurrians, some of whom settled around Nippur,[1] where they are found afterwards. The irruption of these less civilized highlanders is generally considered to be the reason for the sudden cessation of historical sources and for the evident decline of Mesopotamian culture in this period.

From the native evidence alone it is difficult to estimate the influence these events had on the history of Elam. Undoubtedly there was an abrupt change in the locality of our sources. It is no longer at Mālamīr, in Susiana, but at Liyan, several hundred miles to the south-east, that the next Elamite texts reappear. We have no means of estimating the lapse of time involved here, as the indigenous sources do not indicate a gap of any importance. The later texts which begin with the names of earlier kings do not show a break in the succession of the dynasties.

* An original version of this chapter was published as fascicle 16 in 1963.
[1] Some earlier Hurrian elements were already there in the Sargonic period; see §I, 2, 187 ff.

Elamite chronology depends, however, on Babylonian chronology. We know that Ammiṣaduqa and Kuknashur were contemporary,[1] and that the texts of Mālamīr overlap the end of the First Dynasty of Babylon. Events occurring just before the foundation of the new Elamite dynasty are known to us through the texts of Kurigalzu II. Therefore the interval between these two periods in Elamite history depends on the dates assigned to Ammiṣaduqa and Kurigalzu II and there is little agreement on these dates. Some authors consider that at least four centuries separate the two kings, thereby leaving a blank of over four hundred years in Elamite history, whereas others reduce the gap considerably by lowering the date of Hammurabi and adopting a less rigid chronology for the early Kassite kings. As the documents of Mālamīr and of Susa overlap considerably the end of the First Babylonian Dynasty, the gap between the two periods would be greatly reduced by the latter chronology. The Mālamīr texts show that there were about ten of a dynasty, known by the titles *sukkal* or *sukkalmaḫ*, who ruled in Elam after Kuknashur I, the contemporary of Ammiṣaduqa. It is in this period that the texts of Mālamīr are to be placed.[2] These are more or less homogeneous and date from the same period.[3] To judge from their syllabary, they belong to the time of Tan-Uli or Temti-khalki— that is, according to the chronology here adopted, to the middle of the seventeenth century. And lastly the recent excavations in Susiana would seem to indicate that the intervention of Kurigalzu in Elam occurred very soon after the end of the period of the *sukkalmaḫ*. From this we can deduce that the fading-out of Susa was short,[4] and certainly much shorter than the obscure period in contemporary Mesopotamia.

Despite this, the texts from Mālamīr do not fail to reflect the ethnic changes that were taking place throughout the entire Near East. Even though Babylonian traditions are still prevalent, the proper names bear witness to new elements. Certain of the attested names could be Hurrian, while others could be Kassite, Lullian, Gutian or Subarian. They indicate that Susiana was directly affected by the invaders, and it is likely that there was a considerable Hurrian proportion among these.

Excavations in Iran have not, indeed, as yet discovered the

---

[1] See §1, 8, 2 ff., and *C.A.H.* I³, pt. 1, pp. 218, 234 f.

[2] *Mém. D.P.* 8, 169 ff., nos. 1–16, re-edited in *Mém. D.P.* 22, *passim*.

[3] Except perhaps no. 15 (*Mém. D.P.* 22, 76).

[4] Mlle M. Rutten (*Mém. D.P.* 31, 155 ff. and table, 166) proposes to cancel this gap altogether.

pottery characteristic of sites on the Khabur, which in other places (Alalakh or Ras Shamra), seems to trace an expansion of the Hurrians. But their presence in Elam seems to be proved by certain particularities of the Elamite syllabary shortly after this period,[1] perhaps by the seals,[2] and certainly by the proper names.[3] Moreover, certain native princes already have names with the component -ḫalki,[4] which, whatever its origin,[5] evidently belongs to the Hurrians. The question of these foreign elements, their actual proportion, their influence, and how they arrived in Elam, remains to be answered.

Such information as we possess concerning Elam, from the intermediate period, is of only the slightest importance for history. It concerns an assault upon Elamite territory made by the last king of the Sea-Land, Ea-gamil, who was later defeated by the Kassite Ulamburiash, brother of Kashtiliash.[6] Such a brief allusion certainly does not warrant the hypothesis[7] that Ulamburiash, at this opportunity, took possession of Elam and extended Kassite rule even to the extreme south of the country.

It is not in fact until the time of Kurigalzu II that Elamite history comes to light again. A late Babylonian chronicle tells of a conflict between Kurigalzu II and the contemporary 'king of Elam' Khurpatila.[8] Whatever misgivings we may have about the way the chronicle presents these events, the facts themselves are above suspicion, since the victorious campaign of Kurigalzu II against Susa and Elam is known from other sources.[9] It is rather the figure of his opponent Khurpatila which raises doubts. Neither his name nor his reign are given in later dynastic lists, and the passage in the Chronicle is the only mention we have of

---

[1] In particular the use of *qa* for *ka*, which is characteristic of the Akkado-Hurrian syllabary.

[2] Mlle M. Rutten tells me that there is an unpublished seal from Susa in the Louvre of Hurrian origin or inspiration.

[3] For example, Akkamaneni, *Mém. D.P.* 22, 86, nos. 73, 27.

[4] Ike-khalki, Temti-khalki; and cf. Atta-khalki (*Mém. D.P.* 22, 75, 17; 149, 4, etc.).

[5] For a Hurrian origin: J. Friedrich, *Hethitisches Wörterbuch*, 147; for Indo-European: H. Pedersen, *Hittitisch und die anderen indo-europäischen Sprachen*, 177; E. Laroche in *R.A.* 47 (1953), 41.

[6] See §1, 5, ii, 22 ff.

[7] See G, 6, 331 a.

[8] Chronicle P, III, 10 ff. (F. Delitzsch, *Die babylonische Chronik*, 45). Khurpatila is there called 'king of Elammat', whereas Elam is written with the ideogram ELAM.MA.KI in the rest of the text. For the name of Khurpatila see recently §1, 1, 54.

[9] *R.A.* 26, 7.

him.[1] However, we have at present no valid reason to reject this evidence. Khurpatila, as his name indicates, might have sprung from one of those groups of Hurrians whose existence in Susiana is revealed by study of the names. It is possible that he was able to create a short-lived kingdom on the western border of Elam, and the fact that he challenged Kurigalzu implies that he had designs on southern Babylonia, perhaps towards Nippur, around which other groups of Hurrians had already settled. Indeed, that city seems to have been somehow the prize at stake, for after his victory Kurigalzu took care to leave there, no less than at Susa, concrete evidence of his success.

Khurpatila did not strike forthwith into Mesopotamia but massed his troops instead at the stronghold of Dūr-Shulgi, on the other side of the Sea-Land, from which position he defied the Kassites to attack. In the ensuing battle he was defeated and his army routed. He then took refuge in Elam but was unable to unite an army powerful enough to oppose the advance of Kurigalzu who, taking advantage of the situation, ravaged Barakhshe and Elam and captured Susa. Khurpatila was forced to surrender. Kurigalzu celebrated his victory in Susa itself by offering an agate scaraboid to the god Ishataran[2] and the pommel of a sceptre to Enlil.[3] On the acropolis of Susa, he dedicated a statuette of himself bearing an inscription recording the different phases of his conquest.[4] When he returned to Babylonia, he brought back from Susa an agate tablet which had once been dedicated to Inanna 'for the life of Shulgi' and presented it to the god Enlil of Nippur[5] with a new dedicatory inscription.

Despite the wide extent of Kurigalzu's victorious campaign and his occupation of Susa, the interior provinces of Elam seem to have escaped this fate, the political conditions of Elam being different from those in Mesopotamia. The geography of Elam does not lend itself to political unity, and as soon as the bond of a firm central authority holding the country together disappears or is relaxed the different provinces tend to separate and to live their own lives. These conditions probably prevailed during the period for which we have no texts and indeed at the time of

---

[1] E. Unger, in *Forsch. u. Fortschr.* 10 (1934), 256, purported to have found the existence of Khurpatila proved by its occurrence upon a business document from Nippur which he believed to be dated by his fourth regnal year as 'king of Babylon'. But F. R. Kraus, in *J.C.S.* 3 (1951), 12, has shown that the reading was wrong, and that there is nothing about Khurpatila in that text.

[2] *Mém. D.P.* 6, 30; 7, 135. The god's name is written KA.DI.

[3] *Mém. D.P.* 14, 32.

[4] *R.A.* 26, 7.   [5] §1, 3, no. 15, no. 73, and p. 31.

Khurpatila himself. This prince of foreign origin could hardly have ruled over more than Susiana and the western borders of the country, notwithstanding his title 'king of Elam', because for the Babylonians 'king of Elam' meant simply the ruler of Susa. Moreover, Kurigalzu's campaign in Elam, other than at Susa, must have passed over Barakhshe and some other districts like a sudden but momentary shock, so we are not surprised that, almost on the morrow of the defeat, there was already a resurgence of nationalism in the interior of the country which would soon, under vigorous leaders, give birth to a new native dynasty. Extending their authority step by step, successive rulers found their own advantage in restoring the unity of Elam, and out of this they created an empire which soon made its weight felt in the balance of powers arrayed in the Near East. This national resurgence was also to be favoured by circumstances, for the Babylonians became uneasy at the fresh aggressive tendencies of Assyria under Arik-dēn-ili (1319–1308) and Adad-nīrāri I (1307–1275) and turned their gaze away from a land which they might think subdued towards frontiers more immediately threatened.

Later native sources attributed the founding of this dynasty to a certain Ike-khalki. Seeing that the dynastic lists name him only as the father of the first two actual kings he was probably a local chieftain who never himself came to the throne. His native country is unknown although certain indications point to the region of Mālamīr. The texts from this place contain several allusions to a person called Attar-kittakh, son of Atta-khalki,[1] and these names seem to belong to the same family descent as those of Ike-khalki and his second son Attar-kittakh. The name of the father, Ike-khalki, might suggest that the new royal family was, as in the case of Khurpatila, closely related to the Hurrians of Elam.

In any case, the real founder of the dynasty was Pakhir-ishshan, a son of Ike-khalki: he ruled probably during the time of Nazimaruttash (1323–1298). He has left no inscriptions of his own but we know from later texts that he was active in the district of Aakhitek[2] (still unlocated), and that he erected some monument in honour of the god In-Shushinak. The stele of dedication was transported to Susa by one of his successors, Shilkhak-In-Shushinak.[3]

---

[1] *Mém. D.P.* 22, 75, 17; 149, 4, etc.

[2] Inscription of Shutruk-Nahhunte, §1, 4, no. 28, line 24. The nature of this activity is still uncertain; the hypothesis of G, 2, 106, n. 6 (transport of valuable timber) is difficult to accept, for the word under discussion can designate only living beings or objects assimilated to these. [3] §1, 4, no. 49; §1, 6, 26 ff.

Concerning his brother and successor Attar-kittakh, who was probably contemporary with the Babylonian king Kadashman-Turgu (1297–1280), the same later texts show that he extended to Susa the operations which his brother had confined to the province of Aakhitek. Two maces have been found at Susa[1] inscribed with his name. On the first he styles himself 'king of Susa and Anzan'; on the second, an original inscription—'Attar-kittakh, son of Ike-khalki'—is partly covered by a later dedication inscribed at the command of Untash-(d)GAL.

It was during the reign of his son, Khumban-numena (c. 1285–1266), that this Elamite renewal proved itself decisively. The name of this king is frequently mentioned by his successors who, symbolically, attach him to the great royal line issuing from the great and glorious Shilkhakha. Several of his royal inscriptions, in Elamite, are known to us and his titles attest the extent of his personal power.[2] His title in western style—'king of Anzan and Susa'—is here preceded by a series of native titles (merri, katri and halmeni of Elam), which no doubt define the nature of the sovereignty he exercised over the provincial tribes. The epithet 'expander of the empire' is probably more characteristic, as it alludes to the victorious campaigns which allowed him to extend the kingdom that he inherited. Susa was already part of this empire as is indicated by the title 'king of Anzan and Susa', which was also used by his father. A bead inscribed with his name was found in a well of the sixth city of Susa, and the later texts show that he had a temple built in honour of In-Shushinak in Susa. However, it was some four hundred kilometres to the south-east, at Liyan, that his inscriptions were found; they are foundation-deposits celebrating the construction of various sanctuaries. This does not prove that Liyan was the capital of the kingdom, as archaeological evidence discloses that it was a place of little importance, established in an area of backward culture, probably no more than a stronghold designed to protect the southern frontier of the empire. Susa was probably not at that time the real capital of Elam, and the site where Khumban-numena established his capital is as yet unknown, though it may have been in the province of Anzan, the position and extent of which is still a subject of dispute.

Khumban-numena was succeeded by his son, Untash-

---

[1] I am indebted to Mlle M. Rutten for this information.
[2] G, 1, 1, no. 4c (= Mém. D.P. 15, 42 ff.); Z.D.M.G. 49, 693 ff. and various fragments in Berlin.

(d)*GAL*[1] who was probably the contemporary of Shalmaneser I of Assyria (1274–1245) and the Babylonians Kadashman-Enlil (1279–1265) and Kudur-Enlil (1263–1255). It was during his reign, which probably lasted some twenty years that the dynasty founded by Ike-khalki reached its apogee. Numerous temples and many stelae and statues are proof of his building activities. Some of these stones were found at Susa[2] but even more at Chogha-Zanbil,[3] 42 kilometres to the south-east, where the city of Dūr-Untash is situated, founded by and named after Untash-(d)*GAL*. This is confirmed by a foundation-deposit recently discovered in its ruins.[4] A holy city built around a monumental sanctuary, Dūr-Untash was undoubtedly the religious centre of that period and the main residence of Untash-(d)*GAL*. Despite this Susa was not neglected. It grew continually in importance during his reign and consequently the kingdom opened out more and more towards the west. His predecessors seem to have entertained a fear of their western neighbours and thus refrained from making any show of force along these frontiers, but Untash-(d)*GAL*, much more confident in his might, did not hesitate to restore to Susa something of its ancient glory. He had, perhaps, always foreseen Susa, as did the ancient kings, as a base for future operations against Babylonia. For the greater part of his reign, however, Elam seems to have been at peace with its neighbours and there is no proof, at present, that the material wealth which he must have possessed for his extensive building projects in the cities of his realm resulted from booty taken in successful wars.

If so, Untash-(d)*GAL* was biding his time. The reign of Kashtiliash IV and the subsequent apparent weakening of Kassite strength gave him the opportunity of sweeping into Mesopotamia. A mutilated statue of a Babylonian god, brought

---

[1] The second element of the name Untash-(d)*GAL* is a logogram meaning 'God-Great'. It is probably the epithet of a major god in the Elamite pantheon. Some scholars (in particular, §1, 4, 95) assert that the god is *Khu(m)ban* and that therefore the name of the king should read Untash-*Khu(m)ban*. This is probably true, but not certain (see below, p. 404). Because of this doubt I continue to use the formal writing Untash-(d)*GAL* and Unpatar-(d)*GAL*.

[2] Their Elamite inscriptions are collected and transliterated by Hüsing in §1, 4, 44 ff., nos. 5 ff. For their Akkadian inscriptions see below, p. 386, n. 3.

[3] *Mém. D.P.* 28, 29 ff., nos. 16 f.; *Mém. D.P.* 32, 19 ff., nos. 3 ff. Since this publication by M. Rutten around twenty new texts have been found in the latest excavations and they will be published in a future volume of *Mém. D.P.*

[4] Excavations of 1958–9. The inscription on this stone seems to prove that Chogha-Zanbil is actually Dūr-Untash: 'I built the city of Untash-(d)*GAL* and (its) *siyankuk*' (for the possible meaning of this term see below, p. 410, n. 2).

back as booty by Untash-$(d)GAL$, has been unearthed in the ruins of Susa,[1] provided with an Akkadian inscription to commemorate its capture. In addition to the name of the god Immeria (Imerum, a local form of the god Adad), the inscription mentioned its origin or to whom it belonged. But this name is broken and only the following can be seen, . . . *li-ia-aš*. It has been commonly held that it is the end of the name of the Kassite king Kashtiliash IV and that Imerum was his personal god. This interpretation is far from being certain, for a reading [Tup]liash (a Babylonian city) is also possible and perhaps preferable.[2] If so, it would mean that booty was brought back from a victorious expedition led by the Elamite king against the border province west of the Uqnû river, the present Kerkhah. Even if this were only a swift raid without lasting results it proves at least that Elam had emerged from its long isolation and was not afraid to confront its western neighbours.

Elam was once again open to Semitic influence. Babylonian deities formerly worshipped were not excluded from the national pantheon and the native gods had Akkadian epithets. The temples were modelled on the massive stepped towers of the holy cities of Mesopotamia. Many official documents were written in Akkadian, the international language of the day.[3] If their syllabary includes a few local variations, their syntax is none the less classical and shows a high degree of Mesopotamian culture on the part of the Elamite scribes. This borrowing from a foreign civilization does not mean that national sentiment weakened. The native language was preponderant in dedications proclaiming the piety and greatness of the 'king of Anzan and Susa'.

Untash-$(d)GAL$ was succeeded by Unpatar-$(d)GAL$, who was not his son. The later dynastic lists give one Pakhir-ishshan as his father, without indicating whether or not this was the same person as the like-named grandfather of his predecessor; if so Unpatar-$(d)GAL$ would have been the uncle of Untash-$(d)GAL$. This is not impossible but very unlikely, for Kidin-Khutran, the

---

[1] *Mém. D.P.* 10, 85.

[2] This suggestion of Dr E. Reiner was communicated by Dr M. Rowton; see *C.A.H.* I[3], pt. 1, p. 218. A synchronism with Kashtiliash would require the reign of Untash-$(d)GAL$ to be lowered in time by some twenty years. The *kudurru* of Agaptakha may best be dated in this king's reign, as indicated below in relation to Kidin-Khutran.

[3] *Mém. D.P.* 28, nos. 16, 17, p. 32, nos. A, B, C (= *Mém. D.P.* 32, I and II). Since this last publication ten or so Akkadian texts have been found at Chogha-Zanbil. The inscription of Untash-$(d)GAL$ on a statue of the god Immeria is also in Akkadian.

brother and successor of Unpatar-(*d*)*GAL*, would also have been a son of the same Pakhir-ishshan, and the interval seems too long. There is no evidence that dynastic changes were caused by internal upheavals following upon the death of Untash-(*d*)*GAL*, nor is there proof that the queen Napirasu ruled over Elam for a year after the death of her husband. We have only one inscription of hers, upon her bronze statue.[1] Apart from the usual maledictions against profaners, it gives only her name and her title 'wife of Untash-(*d*)*GAL*'.

Whether owing to old age or a short reign, Unpatar-(*d*)*GAL* (*c.* 1245) was not as active as his predecessor. He was incapable of intervention in events taking place even a short distance from his borders. In this period Assyria was forcefully renewing its policy of expansion in the Zagros and towards the Persian Gulf. Tukulti-Ninurta I led a victorious expedition from the mountain Tarsina, on the southern bank of the Lesser Zab, as far as the land of Guti, between the regions Zuqushki and Lallar.[2] He then marched south into Babylon, attacked Kashtiliash and took him prisoner, annexing to his own land a whole series of cities which had been the subject of rival claims by the Babylonians and the Elamites. Elam had to abandon to Assyrian control the cities of Turna-suma, in the region of Me-Turnat, and Ulaiash near the source of Kerkhah, not far from the present-day Mandali.[3] All these events are known to us from Assyrian sources. The only Elamite sources for the reign of Unpatar-(*d*)*GAL*, two texts of a later date, mention only the restoration of a sanctuary of In-Shushinak at Susa, on which work had been done by several previous kings.

On the death of Unpatar-(*d*)*GAL*, his brother Kidin-Khutran came to the throne and ruled for some twenty years (*c.*1242–1222). Either because he succeeded in rallying the military forces of his kingdom or because he was less faint-hearted than his brother, the new king reverted to the aggressive policy of Untash-(*d*)*GAL* and openly opposed the Assyrian conqueror. Tukulti-Ninurta had installed one of his followers, Enlil-nādin-shumi, on the throne of Babylon after the death of Kashtiliash. Kidin-Khutran, taking advantage of this puppet ruler, swept suddenly into lower Mesopotamia. He crossed the Tigris and, marching towards the centre of the country, seized Nippur and massacred the population; then, turning north, he recrossed the Tigris and sacked Dēr,

[1] *Mém. D.P.* 8, 245 ff. and pl. 15; *Mém. D.P.* 5, 1 ff., no. 65; §1, 4, 50, no. 16.
[2] Cf. §1, 9, 1, iv, 25 ff.; 17 ff., etc.
[3] §1, 9, 16, 73 ff., and 27 f., note (ll. 66–82).

destroying the famous temple E-dimgal-kalamma and taking the inhabitants into captivity. The Babylonian king was forced to flee and lost his sovereignty over this whole area.

But the Elamite victory was short-lived. Tukulti-Ninurta took immediate counter-measures and re-established the position in Babylonia to his own advantage. After installing first the Kassite Kadashman-Kharbe, and then, eighteen months later, the Babylonian Adad-shuma-iddina (1224–1219), he kept a constant vigil over this land which he regarded as a kind of Assyrian protectorate. For this reason presumably Kidin-Khutran avoided any further aggressive action. It was only when Adad-shuma-uṣur (1218–1189) had become king in Babylon that he judged the time ripe for a new attempt. On this occasion, encouraged by his previous success, he advanced further, crossed the Tigris, seized Isin and went north as far as Marad, west of Nippur. There alone, it seems, did he meet resistance but he defeated his adversaries and returned to Elam without encountering further resistance.

It was probably during his first or second campaign in Babylonia[1] that he brought back as booty to Susa the *kudurru*[2] on which were inscribed the proprietorial rights to a domain near the city of Padan that Kashtiliash had granted to a certain Agaptakha. We know that this city is to be located between the Turnat (Diyālā) river and the mountain Yalman; that is, on the north-eastern border of Babylonia. Previously the Kassite king Agum-kakrime had asserted his suzerainty over the city by calling himself 'king of Padan and Alman'. But the Elamites had never ceased to claim that this territory was an integral part of greater Elam and in taking this stele the Elamite king was probably reasserting, symbolically, his suzerainty over the territory constantly in dispute between the Babylonians, Assyrians and Elamites.

This reconstruction of the course of events has to be based on Assyrian and Babylonian sources.[3] As yet no contemporary Elamite documents of the time of Kidin-Khutran have been found in the excavations. Some later references mention only the restoration by him of the temple of In-Shushinak at Susa and the temple of Kiririsha at Liyan.[4] If the interpretation of this latter, mutilated,

---

[1] See, however, p. 386, n. 2.
[2] *Mém. D.P.* 2, 95 and pl. 20.
[3] Chronicle P, IV, 14 ff., now in §1, 9, no. 37.
[4] §1, 4, no. 48 (*Mém. D.P.* 5, no. LXXI, 29 f.; §1, 4, no. 48 B (*Mém. D.P.* 5, no. XCVI), 37; §1, 4, Liyan (?), no. 49 (*Mém. D.P.* 5, no. LXXVI), 12.

text is correct it would tend to prove that Kidin-Khutran had firmly re-established Elam up to its southernmost borders. This would account for the boldness of his enterprises in Babylonia. He challenged, in fact, not merely the Babylonians, whose weakness at this time is well known, but Assyrian power, impelled by Tukulti-Ninurta, whose aim it was to establish his influence as far as the shores of the Persian Gulf. In the clash of these two ambitions, Kidin-Khutran was twice successful, due probably to the advantage of surprise attack, but the issue was finally decided in favour of the Assyrians. Tukulti-Ninurta lost no time in avenging his early setbacks and marched triumphantly 'to the southern shores of the Lower Sea'.

It is possible that this expedition brought Kidin-Khutran's reign to an end, perhaps by giving rise to a revolt in Elam. He disappears, in any case, from the political scene and several years passed before a new king ascended the throne. With him, the Anzanite dynasty founded by Ike-khalki came to an end, in all probability overthrown.

II. ARCHITECTURE AND THE ARTS

All the information concerning military and political affairs during this period of Elamite history comes, as has been stated, from foreign sources. It is very likely that Elamite kings had accounts of their victorious campaigns inscribed on stelae as their successors did later, and there is mention of several such campaigns in later inscriptions; but so far no such document has been found and only bricks recording the foundation of buildings have been discovered. These enable us to form a fairly precise idea of a different aspect of the rule of these kings—their building activities, an important guide to the development of civilization in the land. Although we know that nearly all the kings of this dynasty built or restored temples at Susa or in the other cities of the empire, the only inscribed bricks found belong to the time of Khumban-numena and Untash-(d)GAL and they all concern the construction or the repair of religious buildings. The bricks themselves, especially those of Untash-(d)GAL, are beautiful, well-baked and superior in manufacture to those of the period of the *ensi* and *sukkal* rulers.

At Chogha-Zanbil there are whole friezes of these very fine bricks which, inside and outside, follow the contours of the walls. The number of the inscribed bands varies according to the height of the building. They are usually repeated at every ten layers of bricks.[1] The inscription on these bricks is always short and identical, giving the name of the founder, his genealogy, title, and the simple statement 'I have built such and such a building for such a deity and have given it to him'. Sometimes they have curses against anyone who might desecrate the building, an invocation of the god's blessing upon the king's work, or even a prayer for the prosperity of his reign and a long life.

We have several of such documents of Khumban-numena. We learn from them that this king built a sanctuary in the city of Liyan dedicated to the god Khumban (*GAL*) and his consort Kiririsha, and to the Pakhakhutep who were probably old protector-gods of the place. Several later kings, especially Shilkhak-In-Shushinak, refer to this foundation and also mention a chapel built at Liyan by Khumban-numena, dedicated exclusively to Kiririsha, and repairs done at Susa to the temple of In-Shushinak.

The pious works associated with the name of Untash-(*d*)*GAL* were a good deal more numerous. At Susa, if the bricks found there all actually belonged in buildings erected in the city, he built or restored some twenty sanctuaries. As much attention was paid to Babylonian gods, traditionally worshipped in the city— Nabu, Sin, Adad, his consort Shala, *NIN-URU*—as to the Elamite deities—In-Shushinak, Khumban, Nahhunte, Pinikir, Khishmitik, Rukhuratir, Pelala, Napratep, Shimut, Nazit, Upurkupak, and so forth.[2] For each of them he had a new statue sculptured in stone or cast in metal placed in the appropriate temple. Of these temples about a dozen already existed in the city, for Untash-(*d*)*GAL* states that he had them rebuilt on their original sites. In about an equal number of cases it is not clear whether the inscription records a new foundation or not; but at any rate in the case of the goddess Upurkupak he claims to have been the first to build a temple expressly for her, as there had never been one in the capital, and he made several additions to the temple of In-Shushinak. A certain number of these sanctuaries must have been of modest proportions, built most often of sun-dried brick, sometimes with a glazed-brick façade. Some, indeed, were no more than secondary shrines, small chapels which were part of the interior plan of one of the great temples. Of these the most important was certainly that dedicated to the combined cults of Khumban and In-Shushinak.

---

[1] In the zikkurrat there are seven of these inscribed friezes in place, and three on the walls of another building.

[2] For references, see G, 2, 102 f.

Dominating all of these sacred buildings by its size was the zikkurrat of Susa which stood at that time on the acropolis of the city. It was built along the lines of the zikkurrats of Nippur, Babylon and the other sacred cities of Mesopotamia. The presence of numerous inscribed bricks identical with those that can still be seen in the walls of the zikkurrat at Chogha-Zanbil prove that Untash-(d)GAL built or restored a like structure at Susa. At its top stood the upper temple which the Elamites called *kukunnu*, a name which could also be applied to the whole zikkurrat.[1] This edifice had existed at Susa for a long time before that date. A predecesor, Kuknashur, claimed that he built or restored 'a *kukunnu* of baked bricks on the acropolis of In-Shushinak'.[2] The merit of Untash-(d)GAL was to have replaced this covering of baked bricks by enamelled plaques in iridescent colours.[3] In the upper chapel he had erected, as well as a statue of the god, a statue of himself on the pedestal of which was a bilingual inscription commemorating the restoration of the edifice and consigning any profaners to the wrath of the gods. The acropolis was surrounded by a sacred wall and one of its towers was called, as at Chogha-Zanbil, *nūr kibrāti*, 'light of the (four) regions (of the world)'.

The building activities of the king were not confined to Susa. It would appear in fact that the greater part of his pious pre-occupations were in another important religious centre of his kingdom, at the city that he founded and to which he gave his name, Dūr-Untash, on the site now called Chogha-Zanbil. All of the many bricks found there have his name on them and many of them commemorate the building of the city's monumental stage-tower. As at Susa, it was dedicated to the joint cult of Khumban and In-Shushinak, but each had a private chapel as well. It was this zikkurrat that Untash-(d)GAL described thus: 'I built and dedicated to the gods Khumban and In-Shushinak a *kukunnu* with bricks enamelled in silver and gold, and with white obsidian and alabaster.'[4] In one of the rooms he hung a lyre to which he gave the significant style 'glorification of my name'.[5]

Other bricks from here mention sanctuaries dedicated to the

[1] For this Sumerian loanword which corresponds with the Akkadian *gigunû*, cf. *C.A.D.* 5, 67 ff.

[2] *Mém. D.P.* 6, 28, 5.

[3] Resembling those used at Chogha-Zanbil (*Mém. D.P.* 28, 31, no. 17).

[4] *Mém. D.P.* 28, no. 17 (= *Mém. D.P.* 32, no. 11; cf. *C.A.D.* 5, 68 *b* for this text).

[5] *Mém. D.P.* 28, no. 16 (= *Mém. D.P.* 32, no. 1; cf. W. von Soden, *Assyr. Handwörterbuch*, 98 *b* (lyre or harp).

goddesses Ishme-karab, Kiririsha, Pinikir, Manzat, Inanna and Bēlit; to the gods Napratep, Nabu, Shiashum, Khumban, Sunkir-Risharra, Kilakh-supir, and to the divine partners Khishmitik and Rukhuratir, Shimut and *NIN-URU*, Adad and Shala, Shushmushi and Bēlit.[1] As at Susa, some of these chapels were certainly situated within the big temple. There were also other chapels outside the first wall and especially in front of the north-west side. There, in a conglomeration of ruined buildings, a bronze hoe dedicated to the god Nabu was found, thus indicating the location of this god's sanctuary.[2] Further on, an important building was dedicated to the goddess Kiririsha and an adjoining building of similar importance to the goddess Ishme-karab. This sacred complex formed the acropolis of Dūr-Untash and was undoubtedly called *Siyankuk*.

At Liyan, M. Pézard carried out excavations on a mound where Dr Andreas had previously discovered inscribed foundation bricks in the remains of two walls forming a corner. These walls have since disappeared and the archaeological results were meagre. Apart from traces of pavements consisting of plain slabs, there were only remains of very roughly constructed walls; the building work done there was inferior to that in Susiana. The impression thus conveyed is confirmed by the presence of primitive-looking rows of stones which perhaps once formed the backing for mere banks of rammed earth. In general, the remains point to a provincial or archaic technique, or to the work of a local population not far advanced above the stage of barbarism.[3]

At Susa, bricks of Untash-(*d*)*GAL* were found inserted in the walls and pavements of a later date, contemporary with Shilkhak-In-Shushinak; the positions in which they were found show that they were not serving their original purpose but had been gathered from older buildings when these were demolished to make way for new temples. The foundation levels of buildings put up by Untash-(*d*)*GAL* ought then to be found more or less immediately below the level in which these bricks were placed, but the excavations revealed only insignificant remains at that depth. The most important of these remains was simply a long wall, without inscriptions, 2 metres high, with panels jutting and

---

[1] A certain number of these names should be added to the list of deities of Chogha-Zanbil published by M. Rutten in *Mém. D.P.* 32, 8–9. The non-existent name *Akkipish is a misinterpretation of *Mém. D.P.* 32, xviii, no. 1, 3 and should be eliminated.

[2] R. de Mecquenem and G. Dossin, 'La marre de Nabu', in *R.A.* 35, 129 ff., and cf. *Mém. D.P.* 33, 56 f. See below, pp. 409 f.

[3] M. Pézard, 'Fouilles de Bender-Boushir (Liyan)', in *Mém. D.P.* 15.

recessed to an extent of 20 centimetres; this may have been the façade of a wall of unbaked brick. The decoration, either within or without, can only have been slight, for the fragments of decorated relief that can be attributed to the time of Untash-$(d)GAL$ are few and of very little interest. However, it is possible that the other ornamental motifs and the enamelled decorations were, like the inscribed bricks, pulled out and collected for re-use by later kings.

A much more impressive sight, even today, are the ruins of Chogha-Zanbil. Even in Babylonia there are few sites possessing a zikkurrat as grandiose and as well preserved.

The city is located forty-two kilometres south-east of Susa; built on a prominence, it dominates the meandering river Āb-i Diz. The remains, which were found in 1935, at first received only a few superficial soundings. A zikkurrat was identified in the débris of a large mound and along its north-western side a number of other buildings were superficially unearthed. These were later seen to be part of a complex of temples.[1] It was not until 1951 that this site was systematically excavated under the direction of R. Ghirshman. As yet the complete results have not been published but the preliminary reports and articles by R. Ghirshman[2] give us a fairly clear idea of the site. It takes the form of three concentric enclosures. The outer wall, a quadrangle, measures about 1200 by 800 metres and was probably the defensive-wall of the city. Back from this is a square (400 metres square) within which again was the third enclosure which contains the zikkurrat and its surrounding parvis. It is with the zikkurrat that the excavations started and it is completely unearthed today.

It was seen almost immediately that the zikkurrat of Chogha-Zanbil was quite different from the zikkurrats of Mesopotamia.[3] These differences arise both from the method of construction and the planning of certain parts. At Chogha-Zanbil it is an almost perfect square which measures 105 metres each side and it is oriented by its angles. Two storeys and part of the third were uncovered from the surrounding rubble, thus allowing a reconstruction of its original height and showing the stages of its construction. A sort of foundation, 1 metre high and 3 metres wide, encloses the zikkurrat at its base. Solidly constructed, it could be an actual foundation but its real purpose was to protect

---

[1] The results of these first excavations were published by R. de Mecquenem and J. Michalon, 'Recherches à Tchoga-Zembil', in *Mém. D.P.* 33.

[2] See §11, 1; and see Plate 156 (*e*).

[3] Already during the third campaign, cf. R. Ghirshman in *Arts Asiatiques*, 1 (1954), 83 ff.

the base of the zikkurrat against the infiltration of water. Above this, in successively receding steps, stood four storeys, the fourth of which supported the upper platform and the temple which crowned the edifice. At each storey the base of the wall was protected by a smaller version of the foundation at the base of the zikkurrat.

The first storey rises 8 metres above the parvis; the second 11·55 metres, and the third and fourth, which no longer exist, were probably of the same height.[1] Thus the bottom of the temple on the summit was about 43 metres above the ground, and the whole structure must have been about 52·60 metres in height.[2] The upper storeys were solid masses 8 metres thick, consisting of a core of crude bricks with a facing of baked bricks. But the first, the lowest, storey is of a quite different design, and the discovery of rooms made within the mass has revealed the different phases in the building of this tower.

Originally the edifice which was to be the first storey was a quadrilateral built around a courtyard. The north-east side, thicker than the others (12 metres instead of 8), contained a double row of rooms, with the inner rooms opening through a doorway into the courtyard. Another group of rooms lay in the southern part of the south-east side, and communicated with the courtyard by another monumental door. Inscribed bricks found in the walls here show that this group of rooms formed a temple of the god In-Shushinak. To the east of this side there was another sanctuary of the god, opening this time not upon the courtyard, but externally upon the parvis of the zikkurrat. Apart from these two temples of In-Shushinak the other rooms cannot be identified and we have no texts concerning them. The other rooms do not have windows and those which have no doors to the court are entered by a narrow stairway from above. The walls were white-washed with great care. Most of the rooms were empty but one had jars in it and two others, in the north-west corner, were filled with baked clay objects shaped like mushrooms with glazed heads.

The existence of the temple of In-Shushinak with its façade of inscribed bricks thus shows that the original construction was limited to this one storey and that it was not until some time later that the other storeys were added. When the other storeys were constructed those rooms that open into the courtyard were

---

[1] See §II, 3, 25.

[2] If the Elamite cubit—deduced from the dimensions and proportions of Chogha-Zanbil—was in fact 0·526 metre. Thus the zikkurrat should have measured 100 cubits in height and 200 cubits on each side at the base.

condemned and filled in with unbaked bricks and their doors were closed off by the mass of the zikkurrat.

At its finished height its last storey must have measured 35 metres on each side, which was large enough to accommodate the temple that crowned the construction. Nothing is left today of this upper part of the zikkurrat, but its remains are strewn along the slopes down as far as the parvis where they can be found today.[1] In particular, inscribed bricks from the summit of a special form. have been found, which commemorate the construction of the *kukunnu*.[2] The precious materials of which they speak, bricks of gold and silver, are undoubtedly the bricks glazed with metallic hues, fragments of which were found in the débris. The upper temple was plainly the residence of the god.

Communication between the parvis and the top of the tower was by a series of stairways opened in the zikkurrat. A door was built in each of the four sides. But only the stairway on the south-west side went beyond the first storey, thus giving access to the second storey. The rest of the ascent was probably made alternatively by each of the other sides. This means of ascent differentiates it clearly from the Mesopotamian zikkurrats. There are other but less important differences. For instance, the drainage system depends on a vertical system of gutters at each landing which channel off the rainwater from the zikkurrat; in Babylonia drainage is effected by successive layers of reeds. The clay of the bricks is homogeneous and not reinforced with débris and sherds as in Babylonia. The door arches are constructed in an original manner by an irregular alternation of wedge-shaped bricks and complete bricks.

The zikkurrat is surrounded by large paved parvises of different kinds which are about 20 metres wide. On the north-east side, near the central stairway, there is a ramp between the parvis and the base of the tower. At the northern angle of this ramp there is a circular construction, which can also be found at the north-western and south-western doors. These have four symmetrically placed niches and the whole is decorated by rings of inscribed bricks. The wording of these bricks does not help us to identify their purpose.[3] Another problem is set by the fourteen small square socles, made up of five bricks, one of which forms the top, which

[1] *Mém. D.P.* 32, nos. II, VI–IX.

[2] In the Akkadian inscriptions, at least, this is the word used. The corresponding Elamite word is *ulḫi*, which is applied to the royal residence in the Achaemenid period. It is difficult to say whether these two words have the same meaning.

[3] *Mém. D.P.* 32, no. V.

face the south-east stairway. They are probably too small and too fragile to be used as tables or altars for sacrifices. The zikkurrat and the parvises are surrounded by an enclosure with angular projections. On the north-west and the south-west sides the enclosure wall is double and forms rooms. Between these rooms, where there is a single wall, the resulting opening is like a gallery which faces the ramp rising from the parvis to the second storey.

On the north-west side, starting from the northern angle, three temples as a group break the line of the enclosure and spread out over the parvis. The first, completely outside the enclosure, is a sanctuary of the 'Great God', (d)GAL; a paved passage runs between it and a large door which opens out on to the parvis. The two others, farther west and straddling the line of the enclosure are large adjoining temples dedicated, respectively, to the deities Ishme-karab and Kiririsha. These two temples are separated by three rooms in the form of a T. It was here that the bronze hoe of Nabu was found during the first excavations.[1] These three temples in their simplest form are planned in the same way: a courtyard, on one side of which there is the ante-cella and cella and on the other side a number of annexes. In the temple of Kiririsha, other buildings—probably workshops and storehouses—were added.

Outside the inner enclosure which surrounds the zikkurrat is another area, 130 metres in breadth, which is circumscribed by the second wall. This wall has three gates, one on the north-east line, the second on the south-east side and the third on the south-west side. The latter two, called the 'Royal Way' and the 'Gate of Susa' by the excavator, both have the same inscription which seems to give a list of the various royal foundations in this holy quarter of the city. Towards the south there is a tower with its frieze of inscribed bricks still in place. They seem to indicate that this tower was the 'Light of the Regions'.[2]

The remains of four other temples were found in the eastern corner and their inscriptions allow us to identify the gods to whom they were dedicated. The first is the sanctuary of the goddess Pini-kir; the following two of the divine pair, Adad—Shala and Shimut—NIN-URU; and the fourth of a divine group, the Napratep. From the results of the excavations it might be concluded

---

[1] Mém. D.P. 33, 57.

[2] nūr kibrāti. It is consequently very doubtful whether this term means the zikkurrat, as has been supposed. The text was published in Mém. D.P. 32, no. III. The same inscription has been found on bricks at Susa, cf. Mém. D.P. 3, no. XVIII and p. 32.

that the area between the two inner walls was reserved for religious buildings.

Between the second wall and the outside enclosure was the site of the city itself or at least this space was reserved for it, for it seems in fact that the city was never finished. In this whole area the only things found were the remains of three palaces, the remains of a private house (near the northern angle of the area) and a few individual or family tombs. These tombs look like a well but they branch off at the bottom into a vaulted room. The first palace (I)[1] was a building of very large dimensions. Its rooms, one of which contained some beautiful ivories, give on to a large courtyard which is partly paved. On the west side, contrary to the usual disposition, the rooms have their long side on the courtyard, and it was under some of these rooms that the most remarkable discovery was made. Several stairways leading into subterranean rooms were found, access to them being very carefully disguised by a filling of baked bricks, the last courses of which were cemented by a thick coat of plaster and bitumen. Six metres below, the stairs lead into vaulted rooms about 17 metres long and 4 metres wide and high. The vault as well as the head of the door are fully arched and made of matching baked bricks which are covered with a layer of plaster. There is a sort of brick funerary couch in one of these tombs on which there was an intact skeleton and the remains of two burnt bodies. In a neighbouring tomb were some small heaps of ashes and bones of carbonized bodies placed directly on the floor in groups of two, four and five. This is the only evidence we have of cremation in Elam.

The other two palaces are in the eastern angle of the area. Although they do not have underground rooms their general aspect indicates that they were much larger than the first. Each one contains two large courtyards around which are situated four suites with several rooms in each. One of these was a bathroom with a low plaster-covered basin, the drains passing out under the walls. Near the third palace a trench containing different-sized and well-preserved alabaster urns was found.

To the south-west of palace I are the remains of the only religious building found in the 'urban' zone. This building, the inscription of which shows that it was dedicated to Nusku, is rather odd in appearance, being built like a T. The bar of the T is a long vestibule while its leg is a paved court with a pedestal of unbaked brick at the far end. It seems, judging from the distance

[1] Discovered in 1958–9.

between the walls and the lack of remains, that this building did not have a roof.

The outer wall had only one monumental gate, situated near the eastern angle of the wall, and made up of two gate-houses which face each other across a large paved square courtyard. In each gate-house there is a long paved room which was perhaps the guard room. On large bricks the inscriptions 'gate of the king', 'great gate' and 'gate of justice' were found. On the north-west face of the wall there was an ingenious system for bringing in water; along the outside of the wall was a reservoir which received water from a nearby canal. A system of small pipes, in nine steps, brought the water up from the reservoir under the wall into a basin along the inner side of the wall. The surface of the reservoir and the basin are at the same level, but the basin is not as deep as the reservoir. Thus by using the principle of water seeking its own level they were able to bring up water from one to the other while leaving any sediment behind.

The excavations at Chogha-Zanbil have furnished us with much precious information on Elamite architecture at the time of Untash-(*d*)*GAL*, on building materials, planning, systems of measurement, use of the arch and the vault. In the other Elamite arts of this time it is not always easy to date remarkable examples of jewellery or figurines found in the excavations, but stone sculpture and bronze-working reach a high level. The composition and carving of a stele bearing the name of Untash-(*d*)*GAL*, now in the Louvre, is an example of contemporary Elamite sculpture in relief. Although it has survived only in a fragmentary state, it has proved possible to reconstruct the general scheme. Two long serpents with winding coils form a frame for several superimposed panels. In the uppermost the king stands with his hands outstretched to a seated goddess wearing a head-dress with three pairs of horns. The king is also represented in the next panel, in company with his queen, Napirasu. In a lower panel are semi-divine guardians. One of them preserved in its entirety is a female creature, a sort of siren, the head adorned with a pair of horns, the scaly lower body ending in two little fins that serve as feet. She holds against her breast two streams of flowing water issuing from four vases so disposed as to frame the subject, two balanced on the back-turned tips of her tail, the other two at each side of her head in the upper corners. In the bottom panel is another such semi-divine creature, with a rectangular beard and hair falling in tresses at the back; the lower part of the figure is broken off, but the end of a tail curving backwards shows that it is another type of hybrid, half human, half animal.[1]

Remains of a great many stone figures in the round have been found but so mutilated as not to allow of a just appreciation. Many limestone statues date from the time of Untash-(d)GAL. One of these represents the king, the lower part alone being extant with a bilingual inscription in Akkadian and Elamite; another statue of the king is in diorite.[2]

Elamite mastery of the technique of bronze-working is well illustrated for this period by the celebrated statue of the queen Napirasu.[3] The headless figure stands 1·20 metres high and weighs not less than 1750 kilogrammes. The procedure used for casting such a large figure is not known and we cannot but admire the results obtained. Not having our modern high-temperature furnaces they must have had to use a considerable number of small crucibles in order to pour such a large quantity of molten metal, and it is astonishing that they could maintain a more or less constant temperature for each melting. The interior is not perfect but the exterior is remarkably well done, and this statue is a real masterpiece of ancient metallurgy. The queen stands with crossed hands, clothed in a fine embroidered dress which closely fits her shoulders and breasts. A long skirt wrapped round her waist and hanging to the ground covers the feet. The folds of the material, the embroidery, the bands and the incrustation are executed—like the jewellery on the fingers and the wrists—with great delicacy. On the flounce of the skirt an Elamite inscription invokes the anger of the gods upon anyone who may destroy, mutilate or remove the statue or efface the queen's name.

It will therefore appear that Elam was scarcely inferior in the practice of the arts to Babylonia and Assyria at this period, if the combined evidence of the extant objects and of the texts be considered; this was the prelude to the age of Shilkhak-In-Shushinak, the true apogee of Elamite civilization.

III. RELIGION

About one other aspect of this civilization the documents, in spite of their terse character, also provide information: the religion.

[1] G, 8, 41, n. 1; *R.A.* 13, 120; *R.A.* 17, 113 ff.; G, 4, col. 932; § III, 6, 98 and fig. 52.

[2] *Mém. D.P.* 10, 85 pl. x; *Mém. D.P.* 11, 12 and pl. III, nos. 1–2; G, 8, 64, nos. 61–64.

[3] *Mém. D.P.* 8. 245 ff.; § III, 2, vol. II, 914 ff. See Plate 157 (a).

All of the bricks from the time of Untash-(*d*)*GAL* and his predecessor contained many references to the gods and their
sanctuaries, and invocations of the gods in documents of all the
Elamite kings are ubiquitous. But while in Babylonia very many
rituals, incantations, prayers and the like have been found, in
Elam not a single text with this kind of purely religious content is
yet known. Almost all that can be done at present is to enumerate
the divine names with such explanations as are provided by
incidental phrases in the Elamite texts or by Akkadian god-lists
and references in Babylonian and Assyrian inscriptions dealing
with Elam.

The principal native sources, apart from the inscribed bricks of
Khumban-numena and Untash-(*d*)*GAL*, are either earlier or
later than this period. A treaty of alliance concluded between
Naram-Sin of Agade and a prince of Awan includes a list of deities
cited as witnesses and guarantors. In the documents of the time
of the *ensi* and *sukkal* rulers there are divine names included in the
theophorous personal names, and those invoked in oaths. After
the reign of Untash-(*d*)*GAL* the evidence lies in royal inscriptions
of the dynasty of Shilkhak-In-Shushinak, of the last native
Elamite kings at Susa and at Mālamīr, and in references to
Elamite gods occurring in Akkadian literature. In this last class
are divine names occurring in the god-lists and in the Babylonian
magical series called *šurpu*, as well as the account of the sack of
Susa given in Ashurbanipal's annals describing temples and
statues which his soldiery plundered or destroyed. As the inscriptions of the time of Shilkhak-In-Shushinak are more numerous
and more varied in type than previously, it might seem that a
general study of the religion should be attempted only for his
period; but the pantheon was more or less formed at the time of
Untash-(*d*)*GAL* and this period furnishes a good vantage-point
to observe the evolution through which, in the course of centuries,
this religion passed. When the statements of the different sources
are compared, there is a notable divergence between the resulting
lists of gods, according to the date or origin of the source.

Historically it appears that the order of the pantheon underwent important changes. Originally the dominating figure seems
to have been the great goddess Pinikir, the first name invoked in
the Naram-Sin treaty, while In-Shushinak was secondary. This
predominance of a supreme goddess is probably a reflexion from
the practice of matriarchy which at all times characterized Elamite
civilization to a greater or lesser degree. Even when the supremacy of a male was fully recognized in the pantheon, perhaps

under the influence of western ideas, the cults of the goddesses always preserved their popularity in all parts of the empire. Nevertheless the progressive decline of the great goddess in favour of the major gods is one characteristic of religious evolution in Elam. Another, and of no less general significance, is the rise in importance of In-Shushinak the god of Susa; from a purely local god there developed step by step the great national god, who gradually eclipsed the principal ancient deities. In the time of Untash-(d)GAL he was already the equal of the 'Great God', with whom he is frequently associated; a century later, in the time of Shilkhak-In-Shushinak, he supplanted that god completely.

If, again, the documents are studied with regard to their provenance, Awan, Susa, Mālamīr, or Liyan, a clear differentiation of the worship in the different localities can be observed. Apart from certain great gods worshipped throughout the country, most of the deities clearly present provincial features. It would seem that there never was, in Elam, a unity of religious belief worthy of the name. Even in his most formal inscriptions Shilkhak-In-Shushinak invokes 'the gods of Elam', 'the gods of Anzan', 'the gods of Susa', as divine communities fundamentally distinct. Still another group, 'the gods of Aiapir', occurs in other inscriptions, while Tirutir, frequently invoked by Khanni at Mālamīr, appears nowhere else. Yet the name of Shimutta is always followed by the epithet 'god of Elam'. It is perhaps above all in the cults of the goddesses that this geographical differentiation can be observed. Although Kiririsha and Pinikir each had a sanctuary at Chogha-Zanbil, Kiririsha—'the lady of Liyan'—was worshipped more in the south, while Pinikir was worshipped in the north; Parti is essentially the goddess of Mālamīr, although known at Susa also by the name Partikira, according to the annals of Ashurbanipal. The variations of one and the same name are equally revealing as an indication of provincialism; in one place a god is called Lukhuratil, in another Rukhuratir, in one place Manzat, in another Manzit, in one place Khutran, in another Uduran or Duran, and so forth.

These fundamental differences can be explained by the fact that greater Elam was never anything but a political concept realized by a few energetic or ambitious kings. It was always a tribal federation constantly on the verge of breaking up, and with each tribe retaining its own gods. The nationalization of the local cults was one of the means used by the kings of the great dynasties to cement the precarious hold they had on the country. It was with this in mind that they made their capitals—Susa or

Dūr-Untash—into sacred capitals where they tried to group together the provincial gods but avoided attempts at complete assimilation. These cities must have fulfilled much the same purpose as did pre-Islamic Mecca, that of a 'resting place' for the divinities of the different tribes.

Besides regional figures the Elamite pantheon also included gods of peoples who lived in or passed through the Zagros as well as, during the whole of Elamite history, many Babylonian deities. These were worshipped throughout the empire, not in the way that captured deities might be, in that the conqueror sometimes made offerings to such in order to avoid their wrath, but as gods who formed an integral part of the pantheon. Susa, where a large Babylonian colony was established, was always quite open to influence from the west; this would account for the acceptance there of these foreign gods, but the worship of them spread far beyond the area round the city. In the time of Untash-$(d)GAL$, for example, certain Babylonian gods had their own shrines in the new sacred city at Chogha-Zanbil. The influence of Babylonia on the religion can be seen also in the use of Akkadian epithets for the deities, in the form of temples, and perhaps in certain ceremonies such as that which seems to bear the Akkadian name, *ṣīt šamši*, the rite at 'sun-rise'. It is almost impossible to discern why some Babylonian gods were accepted in Elam while others, no less important, were never admitted. The reasons were probably not political. Formerly the Third Dynasty of Ur and the sovereigns of Akkad exercised a firm sovereignty in Elam and this had a very deep influence on the culture of the country, whereas the cults of Ur and Akkad left only slight traces in Elamite religion. Instead of these Susiana was imbued with the doctrines of the great religious centre at Eridu, the holy city of Ea. Various phenomena might be explained on this assumption; the fantastic half-antelope half-fish or half-human half-fish figures of semi-divine beings on reliefs or seals,[1] the ideograms that are used for some divine appellations such as *A.É.A.LUGAL, NUN.LUGAL*, recalling the supreme name of Ea, *ENKI.LUGAL*, or the rites of ablution and lustration to which the many finds of great bowls and ritual basins in the ruins of Susa testify.

Eridu was certainly not the only Mesopotamian sanctuary which influenced Elam, for the goddess Ishtar of Uruk was also of importance. Thus we know of the gift of three richly bedecked white horses sent to her by the king Tammaritu (a contemporary

---

[1] M. Rutten, 'Une cuve décorée provenant de Suse', in *Mém. D.P.* 30, 220 ff.

of Ashurbanipal),[1] and no doubt intended to draw the chariot of
the goddess in processions. Nevertheless, the lack of documents
prevents our knowing whether this assimilation of foreign ideas
penetrated the more distant provinces of the empire. Extensive
though it may have been, the influence of Babylonia on Elamite
religion is not such as to justify the opinion that the introduction
of these new cults ended in the superseding of the old indigenous
religion by purely Babylonian beliefs and practices. The fact that
divine names are written with logograms borrowed from Mesopotamian divine lists does not mean they should be read as Akkadian gods: in most cases they represent the name of a native god.

One more feature of the Elamite pantheon is shared, no doubt,
by other pagan religions in ancient Western Asia, though it
seems to be of wider application in Elam than elsewhere; that is
the ill-defined character of the individual gods and goddesses.
This want of formal distinction is due not merely to a defect of
our knowledge but to the ideas that seem to have been current
among the Elamites about their deities. Most of them were not
only ineffable beings whose real name was either not uttered or
was unknown, but also sublime ideas, not to be exactly defined by
the human race. This may be the reason why Akkadian scribes
experienced obvious difficulty in identifying them with their
national gods; Ninurta, according to their account, corresponded
with no less than eight members of the pantheon at Susa, Adad
with three, and Shamash with two. The names used in the native
language also illustrate this position. When Elamite gods are
not called simply *napir*, 'the god', *zana, zini, sina*, 'the lady',
temti, 'the protector', they often bear only an epithet indicating
local origin or a particular quality, or else a description containing
the elements *nap*, 'god', *zana*, 'lady', *kiri*, 'goddess', or *GAL*,
'the Great'. Even the name of the august Kririsha means no
more than 'the great goddess', while that of In-Shushinak
derives from his position of 'lord of Susa'. There were, moreover, groups of gods known only by a collective epithet, such as
napratep, paḥaḥutep, paḥakikip, or the ancient protecting deities
whom Shilkhak-In-Shushinak invokes: *e nap paḥappi aktip
nappip*—'O protecting deities, ancient deities'.

These general observations provide the background to any
review of the gods and goddesses in the inscriptions of Khumban-
numena and Untash-$(d)GAL$ at this period. The most important
deities are unquestionably *GAL*, In-Shushinak and Kririsha. The
god with the simple epithet *GAL*—'the Great'—is frequently

[1] R. F. Harper, *A.B.L.* no. 268.

associated with In-Shushinak and always precedes him in the enumeration of their names. Their statues were placed side by side in the same temples, and together they are called 'princes of the gods'. The reading Khumban has been proposed for the logogram *GAL* and this is probably right.[1] There is some doubt, however, for beside the many mentions of *GAL* and In-Shushinak, either together or separately, there is one isolated mention, on a brick at Chogha-Zanbil,[2] where Khumban is written syllabically. Despite this, Hüsing's arguments still seem conclusive, until a more definite reason can be brought against them, that *GAL* and Khumban represent one and the same god. This god was, from the time of the earliest texts, the supreme male god in Elam. It is not impossible that he was also worshipped by other peoples more or less related to the Elamites. Even if it be granted that he was himself originally subject to the supreme power of the great goddess, his spouse, he displaced her immediately the idea of the superiority of the female principle began to lose its hold on the religious ideas of the Elamites. There is evidence that this cult was practised in all the provinces of the empire. With his name, Khumban or *GAL*, 'the Great', such epithets as 'the king', 'the greatest of the gods', 'the great protector', 'the sublime divine protector', 'the one creating stability', are constantly associated. The Babylonians treated him as the equivalent of their own Marduk, the creator, lord of Babylon. Although in certain parts of the kingdom he gradually yielded place to In-Shushinak, whose cult continually spread, he never ceased to be the personal god of the kings of that dynasty. Moreover, although 'the lord of Susa' displaced him, that god's pre-eminence was due essentially to political events. In the strictly religious aspect Khumban always kept his proper position in comparison with his rival; his name is always invoked first, and In-Shushinak, alternately with the goddess Kiririsha, appears only in the second place.

The prestige of In-Shushinak continually increased as the centuries passed. His position was closely linked with that of his city, Susa, which began as a provincial city and ended as the capital of an empire. In the early treaty with Naram-Sin his name is mentioned only in seventh place after those of Pinikir, Pakhakikip, Khupan (Khumban), *A.MAL*, Sit and Nakhiti,

---

[1] §1, 4, 95. See above, p. 385, n. 1.

[2] From this, one could suppose that there was one temple (or several) of *GAL* and a temple of Khumban. It should also be noted that in Khumban-numena, Khumban is always written syllabically whereas in the names of his successors Untash-(*d*)*GAL* and Unpatar-(*d*)*GAL*, the divine element is always written with the logogram *GAL*.

while in the time of Untash-(*d*)*GAL* and his predecessor his cult
was already recognized outside the limits of Susiana, for he is
mentioned on the inscribed bricks of the temple which Khumban-
numena built in the island of Bushire.[1] The extension of his cult
reached its maximum in the reign of Shilkhak-In-Shushinak who
instituted, or re-instituted, his worship in numerous cities: Susa,
Ekallatum, Marrut, Peptar, Shakhan-tallak, and others. A
damaged stele with an inscription of this king mentions twenty of
his foundations: out of the fourteen still legible, ten are dedicated
to In-Shushinak, while Khumban, Pinikir, Sukhsipa and Lakamar
are honoured with only one each.

The Assyrians identified 'the divine lord of Susa' with the
Babylonian gods Ninurta and Adad, but he was most often
invoked as 'god of the king' rather than in his character as a
storm-god or fertility-god or war-god. He was, like Khumban,
called 'the great god', 'the great protector', but the epithets
which are much more indicative of his nature are 'the protector of
our city', 'my god, my king, my ancestor', as the kings describe
him; they hold their royal authority by his grant, they thank him
for the aid he lends in war and in their peaceful enterprises. But
this 'protector of the city', this 'god of the king', was for the
Elamites a power as mysterious and as concealed as the other
deities. In his description of the sack of Susa, Ashurbanipal says:
'I bore In-Shushinak away to Assyria, the god of their mysteries,
who dwelt in a secret place, whose divine acts none was ever
allowed to see.' In spite of the extension of his worship, In-
Shushinak always remained in essence the god of Susa and Chogha-
Zanbil. He was never regarded as a 'god of Elam' and the rock
inscriptions of Mālamīr do not mention him.

The goddess of the supreme triad at this time was Kiririsha,
specially celebrated as 'lady of Liyan' where Khumban-numena
erected not only the temple that she shared with Khumban and
the protecting deities of the locality, but also a private sanctuary
which subsequent kings maintained. Although there is no
evidence that Untash-(*d*)*GAL* consecrated a temple to her at
Susa, it is known that she had a sanctuary at Chogha-Zanbil
which she shared with another goddess, Ishme-karab. These
buildings seem to have occupied a privileged place in the holy
quarter. In his curses on possible violators of his pious works, the
king never omitted to invoke her, together with (*d*)*GAL* and
In-Shushinak. Some have thought that she was essentially a

---

[1] [On the 'island' of Bushire, see now E. Sollberger and J. R. Kupper, *Inscr.
royales sum. et akk.*, Paris, 1971, p. 283, n. 1. (Ed.)]

chthonic deity, the ruler of the kingdom of the dead,[1] as they translate an epithet, *Kiririša Liyan laḥakara* by 'Kiririsha of the dead city of Liyan'. But this translation is probably wrong and the epithet means rather 'who dwells at Liyan'. Other texts merely call Kiririsha 'the Great' or 'the divine mother'. Although her name is invoked by Khanni in the inscriptions at Mālamīr, she is not mentioned in the Naram-Sin treaty, or in the documents of the early dynasties at Susa. These facts, combined with the absence of any record of her cult in the inscriptions of Untash-(*d*)*GAL* at Susa seem to be good reason for assuming that she was essentially a deity of the interior, especially the southern provinces of the empire.

In the north, on the other hand, the great goddess was Pinikir, whose cult seems to have been unknown at Mālamīr and Liyan. The primitive importance of this great goddess in the Elamite pantheon has already been mentioned; as the centre of the kingdom gradually shifted southward, she became less important, and gave place to the 'lady of Liyan', Kiririsha. At Susa, however, there was a temple dedicated to her alone at a very early date. Untash-(*d*)*GAL* restored it and added to it another construction called *aštam*.[2] At Chogha-Zanbil he also built her a sanctuary which seems less important than those of Ishme-karab and Kiririsha. The cult of Pinikir was observed throughout the centuries in Susiana, for Shutur-Nahhunte still invoked her as 'sovereign of the gods' and Ashurbanipal names her among the deities whose temples he destroyed. Assyrian lists of his time identify her with Ishtar, the supreme goddess of the Babylonians and Assyrians.

At least two other local goddesses were particularly honoured in the time of Untash-(*d*)*GAL*, called Upurkupak and Ishme-karab, but little is known of either of them. Upurkupak must be a provincial goddess, for the king boasted of having built a temple for her at Susa where none had been in the time of his predecessors. At a much later date Khutelutush-In-Shushinak seems to have been particularly devoted to this goddess, for he built a sanctuary for her in the town Shalulikki where her cult had not previously been observed. Ishme-karab, on the other hand, had been worshipped at Susa since the time of the *sukkal*-rulers. Yet it was not at Susa, but at Chogha-Zanbil, that Untash-(*d*)*GAL* dedicated a temple to her. Next to the temple of Kiririsha it occupied, as we have seen, a privileged place directly on the enclosure around the

---

[1] §1, 7, 101 ff.

[2] It would not seem at present that the Elamite word *aštam* is to be identified with the Akkadian *bīt aštamme*.

zikkurrat. Later, Shilkhak-In-Shushinak restored one or two of her sanctuaries, but the broken text recording them does not allow of our knowing where.

To another important member of the pantheon, the god Nahhunte, Untash-(d)GAL built a new temple at Susa[1] and Chogha-Zanbil,[2] in which he placed a statue to thank the god for having heard his prayers and performed his desires. This god, like Shamash, with whom the Babylonians compared him, was the Elamite god of justice, the Sun. His cult was always a flourishing one in Elam and at Susa his temple was among the most ancient sanctuaries. Some kings call themselves 'servants of Nahhunte' and invoke him as their 'protector' and their 'ancestor'. The kings of the dynasty of Shilkhak-In-Shushinak devoted special attention to him as is shown by his appearance in several personal names of this house. This sun-god is invoked for a specific reason in the curses on possible violators: 'May Nahhunte...deprive him of descendants.'

Other gods whose names occur on inscribed bricks of this period are less known and less important; such are the divine Shimut and his consort, the two associated gods Khishmitik and Rukhuratir, Pelala, Nazit, Shiashum, Sunkir-Risharra, Kilakhsupir, Shushmushi[3] and the Napratep. Shimut, although expressly called 'god of Elam', is known to have been worshipped at Susa, Mālamīr and Awan. If an Assyrian text which mentions a star of the same name can be relied upon, he was perhaps an astral deity; his cult was much in favour in Elam, and never ceased throughout the centuries. In the Naram-Sin treaty he was invoked immediately after In-Shushinak. In the personal name of a *sukkal* called Shimut-wartash he has the character of a tutelary god. He had a temple on the acropolis at Susa before the reign of Untash-(d)GAL and that king, not content with restoring this traditional sanctuary, built another for him at Chogha-Zanbil. When, a century later, the temple at Susa had again fallen into ruin, Shilkhak-In-Shushinak, one of whose brothers was called Shimut-nikatash, rebuilt it completely of more durable material. It survived till the days when the destructive fury of Ashurbanipal's soldiery reduced it to ashes.

[1] *Mém. D.P.* 3, no. xiv.

[2] A brick like *Mém. D.P.* 3, no. xiv, was found at Chogha-Zanbil during the excavations of 1958–9.

[3] These last two gods are mentioned on bricks that were found since the publication of the list of deities given by M. Rutten in *Mém. D.P.* 32, 8 f. The non-existent *Akkipish should be removed as it is the result of a misreading of *Mém. D.P.* 32, xviii, no. i, 3.

In all these sanctuaries Shimut was worshipped with his divine spouse. At Susa and Chogha-Zanbil she was called at this period *NIN.URU*, 'lady of the city'. It is not certain whether this logogram is to be read in Akkadian, Bēlit-āli, or whether this is simply an epithet of Manzat, who is later constantly associated with Shimut as his spouse. Manzat, 'the great lady', was a very ancient deity whose name is found on a business document of the Agade dynasty, and it occurs several times in personal names of the Third Dynasty of Ur. Likened to a leonine Ishtar by the Akkadian scribes she was worshipped not only in Susiana but also, as Manzit, at Mālamīr. She certainly had a sanctuary at Chogha-Zanbil[1] and at Susa, her temple, or perhaps the chapel she occupied in the sanctuary of Shimut, was restored first by Shutruk-Nahhunte and then by Khutelutush-In-Shushinak. She probably had another temple as well not far from Chogha-Zanbil on the other side of the Āb-i Diz on the unexplored mound now called Deh-i Now.[2] A brick found on this site states that a temple of Manzat stood there at the time of Shutruk-Nahhunte.

The two deities Khishmitik and Rukhuratir shared, both at Susa and at Chogha-Zanbil, a common temple built for them by Untash-(*d*)*GAL*. Khishmitik, also written Ishmitik, is known only from inscribed bricks of that king, but Rukhuratir is found more often. His cult existed at all periods, and must have been widespread in the country, as shown by various spellings of his name. In the contracts from Mālamīr he is joined with Shamash as a god before whom oaths were sworn. Assyrian scribes regarded him, together with In-Shushinak, as identical with the god Ninurta, and he appears in the series of incantations *šurpu* as potent to protect against witchcraft.

Of other individual gods little is known. Pelala is named in the contracts from Mālamīr and in the annals of Ashurbanipal, but we are left without information as to the part he played in the Elamite pantheon. The personality of Nazit is equally obscure. His chapel at Susa, mentioned on an inscribed brick of Untash-(*d*)*GAL* may have been part of the joint temple of *GAL* and In-Shushinak, for these two are invoked in this dedication. Only on bricks from Chogha-Zanbil are found the deities Shiashum,

---

[1] The brick mentioning this was found after the publication of *Mém. D.P.* 32, 8 f.

[2] This site was certainly occupied for a long time as bricks dating from the Third Dynasty of Ur to the times of Shutruk-Nahhunte and Shilkhak-In-Shushinak were found there.

Sunkir-Risharra, Kilakh-supir and Shushmushi, of whom nothing more is known than their names, although the first is mentioned in the Naram-Sin treaty. The name of the second is simply an epithet, 'the great king'. All we know about the last, Shushmushi, is that he was coupled with a *bēlit*, a 'lady', who is otherwise unknown. As for the Napratep, worshipped both at Susa and Chogha-Zanbil, we know only that they constituted a group, for the form is plural, as in Pakhakhutep, gods to whom Khumban-numena dedicated a great temple at Liyan. It is not clear whether the former, like the latter, were old, more or less anonymous, protecting deities, or whether it was a generic for several known gods such as the Igigi or Anunnaki of the Babylonian pantheon. The first element means simply 'god' but the second, *ratep*, cannot be interpreted although it formed part of the personal name of a prince of Awan, Khishep-ratep.

In addition to these indigenous gods, the Elamite documents of this period mention many Babylonian deities for whom Untash-(*d*)*GAL* had temples built both at Susa and at Chogha-Zanbil. They are Nabu, Sin, Adad and Shala, Inanna and Nusku. Earlier inscriptions show that a number of Babylonian gods had long been worshipped in Susiana, but it is worthy of note that these cults, adopted from the west, remained in existence at this time when the country took an independent course and displayed a certain chauvinism in the persistent struggle for a national policy and an internal development of civilization. Since many names such as Sin and Adad were written with logograms the question arises whether these should not be interpreted in the same way as the logogram, *UTU*, to be read Nahhunte, that is to say, as true Elamite names. Assyrian lists in fact inform us that Sin was called Dakdadra in Elam, and that Adad corresponded to both Shunnukushsha and Sihhash, as well as In-Shushinak. But Sin and Adad are so well attested in Elam in other periods that there is no *a priori* reason for excluding them from the Elamite pantheon of this time. That Adad and Shala were worshipped in their own names is proved by syllabic writing, and this is another reason for maintaining that the other Akkadian names were used.

It is a pertinent question whether these Babylonian deities preserved in this foreign land the characteristics and qualities which they had in their own country. A votive hoe has been found at Chogha-Zanbil, with its handle in the form of a serpent and bearing the inscription '*marru* of Nabu'. The *marru*, probably borrowed from the symbols of Marduk, is not an emblem of his cult-centre Borsippa, whereas the serpent, on the other hand, seems to indicate that in Susiana Nabu was connected with the chthonic powers which that reptile symbolizes. Again, the goddess Shala was in Babylonia the traditional spouse of Adad. Her cult appeared in Elam immediately after its adoption in Babylonia by the Semites of the Amorite dynasty; but in the contracts of Susa she appears independent of Adad as one of the gods before whom oaths were taken.[1] It was not until later, in Susa as in Chogha-Zanbil, that she was closely associated with the cult of Adad. However this may be, in the dedicatory inscriptions of Untash-(d)GAL, no distinction seems to be made between the foreign and Elamite gods. They were all 'gods of Siyankuk'[2] whom the king implores to accept his pious works and bless his kingship in exactly the same terms. The foreign, like the native, gods receive the tribute of new statues in the restored temples. And to these Babylonian gods, fully accepted in Elam, there is no doubt that Bēltia, 'my lady', should be added. She occurs in the inscription on the statue of Napirasu and it is certain that she was the Ishtar of Babylon, for one of the successors of Untash-(d)GAL describes her as zana Tentar, 'the lady of Babylon'.

In spite, then, of the brevity and monotony of the formulae on the bricks of the kings of this dynasty, a broad reconstruction of the Elamite pantheon in this period is possible, but it would be an exaggeration to treat the list as exhaustive. The excavations of Chogha-Zanbil and Susa have not as yet revealed all there is to know about these two cities. Other cities and other temples are still hidden under the débris of unexplored mounds. Moreover, there were certainly other temples, at Susa and elsewhere, which did not need repairs at that time, and consequently do not appear in the kings' inscriptions, Khutran is a case in point; he was an ancient deity of the national pantheon, closely associated with the divine pair Khumban and Kiririsha, perhaps their son, if an invocation of Shilkhak-In-Shushinak, which calls him 'the chosen descendant' of these two, can be said to prove that. A tutelary god, his name occurs frequently in personal names such as Khutran-temti, Kidin-Khutran and the like. Although his cult

---

[1] It is doubtful whether the personal name Shala on the tablets of Mālamīr refers to this goddess. The name is never preceded by the divine determinative and once (Mém. D.P. 8, 16 = Mém. D.P. 22, 76) instead of Shala we find the personal name Tepti-akhar, which is also on a tablet from Susa (Mém. D.P. 23, 248, 18).

[2] According to the brick cited above for the identification of Chogha-Zanbil with Dūr-Untash, it seems that siyankuk, in which there is the word siyan 'temple', designated a part of the holy city, probably the group, temples and zikkurrat, within the two inner enclosures. It seems to have the same meaning at Susa.

originated perhaps in Awan, he had a temple at Susa which Ashur-banipal was to destroy in the sack of that city. Two other native divinities, Lakamar and Narundi, as well as the Babylonian gods Nergal, Shamash, and Nin-khursag, are in the same situation; no texts from this period mention them, but there is no reason to suppose that their cults fell into disuse at this time, for they occur both earlier and later. It may be that they are disguised under names given to many gods as yet unidentified.

The results of this review of Elamite religion sufficiently demonstrate the inadequacy of our sources. An enumeration of the deities worshipped by a people is not a sufficient guide to the true substance of the religion. We do, however, have other evidence than the dedicatory inscriptions and god lists. There are the monuments, reliefs and sculpture as well as the seals from Elam. Despite the fact that they are difficult to interpret because of their particular symbolism, some of them may illustrate certain fundamental ideas of Elamite religion. The archaic seal impres-sions[1] seem to show that Susa and Mesopotamia had the same primitive concepts about the gods. Each city-state worshipped a patron god who was partnered by his consort, either one being pre-eminent. A pantheon, even regional, does not seem to exist until pre-Sargonic times. There is seen also the king-priest standing beside a temple with a high terrace.[2] According to similar pieces from Uruk these motifs seem to be related to the neo-Sumerian concept of the divine king. Another seal, slightly earlier than the dynasty of Agade, illustrates a feature which we consider distinctly Elamite: the multiplicity and the eminent position of goddesses. A very curious sort of feminine pantheon is evoked by a line of goddesses taking part in a mythological drama which seems concerned with vegetation.[3]

There has already been occasion to mention rites of ablution, which were perhaps due to the influence of the cult of Ea on Elamite religion. These rites are known through the discovery at Susa of many containers and basins, one at least of which is decorated with the representation of an intertwined cord, the symbol of the flowing waters, and with the half-antelope, half-fish figures. Other such rites are illustrated by the votive bronze model called *ṣīt šamši*; two naked figures, perhaps a priest and his acolyte, kneel face to face before a temple and, presumably at

[1] Period of Uruk V–III. As well as a style similar to that of Uruk, there was an original style which shows that Elamite art was not simply a borrowing from Meso-potamia, cf. §II, 2, 105 ff. For the documents of Uruk cf. §III, 8.

[2] See §III, 1, 41.   [3] §III, 3, 1, pl. 45, 11–12 (S. 462), and p. 57.

dawn, are about to commence ritual ablutions with the water
contained in a vase of a form not unlike the *agubbu*, the vessel
containing holy fluid, used by the Babylonians.[1]

These two objects are later in date than the time of Untash-
(*d*)*GAL* but the stele carved in relief that bears his name provides
other religious motifs that are no less instructive. The flowing
streams recur on this stele and the gesture of prayer is shown, a
deity is replaced by a symbol, and the Elamite belief in fantastic
creatures half man, half animal is illustrated, together with the
religious importance of the serpent. Most of these features can
also be found in a rock relief at Kūrangān,[2] between Susa and
Persepolis. This depicts seated deities, groups of worshippers, the
flowing streams, the serpent figure. In this religious scene
there is a theme which adds to the interest, the advance of a procession towards the 'high place' where the divine pair sit.[3] The
worshippers, marching in a column, hold their hands out towards
the god, the gesture of prayer, which does not differ from the
Babylonian act of adoration. The supernatural character of the
gods is symbolized as in Babylonia by the triple row of horns on
the head-dress; even semi-divine beings or demons are sometimes so distinguished, but in their case a single pair of horns for
their leaders is usual. One detail, however, which may also be
found on certain North Syrian reliefs of the 'Hittite' style, dis-
tinguishes these representations of the gods from the Babylonian
tradition: whether the god's head is in full face or profile, the
horns are always full face. But the motif of the flowing streams
leads us back again to the direct Babylonian influence. On the
stele these have the appearance of two long wavy tresses crossing
one another, which join heaven and earth; in the middle they are
held by a semi-divine being, half human, half fish, who holds
them tight against his chest. At Kūrangān, on the other hand, it
is the god himself who lifts in his right hand a bellied vase from
which the two streams flow; the water, curving backwards and
forwards, falls on two groups of worshippers. The comparison
with the frequent use of this *motif* in Babylonia shows a close
connexion with fertility rites.

---

[1] This bronze model is studied in detail below, pp. 496 f.   [2] See Plate 53 (*b*)–(*c*).
[3] See the end of this chapter, and also compare *C.A.H.* I³, pt. 2, pp. 673 f.
N. C. Debevoise, 'The Rock Reliefs of Ancient Iran', in *J.N.E.S.* 1, 72, dates this
relief in the third millennium, but § III, 2, iv, 2139 prefers the middle of the second.
Neither of these dates is certain. It could also be dated to the neo-Sumerian period
by comparing it with a seal-impression found in the Ur III level (*Mém. D.P.* 25,
233, fig. 53) and with the different representations on the seals of Susa B (see *R.A.*
50, 135, no. 4).

The form taken by the semi-divine creatures likewise belongs to a common set of ideas. In the earliest periods of Elamite civilization these supernatural beings had the strangest forms— half human, half plant; half human, half serpent; half human, half goat; and so forth. This was probably common to Elam and Babylonia, but the Elamites seem to have been much more imaginative. They created the griffon, as a temple guard, which was unknown to the Sumerians.[1] Contrariwise, the nude hero 'Gilgamesh', the usual acolyte of the god Ea, was unknown in the glyptic art of Susa.[2] Later, Babylonian influence restricted and regularized the types; to an upper body in human form there was added either the tail end of a fish or the hind quarters of a bull. They are thus represented either in the midst of the interlacing streams, or beside a palm-tree, or on either side of a stylized 'tree of life'. Themselves producing and protecting the fertility of the land, these creatures were also, in Elam as elsewhere, the guardians of sacred buildings. Ashurbanipal mentioned in his annals the šēdū and lamassū which guarded the temples at Susa and the figures of wild bulls which watched over the gates. There is no doubt that the Elamites believed in the existence of evil demons as well as of these beneficent deities. Their Babylonian neighbours in fact regarded Elam as specially the land of witches and of demoniac creatures; the typical demoness Lamashtu herself, though often called 'the Sutian',[3] is just as often named 'the Elamite'. Even if it cannot be denied that Babylonia exercised a controlling influence on Elamite art in the representation of semi-divine beings, it is none the less certain that many of these fantastic creatures were directly due to Elamite imagination.

As well as good and evil demons the Elamite engravers also invented others which seem to personify cosmic ideas and have nothing to do with the notions of good or evil. The scenes that they depicted, most often in a style of caricature, are more probably taken from myth than from stories or fables. There are not only animals parodying men,[4] but Atlas-figures holding up the world,[5] and successions of gigantic animals, perhaps symbolizing

---

[1] This is later found in Egypt; see § III, 1, 42, and fig. 5.

[2] This is the more curious in that the seals of an older period (Susa I) display figures of conquering heroes who anticipate 'Gilgamesh'.

[3] I.e. one who haunts the Syrian desert.

[4] Dog-ploughmen or farmers (*Mém. D.P.* 16, nos. 196, 260, etc.); antelope holding a bow and arrows (§ III, 5, no. 775), etc. Cf. the statuettes from Susa showing drinking and sitting animals (*Mém. D.P.* 13, pl. xxxix, 2–3); cf. M. Rutten in *Rev. ét. sém.* (1938), 97 ff.

[5] *Mém. D.P.* 16, 266, 267, etc.; P. Amiet in *R.A.* 50 (1956), 125 f.

natural cycles, victorious over each other alternately in strict order.[1] These themes conjure up a 'land of fable' from which man is absent, and mysterious domains where the cosmic balance is in operation.

The most important motif in Elamite religious art is the serpent.[2] Our attention has already been drawn to this recurring theme by the two long serpents which frame the stele of Untash-(d)GAL. Actually the serpent appears on very ancient objects, notably on seals that belong to the time of the Third Dynasty of Ur. It is represented on the stele of Puzur-Shushinak, in the rock relief of Kūrangān, and in another relief cut in the rock at Naqsh-i Rustam. It is the essential theme on the celebrated 'altar with serpents', a masterpiece of Elamite metal work dating from the period after Untash-(d)GAL, and bodies of reptiles frequently form the butt of votive sceptres or the handle of a marru dedicated to the god Nabu.

All these examples, together with many others that need not be quoted here, whether the serpent is depicted naturally or as a symbol, are simply representations of a very ancient deity, the serpent god, or rather, a god of which the serpent is the symbol, the captive, and the guardian of his subterranean realm. Undoubtedly the theme of the serpent was popular in Mesopotamia at different times, and even had an influence on Elamite tradition. Thus, during the dynasty of Agade, Susa as well as Babylonia[3] used on their seals a representation of the serpent-god that had been worked out by Agadean artists. In the same way the serpent on the stele of Untash-(d)GAL can be compared with similar representations on several Kassite kudurru.[4] But the serpent was always more important in Elam than in Mesopotamia, and the Elamite artists created a type of human-headed serpent that was typically Elamite.[5] This originality is of special importance from a religious point of view, as it shows a deification of the

---

[1] Mém. D.P. 16, no. 330. (An enormous bull mastering two small lions is counterpoised with an enormous lion subduing two small bulls.) Another seal, now lost, shows two antithetic scenes: a lion theatening a kneeling bull with his bow and the same bull, this time standing, holding a club over the head of the now crouching lion. The same kind of alternation and balancing of forces can be seen in the document Mém. D.P. 16, 335, studied by E. Porada, 'A Leonine Figure...', in J.A.O.S. 70 (1950), 225.

[2] P. Toscanne, 'Études sur le serpent...dans l'antiquité élamite', in Mém. D.P. 12, 153 ff. and 25, 183 ff., 232 f.; and cf. §III, 7, 53 ff.

[3] Cf. R.A. 44 (1950), 172, nos. 30, 31.

[4] See §III, 4, pl. I, pl. LXVIII, 1; pl. LXXXIII, 1.

[5] See §III, 3, 1 S. 105; R.A. 19 (1922), 148, no. 11.

serpent little known in Mesopotamia. This deity tends to become less and less animal. Sometimes it has the head and shoulders of a man and from the torso downwards the body becomes the winding coils of a serpent. Sometimes, however, the serpent is no more than an attribute of the deity, as in the relief of Kūrangān, where the god, entirely human in form, holds the head of the serpent in his left hand while its body, folded coil upon coil, serves as his seat. This serpent-god, the origin of whose cult is lost in the mists of time, is rather a mysterious figure, a symbol perhaps of all those dark powers that are hidden in the depths of the earth, or spring up from the ground, sometimes beneficent, sometimes terrifying, bringing sometimes fertility, sometimes destruction. It is thus not surprising that many representations of serpents have been found in foundation deposits. Heads or bodies of these reptiles were a common form for ex-votos, buried to secure the protection of the chthonic deities for the foundations which descend into their dark realm.

One other religious motif in the relief at Kūrangān deserves special notice. On the rock surface to the left, slightly overhanging the face with the principal relief, where the god with the serpent and the seated goddess beside him form the central group, the procession represented seems to be moving towards the divine pair. Such long files may be seen recurring on the rocks of Kul-i Fir'aun, at Mālamīr, in the rock reliefs carved in honour of Khanni, the ruler of Aiapir.[1] The custom of religious processions, with their trains of priests and worshippers, was common in Mesopotamia from a very early date. Certain of these processions, in particular those of the New Year, even left the environs of the temple and filed out into the surrounding country. But here the worshippers did not accompany their god but came from afar to pay homage. The scene is more reminiscent of a pilgrimage than of a procession, and this form of worship is very rarely known in Mesopotamia. On the other hand, the fact that their goal was a high place, the seat of chthonic deities, rather recalls certain aspects of Anatolian cults, where may also be found these three features: a high place, a procession, and chthonic deities.[2]

It will be apparent from these remarks on Elamite religion that it is still difficult for us to form any precise idea of this

[1] The seals only seldom depict religious ceremonies. The most striking example is the amusing scene which shows a line of sedan-chairs and standard-bearers on the document in *Mém. D.P.* 29, 20, fig. 16 (12). Unfortunately this scene, like many others, is difficult to interpret.

[2] See § III, 2, iv, 2139.

people's beliefs. Certainly we know the name and often the nature of the greater proportion of their gods, certainly also their beliefs contained ideas common to most of the primitive religions of the Near East, together with obvious influence from Mesopotamian cults. But the original bases of the native religion still escape our knowledge. Until future excavations have put at our disposal specifically religious documents, especially prayers and rituals, it will be impossible to attempt a comprehensive account of Elamite religion.

CHAPTER XXX

PHRYGIA AND THE PEOPLES
OF ANATOLIA IN THE
IRON AGE

THE Hittite Empire collapsed in ruins in about 1200 B.C., at the hands of the invaders, among whom their traditional enemies on the eastern frontier, the Kaska peoples, were surely numbered, and a horde or series of hordes flooded over the land; excavation has revealed a level of destruction by fire in the east, at the Hittite capital of Boğazköy, at Alaca and at Alişar.[1] Written records of the Hittites, hitherto our most important source of historical information concerning Anatolia, cease abruptly with the reign of Shuppiluliumash II. At Alişar there was a brief occupation by a people who, it is thought, may have been the Luwians and who may have played an important part in the destruction. When the curtain rises again, central Anatolia is ruled (or at least, occupied) by an invading people, a horse-rearing military aristocracy called the Phrygians (as they were known in the West to the Greeks through Homer), or the Mushki and Tabal (as they were known to the Assyrians in the East). According to the traditions preserved among the Macedonians, says Herodotus (III. 73), the Phrygians crossed the straits into Anatolia from Macedonia and Thrace, where they had until then been known as Bryges or Briges. The Greeks in general believed that this event took place before the Trojan War, enshrining it in legend; though Xanthus, a Lydian historian, held it took place after that event, in a joint invasion with the Mysians.[2] According to one such Greek tradition, the royal house of Priam was connected with Phrygia by marriage, since Hecuba was daughter of the River Sangarius.[3] Another tale (*Iliad*, III. 184 ff.) tells how Priam, king of Troy, fought as an ally of the Phrygian leaders Otreus and Mygdon when they battled against the Amazones on the River Sangarius.

---

* An original version of this chapter was published as fascicle 56 in 1967; the present chapter includes revisions made in 1973.

[1] Boğazköy (Büyükkale): §III, 7, 27, 67 ff.; Alişar, §III, 24, esp. 289 (destruction in Level 5 M); Alaca, §III, 18, 179.

[2] Xanthus: F. Jacoby, *Frag. Hist. Graec.* 765 F14.

[3] Schol. on Homer, *Il.* XVI. 718.

Some scholars see in this battle that which Tudkhaliash IV fought against twenty-two states in the 'Land of the city of Assuwa'.[1] This assumes that the Amazons were the Hittites[2] (which is nothing but a guess) and, what is perhaps more likely, that Assuwa is 'Asia', i.e. north-west Asia Minor.[3] In fact, if the memory of the Amazons refers at all to a historical people, they are more likely to have been one of the peripheral peoples of the Hittite Empire nearer to the Greeks: Luwians or other races of Arzawa, e.g. Mira, Kuwaliya, Kaballa, who acted as buffer states between Hittites and Greeks; perhaps they were the armed priestesses of some goddess of war such as Ma of Comana. It would be a mistake to base much in any direction on these legendary Greek traditions (though they may well contain a germ of fact), unless and until they are confirmed by some new discovery. However, recent excavation in Troy VII b has revealed the introduction, after a destruction of the city by fire,[4] of a new population using a coarse ware apparently of central European origin, and this may reasonably be held to mark the passage of the Phrygians and Mysians. At Gordion, hand-made black pottery suddenly appears at a corresponding level, then disappears as if its makers had been absorbed.[5] In fact, the area in which the Mygdones, the tribe of the eponymous Phrygian hero Mygdon, traditionally lived was round Lake Ascania, by Nicea, close by the last curve of the River Sangarius: and this may very well mark the earliest Phrygian area of settlement, while the Mysians occupied the Troad and Propontis. Within a short time, presumably during the twelfth century B.C., the Phrygians flowed over most of the western Anatolian plateau, isolating the Luwians of the western plateau (who had withstood them, to form the kingdoms of Lydia and Lycia), perhaps driving others before them to safety beyond the Taurus and absorbing the rest. At Beycesultan[6] the city was destroyed about 1000 B.C. It has recently been suggested that the newcomers were at least partly nomadic in their way of life; and this may account for the interruption in the life of the central plateau which seems now to occur over a long period of at least a century or more.[7]

[1] But for a much earlier dating of this episode see *C.A.H.* ii², pt. 1, pp. 677 f.

[2] See article 'Amazones' in *P.W.* 1 (1894). It is noteworthy that, as Akurgal points out (*Späthethitische Bildkunst*, Ankara, 1949, p. 14 and n. 107), on the frieze of the Hellenistic Temple of Hecate at Lagina, Amazons are represented wearing helmets of the type worn by Hittite soldiers at Carchemish.

[3] §1, 3, ch. 1, 'Asia, Isj.j, Assuwa'.   [4] §III, 9.

[5] M. J. Mellink, review of §III, 9 in *Bi.Or.* 5/6 (1960), 251.

[6] §III, 20, 94.   [7] G, 5, 64; §II, 9, 52; §III, 16.

I. GEOGRAPHY

In Greek times, the Phrygians' most north-westerly settlement, according to Xenophon,[1] was Keramon Agora, where a branch of the Royal Road left Lydia to strike northwards. The southern limit of the Phrygians' conquests is obscure, but it is worth noting that another Lake Ascania is found in Pisidia near Sagalassus, north of which was located the tomb of Mygdon, on the road running south towards Lycia; while the inland area beside the River Caÿster, through which ran south-west the road to Iconium and Barata, was later called the Phrygian Paroreia.

But the area which was especially sacred to them, where we find their principal religious monuments, is the hilly area, still well forested today (in Hellenistic times called Phrygia Epictetus or Little Phrygia), rising to four thousand feet above sea level, between modern Eskişehir and Afyon Karahisar, where rise several rivers sacred in myth and religion, such as Parthenius, Tembris, Sangarius, Rhyndacus,[2] and which includes the sacred city of Pessinus and that today called after its most notable inscribed monument 'Midas City' (evidently called in antiquity Metropolis, the 'City of the Mother', because dedicated to the mother goddess, Cybele).[3] On the east adjoined the areas of the Sangarius and the ancient (western) capital Gordion, around which are still to be seen as many as eighty great tumuli, once containing the rich burials of the Phrygian nobility and associated with the names of famous Phrygian kings, Gordius and Midas. Another important area of Phrygian settlement lay still further east around Ancyra (mod. Ankara), where typical Phrygian burial tumuli and temples and other remains of the eighth to sixth centuries have been found,[4] linking the westerly settlements with other Phrygian centres further east beyond the Halys, at Pteria (by some identified with Boğazköy, the former Hittite capital),[5] Pazarlı,[6] Alişar,[7] Alaca[8] and Kültepe.[9] In fact, pottery associated with Phrygians is found at a number of points all over the plateau.[10]

[1] *Anab.* I, ii, 11.
[2] §III, 4; G, 7.
[3] §III, 13, 14; §IV, 4; 14. The identification of Metropolis with Midas City is not accepted by all scholars. See Plate 157(*b*).
[4] §III, 1.   [5] §III, 3, 7; 6, 52; 7, 78, 120; 8, 6.
[6] §III, 19.   [7] §III, 24.
[8] §III, 3; 18.   [9] §III, 25.
[10] Find-spots of Phrygian pottery marked on G, 1, Map 6; §III, 6, pl. 4; §IV, 8.

II. THE NEWCOMERS AND THE
CLASH WITH ASSYRIA

Assyrian sources name as the occupants of this area, in particular that east of the Halys, in the Iron Age from the twelfth century B.C., not Phrygians but Mushki.[1] The Assyrians sometimes speak of the Mushki and Tabal as if linked with Kashku, i.e. the Kaska peoples, formerly the great enemies of the Hittite kings on the latter's east and north-east frontiers, and this alone suggests that the Mushki may have been allied with them in some way, joining them in finally overthrowing the Hittite Empire. It is possible, too, that the mention in the latest records of the Hittite Empire of an unfriendly prince named Mita of Pakhuwa[2] (a city tentatively located west of the upper Euphrates, probably near Divriği), may point to a Phrygo-Mushkian thrust already then developing on that easterly frontier under an early bearer of an afterwards famous royal Phrygian name. It is tempting, in any event, to connect the Mushki on the one hand with the Georgian tribe of Mes'chi (known from about the fifth century A.D. around Lake Çildir beside the present Russo-Turkish frontier), and on the other, perhaps more plausibly, with the tribes recorded by the Greeks as Moschi and Tibarani, who dwelt beside the iron-working Chalybes, near the Black Sea coast around Cerasus, between Themiscyra, the reputed home of the Amazones, and the 'Moschian Mountains'. These Moschians and Tibaranians were still brigaded together in Xerxes' army. We assume that these tribes swarmed southwards from the direction of the eastern Pontus over the central plateau into the Halys bend, joining hands with the Phrygians advancing from the north-west. From the Assyrian royal annals[3] we learn that about 1160 B.C. a great army of Mushki swept on southwards through the Taurus Mountains and settled in the provinces of Alzi and Purukuzzi, 'where no man had vanquished them in battle', but acknowledged Assyrian overlordship by paying tribute. Fifty years later, the Assyrian king Tiglath-pileser I (1115–1077) accused the Mushki of having wantonly invaded the·province of Katmukhi[4] with an army of twenty thousand men, i.e. implying that they were moving south-east threateningly. He may of course have been, and probably was, simply picking on their action of fifty years

---

[1] §II, 3, vol. I, §§220, 221.   [2] §I, 4; 5.
[3] §II, 3, vol. I, §221.
[4] The identification of Katmukhi and Kummukh (Commagene), formerly proposed by some, is impossible.

before as a *casus belli* to justify an attack on them. In any event he attacked, and defeated them in a pitched battle, annexed Alzi–Purukuzzi as a province and carried off six thousand Mushki as captives to a district,[1] probably in north-east Syria, where in Strabo's time they were still known as 'the Mygdones around Nisibis'.[2] Strabo's allusion, if it is to be trusted, is particularly interesting as implying that the original deep south-eastern thrust included also western Phrygian elements (Mygdones).

As the number of captive Mushki claimed is about one third the number of those who were said to have invaded the area, it may be accepted as possible. We are, however, told that the Mushkian army was led by five kings, implying that their horde consisted of at least five tribes; and it is likely that the ultimate Phrygian Empire as a whole was a federation or coalition of several tribes or elements. In this confederation the Phrygians seem to have represented the western element, with their capital at Gordion; the eastern was formed by Mushki with their capital at Mazaca (later Caesarea Mazaca, modern Kayseri), 'said to be derived from Mosoch, the ancestor of the Cappadocians', (Eusebius),[3] and Tabal. Tabal formed a neo-Hittite state, called by the Assyrians Bīt-Burutash, lying east of Niğde and Kayseri. Mushki and Tabal correspond with the names of Meshech and Tubal, two of the sons of Japheth, symbolizing Anatolian origins to Biblical writers (Gen. x. 2; Ezek. xxvii. 13, and xxxii; Ps. cxx. 5). This Anatolian figure of myth, Japheth, is most probably the same as that preserved in Greek legend as Iapetus, one of the Titans.

The eastern group of Mushki in the Euphrates valley seems to have been under partly Hurrian leadership, as the Katmukhian king's name, Kili-Teshub, son of Kali-Teshub, shows (he is also called Irrupi, Hurrian for 'my lord');[4] but possibly they were also partly Indo-Iranian, for kings of Katmukhi, presumably descended from the invaders of 1160 B.C., bear such names as Kundashpi or Kushtashpi still in the ninth and eighth centuries B.C.[5] (Or are we to interpret this ethnic element as a pre-existent Iranian native element, perhaps deriving from Mitanni, which survived the Mushki pressure?) Certainly in Hellenistic times the kingdom of Commagene represented a deeply conservative western

---

[1] §II, 3, vol. I, §221; see below, pp. 457 f.
[2] Strabo, XI. 14. 527; XVI. 1. 23.
[3] *Hist. Eccles.* IX. 12; §I, 7, 303.
[4] G, 4, 91, 178.
[5] §II, 3, vol. I, §§610, 769, 772, 797, 801,

outpost of Iranian religion, albeit in a mixed form,[1] under a diadochic dynasty claiming Achaemenid origins, but possibly with
much older roots.

Though at this point the chronological limit of the present
volume of this *History* has been reached, it is convenient to continue summarily the history of the Phrygian Empire to its end.

Between the twelfth and ninth centuries B.C. the empire of the
Phrygians, Mushki and Tabal spread southwards over the whole
of the vast Anatolian plateau. Tabal seems to represent the older
Luwian elements that survived the Hittite collapse north of the
Taurus, and to have been the new name particularly adapted for
the area formerly called 'Lower Land' by the Hittites. This is the
later Lycaonia and Cappadocia, the area south of the Halys river
as far as the barrier of the Taurus. Here the Tabalians were con-
fronted and held back by the kingdom of Que or Khilakku
(Cilicia) in the eighth century B.C.,[2] while further east a coalition
of small Hittite principalities was formed called 'Land of Khatti',
centred around the old Hittite fortress of Carchemish on the
Euphrates. Til-garimmu (Hebrew, Togarmah; modern Gürün,
classical Gauraina) marked the eastern frontier of Tabal.[3] The
south-eastern limit of Tabal seems, however, to have been at
some time in part pushed by some tribes even beyond the Taurus,
for in the time of the proconsulate of Cicero (51 B.C.) the minor
passes of the Taurus were held by fiercely independent brigand
tribes called Eleutherokilikes ('Free Cilicians'), with a capital
at Pindenissus, controlling some of the Taurus passes, while their
allies the Tibarani (i.e. Tabalians) held the Amanus route. Cicero
soon disposed of their pretensions.[4] Yet it is astonishing how long
such groups preserved their identity, for in the seventh century
A.D., the Mardaites, or *Jarajīma*, apparently preserving the name
of Gurgum (a north Syrian mountain principality of the ninth
century B.C. located at Maraş in the Amanus Range[5]), were still
renowned as fighters in early Muslim times. The Mushki remained
in contact with Assyria, being invaded by Tukulti-Ninurta II
and acknowledging the authority of Ashurnaṣirpal II by sending
him gifts of copper vessels, cattle and wine in about 883 B.C.[6]
But the latter's son and successor, Shalmaneser III, took a more

---

[1] For Nimrud Dağ, see K. Humann and O. Puchstein: *Reise in Kleinasien und
Nord-syrien* (Berlin, 1890).

[2] §II, 3, vol. 2, §349.   [3] *Ibid.* §§290, 349.

[4] Cicero: *Ad Fam.* xv, 4.

[5] H. J. Lammens, *La Syrie* (1921), pp. 81 ff. See now U. B. Alkım in *Anadolu
Araştırmaları*, 1965.   [6] §II, 3, vol. 1, §442.

active line, sending an army in his twenty-second year (836 B.C.) as far as Mount Tunni, 'the copper mountain', perhaps the site of Tunna located near Bulgar Maden[1] and Mount Muli, 'the marble mountain'. Whereas Mushki was previously described as being under five kings, he records now that Tabal was made up of twenty-four 'kingdoms', which submitted to him, sending him tribute in his twenty-second and twenty-third years;[2] the surrender of the cities of Perria (perhaps modern Peri near the Euphrates) and Shitiuarria and twenty-two others is mentioned. After that we hear nothing of the history of inner Anatolia for fifty years.

The Tabalian princes, however, owed only reluctant allegiance to the Assyrians, preferring the protection of the kings of Urartu, and willingly forming part of the latter's sphere of influence. In fact we find in the eighth century B.C. Urartian influence steadily encroaching upon Eastern Anatolia. The Urartian king Menuas (c. 810–785) claims to have conquered the principality of Malatya as far as the modern Murad-Çay, and to have made its ruler Sulehawali or Sulumel[3] his vassal. At the same time he also attacked Khilaruada, 'king of Khate'. Menuas's successor, Argishtis I, claims in his third year c. 775 B.C. the conquest of a descendant of Tuate, king of Malatya, possibly the same as King Tuwatis mentioned in Hittite hieroglyphs, whose authority extended as far west as Topada near Nevşehir.[4] Sarduris III of Urartu c. 750 claimed as his vassals Kummukh (Commagene) and Tabal, and attacked Khilaruada, son of Sakhu king of Malatya, capturing his capital, Sasi, and annexing nine of his fortresses along the line of the Upper Euphrates. Their names are given as: Khazani, Ugarakhi, Tumeiski, Asini, Maninu, Arusi, Qulbitarri, Tase, Queraitase, Meluiani.[5] As a proof of this expansion of Urartian influence into Syria south of the Taurus we see in the sculptured doorways of palaces at both Zincirli and Sakcagözü figures of lions and reliefs which suddenly appear in a purely Urartian style. Further north, recent discoveries indicate that an Urartian principality, probably Dayaeni, extended its control into the Anatolian plateau westwards in the eighth and seventh centuries as far as Altıntepe, between Erzincan and Erzurum.[6]

---

[1] See below, p. 424, n. 6.   [2] §11, 3, vol. 1, §§579, 580.

[3] §11, 4, no. 25 (Palu Inscription); §11, 1, 153.

[4] §11, 4, no. 803 (Van Annals); §11, 2, 161 ff.; §VII, 24, xxix and 114. An earlier Tuate, spelt Tuatti, is mentioned as king of Tabal by Shalmaneser III; cf. J. Læssøe, *Iraq* 21 (1959), 155.   [5] §11, 4, nos. 102, 104 (Izolu Inscription); §11, 1, 176.

[6] G, 4, *passim*; §III, 26.

When, about 770 B.C., we look into the history of Carchemish, the key position at the crossing of the Euphrates, we find that a new dynasty is installed under one Araras as prince of Carchemish, and from his own inscriptions it is clear that he was a usurper who claimed some authority over Mushkians and even Lydians (of the latter this is the first contemporary mention).[1] It is a fair inference that he was established with Urartian help, to subdue the Tabalian league. Kamanas (c. 750), the son of Araras, is explicitly stated to be the vassal of Sasturas, apparently to be identified with Sarduris of Urartu in an inscription found at Cekke between Aleppo and Carchemish.[2] An uneasy balance of power on the Anatolian plateau lasted until the accession in 745 B.C. of Tiglath-pileser III of Assyria, who in his conflict with Urartu found himself steadily drawn forward into Anatolia. After inflicting a severe defeat on Urartu and accepting the consequent submission of Pisiris of Carchemish in 738 B.C. Tiglath-pileser III found his advance into Asia Minor barred by an alliance of four Tabalian kings, Ushkhitti of Tunna, Urpalla of Tukhana, Urimme of Khupishna, and lastly Tukhamme of Ishtunda, with their allies Urikki of Que, Sulumel of Melid and Dad-ilu of Kaska.[3] The domains of these four major rulers evidently consisted of the valleys descending to the north from the principal passes of the Taurus, which they controlled. Urpalla's Tukhana is Tyana; his portrait, showing him worshipping his god Tarkhundas, with his inscriptions in Hittite hieroglyphic script, survives carved on the rock at Ivriz; other texts mentioning him are found at Bor, at Bulgar Maden in the Taurus, and on a stone found at Andaval near Niğde.[4] His was the central position, controlling the road through the Cilician Gates. Tunna is identified with Zeyve-hüyük near Bulgar Maden[5] but Khupishna is most probably Cabissus in the Saros valley (not, as often proposed, Cybistra), while Ishtunda or Ishtuanda is apparently just the Assyrians' spelling of the name of Azitawatas. This city, named after its founder Azatiwatas, Tukhamme's predecessor of the ninth century B.C., has been discovered and excavated at Karatepe, in the Ceyhan (Pyramus) valley.[6]

All four kings, Ushkhitti, Urpalla, Urimme and Tukhamme, acknowledged allegiance to Wassurme (= Wasu-Sarma) 'great

---

[1] §III, 15c, 262 ff.
[2] §III, 15, Part III, 262 ff.; §II, 8; §VII, 6; A, 5, 105.   [3] §II, 3, vol. 1, §772.
[4] Andaval, Bulgar Maden, Bor, §VII, 24, xxi, xxii, xxiii.   [5] By H. Bossert, §VII, 7.
[6] See above, pp. 364 ff. The identification of the city of Azitawatas with Ishtunda was first made by Landsberger and Bossert, §III, 11, part 2, 30.

king' of Tabal, the son of Tuatis mentioned above, who, while remaining in the background, is discernible as the Assyrians' real opponent, and who is mentioned in hieroglyphic Hittite inscriptions at Topada, Çiftlik and Suvasa, south of the Halys, at Kayseri (Sultan Han) and Kululu near Kültepe, probably Wassurme's capital, the name of which is given as Bīt-Burutash or -Burutish.[1] In about 730 B.C. Tiglath-pileser deposed the hostile Wassurme, replacing him as king of Tabal by one Khulli, 'son of nobody', who provided in return a vast tribute of ten talents of gold and one thousand of silver.[2] Khulli, however, after reigning some years, likewise defected from the Assyrian side. On the death of Tiglath-pileser III, there was a shift once more in the balance of power on the unstable Anatolian frontier. Trouble was caused by a princeling of Tabal named Kiakki of Shinukhti, who seems to have alienated Khulli from his loyalties to Assyria. He was joined by Pisiris, king of Carchemish, and a new figure, Mita of Mushki, otherwise Midas the Phrygian of Greek legend, all three making a formidable coalition.[3] Two years later (718), Sargon's army marched against the city of Kiakki, which was given to Matti of Tunna.[4] Mita advanced into Que (Cilicia) and seized three of its towns: but in 717 Sargon II's army marched against Carchemish and deposed Pisiris, carrying him off as a prisoner, and making Carchemish an Assyrian province. Khullu was deposed as king of Bīt-Burutash and replaced by his son named Ambaris (or Amris or Ambaridi—the name is variously written) who stood in high favour with Sargon at Nineveh. Ambaris was given an Assyrian royal princess named Akhatabisha to wife, with Khilakku (a part of Tabal immediately north of the Taurus) for dowry.

But a dramatic turn of fortune's wheel now took place. In 714, the Cimmerians, the Biblical Gomer, from beyond the Caucasus, a horde of fierce barbarians from south Russia, suddenly bore down on the confines of Urartu, driven out, according to Greek tradition,[5] by the Scythian tribes down the central passes of the Caucasus, the ancient military road. Rusas of Urartu met them at Uesi (probably Baş-Kale), was decisively defeated, and committed suicide, while in 714 Sargon marched through the now defence-

---

[1] §VII, 24, xx–xxiii; for Bīt-Burutash see §II, 3, vol. 2, §§24, 25, 92, 118. For excavations at Kululu, see T. Özgüç, *Kültepe and its vicinity in the Iron Age* (Ankara, 1971).   [2] §II, 3, vol. 1, §802.

[3] G, 6.   [4] §II, 3, vol. 2, §§24, 25, 55, 118, 137.

[5] Herodotus, IV. 9; for a discussion of Cimmerian remains in Anatolia see G, 2, 53 ff.

less country and sacked Muṣaṣir.[1] In 713 it was Ambaris' turn; he, too, was accused of playing Assyria false and, in order to strengthen himself, of having sought alliance with Rusas of Urarṭu (now dead) on the east and Mita of Mushki on the west, and 'conspiring to seize Assyrian territory'. Ambaris and his family and court were carried off to Assyria as prisoners and the Assyrian frontier was advanced once more to make Tabal an Assyrian province; the fortresses of Usi, Usian and Uargin were set up on the Mushkian frontier,[2] and Ellibir and Shindarara (Shalmaneser's Shitiuarria?) and ten other fortresses were seized from Meliddu. Midas made an offer of treaty with which Sargon played and temporized.[3] Tabal was made into a province; Khilakku and Que, respectively north and south of the Taurus, into another.

From Urarṭu, the Cimmerians appear to have turned westwards against the Urarṭians' allies, the Phrygians, whose ruler Midas, like Rusas, is also said to have committed suicide. The great tumulus at Gordion, excavated by the Americans in 1957,[4] produced a burial rich in gifts, surrounding the body of a small elderly man of over sixty years of age. None of the gifts included gold which, it has been ingeniously suggested, had all been surrendered to the invaders. At the same period the Phrygian city appears to have been violently burnt, though it revived. The Cimmerians are reputed to have ravaged Ionia, probably attacking Smyrna and Miletus and other cities such as Sinope (Herodotus IV. 12) and Antandrus, but the chief effect of their invasion which terrorized Asia Minor for eighty years was to destroy the Phrygian Empire, the heart of which they appear to have occupied. In 679 B.C., under their king Teushpa, they were defeated by Esarhaddon and thrown back from the Taurus after a pitched battle at Khupishna.[5]

III. PHRYGIAN ART AND ARCHAEOLOGY

The earlier history of the Phrygian state is lost in darkness, but it is evident that, in spite of great interruptions, it eventually gathered up and preserved much of the arts and culture of the

[1] §II, 6.

[2] P. Meriggi, 'Una prima attestazione epicorica dei Moschi in Frigia', in *Athenaeum* 42 (Pavia, 1964), 52 ff., reading the name of the Mushki in the Hittite hieroglyphic rock-inscription of Kızıldağ near Konya, identifies this site and that of Karadağ nearby with two fortresses of Midas.

[3] See M. E. L. Mallowan, *Nimrud and its Remains*, 1, 205, and cf. now A, 10, 21 ff.   [4] §III, 28.   [5] II, 3, vol. 2, §516.

older Hittite world, having been partly built on the ruins of the kingdom of Arzawa and its smaller neighbours.

The Phrygians, while they superposed a new society in the form of a social order of horse-rearing aristocrats ruling over the older natives, became associated with a vast and powerful land-owning priesthood such as that of Pessinus,[1] of a conservative type, having pre-Phrygian origins. Gordion took the place of a Hittite township, the cemetery of which has been found.[2] Phrygian pottery, though not derived from that of the Hittites, is basically Anatolian in inspiration and derivation. It is of two main kinds: east of a line drawn from the Sangarius through the centre of the Konya Plain to the Taurus, it is polychrome, with geometric animals and designs—a style, called Alişar IV from the type-site, employing a technique which has very ancient roots in Central Anatolia; to the west, it is mainly grey or red monochrome (*bucchero*), a type which can also be followed back to the Bronze Age. Some gaily decorated plastic vases of polychrome ware were also found at Gordion and are particularly notable. It has been suggested that these are imports, and that the polychrome style belongs to Tabal and the Luwians of the east, while the grey *bucchero* alone is purely Phrygian.[3]

The Tabalian campaign of Tiglath-pileser III (conducted by his *rab šāqê*, a high-ranking military officer) is apparently depicted both in reliefs from Tiglath-pileser's palace at Nimrūd[4] and in polychrome frescoes from the governor's palace at Tell Aḥmar (Til-Barsib in North Syria).[5] These show us the earliest representations of the Eastern Phrygians or Moscho-Tabalians; they are men with fine, somewhat Greek features and black or sometimes red curly hair and close beards, wearing earrings of Lydian type,[6] long shirts with horizontal coloured bands and tassels at the corners, and high buskins identical with those typical both of Phrygians and Paphlagonians, 'reaching to the middle of the calf', as described by Herodotus (VII. 72, 73). In his day, Phrygian military equipment was completed by plaited helmets, small spears, and shields common to other central Anatolian tribes. Such is the armament of the Phrygian soldiers depicted on the coloured clay tiles found at the early sixth-century East Phrygian site of Pazarlı.[7] The women shown at Til-Barsib are unveiled and wear

[1] §I, 6, 39 ff.   [2] §III, 21.
[3] §VI, 8, including a distribution map. See Plate 158(*a*).
[4] §II, 2, xx–xxiii and pls. XLV–LV.
[5] §II, 7, pl. XLIX; §IV, 12, frontispiece, XV–XVII, pls. I, 109–20, 266, 336–48.
[6] §III, 10, figs. 157–8; §VII, 2, 17, 18, 23.   [7] §III, 19, pls. LIV, LV.

long shirts, gaily striped horizontally, and short coats similar to those of the men, with bell-shaped tassels. A sculptured stone figure wearing a dress of this type was found near Maraş.[1] To secure their dress, Phrygian men used a large ornate fibula of bronze, the best illustration of which is that worn by Urpalla in the relief at Ivriz.[2] A hundred and forty-five of these fibulae were found at Gordion in the Great Tumulus.[3] On the reliefs of Sargon,[4] Phrygian tributaries are represented wearing this large bow-shaped fibula on their long dresses; the fashion spread both southwards and eastwards to Maraş,[5] Zincirli[6] and Carchemish.[7]

The rise to power of Midas's kingdom in western Phrygia is the most significant event in the later eighth century in Anatolia. Midas, son of Gordius, perhaps a usurper, was a legendary figure of such wealth, in the memory of the Greeks, that he was popularly thought by them to have possessed the power of turning all he touched to gold. By the late eighth century, Phrygia was supreme over the ancient kingdom of Lydia, through which roads (forerunners of the Persian Royal Road)[8] ran from the interior to the Greek cities and ports of the Ionian coast. Midas is said both to have taken to wife the daughter of Agamemnon, the king of Cyme in Aeolis (a valuable testimony to the importance of the city at that time) and to have been the first of the 'barbarians' to make an offering at the great shrine of Apollo at Delphi, presenting nothing less than his royal throne (Herodotus, I. 14). This is only one example of a close interchange of goods and cultural influences which took place at this period between the two countries. But the excavators of Gordion have also found evidence of contacts with North Syria and Urartu.[9] 'Cups of Tabal with ears of gold' and 'censers of Tabal' were exported as far as Muşaşir.[10] It is evident that Midas was bidding for the support of the Greek cities as well as of Urartu in his trial of strength with the Assyrians.

Phrygian ring-handled bowls[11] were exported to the Ionian cities, and *phialai mesomphaloi*, bowls with a central thumb-hold used in Anatolia for making libations especially in the cult of the Great Mother, were carried to the mainland of Greece.[12] Remains of great wine-mixing bowls decorated with 'bird-women' set on

---

[1] §IV, 11, fig. 63.   [2] §III, 10, fig. 796. See Plate 159(*a*).

[3] §III, 28; §IV, 10. See Plate 158(*b*).   [4] §IV, 2, pl. 106 *bis*. See Plate 159(*b*).

[5] §III, 10, fig. 805.   [6] §III, 10, fig. 953; §IV, 7, vol. IV, pl. LIV.

[7] §III, 15, part III, pl. B, 64C.   [8] §I, 10.

[9] §IV, 10.   [10] §II, 6, lines 358, 361.

[11] See Plate 158(*c*).   [12] §IV, 13.

tripod stands[1] have been found in many Greek shrines. Although these bowls and stands originated in Urarṭu, it is likely that the Phrygians helped to convey them to Greece. The earliest Greek object found at Gordion as yet is a 'bird bowl' of East Greek ware, to be dated *c.* 650 B.C., but Phrygian objects of the eighth century B.C. have been recognized at Delphi, Olympia, Perachora, the Argive Heraeum, Aëtos (Ithaca), the Temples of Aphaea (Aegina) and Orthia (Sparta), Mitylene, Rhodes and Ephesus.[2]

Phrygian architecture was well developed. Vitruvius (II. 1, 68) describes their houses as built of wooden logs laid in a trench excavated in a mound and then covered with reeds, brushwood and earth; this exactly recalls the construction of the funerary tumuli excavated at Gordion. That such log huts were not just made to be buried in tumuli but were also built as habitations is as yet otherwise unattested, but it seems perfectly possible. Houses of the late eighth century at Gordion were built sometimes of stone, sometimes of crude brick, using a half-timber structure, and the walls were sometimes bedded on parallel logs. As to ground plans, excavations at Gordion have revealed the existence in the pre-Cimmerian levels of a building of *megaron* type, a plan of great antiquity in Anatolia; the Gordion *megaron*, which may have been a palace, possessed an upper floor or gallery. Floors were covered with pebble mosaics as early as 750 B.C. at Gordion. Simple wall frescoes were attempted.[3] The appearance of Phrygian houses may be gauged from the carved rocks representing the façades of elaborate buildings, probably temples, and illustrating them in stone at Arslankaya, Bahşayiş, Demirkale or Midas City.[4] These and some valuable, if childlike, 'doodlings' scratched at Gordion[5] confirm that the Phrygians' houses possessed pitched roofs (known also in Urarṭu) of a type made of a framework of wooden beams supporting a covering of reeds and clay. Their gables were crowned by large horn-shaped finials, a stone example of which has been found at Gordion, but which were perhaps more usually of wood. As houses with friezes supported on dentils and similar, though simpler, finials are also depicted in Lycian house-shaped tombs,[6] it may be inferred that these types of timber dwelling in both localities go back to a common original parent, a type of Western Anatolian (Luwian) house of the late Bronze Age that still awaits discovery. The doorways of Phrygian houses, to judge from the rock-cut

[1] §III, 23.
[2] §IV, 10; §I, 2, 186; §IV, 13, pls. 52–5; §IV, 5.
[3] §IV, 16, parts 1 and 2.
[4] §III, 10, figs. 1026–31, 1033; §IV, 14.
[5] §IV, 16, part 1.
[6] §III, 10, figs. 232, 242, 244.

façades, seem to have been hidden under, or at least flanked, by a large geometrically patterned screen, perhaps formed of wood-work employing marquetry, perhaps formed by a hanging carpet; in both these crafts the Phrygians were traditionally most skilled. By the sixth century such screens on buildings were replaced at Gordion, Pazarli[1] and elsewhere by ornamented revet-ments fixed to the *antae* and made of baked clay tiles, moulded in low relief; they are painted in gay polychrome with figures of men or animals, and are obviously related both to Greek and to Oriental art. It is perhaps not insignificant that tradition ascribed the invention of the frieze (Latin: *phrygium*) to the Phrygians.

No city plan has yet been excavated, but remains of a massive city wall of crude brick have been found at Gordion, forming part of an entire fortified citadel dating from the eighth century B.C.[2] Its gateway was built of hewn stone with a slight inward batter and was placed diagonally to the line of the streets. An Assyrian bas-relief depicting an Anatolian town[3] suggests that a star-shaped city plan formed with re-entrants and pointed pro-jecting bastions may have already existed, thus anticipating Vauban. Clearly this great Phrygian architectural tradition, like Phrygian skills displayed in other fields, could not have failed to exert great influence on the archaic Greek cities of the littoral. These and many other powerful cities were built along trade routes connecting, as we have said above, Phrygia with Greece and the west on the one hand and Assyria, Urartu and Iran on the other. To Greece brazen Urartian cauldrons with their tripod supports and ornamented handles were exported, their handles shaped in the likeness of woman-headed birds overlooking the rim inwards, fabulous creations which may have suggested to the Greeks the story of the unhappy Phineus and the Harpies.[4]

IV. PHRYGIAN LIFE AND CULTURE

The best known feature of Central Anatolia was the so-called 'Royal Road', established by the Persian Kings, running from Ephesus to the Cilician Gates and thus on to Susa, being divided in Lydia and Phrygia into 'twenty $\sigma\tau\alpha\theta\mu o\acute{\iota}$ (stations)' within a distance of ninety-four and a half parasangs (Herodotus, v. 52). But there was certainly an equally important parallel line farther north running through Smyrna.[5] The 'Royal Road' crossed the Halys by a bridge (Herodotus, i. 75) made of rough stonework,

---

[1] §III, 17; 19.   [2] See Plate 160.   [3] §II, 2, pls. XLV, XLVI.
[4] §IV, 17; §VI, 1.   [5] §I, 7, 27 ff.; §I, 10.

remains of which still exist at Çeşnir Köprü.[1] It was really a trade-route of immemorial antiquity going back to Hittite Imperial times. At Pteria (Boğazköy) it met a cross artery that ran north-wards to the sea at Sinope, or southwards through Mazaca and through the Taurus to the Euphrates and Syria. A section of it, surfaced with cut stones, leading from Gordion to Ancyra, has been uncovered near Gordion by the American excavators.[2] These ancient trade-routes lent Phrygia a particular importance to her neighbours, because of her natural assets. Of these, the first was the quality of her grasslands, which supported large flocks of fine sheep. The Anatolian sheep bore the best wool, and Aristagoras remarked on the Phrygians' wealth in sheep (Herodotus, v. 49). Even today the Ankara goat's wool, known as mohair, is world-famous. The conversion of these fleeces into textiles, tapestries and carpets was a traditional craft. Patterned or embroidered textiles may be seen in the fine dress of Urpalla of Tyana depicted at Ivriz.[3] Timber was also an important economic factor. The neighbourhood of Midas City still harbours valuable forests. At Gordion, the following woods have been noted by the excavators as used in building, cabinet-making and inlaying of furniture: cedar and Syrian juniper (logs), pear, box, maple, poplar, black pine, pine, and yew. Some of these woods still grow in the vicinity of the site.[4] Lastly, by the time of the Early Iron Age the mineral deposits of Anatolia had already been famous for one thousand years, having been exploited since the times of the Assyrian merchants of Kültepe. The ancient silver and lead mines of Bulgar Maden, and haematite, were important natural resources. Crystal, onyx,[5] mica came from Phrygia. *Miltos*, red earth or ochre used for paint, was obtained from Cappadocia, but, being exported through Sinope, was called 'Sinopic earth'.[6] Sinope also produced red lead; bronzes and slaves were exported from Meshech and Tubal, and horses and mules from Togarmah (the Assyrian Til-garimmu) according to Ezekiel (xxvii. 13 f.)

The excavations at Gordion conducted by the Körte brothers in 1901 and since 1950 by the University of Pennsylvania[7] showed from actual finds that the Phrygians had reached con-siderable mastery in several crafts, whether as bronze-workers accomplished in both casting and raising, or as expert cabinet-makers and weavers, as workers in ivory, as makers of woollen felt

---

[1] §IV, 6, 2.   [2] §I, 10.   [3] See Plate 159(*a*).   [4] §IV, 16, part I.
[5] K. Kannanberg, *Kleinasiens Natürschätze* (Berlin, 1897), p. 207.
[6] §I, 7, 28.   [7] §III, 17 and 28.

or as weavers of linen, hemp, mohair, and perhaps also tapestry.[1] Phrygian carpets (τάπητες), direct ancestors of the Turkish carpet, were famous—the word is still preserved in the French *tapis*.[2] The influence of their designs and techniques, especially in woodwork, textiles and tapestry, was certainly carried far afield and influenced early Greek art, Phrygian patterns being clearly recognizable in East Greek painted pottery of the seventh century.[3] Embroidery, especially in gold threads, is said to have been a Phrygian invention, the Latin word for an embroiderer being *phrygio*. Fragments of a woven garment, evidently a royal robe, made of woven threads strung with tiny gold beads were found at Carchemish.[4] Many of the craftsmen practising these arts clustered round the royal palace, being organized very closely into craft-guilds of great antiquity.

Throughout the Phrygians' art, great play in ornament is made with interlacing or isolated geometric patterns, and swastikas, maeanders, mazes, lozenges—with this was doubtless connected their interest in Maze games,[5] the *ludus Troianus*. But their human figures are weak: their animals with stylized muscles, their limbs often bordered by rows of dots, but influenced by Mesopotamian, Urartian and Phoenician ideas of art, are more effective.

The Phrygians also appear, however, to have preserved a tradition of free-standing sculpture, though the earliest surviving example (at Palanga) is not earlier than the seventh century;[6] it bears inscriptions in late Hittite hieroglyphs. At Boğazköy, in the gateway, was found a remarkable statue of the goddess Cybele wearing a high headdress and holding her nude breasts, but clad in a skirt. She is flanked by two youths who play the chief musical instruments of her cult, the double *aulos* and lyre respectively, the *aulos*-player's cheeks being comically puffed out—these are the very instruments on which Marsyas and Apollo vied with each other before Midas as the unlucky spectator. This remarkable group is attributed to the sixth century B.C.[7] A fragmentary torso representing the goddess Agdistis was also found at Midas City.[8]

[1] §III, 5.
[2] O. Bloch and W. von Wartburg, *Dictionnaire étymologique de la langue française* (Paris, 1950), p. 595.
[3] §VII, 2, n. 50; §III, 2, fig. 67.   [4] §III, 15, part III, 250 ff., pl. 63.
[5] W. F. J. Knight, 'Maze Symbolism and the Trojan Game', in *Antiquity*, 6 (1932), 115 ff.
[6] §III, 10, fig. 786.
[7] §IV, 3. G. Neumann, *Nachr. Göttingen*, 1959, 101 ff., has suggested that the flanking figures represent two Daktyloi, Titias and Kyllenos. See Plate 159(c).
[8] §III, 10, figs. 1108–9.

In some of these works the human body is columnar in appearance, even basically resembling a cylinder, and one has the feeling that this school of human sculpture is created from a tree-trunk, not, as in the East, from a cube of stone. Such works afterwards obviously were connected with, or perhaps moulded, the ideas of some early Ionic Greek sculptors such as those of Samos and Naxos, where the dedicator of a well-known cult statue of the goddess Hera bears a purely Asiatic name, Cheramyes.

The Phrygians' skill in rock-carving, inherited from the stone-masons of the Bronze Age, enabled them to carve the representations of architectural house- or temple-façades which have been already mentioned. Smaller works, too, exist in the form of shrines showing the goddess Cybele from Ankara;[1] but a series of slabs of red andesite showing heraldic animals, now in the Ankara Museum, betray North Syrian influence, and may be by North Syrian or Urartian artists.[2] They were found scattered but come from some Phrygian palace or shrine, probably at Yalincak, 15 km. from Ankara. The Phrygians even seem to have been gardeners, for Midas is said to have 'discovered' roses and to have possessed a rose-garden on the Phrygian Mount Olympus.

Proofs of the Phrygians' accomplishments in the more abstract and intellectual arts are inevitably intangible and harder to show. But here the Phrygians were also evidently of importance, being reputedly great musicians, the inventors of the mode which bears their name. The Phrygians are credited by Greek tradition with the invention of cymbals, flutes, the triangle and syrinx, though this need mean no more than that they inherited some of these from their Hittite predecessors and taught their uses to the Greeks. But in the Bible (Gen. iv. 22) Tubal-Cain, i.e. 'Tubal-the-Smith', who bears the name of the Tabalians, is the brother of Jubal, inventor of lyre-playing and flute-playing. Some of these claims may be partly factual. At Boğazköy, as mentioned above, a fine Phrygian sculpture of the Mother Goddess was found, accompanied by two figures, a double-clarinet (*aulos*) player and a lyre (*cithara*) player. In the diffusion of the alphabet to the west, however, usually attributed to the Phoenicians, the Phrygians certainly played a most important role. One of the bronze vessels found in the Great Tumulus at Gordion, which must be dated before 700 B.C., bears in wax a short inscription in the Phrygian language, written in the Phrygian form of the alphabet. This use of wax for inscribing messages suggests that wax-covered writing tablets were already in use here as in Assyria. It is common know-

---

[1] §IV, 15. See Plate 159(*d*).   [2] §III, 10, figs. 1053–6.

ledge that the Phrygian alphabet, no less than the Ionic and other Greek alphabets, is derived from the Phoenician. But that the Phrygian letters most closely resemble both the earliest Greek examples as yet known—those from Crete, and those on Late Geometric vases found in Attica—has aroused little attention. The system of writing lines in alternate directions, called *boustrophēdon* ('as the ox turns in the plough'), which is used in early Greek scripts, is apparently derived through Phrygia from the Hittite hieroglyphs. A Phrygian inscription mentioning Mita (Midas) was found as far east as Tyana;[1] another occurs at Midas City on a rock façade, and it seems that the mixing of races and cultures at Midas's court permitted the evolution there of a script more flexible than the cumbrous Hittite hieroglyphs used elsewhere in Anatolia.[2] Inscriptions in the Phoenician alphabet were written and read no farther away than at Karatepe in the Taurus. In short, the Phrygian alphabet may well prove to be a parent of those of Greece, and Gordion the place of its invention in the mid-eighth century B.C.[3] The relation of the Phrygian script to other Anatolian alphabets such as those of Lydia, Lycia, and Pamphylia has scarcely been studied, but must be close. Though the surviving examples of these scripts are not earlier than the fifth century B.C., their origins must go back much farther. As yet, the Phrygian inscriptions cannot really be understood, as the material is too scanty; that the Phrygians possessed a literature is unprovable, but a precious Greek tradition, which declared Aesop to be a Phrygian, ascribed to them the invention of the animal fable, a form of folk-literature of great antiquity in the East and usually unwritten. The home of the animal-fable, in which the normal roles are reversed and animals play the parts of men, is, *par excellence*, India; but traces of it can be detected in Sumer in the third millennium B.C. in the Royal Graves of Ur in the scenes decorating a lyre, and in a relief at Tell Halaf in North Syria in the tenth century B.C., in the motif of the 'Animal Orchestra', a theme which lived on into modern times to enter into the Grimm Brothers' tales in the form of the *Musicians of Bremen*. Similar satirical animal fables are depicted in New Kingdom Egypt, but have not yet been found in Hittite sources. These might still, however, prove to have been the missing medium of transmission of such stories from Sumer to the Phrygians.

[1] See J. Garstang, *The Hittite Empire* (1929), pl. IV and p. 14.
[2] A, 15.
[3] See A, 15, but *contra*, J. Naveh, *A.J.A.* 77 (1973), 1 ff., who argues that the Greeks borrowed their alphabet direct from the Proto-Canaanite script, *c.* 1100 B.C.

V. THE PHRYGIAN LANGUAGE

The Phrygians' origins remain something of a mystery, and so does their language. In the eastern half of the plateau chiefly, the Hittite hieroglyphs were used to write the Luwian tongue but from the late eighth to fifth century B.C. a handful of very short Phrygian texts survives which, as they are written in their alphabet of Greek type, can be read though they cannot be understood.[1] Lexicographers and other writers have preserved for us the alleged meanings of some hundred Phrygian words, but all this is hardly enough to permit the re-creation of even the most rudimentary grammar or syntax. In fact, survivals of the Phrygian language linger into Roman times, occurring in bilingual form with Greek translations on tombstone inscriptions from the region south of the thirty-ninth parallel. These are called 'Late Phrygian' texts in contrast to the earlier group known as 'archaic'.[2] But their value as aids in interpreting those texts of nine hundred years before is naturally debatable. The opinions of scholars, therefore, as to the affinities of the archaic Phrygian language are, not surprisingly, divided: some have claimed it as an Indo-European language of the *satəm* branch and have declared it closest to Armenian; and this would consort well with, and is perhaps influenced by, the dictum of Herodotus who calls the Armenians ἄποικοι τῶν Φρυγῶν.[3] But this view is now rejected by scholars[4] who have shown that Phrygian is not a *satəm* speech but basically an Anatolian language, connected with Hittite or, it may yet be shown, with Luwian.[5] If this is so, it will imply that the true original, native tongue of the Phrygian invaders has probably been absorbed into a patois of their subjects—a by no means improbable conclusion.

VI. PHRYGIAN RELIGION

The Phrygians' religion clearly consisted of at least two strata: primitive Anatolian and Indo-European.

The oldest, most basic and characteristic worship of Phrygia was the cult of the Great Mother of Nature, called Kubaba by the Luwians east of the Halys, Kybele or Kybebe by the Lydians, *Kubile* or *Matar Kubile* in Phrygia, Cybele by the Greeks; she was

---

[1] §v, 3, 7, 8, 14; G, 7.   [2] §v, 1, 12, 13.   [3] §v, 5, 11.
[4] §v, 4; §vii, 13, 123 ff.; §vii, 29, 6, 7. See also A, 14.
[5] §v, 6; *C.A.H.* I³, pt. 1, pp. 142 f.; but see O. Szemerényi, in *J.R.A.S.* (1965), pp. 134 ff.

also called Agdistis ('she of the rock', from *agdos*, meaning 'rock' in Phrygian) by the Phrygians. She and her youthful male consort were evidently worshipped from primeval antiquity in Anatolia, at least from the Neolithic Period, as is shown by finds of the seventh millennium B.C. of clay statuettes of the goddess seated with her lions (or perhaps leopards), at Hacılar near Lake Burdur.[1] Her worship (as a bisexual figure) appears to have spread far east and south through Anatolia and north-west Syria, where it appears at an early date in Bambyce-Hierapolis as Kombabos or in the Legend of Gilgamesh Khumbaba.[2] In Roman times one of her great shrines was at Pessinus, where one version of the story of Agdistis–Cybele was told and recorded by Arnobius. Her worship there was sufficiently important for her cult figure, a black stone, to be transferred from there to Rome under the title of 'Bona Dea' in 204 B.C. The latter is perhaps again an illustration of religious continuity in Anatolia, for a deity called the 'Black Goddess' was worshipped by the Hittites.[3]

Several myths were current concerning the Great Goddess of Nature and her lover-consort Attis, and formed the ἱερὸς λόγος which explained or justified the enactment of an annual cycle of ritual. According to one version, Agdistis was a bisexual monster who fell in love with the beautiful Attis, son-in-law of the king of Pessinus, destroyed him and his city and castrated itself, thus becoming female.[4] Such barbarous themes of monstrous gods born from a rock, of gods and demigods mutilating or slaying one another, or their own parents or offspring, are found in Hittite texts of the Bronze Age such as the 'Song of Ullikummi'. A milder version of the story, much abbreviated, describes Agdistis's love for Attis who, in the flower of his youth and beauty, is killed in a boar-hunt. But by dint of his worshippers enacting an annual spring ritual of passionate lamentation, including self-mutilation, he is annually resuscitated, thus reviving the flagging forces of nature. In the course of the ritual, excitement rose to such a pitch that the most fervent devotees of the goddess castrated themselves in honour of her and of Attis, and became his and her priests, as described in a moving poem of Catullus. This ferocious cult of the goddess, for whose sake her handsome lover suffers and dies, filtered early westwards to Ionia, but was reflected in a softer and, indeed, more romantic form in various Greek myths connected with Asia Minor. In these recurs a theme of a youth beloved by a goddess, who brings misfortune on him by her love; such is that of the Moon and Endymion on Mount

---

[1] §VI, 8.   [2] §VI, 1, 7.   [3] §VI, 6.   [4] §VI, 5.

Latmus or that of Aphrodite and Anchises on Ida.[1] These themes appear to be derived from aspects of the worship of an ultimately bisexual deity.[2]

Being a fierce and implacable goddess of the rocks, Cybele's centres of worship were most often located on mountains after which her local cults were commonly named (e.g. the Berecynthian, the Dindymene, Sipylene or Lobrine Mother). At her sanctuary on Sipylus near Smyrna was a rock-carved statue of the goddess, which still survives; it was interpreted by the Greeks as a figure of Niobe weeping for her children, slain by Apollo and Artemis; it has been identified as the central feature of a possibly Bronze Age water-sanctuary.[3] In fact, Cybele was regularly believed to issue from bare cliffs beside which fresh water rose, and between the eighth and sixth centuries B.C. great façades representing her temples were carved on such rock faces in the specially sacred plateau between Eskişehir and Afyon Karahisar, where the sacred Phrygian rivers rise. These façades, the most famous of which bears an inscription containing the name of Midas, are to-day among the most remarkable antiquities of Anatolia.[4] That at Arslankaya shows the goddess herself, represented standing facing frontally, in a niche between rampant lions—an association of the goddess with lions which is repeated throughout antiquity in her cult. Other rock carvings merely show a house or temple front, decorated with elaborate geometrical patterns representing a carpet or tapestry.

According to some ancient authorities the cult of the Kabeiroi, which included that of Dionysus, son of Zeus Sabazius and Semele, was introduced to Miletus and other Greek cities from Phrygia.[5] There are good arguments for thinking that the worship of the Kabeiroi derives from the world of the Hittites. To the Indo- European stratum in the religion of the Phrygians, we may assign a cult of Zeus called Mazeus (cf. the Iranian *Mazda*), also called Bagaios (Iranian *baga*='god') or Papas ('Father')— a general term equally applicable to Attis or other gods;[6] also that of Mēn, an equestrian male Moon god. These, however, might perhaps be explained as relics of the Achaemenid Persian rule.

Some other figures are little more than names, but imply some degree of cult. Aristaeus, another fertility figure, in reality (in the writer's opinion) may be but a form of *Agdistaeos (*d* and *r* being

---

[1] §VI, 1; §VII, 4.
[2] The variations on this theme and its origins are explained in full in §VII, 4, 217 ff.　　　　　　　　　[3] §III, 4.
[4] §III, 10, 1023–33; §III, 13; §IV, 4, 14. See Plate 157(*b*).　　[5] §VI, 9.　　[6] G, 6.

to some extent interchangeable in Hittite hieroglyphs), meaning
'he who belongs to Agdistis';[1] Marsyas was a river god, inventor
of the *syrinx*, who, after failing in a music contest with Apollo,[2] was
slain, presumably to revive; Lityerses was a rather ferocious form
of John Barleycorn, slain by Heracles and annually lamented by
the reapers. A hero, Tyris or Tyrimnus, is also mentioned but
really appears to belong to Lydia, where he is equated with
Apollo–Helius. Ascanius, or Ascaënus, is identified with Mēn.
Telesphorus is a dwarf-like, hooded figure who appears first in
Hellenistic times.

The Phrygian pantheon, as envisaged in Roman times at least,
is depicted on a rustic rock-relief at Asi Yozgat, about sixty kilometres east of Ankara. It consists of Cybele on her lion, Heracles,
a seated figure (Attis?), Asclepius, Telesphorus, and finally a
figure in a shrine with an eagle who represents either Cronus or
Zeus. A goat (Amalthea or perhaps the goat which suckled Attis)
is also represented[3] in the group.

There were Phrygian 'mysteries' of Attis, involving initia-
tions, at least in late times. Of them we know virtually nothing.[4]
In short, the Phrygians' religion, like their empire, remains vague,
amorphous, barbaric and mysterious.

VII. THE NEIGHBOURS OF THE PHRYGIANS

But Anatolia did not consist only of Phrygians. What do we
know of their neighbours in the west during this dark period?
From historical sources, very little; nor is there any great prospect
of increasing our information, save by fortunate archaeological
excavation. We find the western slopes descending from the
plateau along the Maeander River valley inhabited by the
Lydians, alias Mēïoi, Māïoi or Maiones, whose origins and
early history are lost in legend. Perhaps these may be the same as
a people called by the Hittites Masha, whose name may, it has
been suggested, be reflected in that of the ancient Lydian eponymous hero Masnes.[5]

The Heraclid (otherwise Tylonid) Dynasty, ending with
Myrsilus, *c.* 700 B.C., was said to have reigned for 505 years; this
brings us to a date *c.* 1205 B.C., shortly before the fall of the
Hittite Empire. The Lydians' surviving inscriptions are relatively
late, but they are partly bilingual and seem to show a relation
between their language and Hittite, or perhaps Palaic.[6] Their

---

[1] §vii, 4.   [2] See above, p. 432 n. 7.   [3] §vi, 1.   [4] §vii, 17.
[5] §vii, 17.   [6] (Lydian and Palaite) §vii, 8, 13, 26, 27.

chief goddess is called by them *Artimu*, in Greek Artemis, and was identified by them with the Luwian Kubaba (Herodotus, v. 102). Her world-famous shrine at Ephesus was traditionally founded by the Amazones; it is clearly pre-Greek. The cult of Dionysus, god of wine, appears also to have been largely native to Lydia under the name of Bacchus, and to have been imported from there to Greece.[1] Local Lydian worships disclose, otherwise, principally the adoration of a triad, the Mother Goddess, a male god often equated with Zeus, and Mēn—the equestrian Moon god.[2]

No early Lydian settlements, and until now no Lydian works of art earlier than the seventh century B.C., have as yet been identified, though discoveries may reasonably be hoped for in the excavations now in progress at the site of Sardis. But it seems that the Lydians preserved a direct tradition of civilization more or less unbroken from the Late Bronze Age (although backward tribal communities remained in some areas until Hellenistic times). This is hinted at by Herodotus who carries back the pedigree of the ruling family to Heracles, or even Atys son of Manes (Masnes), i.e. to a dim heroic age; the last member of the dynasty bore a name, Myrsilus, which closely resembles the Hittite name of Murshilish. Hittite rock-carvings accompanied by Hittite hieroglyphs, belonging to the Hittite Empire, exist at Karabel (Nymphi) and Sipylus, both being well known in antiquity. To the Greek mind the Lydians were aliens, depraved Orientals; nevertheless, the Lydians were famous as horsemen, musicians, traders, and bankers, who used the natural wealth of their land in precious metals and the gold washings of Pactolus for their momentous gift to mankind, the invention of coinage.[3]

Of the Carians and Lelegians, almost nothing specific is known except that the Carians made good soldiers and left their graffiti in Egypt, where they served as mercenaries in the seventh and sixth centuries B.C.[4] The Carians, like the Pamphylians, had a script and language of their own; it is partly legible but cannot be understood at present. It is possibly Hittito-Luwian in origin.[5] The Carians claimed to be autochthonous inhabitants of Anatolia, and to be related to the Lydians and Mysians. Their custom of

---

[1] §vi, 1.   [2] §vii, 22.   [3] See A, 4, 310 ff.

[4] §v, 3; §vii, 9; A, 7. An important addition to the corpus of Carian inscriptions from Egypt is the group of Carian–Egyptian tomb-stones found at Memphis by W. B. Emery; see *J.E.A.* 56 (1970), 6 ff., pls. x, xv.

[5] §vii, 13; A, 11.

having queens to rule over them recalls the important place given to women among the Lycians. According to Thucydides, in the Late Bronze Age they were active pirates and colonists of the adjacent Aegean islands, repressed by Minos of Crete, but of this there is no archaeological confirmation whatsoever. But at Müskebi, on the Halicarnassus peninsula, a rich Mycenaean cemetery has been found, while at Dirmil another cemetery of the Protogeometric Age has been uncovered, showing that Greek penetration of this area certainly took place in the Late Bronze Age and survived into that of Iron.[1]

With Lycia we fare a little better, although over the origins of the Lycians the greatest obscurity still hangs. But it is now certain that they were an Anatolian people of great antiquity, also related to the Hittites, and thus can trace their history in Asia Minor back into the Bronze Age. This much is clear from their language, with examples of which in inscriptions, some bilingual, albeit no earlier in date than the fourth century B.C., we are fortunate enough to be provided.[2] As a result, it has recently been identified successfully as a dialect of the Luwian language, known (though poorly) from cuneiform texts found in the library of the Hittite kings, and Luwian deities can be identified in Lycian personal names.[3] It is assumed too (plausibly enough) that the Lycians were descended from the people called Lukka, who are mentioned in the Late Bronze Age and figure among the Sea Raiders of Egypt. In the Iron Age the Lycians' chief cities were Xanthus, Pinara, Myra, Phellus and Antiphellus, but as yet no notable remains of occupation have been found, either in the recent French excavations at Xanthus or elsewhere along the rocky Lycian coasts, to occur earlier than the eighth century B.C. But recent finds near Elmalı further inland strongly point to early Lycian settlement there in the Early Bronze Age.[4] Like that of Caria, Lycian society was organized to give an important place to women, through whom inheritance seems to have been reckoned on a matrilinear basis.[5] The Lycians appear to have preserved a spirit of national organization from the Heroic Age sufficiently strong to resist any Greek settlements being planted in Lycia, and to enable them to retain their national script and language till the fourth century B.C.

Other traces of Luwian speech surviving into Roman times

---

[1] §VII, 33.   [2] §VII, 13, 21. See also A, 8.
[3] §VII, 19; cf. §VII, 27, 29, 31, 32.
[4] M. J. Mellink, 'Excavations at Karataş-Semayük in Lycia, 1963', in *A.J.A.* 68 (1964).
[5] See now S. Pembroke in *J.E.S.H.O.* 8 (1965), 217 ff.

have also been found in Cilicia Aspera.[1] A native language also survived in Pamphylia, to be recorded in a peculiar script at Side in the fourth century B.C., but it is as yet not sufficiently clearly understood to be identified. But in the period of the Phrygian Empire, the most important Luwian-speaking area was clearly south-eastern Anatolia where, as mentioned above, a cluster of principalities, called 'Land of Khatti' by the Assyrians, survived the collapse of the Hittite Empire. These principalities, the most important of which were Kammanu (Malatya), Gurgum (Maraş), Kummukh (Commagene) and Unqi (the 'Amūq), spoke a Luwian dialect, and wrote it in Hittite hieroglyphs.[2] They were allied with the Phrygians, and guarded the mountain roads of the Taurus which led from North Syria to the Anatolian plateau. Beyond them lay Carchemish; this great site was partly excavated by a British expedition before 1914.[3] Its period of importance thereby disclosed seemed to be late Hittite, but it is now seen from documents found at Ras Shamra to have been the seat, in the Late Bronze Age, of the viceroy of the Hittite Emperor, from which he ruled over most of the states of Syria. Carchemish was rightly considered by the Assyrians as the chief of the Hittite states, controlling the great road and ford across the Euphrates leading to Mesopotamia.

To help us form a picture of these diadochic principalities, we may note their actual pedigrees. That of the kings of Gurgum, recorded in their Hittite hieroglyphic inscriptions, can be traced back to one LA+ī−mas; that of Carchemish to Sukhis I (formerly read as Lukhas), both c. 950 B.C. Beyond these names are to be placed some obscure kings known at Carchemish from single references, probably to be assigned to the period 1200–1000 B.C.; at Malatya they go back to the eleventh century B.C., to which date the fine sculptured palace gateway at Malatya belongs.[4] It is clear that these Luwian principalities dated their independence from a time following soon after the collapse of the Hittite Empire. Until then, they had been for some centuries dominated by the kings of Khattusha; but when the storm passed, they revived and carried on into the Iron Age the customs, arts, cults, and traditions of the Hittite Empire of which they were the veritable heirs.

But their position in south-eastern Anatolia was not uncontested. Towards the vital centres of the Amanus and Taurus passes thrust other national groups. A figure known to Greek mythology as Mopsus, king of Colophon, possibly the same as a person of the fourteenth century B.C. known in Hittite records as

---

[1] §VII, 19.   [2] §VII, 24.   [3] §III, 15.   [4] §III, 12.

Mukshush, a western freebooter, appears to have led his followers through Pamphylia to settle finally on the slopes south of the Taurus at Ishtunda, and establish there his dynasty as the kings of the Danuniyim or Danuna, i.e. the Danaoi, with their capital at Adana;[1] their existence is disclosed by the finds at Karatepe and Domuz Tepe.[2] Mopsus was perhaps a Lydian or a half-Greek; in any event, he is the first figure of Greek mythology to emerge into historic reality. The Danuniyim were clients of the kings of Que (Cilicia). At Sam'al (Zincirli) on Mount Amanus was installed the Aramaean dynasty of Gabar, which claims to have been in conflict with the Danuniyim in the ninth century.[3] This dynasty goes back probably to the tenth century, about 900 B.C., giving us the earliest indication of the most northerly thrust of the Aramaean people. Excavations at Zincirli by the German Oriental Society before the First World War have thrown much light on the importance of this site, where they found a series of palaces. Phoenician cultural influence was very powerful in this area and probably radiated from some local colony not yet discovered.

These principalities, then, were the actors who played out their roles on the stage of history in the Dark Age of Anatolia, from the Bronze into the Iron Age. Though little chronicled, we can now see that these roles were dramatic and important. Surviving the collapse of the Hittite Empire and the blows of the Land and Sea Raiders, their kings made terms with the immigrant Phrygians and other tribes, stood firm on the Taurus and Amanus line, and succeeded in passing on to the West the tradition of Anatolian arts and culture until they were successively pressed back, then finally defeated, destroyed and obliterated by the Assyrians, whose custom, as was later said of the Romans, was 'to make a desert and call it peace'.

[1] §vii, 3; see also below, ch. xxxviii, sect. iii.
[2] §iii, 11; §vii, 5.   [3] §iv, 7; §vii, 25.

CHAPTER XXXI

ASSYRIA AND BABYLONIA,
c. 1200–1000 B.C.

I. THE END OF THE KASSITE DOMINATION

WHEN Tukulti-Ninurta I had abducted Kashtiliash in fetters to Ashur the way was open once again for direct Assyrian control of Babylonian affairs. Resistance, however, continued and Babylon itself was surrounded, the city-wall being breached by siege-apparatus. Entry was resolutely opposed until the troops had robbed the temples and city treasury. Yet the greatest blow to Babylonian morale was the removal of the statue of Marduk to Ashur as a mark of the complete subjugation of the country to Assyria. According to the Chronicle P 'Tukulti-Ninurta installed his governors in the land of Babylon and for seven years he gave orders to Babylonia (Karduniash)'. This source lists as the next ruler Adad-shuma-uṣur whom the Babylonian nobles 'seated on his father's throne' after a country-wide rising against their Assyrian overlords.[1] On the other hand, the King List A follows Kashtiliash by three names; Enlil-nādin-shumi, to whom a reign of '1 year 6 months' is ascribed; Kadashman-Kharbe (one year six months) and Adad-shuma-iddina (six years).[2] From this it has been assumed that these were vassal-kings who followed an Assyrian interregnum of seven years for which Tukulti-Ninurta's name was not given for political reasons. However, if the chronological entries are to be interpreted as '1 year (that is of) 6 months (only)' then these rulers comprised the seven years of Tukulti-Ninurta on whose behalf they exercised power.[3] On this theory the Babylonian chronicler, not wishing to acknowledge the Assyrian domination, entered the names of his puppet rulers, much as was later done for Kandalanu and other Babylonians who held similar positions under northern masters.

It is possible that Enlil-nādin-shumi represented only one party in the capital. When the Elamite Kidin-Khutran raided

---

* An original version of this chapter was published as fascicle 41 in 1965; the present chapter includes revisions made in 1973.

[1] §1, 10, 96 (Chron. P, IV, 6–8); G, 6, 46.   [2] G, 22, 41, nr. 37, 7 ff.
[3] G, 2, 79; cf. A, 3, 77, 86; §1, 12, 137; §II, 7, 73 ff.

lower Mesopotamia, seizing Nippur and sacking E-dimgal-kalamma, the temple of Ishataran at Dēr, his aim was to restrict the hold of Babylon over the East Tigris area and to challenge the Assyrian in the Diyālā region by looting Padan[1] and removing a stela.[2] The Elamites seem to have supported the pro-Kassite Babylonians, one of whom, Kadashman-Kharbe II, claimed descent from Kashtiliash. He may well have gained control as a result of the Elamite action and have been a rival and contemporary claimant to the throne in Babylon.[3]

When Adad-shuma-iddina gained the ascendancy it would seem that once again a Babylonian, to judge by the name, held the reins of government. He may, however, have been pro-Assyrian, for after six years he was killed, or taken prisoner, in another Elamite raid.[4] This time their objective was the city of Isin which was seized, perhaps in an attempt to reinstate Enlil-nādin-shumi, who reappeared with the attackers in Babylonia when they crossed the Tigris and advanced on a wide front as far as Nippur.

Loyalty to the local Kassites was by no means dimmed, for the nobles of Akkad and of Babylon chose this critical time to initiate a widespread agitation to seat Adad-shuma-uṣur on his father's throne. As the popularly elected son of Kashtiliash IV and installed with Elamite approval, his long rule of thirty years (1218–1189) and the absence of further Elamite raids enabled the king to gain firm hold of Babylonia. The revolt was possible and successful only because Assyria was weakened through the court intrigues which marked the closing years of Tukulti-Ninurta's reign. After that king's death the Babylonian court tried to intervene in Assyrian affairs but faced with some disaster, plague or fire in their camp, Adad-shuma-uṣur's forces were forced to withdraw to Babylonia after a battle with Enlil-kudurri-uṣur.[5] There is no certain evidence that this action was taken in fulfilment of treaty obligations.[6]

At home, such few indications as remain show the country to be at peace within its borders. At Nippur, this king restored the inner wall of the zikkurrat in the rebuilding of E-kur,[7] while a fragmentary kudurru-inscription tells of a royal grant of land near Daban in the Dullum region.[8]

The same Kassite family continued to hold the country firmly in its power in the person of Meli-Shikhu,[9] 'son' of Kurigalzu,

---

[1] See above, pp. 387 f. [2] G, 15, 2, 95 and pl. 20. [3] G, 20, 287.
[4] Cf. A, 3, 87, n. 451. [5] §1, 12, 131. [6] G, 20, 238.
[7] §1, 7, 81, 34. [8] G, 15, 2, 97; §1, 8, no. 4, 17; §1, 11, nr. 156.
[9] For this reading against Meli-Shipak see §1, 1, 70 and 114; but cf. A, 4, 238 f.

during the next fifteen years (1188–1174).[1] The absence of records
mentioning external affairs may give a false impression of the
internal harmony conveyed by the references to this ruler in
contemporary economic documents. On one *kudurru* the king is
shown introducing his daughter Khunnubat-Nanā to the goddess
Nanā, probably on the occasion of her installation as a priestess.[2]
The king farmed royal estates outside Babylon and granted
fields from his own irrigated lands in Shaluluni,[3] by the royal-
canal at Agade and in the provinces of Bīt-Marduk[4] and Bīt-Piri'-
Amurri (attested by the governor of the Sealands and the high-
priestess of Agade).[5] The continuity in the recognition and rule
of law is most clearly seen in a complicated legal case which came
before the king concerning an estate, Bīt-Takil-ana-ilishu, near
Nippur. The original owner had died in the reign of Adad-shuma-
iddina and the estate passed to an adopted son whose title had been
upheld before Adad-shuma-uṣur. Copies of attested documents
from these reigns were now produced as evidence in quashing
the claim of the descendants of disappointed rivals.[6]

Marduk-apla-iddina I, son of Meli-Shikhu, claimed, like his
father, descent from Kurigalzu. Indeed, he seems to have kept
court in Dūr-Kurigalzu itself, for tablets found in the fire-
blackened ruins of the Tell-el-Abyaḍ quarter (Level I A), which
marked the later Elamite destruction of the city, are dated in the
first two of his thirteen-year reign (1173–1161).[7] These indicate
normal economic relations with Babylonia's western and eastern
neighbours, Subarians and Elamites, whose singers entertained
the royal household.[8] Thus a field, on the Elamite border, east
of the Tigris near Khudada, which Meli-Shikhu had left un-
recorded was now disposed of freely, as were other plots near
the river Radanu.[9] Allocations of land in the district of Kār-Bēlit
between the Euphrates and the Shum-ili canal and at Dūr-
Napshati in the province of E-ugur-Ishtar on the Tigris[10] and
reconstruction work at E-zida of Borsippa show that royal lands
were maintained and held in north Babylonia throughout this
reign.

[1] G, 21, 70 f. (Assur 14616c, 11).
[2] G, 15, 10, pls. 10 ff., pp. 87 ff. See Plate 161(a).
[3] G, 12, no. IV, pls. xxiii ff.
[4] §1, 11, nos. 38, 57; see also 47.   [5] G, 12, no. III, v, 20 f.
[6] G, 12, pls. v ff., pp. 7 ff.
[7] G, 18, 272 (King List A, ii, 13); §1, 9, 260 ff.; §1, 5, 54.
[8] §1, 3, 9; §1, 4, 89; §1, 6, 89 (another text).
[9] G, 15, 6, 6–11; §1, 8, nr. 10 f.; §1, 11, 62, 49.
[10] G, 12, 24 ff., pls. xxxi f.; §1, 9, 261.

This apparently peaceful situation was radically altered in the accession year of the succeeding Zababa-shuma-iddina (1160). His brief reign is recorded only in King Lists[1] but the Synchronistic Chronicle tells how the Assyrian, Ashur-dan, marched from Ashur across the Lesser Zab to capture the towns of Zaban, Irria and Ugarsallu and remove the loot to his capital. This raid was in continuance of the Assyrian policy to maintain control of the trade-routes linking the Diyālā river-plain and the Iranian plateau. His failure to press into the Lower Diyālā itself was the signal for Shutruk-Nahhunte, who had by now brought together the forces of Elam, to make a move for the control of this same disputed border region. The Elamites crossed the Ulai river and moved through Mara and Eshnunna to loot the north Babylonian cities of Sippar, Dūr-Kurigalzu, Dūr-Shar[rukēn], Opis and perhaps Agade. From Eshnunna two statues, one of Manishtusu, and from Sippar the stela of Narām-Sin recounting his victory over the Lullubi and a stela bearing a copy of the laws of Hammurabi were added to the spoils of war taken to mark the supremacy of Elam's own deity.[2]

The resistance of the Kassites was not yet at an end. One Enlil-nādin-akhi was claimed as 'king of Sumer and Akkad' and maintained the struggle against the Elamites for a further three years (1159–1157).[3] By this time Kutir-Nahhunte, the eldest son of Shutruk-Nahhunte, had been installed as Elamite overlord of North Babylonia, unrecognized as such by the Babylonian Chronicler as by the inhabitants of the south. The struggle was long and fierce. Finally the Elamites met the Babylonians in battle by the Tigris pursuing them via Khuṣṣi to the Euphrates[4] and Nippur. They then robbed the capital and other cult-centres and, in an act of impiety never forgotten or forgiven by the Babylonians, Kutir-Nahhunte removed the statue of Marduk from E-sagila to Elam. Though this sacrilege had been committed by the Hittites and the Assyrians it was now 'far greater than that of his forefathers, his guilt exceeded even theirs'.[5] The statue of Nanā of Uruk was also among the loot taken to Susa to await its release by Ashurbanipal's arms more than five hundred years later. Many of the nobles were taken captive to Elam with the king. With the death in exile of Enlil-nādin-akhi there ended

---

[1] G, 18, 273 (King List A and Assur 14616c, ii, 10′); A, 4, 245.
[2] See below, p. 486.   [3] §1, 12, 137; cf. A, 4, 245 f.
[4] Some assign this attack to a later year of Shilkhak-In-Shushinak (see below, pp. 447 and 492).
[5] §1, 12, 137 f.

an enlightened and, on the whole, successful régime whose thirty-six kings had maintained authority for 576 years and 9 months.

That the Kassites strengthened and continued the ancient Babylonian customs and culture cannot be denied, though the extent of their influence on Babylon and Assyria, apart from the political adroitness of the ruling family is much debated.[1] Long after they had lost political control the Kassites remained a strong foreign element in Babylonia and provided the chief element in the Babylonian armed forces till the ninth century.[2]

II. THE SECOND ISIN DYNASTY

Except for one possible raid to the Euphrates by Shilkhak-In-Shushinak,[3] the successor of Kutir-Nahhunte, the Elamites now turned their attention again to their border with Assyria in the Upper Diyālā. In a series of campaigns they aimed to gain control of the area between the Tigris and the Zagros and to open the way to trade and influence further north. One expedition to the Kirkuk area to win the mountain passes may have been influential in stimulating the revolt that ended the reign of Ashur-dan.[4]

This failure to follow up the Elamite control of territory normally held to lie in north-east Babylonia enabled the peoples of the south to rally round the nobles of Isin whose influence had already been extended to support one of the rival claimants to the Assyrian throne on the death of Ashur-dan I.[5] Marduk-kabit-ahhēshu of Isin who, according to Babylonian tradition followed Enlil-nādin-akhi without any Elamite interregnum, founded a new dynasty in which eleven members of the line were to rule Babylonia for 132 years and 6 months.[6] For eighteen years (1156–1139—King List C)[7] or seventeen (according to the less contemporary King List A which may omit the accession year)[8] this new contender for Babylonian independence held sway. Isin was an influential city, judging both by the preferential references to governors of the city as witnesses to *kudurru*-inscriptions at this time, and by the fact that the King List names the dynasty after it.[9] The absence of contemporary records does not necessarily imply, as has been argued, that the economic state of the country following the Kassite régime was such that the ruler had to devote

---

[1] G, 9, 109. [2] G, 20, 295. [3] See above, p. 446.
[4] §1, 13, 7; see below, pp. 491 f. [5] §1, 13, 7.
[6] §1, 15, 146 (*C.T.* 36, 4); G, 18, 273 (King List A, iii, 5).
[7] §11, 6, 3. [8] *C.A.H.* 1³, pt. 1, pp. 198 f. [9] G, 2, 113.

attention exclusively to internal affairs during his early years. Marduk-kabit-ahhēshu is named by his son Itti-Marduk-balāṭu who, in true Babylonian fashion, styled himself 'king of kings, viceroy of Babylon' and king of two cities the names of which are now lost (though one was presumably Isin).[1] *Kudurru*-inscriptions of this reign record the sale of plots of land in Bīt-Udashi, Bīt-Sapri and Bīt-Naniauti, probably to be located near Babylon. Business documents show that provisions were distributed from the royal stables at Dūr-Sumulael on the Imgur-Ishtar canal near Babylon. Grain was received and slaves hired in the king's first year.[2] It is likely therefore that Babylon was occupied as the capital without a break after this reign.

According to the reading proposed for an Ashur text,[3] now lost, the name of Itti-Marduk-balāṭu was inserted after that of Marduk-nādin-ahhē, the sixth king of the dynasty. This reading has never been verified.[4] Such a position would identify the person of this name with the father of Adad-apla-iddina as listed in the Babylonian Chronicle.[5] The order of names in the Chronicle C is to be preferred. This allots Itti-Marduk-balāṭu eight years (1138–1131) before he was succeeded by Ninurta-nādin-shumi, whose relation to his predecessor is unknown. According to one King List he ruled for six years (1130–1125).[6] So far had the Babylonian fortunes revived that they were once again strong enough to challenge Assyria for the disputed border districts east of the Tigris. He led the Babylonian troops as far north as the vicinity of Irbil only to withdraw on the approach of Assyrian shock-troops who were supported by chariots.[7] This incursion was yet one more attempt to master the disputed upper Diyālā border region. A bronze dagger, inscribed with the name of Ninurta-nādin-shumi, bears the claim to sovereignty over all Babylonia.[8] Like the many daggers, spear- and arrow-heads bearing brief royal inscriptions of this period, it was probably a votive offering originally dedicated to a temple in Babylon as a thank-offering for safety, if not always of success, in battle.[9] If, as has been suggested, the raid by the Elamite Shilkhak-In-Shushinak on Nimitti-Marduk is to be dated to this time as a reprisal for such Babylonian audacity, then it shows the Babylonians were

---

[1] The title 'king of kings' was in use at least a generation earlier by Tukulti-Ninurta I (G, 22, 18, i, 3).   [2] §II, 1, 49 ff.

[3] G, 21, 70; G, 18, 273 (Assur 14616c, ii, 18'); §VI, 15, 216.

[4] §II, 8, 383, n. 1; cf. G, 21, 70; A, 3, 41.   [5] G, 13, II, 59.

[6] §II, 6, 3.   [7] G, 22, 58 (nr. 70).

[8] §II, 2, 151, n. 2.   [9] §II, 5, 95.

by now strong enough to resist the last attempt by this non-native dynasty to interfere in their affairs.[1]

In a fragmentary letter written by a Babylonian king he chides his Assyrian counterpart with failure to meet him as arranged at the border town of Zaqqu.[2] The writer implies that the Assyrian is not in full control of his court and threatens to reinstate on the throne Ninurta-tukulti-Ashur, whom his father had welcomed as an exile, if relations between the states do not improve. The deportation of the Assyrian had taken place in the reign of Mutakkil-Nusku,[3] but it seems unlikely that the letter was written to him as co-regent of Ashur-dan or early in the reign of Ashur-rēsha-ishi before the clash at Irbil. If the writer was Ninurta-nādin-shumi it would imply that he was in the direct line of succession, a fact otherwise unknown. On the other hand, if the writer was his son, Nebuchadrezzar I, this would explain the confident tone in which the challenge is couched. At the same time, if such a hypothesis is accepted, it emphasizes the independent position and power of the Babylonians in Ninurta-nādin-shumi's day. The evidence would therefore seem to fit best if Ashur-rēsha-ishi is considered the recipient.[4]

III. DYNASTIC TROUBLES IN ASSYRIA

While the Babylonians were defending themselves against the Elamites and the new ruling house of Isin was establishing control over the southern tribes, the Assyrian court was the scene of intrigues which detracted from its ability to play a leading role in Mesopotamian affairs at this critical juncture. Tukulti-Ninurta I had been murdered by a son in his residence at Kār-Tukulti-Ninurta, a town of his own creation upstream from the ancient capital of Ashur. If a stela at Ashur can be attributed to him the assassin was Ashur-nāṣir-apli who had only a brief reign, giving his name as eponymn to a single year.[5] If this name stood in the Synchronistic Chronicle it is now broken away,[6] though it is certainly omitted in another list. It may be that his name was deliberately erased from a royal stela after he had been acclaimed by only a few followers who were soon crushed,[7] or, less likely, that his name is a scribal error for another son, Ashur-nādin-apli,

---

[1] See below, pp. 492 f.
[2] §1, 13, 2 ff.; §11, 2, 149 f.; G, 22, 53; cf. below, p. 456.
[3] G, 10, 218 f. (iii, 34–6).   [4] §1, 12, 136 and 140.
[5] §111, 1, no. 10; G, 19, 487 ff.; cf. below, p. 469, n. 11.
[6] G, 20, 391; §111, 7, 71; §1, 10, 99.   [7] §111, 1, 18 ff.

who may have been the murderer.[1] The latter ruled for four years (1207–1204 B.C.) claiming, as son of Tukulti-Ninurta, the full royal titles as 'king of all peoples, king of kings'. He repaired the royal treasury at Ashur[2] and erected a statue on the river bank outside the vulnerable north-east corner of the city, that the gods might for ever look upon it and protect the city from flood-damage. This was in answer to his prayer to Ashur and Shamash for help when, in the eponymate of Erība-Sin, the Tigris had swept away 600 acres of rich fields around the city.[3] This may indicate that the foundation of Kār-Tukulti-Ninurta had been in part dictated by the unpredictable manner in which the river was wont to alter its course outside the walls of Ashur, which depended on its flow for water-supplies.

Ashur-nādin-apli was succeeded by his son Ashur-nīrāri III who, according to the Babylonian Chronicle, ruled for six years (1203–1198). The only glimpse of him is afforded by a letter written by the Babylonian Adad-shuma-uṣur who addresses him and Ili-khadda as 'kings of Assyria'.[4] The latter, as a descendant of Erība-Adad I, represented a family whose claims at Ashur were later actively supported by Babylon. He was formerly a vizier and ruler of the province of Khanigalbat.[5] The peremptory note in this letter is, of itself, insufficient evidence for the assertion that Assyria was now a vassal-state of Babylon. Had she been this, the return of the statue of Marduk would surely have been claimed.

Enlil-kudurri-uṣur, another son of Tukulti-Ninurta, next had sufficient backing to hold the throne unmolested for five years (1197–1193 B.C.). At the end of this time he clashed with the Babylonians in a battle in which he was heavily defeated by Adad-shuma-uṣur. Meanwhile, Ninurta-apil-Ekur, a son of Ili-khadda who, as co-regent or claimant to the throne had earlier been defeated by his rival, had fled for refuge to the Babylonian court. He now took the opportunity to re-enter Assyria, rally his many adherents and seize the throne.[6] Enlil-kudurri-uṣur was killed in his stronghold, perhaps Ashur itself, since the city was captured in the uprising.[7] Though Ninurta-apil-Ekur claimed to have 'guarded all the people of Assyria, with wings like an eagle spread out over his country',[8] he doubtless owed his continued

---

[1] G, 14, 1, § 206.   [2] G, 16, nr. 62.
[3] § iii, 9, no. 71; G, 22, 46 f.; § iii, 17; § i, 14, 116 for date.
[4] Or, Ilu-ikhadda (G, 1, 99), a name formerly read as Nabu-daian (G, 10, 211, cf. G, 19, 56 ff.).   [5] G, 22, 50 (nr. 48); § iii, 1, 129.   [6] G, 22, nr. 44.
[7] Not in battle with Adad-shuma-uṣur as was previously assumed (§ i, 12, 131).
[8] G, 4, 94 (vii, 55–9).

position to the support of his southern neighbours. For thirteen years (or three if the variant of Chronicle B is accepted) he carried on the ancient royal traditions.¹ His daughter Muballitat-Sherua? was dedicated as high-priestess with gifts of inscribed vases, gold and lapis-lazuli chains and other ornaments from the palace treasures to the main temple.² Once again, the dearth of sources may give us an imperfect picture of events. Already the pressure of the nomadic tribes towards the Euphrates in the west and in the north was being felt, as in their turn they were forced out of their former grounds by the movement of peoples following the disintegration of the Hittite power. The loss of trading-facilities, combined with poor harvests, was to bring Assyria and Babylonia to one of their weakest states in a long history. At this same critical time Elam again threatened the trade-routes through the Zagros and Diyālā. Ashur-dan, the next holder of the Assyrian throne, made the first move to forestall the Elamites on his south-eastern frontier during the brief reign of Zababa-shuma-iddina of Babylon. He marched c. 1160 B.C. towards the Diyālā capturing Zaban, Irria and Ugarsallu, deporting the inhabitants to Assyria.³ These unfortunates would have been replaced by other deportees, loyal to the Assyrians amid their alien surroundings, who could be relied upon to warn of any encroachments on their territory, for such was the policy of later Assyrian militarists. If a statue dedicated for the life of Ashur-dan by the scribe Shamshi-Bēl in Irbil refers to this king rather than a later monarch of the same name it would imply that he paid close attention to the needs of this frontier.⁴ His descendant, Tiglath-pileser I, writing sixty years later, says that Ashur-dan pulled down the Anu-Adad temple at Ashur but did not rebuild it.⁵ This incident may have occurred towards the end of the long reign of forty-six years attributed to him both by the Babylonian Chronicle and by his heirs. There is no proof that he failed to show the customary respect to the cult-centres for he undertook other constructional work at Ashur⁶ and probably at Nineveh, where early in his reign an earthquake had destroyed part of the Ishtar temple.⁷ There are also records of weapons dedicated at other temples.⁸

---

¹ Note the number of royal edicts extant from this reign (§VIII, 14, 277 f.).
² §I, 14, 127, n. 3; G, 22, 51 (nr. 49); G, 16, II, 76.
³ G, 22, 51.   ⁴ G, I, 100.
⁵ G, 22, no. 60.   ⁶ §III, 16, 209.
⁷ §III, 11, 99; §III, 12, 97.
⁸ §III, 18, 326; §III, 4, 91 ff., and 145; §III, 15, 133.

The closing years of Ashur-dan's long tenure of the throne are obscure.[1] Ninurta-tukulti-Ashur,[2] his son, who may have been co-regent in the last years of his father's reign, 'exercised the kingship for his *ṭuppu*'. This term has been variously interpreted. It may denote an unspecified period of time[3] or the reign of a king who did not hold, and therefore give his name to, the office of eponym, that is one who did not hold the throne for longer than twelve months. Such reigns were therefore marked but accorded zero years in length.[4] Alternatively it may denote a precise twelve-month reign.[5] This last view finds support in official documents and memoranda from Ashur of this reign, some bearing the seal of Ninurta-tukulti-Ashur and of his wife Rimeni, dated by eponyms who cover a full twelve months. These tablets show that tribute and offerings in large quantities were rendered to Ninurta-tukulti-Ashur, perhaps while he acted as regent for his aged, and perhaps sick, father towards the end of his long reign.[6] He is nowhere given the title of king in these texts. Since it is clear that subordinate officials in Ashur controlled an area from Nisibis to the Zagros mountains, and Sutu to the west is a discernible administrative district in these texts, there is no evidence that Ninurta-tukulti-Ashur held an insignificant position.[7] That he was a usurper has long been contradicted, and the Khorsabad King List states that he was son of Ashur-dan who, after 'exercising kingship for a *ṭuppu*', was defeated by his brother, Mutakkil-Nusku, who in his turn held the throne for a *ṭuppu* before disappearing.[8] If the *ṭuppu* were an indeterminate length of reign it would be necessary to suppose that the chroniclers suppressed the length of the reign of the two royal brothers out of a sense of shame at the strife, a motive not observable elsewhere in the same text. When Mutakkil-Nusku overpowered his brother it would seem that the latter fled as an exile to Babylon rather than reached there as a deportee.[9] According to a broken Babylonian prism Ninurta-tukulti-Ashur restored the temple of Erragal in Sirara, reinstating the statue of the deity which had been removed by Tukulti-Ninurta I.[10] He was evidently in sufficient accord with the Isin dynasty at Babylon both to receive a welcome and to be supported as a potential reclaimant of the

[1] G, 22, 51 (nr. 50).   [2] On the name see G, 19, 2, 66 f.
[3] *C.A.H.* I³, pt. 1, p. 203; §III, 4, 265 ff.   [4] G, 22, 52; §I, 13, 9 ff.
[5] §I, 13, 10; G, 9, 90.   [6] G, 9, 92 f.
[7] §I, 13, 22; G, 19, 2, 62.
[8] G, 19, 2, 63; no inscriptions from the latter reign are known (G, 1, 102). Cf. p. 453, n. 2.
[9] G, 19, 2, 63; G, 13, 218 f.   [10] §III, 9, no. 80; G, 1, 100 ff.

Assyrian throne.[1] Although only a few administrative documents from this reign have been recovered as yet, they imply a steady and careful administration which, as marked later by his grandson, paved the way for the long reign of his son Ashur-rēsha-ishi I (1133–1116), who followed the brief rule of his father Mutakkil-Nusku,[2] and led to a restoration of Assyrian prestige.

Ashur-rēsha-ishi claimed, as 'avenger of Assyria', to have shattered the wide-ranging groups of Akhlamu to the north and west of the country.[3] These were primarily semi-nomadic raiders from Sukhi to Carchemish on the Euphrates who, pressing eastwards, now intensified the incursions into the Tigris valley which were to become an important factor in the next reign.[4] Changes in military equipment and technique, in this era of the development of iron, had by now affected the strategy and employment of both Assyrian and Babylonian armies. These were able to build on the military experiences of Shalmaneser I and Tukulti-Ninurta, and now adapted their warfare to combat better-armed opponents whether in the desert or mountain, in the open or in siege-warfare.[5]

Experience would now seem to have led the Assyrians to develop a strategic plan, at first directed to maintaining their existing borders but soon to be extended in offensive operations to control all the main routes into their home lands and to maintain the border along defensible terrain.[6] Fortresses were strengthened to withstand attacks by powerful siege-engines. In the north Ashur-rēsha-ishi improved the defences of Apku, west of Mosul,[7] to maintain control of the district of Khanigalbat and to meet the growing menace from the well-armed Mushki tribe and their confederates in the northern hills. In addition to the construction of a royal residence here, the king undertook a programme of restoration work at Nineveh itself where a new palace was built with an extensive armoury (*bīt kutalli*), storehouses and other depot facilities and repairs made to the Great

---

[1] See above, p. 449.

[2] This king seems to have reigned long enough to undertake constructional work on a palace at Nineveh (§III, 11, 100).

[3] G, 4, 19, l. 6.

[4] See below, p. 460. For the earlier history of nomadic groups in the area see *C.A.H.* II³, pt. 1, pp. 24 ff.

[5] §III, 8, 137 ff.

[6] §III, 8, 141.

[7] G, 20, 297; located at Tell Bumariya (§III, 2, 5) or Abu Mariya (§III, 6, 135). Excavations at Tell er-Rimah in 1965–8 show that the area further west was abandoned by *c.* 1200 B.C. See A, 12, 71; A, 13, 2.

454 ASSYRIA AND BABYLONIA, c. 1200–1000 B.C.

Gate of the Ishtar temple.[1] The temple of Ishtar, severely
damaged by earthquakes in the time of Shalmaneser I and of
Ashur-dan, was the object of much care, the great court and its
gate-towers being restored. Apart from the fulfilment of religious
obligations, this was doubtless part of the plan to provide a firm
base for operations in the north-eastern hills. The Lullubi (or
Lullumi) and Quti were raided and their subjugation claimed. It
may be that Nineveh was also the base from which the king called
out his élite troops (ḫurādu) to march to Irbil as the first stage
of a renewed offensive in the disputed Zagros hills. This action
roused Babylonian opposition, for Ninurta-nādin-shumi (or
-shumāti) mustered his own forces.[2] The broken text implies a
defeat for the southerners who, under Nebuchadrezzar I, were
destined to renew their hostility with Assyria and thus divert
their forces at a time of crisis due to increasing pressures from
the west. However, at first Ashur-rēsha-ishi was able, by the
despatch of a mixed group of chariots and infantry, to force
Nebuchadrezzar to withdraw from Zaqqu with the loss of
valuable siege equipment which he had to set on fire. A later
Babylonian attack, this time with a more mobile force, was beaten
off at Idu (Hīt?) by a similar Assyrian column which captured the
Babylonian general and his baggage-train.[3] With the defeat of
Nebuchadrezzar, some time after the end of Ashur-rēsha-ishi's
eighteenth year of office (1116 B.C.), military conflict between the
neighbours ceased.

IV. NEBUCHADREZZAR I

By this time the control of Babylonia was firmly in the hands of
one ruling family who were to hold the throne for over fifty years.
Nebuchadrezzar, whose very name implies the continuance of the
line, succeeded Ninurta-nādin-shumi and was to rule for twenty-
two years (1124–1103).[4] With the backing of a majority of the
tribes he was in a position to avenge the humiliating defeat
inflicted by the Elamites when Kutir-Nahhunte had sacked the
larger northern cities and removed the statue of Marduk from
E-sagila at the close of the Kassite period. This act of sacrilege
was long remembered as one of the greatest defeats Babylon had
ever suffered. Yet the Elamites still raided the fertile regions east
of the Tigris, perhaps in support of a few remaining adherents
of the old régime which Nebuchadrezzar, as 'spoiler of the

---

[1] §III, 13, 100; §III, 12, 114; §III, 11, 100.   [2] G, 22, 70.
[3] G, 22, 71; G, 4, 216.   [4] §II, 6 (King List C), 4.

Kassites', claims to have crushed finally.[1] An early counter-raid
by Nebuchadrezzar failed when his troops were smitten by plague
and the king himself only narrowly escaped death in the headlong
retreat which followed.[2] Another account, which may refer to
this same event, relates a battle near the river Kerkhah in which
the Babylonian troops were forced to retreat to Dūr-Apil-Sin,
implying that the Elamites no longer controlled the west bank
of the Tigris.[3] This episode may date from the earlier Isin kings
though it fits well into this contemporary situation. It was
certainly later in his reign that Nebuchadrezzar received favourable omens, in response to repeated appeals to the gods, to launch
a further attack.[4] This he did in the month of Tammuz, high
summer, when 'the axes (held in the hand) burned like fire and
the road-surfaces were scorching like flame. There was no water
in the wells and drinking supplies were unavailable. The strength
of the powerful horses slackened and the legs of even the strongest
man weakened.'[5] The march lay through difficult country for
30 *bēru* (*c.* 320 km.) south-east of Dēr before the Elamites were
encountered on the banks of the Ulai (River Eulaeus, modern
Kārūn) near Susa. Although the Babylonians may have had the
benefit of the element of surprise, the battle was hotly contested,
the dust of the affray blotting out the sun. The Elamite Khutelutush-In-Shushinak fled and soon thereafter died. According to
the account by Lakti-Marduk,[6] the shaikh of Bīt-Karziabku, the
action which decided the day was that of the chariotry on the
right wing. For this their commander was rewarded with a
generous grant of land and freedom from local taxes and labour-
service in the province of Nawar[7] and thus formed, like the similar
colonies of deportees in Assyria, a pro-Babylonian nucleus on the
disputed border.

The outcome of the battle was of greater significance for
Babylonian morale than for any political or territorial gain.
Nevertheless, it marked the end of Elamite domination and of
their raids into the plain for many years. Above all, the cult statue
of Marduk was restored to E-sagila amid much popular rejoicing

---

[1] G, 12, 96 ff.

[2] This reconstruction of events follows G, 2, 132 f. Cf. A, 3, 105 f.

[3] See below, pp. 501 f.; A, 3, 106.

[4] §IV, 1, 44; §IV, 4, ii, 4 f., dates this to the sixteenth regnal year.

[5] G, 12, 29 f., no. 6, i, 16 ff.

[6] G, 12, 32, i, 35. On the name formerly read 'Ritti-Marduk' see below,
p. 502, n. 1, and A, 3, 107 where a possible reading Shitti-Marduk is suggested. See
Plate 161(*b*).

[7] G, 12, 32 f. (i, 36–ii, 10).

and elaborate ceremonies.[1] It may be at this time too, rather than in a separate campaign, that the statue of a lesser deity, Eriya of Dīn-sharri on the same border, was brought first to Babylon and then settled in Khuṣṣi near Bīt-Sin-asharēdu.[2] The priests, Shamua and his son Shamaia, were endowed with land sufficient to maintain the cult in an area less exposed to Elamite marauders. Succeeding generations were to laud Nebuchadrezzar as a national victor and hero. He was the subject both of heroic poetry and of historically based omens, one astrological series of the seventh century being entitled 'when Nebuchadrezzar crushed Elam'.[3] It is possible that this notable event played a decisive part in the elevation of Marduk to be the supreme national deity of Babylon.[4] Subsequently one Neo-Babylonian ruler and two short-lived insurgents who were faced with the prospect of the domination of Babylonia by their eastern (then Persian) rivals, were to adopt this honoured throne-name.

Nebuchadrezzar was less successful in his relations with Assyria, but it is the Assyrian account of events between them which alone survives. If Nebuchadrezzar was the author of the letter to Ashur-rēsha-ishi threatening to reinstate Ninurta-tukulti-Ashur[5] then he would seem to have followed up with an attack on Zaqqu, at which border-crossing his rival had failed to meet him for discussions. His defeat here and later at Idu (Hīt?)[6] may indicate action against invading Amorites whose subjugation Nebuchadrezzar claims. A complaint by a semi-nomad, Kharbi-Shikhu, a frontier-official, that the king's envoys only waited for him a day in Zaqqu territory, is answered by reference to the need for care and mediation between Babylonia and Assyria. The letter is broken and the part played by a certain Ashur-shum-lishir in these events cannot now be understood.[7] There is no reason to doubt the explanation given for this defeat by the Assyrian-biased Synchronistic History as a repulse by the Assyrians of Babylonian border raids.

The Babylonians, like the Assyrians, claim victories over the Lullubi in the disputed Zagros mountains. This may be no mere desire to repeat the activities, or claim the titles, of illustrious predecessors but may be a historical reference to a campaign on the north-eastern border of which no record has survived. Within Babylon, the royal residence, the king refurbished E-sagila, now

[1] §IV, 4, 339 ff.; §IX, 17, 10.   [2] G, 12, 96 f. (no. 24, 14 ff.).
[3] §IV, 8, 542 f.   [4] §IX, 17, 9.
[5] See above, p. 449.   [6] G, 22, 59.
[7] G, 20, 295; §VI, 11, 59 ff.; §IV, 7.

restored to its primary place as the seat of Marduk. A dagger bearing his name and titles may originally have been part of the endowment.[1] In the western city a shrine of Adad, E-kidur-khegal-tila, was restored following one successful expedition.[2] At Nippur care was bestowed on the E-kur temple, the chief priest of Enlil being granted an adequate revenue from land in adjacent Bīt-Sin-shemi.[3] This 'pious prince' followed the custom of dedicating objects of gold and silver to the Sin-temple at Ur[4] where a stela of an $ēntu$-priestess from the sacred cloister, recovered by Nabonidus more than five hundred years later, may imply that a royal princess had been installed in that office.[5] Moreover, this may but reflect other activity in the south noted by the scribe who counted this reign as falling 696 years after that of Gulkishar, king of the first Dynasty of the Sealand.[6] Inaccurate though this computation may be, Nebuchadrezzar left his mark as a heroic leader, 'king of Sumer and Akkad', who could claim to be 'the sun rising over the land as in a new day'.[7]

V. TIGLATH-PILESER I

It was as well that the Babylonians had neutralized the Elamites and taken a part in controlling the raiders both from the Lullubi tribes in the eastern hills and from the nomadic tribes of the western desert. Tiglath-pileser I (Tukulti-apil-Esharra of Assyria) (1115–1077) was thus free to face the growing storm clouds in the north in his accession year. Although the annals and historical records afford only summaries of his campaigns on all fronts it would seem that he at least developed and followed an overall strategic plan for dealing with his enemies and extending Assyrian influence.[8] His attention was first directed to the north where the Mushki—perhaps to be identified with the Phrygians, and linked with the Kaska (Gasga) peoples who had broken up the Hittite empire[9]—had crossed the Taurus with a large army ('20,000 men') and were making their way down the Tigris valley towards Nineveh. The threat of the loss of fine agricultural land and the copper-mines paying annual dues to Ashur was serious. For fifty years the Mushki had controlled the rich valleys of Alzi and Purukuzzi, former tributaries of Ashur. They now

[1] §II, 2, 152 (no. 4).
[2] §IV, 1, 43.
[3] §I, 8, ii, 2 ff.
[4] §IV, 3, 143.
[5] §IV, 2, 45.
[6] §I, 7, 83.
[7] G, 12, 31, i, 4.
[8] §III, 8, 141. See Plate 162(b).
[9] See above, p. 420.

raided beyond Katmukhi and dominated the countryside west of the upper Tigris fomenting revolt. Tiglath-pileser resolutely met the tribesmen, headed by five chiefs, in the plain beyond the Kashiari hills (Ṭūr 'Abdīn).[1]

The Assyrians adopted their old practice of displaying the hands of the vanquished at the city-gates and of plundering the rebel towns and villages which had sided with the attackers. More than 6000 prisoners and much booty were carried off. Since many of the tribesmen had fled north-east to Sherishe on the east bank of the Tigris, the Assyrians mounted a punitive expedition. Pioneering a track across the mountains for the passage of their chariots, they captured the city and dispersed the Papkhi who had come to the help of Kummukh. In a series of clashes in the mountains Kili-Teshub, son of Kali-Teshub, and possibly descendant of a Hurrian family, who also bore the native name of Irrupi, was captured with his family and much loot.[2] News of the Assyrian advance north-eastward caused the people of Urraṭinash on Mount Panari to take to more distant hills while their ruler Shadi-Teshub, son of Khattukhe, came to make terms with the Assyrian leader. In accordance with ancient practice the suppliant was made a vassal; his sons were taken as hostages to Ashur together with an initial payment of tribute, more than 60 large bronze vessels, 120 slaves and many head of cattle. The bronzes were dedicated to Adad in gratitude for divine favour in this campaign.

In the following year Assyria won back Subartu. The army, equipped with 120 chariots with teams of yoked horses in the Hittite manner, marched through Alzi and Purukuzzi which were again laid under tribute. These tribes were now weak and without help from the Mushki. The force moved up the Tigris valley and across mountainous terrain between Mounts Idni and Aia to invade Kharia and meet rebels from the Kaska (Gasga) who had formerly defeated the Hittites but were now aiding a coalition of the Papkhi tribes. Whether with the same force or another column moving eastward, the Assyrians broke up the opposition at Mount Azu and fired villages in the foothills towards the Zab river. Men of Adaush submitted but those of Saradaush and Ammaush on resisting were defeated at Mount Aruma, at Isua (previously Ishua) and Dara. Another force, led by the king in person, marched up the Zab to engage the more easterly

---

[1] G, 4, 35 f., i, 62 ff.
[2] G, 4, 40, ii, 25 f. The second name may have been an Assyrian misunderstanding of the Hurrian 'lord' (§v, 3, 177).

tribes. Murattash was captured and burnt in a dawn attack as the troops pressed through Saradaush in the Asaniu and Atunu hills to reach the Sugi district of Khabkhi.[1] Here the Assyrians were checked for a time by a stand on Mount Khirikhu of 6000 men from five of the tribes of eastern Papkhi (Khime, Lukhi, Anirgi, Alamun and Nimni). In the event Sugi was finally made a vassal state, the statues of twenty-five of the local deities being carried off as hostages to stand beneath the eye of Ashur in his temple.[2]

With the dominance of the Mushki and Papkhi over the smaller tribes now broken Tiglath-pileser was free in the next year (third campaign) to make a drive north against the Nairi hill-folks west of Lake Vān. His route lay through regions which he claims, probably justly, had never been traversed by his predecessors. Sixteen mountain ridges were crossed as he moved via Mount Amadana, near Diyārbakr, to bridge the Upper Euphrates near its source. Despite abundant geographical detail given in the royal annals the precise route cannot yet be determined. It would seem that the Assyrians marched by Tunube (Turubun) east of the Tigris to the south-west of Lake Vān.[3] A coalition of 23 Nairi chiefs was defeated, 120 of their armoured chariots being taken and 60 other tribal groups chased northwards.[4] The decisive battle took place to the north and north-west of Lake Vān. At the point farthest north on this expedition, Melazgirt, Tiglath-pileser had an inscribed victory stela set up.[5] Once again hostages were taken and an annual tribute of 12,000 horses and 2,000 head of cattle imposed on the conquered tribes. Sieni of Daieni, the leader who refused to submit, was brought as a captive to Assyria. It was in the westerly course of this campaign that the rebel stronghold of Milidia was visited and made to produce an annual due payable in lead-lumps. This is almost certainly to be identified with modern Malatya. Tribute was claimed from Milidia and from neighbouring Enzate and Sukhme. Thus, by the end of three campaigns Tiglath-pileser had carried Assyrian arms further into the Anatolian hills, and laid more of the hill-tribes under duress, than had any of his predecessors. Most of his opponents in the extensive lands of the Nairi from Tumme to

[1] Rather than Kirkhi, see G, 16, 11, 83, v, 6; §1, 13, 20.
[2] G, 4, 41 ff. (cols. ii, 36–iv, 39).
[3] §v, 3, 170.
[4] The 'Upper Sea' must here be the Black Sea, a term used as a designation of general direction northward.
[5] §v, 3, 171.

Dazaeni, Khimua, Paiteri and Khabkhi,[1] who now owed allegiance and taxes, are only to be encountered in the annals of this reign. While pressure on the sources of raw materials and the trade-routes which linked them was at least temporarily alleviated, and the internal economy strengthened by the new sources of revenue, the seeds of future dissension were being sown. On these hill frontiers especially the peoples, by nature and location independent, would henceforth be forced to group into larger defensive units. In times of weakness in Assyria they would harass the plain and, five hundred years later, play a decisive part in the overthrow of the southern state. Further, a course had been set from which no subsequent ruler could afford to turn back. Yet the periodic incursions needed to control the tribes and recoup overdue taxes would severely drain the sources of manpower and wealth of the very country they were intended to strengthen.

Tiglath-pileser now aimed to extend his jurisdiction to the trans-Tigridian country of Muṣri.[2] Since Muṣri had received help from the land of Qumani, the Assyrian laid siege to the city of Arini, at the foot of Mount Aisa. The siege was raised on promise of submission and regular tribute-payments. By this means, and because in the second campaign the men of Urumma and Apishal[3] had been defeated, the route westwards was now possible. Moreover, Tiglath-pileser had taken bold action against the Akhlamu —an Aramaean tribe or group dominating the Euphrates between Carchemish and Sutium which often raided to the Tigris. In a single day, so he claims,[4] he raided their territory penetrating beyond the Euphrates, which had been crossed on inflated skin rafts (keleks), to the Bishrī hills where six of their villages were burned out. This was but the first action against the semi-nomads of Syria which necessitated the Assyrian army repeating the Euphrates crossing no less than twenty-eight times, twice in one single year. Such constant pressure gives substance to the Assyrian claim to have subdued the Akhlamu—forerunners of the coming Aramaean raiders—from Tadmor (Palmyra) to 'Anah and even as far south as Rapiqu on the frontier with Babylonia. In Sukhi itself the island towns of Sapinata ('Boats') and Khindanu were sacked and ruined by the destruction of their palm-groves. The statues of the local deities were carried off to Ashur as a final disgrace and to mark their reduction to impotence.

---

[1] The tribes here enumerated occupied lands between Erzurum and Lake Urmia.

[2] For the location of Muṣri, see now A, 16, 145 f.   [3] §v, 1, 71.

[4] This is probably to be interpreted as 'at one time', in a single expedition.

With the intervening tribes under close surveillance Assyria could now aim to control the main trade-route to the Mediterranean itself. Tiglath-pileser directed his march to Amurru, which at this time extended from Tadmor to Ṣamuri and included Byblos and Sidon.[1] His march lay to the coast at Armad (Arvad). Here the king embarked on a ship to sail up the Mediterranean littoral to Ṣamuri. On this journey of three *bēru* (c. 20 kms.), he hunted a narwhal (*nāḫiru*).[2] The first Assyrian king to venture across the Lebanon in force was brought gifts by the neighbouring rulers of Byblos and Sidon, while the Egyptian king sent him a crocodile as a present. Before turning homewards Tiglath-pileser had massive cedars cut down for use in his renovation of the Anu-Adad temple at Ashur. An annual tax requiring further supplies of timber was imposed on Ini-Teshub, king of Khatti (N. Syria), who paid homage at this time. Thus by the end of his fifth regnal year Tiglath-pileser was able to boast of his conquest of forty-two lands and their rulers between the Lesser Zab and the Euphrates and along the northern hills as far as the Mediterranean.[3] This wide-ranging activity was possible because all was quiet on the southern borders. It was not until well on in the reign of this long-lived Assyrian monarch that Marduk-nādin-ahhē[4] of Babylon raided across the Lesser Zab and carried off the gods Adad and Shala from Ekallate, a royal city not far from Ashur itself.[5]

Owing to preoccupation with the west it was at least a decade before the Assyrian was able to strike back. According to the Synchronistic Chronicle there were two actions involving Assyrian chariotry.[6] The first crossed the Lesser Zab to ravage Arman in the district of Ugarsallu[7] and marched via Lubdi (south of Arrapkha) and over the Radanu river (Shaṭṭ el-'Adhaim) to plunder villages at the foot of the Kamulla and Kashtilia hills. This was a continuation of the struggle for mastery of the upper Diyālā route, now firmly in the hands of the Babylonians. The second force was directed to northern Babylonia itself and, marching along the customary route taken by such raiders down the eastern Tigris bank through Marritu,[8] it crossed to Dūr-

---

[1] G, 16, 11, 68, 71. The area to the north of this, bounded on the east by Araziq and Carchemish on the Euphrates, was now included in Khatti.

[2] §v, 10, 355 f.   [3] G, 4, 82 f. (vi, 39 ff.).

[4] See Plate 162(c).

[5] The location is disputed. Adad and Shala had a shrine at Kalkhu (Nimrūd).

[6] §v, 10, 351.

[7] Or the 'irrigated district of Saluna'.

[8] Or Gurmarritu. It has been suggested that this may be Sāmarrā, usually written Surmarrāti (see §v, 11, 309).

Kurigalzu ('Aqarqūf), Opis and Sippar of Shamash (Abu Ḥabbah) and of Anunitum to reach Babylon. The cult centres were over-run despite attempts by the Babylonian cavalry to divert the enemy advance. The Assyrians claimed an outright victory setting fire to the royal palaces of Babylon before withdrawing.[1] Marduk-nādin-ahhē remained in control of Babylon and still held the captured statues of the Assyrian deities, presumably having removed them for safety to Nippur or the south.[2] There is no evidence that Assyria either intended or gained any lasting hold over northern Babylonia at this time. Indeed, a fragmentary Assyrian chronicle which records the death of Marduk-nādin-ahhē describes a dire famine in an area usually thought to be in Assyria itself, when Aramaean invaders drove the Assyrians into the northern hills round Kirruria. If this does not refer to events outside the Assyrian home-land or to the Assyrian attack on the north-eastern Babylonian province of Irria,[3] then it would imply that in the closing years of the reign of Tiglath-pileser, who is still named in the text after this event, the Aramaeans were now strong enough to turn on their Assyrian conquerors despite having been so frequently raided. The same text would then imply that Tiglath-pileser outlived Marduk-nādin-ahhē.[4]

Whatever the reasons which led to the retreat of the Assyrian invaders their failure to follow up a military operation was a grave weakness displayed in several campaigns of this reign. The initial successes achieved in constant expeditions over a wide front were only rarely exploited. Tributes and taxes were imposed but not regularly collected. Prisoners do not appear to have been used in major building or resettlement projects as was done by later Assyrian leaders. Nor were they settled to replace rebellious inhabitants at other parts of the dominion. Although the trans-portation of conquered people is mentioned in the annals it was probably no innovation and there is no sign of the establishment of a system of control of newly overrun areas such as followed the later setting up of provinces and administrative districts. The very scale of Assyrian success therefore paved the way for a swift denial of the Assyrian overlordship and thus for the loss of the hard-won territories if ever the central government was weak. The new trade-routes opened into Syria and the mineral wealth of Anatolia brought an immediate if passing economic advantage. The new weapons and tactics, contrived in imitation of, and

---

[1] §v, 10, 351 (ll. 48 f.). A, 3, 125 interprets this as a mere raid.
[2] Unless the Ekallate raid was itself a later reprisal for this attack, see p. 464.
[3] §viii, 1, 235, n. 2.   [4] G, 2, 133 f.; A, 3, 75.

reaction to, those of their powerful neighbours, had been well tried in an age of technological innovation. The personal exploits of Tiglath-pileser, like those of his contemporary Nebuchad-rezzar, were to be long remembered and imitated.

The king showed much prowess in battle and skill in hunting. During campaigns in the Khabur valley, near Harrān and at Araziq on the Euphrates the jungle provided much sport. He slew four wild aurochs, four bull elephants and no less than 920 lions, more than a hundred of which were hunted on foot with the bow or the newly invented iron spear.[1] This claim, especially of elephants, is small compared with that of Tuthmosis III in the same area, and may indicate that already their numbers were declining owing to the predatory activities of the Akhlamu. But these hunts were not without other purposes. Horns, tusks and hides contributed to the economy, live animals and birds stocked the zoological gardens where they were bred for the chase and so that their young could be offered in sacrifice. The first Assyrian to include such details in the royal annals, this king sought to prove his superiority over wild beasts and so demonstrate the unique power granted him by the god of war to overcome any evil or enemy in the field. Such a ritual hunt is attested elsewhere in the Near East at this time. The king was also the first to record the institution of botanical gardens stocked with specimens collected during his widespread expeditions.

The more unusual victims of the hunt, such as the narwhal harpooned off the Mediterranean coast or the wild bull caught in the Lumash Mountains, were reproduced in bas reliefs to decorate the entrances to the restored royal palaces at Ashur.[2] Here, according to many inscriptions, the Anu-Adad temple with its adjacent twin zikkurrats was restored, the temple being re-roofed with Lebanon cedars, the terrace resurfaced and the associated cult buildings (bīt šaḫuru and bīt labbuni)[3] enlarged and repanelled with cedar and pistachio woods. This work of building the temple, according to Tiglath-pileser, had not been completed; though sixty years earlier Ashur-dan had relaid the foundations of a building first constructed by Shamshi-Adad (III), the son of Ishme-Dagan (II), 641 years earlier.[4] Of similar chronological interest is the claim that the walls of the new city, built by Puzur-Ashur III (c. 1500 B.C.), had been neglected for about two centuries since the time of Ashur-nādin-ahhē I (1452–1433). These were now reinforced by a great earth rampart

[1] G, 4, 85.   [2] §v, 10, 356 f.
[3] Ibid. 354 f.   [4] G, 4, 95 (vii, 60 ff.); G, 19, 1, 303; G, 20, 359.

between the Tigris Gate and the inner town.[1] In Nineveh Tiglath-pileser had work carried out on the city walls, which were reinforced with stone, and on the royal palace built by his father between the Ishtar and Nabu temples to which attention was now also given. Water was diverted from the River Khosr both to the city and to a newly set out park.[2] Similar work was carried out at other cities and there is every indication that, despite the irony that Tiglath-pileser is best known from the accounts of his wars, his claim at the end of his reign to have 'made good the condition of my people and caused them to dwell in peaceful habitations' was justified. He left behind also a legacy of literature collected in what must be one of the oldest extant libraries.[3]

VI. PRESSURES FROM THE WEST

Meanwhile in Babylonia, according to the King List,[4] Nebuchadrezzar I had been succeeded by a son, Enlil-nādin-apli who reigned for four years (1102–1099). Little is known of his activities though in his fourth year he ordered the governors of the provinces of Bīt-Sin-māgir and the Sealand to investigate a dispute of title to some land,[5] an indication that the central government still controlled the southern tribes. While the reason for the change is at present unknown he was succeeded by his uncle Marduk-nādin-ahhē, son of Ninurta-nādin-shumi and a younger brother of Nebuchadrezzar.[6] Thus the gains of the previous years were initially consolidated in a stable government with power held within the same family. His rule was recognized at Nippur and at Ur, where he undertook a considerable building programme, restoring the E-(ga)nun-makh and neighbouring buildings.[7] However, it was in the north that the vigour of the southerners was seen. According to Sennacherib 'Marduk-nādin-ahhē, king of Akkad had captured the gods of Ekallate, Adad and Shala, in the time of Tiglath-pileser, king of Assyria, and carried them off to Babylonia. 418 years later I removed them from Babylon and restored them to their shrines in Ekallate.'[8] This implies a date of 1105 B.C.[9] but the exact year when the raid on Ekallate took place within this reign is uncertain.[10] Sennacherib's calculation is to be taken as an error since it would clash

---

[1] §v, 10, 344 (ll. 34 ff.).   [2] §v, 7, 142 f.; §iii, 11, 100; §v, 5, 122.
[3] See below, p. 477.   [4] §ii, 6, 3 (King List C, 5).
[5] §i, 7, 83.   [6] §ii, 6, 3 (King List C, 6); §ii, 3, 309, n. 3.
[7] §vi, 3, no. 306; §vi, 16, no. 101 (pl. xxv); A, 3, 330 ff.
[8] §vi, 9, 83 (ll. 48 ff.).   [9] A, 3, 83 ff. Cf. G, 20, 354.   [10] A, 3, 124 ff.

with the synchronism Ashur-rēsha-ishi–Ninurta-nādin-shumi.[1]
The economic texts imply that the Babylonian king controlled the
border up to the Lesser Zab until his thirteenth year and a *kudurru*-
inscription of his tenth year refers to a defeat of Assyria and a
grant of land at Irria, east of the Tigris.[2] The carefully planned
expedition would seem to have taken place perhaps in the ninth
or tenth regnal year when Tiglath-pileser was preoccupied with
the west, and unable to retaliate. The Babylonian clash with the
Assyrians at Rapiqu earlier in the reign may have been caused
by some anxiety over the mastery of the Euphrates around the
valuable bitumen deposits of Hīt and the control of the waters
at the border. It is unlikely that these Babylonian expeditions
took place after Tiglath-pileser's raid on Upper Babylonia, for
no permanent results followed from them[3] and Marduk-nādin-
ahhē remained in control though the economy was much
weakened. In his eighteenth year severe famine struck Babylonia
and the inhabitants of the cities were reduced to eating human
flesh. Aramaean semi-nomads pressed in from the desert and
the Babylonian ruler 'finally disappeared', no detail being known
of the manner of his death or retirement after a reign of eighteen
years (1098–1081). This Aramaean invasion may have been
part of the same incursion which distressed Assyria towards the
end of Tiglath-pileser's reign and after the death of Marduk-
nādin-ahhē.[4] An attempt has been made to identify five unnamed
kings in an Akkadian prophecy with Marduk-nādin-ahhē and his
four successors[5] but this is very doubtful.[6]

Marduk-shāpik-zēri, who ruled for thirteen years (1080–
1068),[7] came to the throne in circumstances which are still
obscure and his relation to his predecessor is uncertain. A later
commentator compares his accession with that of Esarhaddon so
that he might have been a younger son of Nebuchadrezzar or of
Marduk-nādin-ahhē who gained the throne after a struggle.[8]
That he was contemporary with Ashur-bēl-kala of Assyria in the
opening years of the latter's rule is certain from the Assyrian
Synchronistic History which records that 'Marduk-shāpik-zēri
pledged mutual peace and good will. At the time of Ashur-bēl-
kala Marduk-shāpik-zēri finally disappeared.'[9] The New Baby-

---

[1] See above, p. 454; G, 2, 149.   [2] G, 12, 45 (no. VIII, ii, 27).
[3] See above, p. 462; also Ashur-bēl-kala had to attack Dūr-Kurigalzu again (G, 4,
133).
[4] §II, 8, 384, 2'; §I, 12, 133 f. A, 3, 125 implies that he disappeared during the
invasion.   [5] A, 9, 231 f.; A, 1, 118; A, 8, 9.
[6] A, 3, 129, n. 762.   [7] §II, 6 (King List C, 7); A, 3, 6 f.
[8] §II, 8, 384.   [9] G, 18, 272 (King List A).

lonian Chronicle, after an obscure reference to 'heavy spoil', says that 'Marduk-shāpik-zēri established friendly relations (i.e. a treaty) with Ashur-bēl-kala of Assyria'.[1] It appears to indicate that the Babylonian took the initiative after he had built a defended place, the name of which is now lost, or had won a victory, perhaps over the Aramaeans, for the presence of 105 chiefs or rulers at special (treaty) celebrations is noted. On the other hand, the Chronicle continues, 'at that time the king came from Assyria to Sippar'. This might imply that Marduk-shāpik-zēri had gone to Assyria to establish the international agreement or to receive support for his claim to the throne. This act of reconciliation was probably forced on the parties by their mutual desire to present a united front against the desert tribes. It is possible that it was the Assyrian who came to Sippar, rather than to Babylon which had so recently been the scene of invasion, though Sippar was not necessarily the capital at this time.[2] Extensive repairs to the city-walls and city-gates at Babylon were being undertaken.[3] The temple of E-zida at Borsippa was restored and gifts made to the temples at Ur,[4] Nippur,[5] and other cult-centres.[6] The normal legal procedures for establishing the ownership of land and a list of prices current in the twelfth year of this reign do not indicate any political disturbance at this time.[7] This has, however, to be deduced from the seizure of the throne by an Aramaean usurper, Adad-apla-iddina, which brought the long control of Babylonia by a distinguished family to an end. That the new ruler was to hold the throne for twenty-two years (1067–1046)[8] and himself to be the object of Aramaean attacks makes it unlikely that he was a victorious Aramaean invader.

Adad-apla-iddina styled himself 'King of Babylon, son of Nin-Isinna and son-in-law of Nanna'[9], to assert his divine title to the throne. The Synchronistic History claims that someone, whose name is now lost, 'appointed Adad-apla-iddina, son of Esagil-shaduni, son of a nobody, to rule over them'.[10] While this may mean no more than that he was a native of Babylonia but of non-royal stock, the New Babylonian Chronicle calls him 'son of

[1] G, 13, ii, 58 f., 4 ff.   [2] G, 13, i, 191; G, 2, 159.
[3] §i, 7, pt. ii, 148.   [4] A, 5, 334.
[5] A, 6, 16 (no. 56).   [6] §iv, 3, 143, 15; §vi, 10, 7 f.; A, 2, 247.
[7] G, 12, 80 f.   [8] §ii, 7, 86 f.; §ii, 6, 20.
[9] §vi, 3, 166 f., 1–5; the first title may not be a divine ascription since the name of Nin-Isinna is given before that of his divine father. See §vi, 2, 27 f. and *contra* §vi, 13, 103; cf. also A, 3, 136 f.
[10] G, 3, 90 (King List A, ii, 31–32); G, 2, 161, n. 222, thinks this was Ashur-bēl-kala. Cf. A, 3, 136.

Itti-Marduk-balāṭu, an Aramaean, a usurper'.[1] This ancestral name is common and need not refer to the second ruler of the Isin Dynasty; if such was his forebear the conservative Babylonian chronicler would scarcely have classed him as an Aramaean. That he usurped the throne is almost certain, but that he was opposed in this is unlikely since he continued his predecessor's policy of close ties with the Assyrian king, to whom he had married his daughter. The initial goodwill did not last. The Babylonian devoted himself energetically to the now traditional endowment of the principal religious foundations. Nabu's statue at Borsippa was ornamented, and the shrines of E-meteursag at Kish and E-kishnugal at Ur restored.[2] The Imgur–Enlil wall at Babylon was repaired as was the outer city-wall of Nippur.[3] However, relationships with powerful neighbours soon deteriorated and Ashur-bēl-kala, perhaps sensing Babylonian support for his rebel brother, attacked northern Babylonia. If the so-called 'Broken Obelisk' is assigned to this reign, then Dūr-Kurigalzu was attacked and its governor, Kadashman-Buriash, taken captive.[4] Once again this district was laid open to incursions from the desert, the Aramaean tribe of Sutu sacking Sippar and causing the regular services in the temple to cease for more than a century.[5] If the Era Epic reflects this disturbed period then there was civil war in Babylon and the Sutu joined in the raid on Dūr-Kurigalzu and Dēr.[6]

As so often after a long and distinguished reign, there would seem to have been family controversy on the death of Tiglath-pileser I. Asharēd-apil-Ekur reigned only two years (1076–5).[7] The reading of the Synchronistic Chronicle (Assur 14616c) which held him to be a contemporary of Itti-Marduk-balāṭu[8] has been disproved.[9] His origin, accession, and end are obscure since no contemporary records have survived. He did not commence his reign until after the accession year of Marduk-shāpik-zēri of Babylon, who reigned for thirteen years.[10] This synchronism, subject to a margin of error of only three years either way, makes it probable that Ashur-bēl-kala who succeeded him came to the throne about the seventh year of Marduk-shāpik-zēri.[11]

According to his annals, Ashur-bēl-kala had first to campaign

[1] G, 13, II, 59, l. 8.
[2] §VI, 2, 30; §VI, 7, 65; §VI, 3, 166.
[3] §VI, 12, II, 308; A, 3, 140.
[4] §VI, 5, 209 f.; G, I, 135.
[5] G, 12, 121, i, I ff.
[6] §VI, 6, 398; A, 3, 285 f.
[7] §VI, 15, 21, III, 13–15.
[8] G, 18, 273; G, 21, 70 f.
[9] A, 3, 41.
[10] §VI, 14, 21.
[11] C.A.H. I³, pt. I, pp. 204 f.; cf. A, 3, 75 f.

in Uruaṭri which was itself being troubled by the Aramaeans who by now had reached the Tigris north and north-west of Ashur.[1] The campaigns form the principal subject of the 'Broken Obelisk' from Nineveh which also includes some of the exploits of Tiglath-pileser I.[2] There have been many theories as to the date and ascription of this monument in which the name of the king, who must have reigned for at least five years, is now missing.[3] That it is to be attributed to this reign rather than that of Tiglath-pileser I is evident from the progress made by the Aramaeans who had hitherto been largely confined to the west of the Euphrates. It would seem from the text that Ashur-bēl-kala, if this assignation is correct, began to take vigorous action against the Aramaeans in his fourth or fifth year. Two campaigns were directed against these tribes, now called *Arime*, in Ṣaṣiri. A further expedition reconquered Turmitta in Muṣri, deporting dissident tribesmen, and fought Aramaeans in Pausa at the foot of the Ṭūr 'Abdīn; at Nabula, north-east of Nisibis, at a place [. . .]tibua on the Tigris, in Lishur-sala-Ashur (Sinamu district), and Murarir, all places north and north-west of Ashur between Erishu of Khabkhi and Harrān.[4] This prepared the way for a thrust further west in the following year to Makrisi, near the junction of the Khabur and Kharmish rivers by the Yari hills.[5] Once more Assyrian arms crossed the Euphrates[6] and pressed beyond into the Khani territory where Gulguli was captured.[7] If this Broken Obelisk is a description of Ashur-bēl-kala's campaigns, then he claimed to have reached the Mediterranean and emulated his father's hunting adventures both on land and sea.[8] It may be that it was in thankfulness for help in averting the Aramaean danger at this time that the king dedicated a statue of a nude female, perhaps of some captured goddess, at Nineveh. His inscription ends with a curse, that the gods of the West Land might smash anyone who should damage it.[9] Part of the obelisk inscription is devoted to the building activities of the king and his numerous works of renovation in Ashur. The great terrace of Ashur-nādin-ahhē, the canal of Ashur-dan which had been waterless for thirty years and the quay-wall erected by Adad-nīrāri all received attention. Finally, the king completed the

---

[1] §v, 6, 75 f.
[2] G, 4, 128 ff.; G, 14, 1, 118 ff.; §ix, 10, 123. See Plate 162(a).
[3] Summarized in §vi, 5, 206, n. 1; 208.
[4] §vi, 5, 211 f.   [5] §vi, 5, 212.
[6] At the conjunction with the Sajur: A, 11, 169.   [7] G, 4, 137.
[8] G, 8, 1, pl. 33a.   [9] G, 4, 152; G, 14, 1, 340.

Apku palace begun by Ashur-rēsha-ishi and a palace-terrace of Tukulti-Ninurta.[1] On his death the king was ceremonially buried in the capital to which he had devoted so much attention and had kept free from invasion.[2] As on the death of his illustrious grandfather, there would seem to have been some confusion at the end of Ashur-bēl-kala's reign. An Aramaean Tukulti-Mer, a king of Khana and Mari, son of Ilu-iqīsha, claims in his inscriptions to be king of Assyria and to have campaigned against the Papkhi.[3] Whether this claimant was active at the death of Tiglath-pileser or Ashur-bēl-kala must remain uncertain, though the latter is more likely. An inscribed stone mace dedicated to Shamash of Sippar might imply that he was an Aramaean leader who moved into Babylonia as did the Sutu towards the end of the life of Ashur-bēl-kala and during the long reign of a fellow Aramaean Adad-apla-iddina.[4]

Another claimant to the Assyrian throne at this time was Erība-Adad II, whose broken inscriptions also imply intense military activity along similar lines to those followed by Tiglath-pileser.[5] He restored the temple of E-khursag-kurkurra[6] and continued the religious traditions.[7] However, another son of Ashur-bēl-kala, Shamshi-Adad IV, came up from Babylon and with the support of the Aramaean usurper there, Adad-apla-iddina, deposed him and held the throne for four years (1054–1051).[8] He claimed the title of 'great king' though nothing is known of his political activities.[9] At Nineveh the Ishtar temple was once more renovated according to building and other dedicatory inscriptions, while at Ashur the gate-tower (*bīt nāmeru*) received similar treatment.[10]

The line of Tiglath-pileser continued to dominate Assyrian affairs in the son of Shamshi-Adad, Ashur-nāṣir-apli (Ashurnaṣirpal I) who ruled for nineteen years according to the King and Eponym Lists.[11] Regrettably, only a brief brick-inscription records the residence of the king in the palace which lay between the south-west front of the zikkurrat and the Anu-Adad temple in Ashur.[12] For him as for his predecessors, royal hymns were

---

[1] §vi, 5, 206. [2] §vi, 4, 177; G, 8, i, Tf. 33.
[3] G, 20, 308 and pl. xviii.
[4] G, 16, ii, 77. [5] G, i, 145. [6] G, 14, i, §344B.
[7] §vi, 8, 323. [8] G, 10, 220. [9] G, i, 145.
[10] G, 4, 150 f.; G, 14, i, §343; §iii, 12, 98 (no. 222); G, 16, ii, 79.
[11] G, 17, 9. If the Ashurnaṣirpal who may have been the murderer of Tukulti-Ninurta is counted as holding the throne (see above, p. 449), then this was the second ruler of Assyria to bear this name. §vi, 15, 21, iv, 4.
[12] G, 8, i, 214; G, 14, i, §345.

composed. One of these implies that he had been born in exile and suffered from some dire disease for which he implored the help and healing of Ishtar of Nineveh.[1] If the historical allusions in these later compositions may be trusted the land had been subject to invasion and the cult overthrown only to be restored by this king who duly gives thanks to his protecting goddess. If a much defaced 'white obelisk' is attributed to this Ashurnaṣirpal, rather than to the later Assyrian ruler of the same name, it would be proof of vigorous and successful military activity on a wide front, aimed to restore the border in the eastern hills. But this ascription has been doubted.[2] The succession of his son, Shalmaneser II, who ruled for twelve years,[3] supports the view that at this time the régime was not only strong enough to withstand outside pressures but was already able to take the first steps to make Assyria once more a dominant power. This is seen more clearly when their descendant Adad-nīrāri II and his successors defeated the Amorites and reopened the traditional trade-routes; but at present all this can only be surmised from the unbroken line of rulers known from the official lists, but of whom few, if any, other records remain. Shalmaneser himself tells of work done on the temple of Anu and the temple of Adad at Ashur.[4] He was followed by Ashur-nīrāri IV (1019–1014),[5] Ashurrabi II (1013–973),[6] Ashur-rēsha-ishi II (972–968)[7] and Tiglath-pileser II (967–935).[8]

Meanwhile in Babylonia the equally long-lived Isin dynasty was coming to an end. In this, according to the King List tradition, eleven kings ruled for a total of 132½ years. This is itself a testimony of stability in an age when no single major power dominated the political scene throughout the Near East. The activities of the last two kings of this line are little attested. Marduk-ahhē-erība, whose name implies that he was not the eldest son, ruled for a year and six months (1046–1045) as a contemporary, according to the Synchronistic Chronicle, of Ashur-bēl-kala of Assyria.[9] His relationship with his predecessor and successor is undefined in the solitary *kudurru*-inscription which simply calls him 'king'. He gave instructions to district governors in the north-eastern province of Bīt-Piri'-Amurri which

---

[1] G, 16, 11, 109; §ix, 7, 107, 358; §vi, 11, 72 ff.
[2] §ix, 10, 243, n. 16. [See now E. Sollberger in *Iraq* 36 (1974), 231 ff. (Ed.)]
[3] G, 14, 1, §346 f.; G, 16, 11, 80 f.   [4] §iii, 1, 23 f. (nr. 14); G, 19, 1, 303.
[5] G, 21, 71; G, 17, 9 (ll. 21); §vi, 15, 21 (iv, 18 ff.).   [6] G, 17, 10, 17.
[7] G, 17, 10 (ll. 25 f.); §iii, 1, 22 (nr. 12); G, 14, 1, §348.   [8] §iii, 1, nr. 11.
[9] G, 18, 273 (Assur 14616c, ii, 22'; cf. King List A, iii, 2').

was thus still under firm Babylonian control.[1] For his successors we have but the evidence of the King Lists; Marduk-zēr-[x] who ruled for twelve years (1044–1033)[2] and was in his turn succeeded for eight years by Nabu-shumu-libur whose name and titles are also found on an inscribed duck-weight.[3]

VII. THE SECOND SEALAND AND BAZI DYNASTIES

The ruling house which followed the Second Dynasty of Isin is designated 'ruling succession of the Sealand' in the King List A. This comprised three chiefs who held the throne of Babylon for 21 years and 5 months.[4] It is common to designate this the Second Sealand Dynasty to distinguish it from the earlier family, sprung from the same Persian Gulf tribes, who under Gulkishar had dominated the whole of Babylonia.[5] The Sealand was the title of an administrative province which had owed a loyal, if loose, allegiance to Babylon for more than a century and a half.[6]

Simbar-Shikhu, founder of the Dynasty reigned for eighteen years (1024–1007).[7] It is unlikely that his name can imply a Kassite renaissance for he was the son of Erība-Sin, a military captain who as 'a man of the ruling-line of Damiq-ilishu' may have claimed remote descent from the First Isin Dynasty.[8] According to Nabu-apla-iddina this predecessor had searched in vain for the reliefs and insignia of the deity among the ruins of E-babbar, the temple of Shamash at Sippar, which had been sacked by the Sutu raiders. This would seem to imply that the temple-furnishings were thought not to have been looted. He tells how Simbar-Shikhu, failing to rediscover the earlier cult-statue, built a new enclosure and re-established regular offerings and ceremonies under a priest Ekur-shuma-ushabshi.[9] He also dedicated a throne for Enlil (Marduk) in E-kur at Nippur.[10] As would be expected he continued to hold the Gulf area and this is shown by an inscription of his twelfth year dated at the town of

---

[1] §IV, 2, 149; §IV, 5, 188 f.
[2] A, 3, 146; G, 21, ii, 23'; G, 18, 273 (King List A, iii, 3').
[3] G, 21, 66 f. (14616c, ii, 24'); cf. G, 18, 272 (King List A, iii, 4'); A, 3, 147.
[4] G, 18, 272 (King List A, iii, 9).   [5] §I, 7, 83, 6; cf. G, 13, II, 22, r. 11.
[6] G, 18, 272 (King List A, iii, 6); G, 13, II, 61, l. 12; §VII, 2, 30.
[7] The reading '18' as opposed to '19' is supported by recent collation of the text (G, 3, 92, n. 12).
[8] G, 13, II, 61 (Religious Chronicle, i, 16'); §VII, 2, 28 f. See now A, 3, 151.
[9] G, 12, 121 f., ll. 1–23.   [10] A, 7, 122; G, 13, II, 61, 13'.

Sakhritu in the marshes when a private transaction for land was witnessed, among others by a tax-collector from Kissik and Ea-mukīn-zēri, son of Belani, a priest from Eridu.[1] Two texts, if rightly assigned to this reign, would give glimpses of far different activities. Ashurnaṣirpal II of Assyria, campaigning against Zamua 250 years later tells how he restored the town of Atlila which had been razed by one 'Sibir, king of Karduniash'. If this should be this Simbar-Shikhu, rather than a ruler of the little-known eighth dynasty, it would seem that he must have continued the strategy of his predecessors to contain the hill tribes to the north-east.[2] The Religious Chronicle records an eclipse of the sun associated with abnormal floods and incursions of wild animals on the twenty-sixth day of Siwan of the seventh year of an unnamed king who ruled at least seventeen years.[3] Calcula-tions point to this reign as a possibility (9 May 1012 B.C.), but absence of other supporting evidence makes it a tentative rather than fixed chronological point in the history.[4] Simbar-Shikhu died by the sword and 'was buried in the Palace of Sargon' which phrase may indicate an honourable funeral at the royal mauso-leum.[5] It was probably the act of an assassin, since his successor Ea-mukīn-zēri is called a usurper from Bīt-Khashmar.[6] He was buried in the swamps of his native country after a brief reign of three or five months.[7] Since his home was probably in the south his identity with the priest of Eridu named six years earlier is not improbable, as is the view that he may have met his death in the suppression of a rising.[8] His tenure of office appears to have been too brief for notice in the Ashur chronicle.

Kashshu-nādin-akhi, son of Sappaia, may have led the oppo-sition to Ea-mukīn-zēri and, since he was given a royal burial after a three-year reign (1006–1004), it may be presumed that he was of the ruling family. This may be supported by the refer-ence to him by Nabu-apla-idinna, over a century later, when describing the varying fortunes of E-babbar of Sippar. 'During the distress and famine under Kashshu-nādin-akhi those regular food-offerings were discontinued and the drink-offerings ceased' until restored by E-ulmash-shākin-shumi, his successor (1003–987).[9]

The new family to direct the fortunes of Babylonia for the next

---

[1] G, 12, 101 f.
[2] G, 4, 325; cf. G, 11, 258, n. 2; A, 3, 154.   [3] G, 13, 1, 213, 11, 70 f.
[4] §VII, 4, 106; G, 11, 237, n. 3; A, 3, 68, n. 345.   [5] G, 2, 187, ii, 5'–6'.
[6] This must differ from the Khash(i)mar located in the north-east of Babylonia (§I, 1, 94). On the name of Ea-mukīn-zēri (not -shumi), see G, 8, 11, 259.
[7] G, 18, 272 (King List A, iii, 7); cf. G, 13, 11, 52 (Dynastic Chronicle).
[8] G, 2, 187, n. 338.   [9] G, 12, 122, i, 24–ii, 17.

twenty years and three months came from Bīt-Bazi, which lay east of the Tigris, perhaps to the north-east in Lullu territory.[1] Members of this family had held high office under Marduk-nādin-ahhē.[2] The days were again marked by civil disturbances, perhaps due to famine and the consequent incursions by the neighbouring tribes from the deserts. With the conflicting statements of the King List A and Dynastic Chronicles which allot a span of seventeen and fifteen years respectively, the reign of E-ulmash-shākin-shumi is shrouded in obscurity. Nevertheless, he claimed to be 'king of the world', which formerly implied wide territorial assertions.[3] The religious devotion marked by his restoration of worship at Sippar seems to be tempered by the cryptic notes of the New Babylonian Chronicle—'within the shrine'—probably an indication of the failure to hold the New Year festival in Babylon in his fifth and fourteenth years.[4] This interruption in the ritual was usually the result of political instability. The king was buried in the palace at Kār-Marduk, which may have been the family seat since his successor, a member of the same tribe, held sway there.[5] Ninurta-kudurri-uṣur ruled for two full years as a contemporary of Ashur-rabi IV of Assyria.[6] He maintained the traditional practices of dedications to the main temples.[7] A later *kudurru*-text recounts a lawsuit in the second year of this king, in which he had awarded seven female slaves to Burusha, a jeweller, as recompense for the murder of one of his own slaves.[8]

Shirikti-Shuqamuna of Bazi 'exercised the kingship for three months', a time confirmed by a later extract Chronicle which, however, described him as brother of Nabu-kudurri-uṣur, probably an error for Ninurta-kudurri-uṣur whom he succeeded.[9] The Ashur Chronicle makes him the last king of the Bazi line and a contemporary of Ashur-rabi II of Assyria (1013–973).[10] The king was given a royal burial. Only brief references tell of his successor Mar-bīti-apla-uṣur. From them it appears that he was descendant of an Elamite family who ruled six years before

[1] For the location see G, 20, 208; cf. G, 2, 191. For the King List see G, 18, 272 (A, iii, 10); G, 13, 55 (Dynastic Chronicle, r. ii, 9 ff.).

[2] G, 12, 44, i, 30; A, 3, 160.

[3] The name is also written Ul-mash-shākin-shumi, see §VII, 1, 29; §II, 3, 160.

[4] G, 13, II, 61 f; A, 3, 611.   [5] G, 12, 58, 23 f.

[6] G, 18, 272 (King List A, iii, 11′), 273 (Synchronistic Chronicle, iii, 6); G, 13, II, 54 (Dynastic Chronicle, r. ii, 10′–11′).

[7] As evidenced by the inscribed arrow heads (G, 3, 93; §II, 2, 160).

[8] G, 12, 57, 1–12.   [9] §VII, 3, 30.

[10] G, 18, 273 (Synchronistic Chronicle, iii, 7).

being 'buried in the Palace of Sargon'. Though there is no evidence that he was also ruler of Elam at this time, it seems an irony of fate that a person of such a race should be in control of the country which for two centuries had striven to maintain its independence of its eastern neighbours. In Nisan of his fourth year some unspecified event occurred which, like that noted for previous kings, may be a mark of the failure to maintain the New Year festival.[1] With his passing the period of uncertainty and of brief reigns, indicative of internal dissensions, gave way to the stable rule of Nabu-mukīn-apli (977–942) who inaugurated the 'eighth' Dynasty at Babylon. Despite continuing pressures from Aramaean raiders the new government in Babylon was strong enough to maintain order among the southern tribes, as had the preceding régimes. This stability in the southern state in turn left Assyria free to rebuild her own forces, to regain her hold over western Asia, and later to attempt to assert control over Babylon itself and her neighbouring sacred cities.

VIII. LAW AND ADMINISTRATION

The few surviving Babylonian administrative documents, mainly *kudurru*-inscriptions, confirm this general picture of the country unified under the king during the twelfth and eleventh centuries. As with the language, religion and customs, so the administrative machinery continued unchanged between the Kassite and Isin régimes. The land was divided into at least twenty small districts or provinces (*pāḫatu*), each with a local government responsible directly to the king in Babylon. The areas were named after the principal city within them (Babylon, Dūr-Kurigalzu, Isin, Nippur) or after hereditary tribal lands (Bīt-Piri'-Amurri, Bīt-Sin-māgir) and the provinces stretched from the Persian Gulf (Sealand) to the Lesser Zab (Namar, Irria and Bīt-Ada). Since the majority lay to the north of Nippur it would seem that the southern marshes were sparsely inhabited as in later times.

The governor (*šaknu*) could be posted at the king's direction and was the normal channel for royal commands reaching his secretary or the lesser officials responsible for law and order, the collection of taxes and control of public works, mainly irrigation.[2] In the remoter regions and on the border with Elam tribal chiefs made nominal acknowledgement of the royal suzerainty and held office as independent governors. The king, the final authority

---

[1] G, 13, 1, 185 f. (New Babylonian Chronicle).
[2] §VIII, 1, 328 lists these functionaries and the older designations now obsolete.

and court of appeal, made frequent grants of land. If crown-land it might be used to reward outstanding service in battle or endow a temple and its officials. Such grants were made by charter or by instruments drawn up locally on the instructions of the king. The land was carefully surveyed and recorded, and, though usually granted in perpetuity, private land could revert to the crown.[1] Land was also owned by individual temples, cities, villages, and tribes as well as by private individuals, and if the king wished to grant such land he had first to purchase it. The king personally heard litigants and ordered investigations into the precedents of each case. From Ur to the Lesser Zab and from Rapiqu in the west to the mountains in the north-east there was stable government broken only by the relatively infrequent incursions of the enemy across the border.[2]

Similarly, economic texts of the eponym year of Sin-Sheya show that in the reign of Ninurta-tukulti-Ashur the Assyrian king controlled affairs through the central government at his royal palace in Ashur. At Nineveh Iqīshanni collected provisions from neighbouring towns (Khalahhi and Isana) and dispatched them to the capital.[3] The *abarakku*-intendant of Amasaki, south of the Ṭūr 'Abdīn, and the town-governors of Nakhur,[4] Arbail and Arrapkha also sent supplies from their predominantly agricultural communities.[5] While there is yet no evidence of the elaborate provincial organization which was the basis of the later Assyrian economy and colonial expansion this now existed in embryo, since Shalmaneser I had incorporated Khanigalbat into Assyrian home territory. Frontier posts were established and the governors on whom fell responsibility for the imposition and collection of taxes and the disposition of prisoners of war were responsible to the king as in the days of Tukulti-Ninurta.

Royal edicts formulated since the time of Ashur-uballiṭ were collected by Tiglath-pileser I and, with regulations for the harim and court at Ashur, show a long tradition found also among the Hittites. The king as overseer of the royal household held authority over his subordinates in written agreements. Tiglath-pileser also continued and copied the legal traditions of the pre-ceding centuries, and it would seem that he was no legal reformer or innovator.[6] A series of laws and legal decisions compiled in his reign show that as the ultimate authority his 'word' was final. The laws which relate in particular to the status, rights and duties of women and land tenure applied to the city of Ashur and its environs and to 'Assyrian' men and women. This compilation, incorporating earlier material, shows marked contrasts with the laws of Hammurabi, which were also copied by the scribes of this period.[1] In addition to the usual form of marriage by which a woman left her father's for her husband's family there was an *erebu*-marriage by which a woman could remain with her own tribe or family to be visited there by her husband.[2] This non-Semitic custom reflects the mixed population and customs in Assyria at this time, as does the levirate type of marriage, known from the Hurrians of Nuzi in the fifteenth century and practised on a more extensive scale in Assyria than among the Hebrews during these same centuries. By this, after the death of her husband or fiancé, a woman would be given in marriage by her father-in-law to another of his sons or family. Other customs, including the right of the first-born to a double share of the inheritance, as evidenced in the west at Alalakh and Mari, still survived, as did the old Babylonian class distinctions of freeman, state-dependent and slave.[3] Semi-free men (*ḫupšu*) were required to engage in the militia and their personal names attest the continued virility of this social group in Assyria as in the west with its Semitic or non-Semitic elements.

In general the laws, like the few surviving administrative texts, imply a period of stable government over a predominantly agricultural community. Penalties, apart from death, trial by river ordeal and physical mutilation already enforced in old Babylonian days, included hard labour for the State and payment of heavy fines. The latter were payable in tin or lead, at this time a more common means of exchange than silver or gold. This emphasizes the importance of the campaigns directed to safeguard the trade-routes to the north.[4] If the stamped roundels bearing an Ishtar-symbol found at Ashur were used for this purpose they would be the forerunners of a more highly advanced form of currency.[5]

Until the reign of Ninurta-tukulti-Ashur the old Assyrian calendar was in general use, but by this time the omission of intercalated months, the lack of reference to month subdivisions or *ḫamuštum*-periods of five or ten days and the commencement of the new eponymy coinciding with the beginning of the month

---

[1] §vIII, 2, 4 f.; G, 20, 319.

[2] [For a contrary view, see now G. Cardascia, *Les Lois assyriennes* (Paris, 1969), 63 ff. (Ed.)]

[3] §vIII, 13, 122.

[4] G, 20, 324 and pl. xiv *d*.

[5] §vIII, 10, 4 f.

Sippu, led to obvious calendric confusion.[1] The Assyrian year, like that of the Babylonians, now began at the spring equinox and their calendars coincided. By the time of Tiglath-pileser I the old month names were already virtually displaced by those of the Babylonian (Nippur) calendar,[2] whether as a conscious innovation by the Assyrians or owing to the gradual insistence of traders and Babylonian-trained scribes is not known.

The Assyrians continued without interruption to date their years by the name and style of leading officials in rotation.[3] In this eponym-system the king gave his name to the first full year of his administration and, if still occupying the throne, again in his thirtieth year (as did Tiglath-pileser II).[4] This may imply, as in Egypt, a periodical renewal of kingship.

In Babylonia also, these centuries are marked by a continuity of legal tradition, despite changes in the ruling houses. No collections of laws or legal decisions have survived,[5] but the few indications of the Middle Babylonian legal procedure seem to imply the same general tradition as revealed by the laws of Hammurabi, as when Nebuchadrezzar I claimed the title of 'upright king who passes just judgments'. Practices and penalties varied with local circumstances though decisions made by one king could be upheld by successors even though they were of a different family.[6]

IX. LITERATURE, RELIGION AND THE ARTS

In literature, as in law, the Assyrians continued older traditional forms. Babylonian influence predominated and there were few innovations. The Kassites had given a new impetus to historical inquiry and literary composition in what has been described as the last great creative period of Babylonian literature. Throughout the fourteenth and thirteenth centuries the Assyrians continued to employ scribes trained in Babylonia.[7] Tukulti-Ninurta I had used the occasion of his sack of Babylon to increase the small number of original texts of the Hammurabi–Kassite period in his possession.[8] These, supplemented by collections of omens, hymns, prayers and lexicographical texts made in the earlier reign of Shalmaneser I, were the basis of the library built up in the Ashur temple at Ashur by Tiglath-pileser I while crown-prince,

---

[1] §1, 13, 28; G, 9, 92, n. 18. [2] §1, 13, 27; §viii, 7, 46.
[3] §v, 9, 283. [4] §viii, 11, 456; *C.A.H.* 1³, pt. 1, p. 199.
[5] The 'seisachtheia' (§ viii, 6) being now dated to the Old Babylonian period. Government by royal edict, however, continued.
[6] G, 12, 29 f. (i, 6'). [7] G, 9, 109. [8] §v, 8, 199.

with accessions during his later successful career.[1] Among the literary works were copies of the tales of Tukulti-Ninurta, the 'Babylonian Job' (*ludlul bēl nēmeqi*), the Etana myth, and other classical epics which had been composed under the Kassites or their contemporaries. This literary activity may have been occasioned by some desire to preserve the different traditions at other temple-schools which were now dominated by Babylon itself. The 'authors' were royal scribes, some of whom claimed descent from the learned Arad-Ea who flourished at Babylon in the fourteenth century or earlier.[2] The 'Babylonian Theodicy', in which a sufferer and his friend discuss current oppression is a document of social interest. It may reflect a conflict of political and religious ideologies caused by the times of economic stress resulting from the Aramaean incursions. There is evidence that this text, in its present form, was composed by Saggil-kinam-ubbib, a scholar of Babylon contemporary with the Aramaean usurper Adad-apla-iddina.[3] Since few literary works of this period have survived, the tendency is to hail them, being of high merit, as a literary revival. Certainly the account of Nebuchadrezzar I's victories over Elam and the highly poetic descriptions in his royal inscriptions and *kudurru* are noteworthy.[4] Although not strictly in the same genre as the royal hymns of the Third Ur and First Babylonian dynasties, the recrudescence of hymnography in the time of Nebuchadrezzar I,[5] Ashur-bēl-kala and Ashurnaṣirpal I may similarly have served to clarify separate traditions at Babylon and Ashur.[6]

The political and geographical history underlines the fact that Assyria more than Babylonia was the meeting-place of various traditions. How far the literature, as art, was given a new life by intercourse with the Hittites is hard to judge. Assyrian epigraphy shows that the large and distinctive square hand of the north and west is now refining under Babylonian influence. From at least the reign of Arik-dēn-ili the accumulation of personal details was the first step to prose writing in historical annals.[7] In the military and hunting narratives this development was taken further by Tiglath-pileser I, who was in this respect closely followed by Ashur-bēl-kala.[8] This style has often been attributed to the Hittites, but is as likely to be Babylonian, since the Chronicles presuppose the existence of detailed and continuous

---

[1] §v, 8, 197.　　　　　　　　[2] §ix, 14, 2, 9 f., 112.
[3] §ix, 16, 14, 1; §ix, 15, 71; A, 3, 141: (Esagil-kini-ubba).
[4] E.g. G, 12, no. 6.　　[5] §ix, 7, nos. 107, 358.　　[6] §ix, 12, 113.
[7] G, 20, 335.　　　　　　　　[8] G, 1, 125; §viii, 8, 169 f.

historical records. The Assyrian royal inscriptions would seem to have preserved for us the style of the Babylonian court and scribal schools.[1] This too may mean that the Assyrian court relied upon Babylonian scribes or Assyrian scribes who wrote in a local dialect of Middle Babylonian.

As with literature new religious, as distinct from traditional, trends are hard to judge in the absence of dated religious texts from this period. The onomastic material in the Middle Assyrian contracts may reflect the rise and fall of different members of the pantheon in the northern kingdom. This shows a growing cosmopolitanism accompanying the renewed expansion of the Assyrian Empire. While Ashur as supreme national god supplants the Babylonian Marduk in the local version of the Epic of Creation, Adad as the god of conquest with universal affiliations (like the Hurrian Teshub) appears side by side with him in the twelfth-century texts.[2] Hurrian influences became more pronounced in the thirteenth–twelfth centuries than in the preceding period and Hurrian names are held by persons in all walks of life. Babylonian influence too may be seen in that names compounded with the moon-god Sin are more popular than those with the sun-deity Shamash.[3] This may reflect Babylonian religious and magical ceremonies which were practised in the north without interruption despite hostilities.[4] The New Year festival honouring Marduk at Ashur was no slavish copy of its Babylonian counterpart but an adaptation to local feeling.[5]

In Babylonia, following the Kassites who had accepted the local Babylonian language, religion and customs, Kassite local deities, as Erriya and Shuqamuna and Shimaliya—the creator gods— and Tishpak of Dēr were invoked alongside native Mesopotamian deities. There is some evidence of a gradual change to a monotheistic tendency with the rise to national supremacy of a local southern deity, Marduk. Adad-shuma-uṣur nominated Marduk to second place after Anu and Enlil from a position among the lower group of deities in the official pantheon. Marduk-apla-idinna I, who rebuilt E-zida in Borsippa, was followed by at least six kings who bore this divine name. This shows that even before the unusual popularity accorded to Marduk after his restoration by Nebuchadrezzar I to E-sagila in Babylon from captivity in Elam he had been an influential god.[6] It is in the official documents of Nebuchadrezzar I that Marduk's kingship over the gods and exaltation over Enlil, reflected in the editions of the

[1] §VIII, 9, 159.   [2] G, 9, 103.   [3] G, 9, 105.
[4] §IX, 8, vol. 20, 399 ff.   [5] §IX, 13, 192.   [6] §IX, 17, 8, 10.

literary epics composed in these centuries, are clearest seen.[1] It is, however, likely that a tendency to view gods as remote from men had been present for some time, for at the end of the Old Babylonian period cylinder seals sometimes omit any representation of the deity, as does the altar of Tukulti-Ninurta I. In Middle Assyrian art gods, when rarely represented, are set on a pedestal or, as Ashur, partly invisible in the clouds of his heavenly winged-disk. A distinction was made between the deity himself and his statue. Art and literature combine to emphasize the numinous in religion, and symbols have again particular importance and attraction especially in their protective value, enhancing the traditional curses against anyone who should violate the agreements recorded on the *kudurru*-stones.[2]

The architecture of these centuries also illustrates the new religious tendency. In the temples the gods were set on high niches or platforms approached by steps from a long cella entered from the side, emphasizing their remoteness from human affairs. Tiglath-pileser I restored both the Old Palace and a New Palace, founded by Tukulti-Ninurta I who used the material and human booty of his numerous campaigns, the triumphs of which were thus permanently enshrined. In the doorways representations of victories in the hunting of unusual creatures as well as of bull-colossi show the development of an early Babylonian trend which was to become more common in the Neo-Assyrian palaces. The mainly decorative murals from the palace of Kār-Tukulti-Ninurta—scenes of the hunt and of war in mountainous terrain, the small reliefs of the 'Broken Obelisk', depicting the king and his vanquished foes, like those on the earlier altar of Tukulti-Ninurta I—these already show a distinctive Assyrian style.[3] This was, in part, a development from earlier Hurrian *motifs*, perhaps inspired by renewed contacts with these northern peoples and their descendants. Since their art-forms are often akin to those of the more easterly Kassites it is difficult to attribute the sources of influence with any certainty. This also applies to the locally adapted technique of lead-glazed pottery, glazing, painted and glazed bricks used for façades at this time. This may be of Hurrian origin[4] but, like the contemporary Kassite examples in Babylonia which were imitated during these centuries, both may be but local offshoots from a single and earlier development.

In sculpture the fine modelling of the figures on the Tukulti-

---

[1] §ix, 16, 4 f.; §ix, 17, 6.   [2] G, 12, viii.   [3] See Plates 155, 162(*a*).
[4] Less likely Egyptian or Cypriote (G, 20, 332).

Ninurta socket as on the better examples of the Babylonian *kudurrus* would point to no diminution in skill following the renaissance of art, as of literature and architecture, which began with that Assyrian king.[1] The rare examples of the glyptic art on dated documents of the period show, however, that Assyria continued to be the home of mixed traditions. The formally presented bearded figures between borders and long dedicatory inscriptions were common in Babylonia in Kassite times. Other seals continued the thirteenth-century styles of contest scenes, mostly of single combat, originally derived from Mitannian glyptic. Babylonian influences can be seen in the full-faced sphinxes and heroes holding lions.[2] By this time figures were carefully modelled with that emphasis on the muscles which was to remain an abiding feature of Assyrian art.[3] The incidental elements, as for example the trees, are transformed into landscapes giving the effect of relief—a realistic tendency found in the contemporary art of Egypt and the Aegean. In the twelfth century the remnant of the earlier Akkadian and Kassite styles gradually gave way to larger seals on which the taller figures and heavier modelling led to the omission of detail and loss of the landscape effect.[4]

The favourite scenes of the period are those of animal life or of the hunt as on the seal of Ninurta-tukulti-Ashur.[5] This may reflect renewed interest in the royal ritual and hunt and, since they are set in mountainous country which was the scene of the major campaigns, in the national fortunes. Court scenes also reappear as do other examples of earlier styles, the Early Dynastic 'textile friezes',[6] Mitannian stylized trees and eagle-headed men fighting bulls or centaurs.[7] Alongside the modelled style shallow, yet precisely, cut seals were in use. Few seals can be definitely assigned to Babylonia in these two centuries, but the dated *kudurru* show unmistakably that in the southern kingdom the arts must have flourished as vigorously as among their northern neighbours. If this long period is still little known, there is sufficient evidence extant to show that, despite occasional internal dissension or pressure from outside, the natural vigour of the inhabitants of Assyria and Babylonia was unabated. Politically, economically and culturally the way was already being prepared for that expansion of territory and influence which was to mark the high point of Assyrian civilization in the following three centuries.

---

[1] See Plate 155 (*c*).
[2] §ix, 18, 50 ff.; §ix, 19, 23 f.
[3] G, 20, 330, pl. xxxi.
[4] §ix, 22, 67. See Plate 156 (*a*)–(*c*).
[5] §ix, 21, 49. See Plate 156 (*d*).
[6] §ix, 9, 191.
[7] §ix, 19, 25.

CHAPTER XXXII

ELAM AND WESTERN PERSIA,
c. 1200–1000 B.C.

I. SHUTRUK-NAHHUNTE AND
KUTIR-NAHHUNTE

WITH the disappearance of Kidin-Khutran the internal history
of Elam seems to have witnessed several political disturbances.
The later native sources mention, after him, a certain Khallutush-
In-Shushinak not as the successor of Kidin-Khutran but as the
father of the king Shutruk-Nahhunte. As no reference is made to
any parental ties between this Khallutush-In-Shushinak and one
of the sovereigns of the preceding dynasty, nor to his own reign,
there is no reason to suppose that he belongs to the royal line or
that he ever held power. We are therefore obliged to admit a break
in the dynastic line between Kidin-Khutran and Shutruk-Nahhunte. This break can be explained only by supposing that a new
line of princes took control, aided by internal troubles of the times.
Whence came this family? This cannot be decided from the texts.
The only hint we have is onomastic. Whereas the names of
sovereigns of the previous dynasty were particularly devoted to
Khumban and Khutran, the name of Khallutush-In-Shushinak
and those of at least two of his successors were placed under the
patronage of the god of Susa. One can suppose that this choice of
In-Shushinak as patron god perhaps indicates that this new royal
house was somehow linked with Susiana.

However this may be, one thing is certain—with the reign of
Shutruk-Nahhunte begins one of the most glorious periods in
Elamite history. During a space of almost seventy years five
kings succeed to the throne: Shutruk-Nahhunte, Kutir-Nahhunte,
Shilkhak-In-Shushinak, Khutelutush-In-Shushinak and Silkhina-
khamru-Lakamar; the first three of these at least were destined
to win fame. Their personal qualities were to make Elam
one of the greatest military powers in the Middle East for a
period lasting over fifty years. This Elamite renaissance was
aided by a fortunate juncture of international conditions.

With the tragic death of Tukulti-Ninurta I (1208) came a

* An original version of this chapter was published as fascicle 23 in 1964.

sudden decline in Assyrian military power, and the country was torn by internal troubles. For several years two kings, each supported by his own faction, struggled for mastery. These struggles continued after them, and were exploited by the Babylonians, whose king Adad-shuma-uṣur (1218–1189) laid siege to Ashur and fought against the Assyrian king Enlil-kudurri-uṣur (1197–1193). During these hostilities another Assyrian prince Ninurta-apil-Ekur (1192–1180), until that time an exile in Babylon, seized the Assyrian throne[1] and reigned with the support of the Babylonian king, who had made Assyria into a kind of protectorate. The Assyrians at that time had not—nor had the Babylonians—leisure to take any interest in Elam. The western frontier of Assyria was threatened by the Mushki, and the Aramaean danger in Upper Mesopotamia was becoming more and more pressing.

It was not until 1160 that the new king of Assyria, Ashur-dan I, thought that Assyria was strong enough to take up an aggressive foreign policy again. He threw off Babylonian domination by a raid on Babylonia which was not revenged by its king Zababa-shuma-iddina. But the Assyrian had counted too much upon his strength, for he was unable to push back the Mushki who had crossed the frontiers and installed themselves on the upper Tigris. The weakness of Babylonia and Assyria was thus revealed. Elam under the leadership of capable and energetic kings could take advantage of this situation, first to establish their new strength, and then to wait for a favourable time when they could intervene decisively in Mesopotamia.

Our sources from Mesopotamia at this period are a fragmentary chronicle, a detail from a letter and a few other texts which must be used with caution. These do, however, give us several important synchronisms. We know hereby that Shutruk-Nahhunte was the contemporary of the Babylonian kings Zababa-shuma-iddina (1160) and Enlil-nādin-akhi (1159–1157) as well as the Assyrian king Ashur-dan I (1179–1134). They also inform us that the last years of Khutelutush-In-Shushinak coincide with the beginning of the reign of Nebuchadrezzar I (1124–1103).

The native sources from Elam are more numerous and more varied in nature than those of earlier periods. To the foundation bricks can be added not only the inscriptions engraved on numerous war trophies that the Elamite conquerors brought back to Susa, but the detailed inscriptions engraved on stelae, which enumerate their peaceful operations as well as lists of foreign

[1] §1, 7, 131.

countries and cities which they conquered It is unfortunate that our knowledge of the Elamite language, still very imperfect, does not allow us fully to understand these texts.

For the few years preceding the reign of Shutruk-Nahhunte we know practically nothing about the happenings in Elam, but can suppose that the Elamites were not satisfied with being simple spectators of a drama preluded by the violent death of Tukulti-Ninurta I. It is not possible to say whether the Elamites instigated or had anything to do with the plot that Ashur-nādin-apli, with part of the Assyrian nobility, laid against his father, depriving him first of liberty and then of life.

However this may be, the Babylonians, when Shutruk-Nah-hunte ascended the throne, were looking for means of profiting from the state of affairs in Assyria and were not, therefore, much interested in Elam. It was during this calm period that he established his authority and made Susa the recognized capital of the new empire. Probably with this in mind he brought to Susa various stelae left in different parts of the kingdom by his predecessors, and solemnly dedicated them to his god In-Shushinak. One of the stelae, the work of Untash-(d)GÁL, probably came from Chogha-Zanbil.[1] Another, which came from Anzan where it had been set up by a king whose name he admits not to have known, had its itinerary minutely described in another inscription. The following stages in the journey are mentioned: perhaps the districts (?) of Kutkin and Nakhutir, and certainly the cities Dūr-Untash, on the river Khitkhite, and Tikni.[2] Another document of special importance mentions a third stele which was brought from Aia.[3] The collecting of these, until then dispersed, monuments of Elamite history seems to show the centralist tendencies of Shutruk-Nahhunte and his desire to make the city of In-Shushinak the political and religious centre of the kingdom. Despite this he had temples built in all the principal cities of the kingdom.

He constantly excited, in all respects, Elamite nationalism by pointing out the unity of the empire as well as its lasting tradition. It was undoubtedly this desire that caused him, when he restored the temple of the goddess Manzat, to collect and place next to his own the foundation-bricks of his predecessors who had already done work on this sanctuary.[4] Parallel to this, in the political sphere, he carried on his work of unification and pacification. He imposed his authority even in the far-removed parts of

[1] G, 8, 52, no. 21.   [2] G, 8, 52, no. 20.
[3] G, 8, 54, no. 28.   [4] G, 1, no. 42; G, 8, 86, no. 63; §1, 2.

the kingdom; he was able to subjugate the semi-nomads and obliged them to give back any booty they had taken. And he was no doubt justified in claiming to have been present and active in places where formerly Siwe-palar-khuppak, Pala-ishshan, Pakhir-ishshan and Attar-kittakh had left their marks, as well as in remote districts which none of his predecessors had known, and where his own name had not till then penetrated—such as Shali, Mimurasi, Lappuni, and others.[1]

Towards the south along the Persian Gulf his empire extended into the southernmost parts of Elam. At Liyan, on the island of Bushire,[2] one of his inscribed bricks has been found. In this inscription he boasts of having restored an ancient sanctuary dedicated to the goddess Kiririsha.[3] Susa, as would be expected, had a large share in his religious works. Besides the temple of Manzat he restored a temple dedicated to In-Shushinak which he decorated with baked bricks and possibly a hypostyle room. He offered stone basins for the cult of Sukhsipa as well as In-Shushinak.[4]

Having restored and consolidated the might of Elam, Shutruk-Nahhunte was ready to play an important part on the international scene. He had not to wait long. In Babylon Zababa-shuma-iddina (1160) had succeeded Marduk-apla-iddina on the throne. The new king was a weakling, incapable of maintaining Babylonian domination in Assyria. The Assyrian king, Ashur-dan I, had taken—as we have seen—Zaban, on the Lesser Zab, Irria and Ugarsallu from the Babylonians in 1160. This ineffectual victory which showed the weakness of both sides could only encourage the Elamite. He was all the more tempted because the lower Zab and the Diyālā represented a crucial zone for Elam itself. North and south of the Diyālā pass two important caravan roads which link the Mesopotamian plain to the Iranian plateau.

At the head of a large army Shutruk-Nahhunte and his son Kutir-Nahhunte invaded Mesopotamia. Several stelae, unfortunately in bad condition, record in Elamite the extent and the success of this campaign, as well as details about the tribute extracted from the conquered cities. A fragment of a stele[5] states that after having crossed the Kārūn river (the ancient Ulai) and stopped at Eli he captured many settlements, 700 before arriving at Mara, which is perhaps to be identified with Marriti,[6] and several hundreds more on the other side of Mara. Another fragment[7] gives a list of tributes which several large captured cities were

---

[1] G, 8, 54 f., no. 28; G, 2, 106, n. 26; G, 9, 332b.　　[2] See above, p. 405, n. 1.
[3] G, 8, 51, no. 19.　　　　[4] §1, 5.　　　　[5] G, 8, 56, no. 28a.
[6] G, 16, 393.　　　　　　　　　　　[7] G, 8, 88, no. 67.

obliged to pay to the conqueror. It speaks of great sums paid in *minas* or talents of gold and silver, as well as deliveries of bricks and stone. The following places are mentioned: Eshnunna, Dūr-Kurigalzu, Sippar, Dūr-Shar[....], Opis and perhaps Agade, the name of which is partly broken.

To this evidence we can add other information derived from inscriptions upon spoils of war.[1] Shutruk-Nahhunte removed from Eshnunna two royal statues, one of which represented Manishtusu. From Sippar he took the fine sandstone stele celebrating Naram-Sin's victory over the Lullubi, and perhaps together with it the famous monument inscribed with the laws of Hammurabi. From the country called Karindash, probably the present Karind on the caravan-road from Baghdad to Kirmān-shāh, came a statue of the Kassite king Meli-Shikhu (1188–1174).[2] From another place, the name of which is lost—perhaps Kish—he took the obelisk of Manishtusu, and from Agade two statues of the same king.

Although the above information is probably incomplete it gives a fairly good picture of the zone in which Shutruk-Nah-hunte operated. The mention of Karindash, Eshnunna, Dūr-Kurigalzu, Opis and Dūr-Sharrukīn is very significant as they show that his attention was above all directed towards the lower Diyālā and the passes that commanded the area. He separated Babylonia from the north by cutting across the isthmus between the Tigris and the Euphrates near Sippar. After descending on Kish he had only to bring his campaign to a logical conclusion by the capturing of Babylon. He apparently did not encounter any important resistance despite his destructive progress. Even at Babylon he had no difficulty in bringing the one-year reign of Zababa-shuma-iddina (1160) to an abrupt end.

The collapse of Babylon now seemed irremediable, for Shu-truk-Nahhunte, unlike his predecessors, was not content with booty and prisoners, but decided to establish his authority in the country. To this end he set up his son Kutir-Nahhunte as gover-nor of the province he had conquered in Mesopotamia, and then went back to Susa where he dedicated the booty to his god In-Shushinak. It is probable that he died shortly afterwards, as he did not have time to complete all of the dedications that were to be inscribed on the various captured trophies. A vacant space hammered out on the stele of the Hammurabi laws still awaits the victor's inscription.

---

[1] G, 8, 52 f., nos. 22–7.
[2] On the reading of the name, see above, p. 444, n. 9.

Despite his successes Shutruk-Nahhunte left his work in Babylonia unfinished. National resistance, which Zababa-shuma-iddina had failed to head, soon took shape under a Kassite leader named Enlil-nādin-akhi, afterwards entitled 'king of Babylon' by the chroniclers who refused to recognize the Elamite usurper. It took Kutir-Nahhunte three years to overcome this opponent, and the struggle was so violent that it lived long in the memory of the vanquished. A later Babylonian ruler was thus to sum up the misdeeds of the intruder: 'His crimes were greater and his grievous sins worse than all his fathers had committed...like a deluge he laid low all the peoples of Akkad, and cast in ruins Babylon and all the noblest cities of sanctity.'[1]

This resistance lasted only for three years, at which time Kutir-Nahhunte captured Enlil-nādin-akhi and exiled him to Elam[2] where he probably died. The Kassite dynasty which had ruled for so many years came to an end with the death of Enlil-nādin-akhi. Babylonia became the vassal of Elam. After having deported[3] much of the population the Elamite imposed upon the country a governor who was not of native stock and detested the local gods.[4]

Marduk[5] and Nanā of Uruk, who were also victims of this defeat, were themselves deported to Susa. Marduk stayed in Elam only until the reign of Nebuchadrezzar I (1124–1103), but Nanā had to wait the victorious armies of Ashurbanipal.

When Shutruk-Nahhunte died, Kutir-Nahhunte succeeded him. It is possible that he exercised some part of the power with his father. We know that before succeeding to the throne he was responsible for the installation of decorative panels in the temple of In-Shushinak.[6] These panels,[7] forming a dado with recurring pattern, represent a monstrous figure, half-man half-bull, standing beside a stylized palm-tree, and the narrow outline of a woman with a thin triangular face; the scene is topped by a frieze. The general aspect of this[8] is reminiscent of the wall of the temple of Inanna at Uruk which was built during the fifteenth century by the Kassite king Karaindash.[9]

As king, Kutir-Nahhunte continued the decoration of his capital. One of his main occupations was the temple of In-

[1] §1, 7, 137 (K. 2660), obv. 4 ff.   [2] *Ibid.* obv. 12 f.
[3] *Ibid.* obv. 8.   [4] *Ibid.* obv. 14.
[5] *Ibid.* obv. 10.   [6] G, 8, 57, no. 29.
[7] This type of panel is known from other sites; see §1, 3, 123 ff.
[8] The difficult art of moulding these panels was possibly brought into Elam by Babylonian prisoners. The glazed bricks of Darius at Susa are in the same tradition.
[9] §1, 1, plates 15–17.

Shushinak wherein he had a statue of himself placed. These works were not finished during his reign and it was his successor who was to complete them. He did have time to restore a chapel dedicated to the goddess Lakamar at Susa, and a chapel dedicated to Kiririsha by Khumban-numena was restored at Liyan. The inscription relating the restoration asks the goddess to bless his life as well as that of his wife, Nahhunte-Utu, and his descendants.[1] When he died, c. 1140, he left a strong state with borders extending to Bandar-Bushire in the south and into the Mesopotamian plain on the west. But not all of Babylonia was his vassal, for to the south there were still some independent zones. At Isin a local chief was called king of Babylon and it was around him that the resistance to the Elamite invader formed.

II. SHILKHAK-IN-SHUSHINAK

Shilkhak-In-Shushinak followed his brother Kutir-Nahhunte on the throne, and this reign was to be one of the most glorious periods in the history of Elam. His military expeditions to the north-west which went far beyond any of those of his predecessors, collected large quantities of booty. This flow of material and prisoners brought much wealth to Elam. With this Shilkhak-In-Shushinak was to begin a period of construction in Susa and the other cities of the country which surpassed anything done until that time. Local art was encouraged and flourished to a remarkable degree.

His authority was unquestioned and extended over the whole country. The desire to make himself the symbol of Elamite power and unity was more marked in him than any of the other kings. Although he was a fervent devotee of his personal god, In-Shushinak, he always invoked the gods of Susa, Anzan and Elam, as well as the unnamed hundreds of local protector-gods, with the same piety. He wanted his reign to be the culmination of Elamite history and himself to be the legitimate inheritor and continuer of all the dynasties, whether of Simash, Susa, Elam or Anzan. Whenever he restored a sanctuary he was very careful to add to his dedications the names of his predecessors who had restored the sanctuary before adding his own. The historical importance of these 'genealogical' inscriptions is evident.

It was above all in respect of his brother and immediate predecessor, Kutir-Nahhunte, that Shilkhak-In-Shushinak carried out his ideas on the continuation of Elamite tradition and royalty. He married his brother's widow, Nahhunte-Utu, to whom he ever

[1] G, 8, 57, nos. 29–31.

paid respect. With each of his pious works he asked the gods to bless her, and she, their children, and her children from her former marriage, were united in his prayers. He carried on the work started by his brother on the temple of In-Shushinak, and after finishing the temple he replaced in it the statue of his brother to which he added a special inscription.[1]

It is difficult to say whether his peaceful works or his victorious campaigns brought him the more renown, for he was both a great builder and a warrior. Thanks to several stelae inscribed in Elamite we know that there were many military campaigns during his reign; one inscription relates at least eight of these.[2] Although in bad condition, this is very important, for it lists the different cities and villages taken by Shilkhak-In-Shushinak and the different districts that he invaded. In the mutilated text only about a hundred of these names are left but in its original state the list must have contained nearly twice as many.

His first four campaigns must have been in a Semitic district to judge by the names of the villages captured. These are of the type *Sha-barbarē*, '(place) of the wolves', or *Bīt-nappaḫḫē*, 'house of the blacksmiths'. The only township which can perhaps be located is Bīt-Nakiru, which is possibly derived from the name of the tribe Nakri against which Tiglath-pileser III of Assyria later campaigned.

The next part of the text is in good condition. This campaign took him into the district of Ukarsilla-Epekh, probably made up of Ugarsallu, which Ashur-dan had just taken from his Babylonian rival, and the region around the mountain Ebekh, modern Jebel Hamrīn, which is not far from the point where the upper Diyālā is joined by its higher tributaries. Shilkhak-In-Shushinak captured thirty-one localities in this district, of which only the following names remain: Bīt-lassi, Bīt-Sin-shemi, Bīt-Etelli, Matka, Sha-khalla, Appi-sini-piti, Sha-arad-ekalli and Kiprat. A few villages cited before this paragraph possibly belong to the same district; they are, to list a few: Sellam, Tunni, Matku, Bīt-Sin-eriba and Bīt-Kadashman. These names are mostly Semitic with a few Kassite components.

The next campaign took Shilkhak-In-Shushinak further to the north-west. The name of the district is partially broken and only ...*tilla* is left. The Hurrian aspect of this suffix should be enough in itself to locate the district, but the mention of Arrapkha and Nuzu removes any doubt about where it is—the area around modern Kirkuk. Some of the other names are also known from

---

[1] G, 8, 63, no. 43.   [2] G, 8, 74, no. 54.

other texts: Khanbati, Sha-nishē, Titurru-sha-. . . ('Bridge of . . .'). As he took only eleven localities one may suppose that he did not want to spend too much time in an area so far removed from his home bases.

Next came an expedition on a larger scale, directed against four districts: Durun (Turnat), Ebekh, Shatrak-. . . and Yalman (Ḥulwan). He captured forty-one places the names of which are in part Kassite (Sha-purna-mashkhum) and in part Semitic (Bīt-Ishtar, Bīt-redūti—('small' and 'large'). Certain of the names indicate a cult of Babylonian deities (Bīt-Ishtar, Ishertu-sha-Adad, Bīt-rigim-Adad, . . .ten-Sin). The name Reshu which is mentioned in this list is perhaps to be identified with the Aramaic tribe Rashi in the district of the Upper Karkhah which is mentioned later in a text of Sargon II.[1]

His following campaign was also very extended and traversed at least five districts. The names of these are completely lost except Yalman (Ḥulwan), which shows that the Elamite army went once again over a road it had already travelled. Some fifty townships were captured by the Elamites, and certain of these, known from other texts, allow us to trace various stages of this campaign: Murattash, which is located south of the Lesser Zab and between the mountains Asaniu and Atuma: also Tukhupuna, which is to the south of the river Turnat (Diyālā) and the mountains of Yalman. This area seems to have been inhabited by a rather mixed population, but its civilization was markedly Semitic. Many names of place begin with the Semitic *ša* 'of' or *bīt* 'house (of)', and the second element may indicate settlements purely Babylonian, such as Sha-Balikhu, Bīt-Sin-ishmanni, Bīt-barbarē, Bīt-khuppani, Bīt-Lakipu, or communities probably Kassite such as Bīt-Nashumalia, Bīt-Milshikhu, Bīt-tasak-*EŠŠANA*,[2] Bīt-Burra-khutta. Here and there, besides these, are grouped heterogeneous colonies in localities such as Nakhish-bararu, Sha-kattar-zakh, Anakhuttash, etc. Near the end of the list mention is made of Bīt-rigim-Adad, which had been captured during a previous campaign.

The name of the country next invaded cannot be determined but the village-names are clearly Semitic. All that remains of the district itself is . . .-*uk*? -*li*? -*lir-kattar*. The last element of this name might recall the middle element of the name Sha-kattar-zakh

---

[1] If this identification is correct it is important for the history of the Aramaeans.

[2] The last element is the logogram 'king'; in what language should it be read? For the comparison of this name with *Bīt-Tassaki* of the annals of Tiglath-pileser III, see G, 5, 52 *b*.

in the previous list. The Elamites captured more than twenty places of which the following can be read with certainty: Bīt-nankari Tan-silam, Bīt-kunsu-pati, Pukhutu, Nakapu and Bīt-rapiku.

The following campaign also took place in a district which cannot be located as all that remains of the names is *Shi-*.... None of the twenty-six villages captured is known from other sources. Only a few of the names can be read with certainty: Kitan-Kharap, Bīt-[. . .]-kimil-Adad. Some of the others begin with *Bīt-* and one with *Nār-*, 'river'.

With the remains of a last list, where only *Kulāna* and a few others beginning with *Bīt-* can be read, end the victorious campaigns of Shilkhak-In-Shushinak beyond his borders, according to this account. These, however, were not his only campaigns, for new fragments of stelae mention others, in one of which the district of Khalman-Niri[puni?] was captured. This conquest was followed by another campaign during which the Elamites took fourteen localities, in a country the name of which is lost. Two other campaigns can also be discerned; one was in a region which included the district of Niripuni-Shurutukha and the other mentions the capture of the villages Makshia, Shakutu, Assie, Shakilka, Kishshimu and Talzana.[1]

Even a simple list of these geographical names is enough to show the intense military activity of Shilkhak-In-Shushinak. Guided by the localities that can be located we are able to see the strategy behind the king's military campaigns. He evidently wished to control the country between the Tigris and the Zagros which touched his northern borders. His capture of the upper Diyālā, the area around the Jebel Ḥamrīn and around Ḥulwan shows very clearly that he wished to control the route along which Elam could be invaded from the west. It is on this line that the modern Sharābān, Khānaqīn, Ḥulwan, Karind and Kirmānshāh are located.

After having neutralized the Aramaean tribes along the western bank of the Tigris he penetrated even further north. Here he followed another route which ran northward through the high country from Kifri by Kirkuk and Altın-Köprü towards Irbil. It is possible that one of the expeditions was designed to gain control of the Kirkuk area which was a sort of turn-table. Of the different routes that go out from this point the most important is the one leading into the heart of Assyria; but from a strategic point of view that leading through the mountains towards modern

[1] G, 8, 78 f., nos. 54*a* and *b*.

Sulaimaniyyah was even more important. The fact that he should push on as far as the lower Zab shows his desire to bring pressure to bear on Assyria; from this vantage-point the capital Ashur would be only a few days march away. We do not know whether or not the Elamites actually threatened Ashur, but the fact that a revolt, followed by troubles, brought to an end the long reign of Ashur-dan I (1134) seems to suggest that the presence of the Elamites near by was of some consequence in these events.

The one thing certain is that the region of the upper Diyālā was the centre of Elamite attention. It is therefore surprising to find that on another stele there seems to be mention of an expedition directed towards Babylonia.[1] It seemed that Babylonia had been crushed or at least neutralized by Shutruk-Nahhunte and Kutir-Nahhunte and that it was precisely this condition which allowed Shilkhak-In-Shushinak to concentrate his efforts on lands in which Assyria might have been his rival. This seems to show that in a few years there had occurred a noticeable change in Babylonia. Preoccupied with assuring his hold on the region between the Tigris and the Zagros, Shilkhak-In-Shushinak inevitably lost control of the Euphrates. As we have seen, the campaigns of Shutruk-Nahhunte and Kutir-Nahhunte succeeded in controlling only Agade and its immediate surroundings, not lower Mesopotamia. At Isin a new state came into being. This must have grown rapidly in power, for it was strong enough to interfere in Assyria[2] on behalf of one of the sons of Ashur-dan I when the latter died. One can imagine that this attempt to profit, without striking a blow, from the victories of the Elamites was not favourably received by Shilkhak-In-Shushinak, and that the campaign related on this stele was perhaps a reprisal against the Babylonians for their interference in Assyria.

He therefore crossed the Tigris and crushed the first Babylonian resistance on the other bank. Then after capturing the town of Khussi he swept on to the Euphrates, and marched up the river until he reached Nimitti-Marduk, which was perhaps one of the walled fortifications that protected the southern approaches to Babylon. Despite his boast of having once again defeated the enemy, he probably did not capture the city, as it is not mentioned again in the text. His return to Elam brings to an end all Elamite pretensions in Babylonia.

He was now faced by new, although less important, problems on his own borders. The Zagros was inhabited by tribes of warlike plunderers whose raids had to be chastised from time to time.

[1] G, 8, 79, no. 54c.   [2] §II, 7.

Thus the tribe of Palakhutep had raided Elamite territory and carried off booty and prisoners. This tribe is later joined with the tribe Lallarippe in an inscription of the neo-Elamite king Temti-Khuban-In-Shushinak. If the name Lallarippe is derived from the name of the river Lallar, their homeland should be looked for somewhere in the country of Zamua, and that of the Palakhutep was perhaps in the same general area. Shilkhak-In-Shushinak immediately set out in pursuit of them. After having passed via Eli and Susa(?) he cut across Anzan and camped at Ulan and Sha-purna-mashkum. A break in the text does not allow us to follow the rest of the expedition but we know that the booty which the tribe had taken was brought back to Susa and dedicated to the god In-Shushinak.[1]

These expeditions, as well as others mentioned in fragments, come to a large number. The reign of Shilkhak-In-Shushinak must have been long if one considers that the number of campaigns conducted was at least twelve. It is however possible that not all of these were separate, some being perhaps only episodes in wider campaigns. One of the texts mentions the capture of Sha-purna-mashkum, which occurs again in the raid against the tribe Palakhutep. This could also be the case in the campaign where Bīt-rapiqu and *KUN*-Subbati were captured. If we allow that the former is identical with the Rapiqu mentioned in Assyrian texts as being just to the north of Babylon, and the latter as meaning the *KUN* of the Euphrates, then we could suppose that this text actually refers to the campaign against Babylonia.

Because of all of these campaigns, and despite the recession of Elamite power in Babylonia, Shilkhak-In-Shushinak merited the ancient title 'enlarger of the empire' of which he boasted in his inscriptions. His kingdom, which was well protected along the borders of the Zagros and in the north-west, extended beyond Anzan and Susiana to the eastern shores of the Persian Gulf. The important works undertaken by the king on the island of Bushire[2] show that his rule in this distant province was well established. That he controlled the inland areas as well as the coast can be seen by the material remains found in the fertile mountain plain between Rāmuz and Shīrāz.[3] Bricks with the name of Shilkhak-In-Shushinak were also found in the remains of a building on the plateau of the Mamasenni Lurs. But it is doubtful whether the Elamites ever went beyond this point on the plateau where later on Persepolis was to be built.[4]

[1] G, 8, 66, no. 46; cf. §II, 5, 18 ff., col. III, 9–22.   [2] See above, p. 405, n. 1.
[3] §II, 4; §II, 3, 114.   [4] §II, 2; §II, 1, 21 a; G, 9, 333 b.

III. ELAMITE CIVILIZATION, c. 1125 B.C.

All of these territories, despite their cultural differences, were solidly held in hand by Shilkhak-In-Shushinak, as can be seen by the extensive building that he undertook in all parts of his empire. One stele records that temples to In-Shushinak were restored in Tettu, Shattamitik, Ekallatum, Perraperra, Bīt-tumurni, Sha-attata-ekal-likrub, Marrut and Shakhan-tallak; that a sanctuary of Lakamar was restored at Bīt-Khulki; and that a temple of Khumban was rebuilt at Peptar-sian-sit.[1] This list shows that his activities were not confined to Susiana and Anzan but extended even to northern Babylonia, the Sea-Land and probably the provinces of central Elam. In order to conduct such a widespread programme a 'pax Elamitica' was necessary. We should not conclude from the number of references to In-Shushinak that the king was trying to force his personal god on the country as part of his programme of centralization, for all of the above-mentioned temples existed before his time and Shilkhak-In-Shushinak only restored them using a more durable material. But it must be admitted that the list does show a predilection for the god of Susa.

This stele, in which only the peaceful aspect of this 'man of war' is revealed, rightly draws our attention to a very important activity of the king—as a builder. Susa owes much of its splendour to Shilkhak-In-Shushinak. We have many texts which commemorate the foundation or restoration of temples at Susa:[2] there are the traditional foundation bricks inserted in the walls, stelae, votive vases, divine symbols, door sockets, enamelled decorative cones. These texts which are often very long give the name of the deity to whom the temple was dedicated and, if we were able to translate the whole inscription, details about the temple itself. They are also valuable from another point of view, for they give the list of gods venerated by Shilkhak-In-Shushinak, the genealogical line of the ancient kings who had founded or restored the temple, the names of the royal family whom he blesses as well as the text of older bricks which he carefully looked for and had copied at the beginning of his own inscription.[3]

Naturally it is the god In-Shushinak who is the most often invoked. Bricks, stelae and enamelled pommels speak of the

---

[1] §II, 6, no. LXXI; G, 8, 69, no. 48; §II, 5, 29 ff.
[2] G, 8, 58 ff.
[3] §II, 6, no. LXXVIII, pl. 9; G, 8, 60, no. 38; cf. §I, 6.

restoration of the great temple of In-Shushinak at Susa. It was entirely reconstructed with baked bricks by the king. The interior was very richly decorated and on a copper pedestal he placed an altar decorated with the same metal; to this were added vases and other objects in copper which were to be used for the cult. Facing the altar was his own statue, beside which were the statues of his father, his brother, his wife and his children. A long bronze cylinder was placed in front of the altar, and bas-reliefs of enamelled bricks and sculptured panels of bronze ran around the walls. Other masterpieces of Elamite metal-workers, as votive offerings, contributed to the embellishing of this holy place. Another temple, which In-Shushinak shared with Lakamar, was also rebuilt. It had been founded by an ancient king whose name was unknown, despite the efforts of Shilkhak-In-Shushinak to find the original foundation brick.

Despite this preference for In-Shushinak, the others gods were not neglected. A temple was rebuilt for Khumban of baked brick and a stele of alabaster and sacred ornaments were placed inside. The temple or sanctuary of Manzat and Shimut, Sukhsipa, Pinikir, Ishme-karab, and Tapmikir were restored. The chapel of Bēltia, the Lady of Babylon, was also restored and the interior made somewhat like the temple of In-Shushinak. At Liyan he entirely reconstructed with baked bricks the ancient sanctuary of Kiririsha, and also the temple which this goddess shared with the god Khumban. The restorer took this opportunity to honour the ancient founder Khumban-numena, and to invoke the protection of the goddess upon himself and his family.

One is struck by the ostentatious way in which the king describes how he had these temples, formerly built of crude brick, restored with baked brick. He could well take pride in this, even if the baked bricks were used only as a facing of the walls, for the large-scale use of this material is an act of munificence in itself. The clay is a natural product and cheap enough but the baking is very expensive. The necessary combustibles are not common in the country and what forests there are near Susa supply only a brushwood that flares quickly without giving much heat. The manufacture of baked bricks, therefore, necessitated a large number of workers to cut, collect, transport, and tend the fires, as well as the masons and artists who decorated the outward faces.

Another sumptuous feature of these constructions was the wealth of panels and enamelled motifs as well as the large number of copper and bronze objects with which the buildings were decorated. One thinks of the admiration they caused to the Assyrian conquerers when some centuries later they saw 'the zikkurrat of Susa which was covered with lapis-lazuli' and its summit 'which was adorned with shining bronze'.[1] Elam had always produced excellent artisans in bronze but at this period they were pre-eminent. Excavations have brought to light the very fine bronze bas-relief known as the *bronze aux guerriers*, which probably decorated the temple of In-Shushinak[2] (as we have already said). It is composed of three scenes: the top has now almost completely disappeared; the lowest, a scene representing trees and birds, was only partly finished; but the middle register is executed with incontestable mastery. The seven warriors are shown with helmets and a short tunic divided in front. The left hand, kept down beside the body, holds a bow and the right hand brandishes above the head a broad curved dagger. This line of warriors, caught by the artist in the same sculptured attitude, is most striking.

Besides the bronze cylinder, which was more than four metres long and cast in one piece,[3] numerous other products of Elamite metallurgy were found in the ruins of Susa. There is for instance the remarkable 'serpent-altar' which, despite its damaged state, is one of the more beautiful examples of this art. The table, which was supported by five figures, of which only the upper part of the torso and the arms are left, has two snakes encircling it. There are also channels on the table for draining away liquids, and the whole is very well modelled.[4]

If we cannot date this object with exactitude to the reign of Shilkhak-In-Shushinak there is another which is so dated by its inscription. This is the curious bronze tray known as the *šit šamši*, 'sunrise',[5] which merits more than passing attention. An adoration-scene is depicted—two nude figures with shaven heads squat facing each other before an ablution vessel. On either side of the figures are stage-towers, the larger of which has three storeys and is very complicated in design. The other, simpler and smaller, is made up of a central section higher than its width, flanked on either side by two lower cubes. There is also a table for offerings, two round pillars the top of which is incurved to support an

---

[1] G, 12, vol. II, sect. 810. 'Lapis-lazuli' refers only to the blue colour of the enamelled bricks covering the walls of the temple; cf. G, 16, 387, n. 9.
[2] §III, 4, 86; G, 4, 932 f.; G, 8, 62, no. 42.
[3] §V, 2, 37; §II, 6, 39 ff.; G, 8, 64, no. 45; G, 4, 933 f.
[4] G, 4, 933; §III, 3, 164, plate XII.
[5] §III, 2, 143 ff.; §III, 1, 84 ff.; G, 4, 932 f.; G, 8, 81, no. 56; § III, 5, 144 ff.

impost, two rectangular vats, a stele on a platform, two rows of little conical heaps which possibly represent cereal offerings. Finally there are four tree-trunks, their foliage of thin metal almost completely destroyed by oxidization; these probably represented a sacred grove. It was cast in two parts, one in the round together with the tray; the other parts were made separately and then riveted into place.

The interest of this object goes beyond the fact that it represents a remarkable example of native art or that it shows us certain ablution rites, for it is probably a model of the acropolis of Susa, with two of its temples, their appurtenances, their ornaments and sacred grove, at the time of Shilkhak-In-Shushinak. This allows us to complete, to a certain extent, the information we have from the excavations concerning the topography of Susa.

IV. THE TOPOGRAPHY OF SUSA

In the northern part of the mound certain remains of buildings seem by their orientation to correspond with the smaller of the two temples, which appear on the bronze tray. A tablet from the time of Shulgi identifies this as being, at least in earlier days, the shrine of the goddess Nin-khursag. Rebuilt from age to age this temple carried on the cult of the 'Lady of the Mountain' down to the reign of Shilkhak-In-Shushinak, when she perhaps bore a native name. The temple was built on a platform nearly square, 25 metres each side, cut off by a trench more than one metre in depth. The sanctuary can be located by four brick boxes at each corner containing votive offerings. It measured 16 by 8 metres, and rooms of various dimensions gave off from this space. Four more deposits of offerings marked out the 'holy of holies', 6 metres square, at the western end of a wide passage—here was found the statue of the queen Napirasu.[1] Remains of paving indicate the courtyard, and rectangular basins were built into the east and west inside walls, a brick-built channel leading into one of them. On the north side, where the entrance probably stood, lay fragments of statuettes, vases, pedestals, and various objects, among them especially figures of Puzur-In-Shushinak and a stele of Manishtusu. Still further to the north some Elamite stelae were unearthed.[2]

At the west of the mound, where according to the bronze model the three-storeyed building of complicated design was located, stood in fact the great temple of In-Shushinak.[3] Its limits again were marked by eight deposits of votive offerings. To judge from

[1] See Plate 157(a).   [2] §IV, 3, 70 ff.   [3] §IV, 3, 67 ff.

what was unearthed during the excavations, the temple had greatly altered during the years. Votive objects of Shulgi and inscribed bricks of Untash-(*d*)*GAL* and Shilkhak-In-Shushinak were found here and there in the walls and among the paving stones. The building was constructed at the edge of the tell. It measures 40 by 20 metres and was surrounded by a moat 3 metres in depth. The walls on the longer sides still exist and the eastern, which is in a better state of preservation, was built of baked bricks. It was probably the facing of a thick wall of unbaked clay. The temple proper was delimited by four deposits of votive offerings and measured 20·70 by 8·50 metres. It was separated from the secondary buildings, towards the south, by a large paved area which measured 19 by 4 metres and extended towards the west where it touched the enclosure. Inside the temple against the eastern wall the inner temple, which measures about 8 by 5 metres, was delimited by four more deposits of votive offerings. Here and there other pavements were found but being at different levels they were rather difficult to interpret. It seems that there was a large court or parvis on the eastern side and the entrance was probably located here. The parade on which these buildings stood was surrounded by a wall decorated with bas-reliefs and Elamite stelae placed at intervals. Columns of brick or bronze and lion-figures of stone or glazed earthenware were found in the southern part of the area.

Even if the temples of Nin-khursag and In-Shushinak are actually those in miniature on the bronze tray the complete acropolis is not shown there, for the excavations have found remains of several other religious buildings at other places on the mound.[1] A small sanctuary, oriented in a different direction, measuring 4·50 metres on each side, lay to the south of the temple of Nin-khursag, and not far from this was discovered a white marble statue of Puzur-In-Shushinak. Still further towards the south was another building of rather large dimensions. Its long wall was at least 15 metres in length and 1 metre thick. The long covered stairway of at least 120 steps which goes into the mass of the mound between two walls of rammed earth was possibly an element of this building. Towards the east there was another structure of modest proportions, 5 metres square, decorated with glazed bricks. Its entrance, more than 2 metres wide, faced the west, and the far end of the room was paved, where probably had been an altar or a divine statue. A building facing the temple of In-Shushinak towards the south-west was probably of consider-

[1] §IV, 3, 78 ff.

able size. It is difficult to judge its disposition from what remains, but the obelisk of Manishtusu, the victory-stele of Naram-Sin, boundary-stones and pedestals of statues, which were found in this area, suggest that it was a very important temple on the acropolis. In various parts of the site bases of baked-brick columns were found. They were made in a variety of shapes, round, oval and square, and came from a number of buildings on the site, but only those from the temples of In-Shushinak and Nin-khursag could be identified by their inscriptions.

What is left on the acropolis does not give us a complete picture of what Susa must have been in all her glory. The devastating fury of the Assyrian armies, some five hundred years later, and the ravages of time have reduced its buildings to heaps of ruins. At least the bronze tray (*ṣīt šamši*) gives some idea of the splendour that was once the acropolis of Susa. Ashurbanipal was later to describe the shining façade of the great temple of Susa with its wall glazed in blue, its statues of kings and gods, its protective genii of awe-inspiring aspect who guarded the holy places and, finally, its mausoleums of former kings, whose bones and ashes the Assyrian king scattered to the four winds in his desire for revenge on this race of conquerers.

Fountains and woods added to the beauty of the architecture. The many basins and numerous other remains show that there must have been a complex drainage and irrigation system.[1] It was used for the collection of rain-water, as well as for raising water from the canal up to the acropolis itself. This installation supplied water to the sacred groves which protected the acropolis from the burning sun of Susiana. Planting of trees near temples, attested symbolically by the *ṣīt šamši*, was not unknown in Babylonia and Assyria, for references to trees in the vicinity of temples[2] are not to be understood as indicating only artificial imitations.[3] Ashurbanipal in his annals makes this allusion to the trees at Susa: 'Their sacred groves into which no stranger (ever) penetrates, whose borders he never (over)steps—into these my soldiers entered, saw their mysteries, and set them on fire.'[4] Discoveries and texts thus agree in proclaiming the prestige and prosperity of Susa at the time of Shilkhak-In-Shushinak.

---

[1] §IV, 3, 73 ff. and figs. 34–7.   [2] §IV, 1, 16A f.; §IV, 2, nos. 65, 366.
[3] §I, 3, 26.   [4] G, 12, vol. II, sect. 810.

V. KHUTELUTUSH-IN-SHUSHINAK

To maintain Elamite power Shilkhak-In-Shushinak needed a successor who would be worthy of himself. This, unfortunately, was not the case with his son and successor Khutelutush-In-Shushinak. The royal protocol shows two symptoms of his weakness. In his genealogy he speaks of himself as not only the chosen son of his father but of his uncle, Kutir-Nahhunte, and his grandfather, Shutruk-Nahhunte, as well. This seems to be an attempt to support his authority by the use of the ancient Elamite matriarchal concept,[1] if we admit that his mother, who had been married to the two brothers, was also the daughter of Shutruk-Nahhunte. In any case this desire to identify himself as being of the same blood as these three kings and his desire to affirm the legitimacy of the bonds between him and his brothers and sisters seem to show a lack of confidence in himself, which appears even in his titles. Although he called himself 'enlarger of the empire', perhaps only for traditional reasons, he did not take the title *sunkir* 'king' which had been used by his predecessors, but merely called himself '*menir* of Anzan and Susa'. This brings to mind one of the titles, '*hal-menir* of Elam', used by Khumban-numena, and it refers to a feudal power rather than power based on divine right.

If we compare the very small number of inscriptions left by Khutelutush-In-Shushinak[2] with those of Shilkhak-In-Shushinak they appear lifeless. There were no longer trophies taken from the enemy nor victory stelae. A few texts refer to peaceful pursuits, and these were probably on a smaller scale than those undertaken by his father. At the beginning of his reign, when his mother is still mentioned in the final prayer, he probably had work done on the temples of Manzat and Shimutta and a votive inscription was placed on a door socket in honour of Manzat for the occasion. Later, in the city of Shalulikki, he inaugurated a new temple of baked brick in honour of the goddess Upurkupak, for his life and the life of his brothers. Later again a temple was rebuilt at Kipu, in Elam, for the goddess Ishme-karab from whom he asked blessings upon his children, his brothers and himself. He also had a chapel, constructed of flat green-glazed bricks, founded in honour of his father Shilkhak-In-Shushinak. This building has recently been excavated but it cannot be dated.[3] There is also a fragment of a stele from his reign, invoking the gods of Elam and the gods of Anzan, and of these In-Shushinak, Nahhunte, Upurkupak, Khumban(?), and Manzat are named.

[1] §v, 4; §v, 5.   [2] G, 8, 84 ff. nos. 60–5.   [3] §v, 2, 38.

In the absence of historical texts we can glean some politically important information from these dedication inscriptions. The mention of Shalulikki shows that the Elamite king still controlled a part of lower Mesopotamia, or at least the Sealand. It is probable that the distant province of Liyan was no longer held by the king, as none of the bricks from this site mention him; but Elam, Anzan and Susiana remained under his control and their gods are always named in his inscriptions.

There was a certain coherence in the realm. Shilkhak-In-Shushinak had built up a military power which survived him, but his son was unable to take advantage of this inheritance. This state of affairs was greatly aggravated by the energy and ambition of his adversaries in Assyria and Babylonia. The former, under Ashur-rēsha-ishi (1133–1116), awoke from its lethargy. This king began a policy of expansion and conquest that was to be taken even further by his successor Tiglath-pileser I. Babylonia under Nebuchadrezzar I (1124–1103) had also come to life. Unfortunately Khutelutush-In-Shushinak was not the one who could maintain the position of Elam before two such rivals. As he was to show on two occasions, he did not lack courage, but it was his lack of decision and foresight that was to be his undoing. Instead of moving his armies into the plains and mountains along his borders he allowed Nebuchadrezzar to take the initiative, and the Babylonian king was able to carry out a violent and successful attack against Elam.[1] This might have been preceded by an unsuccessful attempt, for a fragment of a chronicle relates an attack against Elam but the names of the kings involved are missing; it may have involved Nebuchadrezzar or one of his immediate predecessors.[2] This Babylonian king, after having sworn that he would rescue his god Marduk from Susa or die in the attempt, gathered his troops at Babylon and then launched a violent attack through the Zagros towards the upper Karkhah. The Elamite counter-attack, although late, was of equal violence. The Babylonian army was forced to retreat and, after an attempt to take refuge in the city of Dūr-Apil-Sin, the Babylonian king and his army were driven out of the country. The text ends with a lamentation of the defeated king.

That the Babylonians could advance as far as the Karkhah, only 150 kilometres above Susa, reveals that the Elamites had already lost control of the western bank of the Tigris. It was certainly so in the time of Khutelutush-In-Shushinak, but probably

[1] §1, 7, 138 f.
[2] *Ibid.* 137.

too at the end of his father's reign, so that the unsuccessful attack recorded by the chronicle may have been made by one of the earliest kings of the Isin dynasty rather than by Nebuchadrezzar himself. But if by the latter, he had learned his lesson, and before launching the attack which was to succeed he made sure of the help of effective allies. By promising Lakti-Marduk[1] of Bīt-Karziabku to free his land of all taxes, statute-labour and service, he was aided by the chariots of this chief. He also welcomed two important persons from the Elamite city Dīn-sharri, Shamua and his son Shamaia, a priest of the god Ria,[2] undertaking to rescue their god and to secure him important privileges. Thus prepared, he began his campaign from Dēr, the modern Badrah,[3] whence an almost impracticable route followed the Gawi river into the Elamite province called Khalekhasta at a later date. The line of attack was now farther south, thus menacing Susa much more than the previous campaign. The aggressor wished also to spring a surprise attack upon the Elamites and therefore, despite the heat of summer and the lack of water, he force-marched his army in a veritable leap to the river Ulai (the modern Kārūn) near to Susa. Here the Elamites counter-attacked, and according to the inscription of Lakti-Marduk the chariots commanded by him saved the day. The Babylonian victory was decisive and the defeated Elamite king fled and died shortly afterwards.[4] All resistance ceased, and the Babylonian was able to conquer the rest of Elam without striking another blow. After pillaging Elam he returned in triumph with his booty as well as the statues of the gods Ria and Marduk, released after so many years captivity in Susa. He then rewarded his allies as he had promised; the income of several cities and villages was given for maintenance of the god Ria, who had been taken from Babylon to the city of Khuṣṣi by Shamua and his son on the order of the Babylonian king.[5]

This Babylonian victory and the death of Khutelutush-In-Shushinak brought Elamite power to an end. A text[6] from a later

[1] §v, 1 proposed the reading *Lakti-Shipak* instead of the usual reading *Ritti-Marduk*. This is correct as to the first part of the name, for the signs *rit* and *lak* are easily distinguished at that date. See, however, above, p. 455, n. 6.

[2] [Or Eriya: see above, p. 456, and cf. bibliography to ch. xxxi, A, 3, 108 (Ed.)]

[3] §vi, 10, 47; §v, 7.

[4] This victory was so decisive that it was remembered in succeeding ages, and had its place among the historical references of the astrologers: §v, 8, no. 200, rev. 5; §v, 10, 176.

[5] §v, 11, 534 ff.; §v, 3, nos. vi and xxiv, and see also §v, 9 and §v, 6, 147 ff.

[6] A brick of Shutruk-Nahhunte II, G, 14, 5, 63 ff., no. 84.

period tells us that the successor was *sunkir* 'king' and that he reconstructed a sanctuary of In-Shushinak at Susa. But as a political power Elam was finished. This period was followed by a dark age of three centuries, during which there are no native texts nor are there allusions to Elam in the Mesopotamian sources. Undoubtedly broken up internally, Elam was not to be mentioned again until 821 when Elamite, Chaldaean and Aramaean troops were defeated by the Assyrian king Shamshi-Adad V.[1]

VI. THE POLITICAL GEOGRAPHY OF WESTERN PERSIA

The elimination of Elam as a major power did not, however, bring peace to the Zagros. The kings of Babylonia and above all the kings of Assyria continued to make war in the region between Lake Urmīyah and northern Elam. Later this was to become one of the principal theatres of operations for the Assyrians. As these became more and more powerful, they were obliged to get a foothold in the mountainous districts along their borders from which they could push their military expeditions much further towards the east.

The Assyrian interest in these high lands went beyond the strategic advantage of allowing them to cut off any invasions that might come through these trails and valleys. Economically they were also very important, for the Zagros and the western approaches to the Iranian plateau were not uniformly poor. The inner plains and some of the valleys were fertile, and there were oases which were highly cultivated or grazing lands with large numbers of horses as well as flocks and herds. They were also an important source of minerals, having metallurgical centres which manufactured bronze, copper, and afterwards iron. Through these regions moved vast quantities of precious stones, copper ore and manufactured copper.

This strategic and economic importance explains the increasing interest of the Assyrians in these regions. To these reasons was soon to be added another; certain movements and migrations of peoples brought a double menace to bear on Mesopotamia, the threat of cutting off supplies, and of possible invasion.

To understand better the changes that were afterwards to take place in this area we must give a short account of its former populations. The sources of our knowledge about this country—texts from Mesopotamia—show that it was inhabited for a long time

[1] G, 12, vol. 1, sect. 726; G, 15, 156 ff.

by four major ethnic groups: the Subarians, the Hurrians, the Lullubi and the Guti. The two latter groups were native to the area. The Subarians and the Hurrians lived mostly in the plains and only a few of their numbers actually in the Zagros.

The Subarians[1] lived in the mountains to the east of the Tigris between Barakhshe, near the Diyālā, and southern Anatolia. They were neighbours of Anzan and Eshnunna. Hammurabi who had defeated them along with the Guti and Elam put them among those countries whose 'mountains are distant and the languages are complicated'.[2] They had a much fairer skin than the Mesopotamians, to whom they long provided an ample supply of slaves. It was also to the east of the Tigris that the Hurrians first appeared. They entered very early into Mesopotamia but some of them stayed in the area to the south and west of Lake Vān, to the east of Irbil and Altın-Köprü or in the Zagros. Of the latter group some went into Elam and others moved towards the Caspian Sea.[3]

The Lullubi and the Guti stayed in the mountains from where they constantly menaced Mesopotamia. Although the Lullubi (Lullu, Lullubu, Lullumi) may be mentioned as early as in the archaic tablets of Fārah their actual homeland is not revealed until the Agade period, when inscriptions were found in their territory. Those of Naram-Sin are at Darband-i Gawr, south of Sulaimaniyyah, and at Darband-i Ramkan, near the plain of Rania,[4] and commemorate his wars against this people. Others are the work of the Lullubi, celebrating a victory of their king Annubanini. These inscriptions are engraved on rocks at Sar-i pul, in the district of Ḥulwan, some 30 kilometres to the south of Qaṣr-i Shīrīn.[5] This is much further south than those above mentioned, and is probably the southernmost point reached by the Lullubi in their attempt to control and cut off the commercial route which runs through southern Kurdistān from the Iranian plateau to the Mesopotamian plain. At a later date, the date-formulae of Shulgi[6] seem to indicate that the Lullubi homeland began in the area immediately to the east of Irbil and Altın-Köprü with its centre at Rania, which undoubtedly remained the focus of their culture in later years.[7] Thanks to the rock inscrip-

---

[1] §vi, nos. 11, 12, and 38.   [2] G, 6, no. 146, col. iv.

[3] §vi, 11 and 12; §vi, 15, 31 ff.; §vi, 16, 61 ff.

[4] §vi, 6; §vi, 20, 184.   [5] §vi, 40, 98 ff. and 187 (bibliography).

[6] For the 26th, 45th and 46th years; see G, 5, 141 f. Lullubum is conjoined with Urbillum and Simurrum.

[7] §vi, 23, 77, 24–5.

tions of Annubanini and the victory stele of Naram-Sin we have some idea of the physical aspect of these warlike mountaineers. Dressed in light tunics or kilts, an animal skin over the shoulders, short beards and braided hair they appear to be of Mediterranean rather than of Armenoid stock. The mention of their 'numerous kings' shows that they had not a centralized state but were divided into small clans directed by independent chiefs, and were united only in times of emergency.

The Gutians, or Qutu, also lived in southern Kurdistān. After their expulsion from Mesopotamia,[1] where they had established a barbarian rule, texts written during the First Dynasty of Babylon define with some clearness their habitation in the Zagros. It was delimited by the boundaries of Subartu, Turukku, Eshnunna, Barakhshe and Idamaraz.[2] Some of them also lived in the region of Rania.[3] Later on it becomes more difficult to localize them, as the Akkadians grouped all of the autochthonous groups under the general heading of Gutians. Because of this such locations as 'the city of Karkhar is situated in front of the Gutian country'[4] are very misleading. From what little we know of their social structure, during the period when they occupied Mesopotamia, we can see that they formed a sort of tribal confederation of rough and simple people. They were led by a military aristocracy which elected a 'king' for a fixed, but short, period of time.

From what has been said above two conclusions follow: we know the western limits of these various ethnic groups but nothing of their eastward extent—the Mesopotamians themselves knew little of these distant regions. We also find that they had no particular territory of their own, but often overlapped one another. This is very clear in the Rania plain at the time of Shamshi-Adad I. There the principal city Shusharra (modern Shemshāra) was under Assyrian control,[5] but the majority of its population was Hurrian. Others of the inhabitants were Lullubi,[6] and more warlike elements of these lived in the vicinity, maintaining economic relations with the city but holding over it a threat of insecurity.[7] The district was also disturbed by raids of Turukkians,[8] and not far away were Gutians, themselves under a Hurrian chief,[9] and also in relation with the city. Out of this hotch-potch

---

[1] By Utu-khegal, prince of Uruk; §vi, 35 and 36; §vi, 43.

[2] Date-formulae for the 30th, 32nd and 37th years of Hammurabi; G, 5, 180 f.; §vi, 1, vol. iv, 25; §vi, 22, 83, n. 1; §vi, 27, 241.

[3] §vi, 23, 32 ff.

[4] §vi, 28, 12, no. 6, line 7.

[5] §vi, 23, 75.

[6] Ibid. 80, lines 45 f.

[7] Ibid. 77 ff., lines 24–36.

[8] §vi, 1, vol. iv, 25.

[9] §vi, 23, 36, no. 8.

of peoples arose a kind of common culture throughout the mountain region, and the evidence of names proves that it extended even into Elam.[1]

The Kassites were soon to enter into this community. We do not know whether they migrated thither or whether they originated in the region at the source of the Elamite rivers. In any case they appear on the scene at a time when the more western approaches of the Iranian plateau were in a period of social and economic change. A new type of pottery appears; cities and townships begin to put up walls; small stock becomes more numerous, perhaps to the detriment of cattle; and the problem of moving the flocks and renewing pasture-lands becomes more urgent. We know that the Kassites invaded Babylonia in very large numbers at the time of the First Dynasty and that they settled down in this new land. But certain groups stayed in the Zagros, and these, along with the Lullubi and the Gutians, were the important elements in the Zagros down to the end of the second millennium.

It is these people that Nebuchadrezzar I (1124–1103) and his contemporary Ashur-rēsha-ishi (1134–1116), king of Assyria, met during their military expeditions in the Zagros. The former boasted of having subdued 'the powerful Lullubi' and raided the Kassites; the latter claimed that he subdued 'the Lullume, all of the Gutians, and the whole mountainous region where they live'.[2] It was settlements of Kassites, mixed with Semites and Hurrians, that the Elamite king Shilkhak-In-Shushinak at the same period listed among his conquests to the north of his country. Linguistically, the geographical names show that the Subarian language was predominant in the region of the Tigris and the Diyālā, and the Lullubian south of the Lesser Zab.[3] The personal and the divine names show interpenetration among these different ethnic groups. Some of the gods that the Akkadians considered as Gutian were in fact Hurrian. Certain Kassite words, such as the word for 'king', were known as far away as the district of the lakes.

This situation in the Zagros was, at the end of the second millennium, on the eve of profound changes, although nothing of these had yet appeared. Gutians and Lullubians continued, indeed, to be named in the annals of Assyrian kings, and scattered groups of Kassites survived into the classical age on the east and north-east of Babylonia.[1] But from the outset of the first millennium there was to begin a complete refashioning of the political geography in these lands.

[1] §vi, 33.   [2] G, 12, vol. i, sect. 209.
[3] G, 12, vol. i, sect. 449 and 457; §vi, 37, 5, line 11.   [4] G, 18.

CHAPTER XXXIII

SYRIA, THE PHILISTINES, AND PHOENICIA

I. THE SEA PEOPLES IN PALESTINE

IN the early twelfth century B.C. Syria and Palestine were flooded by an irruption of peoples from the coasts and islands of the northern Mediterranean. Unfortunately, we cannot fix the exact date of this invasion, since our chief pertinent sources are the reliefs and accompanying inscriptions of Ramesses III at Medīnet Habu; the former are schematic and undated, while the latter consist almost exclusively of triumphal poems in a stereotyped and bombastic style.[1] Moreover, the date of the reign of Ramesses III is uncertain within a possible range of a generation and a probable range of a decade, but the earliest and latest possible dates for his accession are now considered to have been about 1205 and 1180, respectively. To judge from the monuments, it would appear that the first attack[2] on Egypt came by sea and land not long before the sixth year of the king. The first land onslaught is said to have been beaten back in Phoenicia (*Djahy*). The great triumphal inscription of the eighth year was composed in glorification of the second naval victory; land operations are also mentioned, but it is not clear how successful they really were.[3]

While the inscription of the eighth year makes it certain that the Egyptians connected this migration with the movement which had brought an abrupt end to the Hittite Empire, it seems evident that they were both part of a greater upheaval. The Hittite Empire was overthrown by land peoples who struck deep into the heart of Anatolia and are said in the inscriptions of the Assyrian king Tiglath-pileser I to have reached south-western Armenia about 1165 B.C. The migration with which we are concerned here included five different peoples, at least two of whom are represented as fighting in ships, some manned by warriors with feathered helmets[4] while others have only warriors with low, horned helmets.

---

* An original version of this chapter was published as fascicle 51 in 1966.
[1] §1, 39, 24 ff.   [2] See above, pp. 241 f.
[3] §1, 14, 53 ff. The phrase *iryw šdt m nȝysn iww* should probably be rendered: '(As for the foreign countries,) they were making a (plundering) raid from their islands'—see G, 5, vol. 4, 561.   [4] See, however, above, p. 372.

All of the warriors in the scenes of land-fighting wear feathered helmets. The land-forces of the invaders employ chariots for fighting and heavy two-wheeled carts drawn by humped oxen for women and children. The use of carts suggests a long overland journey but by no means proves it, since they may have been constructed after arrival in Palestine by sea.[1]

The identification of the five peoples listed in the texts of Ramesses III has long been vigorously debated. In the order of importance indicated by the number and character of the allusions to them, they are the Peleset (*Pr/lst*), the Tjekker (*Tjik[k]al/r*), the Sheklesh (*Shekr/lushe*), the Denyen (*Danuna*), and the Weshesh (*Washeshe*).[2] The first people is undoubtedly to be identified with the biblical Philistines, of whom more below. The second is perhaps to be identified with the Teucrians (or less probably with the Homeric Sikeloi, who occupied Sicily and gave their name to the island).[3] The third seems to be unknown otherwise; all proposed identifications are dubious. The fourth is unquestionably to be identified somehow with the land Danuna of a letter of Abi-milki, prince of Tyre in the Amarna period; the name later appears in Cyprus as the *Yad(a)nana* of the Assyrians[4] and in Cilicia as the land of the *Dnnym*.[5] The Washeshe are unknown unless their name is connected with Carian Ouassos. That all these peoples came from somewhere in the Aegean orbit appears reasonably certain. It is significant that the two distinctive types of helmet at Medīnet Habu appear at about the same time on the so-called warrior-vase from Mycenae.[6] On the vase are two processions of five warriors each; one group wears feathered helmets and the other horned helmets. However, the horned helmet is high, with plumes floating from the crest; it is different from both the low horned helmet of the Mediterranean allies at Medīnet Habu and from the crested, horned helmet worn by the Sherden (Shardina), i.e. Sardinian, corps of the Egyptian army itself (shown at Medīnet Habu only when joining with the Egyptians in land operations).

---

[1] The account in §1, 14, 53 ff. is insufficiently detailed to allow any clear reconstruction of the sequence of events.

[2] For the vocalization see §1, 4, *passim*, and §1, 23, 240 ff.

[3] The vocalization *Tjikar* agrees very well with *Teukr-*; cf. Hebrew *s[u]ran-* (which would be written approximately **tju-ra-n* in New Egyptian) and its later Greek equivalent *turann-*. Teucrians are said in Greek sources to have settled at Salamis in Cyprus after the Trojan War. See above, pp. 276 f.

[4] §1, 5, 171 ff.   [5] *Ibid.* 172. See above, pp. 363 ff.

[6] §1, 8, figs. 265 ff. The differences in shape seem largely to be the result of artistic conventions.

Our knowledge of the archaeological and historical background of Philistine culture is now substantial. It is quite certain that the highly distinctive 'Philistine' pottery found in such quantities in Philistine sites as well as in the towns of the adjacent lowland country (Shephelah) of Judah in deposits of the twelfth and eleventh centuries B.C. has been correctly identified. It springs directly from the LH III c 1 ware of the Aegean basin, and its manufacture seems to have been brought from Cyprus to Palestine not later than the early twelfth century, judging from the remarkable likeness of specifically Philistine pottery to pieces found by A. Furumark at Sinda and by C. F. A. Schaeffer and P. Dikaios at Enkomi, both in north-eastern Cyprus near Salamis.[1] This ware has been called by Furumark LH III c 1 b and assigned to the period between c. 1225 and 1175 B.C. It shows Cypriot influence, so there is good reason to reject the view that it was brought by the Philistines directly from their Aegean home.

Since the inscriptions of Ramesses III repeatedly speak of using captives as troops in his own army and since some of the Sea Peoples (especially the Sherden) had been used as mercenaries or as slave troops during the reign of Ramesses II, many scholars now agree that the Philistines were first settled in Palestine as garrison troops. This has been demonstrated on the basis of the virtual identity of weapons, anthropoid clay sarcophagi, and other artifacts in garrison sites from Beth-shan in the northern Jordan valley to Tell el-Fār'ah in the Negeb of western Palestine, as well as at Tell Nebesha in the Delta and Anība in Nubia.[2] In Philistia proper both Ashdod and Gath have been shown by recent excavations to have been originally fortresses of the *Zwingburg* type; Gath is still most probably to be found at the traditional site of Tel Gat (Tell esh-Sheikh el-'Areini) despite the excavator's doubts, for the alternative site (Tell en-Nejīleh) has yielded no Late Bronze remains, and Ashdod was a similar large fortress in early Philistine times. Another fortress may have been the third Philistine inland town, Ekron.[3] Gaza, and Askalon were already, by contrast, important seaports before the Philistine occupation began.

Evidence for the date of the original establishment of the

[1] §1, 11, 209 f.; for the best previous study see §1, 24, and cf. §1, 7 (1954 and later editions), 114 f. Since some Philistines had probably settled in eastern Cyprus several decades before their occupation of the Pentapolis, this chronological situation would be expected.

[2] §1, 12; 13.

[3] J. Naveh's identification (§1, 28) of Ekron with the large (but poorly fortified) site of Khirbet al-Muqanna' is impossible for a number of reasons, and the site of 'Aqir again becomes highly probable.

Philistines in key fortresses was uncovered by Petrie and Starkey (1927–30) at Tell el-Fārʿah (Sharuhen), and still more important clues have more recently been found by H. J. Franken at Tell Deir ʿAllā (Succoth) some 24 miles south of Beth-shan in the Jordan valley. At Sharuhen the fortified 'Residency' yielded early Philistine pottery in a structure first built by Sethos II (1216–1210 B.C.), as demonstrated by the find of four very large and heavy sherds belonging to a massive jar inscribed in well-carved hieroglyphs with the name of Sethos II.[1] Since these sherds, though found in different places in the 'Residency', fit together, it seems clear that the original jar dates from the foundation of the fortress by Sethos II, who is known from other sources to have built such fortresses in the region between the Delta and southern Palestine. It follows that the Philistines were settled here as garrison troops at some time between the foundation of this Egyptian fortress and its destruction in the latter part of the twelfth century.

The Deir ʿAllā finds are much more remarkable, though not entirely unexpected.[2] On the floor of a sanctuary from the end of the Late Bronze Age, about 1200 B.C., was found a broken faience bowl inscribed with the cartouche of Queen Tewosret, who reigned in the last decade of the thirteenth century B.C. In the same occupation level, 8 m. east of the sanctuary, were found (in 1964) three inscribed tablets and a discarded fourth tablet in two rooms containing the same kinds of pottery.[3] Though the sanctuary is said to have been destroyed by an earthquake, Philistine pottery is reported to have been found in the same stratum and, according to information, is to be dated immediately after the time of the tablets.[4] These contain over fifty characters, grouped into some fifteen words separated by vertical strokes; they resemble elongated Minoan Linear A and B tablets, and some of the characters closely resemble signs of Minoan Linear A though simplified in form and reduced in number. Apparently we have to do with a purely phonetic syllabary, analogous to the Cypriot and in part to the Carian. That the tablets are very early Philistine texts is highly probable, though they might represent the script of some other Sea People.

Decisive evidence has now been found identifying the occupants of the anthropoid sarcophagi of Beth-shan with the

---

[1] §I, 36, 28 and §I, 32, 18 (which Starkey seems to have overlooked).
[2] §I, 7, 185 (1954 ed.).
[3] §III, 19.
[4] See above, p. 336.

Philistines of the Medīnet Habu reliefs of Ramesses III.[1] The faces moulded on the cover pieces of the Beth-shan coffins are surmounted by feathered helmets of the same types as we find attributed to the Philistines at Medīnet Habu, with identical decoration around the lower part of the helmets: (1) a horizontal strip with a single row of little circular projections; (2) a horizontal strip with two similar rows of circular projections; (3) a similar strip with a row of chevrons or zigzag decoration above and a row of circular projections below. A fourth modification appears at Medīnet Habu but not at Beth-shan (where the material is incomparably more limited in amount): a strip with a single row of zigzag or chevron decoration. In view of the way in which the pre-Hellenic and early Hellenic peoples were subdivided into three or more tribes (e.g. the Rhodians were divided into three tribes according to the Homeric Catalogue of Ships) we may rest assured that the insignia in question indicate tribal ties, not military rank. In other words, they correspond very roughly with the *wusūm* marks of the Arabs, but they undoubtedly reflect a much higher level of socio-political organization.

The foregoing data establish the fact that there was an early phase of military garrisons manned by Philistines (and quite possibly by other Sea Peoples), which was followed by a large-scale invasion by sea and land, repulsed by Ramesses III early in the twelfth century. The Philistines and their allies were driven back from Egypt proper but were allowed to settle in Palestine as Egyptian vassals. The Philistines occupied the coastal plain from south of Gaza to north of Ekron; south of them there may have been a Cretan colony,[2] and in northern Sharon the Tjekker were settled, as we know from the Wenamun report. Other groups may have been settled in southern Sharon (the 'Auja valley and Joppa) and the plain of Acre, all of which passed under Philistine control before the second half of the eleventh century B.C. The methodical way in which the Sea Peoples appear to have divided up the coast of Palestine is clear from even a superficial geographical analysis of their division. The Philistines themselves, being the dominant group in the confederation, took the best territory. Though only about 40 miles long and averaging little over 15 miles in width, the Philistine Pentapolis had approximately the same area as the whole of Attica; moreover, most of its land was cultivable, producing splendid crops of grain in normal seasons. In due course they absorbed their Cretan neighbours to the south and expanded northwards to dominate the

---

[1] §1, 12, 57 and much more briefly §1, 13, 156 ff.   [2] §1, 1 and §1, 2, 136 ff.

plain of Sharon. The report of Wenamun, from the early eleventh century B.C., tells us that the Tjekker were then occupying Dor, which probably included not less than 30 miles of sea coast just south of Carmel. This tract, however, is so much narrower and less adapted to agriculture than the Philistine plain that one is scarcely surprised to learn that the Tjekker were still noted for piracy a century or more after their settlement. Between these two areas of settlement is a shorter zone around Joppa and Apollonia (Arsuf), only some 30 by 15 miles in extent, but extraordinarily rich and well watered; we do not know which of the Sea Peoples settled there at first, but it later passed under Philistine control. Nor do we know which people was allotted the rich plain of Acre, or whether any of them settled still farther north on the Syrian coast.

Who were the Philistines originally? Biblical tradition, clearly derived from Philistine sources, brings them from Caphtor (Akkadian *Kaptara*, Crete) and this tradition is supported by the appellation *Minoa* given to Gaza. Just south of Gaza was a Cretan settlement,[1] and David employed 'light-armed' Cretans as mercenaries.[2] As noted above, the Deir 'Allā tablets are written in a script with clear affinities to Minoan A (though greatly evolved and simplified), and the Phaestus disk from a sixteenth-century Cretan palace has a frequently appearing character portraying a male head with feathered headdress. On the other hand, the Lydian tradition as reported by the native historian Xanthus (a contemporary of Herodotus) claims that the Philistines were colonists from Lydia.[3] This conflict of opinion presumably arose from considerations of prestige; the Philistines themselves, before Gyges made Lydia world-famous, claimed Cretan origin, while the Lydians claimed the Philistines as former colonists of theirs.

In 1950–1 a new element was introduced into this previously insoluble debate; the old equation of Philistines and Pelasgians was taken up again,[4] and good evidence was presented for an

[1] See preceding note.

[2] Hebrew *Kᵉrēṯī u-pᵉlēṯī*, 'Cherethites and Pelethites', is the common designation of David's favourite bodyguard. Since the Lucianic recension of the Septuagint (now known from Qumrān Cave 4 to be exceptionally reliable) offers a reading *pheltei*, we may be justified in treating the expression as a typical Semitic hendiadys, in which case the second word **peltī* might be derived from the Aegean source of later Greek *peltē*, 'light shield' (from which comes *peltastēs*, 'light-armed warrior'). The Cretans were known as archers in classical times.

[3] G, 11, 81, n. 1.

[4] See §III, 6, 4; and V. Georgiev in *Jahrbuch für kleinasiatische Forschung*, 1 (1951), 136 ff.

ancient variant *Pelastikon*, etc., for *Pelasgikon*, both of which presumably went back to an older form with a consonant found by the Hellenes difficult to pronounce. Unfortunately, Greek tradition about the Pelasgians is so confused that Eduard Meyer was inclined to reject it almost entirely.[1] This goes much too far, and we have some evidence from Greek sources which seems relatively accurate. According to Homer (Iliad II, 840) the southern Troad was inhabited by 'spear-brandishing Pelasgians', and Herodotus, who was a native of Halicarnassus in Caria, traces both the Ionians and the Aeolians to Pelasgian origins. It is more than likely that his 'Coastal Pelasgians' actually preceded the Ionians in Ionia, not in the Peloponnesus as he states.[2] There is also much confusion in our sources between the Tyrrhenians (Tursha in the lists of Sea Peoples) of Lemnos in the Aegean and the Pelasgians.[3] However this may be, we have onomastic data which confirm the derivation of the Philistines from the general area of south-western Asia Minor. The only certain Philistine names until recently were Goliath (*Golyat*) and Achish (correctly *Ekaush*, or the like), but we also have three names of Philistine chieftains or merchant princes in the Wenamun report: Waraktir (*Wr/lktr/l*), Waret (*Wr/lt*) and Makamar (*Mkmr/l*).[4] It was suggested in 1951 that their names were South-west Anatolian (i.e. Luwian),[5] and this suggestion was confirmed independently in 1962.[6] Perhaps the details should be slightly modified and the names be explained tentatively as *Warkat/dara*, *Ward/ta* and *Mag/kamola*, all with excellent equivalents in the daughter dialects of Luwian (Lycian, Carian, Pisidian, Pamphylian and Cilician, etc.).[7] Heb. *Golyat* was long ago identified with Lydian *Alyattes*, older *Walwatta*; the reciprocal dissimilation offers no problems, and the element *walwi* as well as the formation *walwatta* are both well illustrated in Luwian.[8] In short, the 'Philistines may be identified with Pelasgians of some kind, and their language was a Luwian dialect.[9]

---

[1] E.g. G, 11, 237, n. 1. [2] Herodotus, VII, 94. [3] Most recently §1, 19, 224.

[4] Only the consonants are known with certainty, since the syllabic orthography had become hopelessly confused by the eleventh century B.C.

[5] §1, 6.   [6] §1, 20, 50, n. 25.

[7] On the Luwian daughter-dialects see §1, 37, and on Lydian and its relationship to Luwian see §1, 10.

[8] §1, 20, 49; cf. such pairs as *muwa* and *Muwatta* as well as Lydian *walwes* (*ibid.*, n. 21).

[9] An obvious further deduction would be that these Pelasgians spoke a Luwian dialect, but we do not know enough about the Pelasgians to make such a facile generalization—they may have been a multilingual federation for all we know.

As already indicated, the occupation of the coastland of Palestine by the Sea Peoples was attended by much destruction of Canaanite towns. Ramesses III tells us that Canaanite princes and patrician charioteers (*mryn, mariyanna*) joined the Egyptian commanders in resisting the foes. It appears that there were successive raids during the generation or more (possibly as much as fifty years) which preceded the mass invasion in the eighth year of Ramesses III. The excavators of Ashdod are inclined to date the destruction of the Late Bronze town about the same time as the Israelite conquest of the Shephelah.[1] Askalon shows clear remains of a destruction level between Canaanite and Philistine levels. Gath (Tell Gat) and Tell el-Qasīleh on the Yarqōn river were not founded until after the irruption of the Sea Peoples, and Dor seems to exhibit the same picture that we find at Askalon. Much farther north Ugarit was destroyed soon after the beginning of the Mediterranean raids. Publication of the documents from the Tablet Oven,[2] excavated in 1954, provides a solid basis for dating the fall of Ugarit, which must have occurred within a very short time after the tablets were placed in the oven. Two letters are particularly important: RS 18.38 and RS 18.40. The former contains the text (or translation) of a message sent to 'Ammurapi, last king of Ugarit, from his Hittite suzerain (probably Tudkhaliash IV). It states that 'The enemy has come up against me, the As[syr]ian', using the familiar Ugaritic and Aramaic consonantal spelling of the name. The second letter, written by an Ugaritic official to the king of Ugarit, says that he is in Lawasanda (Lawazantiya),[3] watching the approaches from the east together with the king of Siannu.[4] The latter 'has fled and...was killed'.

The events mentioned in these letters correspond with happenings in the first full year of Tukulti-Ninurta I of Assyria, whose troops crossed the Euphrates and carried off '28,800 men of Khatti' as captives. Since the destruction of·Ugarit did not occur until after the accession of Merneptah, we must fix the accession of his father, Ramesses II, in 1304 instead of in 1290, but at the same time we must date the Assyrian invasion of Syria in 1234 instead of in 1244. The fall of Ugarit then took place in 1234— probably a few months after the victory of Merneptah over the

[1] Personal information.

[2] In Ch. Virolleaud, *Textes en cunéiformes alphabétiques des Archives Sud, Sud-Ouest, et du Petit Palais* (*Le Palais royal d' Ugarit V* = *Mission de Ras Shamra XI*). Paris, 1965.

[3] As identified by Mr M. Astour.

[4] So clearly to be read on a photograph supplied by M. Schaeffer.

Libyans and Sea Peoples in the spring of 1234, possibly in 1233 or 1232. The city was not destroyed by an Assyrian army but probably by a sudden raid of the Sea Peoples at a time when the Ugaritic navy had been sent by the Hittites to another area—perhaps Lycia, as explicitly stated in one tablet.

The destruction of Tyre is presupposed by tradition and that of Sidon (at the hands of a king of Askalon) is explicitly mentioned.[1] In the Shephelah of Judah (especially at Beth-shemesh and Tell Beit Mirsim) there is a gap of a generation or more between the latest imports of Mycenaean pottery (which immediately preceded the disruption of trade by the Sea Peoples during the reign of Merneptah) and the introduction of Philistine pottery from the Coastal Plain.

After the death of Ramesses III the Philistines and their congeners appear to have concentrated on sea and land trade. A century later, not long before the Philistine conquest of Palestine, the Tjekker were still more powerful at sea than the prince of Byblos, and the Philistine prince Waraktir (Warkatara) was in trade alliance (*khubūr*) with Sidon.[2] Since there is no good evidence of any Phoenician overseas colonization before the tenth century B.C., it is practically certain that the Philistines and other Sea Peoples of Palestine controlled the waters of the south-eastern Mediterranean until their defeat by the combined forces of Israel and Tyre early in the same century. Land trade was greatly facilitated by the fact that the Philistines already occupied a number of strategic points in the plain of Esdraelon and the Jordan valley (especially Beth-shan and Succoth) in the period immediately preceding the mass invasion under Ramesses III. The influence of the Philistines on desert trade is illustrated by the discovery at Saḥāb, east of 'Ammān, of an Early Iron Age tomb containing a typical anthropoid clay coffin.[3] The conquest of Israel by the Philistines about the middle of the eleventh century was perhaps dictated mainly by the increasing need of protection for caravans from the desert. It must be remembered that this was less than a century after the great Midianite raids, in which camel-riding raiders appeared for the first known time in the history of south-western Asia. Soon after these raids we find

---

[1] G, 11, 79 ff.

[2] §1, 6, 229 ff., and B. Maisler (Mazar) in *Bull. A.S.O.R.* 102 (1946), 9 ff. See also §11, 5, 359, n. 80. It may be observed that 'partnership' is *ment-shbēr* in Coptic; *shbēr* is the normal Coptic equivalent of Eg. *ḫbr* (*khubūr*), itself a loan-word from Semitic.

[3] See W. F. Albright in *A.J.A.* 36 (1932), 295 ff.

the state of Ammon beginning to make forays into Israelite territory.[1] The very existence of Ammon was dependent on caravan trade with the desert, and the ethnic composition of the Ammonites in the following centuries, as known from proper names on seals, etc., was partly north-west Semitic, partly Arab.[2]

The organization of the Philistine 'empire' was also clearly dictated by the interests of a trading confederacy. So far as we know, the Philistines were always governed by their five 'lords', meeting in council; the word is found in Hebrew only in the plural, s*rānīm[3] or sarney P*lishtīm (which is usually identified with pre-Hellenic turan(nos), 'tyrant', and compared with Tyrrhenian turan, 'lady'). The coastal members of the larger confederation marshalled their forces at Aphek above the source of the 'Auja river north-east of Joppa; this well-watered base of operations, midway between Philistine and Tjekker territory, was admirably suited for the purpose and again illustrates the autonomy of the different Sea Peoples about the middle and just before the close of the eleventh century. Two other items may be cited to illustrate the nature of the Philistine 'empire'. It has been pointed out that the solidly and symmetrically constructed late-eleventh century fortress at Gibeah of Benjamin must be attributed to the Philistines, who had actually built a fortress at Gibeah according to 1 Sam. x. 5.[4] The existence of such fortresses constructed at key points along trade-routes would naturally indicate a high degree of organization. The establishment of an iron monopoly in Palestine (1 Sam. xiii. 19–22), after the earlier Hittite model, served the double purpose of limiting Israelite use of iron weapons and increasing industrial profits. Apparently the Philistine smiths were organized into a guild, like the earlier guilds of Ugarit.[5]

II. THE CANAANITE REVIVAL IN PHOENICIA

Between the late thirteenth and the end of the twelfth century B.C., the territory occupied by the Canaanites was vastly reduced. In

[1] On the early history of Ammon see W. F. Albright in *Miscellanea Biblica B. Ubach* (Montserrat, 1954), 131 ff.; and §1, 25, 66 ff.

[2] In addition to the material already mentioned, cf. my note in *Bull. A.S.O.R.* 160 (1960), 41, n. 25 a.

[3] The original Hebrew vowel of the first syllable is quite unknown and may just as well have been u as a; sarney is a secondary formation.

[4] See §1, 27, 13, n. 19 and G, 2, 50. See also L. A. Sinclair, in *Bi. Ar.* 27 (1964), 56.

[5] See §1, 27, 10 and 13, and for other details concerning the Philistines §1, 7, 114 ff. See above, p. 136.

the Late Bronze Age the entire coast of Syria from Mount Casius to the Egyptian frontier had been inhabited by a mixed people sharing a common language (with minor dialectal differences) and a common culture and religion. Inland this was also true to varying degrees; the narrowest belts of 'Canaanite' territory were in Ugarit and Palestine, and the widest eastward extension was in Phoenicia proper, where it stretched across Lebanon at least as far as Anti-Lebanon. First came the Israelites, occupying practically all the hill-country of western Palestine and much of Bashan (Ḥaurān).[1] The Sea Peoples then occupied the coast of Palestine and possibly coastal areas north of Phoenicia. About the same time came the Aramaeans, sweeping over eastern and northern Syria to establish a culture oriented northward and eastward rather than southward and westward. As a result the Canaanites suffered the loss of half their coast and virtually the entire hinterland except for Lebanon, where almost impenetrable mountain forests blocked aggression from the east. In all they must have lost a good three-fourths of their territory and at least nine-tenths of their grain land.

However, there were compensations for these losses. The coast of Phoenicia proper was ideally prepared by nature to become the home of a maritime people. It is true that there were few harbours like that of Berytus, but in those simple days small natural or artificial breakwaters were sufficient to protect most ships against storms. Two of the five leading Phoenician cities, Tyre and Aradus (Arvad), were on islands; they were thus impregnable fortresses as long as they controlled the sea. The remaining three, Sidon, Berytus and Byblos, were on the mainland; it is scarcely an accident that none of the three had the political significance in the middle centuries of the Iron Age that was possessed by Tyre and Aradus. In the Late Bronze Age, as we know from the Amarna Letters and Papyrus Anastasi No. 1,[2] Tyre was dependent on the mainland for its supply of fresh water. From the twelfth century onwards this dependence was greatly reduced; the rapid spread of watertight cisterns about the beginning of the Iron Age[3] explains not only the sudden expansion of settlement throughout the hill-country of Palestine in early Israelite times, but also the similar development of settlement over Mount Lebanon in the same period. This consequent increase in native population provided a substantial part of the

---

[1] Data mentioned above, pp. 514 f., make it probable that the critical phase of the Israelite conquest was nearly contemporary with the beginning of the Philistine raids.

[2] *C.A.H.* II[1], 326.

[3] §II, 5, 341 and 358, n. 72.

personnel needed to man the merchant fleets and colonize the Phoenician trading settlements in the Mediterranean.[1]

Another factor of great importance in the development of Phoenician maritime power was the destruction of the Hittite Empire in the late thirteenth century B.C.,[2] which ended any serious threat from Anatolia to the growth of Phoenician enterprise. After the death of Ramesses III, Egypt soon ceased to be either an actual or a potential danger. During most of the twelfth century Assyria was unable to expand west of the Euphrates. The brief interlude of expansion under Tiglath-pileser I and his sons, at the end of the twelfth and during the first decades of the eleventh century, can scarcely have constituted a direct threat to southern Phoenicia; in any case it soon passed and it was two centuries before Assyrian power again menaced Phoenicia. Moreover, the collapse of Mycenaean sea power during the late thirteenth century relieved the Phoenicians of any serious threat from the west except the perpetual menace of piratic attacks from the Sea Peoples.

Still another factor contributing to Phoenician maritime expansion may be mentioned: the rapid spread of iron after the fall of the Hittite Empire, which had monopolized it. In the sixth century Babylonian economic texts mention iron from Mount Lebanon, and it seems likely that the Phoenicians had long before discovered these deposits, traces of which still remain. Through trade with Asia Minor it soon became easy to obtain iron, which came into use for ordinary tools in the course of the eleventh century. Iron was far better adapted than copper or bronze for making axe-heads, adze-heads, saws and sledge-hammers; it was also much cheaper, once the markets were opened and the arts of smelting and forging iron had been developed. With the new tools came a great expansion in the use of the fine timber of Lebanon for ship construction. Larger beams and boards could now be manufactured much more cheaply.[3]

The devastation of the Phoenician coast by the Sea Peoples in the late thirteenth and early twelfth centuries B.C. must have virtually ended normal economic development. The Sidonians and the Byblians were the first to recover. The ancient rivalry

[1] For early Israelite participation in Phoenician shipping see e.g. Judg. v. 17 (twelfth century), Gen. xlix. 13 (eleventh century), 2 Kings x. 22 ff. (tenth century), etc.

[2] It is now virtually certain that this event took place much earlier than is commonly supposed.

[3] §III, 16, on the early development of the Phoenician merchant marine.

between Tyre and Sidon had been brought to a temporary halt by the destruction of both cities, followed by the rebuilding of Tyre as a Sidonian town.[1] Thenceforward, until the late eighth century, we find 'Sidonian' used in the Bible, the Homeric Epics, and native inscriptions as a term covering the South Phoenicians in general.[2] Ittoba'al I of Tyre (c. 887–856) appears in the Bible as 'king of the Sidonians'; over a century later Hiram II of Tyre (so entitled in the Assyrian inscriptions) is called 'king of the Sidonians' in a native inscription dedicated to Ba'al-Lebanon; Elulaeus (c. 701) is called 'king of Tyre' by Menander, but 'king of Sidon' in the Assyrian inscriptions (which say, however, that his residence was in Tyre, while Menander says that Sidon was separated from Tyre by the Assyrians). In late Sidonian coins Sidon receives the Phoenician appellation 'mother of Kambe (Carthage), Hippo, Citium and Tyre,' which sufficiently attests the fact that Sidon claimed Tyre and its chief colonies as its own daughters. From these and other data it appears certain that Tyre and Sidon formed part of a single Sidonian state in the twelfth to tenth centuries. Similarly, it is probable that Berytus, which is never mentioned in the Bible or the Assyrian inscriptions, was part of the Byblian state.

After more than a hundred years of complete darkness, the report of Wenamun casts a bright light on Phoenicia at the end of the Twentieth Dynasty under Ramesses XI (1100–1085 B.C.).[3] The Egyptian threat to Asia had ceased, as the king of Byblos delighted in reminding the unfortunate Egyptian envoy. The Tjekker, who had settled in Dor (see above), were feared as pirates. The southern coast of Cyprus, far from being under Phoenician domination, was ruled by an independent queen, whose subjects were allegedly about to put Wenamun and his Byblian sailors to death when the extant portion of the narrative comes to an end. Most illuminating is the description of the organization of Phoenician shipping at that time. Zakarba'al, king of Byblos, says to Wenamun, after scolding him for coming in a second-rate ship with an unreliable captain: 'There are twenty *mns*[4] ships here in my harbour which are in trading association[5] with Smendes (the first Tanite pharaoh), and even in Sidon, which you passed, there must be fifty *br* ships[6] which are in association

---

[1] G, 11, 79 ff.   [2] §11, 5, 347 ff.
[3] §1, 6. The Wenamun report is 'a real report', not a literary work as formerly believed; see §11, 11, 41, n. 8 and §11, 12, 22. See below, pp. 641 ff.
[4] §1, 14, 54, n. 206.   [5] See above, p. 515, n. 2
[6] §1, 14, 54, n. 206. See also §1, 27, 3 ff.

with Waraktir (Warkatara)[1] and are carrying (freight) to his residence.' Here again the reference to Sidon evidently includes Tyre and other ports of the Sidonians, since Tyre itself was mentioned in passing earlier in the same narrative. It follows from the words of Zakarba'al that it was then customary to organize syndicates of trading vessels under the protection of powerful foreign princes, such as Smendes of Tanis and Waraktir (Warkatara, of Askalon?), with whom profits were shared. The reason for such organization of shipping is not far to seek; the syndicates provided both the necessary capital with which to build and fit out trading fleets and the protection against piracy without which they could not have plied their trade. Centuries later the same expression was employed in Hebrew in connexion with the formation of syndicates and trading guilds.

That the word 'Phoenician' (Greek *Phoinix*) was derived from *phoinix*, 'red purple dye', was well known in antiquity, though it has often been denied in modern times. It has been deduced from fifteenth-century documents found at Nuzi that the word 'Canaan' is also derived from an older word for 'purple dye',[2] after which it was shown that the Hebrew word $k^e na' an\bar{\imath}$, 'merchant', was already used in this sense as early as the fifteenth century B.C. and that 'Canaanite' meant properly 'dealer in purple dye', i.e. 'textile merchant'.[3] As late as the time of Job (probably seventh century B.C.) the word *ḥabbār*, 'member of a trading association' (*ḥubūr*), still appears as a synonym of $k^e na' an\bar{\imath}$, 'merchant'. These facts illustrate the basic importance of trade in the Phoenician economy, an importance which was interrupted only temporarily by the crises of the late thirteenth and early twelfth centuries B.C.

It is characteristic of Phoenician as well as of Philistine organization that the power of the king tended to be kept in check by the 'elders', who met as a kind of senate in order to consider matters of importance to the state. In the Amarna Tablets we already have a council of elders (*šībūtu*) at Arce (Irqata) in central Phoenicia.[4] In the Wenamun report Zakarba'al of Byblos called the state council (here designated by the well-known Hebrew term $m\bar{o}'\bar{e}\underline{d}$)[5] in order to consider the demand of the Tjekker envoys for the extradition of Wenamun. In later times the council of state still formed an integral part of the constitutions of Tyre, Byblos

---

[1] See above, pp. 513, 515.
[2] *Language*, 12, 121 ff.
[3] B. Maisler in *Bull. A.S.O.R.* 102 (1946), 7 ff. Cf. §II, 5, 356, n. 50.
[4] Amarna tablet 100, 4. My collation has confirmed this reading.
[5] See A. J. Wilson in *J.N.E.S.* 4 (1945), 245.

and Carthage, as we know from Assyrian, Hebrew and Greek sources of the seventh to third centuries B.C.

Epigraphic material throwing light on Phoenician history is relatively plentiful during the Late Bronze Age, but after the fall of Ugarit in the late thirteenth century it becomes very scanty indeed. The earliest of these texts (aside from a few names and the word *ḥeṣ*, 'luck', 'fortune', on javelin heads)[1] belongs to Ahiram (later Hiram), who was king of Byblos in the early tenth century; his sarcophagus is expressly said to have been made for him by his son Ittoba'al, and cannot be dated in the thirteenth century B.C.[2] Such an early date is disproved both by the character of the script and by the explicit statement of the text. On the other hand, it is quite true that the representations which cover the sarcophagus carry on the artistic tradition of the thirteenth century in many details, though the execution seems to be much inferior. To the tenth and early ninth centuries belong a number of inscriptions from Byblos written in substantially the same script as that on the Ahiram sarcophagus; all are datable by filiation and epigraphic sequence dating. Since two were inscribed on statues of the Bubastite kings Sheshonq (*c*. 935–914 B.C.) and Osorkon I (*c*. 914–874 B.C.), they may be arranged in the following order:

Ahiram *c*. 1000   Abiba'al (son of Yehimilk?)
Ittoba'al, son of Ahiram   Eliba'al, son of Yehimilk
Yehimilk *c*. 950   Shipitba'al I, son of Eliba'al[3]

Ahiram was on the throne within half a century or so after the reign of Zakarba'al, Wenamun's contemporary.

It is evident from the inscriptions on the statues of Sheshonq and Osorkon that Abiba'al and Eliba'al regarded themselves as vassals of the first two Bubastite pharaohs. Since there is no hint in Sheshonq's own inscriptions of any penetration beyond the plain of Esdraelon, it does not seem probable that he subjugated any part of Phoenicia by military occupation. The most natural explanation of the Byblian data is that Byblos had voluntarily accepted Egyptian suzerainty in order to protect itself from Sidonian encroachment. There is some Greek and Cypriot[4] evidence for limited Byblian competition with the Sidonians in colonizing the eastern Mediterranean, and Menander of Ephesus

---

[1] See S. Iwry in *J.A.O.S.* 81 (1961), 30 ff.

[2] §III, 20 *passim*. (For specific references see my criticism of this opinion in §II, 4, 2* ff. notes 4 ff.).

[3] For details see §II, 2 and for the list of kings p. 160.

[4] An unpublished study by William R. Lane suggests dialectal peculiarities of probable Byblian origin in certain Phoenician inscriptions from Cyprus.

tells us that Botrys, north of Byblos, was settled by Ittoba'al of Tyre (c. 887–856 B.C.)—a statement which presupposes a preceding defeat of Byblos by Tyre.

New evidence proves that the raids of the Sea Peoples on the coast of Palestine and Syria began several decades before the massive invasion in the eighth year of Ramesses III. This in turn supports the date c. 1191 B.C. given by Menander of Ephesus, following generally reliable native Tyrian records, for the foundation of Tyre by the Sidonians (after its previous destruction, on which see above).[1] If the Tyrian date is correct, it means that Tyre and Sidon were among the first Syrian seaports to have been destroyed by the Sea Peoples, and that Tyre was rebuilt under Sidonian auspices not long before the final Philistine irruption. By the time of Wenamun, as we have seen, Sidon was still much less important than Byblos, and Tyre is mentioned only in passing. Since Byblos was still inferior in power to the Tjekker, it follows that the dates given from the fourth century B.C. (at least) onward for the foundation of Utica near Carthage (c. 1101 B.C.) and of Gades (Cadiz) in Spain (shortly after the Trojan War) are impossible.

But the obvious impossibility of such high dates does not free us from the necessity of examining their basis. Two points must be borne in mind. First, the Phoenicians and Carthaginians reckoned the passage of time, in the absence of fixed written tradition, by generations of forty years, like the Israelites between the thirteenth and the seventh centuries B.C. and like Hecataeus among Greek historians;[2] in earlier times both Israelites and Greeks (Hesiod) had employed a lifetime as chronological unit.[3] Pityusa (Ibiza) was settled by the Carthaginians 160 years, or four generations, after the foundation of Carthage, according to Diodorus; Arganthonius, king of Tartessus in the sixth century B.C., was said to have lived for 120 years, with his life divided into three periods of a generation each, like the life of Moses. From Carthage we have some long genealogical lists; the longest has seventeen generations of a priestly family.[4] This particular list is undoubtedly historical in substance and probably in detail; most

---

[1] P. 519 and G, 11, 79, n. 2.

[2] On Greek genealogical calculations and their inflationary tendency, see especially §1, 9, and §11, 35.

[3] Well known from Etruria and not so well from Greece (for Hesiod, see §11, 35, 15). For earlier Assyria and Israel see *Bull. A.S.O.R.* 163 (1961), 50 ff.

[4] *Corpus Inscr. Semit.* no. 3778; §11, 26, 305 and Plate 31. Harden dates the stele in the late fourth or early third century B.C., in which case the chronology should extend back to the eighth century soon after the foundation of Carthage.

of the names are otherwise attested and a number of them are hypocoristica. The dedicator's great-great-grandfather bore the good Egyptian name *Pnūfe*, and the earliest ancestor named was called simply *Miṣrī*, 'The Egyptian'. Turning back to the date of the foundation of Utica, which is particularly well attested, we may reckon with an original chronological span calculated on the basis of an exact multiple of forty years, ending at 1101 B.C. Since under the special conditions of colonial adventure we are likely to find some exceptionally long generations, we cannot be far wrong in allowing an average of between twenty-five and thirty years. Being restricted to multiples of forty with a strong probability favouring a whole number of generations, and assuming a starting point between *c.* 600 and 400 B.C., we quickly find that most possibilities cluster about the tenth century B.C. This calculation does not constitute proof, but it fits together with many otherwise known facts to establish a clear pattern.

Thanks to the accumulation of datable epigraphs from different parts of the north-west Semitic world, it is now possible to fix the approximate dates of the earliest known inscriptions from the Phoenician colonies, which include two fairly long texts from Nora in Sardinia and from Cyprus,[1] as well as two small fragments from Nora and Bosa in Sardinia. Both script and language are good Phoenician of ninth-century type; attempts to assign them dates below the early eighth century at latest are quite impossible. The contention that the Nora text was not a complete funerary text but part of a decree which must have covered the face of several stones[2] was rejected by many scholars, but was confirmed and further developed by B. Mazar during a visit to Sardinia in 1962,[3] and he has also shown that the text originally extended farther to the right as well as to the left than had been proposed. The now certain date of the inscriptions in question proves that the beginning of Phoenician colonization in Cyprus and Sardinia cannot well be placed later than the tenth century and that a date after the ninth century is impossible.

A striking confirmation of the early date of the painted pottery in the lowest level of the Tanit Precinct at Carthage, has been obtained by comparison of the published material with similar

[1] §11, 1; and A. M. Honeyman in *Iraq*, 6 (1939), 106 ff.

[2] That it is part of a decree is made probable by the words of the text as well as the relatively huge size of the characters, which would be singularly inappropriate for a funerary stele. In the Mediterranean world we are accustomed to the laws of Gortyn in Crete, dating in their present form from the fifth century B.C. Parallels elsewhere are too numerous to mention.

[3] See provisionally §1, 27, 17 ff., and the excellent photograph published as Fig. 9.

painted ware from Megiddo (which was at the time wholly in the orbit of Sidonian material culture).[1] The Megiddo ware in question is almost all attributed to Stratum V by the excavators, but it is not clear whether this refers to V B (early tenth century) or to V A + IV B (a single stratum of Solomonic date from the second half of the tenth century).[2] If the ware continued into IV A it is even possible that the latest pieces (no longer characteristic) may date well down into the ninth century. We must, of course, assume that this ware was brought to North Africa not later than the late tenth or the early ninth century B.C., and that it continued to be manufactured until the eighth century, some time after it had disappeared in Phoenicia. Such phenomena are exceedingly common.

Art-historical data are also accumulating steadily, even though rather slowly. The finds at Aliseda near Cáceres in western Spain, about half-way up the Portuguese border, carry us back definitely to the seventh and eighth centuries B.C.[3] Much more important are the ivories from Carmona in the Guadalquivir valley near Seville, which have long been known,[4] but are now being dated much too late, after years in which they were accidentally dated correctly—at least in principle. These ivories do not resemble any late ivories from the eastern Mediterranean, but are intermediate in type between the Megiddo ivories (dated by Egyptian inscriptions and stratigraphy between c. 1300 and 1150 B.C.) and the Syro-Phoenician ivories of the ninth and eighth centuries, now known so well from different sites.[5] This intermediate date is particularly obvious when one compares the combs from Megiddo and Carmona, and then compares the Carmona combs with imported pieces from the sanctuary of Artemis Orthia in Sparta, dating roughly between 750 and 650 B.C.[6] The Carmona plaque D 513 has a griffin of Mycenaean type[7] and a warrior with spiked helmet, spear and shield like the well-known figures on the back of the warrior vase of Mycenae (about the end of the thirteenth century B.C.).[8] The coat of mail is Asiatic and the drawing of the head in profile is characteristically Egyptian in style. The last piece suggests a Cypriot prototype. That the Carmona ivories are not of local manufacture is shown by the discovery at Carthage of an ivory comb in precisely the same style, but with the addition of a bull and a female sphinx. In the writer's opinion there is only

---

[1] See provisionally §1, 5, 175 and note.
[2] §1, 5, 175; §11, 4, 5*; §11, 5, 346 ff.
[3] See especially A. Freijeiro in *Archivo Español de Arqueología*, 30 (1956), 3 ff.
[4] §11, 9.   [5] §11, 6; §11, 7; §11, 34, etc.   [6] §11, 16, 222 ff. and Plates cxxix ff.
[7] The late A. J. B. Wace first called my attention to this.   [8] §1, 8, fig. 265.

one reasonable conclusion, that they were made for export in quantity and that they belong to the very beginning of Phoenician trade with Spain in the tenth and ninth centuries B.C. If this is the case it would explain the complete absence of comparable material in western sites known to belong to about the seventh century B.C., as well as the apparent fact that no other foreign imports are known to have been recovered from the Iberian tumuli near Carmona where the ivories were found.

If we relate the evidence described in the preceding paragraphs to Sidonian history, it becomes obvious that it was quite impossible for Sidon and Tyre to expand their sea-trade in the Mediterranean until after the elimination of the Philistine sea and land 'empire' which lasted from the conquest of Palestine c. 1050 B.C. until the destruction of Philistine power by David during the first quarter of the tenth century B.C. (probably about 975). Our information about the succession of Sidonian kings of Tyre begins with Hiram's father Abiba'al at the beginning of the tenth century. It was probably Abiba'al who established Phoenician power in Cyprus,[1] and his son Hiram I (c. 969–936 B.C.), who was closely allied with both David and Solomon, may have continued the search for copper by initiating the serious exploitation of the mineral wealth of Sardinia. Utica also, near Carthage, was probably founded about this time. Before the end of the tenth century the Phoenicians had probably founded Gades, which bears the good Phoenician name *Ha-gader*, 'the walled enclosure'. Whether the Phoenicians or the native Iberians organized the trading caravans which travelled up the Guadalquivir valley past Seville and Carmona, branched off northward toward Cáceres and continued on into north-western Spain we shall not know until there have been systematic excavations along the route taken by these caravans.[2]

The Hebrew designation 'Tarshish ships' for the sea-faring vessels of Hiram's navy probably refers to ore-carrying ships, or perhaps to ships which were sufficiently large and strong to carry loads of copper ingots, like the thirteenth-century ship recently excavated off the southern coast of Anatolia.[3] Such refinery ships seem to have been called *kry* in Ugaritic and Egyptian (plural).[4] There is no direct reference to voyages to Tarshish (originally

---

[1] §II, 5, 348 and 361; §I, 27, 15.

[2] This route was first proposed by B. Mazar in 1957; see §II, 5, 347.

[3] §II, 8, 2 ff.

[4] These words are presumably derived from common Semitic *kūr*, 'smelting furnace'. Ugaritic *wry* should be read *kry*. The Eg. sing. is both *kr* and *ḳr*.

Tharros in Sardinia?)[1] in the narratives about Solomon's reign, but the expeditions sent out jointly by Hiram and Solomon, following the old trade association tradition, into the Indian Ocean certainly required just as large and strong vessels. There is no reason to locate Ophir anywhere except in the region extending from Eritrea to Somalia and possibly beyond it. In this region (Egyptian Punt) were to be obtained the gold, silver, ivory, ebony and two kinds of monkeys which are listed as the principal imports.[2] Excavations at Tell el-Kheleifeh near 'Aqaba make it virtually certain that this is the Ezion-geber which was the expedition's base of operations.[3]

The tenth century was, in any case, the golden age of Phoenician wealth and power, before the entire hinterland was overrun by the armies of the Aramaeans and the Assyrians. Little as we know directly about Phoenicia at that time, our indirect evidence is considerable; we have sketched only certain aspects of it.

III. THE SYRO-HITTITE STATES

After the Hittite Empire had been destroyed by the barbarian hordes from the north-west, towards the end of the thirteenth century B.C., the Phrygians and other Indo-European peoples occupied the central plateau of Anatolia. In the mountainous south-eastern provinces (later Cataonia, Melitene and Commagene), the native population seems to have resisted so strongly that it was allowed to go its own way. Syria was protected by the Taurus range and the tough fibre of the northern mountaineers. The Hittites had established several vassal states in northern Syria during the initial period of their occupation in the fourteenth century B.C. At least two of them, Carchemish and Aleppo, were ruled by princes of the imperial Hittite dynasty. In a third state, Khattina, the reigning princes still bore names derived from imperial Hittite history as late as the ninth century B.C., and the imperial name Mutallu was borne by two kings of Gurgum and one of Commagene who are mentioned in the Assyrian records. In the century immediately following the collapse of the Hittite Empire there seems to have been some tendency to bring the various Hittite states together. The inscriptions of Tiglath-

---

[1] §II, 15, 280 ff.; §II, 5, 361, n. 103.

[2] Both the *qōpīm* and the ткүм (1 Kings x. 22) bear Egyptian names; cf. T. O. Lambdin, in *J.A.O.S.* 73 (1953), 154, and W. F. Albright in G, 9, 11, 252a. s.v., 'Fauna: Primates'.

[3] §II, 25, 89 ff.

pileser I (1115–1077) repeatedly mention 'great Khatti', whose king, Ini-Teshub,[1] was defeated by the Assyrians. Since this name was borne by a king of Carchemish in the thirteenth century, he probably ruled there also, but Melid (modern Malatya) is said to belong to 'the great land of Khatti' under a local prince with a Hittite imperial name.[2]

Through surface finds and excavations in Syria many Hittite reliefs and hieroglyphic inscriptions have come to light. The first such finds were made at Hamath in 1871; in 1879 A. H. Sayce pointed out that the script on these monuments was identical with the writing on several Anatolian monuments and correctly applied the term 'Hittite' to them. Early Hittite monuments have since been found by the Germans at Zincirli, by the British at Carchemish, and by the French at Malatya on the border of Syria and Anatolia; later sculptures have also been found at many other sites.[3] Thanks to careful stylistic analysis of the pictured reliefs, it is possible to divide them roughly into three groups: (1) monuments showing clear affinities with the art of the great Hittite Empire (fourteenth and thirteenth centuries); (2) transitional monuments showing less true Hittite and Hurrian tradition and more affected by contemporary Phoenician and Aramaean art; (3) monuments influenced directly by Assyrian art.[4] This sequence has been best preserved at Malatya, where the monuments of the Lion Gate may safely be dated to the eleventh century and may in part be still earlier.[5] At Carchemish a much fuller chronological series has been admirably demonstrated.[6]

In 1930 Piero Meriggi published the important discovery that certain groups of characters in the Hittite hieroglyphic monuments represented words for 'son' and 'grandson'. The successful decipherment of the script of these monuments began almost immediately after this discovery and has since been carried to a point where most of the syllabic signs can be read.[7] By combining study of the order of royal names with stylistic analysis of the inscribed monuments, system has been brought out of chaos. Of course, there are dangers: little is yet known about palaeography; the same name may be repeated several times in the course of several

[1] Formerly read *Ili-Teshub*, but the name is identical with the thirteenth-century *Ini-Teshub*, transcribed into Egyptian as well as into cuneiform; cf. §III, 2, 154.

[2] *Ibid.*

[3] See especially §III, 7; 11.

[4] §III, 2 with the bibliographic indications in the footnotes.

[5] §III, 1; 2, 153 ff.

[6] §III, 44, *passim*. See also §III, 2, 155 ff.

[7] §III, 28; 35.

centuries; uninscribed monuments may be wrongly attributed. The union of the two methods brings assured results only in the case of monuments which are stylistically of the latest Assyrianizing type and bear royal names attested by Assyrian inscriptions: e.g. Warpalawas (Assyrian Urpalla) of Tyana. Thanks to figured monuments with Aramaic or Canaanite inscriptions, we know that the critical phase of the shift from pre-Assyrian to Assyrianizing art came in northern Syria west of the Euphrates between c. 850 and 825 B.C.[1] If we date the transitional group of monuments between the middle decades of the tenth and the third quarter of the ninth century we can scarcely be far wrong; the archaic group best illustrated by the Lion Gate at Malatya will fall between the late twelfth century and the middle of the tenth.

At Carchemish, thanks to the careful analysis of Barnett, it is possible to distinguish between the sculptures of the Water Gate, which are badly damaged but seem to be roughly contemporary with the Sulumeli reliefs of the Lion Gate at Malatya, and the reliefs of the Sukhis Dynasty in the late tenth or early ninth century B.C.[2] The sculptures of the Water Gate at Carchemish belong to the same general age as the inscriptions of the kings whose names were read provisionally as 'Pa-ī-da' and his son 'GREAT-pa';[3] both are called 'king of Carchemish', 'great king', and may go back to the time of Tiglath-pileser I of Assyria or a little later.[4] The following Sukhis dynasty closed with a king named Katuwas, not long before the time of Sankaras (Sangara of the Assyrian monuments, attested before 866 and until 848 B.C.).

Since it is now possible to analyse the increasing influence of neo-Assyrian art on the West, as the Assyrian arms advanced westward, a few observations on areas just outside of Syria proper will help to illuminate the situation in Syria itself. In the first place neo-Assyrian influence had not yet affected known specimens of Aramaean art in the Euphrates valley in 886 (the stele of Tell 'Asharah south of the confluence of the Euphrates and Khabur) and c. 875 (the slightly later steles of Tell Aḥmar, south of Carchemish).[5] Similarly, it appears certain that the reliefs of Tell Halaf (Gozan), from the time of Kapara, precede the Assyrian occupation of the district in 894 B.C., since none of them show any neo-Assyrian influence whatever.[6] A date about the second

---

[1] §III, 2, *passim*.

[2] §III, 2, 157 (after R. D. Barnett in §III, 44, 260 ff.). See above p. 441.

[3] These names are now read *x-pa-zitis* and GREAT THUNDER (=Ura-Tarhundas). See J. D. Hawkins in *Iraq* 36 (1974), p. 71. (Ed.)

[4] §III, 44, 259.   [5] §III, 2, 147 ff. and 156 ff.   [6] §III, 2, 150 ff.; §III, 3.

half of the tenth century for most of the reliefs of Gozan is, there-fore, clear. Turning to eastern Cilicia, just outside Syria on the north-west, there is absolutely no sign of neo-Assyrian influence on the sculptures of Karatepe, which must, accordingly, date from the ninth century, as it has been observed.[1] They cannot reason-ably be dated in the eighth century—much less in the seventh (as recently attempted by a few classical archaeologists, accustomed to reducing Iron Age chronology as much as possible). It is true that the Phoenician script of the bilingual texts has been dated in the third quarter of the eighth century, but examination of the photographs shows that several late forms of letters do not actually occur on the original; a date about 800 B.C. is highly probable. A substantial lag between the neo-Assyrian style of Kilamuwa in neighbouring Sam'al (Zincirli) and the nearly contemporaneous sculptures of Karatepe may be explained geographically. A date for the sculptures of Karatepe earlier in the ninth century remains, however, possible. The recurrence of the royal name *'Wrk* (*Urikki*) in both the ninth and the eighth centuries offers no problem.

In the present state of our evidence, it seems clear that the refusal of an earlier authority to recognize the existence of any monumental art or architecture in the neo-Hittite states of northern Syria between 1200 and 850 B.C. was entirely wrong.[2] In fact it is now becoming increasingly clear that the eleventh and tenth centuries were the golden age of Syro-Hittite art and architecture. By the end of the tenth century most of the small states of northern Syria had become Aramaized, even though some of them continued to give their kings royal names of imperial Hittite or Luwian (in Sham'al and Gurgum) or mixed character.

IV. EMERGENCE OF THE ARAMAEANS

Aramaean origins are elusive, in spite of the fact that we have much scattered information about early Aramaean political history; the less said about supposed occurrences of the name *Aram* in cunei-form texts of the late third and early second millennium the better. And yet within four centuries of the time when they are first mentioned as a people in contemporary inscriptions, Aramaic had become the *lingua franca* of south-western Asia. We are, however, faced with serious difficulties in trying to locate the region where the Aramaic language—and presumably its original speakers—became differentiated from a common Semitic background. We

---

[1] From oral information given the writer by Dr R. D. Barnett in October 1964.
[2] §III, 20, 164 ff., and against it §III, 2, and §II, 4.

first meet with Aramaeans in the Syrian Desert in the reign of Tiglath-pileser I (1115–1077); they were then called by the Assyrians 'Aramaean bedawin' (*Aḥlamē Armāya*). The earliest inscriptions containing more than a word or two belong to Barhadad and Hazael of Damascus; the former dates from about 850 and the latter from somewhere between *c.* 840 and 800. Both are in standard Old Aramaic, and so are the Zakir inscriptions from Hamath (before *c.* 750 B.C.) and the Sefire treaties from the neighbourhood of Aleppo (*c.* 750 B.C.). On the other hand, the two long eighth-century inscriptions of Panammu from Zincirli (Sam'al) are composed in an Aramaic dialect with Canaanite affinities, which has been termed 'Yaudic'.[1] Panammu's son wrote his own inscriptions in standard Aramaic. In the light of this situation it seems to be reasonably certain that standard Aramaic was originally the language of the kingdom of Damascus, called simply 'Aram' in native inscriptions and Old Testament literature.

Analysis of the relation between Aramaic and the older north-west-Semitic language of the second millennium shows clearly that the former is not a derivative of South Canaanite (Phoenician) or of North Canaanite (Ugaritic) or Amorite, though it has more in common with the two latter than with the former. In sibilant shift it differs from the other three; in the use of *n* dual and plural it agrees with Amorite. In verbal structure it is rather more closely related to Amorite than to the other two. Early Aramaic was strongly influenced by Phoenician in vocabulary and morphology; from the seventh century onwards Assyro-Babylonian influence dominated, as we can easily see from its sentence structure, as well as from hundreds of loan-words. The superficial difference in sound between Aramaic and Hebrew is largely due to the fact that the forward shift of the accent, common to all known north-west-Semitic tongues after the thirteenth century B.C., reached its climax in Aramaic and was extended to include the article (*h*)*a*, which was attached to the end of the noun (just as in Romanian among the Romance languages). In brief, examination of the linguistic situation confirms our first impression that Aramaic developed somewhere in eastern Syria, possibly growing out of Sutu dialects spoken there in the Late Bronze Age.[2]

---

[1] G, 6, 153 ff.
[2] Aramaic is not a direct offshoot of 'Amorite', as sometimes thought, but is rather intermediate in type between it and the proto-Arabic dialects of north Arabia. The relation must, however, have been complex, and later Aramaic was strongly influenced by Phoenician (south Canaanite) and by Assyro-Babylonian (Akkadian).

If we turn to Hebrew and Israelite tradition, we gain some idea of the complex tribal relation which presumably existed. The Aramaean stock must have been so mixed that tradition became hopelessly divergent. In Gen. x. 22–3, Aram is one of the principal Semitic peoples, along with Elam, Ashur, and Arphaxad (the putative non-Semitic ancestor of the Hebrews); its principal subdivisions are listed as Uz, Hul, Gether and Mash.[1] Since the nucleus of the list in Genesis X probably goes back to the tenth century B.C.,[2] these names ought to be very instructive; unhappily only Uz and Mash are otherwise known. In a somewhat later(?) passage, Gen. xxii. 20–4, Aram appears as the offshoot of Kemuel, one of the eight sons of Abraham's brother Nahor. Nahor is now known to have been the eponym of the town by that name, probably east of Harran; Nahor (*Naḫur*) appears frequently in Bronze Age documents from Mari and elsewhere, and is mentioned explicitly as a town in Gen. xxiv. 10. Unfortunately, again, most of the eight names are otherwise unknown: Uz reappears elsewhere in the Bible; Chesed is the eponym of the Chaldaeans; Hazo and Buz are Assyrian Khazu and Bazu, in central or eastern Arabia; Bethuel is the traditional father of Rebecca. Nahor's secondary wife, Reumah, is credited with being the mother of Tebah (Tubikhu of Zobah, in central Syria), Tahash (Takhshu, a district north of the region of Damascus), Gaham and Maachah (west of the region of Damascus). The name of Aram's father Kemuel is archaic in formation,[3] but is otherwise unknown. If we add to these two divergent traditions the fact that in the Patriarchal narratives the family of Abraham is represented as closely related to the Aramaeans of the Harran district, and that the Deuteronomic source speaks of Abraham as a 'wandering Aramaean' (Deut. xxvi. 5),[4] the problem becomes still more intricate. Finally, Amos ix. 7 says that the Aramaeans came from some land called Kir, just as the Israelites came from Egypt and the Philistines from Caphtor;[5] Kir is elsewhere stated to be a region near Elam to which the Aramaeans were exiled!

---

[1] §III, 4, 2 ff.

[2] Most of Gen. x has been attributed by documentary critics to J, which is now increasingly recognized as the chief source of E and partly of P (Noth, Mowinckel, etc.), and is dated by more and more scholars (e.g. the Baltimore school) in the tenth century.

[3] Probably revocalized in Hebrew tradition and actually derived from an original *[Yaq]qim-el* ('May El Be His Champion').

[4] Since '*RMY* meant 'travelling trader' in early South Arabic (Qatabanian), the phrase may possibly have meant 'wandering trader'; cf. G, 7, 34 ff., and *Bull. A.S.O.R.* 163 (1961), 44 ff. and 164, 28.   [5] See above, p. 512.

From the preceding survey of the evidence it is clear that we have to do with a complex process, which may be provisionally sketched as follows. The original speakers of Aramaic were nomads of mixed origin, who began settling down on the fringes of the Syrian Desert in the third quarter of the second millennium. They may then have headed a confederation of tribes which took advantage of the collapse of the Hittite and Egyptian empires, followed by the break-up of the Assyrian empire of Tukulti-Ninurta I, to invade *en masse* already tilled lands. The tribesmen pushed westward into Syria and eastward into the valleys of the Euphrates and its tributaries. Settling wherever possible in the fertile river valleys, they combined sheep-herding with agriculture and probably with caravan trade, after the introduction of camels had given them an extraordinary advantage over donkey caravaneers.[1] Their prestige was such that other nomad tribes joined them from southern Babylonia to the Upper Euphrates, and Aramaic rapidly displaced related dialects, at first for tribal inter-communication and eventually for all purposes. The descendants of the Amorites became Aramaean, a process doubtless facilitated by close dialectal similarities. This process was still at work in Babylonia in the eighth century B.C.; it has been shown that the nomad 'Aramaean' tribes of Babylonia at that time were mostly Arabs who had become assimilated to the Aramaeans.[2]

The original name of the Aramaeans was *Aram* (with two short *a* vowels and the accent on the first syllable), as may be shown by comparing the derived forms in different Semitic languages. The early Assyrian shift between nominative *Arumu*, genitive *Arimi*, and gentilic *Armāyu* resulted from the operation of Assyrian dialectal vowel harmony; it has nothing to do with the original pronunciation of the name. We cannot tell whether the name was at first personal or geographical; the suggestion, sometimes made, that it already appears in Old Akkadian or other early Babylonian texts is improbable.

As already noted, we first meet the Aramaeans in the contemporary documents of Tiglath-pileser I (1115–1077 B.C.). In his fourth year (1112) he launched a simultaneous attack on Aramaean settlements in different parts of the Euphrates valley, from the land of Shuah (Assyrian Sukhu), north-west of Babylonia, as far as Carchemish. Crossing the Euphrates in pursuit of the Aramaeans he burned six 'towns' at the foot of Mount Bishrī (*Bišrī*), that is, in Palmyrēnē. In a later, undated inscription the

---

[1] For recent bibliography see *Bull. A.S.O.R.* 163 (1962), 38, n. 9.
[2] §III, 37.

king claims to have crossed the Euphrates for the twenty-eighth time (twice in one year) in order to pursue the Aramaean bedawin. Here he specifies that the Aramaeans were routed from Tadmor (Palmyra) itself to Anath ('Ānah) in Shuah and even to Rapiqu on the Babylonian frontier. The struggle with the Aramaeans continued under the following kings. If the attribution of a fragmentary unpublished text to Ashur-bēl-kala is correct,[1] that king fought against Aram (*mat Arime*) in 1070. About 1062 Adad-apla-iddina, a usurper who is said by a cuneiform chronicle to have been an Aramaean, gained the throne of Babylonia. Contemporary records now come to an almost complete end in Mesopotamia, but later Assyrian inscriptions give us valuable data. Thus Ashur-dan II (934–912) informs us that the Aramaeans had occupied part of the region between the Lesser Zab and the Ḥamrīn mountains, in the East-Tigris country between Assyria and Babylonia, during the reign of Ashur-rabi II (1013–973 B.C.). Under the same king, according to an inscription of Shalmaneser III (858–824 B.C.), an Aramaean king had stormed the Assyrian stronghold of Mutkinu on the Upper Euphrates, opposite the Hittite town of Pitru (Pethor). Mutkinu had been in Assyrian hands since the time of Tiglath-pileser I, according to this same inscription; its loss evidently made a great impression on the Assyrians. Since Ashur-rabi II was an older contemporary of David, we may safely connect the Aramaean triumph with the situation presupposed in 2 Sam. vii. 3 and x. 16. According to this early source, Hadadezer, king of the Aramaeans of Zobah, was fighting at the Euphrates when David attacked him from the south, between 990 and 980 B.C. It seems only natural to suppose that the Assyrians had a share in turning David's attention to the Aramaeans, since the former were fighting for their lifeline to Syria and might reasonably be expected to look for allies wherever they were available.[2]

The Israelites seem to have first come into hostile contact with the Aramaeans towards the end of the eleventh century in the reign of Saul, who is said to have fought with 'the kings of Zobah' (1 Sam. xiv. 47). When we hear next of Zobah in the reign of David it was ruled by Hadadezer of Beth-rehob,[3] who controlled all eastern Syria from southern Ḥaurān to the Euphrates. Zobah appears as *Ṣubatu* (*Ṣubutu, Ṣubiti*) in Assyrian documents of the

---

[1] §III, 43, 84 f.

[2] §III, 15, 25 ff.; §III, 42, 42 ff.; §III, 31, 82 ff.; §III, 32, 102 ff.

[3] Beth-rehob (inferred from *ben Reḥōb*) was probably not Riḥāb north of Jerash, as thought by H. Guthe, but an unknown place of the same name in eastern Syria.

eighth and seventh centuries; it was then a province of greater Damascus, located in eastern Syria. From the account of David's war against Zobah we learn that the chief cities of Hadadezer at that time were Tebah (Late Bronze Tubikhu), Chun (Late Bronze Kunu, Roman Conna) and Berothai (perhaps Bereitan south of Ba'albek).[1] Though all three towns are in the Biqā', between Lebanon and Antilebanon, there can be no reasonable doubt that the land of Zobah proper lay east and north of Antilebanon, and was roughly equivalent to Bronze-Age Takhshu (Tahash, Gen. xxii. 24). Hadadezer was evidently the most important Aramaean ruler of his day; it may well have been he who stormed the Assyrian fortress of Mutkinu on the Upper Euphrates;[2] 2 Sam. viii. 10 (1 Chron. xviii. 10) states that he and Toi (Tou), king of Hamath, had been at war with one another. According to one account of David's war with Hadadezer, the latter began hostilities by sending aid to the Ammonites, who had provoked David into attacking them. In the course of the resulting war, the Aramaean confederation was roundly defeated; we hear of the Aramaeans of Beth-rehob, Geshur (later Gaulanitis, north of Gilead), Maachah (the district around Hermon, west and south-west of Damascus), Ish-tob[3] and Damascus, as well as of auxiliary forces from beyond the Euphrates. The two accounts in 2 Sam. viii and x are too fragmentary to enable us to reconstruct the course of events in detail. The outcome was decisive; Israelite garrisons were placed in Hadadezer's territory, especially in Damascus, and great booty was seized, including gold, silver and especially copper. Thenceforward, until the death of Solomon, the further rise of the Aramaeans in Syria was effectually checked; but the growth of their power in Mesopotamia became correspondingly accelerated.

During the period of obscurity which settled over Assyria under the two weak kings who succeeded Ashur-rabi II, the Aramaeans gained ground very rapidly. By the reign of the *roi fainéant* Tiglath-pileser II (967–935 B.C.) they had occupied Gidara in the region of Nisibis, half-way from the upper Khabur River to the frontiers of Assyria itself. To the second half of the tenth century belong the palace and reliefs of the Aramaean king Kapara[4] at Guzana (Tell Halaf, Gozan in 2 Kings xvii. 6) at the source of the Khabur river. Kapara calls himself 'son of Khadianu,' the Aramaic form of the name which appears as Hezion in

---

[1] In no case Berytus!　　　　　　[2] See preceding page.
[3] Still enigmatic, though a plausible suggestion connects it with Golan = Gaulanitis east of the Sea of Galilee.
[4] See above, p. 528.

1 Kings xv. 18; the men (or clans) by the name were in any case contemporary. The Aramaean tribe which occupied the territory of Gozan was called Bakhianu (Aramaic *Baḥyān*); its chief was Abisalamu (Absalom) at the beginning of the ninth century.[1]

An inscription of Ashur-dan II (934–912), with whom the Assyrian revival began, mentions the Aramaeans in connexion with campaigns in the west and south-east of Assyria, but it is difficult to form a clear picture. Under his son Adad-nīrāri II (911–891) we have a well-preserved account of the operations against the Aramaeans which occupied much of the king's reign. It is significant, however, that there is no mention of a campaign against the Aramaeans of northern Mesopotamia until about his eleventh year. From then until the end of his reign the Assyrians directed campaign after campaign against the Aramaeans, mentioning particularly various chiefs of the large tribe of Teman[2] which had occupied the region of Nisibis. The military culmination of his reign was reached in 892, when Gozan was captured and the settlements of the Khabur Valley capitulated, one after another. In 877 we have the first mention of the Aramaean state of Bīt-Adini (Biblical Beth-eden), which occupied both banks of the Upper Euphrates below Carchemish.

Meanwhile Solomon had died and Damascus had made good its independence, under an otherwise unknown Aramaean chieftain named Rezon. The latter can scarcely have remained in power long, since early in the ninth century we find Ben-hadad I on the throne; Ben-hadad is said to have been son of a Tabrimmon and grandson of a Hezion, that is, perhaps, member of the clan of Hezion (Khadianu in cuneiform).[3] The new state took over the domination of the northern part of the Syrian desert as political heir of Hadadezer of Zobah; in an inscription from the latter part of Ben-hadad's reign, about 850 B.C., the latter calls himself 'king of Aram', in accord with the practice frequently attested in the Bible and also found in the inscription of Zakir, king of Hamath. It is probably not accidental that the king's personal name was also Hadadezer, like that of his predecessor on the throne of Zobah a century earlier. We may perhaps compare the title 'king of Aram', borne by the princes of Damascus, with

---

[1] §III, 3, 82.

[2] Probably not derived from north Arabic *Teimā* (Babylonian *Tema*, biblical and Qumrān *Tēmān*). The name means simply 'southerner'.

[3] The writer's decipherment of the same names in the Ben-hadad inscription from near Aleppo (in *Bull. A.S.O.R.* 87 (1942), 27 ff.) is disputed, but nothing cogent has been proposed in their place.

the title 'king of all the Arabs', borne by 'Amru 'l-Qais in the inscription of an-Namarah (A.D. 328).

The climax of Aramaean political domination in Mesopotamia may thus be dated between about 950 and 900 B.C.; its climax in Syria did not come until the ninth century, owing partly to the lag caused by the triumph of David over Hadadezer. The remarkable accumulation of wealth in the hands of these Aramaean chieftains, attested in both Hebrew and Assyrian records, was undoubtedly in large part the result of commercial activity. We have already noted that the Aramaeans introduced the use of camels in the caravan trade of Syria and northern Mesopotamia. In keeping with the new importance of the camel, we find representations of riding camels in the late tenth century at both Gozan and Carchemish; references to camels became common in Assyrian inscriptions of the ninth century.

The art of the Aramaeans in the tenth century was still almost purely Syro-Hittite, as we know from the older monuments of Zincirli, Hamath and Gozan. It would be a mistake to assume that the bearers of this Syro-Hittite art were still prevailingly non-Semitic. An excellent illustration is the Melcarth stele of Ben-hadad I, found near Aleppo;[1] though dating from about the middle of the ninth century and inscribed in pure Aramaic, the figure of the god which adorns it does not yet show any clear influence from Assyrian or contemporary Phoenician art; it is still Syro-Hittite. At Hamath we know that Hittite inscriptions continued to be carved under Urkhilina (Irkhulina) as late as the middle of the ninth century, but a century earlier Hadoram, son of Tou, had borne a characteristically Semitic name. We have already noted above that the Aramaeans were actually the dominant people in Sham'al, Gurgum and other old Hittite states at least from the ninth century on and probably still earlier. It was not long before the enterprise of the Aramaeans freed them completely from the dead hand of the Hittite past. This does not mean, however, that the Hittites simply disappeared from this region. There is, in fact, very strong reason to derive the Armenians[2] (who occupied the whole country from Cilicia through Armenia Major until the times of the Arab, Kurdish, and Turkish irruptions) both physically and linguistically from the Hittites.

---

[1] See preceding note.　　　　　[2] §III, 5.